CHRISTIAN WORSHIP
ITS ORIGIN AND EVOLUTION

A STUDY OF THE LATIN LITURGY UP TO THE TIME OF CHARLEMAGNE

BY

Mgr. L. DUCHESNE
MEMBRE DE L'INSTITUT

TRANSLATED BY
M. L. McCLURE

FIFTH EDITION

WIPF & STOCK · Eugene, Oregon

Wipf and Stock Publishers
199 W 8th Ave, Suite 3
Eugene, OR 97401

Christian Worship: Its Origin and Evolution, Fifth Edition
A Study of the Latin Liturgy Up to the Time of Charlemagne
By Duchesne, L. and McClure, M. L.
Softcover ISBN-13: 978-1-6667-3376-1
Hardcover ISBN-13: 978-1-6667-2914-6
eBook ISBN-13: 978-1-6667-2915-3
Publication date 8/10/2021
Previously published by SPCK, 1920

This edition is a scanned facsimile of
the original edition published in 1920.

AUTHOR'S PREFACE.

THIS volume contains the description and explanation of the chief ceremonies of Catholic worship as they were performed in the Latin Churches of the West from the fourth to the ninth century. The title is somewhat ambitious, and is not exactly that which I would have chosen. But I did not feel justified in disregarding the suggestions of my publisher, and have had to relegate to the sub-title the description which I had in view.

The contents represent, in the main, merely notes of my lectures. I have dealt with this subject on two or three occasions in my teaching at the *Institut Catholique* at Paris. My pupils and other persons having expressed a wish to have the lectures printed, I am now able to satisfy their desire.

It is, indeed, but a modest contribution to the subject, and I make no pretension to compare this little book with the great works of the French and foreign liturgiologists, who, from the seventeenth century onwards, have explored every department of this vast domain. Small books, however, have their use, and mine, perhaps, may be welcomed by beginners who want a general view of the subject, or by busy people who are engaged in kindred studies and desire to take a rapid survey of this field of research. Owing, moreover, to the narrow limits which I have prescribed for myself, I have found it always possible to resort at first hand to the original printed texts.

When once we have come down beyond the time of Charlemagne in the West, and a limit almost corresponding to it in the East, we find ourselves confronted with such an immense number of liturgical books that their adequate study and classification would require more lives than one. The great and valuable works of Renaudot and of Martène give merely a faint idea of the material stored up in the manuscripts of libraries. But if we go back to a period anterior to the ninth century, liturgical books are much rarer, and it is not impossible to study all of them, and even to throw light on them, by comparing them with other historical documents. This is what I have attempted to do, without having recourse, it is true, to the manuscripts, which are, unfortunately, widely scattered, but confining myself to the texts edited by Tommasi, Mabillon, Martène, Muratori, and others. The last-named has brought together the principal documents in the two volumes of his *Liturgia Romana Vetus*, a work which constitutes a convenient, though doubtless incomplete, *Corpus* of the ancient Latin liturgical books.

I have devoted myself particularly to the Latin Liturgy, consulting the Greek usages merely for purposes of comparison. Our ancient Gallican Liturgy —that of St. Caesarius of Arles, of St. Germain of Paris, and of St. Gregory of Tours—to which the annals and councils of Merovingian times make such frequent reference, deserves a prominent place among the venerable monuments of our ecclesiastical antiquities. I think I have been able to add some fresh observations to the conclusions of Mabillon and Martène, particularly in that which concerns the ritual of ordination and the dedication of churches. It is, however, specially to the Roman Liturgy that I have directed my researches. Its history is clearly more interesting to us than that of any other, since for centuries it has been the only liturgy of the West.

Although I have not hesitated, when I found it possible, to go back earlier than the fourth century, I have, however, for the most part, confined myself to a less remote chronological period. Attention might be called to very interesting liturgical facts in documents anterior to the time of Constantine, but they are isolated facts, and the documents are few, and rarely explicit. In researches into this period, conjecture has to play too large a part, and it is more profitable, therefore, to concentrate attention on a somewhat later date, where both trustworthy and abundant material is forthcoming.

With regard to these primitive liturgical forms, I have not said all that we might wish to know about them, or, indeed, all that might be made known. My erudition has its limits. On the other hand, as I said before, it was not my intention to write a large book, but a small one. It is for this reason that I have refrained systematically from offering any explanation as to the connection between the present and the ancient usages. Such explanations would be interminable. The same may be said of questions, having a direct or indirect theological import, arising from the consideration of certain rites, such, for instance, as the *epiclesis* of the Mass, the reconciliation of penitents, and ordination. These questions have been carefully discussed by specialists, but in large works commensurate with the importance of the subject and beyond the scope of the task I have undertaken. If at times, when lecturing to an audience previously well prepared, I have been able to offer some solutions of these questions, in furnishing explanations of technicalities and in referring to other writers, these were episodes which I consider out of place in the present work, where it would be impossible to elaborate them in such a way as to make them clear to the ordinary reader.

When once I had resolved to restrict myself solely to the domain of history, it appeared incumbent upon me to avoid a special theological terminology. Not that I ignore such terminology, or do not recognise its utility, but, having no other aim in describing very ancient usages than to represent them as they were practised from the fourth to the eighth century, it seemed best not to speak of them in more precise language than was in use at that date.

Many works of a nature similar to mine are restricted to the study of the liturgy properly so called, that is, the Eucharistic Liturgy. I have adopted a wider scheme, and have extended my researches to other ceremonies, and here it became necessary to make a selection from among the innumerable manifestations of the Christian religious life. Some rites, such as those of initiation and of ordination, are so eminently essential that the choice of them was inevitable from the first. But beyond these, selection became more difficult. I at first thought of taking the seven Sacraments as the basis of my scheme. But this arrangement, important as it is from a theological point of view, and even from that of later history, did not fall in with the chronological exigencies of my plan. The seven Sacraments will, indeed, find a place in this book, but only such a place as they occupy in Christian antiquity, that is, somewhat scattered, and differing from each other in importance. I have consequently adopted another system. I have selected such ceremonies as have, in a somewhat marked manner, the character of collective acts, that is, that are ecclesiastical in the true sense of the word, and have a direct bearing on the life and development of the local church. These are almost always recognisable from the circumstance that they were, as a general rule, transacted in an assembly of the whole Church, and presided over by the bishop, surrounded by all his clergy. It is for this reason that no mention will be found in these pages of funerary ritual, which is of an absolutely private nature, and which, with the exception of special formularies for the Mass, has no very ancient features. For the same reason I have omitted all that concerns ministration to the dying, baptism and penance administered *in extremis*, extreme unction, and prayers for the departing. All these rites, necessarily accomplished apart from any ecclesiastical assembly, lack that publicity which is the ordinary and prescribed condition, for example, of baptism and ordination. If I have admitted marriage, which has rather the aspect of a family ceremony than that of an ecclesiastical act, it is because marriage implies a publicity beyond that of the family circle, and brings together all the members of the local Christian community. The bride and bridegroom are married before the Church, and not solely in the presence of God and their immediate family and friends. It was also necessary to exclude from this work all the forms for the veneration of saints, relics, images, and for the benediction of houses, firstfruits, etc. It would require another volume to deal adequately with these varied manifestations of individual and popular piety, which have received the protection, and indeed the encouragement, of the Church, without having been elevated by her to the dignity of those great rites which constitute the actual procedure of the ecclesiastical authority —that is, of the Christian priesthood. There is no place in this book for the consideration of the forms employed by the individual worshipping God in private. It is concerned solely with the assembly of Christians in the Church, and the prayers dealt with will therefore always have a collective character, in whatever measure the various members of the congregation may join in their outward expression.

To this first limit which I have set myself must

be added a chronological one. As I did not intend to treat of anything posterior to the eighth century, I have been obliged to omit certain ceremonies, some of them even of an imposing character, which were not introduced until a later date, or of which the ritual has come down to us in a form too far removed from its primitive condition. I allude especially to the rites connected with the inauguration of sovereigns, an act of great importance, whether viewed from the political or the religious standpoint. In France this ceremony is not older than the accession of the Carlovingian kings, and if we have reason to believe that it was practised somewhat earlier in the British Isles and in Spain, there is no document extant which enables us to gather the details of the ceremony at that remote date. The various rituals for the consecration of the emperors in the basilica of St. Peter at Rome have been recently classified, but none of them, in my opinion, goes back even as far as the ninth century.

Such is the scope of the present volume. I have thought it necessary to define it, in order that the reader may not look for that which I was neither capable nor desirous of including within its pages. It merely remains for me to add that the work I set myself to accomplish was that of the historian, or perhaps even of the antiquary, and that I had not the least desire to protest against the changes introduced into liturgical usages in the course of centuries or by the decisions of competent authorities. It is possible to take an interest in the history of the Merovingians without being suspected of harbouring a secret animosity against Pepin d'Héristal and Hugh Capet.

Neither was my main object that of edification. This book is by no means one to take to church to help the faithful to follow ceremonial worship more intelligently. There is a work which has been written for this purpose, and which is admirably suited to it—I allude to the *Année Liturgique* of Dom Guéranger. If, however, my volume is merely a text-book, I do not think that its perusal can tend to lessen in the reader, whoever he may be, that reverence and affectionate devotion which the venerable rites of our ancient mother the Catholic Church are entitled to command. If any expression has escaped me which might be construed otherwise, I should deeply regret it. These ancient rites are doubly sacred, for they come to us from God through Christ and the Church. But they would not possess in our eyes such a halo of glory about them had they not also been sanctified by the piety of countless generations. Throughout how many centuries have the faithful prayed in these words! What emotions, what joys, what affections, what tears, have found their expression in these books, these rites, and these prayers! I count myself happy indeed to have laboured in shedding fresh light upon an antiquity thus hallowed, and I gladly repeat with the *neocorus* of Euripides—

> Κλεινὸς δ'ὁ πόνος μοι
> θεοῖσιν δούλαν χέρ' ἔχειν,
> οὐ θνατοῖς ἀλλ' ἀθανάτοις·
> εὐφάμοις δὲ πόνοις μοχθεῖν
> οὐκ ἀποκάμνω.   *Ion.* 134.

TRANSLATOR'S PREFACE.

THE translator has to thank several friends for looking over the proof-sheets while the work was passing through the press, and among them the Rev. Canon F. E. Warren, B.D., F.S.A., whose extensive liturgical knowledge has been freely drawn upon whenever a difficulty arose as to the English equivalents of technical terms.

Since the third edition of this work was published a few weeks ago in Paris, Mgr. Duchesne has contributed some additional notes to the English version, in order to meet certain late criticisms. With these exceptions, and the addition of a few short notes by the translator marked [TR.], the English edition represents the French original in its integrity.

Christmas, 1902.

TRANSLATOR'S PREFACE TO THE SECOND EDITION.

THE text of the second English edition has been revised by the Author, who has made some important additions. The so-called *Peregrinatio Silviae* is now attributed to its real authoress, a Spanish Religious (p. 490), and her description of the services at Jerusalem, given in the Appendix, has been revised from the latest edition of the Arezzo MS, that of Mons. Paul Geyer. In response to several requests, an English translation of this excerpt has been added on p. 547, *et seq.* For this I am mainly indebted to my brother, the Rev. George Herbert, who had the advantage of many criticisms and suggestions from so eminent a scholar as the late Canon Chas. Evans, formerly Headmaster of King Edward's School, Birmingham.

Mgr. Duchesne has also inserted in the Appendix, the text of the *Exultet* of Bari, which will be found on p. 543.

In order not to disturb the pagination of the previous edition, which is uniform with that of the French, the new matter introduced into the text has, when it occupies one or more pages, been distinguished by a letter in addition to the number.

All Saints' Day, 1904.

TRANSLATOR'S PREFACE TO THE THIRD EDITION.

THIS edition represents the fourth and latest French edition, brought out at Paris in 1908. Monseigneur Duchesne has made one or two further additions to the present volume, which will be found on pp. 577A and B. The most important, which reached me just before going to press, is an account of the discovery at Monte Cassino by Dom André Wilmart of fragments of an Uncial MS., which on examination proves to be the earliest example known of a Gregorian missal. Although much mutilated, it is of special interest, as it is of far earlier date than the Sacramentary of Adrian, the script being attributable to *circa* 700.

LONDON,
    Easter, 1910.

TRANSLATOR'S PREFACE TO THE FOURTH EDITION.

MONSEIGNEUR DUCHESNE has carefully revised this new Edition and has contributed several fresh notes, which, in order not to disturb the pagination, have been placed in the Appendix, on pp. 577A *et seq.* He has also epitomised the latest theories with regard to the orthography of the name of the authoress of the *Peregrinatio Etheriae*, and the date of her MS. These will be found in note 1 on p. 547.

ATHELHAMPTON,
    Christmas, 1911.

PUBLISHER'S NOTE TO FIFTH EDITION

THIS edition contains the latest improvements suggested by Mgr. Duchesne, the most important of which is a new Appendix 6, in which extracts from Dom Connolly's book on "The Egyptian Church Order," with an introductory note, are substituted for the old "Canons of Hippolytus." Thanks are due to Dom Connolly and the Syndics of the Cambridge University Press for giving the necessary permission. There are also some fresh additional notes.

In July, 1918, Mrs. McClure, to whose zeal and erudition in translating this book and keeping it up to date English students owe so much, passed away, before she had corrected the proofs. They have been seen through the press with the help of a set of proofs annotated by Dom Connolly. It is hoped that no error of importance has crept in. It has not been possible to incorporate in the Index more than a few references to the new matter.

September, 1918.

THIS VOLUME

IS

DEDICATED

BY THE AUTHOR

TO THE MEMORY OF THE DISTINGUISHED ENGLISH
LITURGIOLOGIST

EDMUND BISHOP

TABLE OF CONTENTS.

	PAGE
PREFACE	iii

CHAPTER I.

ECCLESIASTICAL AREAS.

§ 1. Jewish and Christian Communities	1
§ 2. Local Churches—Episcopal Dioceses	11
§ 3. Ecclesiastical Provinces	13
§ 4. Patriarchates—National Churches	23

CHAPTER II.

THE MASS IN THE EAST.

§ 1. The Liturgy in Primitive Times	46
§ 2. The Syrian Liturgy in the Fourth Century	55
§ 3. The Oriental Liturgies	64
(1) Syria, p 65; (2) Mesopotamia and Persia, p. 69; (3) Cæsarea and Constantinople, p. 71; (4) Armenia, p 73	
§ 4. The Alexandrine Liturgy	75
(1) The Euchologion of Sarapion, p 75; (2) Later Liturgies, p. 79	
§ 5 Later Modifications	82

CHAPTER III.

THE TWO LITURGICAL USES OF THE LATIN WEST.

§ 1 The Roman and Gallican Uses	86
§ 2 Origin of the Gallican Use	90
§ 3 Fusion of the Two Uses ... ,,. ... ,, ,,.	96

CHAPTER IV.

LITURGICAL FORMULARIES AND BOOKS.

	PAGE
§ 1. The Forms of Prayer	106
§ 2. The Lections	112
§ 3. The Chants	113

CHAPTER V.

ANCIENT BOOKS OF THE LATIN RITE.

§ 1. Roman Books ... 120
(1) The Gregorian Sacramentary, p. 120; (2) The Gelasian Sacramentary, p. 125; (3) The *Missale Francorum*, p. 134; (4) The Leonian Sacramentary, p. 135; (5) The Roll of Ravenna, p. 144; (6) The *Ordines Romani*, p. 146

§ 2. Gallican Books ... 151
(7) The *Missale Gothicum*, p. 151; (8) The *Missale Gallicanum Vetus*, p. 152; (9) Masses published by Mone, p. 153; (10) The Lectionary of Luxeuil, p. 154; (11) The Letters of St. Germain of Paris, p 155; (12) British and Irish Books, etc., p. 156, (13) The Bobbio Missal, p. 158; (14) Ambrosian Books, p 160

CHAPTER VI.

THE ROMAN MASS ... 161

CHAPTER VII.

THE GALLICAN MASS ... 189

CHAPTER VIII.

THE CHRISTIAN FESTIVALS.

§ 1. Usual Observance of the Week	228
§ 2. The Ember Days	232
§ 3. Holy Week	234
§ 4. Movable Feasts	235

(1) The Computation of Easter, p. 236; (2) Eastertide, p. 239; (3) Lent, p. 241; (4) Holy Week, p. 247

5. The Immovable Feasts 257
(1) Christmas and Epiphany, p. 257, (2) The Festivals after Christmas, p 265B, (3) The Festivals of the Virgin and St

John Baptist, p. 269; (4) The Festival of the 1st of January, p 273; (5) The Festivals of the Holy Cross, p. 274; (6) St. Michael and the Maccabees, p. 276, (7) The Festivals of the Apostles, p. 277; (8) The Martyrs and other Local Festivals, p. 283; (9) Fasts, Octaves, and Litanies, p. 285; (10) Calendars and Martyrologies, p. 289

CHAPTER IX.

CEREMONIES OF CHRISTIAN INITIATION.

§ 1. Baptism according to the Roman Usage 294
   (1) Rites of the Catechumenate, p. 295, (2) Preparation for Baptism, p 298; (3) Blessing of the Holy Oils, p 305; (4) Baptism, p. 308; (5) Confirmation, p. 314; (6) First Communion, p 315
§ 2. The Gallican Baptismal Rite 316
   (1) The Catechumenate, p. 317; (2) Preparation for Baptism, p 319; (3) Baptism and Confirmation, p 320
§ 3. The Initiatory Rites in the Churches of the East 327
§ 4 Comparison of Rites, and their Antiquity 331
§ 5 The Reconciliation of Heretics 338

CHAPTER X.

ORDINATION.

§ 1. The Ecclesiastical Hierarchy 342
§ 2 Latin Ceremonies of Ordination 350
§ 3. Ordinations at Rome 352
   (1) The Minor Orders, p 352, (2) The Ordinations at the Ember Seasons—that is, of Priests and Deacons, p 353; (3) The Ordination of Bishops, p 359; (4) Ordination of the Pope, p. 362
§ 4. Ordinations according to the Gallican Rite 363
§ 5. Ordinations in the East 376

CHAPTER XI.

LITURGICAL VESTMENTS 379
   (1) The Tunicle and the Planeta, p 379; (2) The Dalmatic, p 382; (3) The "Mappula" and the Sleeves, p 383, (4) The Pallium, p 384; (5) The Stole, p. 390; (6) Shoes and Head-dress, p. 395, (7) The White Saddle-cloth of the Roman Clergy, p 396, (8) The Crozier and Ring, p 397

CHAPTER XII.

THE DEDICATION OF CHURCHES.

	PAGE
§ 1. Buildings consecrated to Christian Worship	399
§ 2. Roman Dedication Rites	403
§ 3 Gallican Dedications	407

CHAPTER XIII.

THE CONSECRATION OF VIRGINS.

§ 1. The Profession of Virgins ... 419
§ 2 The Rites of the *Velatio Virginum* ... 424
  (1) The Roman Use, p 424; (2) The Gallican Use, p. 425

CHAPTER XIV.

THE NUPTIAL BLESSING ... 428

CHAPTER XV.

THE RECONCILIATION OF PENITENTS ... 435

CHAPTER XVI.

THE DIVINE OFFICE ... 446

APPENDIX.

1. The Roman *Ordines* from the Manuscript of St Amand ... 455
2. The Roman *Ordo* for the Three Days before Easter ... 481
3. The Dedication Ritual in the Sacramentary of Angoulême ... 485
4. The Dedication Ritual according to the Use of the Bishop of Metz ... 487
5. Order of the Offices at Jerusalem towards the End of the Fourth Century ... 490
6. The "Apostolic Tradition" of Hippolytus ... 524
7. The *Exultet* of Bari ... 537
Translator's Note. Early Greek form of the *Ave Maria* ... 540
English Translation of No. 5 (Pilgrimage of Etheria (Silvia)) ... 541
Additional Notes ... 572

INDEX ... 577

CHRISTIAN WORSHIP:

ITS ORIGIN AND EVOLUTION.

CHAPTER I.

ECCLESIASTICAL AREAS.

§ 1.—JEWISH AND CHRISTIAN COMMUNITIES.

THE Christian Church arose out of Judaism. It was at Jerusalem that the preaching of the Gospel had its beginning, and it was through the medium of the Jewish communities of the Roman Empire that it reached the pagan world.

These Jewish colonies dated back to the time of Alexander's successors.[1] The Seleucidæ and the Ptolemies, who did so much to Hellenise the East, were not less successful in their efforts to force Judaism beyond its national limits. These two objects were subsidiary to each other. The new towns which were springing up throughout

---

[1] See Mommsen, *Röm Geschichte*, vol. v. p 489, *et seq.*; Schurer, *Gesch. des Jüd. Volkes*, vol. 11 p 493

the East were in need of an increase of population to ensure their prosperity. Since the time of the Exile the Jews had greatly increased in numbers, and colonists could readily be obtained from amongst them. Several dynasties of Asiatic rulers—Assyrians, Babylonians, Medes, and Persians—had already had demonstration of the tractable nature of the Israelites, of their disinclination to play any part in politics, and of their resigned and passive loyalty to their conquerors. No sovereign could wish to have more faithful subjects provided he was careful that their religious customs should not be interfered with. This was of vital importance. The Jews might be brought to live in the midst of Greeks, to speak Greek, and even to forget Hebrew; but to convert them to polytheism was a thing not to be thought of. Antiochus Epiphanes, who attempted it, could not congratulate himself on the success of his endeavour. On the other hand, apart from the question of religious assimilation, it was impossible to make a Jew into a true Greek, a *citizen* of an Hellenic town. This constituted an obstacle to colonisation, but it was surmounted by arranging that the Jewish colonists should not be introduced among the body of citizens, but assigned a privileged position among those who were non-citizens. They possessed an entirely separate administrative and judicial organisation,—a privilege not shared, for instance, by the Syrians of Antioch or the Egyptians of Alexandria. Each Jewish community rendered obedience to its own particular rulers, chosen from among its members; it constituted a sort of subordinate city, occupying an intermediate position between the Hellenic city and the subject population. The religious scruples of the Jews were, moreover, respected by law; they could not be compelled to break the Sabbath, as, for instance, by appearing in a court of justice, and they were exempt from certain burdens which were repugnant to them, such as military service.

ECCLESIASTICAL AREAS.

It was not only, however, into the cities of recent foundation that Jewish colonies were introduced; we find them, and that at an early date, in the Greek cities of the Ægean. There again they played a part amongst the "instruments of government" according to the custom of the Macedonian dynasties Into the midst of this restless population, stirred periodically by the remembrance of their ancient freedom, the Jews imported an element of order and loyalty to the established rule.

Once founded, these Jewish colonies developed rapidly, both by the natural increase of population, and the spontaneous immigration of their fellow-countrymen from Palestine, as well as by proselytism. Proselytism was favoured at this particular moment by the decay of religious belief throughout the whole of Greece. Jewish ideas with regard to the divinity, even if they differed widely from the polytheism of the people, were not opposed to the tenets of the Greek philosophers, which had spread largely among the cultivated classes. In that period of servility, the better spirits within the recently founded cities where the Greek decadence was unhappily allied to the old corruption of the East, might by a moral reaction be attracted towards Judaism. The Jew, moreover, far removed from Jerusalem and the Temple, displayed nothing narrow or exclusive in his faith, and became readily disposed to making converts. Many Jewish books were in circulation, in most cases under fictitious names, setting forth monotheism and a pure worship. Allegory, boldly employed, veiled those features of Hebrew history which might have offended the æsthetic sense of the Greek, and presented them in such a philosophic form as fell in with the fashion of the time. Philo of Alexandria was the most celebrated writer of this school. The principal obstacle to this kind of propaganda was the difficulty of conversion without a change of nationality. However diluted the Judaism of Philo might be, it still remained a religion peculiar to a foreign nation, and it was necessary to become a Jew in order to worship the god of the Jewish people. On the other hand, the Greeks for some time past had combined a respect for the externals of worship with the greatest latitude of opinion as to their efficacy, and even as to the nature of the gods. Philosophical speculation could readily be pursued without abandoning the national religion. Such a state of things, however, was not very favourable, on the whole, to the spread of Jewish belief among the true Hellenic population. There is ground to think that the Jewish propaganda obtained its chief success in another direction, namely, among those subject peoples without home or country, who were legally incapable of citizenship, and for whom union with the Jewish community meant a step upwards politically, while at the same time their initiation into the worship of God meant a step upwards spiritually.

However this may be, it is certain that the Jewish communities in the East, as also in Greece, had attained a considerable development by the time these countries were transferred to the Roman rule. The Romans accepted the situation and maintained and safeguarded the privileges granted to the Jews by the Macedonian rulers This organisation was part of the political machinery, and they were careful not to destroy it. They refrained, however, from importing it into the West. There was no doubt a Jewish colony in Rome, and that at a fairly early date; but it had no privileged position. More than once—under Tiberius in A.D. 19, and under Claudius in A.D. 54—it was broken up, and its members driven out of Italy. Rome, moreover, was at this period a semi-Greek city, and it was among its Greek-speaking inhabitants that the Jews were to be found, a fact which is evidenced by the exclusively Greek inscriptions on their tombs. The Jews never translated the Scriptures into Latin. The influx of their nation into the West is posterior to the early ages of Christianity.

Safeguarded outwardly by their privileges, provided with a recognised organisation, the Jewish communities of Greek-speaking countries were not attached to each other by any external bond. Their connection with the political authorities at Jerusalem was never manifest, not even during the short period in which the Maccabees made the Holy City the capital of a small independent kingdom. But the Jews felt themselves to be closely united together by the strongest ties,—by a common religion, and by a keen patriotic feeling, which, although uninfluenced for the moment by any political hopes, was still fostered by mysterious aspirations. Jerusalem, whatever her temporal rulers might be, always remained the ideal centre, the lodestar of the whole Jewish Dispersion. The ties which bound them to her were the annual tribute of the half-shekel, which every Israelite paid to the Temple of the Lord, and the pilgrimage thither, which every Jew had to make at least once in his lifetime

In contradistinction to the Holy City, Rome assumed in the Jewish mind, before long, the position of metropolis of the pagan world. The Greek kingdoms having passed away, and the ancient Greek cities having been reduced to insignificance, it was to the Italian capital that the spirit of Hellenism turned. The opposition between these centres soon manifested itself. From the time of the persecutions of Epiphanes onward, the Jewish race had been swayed by an undercurrent of hatred against Greek paganism—against the whole Hellenistic spirit, institutions, art, and religion. Jerusalem was the source from whence this undercurrent flowed. Here it was felt, and here it was preached, that there could be no truce between the empire of falsehood and evil, which from this time forward had its throne in the great Babylon of the West, and the kingdom of God, which the Messiah was shortly to set up in the Holy City of David.

We know how these hopes were frustrated. An open struggle at length broke out under the shadow of the Temple between the chief priests and the leaders of the fanatical masses. The triumph of the latter was soon expiated by the destruction of Jerusalem and its sanctuary. Attempts at reprisals under Trajan, and again under Hadrian, were promptly suppressed As a result of these misfortunes, the Jews of the Roman Empire were driven into an increasing antagonism to the world in which they had to live. Becoming daily more isolated, it devolved on the Christians to conduct the propaganda of monotheism. The Jews still, doubtless, constituted a nation, even more strongly characterised than before, and they still preserved, even after the destruction of the Temple, a centre, somewhat theoretical it is true, in the Talmudic school of the Tiberiad. But it soon became evident that the future, or at all events the immediate future, did not belong to them either in the sphere of politics or in the domain of religion.

Their former privileges were, nevertheless, maintained, and in this particular their position was a much stronger one than that of the Christian communities which had separated from them.

This separation was the foundation of the Church. It is not my aim to write here the history of the beginnings of Christianity. The general facts are well known. The apostles of Christ, as soon as they arrived in a locality, placed themselves in communication with the Jewish community, preached in their synagogue, and set forth the object of their mission. It does not appear that they ever were completely successful, and that the entire Jewish colony in any place accepted the Gospel. In most cases, after having recruited a certain number of adherents, they and their disciples were excommunicated by the elders of the synagogue. They then founded a fresh group, schismatical in relation to the older one, with its separate meetings and with a distinctive spirit, doctrine, and government. This was the origin of the local Christian communities, the beginning of the body of the faithful—in a word, the Church of Jesus Christ.

Detached one after another from the Jewish communities, and rapidly increased by an active propaganda among the pagan population, the Christian Churches soon realised that they were united together by a common feeling of faith, hope, and charity. The more they spread and increased in strength, the stronger this feeling revealed itself. It was a new religious brotherhood, a loftier and more ideal nationality looking for its realisation in the near future. Although on the earth, and in the world of reality, its expansion was not that of a race, nor its establishment a national one, for it had no local religious centre answering to Jerusalem and its Temple. It is true that this latter feature, which accentuated so strongly the difference between Jew and Christian, was soon to disappear. The triumph of Titus increased for a moment the resemblance between these two religious nations, both living in the heart of the Empire, and on several points in opposition to it.

Any resemblance and relationship between them was rather the resemblance and relationship of two hostile brothers. The question of privileges made this apparent from the outset. The Jewish communities were recognised; the Christian communities were not. Their existence was in contradiction to the law, and their development soon came to be considered wholly incompatible with the constitution, and even with the spirit, of the Empire. Hence the state of insecurity, and at times, of terror, in which the Christians lived until the reign of Constantine.

I have laid emphasis on the historical tie which connected the first Christian Churches with the Jewish communities scattered over the Greek-speaking world, because so close a relationship could not fail to be an important factor in determining the organisation of ecclesiastical government, and the form of public worship.

The Christian Churches appear before us in the earliest documents as having over them a hierarchy of two or three grades. The lowest grade is that of the ministers, or serving brethren, to whom were entrusted temporal matters, and who exercised the lower functions of divine worship. These were the deacons. Above them were the " elders," *presbyteri*, priests, or the "inspectors," *episcopi*, bishops. It is clear that in early times the use made of these terms was variable, as were also the functions assigned to the persons they designated. At any rate, it is certain that the priests or bishops who directed a local community, recognised the apostles, of whatever order, as possessed of superior authority, and as the founders and spiritual masters not only of an isolated Christian body, but either of all Christian bodies generally, or of those of particular regions. As these great leaders gradually passed away, a definitive hierarchy made its appearance. In each town, all the Christians and all their directors, *presbyteri*, *episcopi*, were ranged under a chief bishop, to whom this name of bishop was shortly after exclusively applied. Around him, and constituting with him a college, were his priest-counsellors; beneath them the deacons, who in their functions, already become varied and numerous, were not long after assisted by a whole staff of inferior ministers.

The question has been raised how far all this organisation grew out of that of the Jewish communities. It appears to me to have had its origin above all in the nature of things. It is indeed difficult to imagine a community of the sort that we are dealing with, without a council, a staff of working functionaries, and a head able to act and direct.[1] This was the hierarchy bequeathed by the apostles, in the dawn of

---

[1] This is an essential element in the constitution of corporations, as defined by Roman Law *Dig*, III., 4, 1.

Christianity, to the Church of Jerusalem, the first in point of time of all Christian Churches, and the most favourably placed in those early days to serve as a model. From this period the question under discussion loses much of its interest. It is one, moreover, somewhat difficult to treat with any degree of precision, owing to the paucity of the information we possess with regard to the organisation of the Jewish communities of the Dispersion. The condition of these differed widely. In some instances, where the Jewish population was considerable, several synagogues were to be found in one and the same town, although the Hebrew community as a whole was under a single ruler. This was the case at Alexandria, where the Jews were under the direction of their *Ethnarch*. At Smyrna, an inscription [1] mentions "the nation of the Jews;" but it does not state whether there also they had an ethnarch or some similar magistrate. If from the organisation of communities regarded as national bodies we pass to that of the synagogues, which in many cases must have served both purposes, the information is still more uncertain. The Gospels and the Acts of the Apostles frequently make mention of the rulers of the synagogue; but the information is rarely definite enough to enable us to determine whether each synagogue had one or several rulers. When they do exceptionally give us the distinct information we require, it is not of such a character as to enable us to infer the existence of a single and universally recognised type. In the district of Galilee, where the raising of Jairus's daughter took place, there were several "rulers of the synagogue." [2] In the locality where the woman with the spirit of infirmity was healed [3] there was only one. The same want of uniformity

---

[1] It deals with the payment of a fine, in a case of the violation of a burying-place, τῷ ἔθνει τῶν Ἰουδαίων. This inscription has been published by M. Salomon Reinach in the *Revue des Etudes Juives*, 1883, p. 161.
[2] Mark v. 22.
[3] Luke xiii 10, 14.

is manifested beyond the limits of Palestine: at Antioch in Pisidia there are several "rulers of the synagogue;" at Corinth, a single one.[1] This diversity in Jewish customs may possibly have contributed to produce that looseness in the use of terms, or in the actual differences, which meet us in the earliest Christian documents when they come to speak of the hierarchy of their newly founded Churches.[2] The real differences may have been very great; the primitive Churches were not all influenced to the same extent by the Christian social ideal. At Jerusalem they went so far as to recognise the community of possessions; but as a general rule they stopped a long way short of this.

The institution of the *Seven,* in the same Church, served later on as a support for the tradition that the number of deacons should not exceed that figure. In other Churches, where the duties to be performed were of a less complex nature, the number of the officials, as far as serving brethren were concerned, was more restricted. There was a similar class of persons employed in the synagogue; they are designated in the Gospel simply as ὑπηρέται (servitors).

In short, whether from imitation of the synagogue, or simply from the exigencies common to any community, the first Christians soon appeared equipped with a hierarchy of three grades. This hierarchy derived its powers directly or indirectly from the apostles themselves. As a rule, the community chose the individual, but the investiture was made either by the local bishop, or, when this office itself was in question, by the superior ecclesiastical authority representing the succession of the apostles.

---

[1] Acts xiii 15; xviii 8, 17

[2] Upon this question compare M l'Abbé Michiels' book, *Origine de l'Episcopat,* Louvain, 1900, and the bibliography attached to it

§ 2.—Local Churches—Episcopal Dioceses.

The ecclesiastical local body was at first constituted and organised on the model furnished by the Jewish communities, or at least under the influence of exigencies similar to those by which the Jewish communities themselves had been instituted and developed. Owing to the continuous advance made in the propagation of the Gospel, there came a time when, as a very early writer has remarked, "the children of the barren woman surpassed in number those of the fruitful woman."[1] The Christian population in each town rose from being an insignificant minority to a respectable minority, became afterwards the majority, and at length embraced the whole population. It passed through these various phases in different localities at widely different dates. Phrygia was almost entirely Christian when Gaul possessed only a very small number of organised Churches. The fourth century witnessed the final stage of this change in nearly every region, at least as far as the mass of the people in the towns were concerned. This immense development modified but very slightly the hierarchical organisation of the Churches. The number of ordained ministers increased; some changes, some specialisation of power arose, but the government remained monarchical throughout. It even tended to become more and more so. The priests continued to be the counsellors, the substitutes, the assistants of the bishop; the deacons and other lesser ministers were still engaged in temporal duties, charitable works, and the minor details of the service of God.

Roman municipal institutions, such as the *curiae*, the *duumviri*, and the *curatores*, furnished no models for imitation

---

[1] II so-called Epist. of Clement. 2.

to the Christian Church. It is a mistake to suppose with some that the documents of the fourth and fifth centuries afford ground for belief that the bishop had a share in the government of the city. It is not only impossible to demonstrate, but absolutely incompatible with the ecclesiastical law of the period with which we are dealing, that the clergy were identified with the curia, and that the bishop, under the title of *defensor civitatis*, took his place among the municipal magistrates. There is not any doubt that moral influence may have made itself felt, and that in the fourth and fifth centuries the religious rulers may indirectly have played a part in the government of the towns. But both in theory and practice the Church and the city, the clergy and the curia, the bishop and the municipal magistrates, continued to keep the limits of their respective domains distinct.

In one respect only, and that an important one, the administrative organisation of the Empire exercised a real influence on the development of ecclesiastical institutions. I refer to the areas of jurisdiction, municipal, provincial, or otherwise.

At the outset no question had been raised with regard to local limits. The Jewish colonies were always confined to the towns, and this was also the case with regard to the early Christian communities. As Christianity spread into the smaller towns and the country districts, it became necessary to know where the territory of each Church began and where it ended. The cities of the Empire, with their territories clearly marked out by the census, here presented limits already defined, against which no reason of a religious nature could be raised. It was admitted generally that each city should have its own bishop, and that its population should constitute a Church by itself. These areas, it is true, were very unequal. In some countries they were really provinces, as, for instance, Poitiers, Bourges, and many others in Gaul. In Africa, on the other hand, in Southern Italy, and in Western

Asia Minor, the towns, situated close to one another, had merely a narrow ring of suburbs. There were countries also like Cappadocia, into which municipal institutions were not introduced till a very late date, while in Egypt they were almost unknown. Such provinces were otherwise subdivided, nomes or *strategiae* forming the components.[1]

Elsewhere, there existed, among the metropolitan areas, immense domain lands, *nullius civitatis*, the rural population of which was ruled by procurators holding office directly under the provincial governors. The city limit was, however, the general rule, and the bishop's jurisdiction was co-extensive with the city, or some equivalent area, in nearly every instance during the fourth century and onwards.

§ 3.—Ecclesiastical Provinces.

But there were other ties between Christians besides those which bound together the members of a single Church within the territory of any one city. From the outset, Christians of all countries, no matter of what race or of what condition, had recognised one another as brethren. Apart from the ties arising from a common faith and hope, apart from the continuous relations established by charity, of which we have evidence in the early pages of Christian literature, there was at the beginning the perpetual intercourse of apostles, missionaries, prophets, and doctors,[2] who were

---

[1] I do not mean to infer that there were bishops of nomes, of *strategiae*, or of *saltus*. A special study of these particular cases has not yet been made, and this is not the place to put forward what I have been able to gather on the subject in the way of texts, observations, and conjectures

[2] *Doctors* is a very comprehensive word. I use it in the acceptation of

not attached in their ministry to any fixed locality, but who came and went from one Christian body to another, moving in all directions, either to carry the Gospel into regions whither it had not yet penetrated, or to encourage, instruct, and defend struggling infant communities.

At the close of the first epoch, when once all this itinerant, unattached, ministry had passed away, there remained nothing but the local ecclesiastical organisations. It was to these organisations that the hierarchical expression of the unity of the Church, and at the same time the provisions for its œcumenical and provincial government, were to owe their respective origins.

Jerusalem had ceased to exist except as a memory. After the destruction of the city under Titus, a small body of Christians were able to re-establish themselves there, but they remained for a long time obscure and unimportant. It was evident that the Holy City was not destined to become the metropolis of Christendom. It devolved on the great Babylon of the West, against whom the Jewish prophets had hurled so many imprecations, to take her place.

Although situated on the confines and even beyond the limits of the Greek world, Rome was, nevertheless, the centre to which that world was gravitating. From the moment that Christianity sought to embrace the whole *Orbis Romanus*, no other capital was possible. Rome was, moreover, as it were, consecrated by the preaching and the martyrdom of the two greatest apostles. The remembrance of them was still fresh. The other missionary apostles, with the exception of St. John, had disappeared, leaving but a vague memory behind them. In the absence of other than very fleeting traditions concerning them, it was all the more natural for them to

---

the Greek term διδάσκαλοι, which would perhaps be best rendered by *catechists*.

become the subject of legend. Rome, the capital of the Empire, the see of St. Peter, a place hallowed by the apostles, became the uncontested metropolis of the Church. The Easterns themselves, in spite of the long sojourn in their midst of the Apostle John, recognised the fact without raising any obstacle. At the end of the first century, the Roman Church, by the mouthpiece of Clement, intervened with imposing authority in the internal conflicts of the Church of Corinth, which was, however, equally of apostolic foundation. Hermas, shortly after, wrote his *Pastor* for all the Churches; and Ignatius, the Martyr Bishop of Antioch, calls attention to the pre-eminence of the Church of Rome. In the second century the whole of Christendom flocked thither—heretical doctors, orthodox travellers, apologists, bishops, inhabitants of Asia Minor, Syrians, people from Pontus, Palestine, and Egypt. Rome was, in short, the visible centre of all Christian activity, whether Catholic or heterodox. The great capitals, Carthage, Alexandria, Antioch, which played an important part hereafter, had not yet risen to any prominence. The Roman province of Asia alone counts for something; but its claims to importance were only secondary, as the conflict at the end of the second century with regard to the keeping of Easter clearly demonstrated.

This hierarchical pre-eminence, this general direction which had its seat at Rome, was, however, exercised without any thought of organising a special staff of officials. It was with the aid of the priests, deacons, and secretaries (*notarii*) of his Church, that the Bishop of Rome dealt with the affairs that came before him, or attended to the temporal and spiritual needs of the Churches which he deemed it incumbent on him to assist.

Among the latter, the communities of Southern Italy, already very numerous in the third century,[1] were bound by

[1] Eusebius, *Hist. Eccles*, vi 43.

close ties to Rome, from which, evidently, they had received their first apostles and their organisation. Metropolis of all Christendom, Rome was yet the centre of what might even then be called a provincial government, or of an ecclesiastical province.

Similar relations had been established, and for analogous reasons, in other countries around certain large towns. Carthage, for example, was always regarded as the centre of African Christianity, both as regards evangelisation and organisation. As early as the beginning of the third century, its bishop had become a primate, or a patriarch.[1] It was the same at Alexandria, and in a lesser degree at Antioch, the oldest of the Christian communities in the Greek world, and the centre of the earliest missions in Northern Syria, Cyprus, Asia Minor, Mesopotamia, and Persia. In Asia the missionary centres were more numerous, and authority was more conflicting, owing to the presence of so many celebrated cities, between whom a rivalry had existed from fabulous times. Ephesus never enjoyed more than a primacy of honour over Smyrna, Sardis, Pergamos, and the other Churches of this region.

These relations between mother and daughter communities may be taken into consideration in themselves, without regard to the internal development of their organisation. We have seen how, in the earliest Christian bodies, the single episcopate appears as the final stage of an hierarchical evolution of varying duration. Before this final stage had been reached, a body of Christians might already have evangelised its immediate and even remote neighbourhood, and formed colonies which were bound to her as to their Mother Church.

---

[1] This local authority, however, was at that time less felt in Africa than the higher authority of the Roman Church. This is particularly seen in the writings of Tertullian.

There was thus a metropolis without as yet a metropolitan. Such was the case, for example, in the Church at Antioch.

When such inter-relations were represented by the episcopate with its hierarchical staff, these are found to correspond with tolerable exactness to certain institutions of the Empire. We may compare the Bishops of Carthage, Alexandria, and Antioch to the Proconsul of Africa, to the Prefect of Egypt, and to the Legate of Syria respectively, but it is certain that there was no imitation intended. The forms of civil government in question arose out of geographical exigencies and from certain historical relations resulting from these exigencies. It was the same with the Christian primacies. The Bishop of Carthage became the chief of the African bishops, because it was from the Church of Carthage that the founders of the Churches of Africa had gone forth, and their starting out from that city was conditioned by the geographical disposition of the country which had made Carthage a natural centre. The same may be said of other *natural* metropolitan sees, which are the most ancient of all.

Beyond this, however, there is no farther resemblance, during the period anterior to the end of the third century, between the areas of the metropolitan sees of the Church and the provincial divisions of the Empire. What little we know of the councils held in those early times is sufficient to prove that there was no attempt to group the Churches according to the divisions of the civil provinces.

These councils, the earliest of which date back to the later years of the second century, constitute a very remarkable revelation of ecclesiastical inter-diocesan relations. At the time that Tertullian wrote his *De Jejuniis* (cir. 220) they were unknown in Africa; in the Greek-speaking countries, on the contrary, they were already an established institution.¹ Very shortly afterwards we find the Bishops of Carthage—Agrippinus, Donatus, Cyprian—gathering around them the bishops of all the African provinces. Mauritania, in the time of St. Cyprian, was not under the Proconsul of Carthage, and it is now known that Numidia, although bound to Africa by certain ties, as, for instance, by a common line of provincial custom-houses, had nevertheless its own governor. In spite of this, we see the bishops of all the African provinces ranging themselves round the Bishop of Carthage without our being able as yet to distinguish any other distribution. The primates of Numidia, for instance, were not instituted until a later date.

In Egypt, where there is no record of councils being held up to this period, the Bishop of Alexandria intervened not only in the affairs of the Churches of his own province,² but also in those of the Libyan Pentapolis, which at this time was under the administration of the island of Crete.³

In Syria, towards the close of the second century, a council held there to deal with the Easter controversy, brought together the Bishops of Cæsarea, Ælia, Ptolemais, Tyre, and others whose sees are not known to us.⁴ Now, Tyre and Ptolemais belonged at that time to the province of Syria (though shortly after to the new province of Phœnicia), while Ælia and Cæsarea were in the province of Palestine. This grouping, therefore, was not in any way conditioned by the distribution of the provinces. It was purely

---

[1] "Aguntur per Graecias illa certis in locis concilia ex universis Ecclesiis, per quae et altiora quaeque in commune tractantur et ipsa repraesentatio totius nominis christiani magna veneratione celebratur." —*De Jejuniis*, 13.

[2] For example, at Arsinoë (Eusebius, *Hist. Eccles*, vii. 24).

[3] Eusebius, *Hist Eccles*, vii 68.

[4] *Ibid*, v 23, 25.

geographical. The bishops of the southern slopes of the Lebanon were nearer to Cæsarea than to Antioch; they therefore went to Cæsarea. It is also noticeable that in their synodal letter, of which Eusebius has preserved a fragment, they state that they are in the habit of referring to the Bishop of Alexandria for fixing the date for keeping Easter. There is no trace of any relations with the metropolitan see of Syria.

This see, on the other hand, extended its influence beyond the boundaries of the province of Syria. Towards the end of the second century we find Sarapion, Bishop of Antioch, exercising his pastoral authority at Rhossos,[1] a town situated in Cilicia. According to the tradition of the Church of Edessa,[2] this same Sarapion had ordained Palouth, third occupant of the Mesopotamian see. In the time of Sarapion and Palouth, however, the town of Edessa had not yet become part of the Roman Empire.

In Asia Minor, about the middle of the third century, we find a Council at Iconium, at which bishops of wholly unconnected provinces—Cappadocia, Galatia, Cilicia, and others —are gathered together.[3]

We have, on the whole, as yet, no traces of a tendency to shape the ecclesiastical on the model of the civil provinces. But there is here and there a local ecclesiastical grouping either around the natural metropolitan sees or into regional councils embracing more or less extensive areas, according to circumstances.[4]

---

[1] Eusebius, *Hist Eccles*, vi. 12. [*Hod.* Arsus —Tr.]

[2] This tradition is preserved in the *Doctrina Addæi*, as well as in the acts of St Barsumas (Tixeront, *Les Origines de l'église d'Edesse* p. 140).

[3] Cypr, *Ep*, lxxv. 7. Iconium and Lycaonia then formed part of the province of Cilicia. See *Bulletin de corresp. Hellénique*, vol. vii. p. 290; vol xi p 351.

[4] It has been often stated of late that the Christian Hierarchy of Bishops and Metropolitans owed its origin to the Hierarchy of the municipal and

20   CHRISTIAN WORSHIP: ITS ORIGIN AND EVOLUTION.

Under the latter category, mention must be made of Antioch as one of such centres from the middle of the third century onwards. On various occasions we find the bishops of all Syria gathered together there, as well as those of Eastern Asia Minor, which shortly after was to become the diocese of Pontus. As early as the year 251 we find mention of a synod, which must have been held at Antioch, on account of Fabius, bishop of that place, appearing to favour Novatianism. The promoters of this council were the Bishops of Tarsus, Cæsarea in Palestine, and Cæsarea in Cappadocia.[1] A few years later, in 256, Dionysius of Alexandria,[2] in enumerating the Churches of the East which had been disturbed by this conflict, mentions those of Antioch, Cæsarea in Palestine, Ælia (Jerusalem), Tyre, Laodicea in Syria, Tarsus, and Cæsarea in Cappadocia. Subsequently, from 264 to 268, the case of Paul of Samosata necessitated the meeting of several bishops at Antioch in the interests of that Church. On each occasion they come from the same provinces, from Pontus Polemoniacus (Neocæsarea) and Lycaonia (Iconium) from as far as Arabia (Bostra) and Palestine (Cæsarea, Ælia). Immediately after the persecution of Galerius and Maximianus, a celebrated council was held at Ancyra, presided over by the Bishop of Antioch, at which some fifteen bishops from the same countries were again present; this time, however, the provinces of Galatia, Bithynia, Phrygia, and Pamphylia are repre-

provincial Priesthood of Rome in the time of Augustus. It is difficult to imagine a more erroneous idea, or one more at variance, both with the documents and the nature of the institutions thus compared. Those who originated such a singular notion have allowed themselves to be misled by an empty resemblance. They have, moreover, refrained from producing any proofs, and have not studied the question seriously When confronted with such a gratuitous statement, I cannot do more here than charitably point out the fruitlessness of their too oft repeated line of argument.

[1] Eusebius, *Hist. Eccles*, vi. 46.
[2] *Ibid.*, vii. 5

ECCLESIASTICAL AREAS.

sented, but Asia, properly so called, still remained outside the group.

The sees above mentioned form, as it were, the nucleus of what was called in the fourth century the Episcopate of the *Orient*, which was perpetually engaged in conflict about certain individuals and formularies with the bishops of the West and of Egypt. The designation which it bore was derived from its undisputed primate, the Bishop of Antioch —that great city at this time the capital of the immense diocese of the Orient, the residence of the *Comes Orientis*, and since the time of Constantius, of the Emperor of the East himself. Shortly before this Nicomedia had been the Imperial residence, and, though Constantine was occupied in planning a great future for his new Rome, the time had not yet come for its realisation. Up to the reign of Theodosius, Antioch remained Queen of the East, the centre to which the Greek Empire and its chief ecclesiastical metropolis gravitated, the ancient Churches of Asia and the Christian communities of the diocese of Thracia being drawn within its circle of influence. Alexandria resisted its attraction. The opposition shown by Athanasius to the councils of the East was warmly supported by the Egyptians. Their hatred to Syria dated back from the very earliest times. The Egyptians had been formerly placed under the rule of the *Comes Orientis*, and a dignitary of no lower rank had now to be granted to them, and hence the prefect Augustal made his appearance there under Theodosius. An attempt was made to impose upon them bishops from Antioch ordained by the metropolitan of that city, but they obstinately refused to recognise them, and at length succeeded in this point also, in spite of all Imperial insistence.

These considerations have carried us somewhat beyond the third century, but they may serve to show that the further Christianity spread the more its limits were conditioned by the same geographical and historical influences which had determined those of the Empire. Some assimilation between the two was therefore inevitable. In the East this took place much sooner than in the West, on account of the vast numerical superiority of the Oriental Christians over those of the latter. At the Council of Nicæa,[1] the classification of bishops according to provinces and their subordination to the bishop of the civil metropolis were already accomplished facts. This arrangement was the basis for legislation in the matter of ordinations and with regard to ecclesiastical jurisdiction, as well as for regulating certain special cases. The provinces with which the Council had to do were those of the time, viz. those that Diocletian had formed out of the older provinces.[2] Ecclesiastical provinces were not instituted by the Council of Nicæa, for they were in existence previously in the East. There was nothing as yet corresponding to them in the West, except perhaps in Africa, where the bishops of the province of Numidia had possessed a senior or primate of their own from the time of Diocletian and Maxentius onwards.[3] But all the provinces of Africa had not arrived at this stage. That of Mauritania Sitifensis remained incorporated with Numidia until the Council of Hippo held in 393[4] These African primates, moreover, must be distinguished from metropolitans, properly speaking. There was no ecclesiastical metropolis in Africa, unless at Carthage. The provincial primate was simply the senior of the bishops of the province, wherever his see might be. It is possible that in Spain there was some organisation of

[1] Canons 4–7.
[2] See Mommsen, *Mémoire sur les provinces romaines*, trans by Picot, Paris, Didier, 1867 (from the *Revue Archéologique* of 1866); Jullian, *De la réforme provinciale attribuée à Dioclétien*, in the *Revue Historique*, vol xix (1882) p 331.
[3] This may be gathered from the documents dealing with the origin of the Donatist Schism
[4] *Cod can Ecclesiae Afr* , c 17

this kind. A somewhat obscure expression in the decrees of the Council of Elvira gives colour to this conjecture.[1] Elsewhere, throughout the whole of the West, up to the Danube and the Adriatic, no trace exists of ecclesiastical divisions according to provinces or of metropolitan jurisdiction in the Eastern sense of the word.

The Council of Nicæa made special provision in its sixth canon for certain cases which did not fall in with provincial distribution. The chief exception was that of the Bishop of Alexandria, who was accredited with powers to settle all ecclesiastical affairs, especially ordinations, throughout the whole of Egypt and in the two Libyan provinces. In support of this exception, the example of the Bishop of Rome was cited, who also exercised jurisdiction over a large number of Churches without the mediation of metropolitans. It is not stated precisely what were the privileges granted in the case of the Bishop of Antioch, but his case was specially considered. The council also mentions other exceptions without indicating them by name. It is possible that these were in Western Christendom, where, indeed, other usages obtained. Moreover, the Council of Nicæa, like all Eastern councils, even when they were œcumenical, legislated mainly for the East, and took but little heed of what was passing in the West.

§ 4.—PATRIARCHATES—NATIONAL CHURCHES.

The organisation by provinces by no means represents the limit of approximation which had been established in

[1] Canon 58: *Placuit ubique et maxime in eo loco in quo prima cathedra constituta est episcopatus, ut interrogentur hi qui communicatorias litteras tradunt.* It is not certain that *prima cathedra episcopatus* does not mean simply the episcopal chair, in contradistinction to the *plebes* or parishes established in the towns or villages

the East between ecclesiastical and civil jurisdiction. Over the governors of provinces Diocletian had established rulers of dioceses, or vicars. In the eastern division of the Empire these dioceses were at first four in number—those of the Orient, of Pontus, of Asia, and of Thrace. About the time of Theodosius, this number was increased to five by the creation of the diocese of Egypt, taken out of the jurisdiction of the *Comes Orientis*. At the Council of Constantinople in 381, these five dioceses were adopted as bases for an ecclesiastical jurisdiction superior to that of the metropolitans and provincial councils.

This superior jurisdiction was assigned, in the diocese of Pontus, to the Bishop of Cæsarea in Cappadocia, and in the diocese of Asia, to the Bishop of Ephesus. In the diocese of Thrace, Constantinople, thenceforward the Imperial residence, gave the title to the see. But the bishops of the Eastern capital were not content to remain long the ecclesiastical rulers of one diocese only. The Council of 381 had given them precedence of the whole episcopate, after the Bishop of old Rome. Constantinople being, from the civil point of view, the exact counterpart of the ancient metropolis of the Empire, the Fathers of the Council considered that, from the ecclesiastical standpoint, it ought also to take precedence over all the cities of the East. This decision, it is true, was not accepted at Rome, and its confirmation seventy years later by the Council of Chalcedon was equally fruitless. The Popes adhered to the ancient traditions, and, in spite of the claims of the bishops of the Imperial city, persisted in maintaining for the ancient sees of Alexandria and Antioch their privileges of antiquity and honour.

The Popes' contention received but scant attention; doubtless some satisfaction was accorded them, but merely as a matter of courtesy. The Bishop of Constantinople assumed more and more the position of a sort of Pope of the Oriental Empire, and the obstacles he met with in so doing were one after another swept away.

The Church of Alexandria was the most energetic in defending its privileges. The obstinacy of ancient Egypt, its extreme centralisation concentrated in its patriarch, the zeal and prestige of its monks, together with the traditional and marked support given to it by the Roman Church, enabled the see of St. Mark to maintain its independence for a long time. Men like Theophilus, Cyril, and the Dioscori on more than one occasion made the bishops of the Imperial city to feel their power. Heresy was the cause of their ruin. The Roman Church on the one hand found itself at length obliged to abandon the successors of Athanasius, and the Council of Chalcedon on the other was the means of humbling the pride of the ecclesiastical Pharaoh. Thenceforward, split up into factions, exposed to internal quarrels and secular troubles which alienated it from the Empire, Christian Egypt fell an easy prey to Islam, and its separation became an accomplished fact.

The remainder of the Eastern world was accustomed to regard the capital as its centre. Antioch having lost this position from the time of Theodosius, the entire East now looked to Constantinople. The three northern dioceses, originally cut off from the ancient capital, were soon seized upon by the new. The Bishops of Constantinople, upheld, it must be admitted, by general opinion, soon began to interfere in the ecclesiastical affairs of neighbouring dioceses. Several instances of this interference, not without resistance in some cases, had already occurred,[1] when the Council of Chalcedon gave the Bishop of Constantinople the right of consecrating the provincial metropolitans of the three dioceses, reserving only to the latter the ordination of their suffragans. The same right of ordination was granted to him in the case of the rulers of those national Churches

---

[1] See Tillemont, *Hist. Eccles.*, vol xv p. 702.

which derived their authority from the three dioceses already mentioned (can. 28). He was invested, moreover, with a jurisdiction coextensive with that of the civil rulers of dioceses (exarchs), enabling him to decide in ecclesiastical cases brought up before the metropolitans (cans. 9, 17).

In this manner the occupants of the sees of Cæsarea, Cappadocia, and Ephesus gradually lost all authority over the bishops of their respective provinces; they at length became mere metropolitans, whose only honours consisted in a few titular privileges and in distinctions of precedence. By the fusion of the three dioceses of Thrace, Asia, and Pontus, the patriarchate of Constantinople thus became established.

It was not, however, in this matter alone that the area of ecclesiastical influence exercised by Antioch had become restricted. It might be supposed that the diocese of Orient, considerably reduced by the withdrawal of Egypt, would have constituted the province of the patriarchate of Antioch. But such was not the case. At the very beginning of the fifth century we find the Bishops of Cyprus defending the independence of their province against the patriarch. Pope Innocent intervened[1] in favour of the claims made by Antioch, but the issue of his action is not known. The Cypriots availed themselves of the opportunity afforded by the Council of Ephesus (431), which was ill disposed towards Antioch and the Syrian bishops, to wrest from that assembly an express recognition of their independence, and of the autocephalic privilege of the island.[2] But at Antioch the question was not regarded as definitely settled. In 488, the patriarch, Peter the Fuller, who had considerable influence at Court and with the Bishop of Constantinople, succeeded in bringing great pressure to bear upon the

---

[1] Jaffé, 310.
[2] VIIth session, Hardouin, vol 1 p. 1619.

insular bishops. Their cause was all but lost when the tomb of St. Barnabas, the apostle of the country, was suddenly discovered near Salamis. This event, which was regarded as an intervention of Providence, brought about a reaction.[1] The ecclesiastical province of Cyprus had its autonomy confirmed, and has remained in possession of it to this day.[2]

Again, it was at the Council of Ephesus that the first official attempt was made to create a patriarchate at Jerusalem. The Council of Nicæa had granted the Bishop of Jerusalem some special honours; but, far from raising him to the position of an arch-metropolitan, the Council had still left him under the jurisdiction of his provincial metropolitan, the Bishop of Cæsarea. A century later, we find the ambitious and somewhat unscrupulous Juvenal, Bishop of Jerusalem, exalting the honorary distinctions granted to his see into a power of jurisdiction, and encroaching boldly on the domain of the Patriarch of Antioch. At the Council of Ephesus he endeavoured to get his action legalised, and persistently claimed half of the Syrian provinces, viz. the three Palestines (Cæsarea, Scythopolis, Petra), together with the Phœnicia of the Lebanon (Damascus), and Arabia (Bostra). His pretensions were not allowed. Twenty years later, however, at the Council of Chalcedon, he returned to the charge. He entered into an arrangement with the Patriarch of Antioch, by which the three provinces of Palestine were made over to him. St Leo, the Pope, though much displeased at the transaction, did not, however, formally annul it, and from thenceforward the arrangement has remained unchanged.[3]

---

[1] Assemani, *Bibl Orient*, vol. ii. p. 81; Theodorus Lector, ii. 2; *Acta Sanct*, June 11th

[2] It is possible that this autonomy existed from earliest times. The Council of Ephesus based its recognition of it on an ancient and well-attested tradition

[3] Council of Chalcedon, *actio* vii , Jaffé, 495

In this way the great ecclesiastical areas of the East were defined, from the middle of the fifth century onwards, viz. the patriarchates of Constantinople, Antioch, Jerusalem, and Alexandria, with the autonomous province of the island of Cyprus.

Outside the patriarchates and beyond the frontiers of the Empire there still existed the national Churches of Ethiopia, Persia, and Armenia. These Churches, founded respectively by those of Alexandria, Antioch, and Cæsarea in Cappadocia, were looked upon as subject to these great sees. That of Ethiopia did not date back farther than the time of St. Athanasius. Its metropolitan, whose seat was at first at Axum, was, and still is, ordained by the Patriarch of Alexandria.[1]

The Church of Persia, far more ancient than the above, had been in existence as early as the close of the second century. Barely tolerated by the Parthian kings, it was often persecuted under the Sassanids. Its ruler resided at Seleucia. When, towards the close of the fifth century, the Nestorians were proscribed, and banished from the Empire, they took refuge beyond the Persian frontier, and Nestorianism, introduced by them, became, after a fashion, the national religion of the Christians of the Sassanid kingdom. This circumstance afforded them increased security, and they availed themselves of their position to found in Malabar, and even in distant China, Churches which exist, or of which traces are preserved, even to the present day.

Christianity was introduced into independent Armenia towards the latter end of the third century. National tradition makes St. Gregory the Illuminator the first apostle

---

[1] The foundation of the Church of Nubia is not earlier than the time of Justinian It, too, occupied the position of suffragan to Alexandria See my *Eglises Séparées*, p 287 *et seq*

of the country, but with no less precision it connects his apostolate with the Church of Cæsarea. As a fact, till about the fifth century, the Armenian Catholicos was consecrated at that place.[1]

Beyond the Danube, which constituted the frontier of the diocese of Thrace and of the Empire, there was also a foreign Church—that of the Goths, the origin of which was connected with the great invasion in the time of Valerian and Gallienus. It was to the missionary efforts of the prisoners, which these Germanic tribes carried away from Pontus and Cappadocia, that they owed their conversion. A Gothic bishop, possibly the only one existing in the country, was present at the Council of Nicæa. Another, the celebrated Ulfilas, who was won over at an early date to Arianism, spread that heresy among his compatriots. When the Arian Goths, in 376, crossed the Danube and settled within the territory of the Empire, they soon came into conflict with Nicæan orthodoxy, which had been restored by Theodosius. This was also the case with the other barbarians, amongst whom, from the close of the fourth century, Christianity in its Arian form had spread with great rapidity. The invasions of the following century renewed not only the conflict of Germanic barbarism and Latin civilisation, but also that of Arianism and orthodoxy.

In the West, at an early date, we meet with two strongly centralised ecclesiastical groups—that of the Italian peninsula and that of the African provinces.

As far back as the year 251, Pope Cornelius was able to

---

[1] Mention must also be made of the little national Church of Iberia, or Georgia, the foundation of which is recorded by Rufinus (*Hist. Eccles.*, i. 10). The Bishop of the Iberians, who at a later date bore the title of Catholicos, or Exarch, resided at Tiflis Albania, to the east of Iberia, had also, down to the tenth century, its own Catholicos.

gather round him a council of sixty bishops,[1] who were mainly Italians from Southern Italy, for, in the North, there were, until the fourth century, very few episcopal sees.[2] Italy was not, as yet, divided into provinces, as the division did not take place till the end of the third century. By that time things had already taken definite shape. The Pope exercised his authority as superior, without any intermediary, over all the bishops of the peninsula. When the Italian islands were brought into connection with the suburbicarian diocese, their bishops naturally formed part of this group. Those of Caralis and Syracuse succeeded in obtaining some special honours for their sees, but that was all. The Pope remained the only real metropolitan of the Italian peninsula and its islands.

I have already spoken of ecclesiastical centralisation in Africa. There, the primacy of Carthage did not prevent a certain provincial grouping of the episcopate around the senior bishop of each province. In the African councils, of which we have so large a number, it is always necessary to distinguish between those that are provincial only and those that are general, convoked and presided over by the Bishop of Carthage. But these different groupings are merely the outcome of the organisation of one large united and vigorously active body No ecclesiastical group is more clearly specialised than that of North Africa, just as no region of the Empire is more clearly isolated from the rest by its natural boundaries.

In Southern Italy, and specially in Africa, the episcopal sees were very numerous. The same cannot be said of the rest of Western Christendom. In the part of Italy watered

---

[1] Eusebius, *Hist Eccles*, vi. 43

[2] The only sees that have any serious claim to an antiquity prior to the fourth century are those of Ravenna (Classis), Milan, Aquileia, Brescia, and Verona The two first appear to have been founded about the beginning of the third century, or even a little earlier.

by the Po, in the Danubian provinces, in Gaul, Spain, and Britain, whether owing to the fact that the cities in these regions included a large extent of territory, or that it was not thought advisable to place a bishop in each, the episcopal areas were more extensive and numerically smaller. This fact probably accounts for the late grouping of them into provinces and assigning them metropolitans. In Northern Italy there was at first one metropolitan only, that of Milan, whose jurisdiction extended over the whole diocese of Italy so called. Towards the beginning of the fifth century this province was made into two by the formation of the metropolitan see of Aquileia. A little later the province of Emilia furnished some suffragans to the Bishop of Ravenna, when this town became the Imperial residence. Ravenna, however, was included within the area of the metropolitan rule of the Pope, and hence its bishop remained a suffragan of the Roman see, although he was himself metropolitan of the sees of the province of Emilia which had been detached from that of Milan.

Britain and the Pannonian provinces were separated from the Empire before the system of ecclesiastical metropolitans could be introduced into them respectively. At all events there is no documentary evidence to the contrary. In the fifth and sixth centuries, what remained of the Upper Danubian provinces was divided between the two Italian metropolitan sees of Milan and Aquileia. Rhætia Prima (Coire) was under the jurisdiction of Milan; Rhætia Secunda (Augsburg, Seben), Noricum (Tiburnia), Pannonia Prima (Scarbantia), formed part of the Council of Aquileia.[1] In Gaul and Spain the metropolitan system was introduced

[1] See the signatures of the Council of Milan, in 451, and those of the Councils of Aquileia, under the patriarchs Helias and Severus, in the *Chronicon Gradense*, and in the History of the Lombards, by Paulus Diaconus, III. 26 (*Mon. Germ Script Lang*, p 397, 107). Cf the letter of the suffragans of Aquileia to the Emperor Maurice (*Greg M. Reg*, 1 16a)

towards the end of the fourth or the beginning of the following century.

Gaul, Spain, and Britain are countries of which the limits are clearly defined by nature. In the fourth century the difference in the degree of civilisation which possibly existed, for instance, between Bœtica and Spain, and between the region of Narbonne and the *Tres Galliæ*, had become considerably less apparent. If the Roman Empire had lasted, it is possible that Spanish, Gallic, and British ecclesiastical groups might have been formed, of which the centre would have been determined by the convergence of the lines of administration. The ecclesiastical province of Arles, which in no way corresponds with the civil province of Vienne, took its origin in that way. But the Barbarian invasions, and the redistribution which followed, put a stop to any development on these lines, and the ecclesiastical provinces of Gaul and Spain remained independent of all superior authority or organisation until they emerged at length as the two national Churches of the Visigoths and the Franks.

We must not, however, ignore the peculiar position which Milan held, towards the end of the fourth century, as a centre of influence, which was felt more in Gaul than elsewhere. For a short but important period it would thus appear that the Western episcopate recognised a twofold hegemony—that of the Pope and that of the Bishop of Milan.

This divided authority became first apparent in the time of St. Ambrose. The see of that illustrious bishop was regarded with a respect that was quite exceptional—without prejudice, of course—to the authority of the apostolic see. The influence of Ambrose made itself felt in the affairs of the Eastern Church—at Antioch, at Cæsarea, at Constantinople, and at Thessalonica, and he it was who was commissioned to provide Sirmium with a bishop at a critical moment of its history. At Aquileia he presided over a council at which the last difficulties connected with the Arian crisis in the Lower Danubian provinces were disposed of. It is, however, particularly in Gaul and Spain that the ecclesiastical authority of Milan seems to have been accepted as a natural and superior tribunal.

About the year 380 we find the Priscillianists of Spain bringing their cause both before Pope Damasus and Bishop Ambrose. Long after the bloody executions of Treves, at a time when the position of the dissentients in Spain was in question again, both sides approached the Bishop of Milan. The Galician prelates, who had remained faithful to the traditions of Priscillian, had been summoned by their colleagues assembled in Council at Toledo to appear before them. They refused to acknowledge the jurisdiction of the latter, but the foremost among the dissentients, Symposius, the aged Bishop of Astorga, and his son Dictinius, repaired to Milan. Ambrose imposed very hard conditions upon them, which, nevertheless, they promised to fulfil. Pope Siricius acted with him in this matter, and advised the same solution of the difficulty. But this decision did not put an end to the conflict. In the year 400, after the death of both Siricius and Ambrose, a fresh council assembled at Toledo, and was successful this time in securing the attendance of the Galician prelates. Several difficulties were then settled, but on some points the council, mistrusting its own authority, or failing to come to an agreement, made a formal appeal both to the new Pope Anastasius, and to Simplicianus, the successor of St. Ambrose.

Not only in Spain, but also in Gaul, Priscillianism had sown dissensions amongst the bishops. Some of these accepted, while others refused, communion with Felix, Bishop of Treves, who had been ordained with the concurrence of the opponents of Priscillian. The contest was carried before the tribunal of the Bishop of Milan in the first instance, probably during the lifetime of St. Ambrose It was, indeed, very likely to deal with this business that the meeting of the Synod of Milan *propter adventum Gallorum episcoporum* was held, which was in session when the news of the massacre at Thessalonica reached Ambrose.[1] The Bishops of Octodurus (Martigny) and of Orange were present.[2] They had already attended, a few years before, in 381, the Council of Aquileia.

Later on, about A.D. 400, the Council of the Bishop of Milan assembled afresh at Turin, to pass judgment this time not on one, but on several disputed points which the Churches of Gaul had referred to it. The following questions were submitted to it—the dispute between the Bishop of Marseilles and the bishops of Gallia Narbonensis secunda, the quarrel for precedence between the Churches of Arles and Vienne, the difficulty as to communion with Felix of Treves, and many other points of discipline and law of minor importance upon which we are imperfectly informed. Upon all these the Synod of Turin gave decrees and judgment without the slightest hesitation as to its competence. Before the Bishop of Milan, the most important Bishops of Gaul felt themselves in presence of a superior authority, and believed themselves bound to accept his decisions. As a fact, the decrees of the Council of Turin were inserted in all the canonical collections compiled in Gaul, and were regarded there as one of the most authoritative texts in the matter of ecclesiastical law.

The Churches of Spain and Gaul, however, were not alone

---

[1] Ambrose, *Ep.* 51

[2] This must have been the council that gave its adherence to the condemnation of Jovinian. The names of Theodore and of Constantius appear at the end of the synodal letter addressed to Pope Siricius (Ambr., *Ep.* 42), though without indication of their sees It is generally admitted that they may be identified with the two bishops of the same names who took part in the Council of Aquileia—that is, the Bishops of Octodurus and of Orange

in appealing to Milan. The Church of Africa also attached extreme importance to the decisions pronounced by this illustrious see. In 393, the General African Council, held at Hippo, thought it advisable to withdraw the prohibition which prevented their clergy from ministering to the Donatists who had received in infancy schismatic baptism. But as this involved the infringement of a general law of the Church, it was thought necessary first to consult the "Church across the sea." Political events interfered with the accomplishment of this project. The question was brought up again in another general council held at Carthage in 397. The decision arrived at by that assembly indicated expressly that Siricius and Simplicianus should be consulted The replies sent from Rome and Milan were unfavourable; but after the death of Siricius and Simplicianus the Africans made a fresh application to Anastasius and Venerius, their successors. The General Council of June, 401, sent as a deputy to the latter a bishop charged to explain to them the desirability of the concession demanded.

There are thus evidences of an universal tendency, about the close of the fourth century, to regard the Bishop of Milan as an authority of the first order, and to associate him with the Pope in the exercise of the functions of supreme ecclesiastical magistrate, that is as judge in important causes, and as interpreter of the laws of general discipline. This extraordinary position ascribed to the Bishop of Milan did not owe its existence to the antiquity of his Church, which did not date farther back than the end of the second century, nor to the celebrity of its founders, for they are quite unknown to us. The earliest facts pointing in this direction are to be referred to the episcopate of St. Ambrose, but the personal merits of that great bishop are not sufficient to account for this attitude of the Latin episcopate towards the see of Milan. There was no lack in the West at that moment of prelates renowned for their zeal, sanctity, and enlightenment. St. Martin and St. Augustine both belong to this period. The real reason was that Milan was the Imperial official residence, the capital of the Western Empire. It had enjoyed this position from the close of the preceding century, on the reorganisation of the Empire under Diocletian and Maximianus. At the period with which we are dealing its supremacy became more and more accentuated. From the death of Maximus, in 388, Treves had ceased to be the second capital. The importance of Ravenna was still a thing of the future, for it was not till 404 that the Emperor Honorius took up his abode there Even then a certain time must have elapsed before his residence could have taken definite effect and have produced its consequences in ecclesiastical circles. Milan was therefore without a rival, and its ecclesiastical position was becoming established on the same lines as that of Constantinople. As early as the reigns of Constans and Constantius several councils had been held there, and it was there, rather than at Rome, that the two Churches of the East and West found a point of contact. Thither the formularies elaborated at Antioch were brought, and there the Latin bishops and their delegates were called together and assembled under the eye of the emperor. Milan was thus, even before the middle of the fourth century, the great centre of ecclesiastical interrelations in the West, and that solely on account of its being the capital of the Empire. Constantius filled the see with an Arian bishop named Auxentius, an able and energetic man, who succeeded in maintaining his position after the defeat of his party in the West, and remained there till 375 the personification of the doctrine of Ariminum. There was doubtless then a lull in the competition of which the Imperial Church was the prize, but the election of St. Ambrose was soon to remove all difficulties and to shed a lustre upon the see which should render it famous for all time

Those who had recourse to Milan at the same time that

they appealed to Rome, or even in preference to Rome, had certainly no intention of creating an opposition between these two great authorities, or even of placing the Imperial Church on a level with the apostolic see. This appeal to them was made simultaneously on the supposition that they could not act otherwise than in concert, and the issue invariably justified this assumption. When the appeal was made to Milan alone, as the Gallican Bishops are known to have done on several occasions, it was only because Milan was nearer to them and for this reason had a better opportunity of obtaining information. Questions continued to be submitted to Rome all the same. We may point out as instances of such appeals, those of Himerius, Bishop of Tarragona, in 384, of Victricius, Bishop of Rouen, in 403, and of Exuperius, Bishop of Toulouse, in 404. We still possess the decretals of Siricius and Innocent,[1] in which they replied to the questions submitted by these bishops of Spain and Gaul.

The pre-eminent position, however, of the see of Milan could not have been further accentuated without in the end establishing a precedent which might be cited against the pre-eminence of Rome. The Popes soon realised this, and neglected no opportunity of defending themselves against this incipient rivalry. It is not known what part they took in the foundation of the metropolitan see of Aquileia, but it is certain that they helped to create the metropolitan diocese of Ravenna, formed at the expense of that of Milan.[2] In a letter addressed to the Bishop of Eugubium, his suffragan, Pope Innocent points out, not without a certain incisiveness

---

[1] Jaffé, 255, 256, 293 We may add the *Synodus Romanorum ad Gallos Episcopos* (Constant, *Epp. Rom Pontif*, p. 685), which it is supposed was drawn up under Siricius or Innocent It is perhaps rather earlier (E. Babut, *La plus ancienne décrétale*. Paris, 1904).

[2] St Peter Chrysologus, sermon 175.

of style, the inconsistency of those who do not follow in all things the usages of the Roman Church. He asks them if they have read anywhere that the Churches of Italy, Gaul, and Spain owe their foundation to others than to St. Peter and his successors. It will be seen further on that this letter testifies, more fully than I can indicate here, to the opposition between the two great Italian metropolitan sees.

Under Pope Zosimus, the successor of Innocent, the primacy of Milan received a blow, which, although of an indirect character, was none the less decisive. I refer to the foundation of an apostolic vicariate for the Gallican provinces, attached to the episcopal see of Arles.[1] The continued advance of the Germanic hordes had caused the great Roman establishment of Treves to be all but abandoned. The higher Roman functionaries had been obliged to retire and to remove their headquarters to a position in the Rhone valley. Arles, which had long been a flourishing city, and had enjoyed the favour of the emperors of the family of Constantine, besides being advantageously situated between the Gauls, Spain, and Italy, became thenceforward the residence of the prefect, the prætor, and all the higher administrative functionaries of the transalpine provinces. For a very short time—that is, during the reign of the "usurper" Constantine (407–410)—it had even been the capital of the Empire. This reign was followed by a violent political reaction directed by the powerful Constantius, the favourite and afterwards the brother-in-law of Honorius, who at length made him his associate on the throne of the Empire. The inhabitants of Arles, in the hope of purchasing pardon for the attitude they had assumed in the late events, banished their saintly bishop, Heros, who had compromised himself in the opinion of the Court of

---

[1] See my *Fastes Episcopaux de l'Ancienne Gaule*, vol i pp 84–144.

Ravenna. They appointed as his successor Patroclus, who was in great favour with Constantius, but who was an ambitious, intriguing, and avaricious man, and at the same time clever and audacious. Pope Zosimus, who had been prepossessed beforehand in favour of this individual and had been deceived as to his moral character, hastened, on succeeding to the pontificate, to grant him letters which invested him with powers superior to all the bishops of the two administrative dioceses of Gaul and of the Seven Provinces. The Pope, by the intermediary of this his vicar, took the effective direction of the episcopate of the Gallic provinces, over which, up till that time, he had not been able to exercise more than a feeble and intermittent influence

This attempt was a failure. Patroclus abused his powers so scandalously that they soon had to be withdrawn. Under the immediate successors of Zosimus—Boniface, Celestine, Xystus III. (Sixtus), and Leo—the efforts of the Bishops of Arles were directed, with varying success, not to the revival of the vicariate, but to secure their being recognised as rulers of an ecclesiastical province of greater importance than the others Pope Hilary attempted to carry out once more the scheme of Zosimus, but less successfully, inasmuch as the Bishops of Arles, despairing of its realisation, had taken a merely theoretical interest in the matter. From the time of St. Cæsarius and down to the end of the sixth century, they were careful to provide themselves with letters of vicariate to which the distinction of the pallium had then been added; but these were merely empty honours, and did not even result in securing precedence for the Bishops of Arles in the councils of the Frankish Empire.

But if the vicariate never became an effective institution, it was nevertheless the occasion of more frequent and regular relations between Rome and the bishops of the Rhone valley. The current of affairs was diverted from

Milan to Rome. The correspondence between Rome and Arles became incessant, and the Bishops of Southern Gaul grew accustomed to proceed to Rome to submit their disputes to the tribunal of the Pope. We note the presence of such bishops at the Roman councils of the fifth century.

If the Western Empire had been able to maintain its existence, an ecclesiastical centralisation similar to that which had made such vigorous progress in the East, would have been established at an early date in the West. St. Leo had placed this ecclesiastical concentration under legal protection by obtaining from Valentinian III. a recognition of his right to compel the bishops of all the provinces to appear before his tribunal.[1] This Western centralising movement was, however, thwarted by the rise of the barbarian kingdoms. Political frontiers were established between Rome and the Churches which lay beyond the Alps and the seas. The laws and functionaries of Ravenna had no longer any influence in Vandal Africa, in Frankish Gaul, and in Visigothic Spain. Whether Catholic or heretic, the barbarian kings regarded with but slight favour the maintenance of regular and frequent communications between their bishops and the Bishop of Rome, a subject of that power at the expense of which their own authority had been established. On the other hand, the Frankish and Visigothic sovereigns soon recognised the necessity of being on good terms with their bishops. The Roman Imperial officials having once disappeared, the bishops were found to be the best qualified representatives of the conquered population, and numberless occasions arose for an appeal to their moral authority. Constant relations were thus established between the various Churches and the sovereign, and the Court of the king became the centre of ecclesiastical as of all other affairs.

[1] *Nov Valent. III.*, 16.

From thence were issued the summonses convening councils, and from the same source proceeded the appointments of bishops. Each kingdom was a centre for itself. There was thus a national Frankish Church and a national Visigothic Church, the former the more centralised, and more closely united to the State, the latter always the more disintegrated of the two, owing to the constant redistribution of territory among the Merovingian princes, and the absence of a capital, either religious or political.

In Italy, the Lombardic conquest had at first still greater damaging effects upon ecclesiastical centralisation and even upon religious unity itself. The Metropolitan of Aquileia, who had become a schismatic after the fifth Œcumenical Council, continued his insubordination for a considerable time within the shelter of the frontier of the Duchy of Frioul. The Churches which had been overthrown at the beginning of the invasion, had not all recovered by the seventh century. Those which were fortunate enough to have done so, found themselves somewhat strained in their relations with Rome. Metropolitan institutions in Italy, however, were too deeply rooted to be easily overturned. Rome, Milan, Aquileia, and Ravenna maintained their respective positions, and continued, in all essentials, to exercise their jurisdictions.

Beyond the Adriatic, Dalmatia constituted a province by itself, under the Metropolitan of Salonæ (Spalatro). Further east. the group formed by the Illyrian provinces, together with Macedonia, Thessaly, Epirus, Achaia, and the Greek islands as far as and including Crete, did not belong to any of the Eastern patriarchates. These countries were included in the jurisdiction of the Pope, regarded as the Patriarch of the West. According to this assumption, the West began at Philippi and Sardica. This demarcation had been determined by the limits of the Eastern Empire under Licinius (314–

323), Constantius (337–350), and Valens (364–378). When Gratian associated Theodosius with him as emperor, he entrusted him with the government of Eastern Illyricum, which extended northwards as far as the Save, and westwards up to the Dalmatian mountains. Connected in this manner with the Eastern Empire, these provinces could not fail to be drawn within the ecclesiastical influence of Constantinople. Greek was spoken throughout most of them, and commercial intercourse and business of every kind caused a much stronger drift in the direction of Constantinople than in that of Rome or Milan. The Popes, anxious not to lose the spiritual direction of so many distinguished Churches, resolved, at an early date, to found a vicariate at Thessalonica, of which that at Arles was merely an imitation. More successfully managed than its Gallican counterpart, it manifested a certain vitality, and for nearly a century produced appreciable results. The schism of long duration connected with Acacius (484–519) inflicted on it a fatal blow. Although we find as late as the sixth and seventh centuries certain acts indicating papal jurisdiction in these regions, they are either isolated instances, or unconnected with the institution of the vicariate. Of the latter nothing remained but the titles, which the Bishops of Thessalonica and some others delighted to parade at councils. In fact, if not in theory, the provinces of Eastern Illyricum had passed under the authority of the Patriarchs of Constantinople.[1]

At the opposite extremity of the West, the Churches of Britain, which had been destroyed by or had suffered severely from, the Saxon invasion, had not long enjoyed, if they had ever known, the metropolitan system.

[1] See *Eglises Séparées*, ch vi

Christianity, which had taken refuge in the West, held its own there as best it could in the midst of a barbarian population, which, though undisciplined, was capable of great religious fervour. Towns no longer existed, but from the monastic centres missionaries spread over their immediate neighbourhood, preaching and carrying spiritual ministrations to the inhabitants of scattered groups of dwellings in these out-of-the-way districts. Many of the Britons emigrated, some to the shores of Armorica in Gaul, others as far as Spain. In the latter country they formed a bishopric which found a place within the organisation of the local Church. In Gaul it was otherwise. The Breton Churches preserved a separate existence, entrenched behind the frontier which separated the peninsula with its national rulers from the Frankish Empire. It was not until the time of Charlemagne that they were at length brought into union with the ecclesiastical body of the Franks, and were incorporated into the metropolitan province of Tours. Even this union, disturbed by political fluctuations, was for a long time lacking in completeness and efficacy.[1]

It was from the Island of Britain that Patrick went forth to be the Apostle of Ireland, then an independent country. The Church which he founded there reproduced, and at the same time exaggerated, all the traits characteristic of British Christianity. It developed rapidly. As early as the sixth century, through the efforts of Columba and his monks of Hy or Iona, it had already spread to the country of the Picts and the Caledonians. Other apostles, free lances of the Irish Church, appeared shortly after on the Continent, and settling on the eastern confines of ancient Gaul, began to spread Christianity in the parts of Germany watered by the Danube and the Main, whence, after the invasions of the fifth

---

[1] *Fastes Episcopaux*, vol ii p. 252.

century, it had been almost completely exterminated. Their somewhat undisciplined foundations there were, a century later, taken in hand and reformed by St. Boniface.

Thus throughout the regions of the West, whatever the political situation may have been, whatever the form or degree of progress of ecclesiastical organisation, there was nothing at the close of the sixth century which could lead us to foresee that the Latin Church would one day be more centralised than ever the Roman Empire had been. Rome continued to be for the whole world the apostolic see, the supreme metropolis of the Church. On the questions of dogma or general discipline which divided the East and the West, it was an understood thing that the Pope had the right to speak in the name of all the Western Churches. The Pope's decretals had the same legal force as the decisions of councils, and were inserted under the same category in the collection of canons. The sanctuaries of the apostolic city, particularly St. Peter's, attracted pilgrims from all countries. No spot in the West was more sacred, and no moral or religious authority could be compared to that of the priest who ministered at those illustrious shrines. But from this universal respect to an ecclesiastical centralisation was a far cry. No one, moreover, not even the Popes themselves, appeared to have felt any urgent necessity for it. They adapted themselves to the existing state of things without attempting to modify it.

The movement towards centralisation had its origin, though indirectly, in the conversion of England under the auspices of the Roman Church. The Frankish Church, which did not possess the missionary spirit in any extraordinary degree, made no effort of any kind to convert their neighbours beyond the Rhine or across the Channel. On the other hand, the zeal of the British in preaching the Gospel was limited by the Saxon frontier. The work in England was begun and successfully carried on by the Roman missions of Augustine (597) and Theodore (668). Between these two the Scots of Ireland had intervened to such an extent, that it would be unjust not to attribute to them a very large share in the success of the enterprise. The Roman mission in Kent, however, retained the direction of the English Church, and in the sum-total of influences, it was the Roman spirit that predominated. From thence went forth the apostles of Germany and the ecclesiastical counsellors of the first Carlovingian princes. From thence, through more or less numerous intermediaries, emanated the reform of the Frankish Church, and later on of the Roman Church itself; and from thence, above all, proceeded that centralising movement which, by relieving the Latin ecclesiastical world of the embarrassments and complications arising from primacies and national Churches, placed their united forces in the hands of the successors of St. Peter.

CHAPTER II.

THE MASS IN THE EAST.

§ 1.—THE LITURGY IN PRIMITIVE TIMES.

WE have seen in the preceding chapter that the local Christian communities for the most part were detached from the pre-existing Jewish communities, and that in consequence of this origin, a strong resemblance existed between the organisation of the Church and that of the synagogue. This resemblance is especially apparent in the sphere of worship. The Christian Liturgy to a great extent took its rise from the Jewish Liturgy, and was, in fact, merely its continuation. But here it is important that we should not confound the worship of the temple at Jerusalem with that of the synagogue. The former did not in any way influence the Christian Liturgy, and the connection which the commentators of the Middle Ages delighted to point out between the ritual of the Pentateuch and that of the Church cannot be taken seriously. Everything that has been said on this point is a matter of mere imagination, and has no basis in tradition. The worship in the Temple was of a national character, and altogether different from the religious exercises joined in by a brotherhood, or a local congregation, in the sacred assemblies of the *Diaspora*, or in the towns of Palestine, or even in Jerusalem itself. The first Christians, at a time in which they were still almost altogether congregated in the Jewish capital, took part in the worship of the Temple, but without prejudice to their own special meetings—those of the new synagogue which they had established at the very beginning. Outside Jerusalem, the highest expression of their collective religious life was for them, as for the Jews, in the weekly meetings of the synagogue.

These meetings took place on Saturday. From a very early period the Christians adopted the Sunday. It is possible that, at the very outset, the choice of this day was not suggested by any hostility towards Jewish customs, but that they observed it merely in order to have side by side with the ancient Sabbath, which they celebrated with their Israelite brethren, a day set apart for exclusively Christian assemblies. The idea of importing into the Sunday the solemnity of the Sabbath, with all its exigencies, was an entirely foreign one to the primitive Christians. This was especially the case in regard to the prohibition of work, but it was true also with respect to worship properly so called. The observance of the Sunday was at first supplemental to that of the Sabbath, but in proportion as the gulf between the Church and the synagogue widened, the Sabbath became less and less important, and ended at length in being entirely neglected. The Christians, like the Jews, had thus one single day in the week set apart for religious meetings, but the Christian day was different from that of the Jews

The religious assemblies of the synagogue involved no bloody sacrifice, no oblation of the products of the soil, no firstfruits or incense. The children of Israel assembled together not only for common prayer, but also to read their sacred books—the Law in the first place, and then the Prophets ; that is to say, the remaining books of the Bible. Besides these readings there were also chants, of which the text was furnished by the Psalter. A less essential but widely used exercise was the homily (Midrash) on a theme supplied by the lections.

These four elements—lections, chants, homilies, and prayers—were adopted without hesitation by the Christian Churches. There was soon to be found on the reader's desk, in addition to the books of the Jewish Bible, the writings of the New Testament, among which a special prominence was given to the Gospel. This was all the change, with the exception, of course, of such modifications as were necessitated, by the new direction given to faith, in the text of prayers and homilies, as well as in the choice of the biblical lessons and sacred canticles.

But if the Church took over *en bloc* all the religious service of the synagogue, it added thereto one or two new elements, which constituted that which was original in the Christian Liturgy. I refer to the Supper, or sacred repast, and the spiritual exercises

These both occupied a very high place in the Christian service, such as we see it in the earliest documents. After the Eucharist, certain inspired persons began to preach and to make manifest before the assembly the presence of the spirit which animated them. The prophets, the ecstatics, the speakers in tongues, the interpreters, the supernatural healers, absorbed at this time the attention of the faithful. There was, as it were, a Liturgy of the Holy Ghost after the Liturgy of Christ, a true liturgy with a Real Presence and communion. The inspiration could be felt—it sent a thrill through the organs of certain privileged persons, but the whole assembly was moved, edified, and even more or less ravished by it and transported into the Divine sphere of the Paraclete.[1]

---

[1] See especially 1 Cor xiv.; and the *Doctrine of the Apostles*, 10, *et seq*.

However frequently these Divine phenomena might occur they were not on that account the less extraordinary, and it is impossible to regard them, properly speaking, as a religious institution. Neither the Christian communities nor their pastors were able to produce them or to obtain them at will. It was very difficult even to regulate them, as we see from the history of St. Paul and the Church at Corinth. Moreover, they soon disappeared, and from the beginning of the second century onwards we find only exceptional and isolated instances of them. The only permanent element, on the whole, which Christianity added to the liturgy of the synagogue was thus the sacred meal instituted by Jesus Christ as a perpetual commemoration of Himself.

The details of this august ceremony are furnished by the synoptic Gospels, and by the passage in which St. Paul treats of the Last Supper. We have, first of all, the act of thanksgiving, or eucharistic prayer, then the breaking of the bread, and finally the distribution of the bread and wine to those present. These constitute, strictly speaking, the principal elements of the Mass in its entirely Christian and original aspect.

It is not my aim to adduce here all the texts of the second or third century in which there is mention made of the Eucharist and of its essential rites. I confine myself to quoting from the most important of them, namely, the description of the Christian meetings for worship on Sunday, which we find in the first *Apology* of Justin Martyr.[1]

---

[1] Justin, *Apol*, i. 6. At its very origin, as we see in the First Epistle to the Corinthians, the Eucharistic celebration was preceded by an ordinary repast partaken of in common. This was what is called the Agape. But this custom allowed of the introduction of too many inconveniences to be lasting. The liturgical Agape disappeared, or nearly so, within less than a hundred years after the first preaching of the Gospel. As for the love-feast (Tertullian, *Apol*, 39), it continued to take place, and survived, especially on the occasion of a funeral, down to at least the fifth century.

On the day of the Sun (Sunday) all who live in towns or in the country gather together to one place, and the memoirs of the apostles or the writings of the prophets are read as long as time permits. Then when the reader has ceased, the president verbally instructs and exhorts to the imitation of the good examples cited. Then all rise together, and prayers are offered. At length, as we have already described, prayer being ended, bread and wine and water are brought, and the president offers prayer and thanksgivings to the best of his ability, and the people assent by saying *Amen*: and the distribution is made to each one of his share of the elements which have been blessed, and to those who are not present it is sent by the ministry of the deacons.

Of the four elements borrowed from the current usage of the synagogue—namely, the lection, the chant, the homily, and the prayer—the only one of which there is here no express mention is the chanting of the Psalms. In another passage of his *Apology*,[1] St. Justin, in explaining the ceremonies of baptism, adds a description of the eucharistic liturgy in terms similar to those just cited, except that he here makes mention of the kiss of peace, which the Christians, he says, give to one another after the prayers, and before beginning the sacred meal, or Eucharist, properly so called.

St. Justin confines himself to the description of the order of service followed in the Christian assemblies: he gives no text, or formulary of prayer or exhortation. His omissions on this point, however, can be made good by the help of very ancient ecclesiastical documents.

The epistle of St. Clement of Rome preserves for us a passage evidently of a liturgical character. We cannot, indeed, regard it as a reproduction of a sacred formulary, but it is an excellent example of the style of solemn prayer in which the ecclesiastical leaders of that time were accustomed to express themselves at meetings for worship.

"May the sealed number of the elect in the whole world be preserved

---

[1] I. 65

intact by the Creator of all things, through His well-beloved Son Jesus Christ, by whom He has called us from darkness to light, from ignorance to the knowledge of the glory of His Name . . . to hope in Thy[1] Name, from whom every creature proceeds. Thou hast opened the eyes of our hearts that they may know Thee, Thou the sole Highest among the highest, the Holy One who rests in the midst of the holy ones. Thou who abasest the insolence of the proud, who scatterest the machinations of the people, who exaltest the humble and puttest down the mighty; Thou who givest riches and poverty, death and life, sole Benefactor of spirits, God of all flesh; Thou whose regard penetrates the abyss, and scans the works of men; Thou who art our help in danger, Thou who savest us from despair, Creator and Overseer of all spirits; Thou who hast multiplied the nations upon earth, and chosen from among them those who love Thee through Jesus Christ, Thy well-beloved Servant, by whom Thou hast instructed, sanctified, and honoured us. We beseech Thee, O Master, be our help and succour. Be the Salvation of those of us who are in tribulation; take pity on the lowly, raise up them that fall, reveal Thyself to those who are in need, heal the ungodly, and restore those who have gone out of the way. Appease the hunger of the needy, deliver those among us who suffer in prison, heal the sick, comfort the faint hearted; that all people may know that Thou art the only God, that Jesus Christ is Thy Servant, and that we are Thy people and the sheep of Thy pasture.

"Thou art He who by Thy operations hast manifested the everlasting harmony of the world; Thou, Lord, hast created the earth, Thou who remainest faithful throughout all generations, just in Thy judgments, wonderful in Thy might and majesty, wise in creation and prudent in the upholding of things created; Thou who showest Thy goodness in saving us, Thy faithfulness to those trusting in Thee. O pitiful and merciful God, forgive us our faults, our injustices, our shortcomings, our transgressions; remember not the sins of Thy servants and Thy handmaids, but cleanse us by Thy truth and direct our steps, that we may walk in holiness of heart and do that which is good and acceptable in Thine eyes and in the eyes of our princes. Yea, O Lord, make Thy face to shine upon us, for our well-being and our peace, for our protection by Thy strong hand and our deliverance from every sin by Thy mighty arm, for our salvation from those who wrongfully hate us. Give peace and concord to us and to all the dwellers upon earth, as Thou didst give them to our forefathers when they called upon Thee with faith and sincerity, in submission to the almighty power and supreme virtue of Thy Name.

---

[1] This change of person is in the Greek text.

"It is Thou, Lord, who hast given to our princes,[1] to those who rule over us upon earth, the power of royalty, by the excellent and unspeakable virtue of Thy might, in order that, knowing the glory and honour which Thou hast conferred upon them, we may submit ourselves to them, and not put ourselves in opposition to Thy will. Grant them, Lord, health, peace, concord, and stability, that they may exercise unhindered the authority with which Thou hast entrusted them. For it is Thou, O heavenly Lord, King of the ages, who givest to the sons of men glory, honour, and power over earthly things. Direct their counsels, O Lord, according to that which is good, according to that which is acceptable in Thy sight, so that exercising peaceably and mercifully the power which Thou hast given them, they may obtain Thy favour. Thou alone hast the power to do this, and to confer upon us still greater benefits. We confess Thee through the High Priest and Ruler of our souls, Jesus Christ, through whom glory and majesty be to Thee now, and throughout all generations, for ever and ever. Amen."[2]

In addition to these documents drawn up at Rome, I will further quote the formularies preserved to us in the *Doctrine of the Apostles*, a very ancient writing, contemporary, at the latest, with St. Justin, but of whose *provenance* nothing is definitely known.

"As to the Eucharist, we give thanks in this wise. First for the chalice: *We, thank thee, our Father, for the Holy Vine of David, Thy servant,*[3] *which Thou hast made known to us by Jesus Thy Servant.*[3] *Glory to Thee for evermore!*

"For the bread:[4] *We thank Thee, our Father, for the life and the knowledge which Thou hast made known to us by Jesus, Thy Servant. Glory to Thee for evermore! As the elements of this bread, scattered on the mountains, were brought together into a single whole, may Thy Church in like manner be gathered together from the ends of the earth into Thy kingdom; for Thine is the glory and the power, through Jesus Christ, for evermore.*

---

[1] Note the spirit in which the Christians at Rome prayed for the emperor on the morrow of the fury of Domitian.

[2] 1 Clem 59–61.

[3] "τοῦ παιδός σου," in both cases, and further on.

[4] "περὶ τοῦ κλάσματος" This refers to the bread as already broken or about to be so.

"Let no one eat or drink of your Eucharist if he is not baptised in the Name of the Lord, for it was of this the Lord said, 'Give not that which is holy to dogs.'

"After you are satisfied[1] return thanks thus: *We thank Thee, Holy Father, for Thy holy Name, which Thou hast made to dwell in our hearts, for the knowledge, faith and immortality which Thou hast revealed to us through Jesus Thy Servant. Glory to Thee for evermore! It is Thou, mighty Lord, who hast created the universe for the glory of Thy Name, who hast given to men meat and drink, that they may enjoy them in giving Thee thanks. But to us Thou hast given spiritual meat and drink, and life eternal through Thy Servant. We give Thee thanks before everything, because Thou art mighty. Glory to Thee for evermore! Be mindful, Lord, to deliver Thy Church from all evil, and to grant it perfection in Thy love. Gather it together from the four winds of heaven, this sanctified Church, for the kingdom which Thou hast prepared for it; for Thine is the power and glory for evermore. May grace come and this world pass away! Hosanna to the Son of David! If any one be holy, let him come; if any one be not, let him repent. The Lord is at hand!*[2] *Amen.*

"Let the prophets then make the Eucharist as long as they may wish."

It is evident that this ritual and these formularies come to us from a sphere widely different from that in which St. Justin and St. Clement composed their writings—from a sphere in which intense enthusiasm still prevailed. The prophets play here an important *rôle*. The minds of the people, too, are excited and feverish in expectation of the kingdom of Christ. I have no intention of entering here into details of the contrast. It is enough to point out that the liturgical language of which St. Clement offers us such an ancient and authoritative example, and the ritual presented by St. Justin as of general use in the assemblies of Christians, are in every respect analogous to that which we encounter three centuries later, at a period when documents abound. The liturgy described in the *Doctrine* has, on the contrary, altogether the aspect of an anomaly; it

---

[1] "ἐμπλησθῆναι."
[2] "Μαρὰν ἀθά."

might furnish some of the features which we meet with in later compositions, but it is on the whole outside the main stream, outside the general line of development both in respect of its ritual and style.

From these monuments of the primitive age we must come down at once to the fourth century. It is about the latter period that we encounter sufficiently numerous examples of the liturgical uses which, completed and varied later on, became eventually that which we see them to-day. Between the two epochs we find only isolated references, passing allusions, scattered among authors of the most divers character. It must be admitted, moreover, that peculiarities in ritual took a certain length of time to become fixed and established. At the beginning the procedure was almost identical everywhere; I say almost, for a complete identity of all the details cannot be assumed, even in the Churches founded by the apostles. It was not in accordance with the practice of early days to attach to things of this nature that importance which would sanction and fix them. Usages developed by slow degrees into rites; rites expanded into more and more imposing and complicated ceremonies, and at the same time a limitation was put upon the subject-matter of the prayers and exhortations. Custom had indicated to the celebrant the ideas which he had to develop and the order in which he had to treat them. A final step was at length taken when fixed formularies were adopted, which left no longer anything to individual caprice, or to the chances of improvisation.

Long before this stage had been reached, local diversities had crept into the ritual. The uses of Rome, Antioch, and Alexandria must, in the third century, have departed widely from the primitive uniformity: *Facies non omnibus una, nec diversa tamen.* In proportion as these great metropolitan Churches widened the circle of their missions, they extended also the area of their special uses, for it is altogether natural that the use of the Mother Church should become a law to the daughter Churches. It was in this manner that the liturgical provinces, if we may use the expression, became identified with the ecclesiastical provinces.[1]

We may refer the liturgies with which we are acquainted to four principal types—the Syrian, the Alexandrian, the Roman, and the Gallican. It might not be impossible, moreover, to trace back the Gallican to the Syrian type, and to infer that the use of Alexandria was derived, as far as a certain portion is concerned, from that of Rome. The four different forms would thus be reduced to two, a division which is analogous to that which obtains to-day, when the uses of Rome and Constantinople have almost absorbed the rest.

But the documents do not carry us so far back. We are certain that in the fourth century there were four types at the very least, for the Syrian type had already given origin to some very marked sub-types.

§ 2.—The Syrian Liturgy in the Fourth Century.

The most ancient documentary sources of the Syrian Liturgy are—

1. The 23rd Catechism of St. Cyril of Jerusalem, delivered about the year 347.

---

[1] On the Eastern liturgies, the works of capital importance now are Swainson, *The Greek Liturgies chiefly from Original Authorities*, Cambridge University Press, 1884, and *Liturgies Eastern and Western*, by F E Brightman, vol. 1, Oxford, 1896, a considerably improved and enlarged edition of a book bearing the same title published in 1878 by C. E. Hammond.

2. The *Apostolic Constitutions* (II. 57 and VIII. 5–15).
3. The Homilies of St. John Chrysostom.

St. John Chrysostom cites frequently in his Homilies passages, and even prayers, taken from the Liturgy. Bingham[1] was the first to form the project of collecting and putting into order these scattered data. This work has been lately undertaken again by several experts.[2] Interesting testimony may be drawn from this source, but the orator nowhere gives a systematic description of the Liturgy in the order of its rites and prayers.

The Catechism of St. Cyril is really an exposition of the ceremonies of the Mass, drawn up for neophytes after their initiation. The preacher leaves out of consideration the Mass of the Catechumens with which his auditors have been for a long time familiar. He assumes that the bread and wine have been brought to the altar, and begins at the moment in which the bishop, having washed his hands, prepares to celebrate the holy mysteries.[3]

In the *Apostolic Constitutions* we must make a distinction between the description given in Book II. from that in Book VIII. The first is somewhat sketchy; it contains merely the description of the rites, without the formularies. The latter furnishes at full length the forms of prayer complete, but only those which occur after the Gospel.

We know now that the *Apostolic Constitutions* represent, in the present condition of the Greek text, a fusion of two similar works, the *Didascalia of the Apostles*, of which we

---

[1] *Origin. Eccles*, xiii. 6.
[2] Hammond, *The Antient Liturgy of Antioch*, Oxford, 1879. Cf. *Zeitschrift für kath. Theologie*, 1879, p 619 (Bickell), and 1883, p. 250 (Probst) Probst makes a distinction between the Homilies preached at Antioch and those delivered at Constantinople Mr Brightman (*lib cit*, p 470) has rehandled the subject, profiting by the labours of his predecessors
[3] Brightman, p 464.

possess only the Latin and Syriac versions,[1] and the *Doctrine of the Apostles,* discovered not long ago by the metropolitan Bryennios Philotheos. The former of these works served as a base for Books I.-VI. of the *Apostolic Constitutions;* the latter, much attenuated, became Book VII. of the same collection. The eighth book [2] must have been added to the other seven by the author of the later redaction of the *Didascalia* and the *Doctrine.* This was the author who interpolated in the seven authentic letters of St. Ignatius six others of his own production. He lived in Syria, either at Antioch or in the ecclesiastical region of which that town was the centre. He wrote towards the end of the fourth century, at a time when the "subordination" theology, of which we have more than one indication in his various works, still enjoyed a considerable reputation. He was the author of the description of the liturgy which figures in Book II. of the *Apostolic Constitutions.* This passage, in fact, is wanting in the Syriac *Didascalia.* Was he also the author of the redaction of the liturgy in the eighth book? We may hesitate to answer this question affirmatively, for there are some differences between this liturgy and that of Book II.

I am now going to describe the Divine Service such as these documents imply it to have been, noting where necessary their divergences from each other.

The congregation has assembled, the men on one side and the women on the other, and the clergy in the apse. The readers at once begin the lections, which are interrupted here and there by chants. A reader ascends the

---

[1] See the edition of all these texts by Funk, *Didascalia et Constitutiones Apostolorum* Paderborn, 1905.

[2] This eighth book itself has as its nucleus the "Apostolic Tradition" of Hippolytus. Cf. Appendix 6.

ambo, placed about the middle of the church, between the clergy and the congregation, and reads two lessons; then another takes his place and chants a psalm. This is sung as a *solo;* but those present take up the last modulations of his chant. This is what is called the respond, *Psalmus Responsorius,* and is to be carefully distinguished from the antiphon, which is a psalm rendered alternately by two choirs. The antiphon did not then exist, and the respond alone was in use. There must have been a considerable number of lections, but we are not informed how many. The series comes to an end with the reading of the Gospel, which is accomplished, not by an ordinary reader, but by a priest or deacon. The whole audience stand up at the reading of this last lection.

The lections and psalms being ended, the priests begin the homilies, each one preaching in his turn,[1] and after them the bishop. The homily is always preceded by a salutation addressed to the congregation, who respond by the versicle, "And with thy Spirit."

After the homily the various classes of persons who are not entitled to be present at the holy mysteries are dismissed. The catechumens are sent away first. At the invitation of the deacon they offer up a silent prayer, while the congregation also prays for them. The deacon formulates this prayer, specifying the particulars of it, giving the petitions in detail. The faithful, especially the children present, answer him by the supplication, *Kyrie Eleison!* The catechumens afterwards rise up, and the deacon invites them in their turn to pray, by joining with him in the form which he employs;

---

[1] This detail is confirmed, apart from the *Apost Const*, II 57, by the *Peregrinatio* of Silvia "Hic (at Jerusalem) consuetudo sic est, ut de omnibus presbiteris qui sedent, quanti volunt praedicent, et post illos omnes episcopus praedicat; quae praedicationes propterea semper dominicis diebus sunt ut semper erudiatur populus in Scripturis et in Dei dilectione, quae praedicationes dum dicuntur grandis mora fit ut fiat missa ecclesiae' (p. 81).

he then invites them to incline their heads to receive the blessing of the bishop, after which they are dismissed.

The same form is observed in regard to the energumens, the competents, that is to say, the catechumens who are preparing to receive baptism, and finally the penitents.

The faithful communicants, who are now alone in the church, give themselves to prayer. Prostrating themselves towards the east, they listen to the deacon while he says the petitions of the Litany: " For the peace and welfare of the world . . . For the holy Catholic and Apostolic Church . . . For the bishops, priests . . . For the benefactors of the Church . . . For the neophytes . . . For the sick . . . For those who are travelling . . . For young children . . For those who have gone astray, etc " The congregation join in these petitions by the supplication, *Kyrie Eleison!* The Litany is brought to an end by a special formulary: "Save us, restore us again, O God, by Thy mercy." Then the voice of the bishop makes itself heard above the silence, pronouncing in a grave and dignified manner a solemn prayer.

Thus ends the first part of the liturgy, that which the Church borrowed from the ancient usage of the synagogue.[1] The second part, the Christian Liturgy proper, begins with

---

[1] In the liturgy of the Second Book the kiss of peace is followed by the Diaconal Litany and by the blessing of the bishop above described. In place of these another prayer of the faithful is indicated in which there must have been reference to the fall of Adam and his dismissal from paradise I believe that this prayer was no other than that which, according to the eighth book, the bishop utters over the penitents at the moment of their dismissal As for the place occupied by the kiss of peace, the direction of the eighth book appears to be confirmed by St. Cyril, who speaks of the *Preface* immediately after the kiss of peace. This is one of the places in which the liturgies differ most widely from each other. In the Greek Liturgy of St James there are two Litanies — one before and another after the kiss of peace; but after the former the procession of the oblation and the recitation of the Creed came immediately. The Syriac Liturgy of St James is on the whole in agreement with St Cyril and the eighth book of the *Constitutions* In the Liturgy of

the salutation of the bishop, followed by a response from the congregation. Thereupon, at a signal given by the deacon, the clergy receive the kiss of peace from the bishop, while the faithful interchange it with each other, the men with the men, and the women with the women.

Then the deacons and other inferior ministers distribute themselves into two bodies, to one being assigned the supervision of the congregation, and to the other the service of the altar. The former take their places among the faithful, arranging the latter according to their rank, the young children being placed at the approaches to the sacred precincts. They watch the doors also, in order that no profane person may enter the church. The others bring and place upon the altar the loaves and chalices prepared for the sacred repast, while two of their number keep waving the flabella to protect the holy oblation from insects. The bishop washes his hands and puts on a festal garment; the priests arrange themselves around him, and together they all draw near to the altar. This is the solemn moment. After a private prayer offered in silence by the bishop, the latter makes the sign of the cross on his forehead, and begins:

"The grace of God Almighty, the love of our Lord Jesus Christ, and the communion of the Holy Spirit, be with you all.

" And with Thy Spirit.

" Lift up your hearts.

" They are with the Lord.

" Let us give thanks unto the Lord.

" It is meet and right.

"It is truly right to glorify Thee, first of all, God truly existing. . . ."

And the eucharistic prayer goes on, starting from the

Constantinople we have in the first place the prayers of the faithful uttered by the celebrant, then the procession of the oblation, the Diaconal Litany, the kiss of peace, and the Creed

majesty of the unapproachable God, passing in review all His benefits conferred upon His creatures, enumerating all the wonders of nature and grace, appealing to the great types of the ancient covenant,[1] and concluding, at length, by a return to the mysterious sanctuary, in which the Divinity rests in the midst of spirits, where the Cherubim and Seraphim sing together the eternal hymn of the Trisagion.

At this point the whole congregation raise their voices, joining with the choir of angels in their hymn, " Holy, Holy, Holy is the Lord. . . ."

The hymn being ended, there is once more silence, and the bishop then proceeds with the eucharistic prayer which had been interrupted .

"Yea, truly Thou art holy . . ." and he commemorates the work of Redemption, the incarnation of the Word, and His earthly life and passion. At this moment the improvisation of the celebrant follows closely the Gospel account of the Last Supper, and the mysterious words spoken for the first time by Jesus on the eve of His death are repeated at the holy table. Thereupon the bishop, taking as his text the last words, "Do this in memory of Me," expands them, recalling to memory[2] the passion of the Son of God, His death, resurrection, ascension, and the hope of His glorious return, declaring that it is truly in keeping of Christ's command, and in commemorating these events that the congregation offers to God this eucharistic bread and wine. Finally, he prays the Lord[3]

---

[1] The formulary of the *Apostolic Constitutions* enumerates, in their historical order, a certain number of miracles from the Old Testament. An interruption then occurs, when after having recalled to memory the fall of the walls of Jericho in the time of Joshua, the formulary stops short. Such an abrupt breach of continuity can neither have been regular nor habitual.

[2] This is what is called in technical language the *Anamnesis*.

[3] This is the *Epiclesis*, or invocation of the Holy Spirit.

to regard the oblation with favour, and to cause to descend upon it the virtue of His holy Spirit, in order that it may be made the body and blood of Christ, the spiritual food of His faithful people, and the pledge of their immortality.

The eucharistic prayer proper comes thus to an end. The mystery is consummated. At the call of His disciples Christ has become present in their midst. He has taken up His abode on the sacred altar under the mystic veils of the consecrated elements. The prayers are resumed, but directed now to the present, although invisible, God. It is no longer the deacon, an inferior minister who speaks and conducts the supplications, but the bishop himself, the head of the Christian community:

"Lord, we pray to Thee for Thy holy Church spread abroad from one end of the world to the other . . . for myself who am nothing . . . for these priests, for these deacons, for the emperor, the magistrates, and the army . . . for the saints who in all ages were enabled to please Thee, patriarchs, prophets, the righteous, apostles, and martyrs . . for this people, for this city, for the sick, for those who are under the yoke of slavery, for the exiles, the prisoners, sailors, travellers . . . for those who hate us and persecute us . . . for the catechumens, the possessed, the penitents . . . for regularity of the seasons, for the fruits of the earth . . . for the absent." At the end of this long prayer is a doxology, to which the whole congregation responds *Amen*, thus ratifying the act of thanksgiving and intercession.

The *Pater Noster*[1] is now recited, accompanied by a new but very short Diaconal Litany, in which some of the subjects already enumerated by the bishop in his long

---

[1] The place of the *Pater Noster* is not the same in all the documents The liturgy of the *Ap. Const* omits it entirely, but St Cyril places it here

supplication are again taken up. After this Litany the bishop again gives his blessing to the people.

This ceremony being ended, the deacon arouses the attention of the faithful, while the bishop says, in a loud voice, "Holy things for holy persons!" The people respond:[1] "One sole Holy, one sole Lord, one sole Jesus Christ, for the glory of God the Father, blessed for evermore, Amen. Glory to God in the highest, peace on earth, good-will towards men. Hosanna to the Son of David! Blessed be He that cometh in the Name of the Lord! The Lord is God; He has manifested Himself to us. Hosanna in the highest!"

It was doubtless at this point that the fraction of the bread took place, a ceremony which the documents of the fourth century do not mention in express terms.

The communion then took place. The bishop communicated first, then the priests, deacons, sub-deacons, lectors, psalmists, ascetæ, deaconesses, virgins, widows, and young children, and at length the whole congregation.

The bishop administered the consecrated bread by placing it in the open right hand, supported by the left, of the recipient. The deacon held the chalice, from which each one drank directly. To each communicant the bishop said, "The Body of Christ." The deacon administered with the words, "The Blood of Christ, chalice of life." The recipients replied by "Amen."

During the communion the psalmists chant Psalm 33 [34], *Benedicam Dominum in omni tempore*, in which the words, *Gustate et videte quia suavis est Dominus* have a special significance.[2]

---

[1] This is the formulary of the *Ap Const* St. Cyril gives only the beginning: "εἷς ἅγιος, εἷς κύριος, Ἰησοῦς Χριστός" Compare the third prayer of the *Doctrine of the Apostles*, given above, p 53.

[2] St Cyril expressly cites them

The communion ended, the deacon gives the sign for prayer, which the bishop offers in the name of all. The people bow to receive his blessing, and are finally dismissed by the deacon with the words, "Depart in peace."

§ 3.—THE ORIENTAL LITURGIES.

The Liturgy of the *Apostolic Constitutions* cannot be considered as the normal and official Liturgy of any distinct Church. It can be proved that its formularies did not pass into the texts adopted later on as the Official Use. But if, from the point of view of its purport, it cannot be considered more than a private composition, it is otherwise with the ritual which it implies, and with the arrangement of the prayers, their style and general tenor. In regard to these, we must recognise in it an exact representation of the use of the great Churches of Syria, Antioch, Laodicea, Tyre, Cæsarea, and Jerusalem. The most trustworthy documents, in that which concerns Antioch and Jerusalem, furnish us with completely convincing evidence. Among these documents we must not only assign a place to the texts of St. Cyril of Jerusalem and of St. John Chrysostom, but we must also take into our reckoning the Syrian liturgies of later centuries. All these are, indeed, of the same type as the Liturgy of the *Constitutions*, allowance being made, as a matter of course, for the additions and the greater complexity of the rites and prayers which have been incorporated into it in the course of time.

This brings me to speak of the area in which the Syrian Liturgy was used, of its spread, to a varying extent, throughout the whole East, Egypt excepted, and finally of the documents containing it.

1. *Syria.*

We have already seen that the original obedience owed to Antioch had been restricted, in the fifth century, through the foundation of the autocephalous province of Cyprus and of the Patriarchate of Jerusalem. It would appear that this rearrangement had no marked influence on the liturgy. At the time in which it took place the use of Antioch had been adopted throughout the whole of Syria, and it continued to be observed there. An event of more grave consequence in this respect was the Jacobite schism of the sixth century. The adversaries of the Council of Chalcedon were then forming themselves, under the instigation of Jacob Baradai, into dissentient Churches absolutely separate from those of the orthodox communion, and provided with a complete hierarchy, from the Patriarch of Antioch down to the inferior orders. These communities maintained their existence side by side with the official Churches (Imperial, Melchites), and attained, especially after the Mussulman invasion, a high degree of prosperity. They exist to this day, but, from the end of the eighteenth century, a considerable number of Monophysites have returned to orthodoxy in attaching themselves to the Roman Church. Hence two groups of "Syrians" have been formed—the Jacobite Syrians or Monophysites, and orthodox Syrians. Their two patriarchs reside, or are supposed to reside, at Mardin in Mesopotamia.[1]

After the Monophysites came the Monothelites. Monothelitism, condemned at the Sixth Œcumenical Council of Constantinople (681), was thereupon abandoned by the official Churches of the Greek Empire, except during a short

---

[1] The Catholic patriarch resides usually at Aleppo

interval when it was restored under the Emperor Philippicus (711–713). It held its ground, however, at the convent of John Maron, in the Lebanon, and within the radius of influence of this monastery. Hence the origin of the religious group of the Maronites, who, after having maintained their dogmatic isolation for five hundred years, entered, in 1182, into communion with the Roman Church—in a somewhat precarious fashion, it is true, for even up to the end of the sixteenth century the union was subject to considerable fluctuations. The Maronites were governed from their monastery, in which a certain number of bishops resided. After many efforts, success at length attended the attempt to substitute for this primitive organisation a sort of ecclesiastical province, with dioceses and fixed episcopal seats. The bishops recognised a patriarch as their head, who took his title from Antioch. Syriac is the liturgical language of the Maronites, as it is of the Jacobites, both Uniats and non-Uniats.[1]

Alongside these national patriarchs, whose origin goes back to the heretical schism, the official and orthodox Patriarch of Antioch maintained his existence, although numerous secessions had much enfeebled his position. His peculiar liturgy was gradually supplanted by that of Constantinople, the only one which is now in use in the Greek Churches of the Patriarchate of Antioch. A

[1] The Maronite patriarchate is therefore quite a modern institution. Its titular patriarchs are in no respect the successors of the ancient Patriarchs of Antioch. This is not the case, however, with regard to the Syrian patriarchs, the Melchite patriarch, and the Greek non-Uniat patriarch. These two last represent—with the difference of communion—the succession of the Greek orthodox patriarchs of Antioch; the Syrian patriarchs, with the same difference, are the inheritors of the Jacobite patriarchal see founded in the sixth century. Strictly speaking, there ought not to be in Syria another Catholic patriarch than the Melchite. The existence of the other two is due to the respect with which the holy see considers it right to regard distinctions introduced centuries ago, whatever their legitimacy may have been at their beginning

number of Syrian Greeks, or rather of the Christian population using the Arabic language and following the Byzantine rite, became incorporated in the Roman Communion at the end of the seventeenth century. These constitute what are called the Greek Melchites. They are organised into a patriarchate,[1] whose titulary resides at Damascus. Their entry into the Roman Communion, however, has had no influence upon their liturgy, which, with a few slight alterations, remains that of the non-Uniat orthodox Christians. They use purely and simply the Liturgy of Constantinople, translated, it is true, into the Arabic language.

The liturgical documents which owe their origin to Syria, that is to say, to the Patriarchates of Antioch and of Jerusalem, as well as to the autocephalous province of Cyprus, are—

1. *The Greek Liturgy of St. James.*—This appears to have been at first the normal liturgy in all these countries, and is analogous to that which is called in the Roman rite the Ordinary of the Mass. At the present day it is no longer in use, except in Jerusalem, Cyprus, and certain other localities, and there only on one day of the year, the Feast of St. James (October 23rd). During the remainder of the year the liturgies of Constantinople are exclusively followed. The most ancient witness to the existence of this liturgy is a mention of it in the 32nd canon of the Council *in Trullo* (692), where it is cited as being the actual production of St. James, the brother of our Lord. It must go back, however, much beyond the seventh century. The fact that the Jacobites have preserved it in Syriac as their fundamental liturgy proves

---

[1] The title was at first that of Patriarch of Antioch. From the time of Gregory XVI, the head of the Melchite Church has been distinguished by the title of Patriarch of Antioch, Jerusalem, and Alexandria. He is represented in each of the two last cities by a vicar.

that it was already consecrated by long use at the time when these communities took their rise—that is to say, about the middle of the sixth century. St. Jerome appears to have known it. It is certain, at least, that he cites a liturgical passage that is found in the Liturgy of St. James.[1] The manuscripts in which it is preserved cannot, unfortunately, lay claim to any antiquity. As it appears in these manuscripts, it contains many modifications traceable to the Byzantine use.[2]

2. *The Syriac Liturgy of St. James.*—This is nearly identical with the preceding, from the Kiss of Peace onwards. The manuscripts which contain it are of the eighth century.[3]

3. *The Other Syriac Liturgies.*—They differ from one another only in the *Anaphora*. The Ordinary[4] is the same in all of them.

To these manuscripts must be added a letter of James of Edessa (end of the seventh century), which contains

---

[1] *Adv Pelag*, ii 23· "Sacerdotum quotidie ora concelebrant ὁ μόνος ἀναμάρτητος, quod in lingua nostra dicitur *qui solus est sine peccato*" These words occur also in the *Memento* for the dead (Brightman, p 57)· αὐτὸς γάρ ἐστιν ὁ μόνος ἀναμάρτητος φανεὶς ἐπὶ τῆς γῆς. In Syriac "Nec ullus est a peccati culpa immunis aut a sordibus purus ex hominibus qui super terram sunt, nisi unus D N. Jesus Christus"

[2] The last edition is that of Brightman, *Liturgies Eastern and Western*, p 31. The most ancient manuscript is a roll of the end of the tenth century, now preserved at Messina, I must further cite the Rossano manuscript (*Vatic*, 1970) of the twelfth century; the *Parisinus* 2509, of the fourteenth century (copy No 303 of the Greek supplement), and the *Parisinus*, Greek suppl. 476, also of the fourteenth century These copies, or their originals, all come from Syria The same may be said of the Sinaitic manuscript of the fourteenth century, from which Mr Brightman has taken a *diaconicon* (the deacon's part) belonging to the Mass of the Presanctified according to the rite of St James (*op cit*, p 494)

[3] Renaudot's translation (*Liturg Orient*, vol ii) has been reproduced by Hammond, and, in the portions common to the Greek and the Syriac, by Swainson (*The Greek Liturgies*: London, 1884). Mr. Brightman gives the text of this liturgy in English

[4] For these texts, see Brightman, p lv, *et seq.*

many details with regard to the liturgy in the Monophysite Churches using the Syriac language.[1]

2. *Mesopotamia and Persia.*

There is no doubt that the Churches of Mesopotamia and Persia were founded by missionaries who came from Antioch. But after these first and remote beginnings, those Churches of the Roman Empire which were more or less connected with Edessa, as well as those of the Persian Empire which had their chief Metropolitan at Seleucia-Ctesiphon, followed somewhat divergent lines in the development both of their liturgical and ecclesiastical institutions. We possess, up till now, very scanty information with regard to the peculiarities of the Liturgy of Edessa compared with the uses of Antioch and Seleucia. We have, on the other hand, a fairly large number of documents on the liturgy of the Persian Church, usually known as the Nestorian Liturgy.

The liturgical books in use at the present time are traceable either to the Nestorians properly so called, who have kept themselves together with their national patriarch in the mountains of Kurdistan,[2] or to the Uniat or Chaldean Nestorians, who have at their head a Catholic Patriarch residing at Mossul. These two dignitaries, who bear the title of Patriarchs of Babylon, are representatives of the succession of the ancient *Catholicos* of Seleucia.[3]

The most ancient documents of the Mesopotamian or Persian use are four Homilies of Narses, the celebrated Teacher of the School of Nisibis at the end of the fifth century.[4]

[1] Assemani, *Bibl. Orient*, vol. i. p. 479. Brightman, p. 490.

[2] His residence is at Kochanes, near Julamerk, a place situated on the Zab, in the mountains to the north of Mossul, a short distance from the Persian frontier.

[3] The Jacobites have also in these countries their own particular organisation, presided over by a "Maphrian"

[4] These and forty-three other homilies by the same author, were published first in Syriac by Alphonse Mingana, at the Dominican Press at Mossul (1905), they have been translated into English with a com-

The following are the texts which are at present known of these liturgies.

1. An *Anaphora* of the sixth century, first published by Herr Bickell[1] and, after re-examination of the manuscript, by Mr. Hammond.[2] It is merely a fragment in very bad preservation, but entitled to respect on account of its antiquity.

2. The Liturgy of SS. Adaeus and Maris, founders of the Churches of Edessa and Seleucia. This is the normal liturgy of the Nestorians, and the only one used by the Chaldean Uniats.[3]

3. The two *Anaphorae* of Theodore of Mopsuestia and of Nestorius, which are used by the Nestorians at certain times of the year.[4]

Nestorian tradition attributes the final fixing of the liturgy in its curtailed form as found in the text attributed to SS. Adaeus and Maris, to the Patriarch Jesuyab III. (644-647).[5]

mentary by Dom R. H Connolly in vol. viii of *Texts and Studies*, Cambridge (1909). One of them (xvii. Mingana) is a Commentary on the Liturgy of the Mass, two others (xxi and xxii) are explanation of the ritual in Baptism, the fourth (xxxii.) treats of the ceremonies of Ordination.

[1] *Conspectus rei Syrorum Literariae*, p. 71, *Zeitschrift der deutschen morg. Gesellschaft*, 1873, p. 608.

[2] *The Liturgy of Antioch*, p. 41. Brightman, p. 511.

[3] Published only in part by Renaudot (vol. ii p. 578). The best text was published in 1892, by the English mission at Urmia (*Liturgia SS. Apostolorum Adaei et Maris, etc*). English trans., Brightman, p. 247. This liturgy is the only one which, in the *Anaphora*, does not contain the narrative of the Institution with the Sacramental words. This omission did not exist in the text which served as a basis for the corrections of the Synod of Diamper in 1599. The history of this special feature has not yet been clearly worked out, but it is evidently very important. For the Malabar text of the Liturgy of Adaeus and Maris, see R H. Connolly, *Journal of Theological Studies*, 1914, pp. 396 and 569.

[4] Edited, together with the normal Liturgy, by Renaudot, in the volume just mentioned.

[5] Bickell, *Real Enc*, vol. ii. p 321. Here, as in other instances, I make no mention of the texts printed for actual liturgical use. Those which are used by the Catholic communities have suffered from alterations which have been made with more zeal than knowledge. It is not to these books, but to

3. *Cæsarea and Constantinople.*

We have previously seen that, towards the end of the third century, and during a considerable part of the fourth, the Churches of Asia Minor, and especially those of Cappadocia, Pontus, and Bithynia, had close and frequent relations with the see of Antioch. It was from Antioch, moreover, that the Gospel was carried towards these regions. Cæsarea had looked to Antioch before owning obedience to Constantinople. It was by the bishops who came from Antioch or Cæsarea—Gregory Nazianzen, Nectarius, Chrysostom, Nestorius—that the Church of Constantinople was ruled at the period when it received its final organisation.[1] It is, therefore, not surprising that its liturgy reproduces all the essential features of the Syrian Liturgy.[2]

This liturgy is now used over an immense area. It has ended by supplanting the older liturgies in all the Greek patriarchates of the East. It is in use in the National Church of Greece and in those of Servia, Bulgaria, Russia, Roumania, etc.[3] It is true that, in these

ancient manuscripts, we must have recourse if we wish to reconstruct antiquity.

[1] The Arian bishop Eudoxus (360–370) also came from the environs of Antioch

[2] The Council of Laodicea, in the fourth century, has preserved for us some interesting liturgical details. *e g.* lections alternating with hymns (c. 17), homilies, prayers, the dismissal of catechumens and penitents, the threefold prayer of the faithful, in silence in the first instance, and twice aloud, and finally the kiss of peace and the oblation (c. 19).

[3] The ecclesiastical groups connected theoretically with the Greek Patriarchate of Constantinople are: 1st, the Holy Synod of Athens (Kingdom of Greece); 2nd, the Holy Synod of Petersburg (Russian Empire); 3rd, the Servian Patriarchate of Carlowitz (Servia in Austro-Hungary);

72 CHRISTIAN WORSHIP: ITS ORIGIN AND EVOLUTION.

latter countries, where the liturgical language is not Greek, translations are employed which are made from the Greek text used in the Patriarchate of Constantinople.

There are now in use two texts of the complete Constantinopolitan Liturgy, besides a Mass of the Presanctified. The two complete liturgies bear the names of St. Basil and St. John Chrysostom. The first was, at the outset, the normal Liturgy. It is now used only on the Sundays in Lent (except Palm Sunday), Holy Thursday, Easter Eve, Christmas Eve, the Eve of the Epiphany, and the 1st of January, which is the Feast of St. Basil. On other days, the Liturgy of St. Chrysostom, considerably shorter than the former, is followed. During Lent, except on Saturdays and Sundays, since the Mass, strictly so called, is not then celebrated, the Liturgy of the Presanctified is used, which has come to be attributed, but for what reason it is not known, to St. Gregory the Great.

The most ancient manuscript known of the Byzantine Liturgy is the *Codex Barberinus*, No. 77, of the eighth or ninth century. It is a *Euchologion*, which contains, besides the three liturgies, prayers belonging to other services,

---

4th. the Metropolitan Province of Cetinje (Montenegro); 5th, the Metropolitan Province of Belgrade (Kingdom of Servia); 6th, the National Bulgarian Church; 7th, the National Church of Roumania; 8th, the Metropolitan Provinces of Hermanstadt (Transylvania) and of Tchernowitz (Bukovina); 9th, the Georgian Church under the Exarch of Tiflis (now absorbed by the Russian Church). In Greece, the liturgical language is Greek; in Georgia, Georgian; in Roumania, and the two provinces of Hermanstadt and Tchernowitz, Roumanian; in the other countries, Slavonic. The Uniats of the Byzantine rite are grouped ecclesiastically as follows · In the Eastern Patriarchates of Antioch, Jerusalem, and Alexandria they are under the Melchite patriarch residing at Damascus, as above-mentioned. In the Patriarchate of Constantinople, the Greek-speaking Uniats have no special organisation; they are under the Latin bishops, as are also the few Greek parishes in Italy and Sicily. Those speaking Bulgarian in Turkey, Roumanian in Hungary, and Ruthenian in Austro-Hungary and Russia, have bishops and even ecclesiastical provinces of their own rite.

such as Baptism, Ordination, etc. The first of the three liturgies, that of St. Basil, is the only one which bears on it the name of its author, the two others are anonymous.[1] In this ancient manuscript the prayers to be said by the celebrant only are given, the litanies to be said by the deacon not being included, nor, of course, the lections and hymns. It contains but few rubrics. This arrangement closely recalls that of the Latin Sacramentaries. The later manuscripts, of the twelfth century and onwards, are much more complete.

There is no doubt that the Liturgy of St. Basil is the most ancient of the three. The text we possess of it is attested as early as the beginning of the sixth century. In a letter addressed about 520, by the monks of Scythia to the African bishops in exile in Sardinia,[2] we find a passage from it quoted at length.

4. *Armenia.*

The Armenian Liturgy, evidently derived from that of Cæsarea and Constantinople, may be regarded as representing, in certain respects, an ancient stage of the Byzantine Liturgy.

---

[1] Mr. Brightman has published (*op cit*, p 309, *et seq*) the three liturgies according to the Barberini manuscript, which gives the use of the ninth century or thereabouts; in addition to this, he gives the two liturgies of St Chrysostom and of St Basil, following the texts now in use. He has also collected and classified (p 518, *et seq*) a certain number of texts which are useful in giving an idea of the development of the Byzantine Liturgy.

[2] Migne, *P. L*, vol lxv. p 449 "Hinc etiam beatus Basilius Caesariensis episcopus in oratione sacri altaris quam paene universus frequentat Oriens, inter caetera *Dona*, inquit, *Domine virtutem ac tutamentum; malos quaesumus, bonos facito, bonos in bonitate conserva. Omnia enim potes et non est qui contradicat tibi Cum enim volueris salvas et nullus resistit voluntati tuae*"

The Armenian use is represented by only a single text, of which the oldest attestation as to its details is a commentary of the tenth century.[1] The Armenian Church, in 491, denounced the Council of Chalcedon, at a time when none of the official Churches of the Greek Empire accepted it. When the latter came into communion with Rome (519), and embraced the faith of Chalcedon, they made several attempts to induce the Armenians to do the same. But their efforts were in vain—in place of reconciling them they only intensified the schism, which made itself particularly noticeable in the matter of ritual.[2]

In the Middle Ages, many Armenians, who had been driven out of their country by various invasions, emigrated into Persia, Syria, Asia Minor, and even as far as Hungary and Poland. In this dispersion, which was similar to the Jewish *Diaspora*, they preserved their language, nationality, and ritual. Their chief ecclesiastical superior has always been, theoretically, the Catholicos of Etchmiadzin, but they have, as a matter of fact, in various countries, an organisation independent of this theoretical authority, placed at the present time under the influence of Russia. During the eighteenth century many of them were received into communion with the Roman Church. Those in Turkey have at their head a national patriarch (Patriarch of Cilicia), residing at Constantinople. In Austria they are under the Armenian Archbishop of Leopol.[3]

---

[1] P Vetter, *Chosroae M. Explicatio precum missae.* Fribourg, 1880. The Armenian Liturgy is given in English in Brightman, p 412.

[2] The Armenians at that time used unleavened bread, and consecrated their wine without any admixture of water. They did not admit the festival of Christmas into their calendar.

[3] It is clear that neither the Armenian-Gregorian Patriarchs of Turkey, nor the Catholic Patriarch of Cilicia, can be placed on the same footing as the representatives of the four Greek patriarchates. The Catholicos of Etchmiadzin, whose jurisdiction in theory extends over the whole Armenian nation, has a superior title to theirs. But, according to the

§ 4.—THE ALEXANDRINE LITURGY.

1. *The Euchologion of Sarapion.*

With regard to Christian Egypt, we possessed, until lately, no ancient liturgical text which could compare with that of the Syrian Apostolic Constitutions.* This want has been supplied by the discovery, in a manuscript at Mount Athos, of a collection of prayers, two of which bear the name of Sarapion, Bishop of Thmuis, a friend and correspondent of St. Athanasius.[1] It is probable that the others are of the same authorship. The collection comprises thirty compositions, connected respectively with the eucharistic liturgy (1-6), with baptism (7-11), with ordination (12-14), with the blessing of the oils (15-17), with funerals (18), and with the office for Sunday (19-30). It is to the latter that a sort of final rubric seems to refer—"All these prayers come before that of the Oblation."

The prayer of the Oblation is the first of the series referred to, and is an *Anaphora*. The text [2] is as follows:—

---

ancient custom, this high dignitary is subordinate to the Archbishop of Cæsarea in Cappadocia; his position is analogous to that of the *Catholicos* of Seleucia and of the Abuna of the Ethiopians. The united Armenians have not even the equivalent of a *catholicos*, for the Archbishop of Leopol is in no way subordinate to the Patriarch of Cilicia. Like him, he is directly under the Pope, without any intermediary

[1] The credit of this discovery is due to Herr G. Wobbermin, who has published these texts in the *Texte und Untersuchungen* of Gebhardt and Harnack (new series, vol 11)

[2] [At the request of Mgr Duchesne, the Bishop of Salisbury's translation from the original is here substituted for his own Speaking of the latter, Mgr. Duchesne dwells upon the word ἀγένητος used in the original, and says], It will no doubt excite astonishment that in this composition of a friend of St. Athanasius, there should be a kind of predilection for the term *ingenitus*, with the corresponding words, *unigenitus, genitus* so much in vogue in the Arianising world In spite of this awkward terminology, perhaps due to custom, the redaction is most strictly orthodox.

* See Appendix, p. 577A.

Prayer of Oblation of Bishop Sarapion.

It is meet and right to praise, to hymn, to glorify Thee the uncreated[1] Father of the only-begotten Jesus Christ. We praise Thee, O uncreated God, who art unsearchable, ineffable, incomprehensible by any created substance. We praise Thee who art known of Thy Son, the only-begotten, who through Him art spoken of and interpreted and made known to created nature. We praise Thee who knowest the Son and revealest to the saints the glories that are about Him: who art known of Thy begotten Word, and art brought to the sight and interpreted to the understanding of the saints. We praise Thee, O unseen Father, provider of immortality. Thou art the Fount of life, the Fount of light, the Fount of all grace and all truth, O lover of men, O lover of the poor, who reconcilest Thyself to all, and drawest all to Thyself through the advent (ἐπιδημία) of Thy beloved Son. We beseech Thee make us living men. Give us a Spirit of light, that "we may know Thee the True [God] and Him whom Thou didst send, (even) Jesus Christ." Give us Holy Spirit, that we may be able to tell forth and to enuntiate Thy unspeakable mysteries. May the Lord Jesus speak in us and Holy Spirit, and hymn Thee through us.

* For Thou art "far above all rule and authority and power and dominion, and every name that is named, not only in this world, but also in that which is to come." Beside Thee stand thousand thousands and myriad myriads of angels, archangels, thrones, dominions, principalities, powers (*lit.* rules, authorities): by Thee stand the two most honourable six-winged seraphim, with two wings covering the face, and with two the feet, and with two flying and crying holy (ἁγιάζοντα), with whom receive also our cry of "holy" (ἁγιασμόν) as we say: Holy, holy, holy, Lord of Sabaoth, full is the heaven and the earth of Thy glory.

Full is the heaven, full also is the earth of Thy excellent glory.* Lord of hosts (*lit.* powers), fill also this sacrifice with Thy power and Thy participation (μεταλήψεως): for to Thee have we offered this living [2]

---

[1] The word is ἀγένητον in the original [Mgr Duchesne rendered the words γεννητός and ἀγένητος by *créé* and *incréé* in the French—at the same time regretting that that language did not permit of his using *devenu* and *indevenu* (the latter does not exist) in an absolute sense.—Tr.]

[2] [The Bishop of Salisbury compares this with the phrase of the Nestorian Liturgy which speaks of the Body and Blood of Christ as being on the altar before consecration (Brightman, p. 267)]

* [The Bishop of Salisbury says there is much similarity in the passage between these asterisks to the parallel passage in the Liturgy of St. Mark, but the differences are also striking]

THE MASS IN THE EAST. 77

sacrifice, this bloodless oblation. To Thee we have offered this bread the likeness (ὁμοίωμα) of the Body of the Only-begotten. This bread is the likeness of the Holy Body, because the Lord Jesus Christ in the night in which He was betrayed took bread and broke and gave to His disciples saying, "Take ye and eat, this is My Body, which is being broken for you for remission of sins" (cp. *Lit. of St. Mark, etc.*). Wherefore we also making the likeness of the death have offered the bread, and beseech Thee through this sacrifice, be reconciled to all of us and be merciful, O God of Truth : and as this * bread had been scattered on the top of the mountains and gathered together came to be one, so also gather Thy holy Church out of * every nation and every country and every city and village and house and make one living Catholic Church. We have offered also the cup, the likeness of the Blood, because the Lord Jesus Christ, taking a cup after supper, said to His own disciples, "Take ye, drink, this is the new covenant, which (ὅ) is My Blood, which is being shed for you for remission of sins (ἁμαρτημάτων)." Wherefore we have also offered the cup, presenting a likeness of the blood.

O God of Truth, let Thy Holy Word[1] come upon this bread (ἐπιδημησάτω ... ἐπὶ τ ἀ.τ), that the bread may become Body of the Word, and upon this cup that the cup may become Blood of the Truth ; and make all who communicate to receive a medicine of life for the healing of every sickness and for the strengthening of all advancement and virtue, not for condemnation, O God of Truth, and not for censure and reproach. For we have invoked Thee, the uncreated, through the Only-begotten in Holy Spirit.

Let this people receive mercy, let it be counted worthy of advancement, let angels be sent forth as companions to the people for bringing to naught of the evil one and for establishment of the Church.

We intercede also on behalf of all who have been laid to rest, whose memorial we are making.

After the recitation (ὑποβολὴν †) *of the names* : Sanctify these souls: for Thou knowest all. Sanctify all (souls) laid to rest in the Lord. And number them with all Thy holy powers, and give to them a place and a mansion in Thy kingdom.

Receive also the thanksgiving (eucharist) of the people, and bless those who have offered the offerings (τὰ πρόσφορα) and the thanksgivings,

---

[1] It is noticeable that, in this passage, which corresponds to the *Epiclesis*, the Divine Word, and not the Holy Spirit, is mentioned.

* The passage between asterisks is suggested by the *Doctrine of the Apostles, vide supra*, p 52

† [The Bishop of Salisbury calls attention to Socrates, *H. E*, vol. xxii. p 296, where ὑποβολεῖς are mentioned with "Readers": see Valesius' note, and the Bishop's Index, p 104]

and grant health and soundness and cheerfulness and all advancement of soul and body to this whole people through the only-begotten Jesus Christ in Holy Spirit; as it was and is and shall be to generations of generations and to all the ages of the ages. Amen.

Five short prayers follow in the manuscript. The first was said at the moment of the fraction; the second, over the people, upon whom there was an imposition of hands [blessing] after the communion of the clergy; the third was the thanksgiving after the communion of the people. Then follows a blessing of the offered oil and water which were to be used in private as phylacteries, and lastly the blessing of the assembly at the moment of dismissal.

As to the formularies which terminate the *Euchologion* (19–30), and which, according to the rubric, preceded the prayer of Oblation, the series begins (19) by a "first prayer for Sunday," which is, in fact, an introductory prayer. Supplication is there made to God for the right apprehension of the Holy Scriptures, and for their right interpretation. The second (20) comes after the homily. I take it that these two prayers presuppose the presence of those who are still outside the pale of Christianity, though they may be disposed to embrace it, or, at least, to be instructed in it. The three ensuing formularies are prayers for the catechumens (21), for the sick (22), and for the fruits of the earth (23). The prayer for the catechumens was doubtless used at the moment of their dismissal. Then follows a prayer for the local Church as a whole (24), then another for its various members, bishops, priests, deacons, sub-deacons, lectors, interpreters,[1] *ascetae* (μονά-ζοντες), virgins, and married people. Next we have (26) a "prayer of genuflection," which deals with the names inscribed in the book of life. Perhaps this had some connection with the recitation of the diptychs. The prayer

---

[1] In Egypt the Greek had to be translated into Coptic.

which follows (27), entitled, "For the People," deals in detail with all the objects and classes of persons prayed for by the Church in her solemn supplications—the well-being of the faithful, the peace of the State, the tranquillity of the Church, for the slaves, the poor, the aged, the travellers, the sick, etc. .The three last accompany the imposition of hands on the catechumens (28), on the faithful (29), and on the sick (30).

I do not believe[1] that these twelve formularies represent the official or ordinary *ordo liturgicus* of the Church of Thmuis, but they are all of a nature applicable to a non-liturgical service, or to a liturgical service before the *anaphora*, or prayer of sacrifice.

2. *Later Liturgies.*

Religious unity in Egypt was broken up after the condemnation of the Patriarch Dioscorus by the Council of Chalcedon. After a century of fruitless attempts to bring the dissentients once more within the pale of orthodoxy, the Imperial Government found itself obliged to acknowledge the coexistence of two Churches within the country. One, the orthodox, supported by the Government and the Byzantine official world, the other, the heretical, upheld by the mass of the indigenous population. This division did not immediately make itself apparent in the sphere of worship, both heretics and orthodox continuing to follow the ancient use of Alexandria. But the official Church modified this use little by little, under the influence of the Liturgy of Constantinople, until a time came when the latter was completely substituted for it.

[1] In this I differ from the Bishop of Salisbury, Dr Wordsworth, who has published the "Prayer-book" of Sarapion in English, with a learned commentary—*Bishop Sarapion's Prayer-book*· S P C K, London, 1899.

The orthodox or Melchite Church continued to use Greek, whereas the Monophysite Church discarded the language of Constantinople, and made almost exclusive use of Coptic, the national tongue of the Egyptian population.[1]

The Church of Abyssinia, which was not definitely formed until after the Council of Chalcedon, was, from the outset, dependent on that of Egypt, and, following its example, embraced the Monophysite confession. Its liturgical language has always been Ethiopic or Gheez.[2]

The texts at our disposal for studying the ancient use of Alexandria are—

1. *The Greek Liturgy of St. Mark*, of which three texts are known, of the twelfth century and onwards. It doubtless was subject to many Byzantine revisions, but the essential parts agree with the style and often with the tenor of the best texts which have reached us from other sources. There is no doubt that it is of great antiquity, going back at latest to the fifth century.[3]

2. *The Coptic Liturgies.*—These are three in number— that of St. Cyril (of Alexandria), of St Gregory (Nazianzen), and of St. Basil[4] They do not differ except in the *anaphora*. The liturgy at present in use is that of St. Basil, and it is to the *Anaphora* of St. Basil that the

---

[1] A certain number of the Copts have entered into communion with Rome They have recently (1895) been organised into a patriarchate.

[2] The Abyssinian Catholics possess no other organisation than that of the Apostolic Vicariate of Abyssinia, under the direction of Latin missionaries

[3] Mr Brightman, working on the results obtained by Canon Swainson, has published this liturgy from the Rossano manuscript (Vaticanus 1970), and from two *rotuli*, one at Messina, of the twelfth century; the other in the Vatican, of the year 1207 (*op cit.*, p. 113)

[4] This liturgy must not be confounded with the Byzantine Liturgy bearing the same name.

Ordinary of the Mass is attached in the liturgical books. The *Anaphora* of St. Cyril, however, is evidently the most ancient. This is clear, in the first place, from the fact that it alone of the three presents certain features characteristic of the Alexandrine Liturgy; and, in the second, because it reproduces often the text of the Liturgy of St. Mark word for word. By joining to the *Anaphora* of St. Cyril the Ordinary of the Coptic Mass, we obtain a Coptic liturgy which is the exact counterpart of the Greek Liturgy of St. Mark.[1] The *Anaphorae* of St. Gregory and of St. Basil are also found in Greek

3. *Abyssinian Liturgies.*—The Abyssinians have as their normal liturgy the Liturgy *of the Twelve Apostles*,[2] which is fundamentally identical with the Coptic Liturgy of St. Cyril. In addition to this they have a dozen or so alternative *anaphorae*.

4. *The Borgian Fragments.*—These were published by the Abbé Hyvernat[3] from Coptic manuscripts ranging in date from the eighth to the twelfth century. These fragments are parts of five different masses. Giorgi had already published a portion of one of them.[4]

Not counting these fragments, and discarding the alternative pieces belonging to the Abyssinians, together with the *anaphorae* of Gregory and Basil, which are rather of the Syrian type, and represent a foreign importation, there remain three texts, viz. the Greek Liturgy of St. Mark, the Coptic Liturgy of St. Cyril, and the Abyssinian Liturgy of the Twelve Apostles, which have each as its source one of the three ecclesiastical varieties of the Alexandrine rite. The texts are fundamentally one, and their variations

[1] Brightman, p 144.
[2] *Ibid.*, p 194.
[3] *Römische Quartalschrift*, 1888
[4] *Fragmentum Evangelii S Johannis* · Rome, 1789. Cf Hammond, *The Liturgy of Antioch*, p. 27.

arise merely from later modifications. If we would reconstruct the ancient Alexandrine Liturgy we must, to begin with, compare these liturgies together and select from them that which they have in common. The works of Egyptian writers containing liturgical allusions may also be profitably examined.[1]

The characteristic feature of the Alexandrine Liturgy is the occurrence of the Great Supplication in the Preface instead of after the Consecration. The *Sanctus*, the words of institution, and the *Epiclesis*, are thus placed much later than in the Syrian Liturgy. This arrangement is not found in the *Anaphora* of Sarapion, but it was pointed out by Jacob of Edessa as early as the end of the seventh century.[2] He remarks also that the Salutation before the Preface is much less complicated than in the Syrian, the celebrant merely saying, *Dominus vobiscum omnibus*;[3] moreover, the acclamation of the people at the *Sancta Sanctis* presents certain peculiarities of form.

§ 5.—Later Modifications.

Even when we have reduced them to their most ancient form—that which they possessed before the schisms of the sixth century, all these liturgies are still far from having the simplicity of those of the fourth century. Many things have been changed, suppressed, and added. The points at

---

[1] They are brought together by Brightman, p 504.
[2] Assemani, *Bibl. Orient*, vol. i. p. 481, *et seq*. They are also to be found in the fragments published by Hyvernat.
[3] The following are the forms in known documents—Lit. of St. Mark: 'Ο Κύριος μετὰ πάντων (Cod. Ross; the *Rot. Vaticanus* has here the Syrian Salutation; in the *Rot. Messanensis* there is a *hiatus* at this point); Lit. of SS. Cyril and Basil: *Dominus vobiscum;* the Æthiopian gives, *Dominus vobiscum omnibus*.

which the modifications have been most marked are as follows :—

In the first place, the entry of the celebrants has become an imposing ceremony. In the Byzantine Liturgy it was accompanied from an early date by a special chant, the Μονογενής.[1] Before the lections comes the Trisagion.[2] The use of this doxology must be very ancient. It is common to all the Greek Oriental liturgies, and occurs even in the Gallican Liturgy.[3] The most ancient testimony for its existence is found in the Council of Chalcedon (451)[4]

The dismissal of the catechumens, energumens, competents, and penitents, which stands out so prominently in the liturgy of the fourth century, had all disappeared at an early date, owing to changes in the discipline regarding these different categories. The Constantinopolitan ritual, however, has preserved to our own day the ceremony of the dismissal of the catechumens.

But it was especially in the preparation of the elements of the sacred feast that a theme was found for the development of rites and prayers. The bread and wine for consecration were prepared, before the entry of the celebrants, at a special table—the table of proposition ($\pi\rho\acute{o}\theta\epsilon\sigma\iota\varsigma$)—standing like the altar within the sacred enclosure and out of sight of the congregation. This constituted a preparatory Mass, the Mass of the Prothesis, which was very long and complicated,

---

[1] Ὁ μονογενὴς Υἱὸς καὶ Λόγος τοῦ Θεοῦ, ἀθάνατος ὑπάρχων, καταδεξάμενος διὰ τὴν ἡμετέραν σωτηρίαν σαρκωθῆναι ἐκ τῆς ἁγίας Θεοτόκου καὶ ἀειπαρθένου Μαρίας, ἀτρέπτως ἐνανθρωπήσας σταυρωθείς τε, Χριστὲ ὁ Θεὸς, θανάτῳ θάνατον πατήσας, εἷς ὢν τῆς ἁγίας Τριάδος, συνδοξαζόμενος τῷ Πατρὶ καὶ τῷ ἁγίῳ Πνεύματι, σῶσον ἡμᾶς.

[2] Ἅγιος ὁ Θεὸς, ἅγιος ἰσχυρὸς, ἅγιος ἀθάνατος, ἐλέησον ἡμᾶς.

[3] In the Coptic Liturgy the Trisagion is placed before the Gospel, and after the other lections. In the Gallican Liturgy we find it also placed before the Gospel, and even after it; but this does not interfere with its being sung at its normal place before the lections.

[4] *Hardouin*, vol. ii. p. 272. For the legend connected with the Trisagion, see Tillemont, *Hist Eccles*, vol. xiv p 713.

especially in the ritual of Constantinople. After the lections and the prayer of the faithful, the oblation was brought with great pomp to the altar. This procession of the oblation [1] constituted the most imposing ceremonial in the entire Mass. It was accompanied in the Churches of the Byzantine, or Byzantinised rite, by a chant or hymn, called the *Cheroubicon*.[2]

It was at this point in the Mass that the recitation of the Creed occurred. According to Theodore the Reader, this custom was first introduced at Antioch by the bishop Peter the Fuller, in 471, and afterwards at Constantinople by the patriarch Timotheus, in 511. Peter and Timotheus were reckoned among the most zealous opponents of the Council of Chalcedon. Their innovation was not, however, abolished after the Eastern Churches came back into the orthodox Communion.[3]

During the procession of the oblation and the ceremonies which followed it—the kiss of peace, the recitation of the Creed, the recitation of the diptychs—the celebrant said his own private prayers. These prayers at length became

---

[1] Dionysius the Areopagite makes mention of this procession, and the custom of chanting a hymn during it, but he does not give the text of the hymn (*Eccl. Hier.*, iii 2)

[2] "Οἱ τὰ Χερουβὶμ μυστικῶς εἰκονίζοντες καὶ τῇ ζωοποιῷ Τριάδι, τὸν τρισάγιον ὕμνον ᾄδοντες, πᾶσαν τὴν βιωτικὴν ἀποθώμεθα μέριμναν, ὡς τὸν βασιλέα τῶν ὅλων ὑποδεξάμενοι, ταῖς ἀγγελικαῖς ἀοράτως δορυφορούμενον τάξεσιν, Ἀλληλούια, Ἀλληλούϊα, Ἀλληλούια" The Liturgy of St James furnishes us with another as fine: "Σιγησάτω πᾶσα σὰρξ βροτεία καὶ στήτω μετὰ φόβου καὶ τρόμου καὶ μηδὲν γήινον ἐν ἑαυτῇ λογιζέσθω. Ὁ γὰρ βασιλεὺς τῶν βασιλευόντων, Χριστὸς ὁ Θεὸς ἡμῶν, προέρχεται σφαγιασθῆναι εἰς βρῶσιν τοῖς πιστοῖς · προηγοῦνται δὲ τούτου οἱ χοροὶ τῶν Ἀγγέλων, μετὰ πάσης Ἀρχῆς καὶ Ἐξουσίας, τὰ πολυόμματα Χερουβὶμ καὶ τὰ ἑξαπτέρυγα Σεραφίμ, τὰς ὄψεις καλύπτοντα καὶ βοῶντα τὸν ὕμνον Ἀλληλούια."

[3] One of the things most urgently insisted upon by the Monophysite party was the abrogation of every formulary of faith later than that of Nicæa-Constantinople It is certain that in the introduction of the latter into the liturgy, they meant to protest against the definition of Chalcedon.

fixed in formularies.[1] One of them was said at the moment at which the veil was withdrawn. There was in fact a veil which, stretching across the altar, or even across the whole apse, shut out the view up to the moment when, after the dismissal of the catechumens and other non-communicants, the celebration of the mysteries in the presence of the initiated only was begun. This veil is still in use among the Churches following the Oriental rite. It is stretched before the central door of the iconostasis; and is drawn and withdrawn at the times enjoined in the ancient liturgies.

We must take note of the recitation of the diptychs in this part of the Mass. The Syro-Byzantine liturgies place it between the Kiss of Peace and the Preface, and this custom is corroborated, at the beginning of the sixth century, by Dionysius the Areopagite. It disappeared afterwards at Constantinople. In the Alexandrine use, the reading appears to have taken place, as it did in the Gallican rite, after the Kiss of Peace.

From the *Sursum Corda* until the end of the Mass the rites, and subject-matter of the prayers, have remained almost the same as they were at the beginning. Some diversities, when we compare one use with another, appear in the position assigned to certain parts, such as the *Memento*, the *Pater Noster*, and the fraction of the bread, but hardly any addition has been made to the primitive ritual. It is necessary to draw attention, however, to the complication introduced in the ceremony of the *fractio*, and of the *commixtio*, that is to say, the mixture of the consecrated bread and wine. A characteristic feature of the Liturgy of Constantinople was the infusion of a little hot water into the chalice immediately before the Communion.

[1] Dionysius the Areopagite makes mention of the prayer said by the bishop at the moment when the sacred oblations were placed upon the altar: this is the εὐχὴ τῆς προσκομιδῆς of the Byzantine Liturgy, the counterpart of the prayer *Super oblata* in the Roman Liturgy.

CHAPTER III.

THE TWO LITURGICAL USES OF THE LATIN WEST.

§ 1.—THE ROMAN AND GALLICAN USES.

THE liturgical uses of the East, varying at first with the patriarchates, or, rather, with the great ecclesiastical groups of the fourth century, gave way at length, one after the other, to the distinctive ritual of the Church of Constantinople. Provincial peculiarities were maintained only among the dissentient Churches outside the sphere of orthodoxy, and beyond the bounds of the Greek language and even of the Byzantine Empire. In the West also diversity of use preceded unity. It is easy to show that towards the end of the fourth century the Latin Churches did not all follow the same use. Judged in the whole, and apart from certain local peculiarities, these different liturgical uses can be reduced to two—the Roman and the Gallican.

There is something strange in this duality. The history of the evangelisation of the West gives support to the assertion of Pope Innocent that it proceeded entirely[1]

---

[1] The presence, in the Church of Lyons, at the time of the Emperor Marcus Aurelius, of a certain number of Christians from the Province of Asia, and from Phrygia, forms no objection to this point of view. All the documents which have come down to us bearing on this ancient Christian community agree in representing it as being in close and frequent relations with the Church of Rome. There is nothing to prove that its founder was from the Province of Asia, rather than a Roman. Supposing even that he was an Asiatic, it was possibly the case that he had lived in the first instance at Rome, and had there received his mission.

from Rome, and that on this ground the Roman Liturgy alone has the primordial right to be the liturgy of Latin Christendom [1] :—

> Quis enim nesciat aut non advertat id quod a principe apostolorum Petro Romanae ecclesiae traditum est ac nunc usque custoditur ab omnibus debere servari, nec superduci aut introduci aliquid quod auctoritatem non habeat, aut aliunde accipere videatur exemplum? Praesertim cum sit manifestum in omnem Italiam, Galliam, Hispanias, Africam, atque Siciliam insulasque interjacentes nullum instituisse ecclesias, nisi eos quos venerabilis apostolus Petrus aut ejus successores constituerunt sacerdotes? Aut legant si in his provinciis alius apostolorum invenitur aut legitur docuisse. Quod si non legunt, quia nusquam inveniunt, oportet eos hoc sequi quod ecclesia Romana custodit, a qua eos principium accepisse non dubium est.

However strange the fact may seem to us, it is none the less certain that, from the time of Pope Innocent, the Roman liturgical use was not the only one followed in the West, or even in Italy itself. The bishop to whom the letter, from which I have just quoted, was addressed was Bishop of Eugubium (Gubbio), in the district of Umbria, which belonged to the metropolitan diocese of the Pope. As an immediate suffragan of the Pope he had special reasons for conforming to Roman customs, and notwithstanding this he was tempted to introduce others. The practice of Rome was thus attacked in its own domain.

The letter belongs to the year 416. The liturgical and disciplinal peculiarities which were therein found to be opposed to the Roman customs are all characteristic of

---

[1] The word *Liturgy* may be used in several senses, more or less comprehensive. It may sometimes be taken to denote the order of the ceremonies and the formularies of the ritual of the Mass, in the special sense of Eucharistic Liturgy. Here it is applied to all the forms of Christian Worship—Baptism, Ordination, the Eucharistic Service, the Consecration of Churches and of Virgins, the reconciliation of penitents, etc.

the use which is conventionally called the Gallican. The latter was, therefore, already in existence at the beginning of the fifth century; it had even sufficient vigour to enter into competition with the Roman Liturgy, and that, too, up to the surburbicarian diocese itself. This use, as is evident from very numerous documents, was followed by the Churches of Northern Italy (metropolitan diocese of Milan)[1] and by those in Gaul, Spain, Britain, and Ireland. From what we can learn, however, from allusions by the Christian orators and synodical decrees of Africa, the use there seems to have been in absolute conformity with the use of Rome and of Southern Italy.[2] We thus find Rome and Carthage on one side, and on the other Milan and the countries beyond the Alps.

In grouping the transalpine countries with Milan, I imply that the Ambrosian Liturgy is identical with the Gallican. This is a view which is not generally accepted. There is no difficulty, on the other hand, in the identification of the liturgy of the Churches of Spain, or Mozarabic Liturgy, up to the eleventh century, with that which was followed by the Churches of Gaul before Charlemagne, and with that which obtained in the British Isles before the Roman missions of the seventh century. With regard to the Ambrosian Liturgy it is, in its present state, very different from other types of the Gallican Liturgy, but we

---

[1] We have no documentary evidence for the uses followed in Aquileia, in the Danubian provinces, and in Dalmatia It is probable that the use observed in Aquileia and the Danubian provinces resembled rather the Milan than the Roman Liturgy. Dom G. Morin has published lately (*Revue Bénéd*, 1902, p. 1) a Lectionary of the Gospels, which probably belonged to Aquileia, and it contains nothing opposed to this view. The Latin liturgical fragments which are included in the Arian texts published by Mai (*Script. Vet*, vol. iii p. 208, *et seq* ; cf *P. L*, vol. xiii. p. 611) are, in my opinion, assignable to the Danubian region. Sig. Mercati has thrown fresh light upon them in a note to his *Studi e Testi* of the Vatican, fasc. 7, p. 47.

[2] See note, p. 572.

must not lose sight of the fact that it has been for centuries subject to continuous modification in the direction of bringing it more and more into conformity with the Roman use. This movement suffered no check from the discovery of printing. Editions after editions of the Ambrosian Missal became more and more Romanised. But the beginning of this process goes back to some time before Charlemagne. It was natural that such should be the case, for Milan was too near Rome to escape from its influence in this as in other respects. It adopted at an early date the Gregorian Canon. In spite, however, of the many modifications it has experienced, the Ambrosian Liturgy preserves sufficient Gallican features to establish clearly its primitive identity, in my opinion, at least, with the transalpine liturgies.[1] The facts I intend to adduce later on will put this in a clear light. I do not bring them forward here because they would lose something of their significance if I isolated them from the comparative analysis of the Gallican rites; but I think no one will regret giving me credit in the mean time.

[1] I ought in truth to say that these views have not been accepted without reserve by the Milanese experts who have taken up the study of the Ambrosian Liturgy. This difference of appreciation would have given me more concern if I did not feel that it was connected with a tendency, very natural and worthy of regard in other respects, to exaggerate the importance of this liturgy. It is not willingly admitted that the Ambrosian rite has been subject to so much Roman revision, and that it is now very far from its primitive form. I fear I have perhaps given offence in presenting it as a combination, somewhat hybrid in character, of the Roman and the Gallican. There is a tendency to regard it as not only relatively pure, but that it preserves in it the ancient Latin rite, of which the Roman is a degraded form. I cannot accept this view of the matter. This does not, however, prevent me from having a deep interest in the Ambrosian Liturgy, and in its preservation and restoration. The Gallican Liturgy may be purer in the ancient books, but, like Roland's mare, which had otherwise such excellent qualities, it is dead. At Milan, however much it may have suffered in its many vicissitudes, it is still living. In this respect there is compensation for many defects.

§ 2.—Origin of the Gallican Use.

Assuming that the domain of the Gallican Liturgy extended up to the metropolitan diocese of the Pope, embracing North Italy, or, at the least, the metropolitan diocese of Milan, the way becomes open for the solution of an obscure and contentious question : that of the origin of the Gallican Liturgy.

The English liturgiologists, who have been much occupied with this question, have in general resolved it as follows: The Gallican Liturgy, according to them, is the Liturgy of Ephesus, of the ancient Church of the Roman province of Asia, and was imported into Gaul by the founders of the Church of Lyons. From this Church it spread throughout the whole transalpine West.

I believe that this position cannot be maintained, and for the following reasons : The Gallican Liturgy, as far as it is distinct from the Roman, is a very complicated affair, and there is something very formal in its complication. While it implies numerous and varied rites arranged in a certain order, it consists of formularies which are identical in theme and style, and sometimes in tenor. It departs widely from those simple and still unfixed forms which can be definitely assigned to, or may be assumed to have existed in, the liturgy of the second century. Its development corresponds at the earliest with the condition of things in the fourth century. It shows an advance upon that of the Apostolic Constitutions. Its importation into, and propagation throughout, the West cannot be assigned to the second century. We have here before us a text which must be ascribed, at the very earliest, to the middle of the fourth century.

Now, in the fourth century, the ecclesiastical influence of Lyons was almost non-existent. This city, after the new provincial organisation under Diocletian, had lost its position as metropolis of the three Gauls. The glory and influence of

Treves, Vienne, and Arles had passed away. The Bishop of Lyons, whatever may have been his importance in the second century, occupied no special prominence after Constantine. He was scarcely more than metropolitan of *Lugdunensis Prima* until the time of Gregory VII., who was the founder of the primacy of Lyons, ineffective as it was. It was not in conditions such as these that this Church could become the model of all Western Churches, the focus of an ecclesiastical radiation sufficiently intense to make itself felt beyond the Pyrenees and the English Channel, and, crossing the Alps, strong enough to withdraw from the area of Roman influence half the Churches of Italy.[1]

It is manifest that another solution of the question must be sought for. The solution I have to offer is based on the assumption that Milan was the principal centre of this development.[2]

I have shown above that the Church of Milan had been,

[1] I am well acquainted with the fact that, towards the end of the sixth century, the Bishop of Lyons seems to have put forward a claim to supremacy over the Bishops of Gontran's kingdom. Gregory of Tours (*Hist. Franc*, v. 20) gives the title of patriarch to St. Nizier. His successor, Priscus, bears the same designation in the national council of 585. He even brings about the decision there that the national councils shall be held every three years, he and the king convoking them The Bishop of Lyons is the first to sign in the councils of Paris (614), Clichy (627), and of Chalon-sur-Saône (about 650). In the years 597 and 692 he consecrates the Archbishop of Canterbury. Cf my *Fastes Episcopaux de l'Ancienne Gaule*, vol. i p 138. But this state of affairs has no sort of relation to that which obtained at the beginning, in the time of Pothinus and Irenæus The history of St. Avitus of Vienne and that of the Vicariat of Arles are sufficient to prove this

[2] We might, in this connection, think of Arles, which enjoyed such a very high ecclesiastical position in the fifth and sixth centuries But this position was attained too late It was to the fourth, and not to the fifth or sixth, century that the liturgical influence belonged of which I am seeking the origin. Arles became at a fairly early date the focus of ecclesiastical law in Gaul. I have shown (*Fastes Episc*, vol 1. p 141) that almost all the *Libri Canonum* in use in Merovingian Gaul were derived from those of the Church of Arles In regard to the liturgy the matter was different. Arles was not of sufficient importance at the time when the Churches of Gaul felt the necessity of regulating the order of worship.

towards the end of the fourth century and in the early years of the fifth, a kind of superior metropolis to which the whole of the West was inclined to look. We have seen that the Bishops of Gaul and Spain were accustomed to proceed thither frequently to procure solutions of difficulties and rules of conduct.[1] The imperial city was admirably situated to afford a model in the matter of worship and of liturgy. What cannot be allowed to Lyons is readily granted in the case of Milan. From the moment when Rome became no longer the centre of attraction, from the moment when inspiration was sought elsewhere, Milan could not fail to have the preference over all other Churches.[2] And it is worthy of note that the time to which we have assigned these relations between Milan and the transalpine Churches of the West corresponds with a period in which a considerable number of these Churches were undergoing an internal organisation and development, or even in process of being founded.[3] This was the time in which the masses in the towns were converted, in which Churches were reconstructed on a larger scale, in which it was necessary to increase the number of the clergy and to lay down with precision the rules regulating discipline and public worship. The influence

[1] The remembrance of this influence is still active in the middle of the sixth century, as we see from a sermon preached at Constantinople by Dacius, Bishop of Milan "Ecce ego et pars omnium sacerdotum inter quos ecclesia mea constituta est, id est Galliae, Burgundiae, Spaniae, Liguriae, Aemiliae atque Venetiae, contestor quia quicumque in edicta ista consenserit, suprascriptarum provinciarum pontifices communicatores habere non poterit, quia constat *apud me* edicta ista sanctam synodum Chalcedonensem et fidem catholicam perturbare" (*Ep Clericorum Italiae*, Migne, *P. Lat*, vol. lxix. p 117)

[2] It is worth while to recall here how the finding of the martyrs at Milan in the time of St. Ambrose called forth in Gaul a responsive feeling. It is to this epoch, and in consequence of these relations, that the dedication of so many Churches in Gaul under the invocations of St. Gervais and St Nazaire are to be assigned.

[3] Many Churches in Gaul were founded in the fourth century, *i e* in the time of Constantine and his sons.

of Milan was asserting itself just at the moment when the
Gallican Liturgy had reached that stage of development
which it possessed when it spread throughout the West,
and at the very moment when the West experienced the
need of a definitely fixed liturgy.

This is not all. It is well known that the Gallican
Liturgy, in the features distinguishing it from the Roman
use, betrays all the characteristics of the Eastern liturgies.
We shall see, further on, that some of its formularies are
to be found word for word in the Greek texts in use in the
Churches of the Syro-Byzantine rite either in the fourth
century or somewhat later. This close resemblance implies an importation. The Gallican Liturgy is an Oriental
liturgy, introduced into the West towards the middle of
the fourth century. Now, apart from the presence of the
Court at Milan, and the numerous assemblies of Oriental
bishops held there, we have to take into account the important fact that the Church of Milan had at its head for
nearly twenty years (355-374) a Cappadocian, Auxentius,
who had been designated by the Emperor Constantius to
occupy the see of St. Dionysius, when the latter was exiled
for the Catholic faith. Auxentius belonged to the clergy of
the Court, who were out of sympathy with St. Athanasius
and the defenders of "consubstantial" orthodoxy. He played
a distinguished part at the Council of Ariminum (359).
After the defeat of the Arianising party which, in the West,
followed closely upon the breaking up of this council, Auxentius maintained his position, and remained fifteen years in
his see, notwithstanding the efforts made to dislodge him.
This would seem to indicate that he had a strength of mind
beyond the common. We can readily believe, therefore, that
during his long episcopate he made some impression upon his
clergy and upon the internal organisation of his Church. St.
Ambrose, his successor, found many customs established which
did not all seem to require correction. His broad-mindedness

on this score is shown by his retention of the whole of the clerical staff left or organised by his predecessor.[1] Possibly, doctrine being safeguarded by the very fact of his elevation to the see of Milan, Ambrose thought it inopportune to introduce useless changes in the domain of ritual. Certainly many of the most important Milanese peculiarities in discipline and worship go back to his episcopate, and, seeing that these peculiarities have a distinctly Oriental character, they could not have been introduced by him. It is more natural to believe that they existed before him, and that he had only sanctioned customs previously imported.[2]

I do not wish to be dogmatic on this point. Milan was in easy communication with Constantinople and Asia Minor through Aquileia and the Illyrian provinces. Auxentius was not the only Greek who in the fourth century may have exercised episcopal functions in a Latin country. His action in the liturgical domain may have been but an episode in a larger movement. Others might have acted as he did in adopting the same models. Nevertheless, it is very difficult to regard the development in Gaul and Spain as having proceeded from a Latin source further removed than Milan.[3]

However this may be, the political position of Milan was not maintained later than cir. 400. The glory of its see was dimmed at the same time, and Rome was thus

[1] This is clear from a contemporary letter from Theophilus of Alexandria to Flavius of Antioch (E. W. Brooks, *The sixth book of the select letters of Severus*, vol. II p. 304).

[2] To those disinclined to accept what would seem to be an Arian origin for the Gallican Liturgy, I would say that Arianism has nothing to do with the question, which deals solely with the Oriental form of the liturgy, a form of earlier date than Arianism in the countries of its origin. I would add that, inasmuch as forms of prayer were in the fourth century much varied and very easily modified, it must be considered certain that St. Ambrose would have left nothing in them which could possibly have fostered heresy.

[3] This does not exclude the direct importations of Byzantine, and especially Palestinian, usages. I shall give several instances later on.

relieved from a competition which might have ended in the establishment of a rival. It was scarcely possible, indeed, to undo an accomplished fact. The Popes no doubt considered that no inconvenience would arise if liturgical usages differing from their own were allowed to continue; in any case, there were more urgent questions seeking solution. They confined their efforts to defending their metropolitan diocese from the invasion of the Gallican ritual, and left the Churches of other provinces to arrange on this point as they felt inclined. Circumstances, moreover, did not favour the development of ecclesiastical centralisation. National barriers soon rose up between Rome and the Churches of the barbaric kingdoms founded in Gaul and Spain.[1]

[1] The above view has, from the first edition of this book, been contested by divers persons. Those among them whose opinion is of weight, put forward another explanation. The Gallican ritual, according to them, is none other than the ancient Roman ritual, which, reformed at Rome in the fourth century, maintained its position in the provinces. They give even the name of the reformer—according to some, Pope Damasus, according to others, St Gregory or some other pope of the sixth century. But in addition to these latter being clearly excluded by the letter of Innocent, it would be impossible to produce any evidence for these supposed reformations. Besides, with this hypothesis, how can we explain that Pope Innocent, far from recognising in the Gallican ritual the ancient use of his own Church, treats it as a foreign importation, *aliunde acceptum exemplum alterius ecclesiae quam Romanae consuetudinem*? How, moreover, can we account for the fact that Africa, so jealous of her individuality, hastened to adopt the Roman reform, while St Ambrose, who was Roman by birth and feeling, refused to introduce it into his Church? Doubtless certain forms of worship must have been propagated in the West by the Roman missions at the actual time of evangelisation. But these missions took place too early to warrant us attributing to them an organised ritual of so complicated a nature as that under consideration. For we must not allow ourselves to be hypnotised by the Canon of the Roman Mass and its possible variations. The differences between the two uses, Roman and Gallican, exist not in the Mass only, but in the various ceremonies as a whole—Initiation, Ordination, Consecration of Churches and Virgins, the arrangement of Festivals, and even in certain disciplinary observances in connection with Christian Worship. The divergence lies in the entire accustomed Use, the *consuetudo ecclesiae*. Why Rome should have changed her own, is what we cannot understand. Throughout

§ 3.—FUSION OF THE TWO USES.

If the countries of the Gallican rite found themselves increasingly isolated from Rome, their liturgical use, deprived of a common religious centre, escaped all regulation and all superior ecclesiastical authority capable of controlling its development. Numerous varieties were the consequence, and many details not settled at the beginning were determined later on without any common understanding. The provincial synods attempted here and there to establish some uniformity: *e.g.* the decrees of the Council of Vannes (cir. 465) may be cited for the province of Tours, those of the Council of Agde (506) for the Visigothic kingdom of Gaul, and those of the Council of Gerona (517) for the province of Tarragona.

The most remarkable results were obtained in Spain, in the seventh century, when that country had attained its religious and political unity. There, at least, there had been, in the Councils of Toledo and in the primacy of that see, a firm basis for legislation and for the reformation of public worship. It was in this country that the Gallican use maintained its hold the longest.

Outside the Visigothic kingdom this use fell into irremediable decadence. Rome, on the contrary, continued always to appear as a model Church, as well regulated in its worship as in its discipline and its faith. Relations between it and the Churches of the West were not impossible, though they had become less close and less easy. The bishops of the regions of the Gallican rite resorted from time to time to the apostolic see, after, as well as before, the invasions of the fifth century, to obtain from it a ruling in their difficulties. When liturgical matters were in question, the

the fourth century, and since that date, the government of the Roman Church has always remained in native hands. It was not so at Milan, where the Episcopate of Auxentius and the almost exclusively Eastern influence of the Court are sufficient to account for a change such as that with which we are dealing.

Popes could not reply otherwise than by sending their own books and recommending their own use. In this manner, little by little, the influence of the Roman ritual made itself felt. The result was at first the combination of the two uses; then the Roman use gained the ascendency over the other until at length it ended by almost completely eliminating the Gallican. The following are the main facts of the history of this change.

In 538, Profuturus, Bishop of Braga, the metropolitan of the Suevic kingdom [1] of Galicia, wrote to Pope Vigilius to consult him on certain liturgical points. We still possess the Pope's [2] reply. Added to this reply were certain appendices containing decisions on matters of discipline, and, in the way of liturgical texts, the order of the baptismal ceremonies and of the Roman Mass. The latter contained merely what we call the Ordinary of the Mass, that is, the part which does not vary, but the Pope notified to the Bishop of Braga that it was customary to add to it in various places formularies peculiar to the solemnity of the day. Of these formularies, which represent the greater part of what is called the *Liber Sacramentorum*, or Sacramentary, Vigilius confines himself to giving only one specimen, that of the festival of Easter. He assumes that the Bishop of Braga could draw up his own Sacramentary for himself, in case he thought proper to conform to the Roman ritual. The Pope gives expression to no order or advice on this point. The liturgical documents sent by him were nevertheless received in Galicia with the greatest respect. This was manifested a little later on, when, after the conversion of the king of the Suevi

---

[1] The Suevi and their king were at this time still Arians. Their conversion dates back only to the year 550, or thereabouts.
[2] Jaffé, 907.

to Catholicism, the bishops of this country considered it opportune to put their ecclesiastical regulations on a definite basis. In the National Council held in 561 the liturgical texts sent from Rome to Profuturus were made obligatory.[1]

From this there must have arisen a mixed liturgy, in which there were naturally blended with the Roman *ordines* of the Mass and of baptism certain other elements either of an indigenous origin, or borrowed from the Gallican Liturgy. As no Suevic Liturgy has come down to us, it is not possible to form an idea of what these combinations were, but they did not at any rate enjoy a lengthy existence. In 588, the Suevic kingdom having been annexed to the Visigothic, the Churches of this country passed under the jurisdiction of the National Councils of Toledo, which were very eager for liturgical uniformity. The Roman usages introduced into Galicia were treated as departures from the normal, and were carefully deleted in favour of the Gallican Liturgy.

The Roman mission which was sent to England at the end of the sixth century naturally introduced the use of the Roman Liturgy into the Christian communities which it had newly founded there. But this first mission was not attended with permanent success. The work of evangelising the Anglo-Saxons was again taken in hand, shortly afterwards, by Irish missionaries from the North, where at Lindisfarne, a small island on the east coast of Northumberland, they had their headquarters. With the advent of these new apostles the liturgy used in Ireland, that is to say, the Gallican rite,

---

[1] *Conc. Bracarense*, c. 4: "Item placuit ut eodem ordine missae celebrentur ab omnibus quem Profuturus quondam hujus metropolitanae ecclesiae episcopus ab ipsa apostolicae sedis auctoritate suscepit scriptum"—C 5: "Item placuit ut nullus eum baptizandi ordinem praetermittat quem et antea tenuit metropolitana Bracarensis ecclesia, et pro amputanda aliquorum dubietate praedictus Profuturus episcopus scriptum sibi et directum a sede beatissimi apostoli Petri suscepit."

was imported into the Anglo-Saxon Churches. Hence arose a conflict as to use between the Irish missions from Lindisfarne and the somewhat inactive mission in Kent, which was always Roman in principle, even if its members were not all Roman. The episcopal succession of Canterbury having come to an end, Pope Vitalian sent to England (668), as its new archbishop, Theodore, a Greek monk of Tarsus in Cilicia. It was to this man, as able and energetic as he was conscientious, that the English Church owed its definitive foundation. He managed to reconcile the various and somewhat conflicting elements which he found in the missions entrusted to his care. By his wise and strong rule he was able to secure unity, and the work of evangelisation prospered in consequence. He doubtless made concessions in liturgical matters, and condoned the customs introduced by the Irish missionaries, for the oldest Anglo-Saxon books by no means contain the Roman Liturgy in an absolutely pure form; they abound, indeed, in Gallican details.

The attitude of Theodore, however, as far as the liturgy was concerned, was in harmony with the instructions which had been given by St. Gregory to his disciple Augustine, the first Archbishop of Canterbury [1] :—

Cum una sit fides, cur sunt ecclesiarum consuetudines tam diversae, et altera consuetudo missarum est in Romana ecclesia atque altera in Galliarum ecclesiis tenetur ?

— Novit fraternitas tua Romanae ecclesiae consuetudinem in qua se meminit enutritam. Sed mihi placet ut sive in Romana, sive in Galliarum, sive in qualibet ecclesia aliquid invenisti quod plus omnipotenti Deo possit placere, sollicite eligas et in Anglorum ecclesia, quae adhuc in fide nova est, institutione praecipua quae de multis ecclesiis colligere potuisti infundas. Non enim pro locis res, sed pro rebus loca nobis

---

[1] *Greg M. Ep*, xi. 64 (56a). On the subject of the authenticity of this letter, see Mommsen, *Neues Archiv*, vol. xvii pp. 390, 395.

amanda sunt. Ex singulis ergo quibusque ecclesiis quae pia, qua religiosa, quae recta sunt collige, et haec quasi in fasciculum collect apud Anglorum mentes in consuetudinem depone.

There were, in England, moreover, even in the lifetime of Theodore, some who were more zealous than he was for the purity of the Roman use.[1] We may gather this much from his disputes with St. Wilfrid. This ultramontane tendency, as we should say at the present time, was introduced on the Continent by St. Boniface, the Apostle of Germany and the reformer of the Frankish Church. It was he who inaugurated that movement towards Rome, which, favoured by later political relations, brought about, among other consequences, the suppression of the Gallican Liturgy in the Churches of the Frankish kingdom.

Even before St. Boniface the influence of the Roman Liturgy had been felt in Gaul. During the seventh century this country was constantly traversed by the Roman missionaries on their way to England. The English converts, on their side, were accustomed to undertake the journey to Rome, from whence they brought back relics, pictures, books, and above all, liturgical documents. Some of the latter may have been dropped on the way, or copies taken of them in the dwellings of the bishops, or in the monasteries where these pious travellers were accustomed to put up. Finally, the monks of St. Columbanus, who did so much to propagate the Benedictine rule,[2] must also

---

[1] In this category an important place must be allotted to the activity of Benedict Biscop, who journeyed five times to Rome, and brought back from thence, for his monasteries at Wearmouth and Yarrow, many personal observations, books, and works of art He even persuaded, in 679, Abbot John, superior of one of the monasteries of the Vatican and arch-cantor of the Roman Church, to follow him to England In this tradition was trained Venerable Bede (Bede, *Hist Eccl.* xciv p. 717).

[2] Cf. the important dissertation by Monsieur l'Abbé Malnory, *Quid Luxovienses monachi ad regulam monasteriorum atque ad communem Ecclesiae profectum contulerint,* Paris, 1894, p. 20.

have contributed to the spread of the liturgical customs of the Roman Church.

The few Gallican books which have come down to us date back to the last period of the Merovingian rule. Nearly all of them contain formularies of Roman origin and Masses in commemoration of Roman saints. As early as the time of Gregory of Tours, the *Hieronymian Martyrology*, a book of Roman origin, though not of an official nature, was introduced into Gaul and adapted to the Use of the country. The Sacramentary of St. Denis, known as the *Gelasian Sacramentary*—a work which is, in fact, fundamentally Roman—was drawn up at the latest in the time of Charles Martel. Some other books, or fragments of books, of both Roman and mixed origin, belong to this period, that is to say, to a time when the influence of St. Boniface had not yet made itself felt in the Frankish Church, at all events, within the limits of ancient Gaul.

That St. Boniface gave a strong impulse to liturgical reform and to the adoption of Roman customs is indubitable. We know little, however, of the details of his activity in this direction. He must have been vigorously supported by the Popes, whose counsellor he was, as well as their legate. There was introduced into the matter, moreover, a zeal and an acrimonious heat far removed from the spirit manifested in the Gregorian document I have just cited. One of the most impressive rites in the Gallican Mass was the benediction of the people by the bishop at the moment of communion. So much importance was attached to this rite that it was retained even after the adoption of the Roman Liturgy. Almost all the Sacramentaries of the Middle Ages contain formularies of benediction; they are even still in use in the Church of Lyons. I quote here a letter to Boniface from Pope Zacharias, which shows how the latter speaks of them.

[1] Jaffé, 2291. The letter belongs to the year 751.

Pro benedictionibus autem quas faciunt Galli, ut nosti, frater, multis vitiis variant. Nam non ex apostolica traditione hoc faciunt, sed per vanam gloriam hoc operantur, sibi ipsis damnationem adhibentes, dum scriptum est: *Si quis vobis evangelizaverit praeter id quod evangelizatum est, anathema sit.* Regulam catholicae traditionis suscepisti, frater amantissime: sic omnibus praedica omnesque doce, sicut a sancta Romana, cui Deo auctore deservimus, accepisti ecclesia.

It was during the episcopate of St. Chrodegang (732-766), and very probably after his return from Rome in 754, that the Church of Metz adopted the Roman Liturgy.[1] Among all the liturgical innovations, the most obvious and most striking was the chant, the *Romana Cantilena*. This has left more traces than any other innovation in the books and correspondence of the time. Pope Paul sent from Rome to King Pepin, about the year 760, an *Antiphonary* and a *Responsorial*.[2] In the same year, Remedius, son of Charles Martel, and Bishop of Rouen, having been sent on an embassy to Rome, obtained permission from the Pope to take back with him the sub-director (*secundus*) of the *Schola Cantorum*, in order to initiate his monks "in the modulations of psalmody" according to the Roman method. This teacher having been shortly afterwards recalled by the Pope, the bishop sent his Neustrian monks to finish their musical education at Rome itself, where they were admitted to the School of Cantors.

These are mere isolated facts. It was owing to a general measure, a decree of King Pepin, that the Gallican Use was suppressed. This decree is not forthcoming, but mention of it is found in the *admonitio generalis* put

---

[1] "Clerum abundanter lege divina Romanaque imbutum cantilena morem atque ordinem Romanae Ecclesiae servare praecepit, quod usque ad id tempus in Mettensi Ecclesia factum minime fuit" (Paulus Diaconus, *Gesta Epp. Mett*; Migne, *Pat. Lat.*, vol. xcv. p. 709).

[2] Jaffé, 2351. This letter is dated between 758 and 763.

forth by Charlemagne in 789.[1] The passage (cap. 80) reads as follows:—

Omni clero.—Ut cantum Romanum pleniter discant et ordinabiliter per nocturnale vel gradale officium peragatur, secundum quod beatae memoriae genitor noster Pippinus rex decertavit ut fieret, quando Gallicanum tulit, ob unanimitatem apostolicae sedis et sanctae Dei Ecclesiae pacificam concordiam.[2]

It was not, therefore, Charlemagne, as has often been stated, but Pepin the Short, who abolished the Gallican Liturgy. This reform had become necessary. The Frankish Church, during the reigns of the latest Merovingians, had fallen into a sad state of corruption, disorganisation, and ignorance. There was no religious centre anywhere, no metropolis whose customs being better regulated and better preserved might serve as a model and become the point of departure for a reformation. The Visigothic Church had a centre at Toledo, a recognised head in the metropolitan of this town, and an unique disciplinary code—the *Hispana* collection. The Liturgy of Toledo was then the liturgy of the whole of Spain. The Frankish Church possessed frontiers only, and lacked a capital. The Frankish Episcopate, except when the king or the Pope took the direction of it, was an acephalous episcopate.[3] Each Church possessed its book of canons and its liturgical use

[1] Bohmer-Muhlb, 292, Hardouin, *Conc*, vol iv p 843 Cf. chapters 53 and 54 of the same work

[2] Page 61 of the edition of Boretius (*M Germ Leges*, Sect. II, vol. i. Part I) Cf the *Epistola Generalis* put forth between 786 and 800 (*ibid*, p 80). "Accensi praeterea venerandae memoriae Pippini genitoris nostri exemplis, qui totas Galliarum ecclesias Romanae traditionis suo studio cantibus decoravit."

[3] This position never varied. It was the case before the Merovingians, and continued so afterwards. Every effort to establish in France an ecclesiastical power superior to the bishops—apart from the Pope or Government—has invariably resulted in failure. The metropolitan authority itself never enjoyed a strong position The archbishops are no longer more than dignitaries, and it would be easy to prove that, with a few isolated exceptions, they have never been anything more.

There was no order anywhere, nothing but the most complete anarchy—a lawless state of affairs which would have been irremediable if the Carlovingian monarchs had made no appeal to tradition and to the authority of the Roman Church.[1]

The intervention of Rome in the reformation of the liturgy was neither spontaneous nor very active. The Popes contented themselves with sending copies of their liturgical books without troubling themselves as to the use which might be made of them. The individuals who were charged by the Frankish kings—Pepin, Charlemagne, and Louis the Pious—with the execution of the liturgical reform did not regard themselves as prohibited from supplementing the Roman books or from combining with them whatever seemed worth preserving in the Gallican rite. Hence arose a somewhat composite liturgy, which from its source in the Imperial chapel spread throughout all the Churches of the Frankish Empire, and at length, finding its way to Rome, gradually supplanted there the ancient use. The Roman Liturgy, from the eleventh century at the least, is nothing else than the Frankish Liturgy, such as men like Alcuin, Helisachar, and Amalarius had made it. It is even extraordinary that the ancient Roman books—representing the genuine use of Rome up to the ninth century—have been so completely displaced by others, that not a single example of them is now to be found.

It would appear that the liturgical reform taken in

---

[1] It was owing to this state of things, and not to ethnographical considerations (see The Prayer Book of Aedelwald the Bishop, commonly called the "Book of Cerne," notes, p. 3), that such diversity of uses as are found in our ancient Merovingian books is explained. If the Roman books present a greater uniformity, it is because they come from one and the self-same Church, and not from various Churches liturgically independent of each other. Why should it surprise us, moreover, that the Gregorian books resemble one another? They were all derived from one copy

hand by the Carlovingian kings never reached Milan. The particularities of the Milanese ritual were not unknown in France, but this important Church, being better governed, doubtless, than those of Merovingian Gaul, seems to have been able to dispense with reform. The use of the Church, moreover, had already approximated considerably to the Roman rite. It was protected by the name of St. Ambrose.[1] The fables related by Landulf[2] as to the hostility displayed by Charlemagne to the Ambrosian ritual are not worthy of credit.[3]

[1] Walafrid Strabo, *De Reb Eccl*, 22 · "Ambrosius quoque, Mediolanensis episcopus, tam missae quam caeterorum dispositionem officiorum suae ecclesiae et aliis Liguribus ordinavit, quae et usque hodie in Mediolanensi tenentur ecclesia". (Migne, *Pat. Lat*, vol. cxlvii p 583).

[2] *Hist. Mediol*, ii 10 (Migne, *Pat Lat*, vol. cxlvii. p. 853).

[3] For the suppression of the Mozarabic Liturgy in Spain, in the time of Alexander II. and of Gregory VII, see Gams, *Kirchengeschichte von Spanien*, x. 4.

CHAPTER IV.

LITURGICAL FORMULARIES AND BOOKS.

BEFORE entering upon a description of the Latin liturgical books, I think it will be useful to discuss briefly the formation of liturgical books in general, and I will deal in the first place with the elements of which they are composed.

§ 1.—THE FORMS OF PRAYER.

Common prayer, especially in large assemblies, was subject at an early date to a certain amount of regulation. Prayer was offered in three different ways, which I may be allowed to specify by the terms *Litany* prayers, *Collective* prayers, and *Eucharistic* prayers.

The Litany was said in the following manner. One of the sacred ministers in a loud voice invited the congregation to pray for divers needs, which he specified one after the other. At each petition he made a pause, during which the whole congregation joined in a short formulary of supplication: *Kyrie eleison, Te rogamus audi nos*, etc. This form of prayer still holds, in the East, an important place in the Liturgy of the Mass. In the West it has disappeared; but we shall see later on that it had a place there in ancient times. In the East the task of enumerating the petitions of the Litany was assigned to a deacon. At Rome this office, together with other analogous functions, was transferred at a somewhat early date from the deacon to the precentor.

The second form of prayer was arranged as follows. The president of the congregation, that is, the officiating minister, invited the faithful to pray to God, indicating sometimes more or less briefly the general tenor of the prayer in which they were to join, and at others confining himself to a short formula of invitation. The congregation then assumed silently the attitude of prayer—that is, they stood with their arms raised up and hands extended. On certain days they were accustomed to kneel, or even to prostrate themselves with their faces to the ground. They remained in this position for some time, praying silently. Then the voice of the officiating minister was heard, expressing in a short formulary a *résumé*, as it were, of the prayers arising from every heart, and the congregation associated themselves with him by the response *Amen*.

We find, it is true, no description anywhere of this ritual. The liturgical books which have come down to us are neither sufficiently ancient nor explicit enough to furnish us with information on the point. The structure of the formularies contained in them is such, however, that we cannot imagine matters to have been otherwise conducted at the outset.

In the Gallican ritual, in fact, the principal prayers are always preceded by an invitatory, in which the officiating minister exhorts the congregation to pray. This invitatory has sometimes the proportions of a short sermon. Several formularies of this kind recall, in all respects, the style of the addresses of St. Zeno of Verona, which were doubtless composed for a similar purpose. A real formulary of prayer follows, in which the officiating minister addresses his supplications to God in the name of all present. The following specimen, taken from the office for the vigil of the Epiphany,[1] will give an idea of the combination referred to :—

Miraculorum primordia quae dominus noster Jesus Christus proferre in adsumptae carnis novitate dignatus est, Fratres karissimi, debita exultatione veneremur ; quia dum se Deum intra humana viscera proferebat, jam de salutis nostrae absolutione tractabat. Homo est utique invitatus ad nuptias ; et quod in nuptiis protulit Deum probavit. Cujus praeconia nec inter ipsa quidem virtutum possumus rudimenta depromere ; sed dum tantarum rerum stupescimus gloriam, temeritatem [2] proferendae laudis ingredimur. Humili ergo oratione poscamus ut per ipsum ad vitam aeternam nobis tribuatur ingressus, cujus nativitatis lumine orbis inlustratus est universus. Quod ipse praestare dignetur qui in trinitate perfecta vivit et regnat in saecula saeculorum.

COLLECTIO SEQUITUR.

Omnipotens et misericors Deus, plebi tuae suppliciter exoranti pia benignitate responde, quam cernis in hoc die fideli devotione gaudere, quo dominus ac Deus noster vera humilitate suscepta sic servilem formam misericorditer ostendit in saeculo ut divinam potentiam suam mirabiliter monstraret in caelo. Qui enim pro nobis puer parvulus fuit, ipse ad se magos officio stellae praeeuntis adduxit. Obsecramus itaque, Domine, clementiam tuam, ut sicut illis dedisti Christum tuum verum Deum in vera carne cognoscere, sic omnes fideles tuos quos materno sinu sancta gestat Ecclesia in praesenti tempore protegas invictae virtutis auxilio [3] et in futuro facias regni caelestis adipisci munera [4] sempiterna. Per ipsum dominum nostrum Jesum Christum filium tuum, qui tecum beatus vivit, etc.

In the Roman Liturgy few formularies of this kind have been preserved. Enough of them, however, exist to enable us to reconstruct the ancient use. I append, as an instance, the following, taken from the solemn prayers of Good Friday.[5]

---

[1] *Missale Gothicum.* Muratori, *Lit. Romana Vetus*, vol. ii p 536.
[2] The printed edition has *temeritatis.*
[3] In the printed edition, *auxilium*
[4] In the printed edition, *munere sempiterno.*
[5] Gelasian *Sacrament.* Muratori, *Lit Rom Vet*, vol i p 560.

Oremus, dilectissimi nobis in primis pro Ecclesia sancta Dei; ut eam Deus et Dominus pacificare, adunare et custodire dignetur per universum orbem terrarum, subiciens ei principatus et potestates, detque nobis tranquillam et quietam vitam degentibus glorificare Deum Patrem omnipotentem. Oremus!
Adnuntiat diaconus: Flectamus genua!
Iterum dicit: Levate!
Omnipotens, sempiterne, Deus, qui gloriam tuam omnibus[1] in Christo gentibus revelasti, custodi opera misericordiae tuae, ut Ecclesia tua toto orbe diffusa stabili fide in confessione tui nominis perseveret. Per [eumdem Christum, etc.]

We must also recall in this connection the *Orate, Fratres*, of the Mass. The Roman invitatory is more frequently confined to the simpler *Oremus!* Something like this must have also been in use in the Gallican ritual, for many prayers therein have no elaborate invitatories, and it is difficult to believe that they were not preceded by any announcement.

The Roman formularies, *Flectamus genua, Levate*, contain, both in books and usage, the only trace of what was at one time the essential element in this form of prayer, viz. the supplication offered up in silence and in a prescribed attitude.

The *Eucharistic* prayer was the most solemn form of all. It was said by the officiating minister alone, and in the name of all; the congregation had merely to listen, to join in it mentally, and to make the response *Amen* at the end. Its general subject-matter is thanksgiving. In the Roman ritual, and indeed in all others, it began always in the same way: "It is truly meet, right, and salutary to render thanks to Thee, at all times and in all places, holy Lord, Father Almighty, eternal God!"

---

[1] *In omnibus in Chr* Gelasian. The Gregorian Sacramentary has not the first *in*.

It comes before us everywhere, not only in the same words, but also invariably preceded by an invitatory in the form of a dialogue between the officiating minister and the congregation—

"The Lord be with you!—And with thy spirit!—Lift up your hearts!—We lift them up unto the Lord.—Let us give thanks to our Lord God!—It is meet and right."

This prayer forms one of the essential parts of the Mass, but it is also found in several other liturgical offices, such as Ordination, the Consecration of Virgins, the Benediction of Baptismal Fonts, etc. In Greek the special name by which the Eucharistic prayer used in the Mass is known is the *Anaphora*. Latin liturgical language has no analogous term, but two names are applied to it which correspond respectively to its two parts. The part of the formulary which precedes the singing of the *Sanctus* is called the Preface (*Praefatio*), and the part following, the Canon (*Canon actionis* or *Actio*). In the Gallican books the Preface has several names—*Contestatio, Illatio, Immolatio*.[1]

These three modes of prayer furnished occasion, at a somewhat early date, for the construction of formularies, which were at length grouped together in special books, called in Greek *Euchologia*, and in Latin *Libri Sacramentorum* (Books of the Sacraments.)[2] These books, which were for the special use of the priest or officiating bishop, do not contain the part of the

---

[1] In the *Anaphora* it is easy to distinguish certain essential parts which are found in all liturgies. Besides the Preface and the *Sanctus*, there is always the *Account of the Last Supper*, followed by the *Anamnesis* and *Epiclesis*, to which reference was made at page 61.

[2] Councils at Carthage in 397 (can. 23) and 407 (*Cod. Can. Eccl. Afric*, c. 103); Gennadius, 68, 79, 80; *Liber Pontificalis* (Gelasius), vol. 1. p. 255; Gregory of Tours, 11. 22. It was probably a book of the sacraments to which the term *Comes* was applied in a charter of the year 471 (*Liber Pont.*, vol. 1 p. cxlvii.*a*).

deacon. The latter had either to know his Litany by heart, or read it from another text.¹ Certain formularies were written in *volumes*, or rolls of parchment, separately. This was the case in the East in regard to the Liturgy of the Mass. We find in Italy similar rolls for the ceremonies of the Benediction of Fonts, of Baptism, and for the *Praeconium Paschale*,² etc. Sometimes the formularies were accompanied by directions as to the order of the ceremonies; forming what is called an *Ordo*. There is the order of Baptism, and those of Ordination, of Penance, of the Consecration of Churches, of Chrism, etc. These *ordines* are either found existing separately, or bound up with other formularies in the body of the *Libri Sacramentorum*. There were also forms which were restricted to details of the rites and ceremonies, the omitted formularies being found by the officiating minister in the Sacramentary.

The Sacramentaries, or *Libri Sacramentorum*, assumed a greater importance in the West than in the East. This arose from the fact that in the Oriental ritual the prayers of the Mass were, with some exceptions, always the same, whilst in the West they varied according to the occasion of the Mass. At Rome there was still a certain fixed element, the formula of the canon being almost invariable. But in the Gallican rite there was hardly anything fixed except the commemoration of the Last Supper, with the words of institution of the Eucharist.

Already at an early date * the custom arose of

¹ A collection of diaconal litanies for the use of some Church in Egypt was published by Giorgi at the end of his work called *Fragmentum Evangelii S. Johannis*, Rome, 1789, and reproduced by Hammond in *The Liturgy of Antioch*, p. 33. Other examples occur in Mr Brightman's *Liturgies Eastern and Western*

² Cf. the essay of E Langlois on *Un rouleau d'Exultet* in the *Mélanges de l'Ecole de Rome*, vol vi p 467. A special term was used at Milan to designate the cleric whose business it was to hold and unfold these rolls before the officiating bishop—that of *Rotularius*.

* See pp. 158 and 577A.

inserting in the Sacramentaries the lections and chants of the Mass. Hence originated what were called *Missals plenary*, or simply *Missals*. These are now the only books in use.

§ 2.—THE LECTIONS.

Lections were, in the first instance, taken from the books of the Bible itself, either as isolated texts or grouped in divers manners. The president of the congregation chose the passages to be read, and he stopped the reader when he thought proper. Later on there was an assigned text, of which the length had been previously determined, for every Sunday and festival. This did not prevent, however, the employment of books with complete texts, in which it was enough to indicate either on the margin, or in a table placed at the commencement, the beginning and end of the lessons belonging to the Sunday or holy day. This table was designated in Greek by the term *Synaxary*,[1] and in Latin by that of *Capitulary*. The custom soon began of extracting from the books of the Bible, and even from the Gospels, the lessons for the different days of the year. Thus there arose in place of the *Evangelium* the *Evangelary*, and in place of the complete Bible, the *Lectionary*. There resulted at length a blending in the same collection of the lessons taken from the Old Testament with those from the Epistles and Gospels, including even extracts from certain other books.[2]

It is manifest that a great number of varieties would thus come into existence, not only in different countries,

---

[1] This is one of the meanings of the word: there are others. Cf *Analecta Bolland*, vol. xiv p. 400.

[2] For details on this point, see the article *Lectionary* in Smith's *Dictionary of Christian Antiquities* Cf. Gennadius. 80.

but even in the same country, these varieties depending on whether the Church was an important one, capable of indulging in the expense of a rich liturgical library, or whether it was a poor country Church which had to restrict itself to what was absolutely necessary. Setting aside the Lectionary of Luxeuil, of which I will treat further on, I am unable to furnish instances of the existence in the West of this kind of book before the time of Charlemagne.* Those of the East are not more ancient. But there is no doubt that the majority of the very ancient manuscripts of the Bible, whether Greek or Latin, which have come down to us, were employed for public reading in Churches. They still bear traces of this use.

§ 3.—The Chants.

The chanting of the psalms was from the beginning, as I have previously pointed out, one of the essential elements of public worship. Its use alternated with the lections, which were read either at the office for vigils, or at Mass before the oblation.

In ancient times, and up to the latter part of the fourth century, the psalms were always sung as a solo, and, doubtless, also with somewhat complicated modulations. The congregation, however, repeated the last words of the chant. The execution of the liturgical chant is described in this way in the *Apostolic Constitutions*.[1] The choir-rules, moreover, prescribe this same mode of chanting in the case of those portions which, in the Roman use, correspond to the most ancient psalmody—I mean the gradual and the other musical pieces inserted between the Epistle and Gospel. These psalms are essentially *Psalmi responsorii*

---

[1] See above, p 58
* See Appendix, p 577A.

(responds), and they were thus called because the congregation made, in fact, a response to them by repeating the final clause.

The Roman custom permitted the use of two kinds of melodies for this class of sacred chants. One of these was designated by a term which has no reference to its musical character. This was what was called the gradual, which was sung at the ambo, or *gradus*, and took from this fact its name of *Psalmus gradualis*. The other was the *Psalmus tractus*, or tract. At the time to which the most ancient documents dealing with these details go back, the *Psalmus tractus* was, like the gradual, sung at the ambo, and not in the choir. Its name of *tractus* can thus be derived only from some peculiarity in its execution. Amalarius tells us, in fact, that the tract differed from the *Psalmus responsorius* in that the choir did not respond to it as they did to the latter.[1]

The custom of singing the *Alleluia* is very ancient in the Church, but the adaptation of this chant to the liturgical service did not take place until late, and then with considerable diversity in its use. At Rome it was joined to the last verse of the gradual psalm. In the East and in the countries of the Gallican rite, it was sung still later in the service, that is, after the Gospel, or at the procession of the oblation.

Towards the end of the fourth century there was introduced side by side with the *Psalmus responsorius* another kind of psalmody, the antiphon, which consisted of a psalm chanted by two choirs alternately. It was at Antioch,[2] in the time of Bishop Leontius (344–357), that this custom was introduced. Under the guidance of two ascetics,

---

[1] Amalarius, *De Eccl. Off*, iii 12. I called attention to this text in the *Paléographie Musicale* of the Benedictines of Solesmes, vol v. p 31.

[2] Theodoret, *Hist. Eccl*, ii. 24

Flavian and Diodorus, who became later on Bishops of Antioch and Tarsus respectively, some pious lay people were accustomed to meet at night in the sanctuaries of the martyrs to pass the time in chanting psalms with two choirs. Bishop Leontius, who favoured the Arianising party, regarded with distrust these meetings, which were held without his sanction. He induced the friends of Flavian and Diodorus to celebrate their pious vigils in the Churches of the city. This circumstance contributed much to making known this new method of psalmody, and it soon spread rapidly. By the time of St. Basil[1] it had already been introduced into the Cappadocian Cæsarea. The pilgrim Etheria (Silvia), in the time of Theodosius, makes mention of nocturnal meetings exactly like those of Antioch and Cæsarea: the antiphon there occupied a place alongside the ancient responsive psalmody: *Psalmi responduntur* (sic), *similiter et antiphonae.* St. Ambrose adopted this practice in 387.[2] It appears to have taken a longer time to get introduced into the Roman Church. A text, somewhat obscure in character, it is true, of the *Liber Pontificalis*[3] refers this introduction to the time of Pope Celestine (422–432).

In the form in which it was adopted at Rome, the antiphon admitted the alternative singing of a complete psalm. All the verses were chanted to the same melody, but the melody varied for each psalm. Before beginning the psalm proper, some musical phrases were first executed, to which certain words, borrowed chiefly from the psalm itself, were adapted. This was what is called the anthem [*antienne*]. It was doubtless performed as a solo by a cantor, in order to give the tone for the following psalmody. The psalm being ended, there was a repetition of the anthem.[4]

[1] Ep. 207.
[2] St. Augustine, *Conf.*, iv 7.
[3] Vol. 1. pp. 230, 231.
[4] See note on p. 572.

It is clear that the word anthem is nothing more than a transformation of the term *antiphona*. I will use the word anthem in its present significance, but to *antiphon* I will apply its primitive sense, viz. that of a psalm sung by two choirs, and with its initial and final modulation.

We shall see hereafter that antiphons were used at Rome, not only in offices other than the Mass, but in the Mass itself, which admitted of two forms of it, the antiphon *ad introitum* and the antiphon *ad communionem*.

Whatever the form of psalmody might be, it was a general custom, in the fourth century, for the psalm to end with the doxology: *Gloria Patri et Filio et Spiritui sancto, sicut erat in principio et nunc et semper et in saecula saeculorum. Amen.*[1]

As was the case with the formularies of prayers, the musical portions of the service were fixed at an early date, and had places assigned to them according to the days and feasts of the year. Hence arose the need of special books. At Rome there were, besides the books which were employed for the day and night offices, two distinct volumes for liturgical use, strictly so called, that is, for the Mass. These were called respectively the *Cantatorium*[2] and *Antiphonarium*. The former was for the use of the deacon (later cantors), who sang the gradual and similar chants from the ambo. The other was a choir-book, which was kept in the place in which the *schola cantorum* was held. It contained, beside the two antiphons already mentioned, the other musical parts of the Mass for every day in the year, namely the offertory, the *Gloria in excelsis*, etc. As far as the antiphons were

---

[1] This is the Roman formulary The slight variations in other uses will be noted elsewhere

[2] *Ordo Rom*, 1 10; Amalarius, *De Officiis*, second prologue; *De Ord. Antiphonarii*, prol.

concerned, it was only necessary to note the anthems, which gave the tone for the psalm, seeing that the choristers either had a psalter in their hands, or else knew the psalm so thoroughly by heart that it was needless to inscribe it in the antiphonary.

Antiphonal chanting of the psalms as it obtains to-day is executed sometimes with a rapid, and at others with a slow, movement and more complicated modulations. The latter method is almost exclusively reserved for the antiphon of the *introit*, while the other is of general use in the psalmody of the office. It is probable that at the beginning the slow movement was that which was more generally followed. There has been a progressive shortening of all the parts of Divine Service, whether prayers, lections, or chants, but it was in the category of the chants that most of the suppressions occurred. We see this clearly in the antiphons of the Mass. In one of these—the *introit*—the psalm is reduced to a single verse, followed by the doxology, while in the antiphon *ad communionem* it has entirely disappeared.

In addition to the psalms introduced between the lections and the antiphons of the Roman Mass, the Eucharistic service admitted other chants, of which I will treat later on. All of them, with the exception of the *Sanctus*, are of relatively recent date. In regard to the *Sanctus*, moreover, it is necessary to distinguish between its words and the musical rendering of them. The present custom of reciting the seraphic hymn in common, and aloud, goes back to the same early date as that assigned to the general subject-matter of the preface and of the canon. The application of melody to the words is probably of later date.

I do not include under the term liturgical chant the recitative or intoning of the lections or such of the prayers as are said aloud. This practice may be very ancient. It was necessarily introduced as soon as the Christian assemblies became very large, and thus rendered it difficult for the officiating minister or reader to make himself heard. The flections of the voice served for a scansion of the text, and thus gave more relief to the intonation. But the slight modulations resulting from this were more akin to accentuated reading than to chanting properly so called.

It was for the same reason—namely, the difficulty of maintaining a high intonation in a large building—that the custom must have arisen of pronouncing in a low voice certain formularies which were evidently intended in the first instance to be heard by everybody. There are two of such in the Roman Mass, viz. the prayer called *Secreta* before the preface, and the Canon from the *Sanctus* onwards. According to the Eastern usage, many other formularies of prayer are said in a low voice by the officiating minister. But in every country these formularies end in what the Greeks call an ecphonesis (ἐκφώνησις), that is, in a raised inflection of the voice at the end, so that the congregation may respond with *Amen*.

CHAPTER V.

BOOKS OF THE LATIN RITE.

ANCIENT books of the Latin rite are much rarer than we might be led to expect. It is useless to look for anything of the kind in the Danubian provinces or in Latin Illyricum, where the Churches of Dorostorum, Sardica, Salona, Sirmium, Siscia, and Savaria once flourished. A wholesale destruction was effected in these countries by the Germanic, Slav, and Finnish barbarians, and though no doubt, these countries have their liturgical history, it begins very late, that is, in the ninth century, at the time when the missionaries from Rome vied with those from Constantinople in evangelising the conquering tribes which thenceforward took up their abode in those regions. Africa, also, has nothing to offer us, unless it be the mention of a *Libellus Sacramentorum*[1] compiled in Mauritania, but now hopelessly lost, and a few decisions, scattered among the decrees of the councils. The ancient Spanish Liturgy has up to the present time been known to us solely by the Mozarabic Missal, which was recovered in 1500 by the efforts of Cardinal Ximenes. With a single exception,

---

[1] Gennadius, *De Script*, 79 · "Voconius, Castellani, Mauritaniae oppidi, episcopus, scripsit adversus Ecclesiae inimicos, Judaeos et Arianos et alios haereticos. Composuit etiam Sacramentorum egregium libellum." About the year 400, ecclesiastical legislation would lead us to suppose that the bishops had, up to that time, considerable latitude in the redaction and use of formularies. Councils of Carthage of 397 (c 23) and of 407 (*Cod.* 103).

which I shall shortly mention, the Liturgy of North Italy is found in no text earlier than the tenth century. Of the manuscripts of the Roman Liturgy, one alone—and that not an official book—has an absolutely indigenous origin, free from any transalpine influence; all the others, and they are legion, are traceable to originals which have suffered more or less from French Carlovingian alterations of the eighth century and onwards. From the British Isles we have merely mixed manuscripts of the eighth century, or earlier, in which local rites are curiously combined with those of the Roman Church. Gaul is scarcely less poverty-stricken, though there a few manuscripts of Merovingian times have been preserved.

I propose to describe in this chapter the ancient liturgical books still extant, which are anterior to the fusion of the Roman and Gallican uses.

§ 1.—Roman Books.

1. *The Gregorian Sacramentary.*

In a letter from Pope Adrian[1] to Charlemagne, written between 784 and 791, it is stated that the king had asked a short time previously that a Sacramentary drawn up by St. Gregory might be sent him from Rome, and that the Pope had despatched it to him by John, a monk and abbot of Ravenna.

As soon as it arrived in France, a large number of

---

[1] "De Sacramentario vero a sancto disposito praedecessore nostro, deifluo Gregorio papa: immixtum vobis emitteremus, jam pridem Paulus grammaticus a nobis eum pro vobis petente, secundum sanctae nostrae ecclesiae tradicionem, per Johannem monachum atque abbatem civitatis Ravennantium vestrae regali emisimus excellentiae" (*Cod Carol., Mon. Ger. Ep.* tom iii p. 626).

copies were made of the Gregorian Sacramentary, and apparently all the Churches were obliged to make it the basis of their liturgical use. A considerable number of the copies executed under Charlemagne and his immediate successors have been preserved till the present time. Monsieur L. Delisle has drawn up a catalogue[1] of them, which will, no doubt, be rendered more complete by further researches, but which is sufficient to give an idea of the rapid propagation of the Gregorian text.

The Sacramentary sent by Pope Adrian was, however, far from containing all the necessary details and formularies. In transcribing it, it was rendered more complete. In some of the manuscripts,[2] its text from one end to the other was combined with the Roman Sacramentary which had been in previous use. In others—and these are the most numerous—the copyist merely inserted, as an appendix to the Gregorian text, the supplementary matter which he considered needful. I doubt whether such a thing exists as a pure Gregorian text without interpolations or additions of any kind.[3]

But this is of little moment, since in the large number of copies in which the Gregorian text is followed by supplements, these latter are separated from it in a very distinct manner, and it is perfectly easy to isolate them. The author of the supplemented edition, very probably Alcuin, has been careful to inform us what were the contents of the Sacramentary properly so called, and the nature of the additions

---

[1] *Mémoires de l'Académie des Inscriptions*, vol. xxxii., 1st part. Monsieur Delisle's catalogue comprises all the Latin Sacramentaries without distinction, but the copies of the Gregorian Sacramentary are by far the most numerous.

[2] For instance, the Sacramentaries of Gellona and of Angoulême (*Paris*, 12048, 886, cf. Delisle, *op. cit.*, pp. 80, 91), and that of S. Rémi of Rheims (Delisle, p. 87), now lost, but known through a modern copy (U. Chevalier, *Bibliothèque liturgique*, vol. vii., pp. 316-357).

[3] See, however, *infra*, p. 573 (note to p. 122).

which he believed it necessary to make. He has prefaced the latter with an explanatory note and a list of the fresh material added. Hence, there can be no difficulty in distinguishing in the Gregorian manuscripts [1] those portions which represent the copy sent by Adrian to Charlemagne.[2]

The Gregorian Sacramentary comprised:—1st, the Ordinary of the Mass; 2nd, the Prayers, Prefaces, and other variable parts of the Mass, recited or chanted by the bishop or officiating priest, on festival and stational days. This series embraces the entire course of the ecclesiastical year, beginning with Christmas Eve. 3rd, Prayers at the ordination of deacons, priests, and bishops. These three parts do not occur always in the same order. In some MSS. the ordination prayers are at the beginning, in others they are inserted

---

[1] This may be seen from M. Delisle's descriptions on pp. 96, 124, 141, 143, 150, 151, 171, etc. In Muratori's edition, a provoking transposition of the text has here been the cause of some confusion; pp. 139-240, which evidently belong to the supplement, ought to follow on after p 272, where we find the end of the *Liber Sacramentorum* sent by Adrian, and, immediately after, the preface to the supplement

[2] For the references to the text of the Gregorian Sacramentary I make use (for want of a better) of Muratori's edition, *Liturgia Romana vetus*, vol. ii. In his notes on the *Book of Cerne* (the Prayer Book of Aedelwald the Bishop, commonly called "The Book of Cerne," ed. by Dom A B. Kuypers, Cambridge, 1902), p 5 of the separate part, Mr Edmund Bishop considers it evident that in my opinion the Sacramentary of Adrian is exclusively represented by pp. 1–138 of Muratori's edition, while, in his opinion, pp. 241–272 and 357–361 should also be included. Pages 357–361 contain the forms of ordination for bishops, priests, and deacons, and it will be seen above, as also in preceding editions of the present work, that I have mentioned these formularies as constituting part of the Sacramentary in question. As far as this point, therefore, is concerned, Mr. Bishop's criticism is without foundation. As to pp. 241–272, I willingly admit with him that they should be added to pp. 1–138, and that they were only separated from them by a mistake in the arrangement of the pages. Even then, with this addition, the Sacramentary is still a very incomplete book, and I adhere to my belief that, taken by itself, it does not represent the entire collection of liturgical formularies in use at Rome during the eighth century. See Appendix, p. 577A, of this volume.

after the Ordinary of the Mass, or are placed at the end of the Sacramentary.

The second part, by far the most important, is the main part of the Sacramentary. As I have said, it contains only the Masses for great festivals and solemn stations. There are none for the ordinary Sundays between the Epiphany and Lent and from the octave of Easter to Advent. Advent with Christmastide, Lent with Easter Week, Ascension Day, Whitsunday, and Ember days are all that is represented by the *proprium de tempore* of later Missals. The festivals of saints which are on fixed days are distributed more or less systematically among the movable feasts, but in such a way that Lent and Easter Week form an uninterrupted series.

The place of the station is always expressly indicated, unless the name of the saint alone is sufficient to designate the Church at which the festival was held. For instance, it was not deemed necessary to say where the station was on the days of St. Marcellus, St. Agnes, St. Sylvester, etc. But for the days of Lent, for the festival of the Holy Innocents, and for that of St. Felix of Nola, the Church is indicated. There are sometimes even two indications when the station is preceded by a general procession; in that case the Church is denoted from which the procession starts, and that also wherein Mass is celebrated. Similar indications are given when there are several stations on the same day, or several stopping-places in a procession, as, for instance, at the festival of Christmas, on the day of the Greater Litany, and at vespers in Easter Week.

We have here, in the main, a book drawn up, not for the Roman use in general, applicable to any country whatever, but for the Roman use as observed in Rome. Moreover, it is an essentially stational Sacramentary, which could hardly have been used unless on festivals and days of solemn assembly. In addition to the Masses for these holy days, it provides no others, except for the day of a dedication festival, for the ordination of a Pope or Priest Cardinal, for a marriage, or the obsequies of a Pope. It furnishes no ritual for a dedication, nor any Mass for Sundays and ordinary days, or for the funerals of clergy or laity. There are no Masses for special needs, such as in time of war, pestilence, tempests, and other visitations; nor for the sick, fishermen, travellers, and so forth. We do not even find in it the formularies[1] connected with the *velatio virginum* and the reconciliation of penitents.

I should therefore hesitate to consider this selection as a complete book, sufficient for all liturgical necessities, even in the time of Adrian. It may possibly have been a copy for the Pope's special use, for it contains, indeed, the prayers which he would be called upon to recite during most of the ceremonies at which he usually presided. It may have been a book with a less restricted use, but in such a case it would be necessary to conclude that it was considerably supplemented by other texts. A priest of Rome, if he were limited to this book, would not have been able to bury one of his parishioners, or officiate on ordinary Sundays, or observe the festival even of any Roman saint outside the very small number who figure in the *Liber Sacramentorum*. The strongest proof of its inadequacy is the fact that when at length it reached France, it was recognised as defective for use, and had to be provided with considerable supplements.

Hence it is a grave mistake to regard it as having been the only Missal in use in the Roman Church at any given

---

[1] The short prayers *Super penitentem, ad diaconam faciendam, ad ancillas Dei velandas*, which figure (Muratori, vol. ii, pp. 265, 266) in Adrian's Sacramentary, cannot be considered as equivalent to the formularies used on these occasions.

date. It is a still graver error to accept it as being the work of St. Gregory himself. This attribution, it is true, was current in the time of Adrian, and finds expression, with slight variations, in the titles of all the MS. copies: *Incipit Liber Sacramentorum de circulo anni expositus, a Sancto Gregorio papa Romano editus, ex authentico libro bibliothecae cubiculi scriptus.* In this form, this title is not earlier than the transcription itself. It is possible, however, that the copyist of Adrian may have already found the name of St. Gregory in the copy he was reproducing, viz. that belonging to the private library of the Pope. It is equally admissible that this name may not have been placed there without a reason, and that the copy in question was taken from some book drawn up by order of St. Gregory or for his use. But to what extent it followed it, is impossible to decide.

It certainly contains a number of prayers which were in use in the time of St. Gregory, and, indeed, long before him. But the author of the supplements added in France had, even in his day, remarked that St. Gregory could not have mentioned his own festival, and he also notes as later additions the Masses for the Nativity and the Assumption of the Blessed Virgin, and those for certain days of Lent. He has further denoted by an obelus[1] whatever he considered to be an interpolation. Indeed, besides the Mass of St. Gregory himself, we must reject those for the four festivals of the Blessed Virgin, not only those for her Nativity and Assumption, but even those for the Purification and the Annunciation, and the festival of the Exaltation of the Cross, these holy days not having been introduced into Rome till during the course of the seventh century. With regard to Lent, the

---

[1] As far as I am aware, the employment of this obelus has not been pointed out in any of the manuscripts still extant.

stations of the Thursdays are not older than Gregory II. (715-731), whereas the stations of Ash Wednesday and the following days, up to the First Sunday in Lent, are more ancient, but at the same time still later than St. Gregory. Another addition is evident in the station of January 1st, given as *ad St. Mariam ad Martyres*, since this Church, that is, the Pantheon, was not consecrated for Christian worship until the time of Pope Boniface IV. (608-615). Its dedication is indicated on May 13th, so that here again we have a festival posterior to St. Gregory. The same applies to the dedication of St. Nicomede, on June 1st, this Church having been consecrated under Boniface V. (619-625). The Churches of St. Adrian, St. Andrew near the Lateran, St. Lucy, St. George, St. Theodore, and St. Apollinaris, mentioned as stational Churches, are, the three first of the time of Honorius (625-638), the others probably later. Finally, the festival of Pope St. Leo, indicated on June 28th, is the anniversary, not of his death, but of the translation of his relics under Sergius[1] (687-701).

These are the only modifications that the information at our disposal has enabled us to verify. But it is possible there may be many others which have escaped us. Any text or rite which appears in this book, but does not figure in any earlier document, may, it is true, go back to a remote antiquity; but it may, with equal possibility, date merely from the eighth century. In these circumstances, and especially when there is a question of the date of a text or rite, it would be hazardous to cite the Gregorian Sacramentary as an authority belonging to the end of the sixth

---

[1] It should also be noted that on the 29th of July we find under the rubric *SS. Felicis, Simplicii, Faustini et Beatricis*, a Mass in honour of St. Felix only. This suggests that the translation of the three other martyrs had already taken place. It occurred under Leo II. (682-683).

century. The best course is to regard it as representing the state of the Roman Liturgy at the time of Pope Adrian. It would be more natural, to avoid all ambiguity, to call it the Sacramentary of Adrian, and this I propose henceforward to do.

2. *The Gelasian Sacramentary.*

I have already said that, immediately after its arrival in France, the Sacramentary of Adrian had been combined with a similar text which had been previously in use, and was far more complete. This text is what is known as the Gelasian Sacramentary. In addition to the forms [1] in which it appears combined with the Gregorian Sacramentary, it is known to us from several manuscripts of the eighth century, the earliest of which is No. 316 of Queen Christina's collection in the Vatican. This manuscript has been published by Tommasi,[2] whose edition is reproduced in the first volume of the *Liturgia Romana vetus* of Muratori. Next in date to this are two manuscripts, one of Rheinau, the other of St. Gall, till lately very imperfectly known through a publication by Dom Martin Gerbert.[3] A complete edition,

---

[1] Cf. *supra*, p. 121. See Appendix, *infra*, p. 577A.
[2] *Codices Sacramentorum*, Rome, 1680.
[3] They are MSS. 30 (Rheinau) at Zurich, and No. 348 at St Gall Cf. Delisle, *op. cit.*, pp. 83, 84. Gerbert has not published either of these Sacramentaries, but only a mixed Sacramentary compiled in the tenth century, *ex triplici ritu Gelasiano, Gregoriano et Ambrosiano*. This Sacramentary came from St. Gall, but in Gerbert's time it was at Zurich. It was MS. 348 of St. Gall which furnished the compiler with the Gelasian text.

based on these three manuscripts and collated afresh, has been published at Oxford.[1]

None of these copies bears the name of Gelasius. Tommasi, however, who applied it to the text which he published, did no more, as will be seen, than revive a designation in use in the ninth century.[2]

In the inventory of the liturgical books at the abbey of St. Riquier,[3] we find Gregorian "Missals," Gelasian Missals, and a mixed Missal, *Missalis Gregorianus et Gelasianus modernis temporibus ab Albino ordinatus*. Walafrid Strabo[4] mentions that Gelasius was supposed to have arranged in order the prayers composed by himself and others, and adds that the Churches of the Gauls made use of his prayers, and that many still continue to do so, but that St. Gregory, struck with the imperfection of Gelasius's book, revised it, and made of it the Gregorian *Liber Sacramentorum*. These two testimonies are both of the first half of the ninth century. Fifty years later, John the Deacon, in his *Life of St. Gregory*,[5] used nearly the same expressions as Walafrid Strabo. It was therefore believed in the ninth century that a Sacramentary of Gelasius had existed, and that the Gregorian Sacramentary was merely a revision of it. By Gregorian Sacramentary was evidently meant the Sacramentary of Adrian, such as I have described it, bearing as its heading the name of Saint Gregory. But what was understood by the Gelasian Sacramentary?

---

[1] The Gelasian Sacramentary, edited by H A. Wilson. Oxford, 1894.

[2] Before Tommasi's time, Morin and Bona had already given the name Gelasian to the text which Tommasi afterwards published, and with which they had a first-hand acquaintanceship.

[3] *Chronicon Centulense*, Migne, *P. L*, vol clxxiv. p 1261. Cf. G. Becker, *Catalogi Bibliothecarum Antiqui*, Bonn, 1885, p 28.

[4] *De Rebus Eccl.*, c 22.

[5] II. 17: "Gelasianum codicem de missarum solemniis, multa subtrahens, pauca convertens, nonnulla vero superadiciens pro exponendis evangelicis lectionibus, in unius libri volumine coartavit"

It was evidently the same text as that used by Cardinal Tommasi, and it is, in fact, under the name of Gelasian Sacramentary that it is quoted in a compilation of the tenth century published by Dom Gerbert. The author of this compilation desired to bring together in one volume the three texts—Gelasian, Gregorian, and Ambrosian. For the first of these he simply copied MS. 348 of St. Gall, which still bears traces of this work of transcription.[1] Walafrid Strabo, who wrote in the neighbourhood of St. Gall, cannot have meant anything else by the word Gelasian. For the matter of that, only two types of Roman Sacramentaries were known in France, namely, that of Adrian, bearing the name of St. Gregory, and when any other type is mentioned, there can be no doubt as to its meaning the Gelasian. This remark is applicable to the designations used in the catalogue of St. Riquier. As to John the Deacon, who lived at Rome, we may imagine that in his case the term *Codex Gelasianus* might be applied to some other form of the Roman Sacramentary. But this supposition must be set aside, since John the Deacon speaks of the Sacramentary anterior to St. Gregory in terms which are exactly applicable to the text which we have now under consideration. It is, indeed, much longer than that of the Gregorian Sacramentary (*multa subtrahens*); the formularies common to both are almost always the same (*pauca convertens*); it is divided into several books, whereas the Gregorian Sacramentary comprises only one (*in unius libri volumine coartavit*).[2]

The question now arises, why the name Gelasian was applied to this *Liber Sacramentorum?* The title in the manuscript of the Vatican and of St. Gall (that of Rheinau

---

[1] Delisle, p 85; cf *supra*, p 125, note 2.
[2] I am not quite clear what John the Deacon means by the words *nonnulla vero superadiciens pro exponendis evangelicis lectionibus*

has no heading) is simply *Liber Sacramentorum Romanae Ecclesiae*, without the name of any Pope. As to the text itself, it contains a great number of things posterior, not only to St. Gelasius, but to St. Gregory. It is therefore not the Sacramentary itself that can have suggested its attribution to Gelasius, neither can I believe that it was handed down by tradition. The Gelasian Sacramentary is derived from official books which were in use in Rome about the end of the seventh century. It is not easy to believe that at that date a Gelasian Liturgy existed at Rome. At that period everything followed the Gregorian tradition, not that there was any shrinking from the introduction of needful modifications, but even when changes were made, they were supposed to follow on the lines of the Gregorian use. It was from this method of representing things that the appellation of Gregorian Sacramentary was applied without the slightest hesitation by Pope Adrian to a book much later than St. Gregory's date. If the Roman books that we find in use in France before the time of Adrian and Charlemagne had borne the name of any Pope, it would doubtless have been that of St. Gregory. We can, however, without having recourse to a far-fetched tradition, explain how the designation of Gelasian Sacramentary arose. It appears to have been first used by Frankish scholars of the ninth century, who moved in a sphere in which liturgical matters and ecclesiastical history were of absorbing interest. The *Liber Pontificalis* was known to these writers, and was regarded as a great authority. When its pages were consulted for information concerning the books of the Roman Liturgy, it was indeed rightly found that St. Leo and St. Gregory had added some words to the canon of the Mass, but that St. Gelasius was the only Pope who is mentioned by his biographer as the author of a *Liber Sacramentorum*. Again, on closer inspection, it is clear that in the life of Gelasius merely prefaces and isolated prayers are attributed to him, and not a systematic and official collection.[1] This, however, proved sufficient to give rise to the idea that Gelasius had put forth a Sacramentary. On the arrival of Pope Adrian's missive, the Franks had found themselves face to face with a Sacramentary attributed to St. Gregory, and differing from that which they had known hitherto. Thenceforward the latter could be as none other than that of Gelasius, and this idea having once taken hold of the minds of teachers like Alcuin and others, it was inevitable that it should spread widely and rapidly. Among the branches of study over which these learned men presided, there were few of greater importance and of more practical application than that of the Liturgy. The Gelasian Sacramentary became a subject of teaching in the schools, and its position thenceforward was impregnable.[2]

In our opinion, no weight can be attached to this designation. By the term Gelasian Sacramentary we must understand a Roman liturgical collection introduced into France some time before Adrian, and certainly subsequently to St. Gregory This conjecture as to the date

---

[1] "Fecit etiam et sacramentorum praefationes et orationes cauto sermone" (*Liber Pont*, vol 1 p 235) In some copies of the *De Scriptoribus* of Gennadius, we find a notice of Gelasius, in which he is said to have written afterwards, "*tractatus diversarum scripturarum et sacramentorum*" (*Ibid*, p 257)

[2] This explanation is a pure hypothesis But in spite of its not having been accepted by all those who are concerned with the subject, no better one has as yet been put forward It has been suggested that the Roman Sacramentary might have been introduced into Gaul by St. Cæsarius, under the name of Gelasius, but this is quite inadmissible St Cæsarius, as is seen by his Homilies, never used any except the Gallican Liturgy Wilson (*op cit*, p lxi) properly remarks, that if Alcuin, or whoever the compiler of the supplements to the Gregorian Sacramentary may have been (*supra*, p. 121), had found the name of Gelasius in the Gelasian Sacramentary, he could hardly have refrained from using it to authenticate his additions.

of the collection may be confirmed by a more careful study of the manuscripts.

The most ancient of them, No 316 of Queen Christina's collection, is, in the opinion of Mons. Delisle,[1] "of the seventh or beginning of the eighth century." This opinion is confirmed by internal evidence. We find, for instance, no mention in it of the stations for the Thursdays in Lent instituted by Gregory II. (715–731). The Roman original was therefore earlier than the death of that Pope. On the other hand, we find in it certain things which could not have been introduced before the seventh century, viz. a *capitulum Sancti Gregorii papae*[2] (I. 21), the Wednesday, Friday, and Saturday stations before the First Sunday in Lent, the four festivals of the Virgin, and that of the Exaltation of the Cross. The latter five festivals are posterior to the time of St. Gregory (d. 604) and earlier than Pope Sergius (687–701);[3] that of the Exaltation must have doubtless been introduced after the discovery of the true cross by Heraclius (628). We cannot therefore determine within a century (628–731) the date of the Roman original of our Sacramentary.

I call it the Roman original. I ought rather to say the Roman model, or framework, for the Gelasian manuscripts are far from having preserved for us a Roman text, free from all interpolations. In the most ancient copy all topographical indications have disappeared. Not one of the basilicas in Rome is mentioned. All the prayers having reference to certain observances peculiar to Roman ritual are likewise suppressed, such as the Mass of St.

---

[1] *Op. cit*, p. 68 Cf *Bibl. de l'École des Chartes*, 1876, p 476.

[2] The name of St. Gregory occurs in the Canon of the Mass, where it could not have been introduced until some time after his death. But these are details which vary in the different manuscripts, and which we cannot trace to the original with any certainty

[3] *Liber Pont.*, pp. 379, 381

Anastasia for Christmas Day, the Greater Litany (April 25), the processions at the Easter vespers, and the collects on certain festivals. These belong to the course of the ecclesiastical year at Rome, and are essentially Roman formularies, though appropriated to the use of other countries.

The Sacramentary known as No. 316 was drawn up in France, probably for the Abbey of St. Denis, whose three patrons are mentioned in the Canon of the Mass, before St. Hilary and St. Martin. The two other manuscripts, those of Rheinau and St. Gall, are also Frankish in origin. It is in France, moreover, that we find the manuscripts which the Carlovingian liturgiologists made use of to supplement the Sacramentary of Adrian. These manuscripts, with the exception of that of St. Gall, agree in employing certain significant variations in the prayers for the Sovereign in the office for Good Friday. The Sacramentary of Adrian mentions the Roman Emperor only, and does not associate with him the Frankish Sovereign. In the Gelasian Sacramentary, the formularies are modified as follows:—
Oremus et pro christianissimo imperatore VEL REGE NOSTRO *illo. . . . Respice propitius ad Romanum* SIVE FRANCORUM *benignus imperium.*[1]

The modifications, however, are not limited to the suppression of peculiarities relating to the city of Rome, and to the region subject to the Empire. There are others, of a purely liturgical nature, which indicate a combination of the Roman and Gallican uses. These are mostly met with in the rite of Ordination. I will merely point out the

---

[1] The correction was not made at first in the text of the Masses *Tempore belli et Pro regibus*, which figure in the third book of the Gelasian Sacramentary under the Nos. 57-62 The prayers in these Masses almost all recur in the supplement of the Gregorian Sacramentary, Nos 83-87 With a single exception, No. 83, the word *Christianus* is always found substituted for that of *Romanus*

principal instances, as 1 shall have to return to this subject later on. At the end of the benediction of the sub-deacon (I. 96) we find a formulary entitled *Consecratio manuum*, which is evidently out of place, for the consecration of hands was never employed in the case of subdeacons. This formulary, moreover, belongs to the rite of the ordination of priests according to the Gallican use. It cannot possibly have been Roman. We know, indeed, from most trustworthy documents, that the consecration of hands did not form part of the ordination rites in use at Rome. We are here confronted, therefore, with a Gallican interpolation

This is not an isolated instance. The whole of the ritual of the minor orders, as it appears in sections I., 95, 96, of the Gelasian Sacramentary, is Gallican from end to end. It is headed by the rubric *Incipit ordo de sacris ordinibus benedicendis*. Next follows an instruction with regard to the conditions of age, etc., for receiving orders, copied from the decretal sent by Pope Zosimus to Hesychius of Salona.[1] Then follow the first ten chapters of the *Statuta Ecclesiae Antiqua*, as to the ordination or installation of bishops, priests, deacons, sub-deacons, acolytes, exorcists, readers, doorkeepers, cantors, consecrated virgins. This document, which is often assigned to the fourth Council of Carthage, is in reality a decree of Gallican origin, promulgated in the province of Arles towards the end of the fifth century. The whole of the above serves as a preface to the *Benedictiones super eos qui sacris ordinibus benedicendi sunt*, benedictions, as we shall see later on, which were not in use at Rome at all. The compiler who inserted this long excerpt, had before him a Gallican text embracing all the various orders. As far as the benedictions are concerned, he restricted himself to the forms connected with the minor orders, those for the major

---

[1] Jaffé, 339, c. 3.

orders being found in another place, but, by an oversight, at the end of the formularies relating to the subdeacons, the compiler has left a fragment of the rite for the ordination of priests.

These interpolations are not isolated instances, as I shall soon have occasion to point out.

In the arrangement of the various festivals, there are often discrepancies between the Gelasian and Gregorian Sacramentaries. The former inserts certain festivals which the latter omits, and *vice versâ*. Now, it must be remarked that in these divergencies the Gregorian has the support of the Leonian Sacramentary, of which I shall speak later on; that is to say, it has on its side a purely Roman compilation, free from any Frankish or Gallican influence. The Leonian never mentions any festival characteristic of the Gelasian Sacramentary. On the contrary, it contains several festivals peculiar to the Gregorian, namely, those of the Seven Brothers (July 10), St Stephen, the Pope (August 2), SS. Felicissimus and Agapitus (August 6), SS. Felix and Adauctus (August 30), and S. Chrysogonus (November 24). It inserts, moreover, although out of its proper place, the anniversary of St. Silvester, a festival unknown to the Gelasian Calendar, and finally, as in the Gregorian Sacramentary, it places the Feast of St. Euphemia on September 16, whereas the Gelasian assigns it to April 13.[1] This last divergence, which is also met with in the Hieronymian Martyrology and in the Mozarabic Missal, may well have been suggested by the Gallican use. The same may be said of the festivals of the Invention of the True Cross and the Martyrdom of St. John Baptist, which are inserted in the Gallican liturgical books, but for which no Roman document can be cited as an authority. I would also point out

---

[1] This is also the day on which this festival is marked in the Calendar of Carthage and in all the Greek calendars

the expression *post clausum Paschae*, applied to the Sundays between the octave of Easter and the festival of Pentecost. This term is found in the *Missale Gothicum* and in the Lectionary of Luxeuil, both of them Gallican books. Gregory of Tours uses it,[1] but it is not met with in the books of purely Roman type.

These details are sufficient to show that the Gelasian Sacramentary cannot be regarded as affording uniform evidence to the customs of the Roman Church. It is, both as regards its origin and its text as a whole, a Roman book, but one which has undergone many modifications in a Gallican direction.

3. *The Missale Francorum.*

The *Missale Francorum* should be assigned a place beside the Gelasian Sacramentary. This manuscript is now in the Vatican,[2] and figures as No. 257 in the collection of Queen Christina. Before it found its way into the Petau Library, from whence it passed into that of the Queen, it had lain for a considerable time in the Abbey of St. Denis, where it was known as early as the thirteenth century. It is written in uncials, and must be attributed to the end of the seventh or the beginning of the following century. Its Frankish origin is undoubted. In the State prayers, the *regnum Francorum* has everywhere been substituted for the Roman Empire.

This manuscript is merely a fragment. It contains, first, Ordinations, the Benediction of Virgins and Widows,

---

[1] *Gloria Conf*, 47
[2] Delisle, *op cit.*, No 4. Cf Wilmart, *Revue bénédictine*, 1911, p. 369. The text has been published by Tommasi (*op. cit.*), by Mabillon, in his *De Liturgia Gallicana*, and by Muratori (*op cit*).

the Consecration of Altars, followed by eleven Masses, of which the first is *pro regibus,* the second in commemoration of St. Hilary, the rest for the common of saints, or for other purposes. The collection ends with the *Canon actionis,* that is to say, the Roman Canon, which breaks off with the manuscript itself at the *Nobis quoque.*

All the Masses contained in this Sacramentary are Roman in style and ritual. Here and there, however, we meet with a few Gallican rubrics, such as *post prophetiam, ante nomina.* At the beginning, the ordination prayers exhibit an unusual complexity, and in this section interesting resemblances may be pointed out between the *Missale Francorum* and the Gelasian Sacramentary. I am of opinion, however, that they have not been taken one from the other, nor that they are both copied from one original.

4 *The Leonian Sacramentary.*

Joseph Bianchini, in 1735, was the first to publish[1] the text of this Sacramentary, which had been found shortly before in the Chapter Library at Verona. It is an uncial manuscript, and, in the opinion of M. Delisle, of the seventh century.[2] The beginning of it is mutilated, so that out of the twelve sections, corresponding to the

---

[1] In vol. iv. of the *Anastasius Bibliothecarius* of his uncle, Fr Bianchini. This edition was reproduced by Muratori in vol. 1. of his *Liturgia Romana vetus* (1748) The brothers Ballerini have published, another, collated with the original manuscript, in their edition of the works of St Leo. This is the edition found in Migne's *Patrologia Lat.*, vol lv Cf. Delisle, No. 1. A new edition, still more critical, and very convenient to consult, has been lately published at Cambridge by Mr Feltoe (*Sacramentarium Leonianum* University Press 1896)

[2] *Op. cit.,* p. 65.

twelve months of the year, nine only are now remaining, and the fourth, that of the month of April, is incomplete. The loss of the first three months is much to be regretted, for these contained the paschal ceremonies, which constitute the most interesting part of the Sacramentaries.

What remains of the month of April is divided into thirty-nine sections, comprising as many [1] Masses in honour of various martyrs. The martyrs are not mentioned by name,[2] so that the formularies may be used in commemoration of any martyr. The month of May contains the Masses of the Ascension, of Pentecost, and of the summer Ember days. In the month of June we have the Masses in honour of St. John Baptist, SS. John and Paul, and the Apostles Peter and Paul. In July the only festival given is that of the Seven Brothers. These are followed by a considerable number of Masses and prayers for divers occasions. In the month of August we find a still greater number of festivals—that of Pope St. Stephen (August 2), that of SS. Xystus, Felicissimus, and Agapitus (August 6), that of St. Laurence (August 10), that of SS. Hippolytus and Pontianus (August 13), and SS. Adauctus and Felix (August 30). In September we have the festivals of SS. Cornelius and Cyprian (September 14), St. Euphemia (September 16), of the dedication of the Church of St. Michael on the Via Salaria (September 30), followed by the autumn Ember days, the prayers used at ordinations and for the *natale* of bishops, priests, and deacons, for the benediction of virgins, and for marriages. There are no festivals in the month

---

[1] And even a few more. The numbers are sometimes incorrectly placed, so that two Masses are given under one heading.

[2] These Masses were, however, drawn up at the outset for the anniversaries of specified martyrs, of whom they originally contained the names But these have been suppressed, although two of them still remain, those of St. Tiburtius (No. 6), and St. Gregory, or rather St George (No 33).

of October, but merely Masses *de siccitate temporis* and *super defunctos* In November we find the festivals of the Four Crowns, of St. Cecilia, of SS Clement and Felicitas, Chrysogonus and Gregory, and also of St. Andrew. There is no entry in the month of December until the Christmas Masses, which are followed by the festivals of St. John the Evangelist, the Holy Innocents, and the winter Ember days.

To what date are we to assign this collection?

It contains, at the end of the month of October, a prayer composed for the burial or funeral anniversary of Pope Simplicius, who died in 483, but this date would, I believe, be far too early.

Many of the prayers, indeed, allude to the times in which the Romans were besieged, surrounded by their enemies, and exposed to massacre and pillage. Others express thanksgiving to God after a victory or a deliverance. Among the latter I would point out one which is the *Secreta* of a Mass occurring in the month of July, and denoted by the number 28. It will be seen that this Mass has no connection with the month of July, but ought to be relegated to Eastertide. This is but one out of numberless instances of the disorder which characterises the whole collection. The *Secreta* is as follows:—*Munera nomini tuo, Domine, cum gratiarum actione deferimus, qui nos ab infestis hostibus liberatos paschale sacramentum secura tribuis mente suscipere.* The besieging and pillaging of Rome by Alaric, Genseric and Ricimer, all took place in the summer months, and therefore it cannot be to these attacks that the prayer under consideration alludes. On the other hand, the long siege by Vitiges, which lasted a whole year, was raised in the month of March. In that year (538) Easter Sunday fell on the 4th of April. The coincidence is noteworthy.

It might be possible to find in the Veronese text of

the Sacramentary other allusions which may be explained far more satisfactorily by attributing them to the anxiety felt during the siege of 537–538 than to any other occasions. Thus we find, for example, in the Preface of another Mass in the month of July (xviii. 6), the following words:— *Agnoscimus Domine . . . ad peccantium merita pertinere ut servorum tuorum labore quaesita sub conspectu nostro manibus diripiantur alienis, et quae desudantibus famulis nasci tribuis, ab hostibus patiaris absumi.* In the year 537 it was the Goths who reaped the harvest on the Roman campagna, and from the tops of the city walls the Romans must have watched with sorrow the operation by which the fruit of their own labour passed into the hands of the besiegers. It is for other reasons quite impossible to assign this prayer to the time of Alaric and Genseric. It was the city rather than the campagna that suffered from the pillaging of the Visigoths and the Vandals. Had it referred to them, we should certainly find somewhere in that long list of Masses *tempore hostili*, some allusions to the sack of public buildings, churches, and private houses. When these invaders, moreover, appeared before the walls of Rome, the season was too far advanced for the harvesting to be still proceeding. On the other hand, everything can be satisfactorily explained by the hypothesis that it refers to the Ostrogoths and the siege of 537–538. On the other hand, however, as the Romans were often besieged during the wars with the Goths, and later on during the Lombardic invasion, I would not like to affirm that it was this particular siege by Vitiges that was actually in question. The latter is the earliest to which we can assign it, and I do not press the point further.

The earliest limit having been thus determined, it remains to be seen whether a more definite one can be found for the latest date than that furnished by palæography. I do not think that we need look later than the time of

St Gregory It is true that the Sacramentary contains the name of a St. Gregory in two places; but even if there be not a copyist's error between the two names *Georgius* and *Gregorius*—an error of frequent occurrence in the manuscripts—it cannot, in any case, be St. Gregory the Pope, as the saint in question is a martyr. Besides this, the Pope of that name decreed that the prayer *Hanc igitur oblationem*, in the Canon of the Mass, should from this time forward conclude with the words, *diesque nostros in tua pace disponas atque ab aeterna damnatione nos eripi et in electorum tuorum jubeas grege numerari*. It is true, indeed, that the Canon of the Mass is missing in the Verona manuscript. It must have been at the beginning, in the part now lost. The prayer *Hanc igitur*, however, occurs a certain number of times in the remainder of the text, yet never once with the Gregorian ending. As we do not find elsewhere any other indication of a date posterior to that of St. Gregory, we shall not be far wrong in attributing the old Veronese Sacramentary to the middle or end of the sixth century.

It must be a purely Roman book, not only because of the absence of any traces of Gallican elements in it, or because in the State prayers it always makes mention of the Roman Empire with peculiar loyalty, but because it exhibits on every page those topographical touches which enable us to distinguish between a text drawn up for the Church of Rome locally, and one which is merely in conformity with the Roman use. The rubrics which announce the festivals of the saints often designate the place of the station with marked topographical precision. Thus we have *VI id. Jul. natale sanctorum Felicis, Philippi*, IN CYMITERIO PRISCILLAE; *Vitalis et Martialis et Alexandri*, IN CYMITERIO JORDANORUM;[1] *et Silani*, IN CYMITERIO MAXIMI, VIA SALARIA; *et Januarii*, IN CYMITERIO PRAETEXTATI, VIA APPIA;—*III non Aug*, *natale sancti Stephani*, IN CYMITERIO CALLISTI, VIA

---

[1] Feltoe, *Sacram. Leon.*, reads JORNARUM and PRAETEXTATAE.

APPIA;—*VIII id. Aug., natale sancti Xysti*, IN CYMITERIO CALLISTI; *et Felicissimi et Agapiti*, IN CYMITERIO PRAETEXTATI, VIA APPIA;—*prid. kal. Oct., natale basilicae Angeli* IN SALARIA. This last festival is that of the dedication of a Church in the environs of Rome. Another dedicatory Mass in honour of St. Stephen is found among the Masses for the month of August;[1] it must be referred either to the Church on the Via Latina, or to that on the Cœlian. The Preface of one of these Masses, in honour of SS. John and Paul,[2] takes for granted that the officiating priest is at Rome and in the Church dedicated to the two martyrs. The same remark is applicable to the Masses in honour of the apostles Peter and Paul, and many others. Among the services for the departed,[3] several formularies presuppose that those present are at San Lorenzo *fuori le mura*, and that the prayers are offered for one of the Popes interred in that Church.[4] It is unnecessary to press the point further. The Roman origin of this collection is clearly evident.

On the other hand, we must beware of regarding it as an official book. It is a private compilation, in which various materials of different age and authorship have been gathered together without much attempt at order. We find in it, indeed, the Stational Masses for the great festivals and for the Ember days, but besides these necessary offices there is a vast amount of superfluous matter. In the other Sacramentaries, the compilers have confined themselves to giving one Mass for each station. In the Gelasian we sometimes find two prayers where the Gregorian gives only one (p. 141), but one of these is merely a variant, or an alternative prayer. In the

---

[1] Muratori, pp 388, 389
[2] *Ibid.*, p 329.
[3] *Ibid*, p. 453.
[4] Zosimus, Xystus III., Hilary.

Verona manuscript the alternatives are far greater in number. There are five Masses, for instance, for the festival of St. Cecilia, nine for Christmas and for St. Stephen's Day, eight for St. Sixtus, fourteen for St. Laurence, twenty-eight for SS. Peter and Paul, and so forth; as to private Masses, they are given *ad libitum*, and are legion.

In this enormous collection there is, as I have remarked, more material than arrangement. Thus the Whitsuntide Mass is inserted among the Masses for the summer Ember days; while under the rubric which announces the anniversary of Pope St. Stephen, on the 3rd of August, we find only the Masses in honour of St. Stephen, the first martyr. These latter, on the contrary, do not appear in their proper place, that is, between the festivals of Christmas and St. John the Evangelist. The Ember days in December are placed after Christmas. Several Masses *pro diversis*, or for the general office of martyrs, are found in impossible months. There are some, in July, which presuppose that the festival of Easter is still being kept. Masses to be said on a vigil are placed after the festival which they are supposed to precede. It would be impossible for an official book to exhibit such a state of disorder.

It should be added that the manuscript contains a certain number of compositions the presence of which is inexplicable in such a book. The brothers Ballerini have pointed out a contradiction between the decree of Gelasius *De recipiendis et non recipiendis libris* and one of the Masses in the Sacramentary in question. It is stated in the latter[1] that the apostles Peter and Paul suffered, indeed, on the same day, but, *tempore discreto*, in different years. Now, the decree of Gelasius holds this belief to be heretical gossip, *sicut haeretici garriunt*. This contradiction would be a serious one if it were certain, as the brothers Ballerini

[1] Muratori p. 344

suppose, that the decree concerning the books is really attributable to Gelasius, or, indeed, to any Pope. As this point appears to me to be difficult of solution, I shall confine myself to pointing out a certain number of prefaces in the Sacramentary which give expression to unexpected and rather startling sentiments. There are actual declamations against monks, unworthy monks it is true, but such declamation in any case is singular. God is called to witness that His Church now contains false confessors [1] mingled with the true; enemies, slanderers, are mentioned, proud ones who, esteeming themselves better than others, harm them, who present themselves under a pious external garb, *sub specie gratiae*, but with the intent to injure. The necessity of guarding against these is urged; the wisdom of the serpent must be joined to the harmlessness of the dove; improvident kindness must not be indulged in; it is right indeed to forgive, but we must also defend ourselves. Sometimes the offensive is assumed. It is urged that these censors are not so worthy as they think themselves. If they do not perceive their own weakness, their own baseness, others can perceive it, and God first of all. It is in vain that they make honeyed speeches, that they wrest the Holy Scriptures; it is known that they go to seek Christ specially in the secret chambers of others. They will be judged by their conduct, and not by their words. These deceitful workers seek to explore the liberty which the Church has in Christ that they may bring it to a shameful servitude. They penetrate into houses, and lead captive silly women laden with sins; apt to appropriate for their own use not only the fortune of widows, but even of married women. To judge of them by their external conduct, what must they not do in

---

[1] Muratori, p 301. "Confessor," in the language of the fourth and fifth centuries, often means an ascetic—a solitary monk

secret? It is a scandal in the eyes of the faithful, and even for the heathen who are thereby deterred from baptism.[1]

I am minimising matters; but it is useless to press the matter further. This manner of putting one's adversaries in the pillory, or worse than the pillory, is clearly foreign to the recognised methods of the Roman Church. The compiler of the Sacramentary could not have invented these strange prayers, for it is scarcely possible for them to have been composed in the sixth century. The use of the word *confessor* in the sense implied, and especially the mention of a still numerous pagan public, carries us back rather to the end of the fourth century—to the time of Damasus and Siricius, for instance, when religious houses for men were almost unknown at Rome, but where, on the contrary, were a considerable number of isolated ascetics, of the type of St. Jerome, Rufinus, or Pelagius. It is well known that St. Jerome did not spare the Roman clergy. One is tempted to believe that they did not allow him to get the better of them, and that his blows were sometimes returned. These disputes must have been frequently renewed, since we find an echo of them even in the pages of the Liturgy.

It is certain, moreover, that such liturgical scandals could only be possible in small communities, in little private conventicles, where the officiating minister, taking advantage of the liberty still allowed to individual caprice in such matters, could give vent to his spite. It was a great mistake ever to have written such things, but to have made a collection of them afterwards and inserted them in a book of liturgical texts was a blunder that we should not be likely to impute to the rulers of the Roman

---

[1] Muratori, p 350, *et seq*

Church. The brothers Ballerini, therefore, were perfectly right in regarding the so-called Leonian Sacramentary as a private collection exhibiting but little intelligence in the manner in which it is drawn up and arranged.

This Sacramentary has nevertheless a very great value. The formularies which I have just mentioned are relatively few in number, and are the exception. With regard to the others, what I have said above throws no doubt on their Roman—indeed, exclusively Roman origin, and proves that they go back to a time anterior, in some cases long anterior, to the pontificate of St. Gregory.

5. *The Roll of Ravenna.*

Signor Ceriani published some years ago[1] a liturgical Roll belonging to the collection of Prince Antonio Pio of Savoy. This parchment, which is 11 feet 9 inches in length, in spite of its being mutilated at the beginning and ending, contains, in large uncial characters, forty prayers, of the Roman type, relating to the preparation for the festival of Christmas. On the back of the manuscript have been copied,[2] in minuscules of the tenth century, seven letters of an Archbishop of Ravenna named John, and another from Pope Sergius III. These eight documents all belong to the period 900-910. The letter of Pope Sergius was written in the interests of the Church of Ravenna, and the archbishop acknowledges, in one of his replies, that he has read it. We have, therefore, ground to believe that the whole of this correspondence came originally from the

---

[1] *Il rotolo opistograja del principe Antonio Pio di Savoia*, in-f°, Milan, 1883 This memoir has been re-edited in the *Archivio Storico Lombardo*, 1884, p. 1, *et seq*

[2] This part of the Roll has been re-edited by Herr S. Lowenfeld in the *Neues Archiv*, vol ix p 515, *et seq*, with an historical commentary

metropolitan archives of Ravenna. The liturgical Roll, on the back of which it was transcribed, must therefore have the same *provenance*. We have here, then, a collection of prayers which had been in use in the Church of Ravenna. One of them only, the twenty-seventh, is found in any known document of the Roman Liturgy. It figures in one of the Masses for Christmas Day [1] in the Leonian Sacramentary, and among a group of prayers for the same festival in the Gregorian Sacramentary.[2] The Ravenna prayers are not arranged in the order observed in the Mass. There is no attempt at any distribution of this kind, for they are simply placed one after the other. They could have served as well for the Office as for the Mass, and this circumstance detracts considerably from the value of the Ravenna Roll.

It is, moreover, difficult to assign a date to it. The uncials are rather coarsely formed, and it may be attributed with equal probability to the eighth or ninth as well as to the sixth centuries.

Mons. Chatelain has published [3] a series of prayers, which are in the script of the seventh or eighth century, and accompanied by a certain number of Tironian notes,* from a manuscript which came from Bobbio.[4] They number seventeen in all, and comprise the *post communio* prayer and the *Secreta;* they are Roman in type, and are found in the Sacramentaries of that use, especially in the Leonian Sacramentary.[5]

---

[1] Muratori, vol i col. 468
[2] *Ibid*, vol. ii col 10
[3] *Introduction à la lecture des notes tironniennes*, Paris, 1900, pl. xiii. p. 229.
[4] *Ambros.*, O 210 sup, fol. 46 verso.
[5] Signor G Mercati, who was the first to draw attention to this text (*Rendiconti dell' Istituto Lombardo*, 1898, p. 1211), has re-edited it with the help of Mons. Chatelain's readings, and commented on it in the *Studi e Testi* of the Vatican Library, No VII, p 35

* [The shorthand of the ancient Romans.—Tr]

6. Ordines Romani.

In the second volume of his *Musaeum Italicum*,[1] Mabillon published some of the *Ordines Romani*, or ritual directions for different ceremonies. All these documents are not of the same date, and it is possible to trace in them modifications which were made in the Pontifical Liturgy from the ninth to the fifteenth centuries. It is only with the most ancient that we have to deal here, and we must of course put aside those which correspond to the Roman Liturgy as it has been modified owing to various influences, whether in France or at Rome, subsequent to the ninth century. I shall therefore select only Nos. I., VII., VIII., and IX. out of the whole series of the *Ordines*. The first of these relates to the liturgy of the Mass, the second to baptism, and the two others to the ceremonies at ordination.

We must, moreover, distinguish between the different parts of the *Ordo Romanus I.* as it is published by Mabillon. The whole of it, indeed, is taken from manuscripts of the ninth century, and it may be taken for granted that all of it existed in the early years of that century. But all the parts do not exhibit to the same extent a Roman impress.

After an introduction relating to the apportioning of the liturgical service among the clerics of the seven regions of Rome, the *Ordo* gives us a description of the stational Mass, presided over by the Pope. This first part comprises Chapters 1–21 of Mabillon.

It is found, with an abrupt break at this point, in several manuscripts cited by Mabillon and others, and especially in that of Verona, published by Fr. Bianchini.[2]

---

[1] In the edition reproduced in Migne's *Pat Lat*, vol. lxxviii

[2] *Anast Bibl*, vol iii p xxxix For this *Ordo*, cf Grisar, *Analecta Romana*, vol i p 195.

Then follow some supplements, referring to peculiarities in the service when the Pope is prevented from being present, and also to special festivals or seasons of the year. These supplements are peculiar to the St. Gall manuscript, which forms the basis of Mabillon's edition To these may be added Chapters 48–51, which are also found in the Verona manuscript, and have the same supplementary character. The description of the ceremonies at the end of Lent and in Holy Week is comprised in Chapters 27–47. Another set of directions for the same ceremonies, but carried on to the end of Easter Week, is added as an appendix to *Ordo I.* in Mabillon's edition. There are two redactions, the second more complete than the first, of the same paschal *Ordo*, but they are not found in the same manuscripts.

About the year 830, Amalarius[1] put forth a work in four books, entitled *De Officiis Ecclesiasticis*. It is a commentary on the liturgical ceremonies and the Divine Office. Among the documents which the writer made use of, there was an *Ordo Romanus*, which he frequently cites as an important authority. We recognise in it the text of Mabillon's *Ordo I.*, including the chapters on the paschal ceremonies. The latter, therefore, must be very ancient, but these ceremonies did not correspond with those in actual use at Rome, as Amalarius had occasion to experience in a journey which he made thither in 832 for the special purpose of pursuing his liturgical studies. Pope Gregory IV. put him into communication with his archdeacon, Theodore, who gave him all the information he required. It is remarkable that on almost every occasion in which he referred to the paschal ceremonies, the information of the

[1] See, for this personage and his various ecclesiastical positions, Dom Morin s articles in the *Revue Bénédictine*, 1891, p 433; 1892, p 337; 1894, p. 241.

archdeacon was contrary to that furnished by the *Ordo*, and poor Amalarius was obliged to acknowledge that his document was not without its shortcomings.[1]

It does not, moreover, require a lengthy examination to see that the paschal *Ordo* does not possess the Roman characteristics of the *Ordo* of the Mass. In taking up the latter, we feel ourselves transported to Rome, into the midst of the Roman clergy, to the city with its seven regions, and its special days of service for each region. The officiating minister is the Pope himself, *domnus apostolicus*, who appears surrounded by the great dignitaries of his court—the *primiciarius*, the *secondicerius*, the *sacellarius*, the *nomenclator*, and others. He starts from his Palace of the Lateran and proceeds on horseback in procession to one or other of the Roman basilicas. It is clearly impossible to refer these details to any other locality. In the paschal *Ordo*, on the contrary, there are no indications of any particular town, while it is an ordinary dignitary—a bishop —who officiates, and sometimes even merely an inferior ecclesiastic. The use is indeed Roman, but Roman as observed elsewhere than in Rome, and combining with it customs unknown to the papal court.

It is therefore impossible to attach the same weight to the paschal *Ordo* as to the rest. It contains, doubtless, many Roman details, but details which in every case require to be confirmed by more trustworthy documents.

Among such documents is a fragment of a paschal *Ordo* found by Signor de Rossi in the celebrated epigraphical and topographical manuscript of Einsiedeln, and published by him in vol. ii. of his *Inscriptiones Christianae*, p. 34

---

[1] His enemies were not slow to take advantage of this admission Florus, *Adv. Amalarium*, i 7 : " Libellum Romani ordinis tantae auctoritatis habet ut eum pene ad verbum nitatur exponere; et tamen statim sibi ipse contrarius asserit hunc Romano archidiacono cuius traditionibus gloriatur ignotum "

It contains merely the three last days of Holy Week, but it is absolutely Roman in character.

Mabillon's *Ordo VII.*, relating to the ceremonies of Christian initiation—the catechumenate, baptism, and confirmation—is as well attested by documentary evidence as the *Ordo I.* Like the latter, it is published from manuscripts of the ninth century. Prior to the death of Charlemagne, Jesse, Bishop of Amiens, wrote a commentary on it, and transcribed a large portion of it in his *Epistola de Baptismo.*[1] It must even be earlier than that, as it figures almost in its entirety in the Gelasian Sacramentary.

With regard to *Ordo VIII.* and *Ordo IX.*, I am unable to give any other external proof of their antiquity than the fact that they occur in manuscripts of the ninth century. They commend themselves, moreover, to us by their import. Like the preceding manuscript, they presuppose that the ceremonies take place at Rome, and are presided over by the Pope in person.

I have found in the Latin manuscript No. 974 in the Bibliothèque Nationale, which came from the Abbey of St. Amand, a whole group of *Ordines Romani*, which appear to me to have escaped, up to the present, the notice of liturgiologists. This manuscript contains some treatises of St. Augustine, and advantage has been taken of the few blank leaves at the beginning and the end to copy the *Ordines* on them. The text of these, like that of St. Augustine's work, is of the ninth century. It comprises: 1st, the description of the stational Mass; 2nd, the paschal ceremonies; 3rd, the order of the Greater Litany; 4th, the ordination of priests and deacons; 5th, the dedication of churches; 6th, the procession at Candlemas. In all these ceremonies the ritual is strictly Roman—Roman of the city itself, for it is taken for

---

[1] Migne, *Pat Lat*, vol cv p. 781

granted throughout that the Pope is present and officiating.[1]

The *Ordo* of the stational Mass, in the state in which it has come down to us, is certainly later than the time of St. Gregory. We find in it several directions which we know to have been introduced by him. For instance, in the Pope's escort defenders of the regions are mentioned, dignitaries whose office was created by St. Gregory;[2] the gradual is sung by a cantor, and not by a deacon, in conformity with the rule laid down by the Roman Council of 595; the *Pater Noster* is placed before the *Pax Domini*, an alteration which St. Gregory himself states that he made.[3] It would not, however, be correct to affirm that the whole of the ritual goes back to the time of St. Gregory and to the beginning of the seventh century. The mention of the deaconries, the designation of the Palace of the Lateran by the name of *Patriarchium*,[4] the marked development of the papal court,—all point to the later part of the seventh century. Moreover, we have the mention of the *Agnus Dei*, and this hymn is known to have been introduced by Pope Sergius (687-701).[5] It is therefore quite to the end of the seventh, if not to the following century, that I should assign the redaction of the *Ordo*, as we possess it. Indeed, we must give even a later date, if we are to include some of the supplements, for in one of these (c. 24) we find the name of Charlemagne, and a reference to the time (already past) of the pontificate of Adrian. If we take into consideration this additional part, the *Ordo* cannot be earlier than 795.

[1] The text of these *Ordines*, and that of Signor Rossi, will be found in the Appendix to the present volume

[2] Ep viii 14 (16)

[3] Ep ix 12 (26)

[4] *Lib. Pontif*, vol i p 364, note 6 The pontifical palace was, in the seventh century, called *Episcopium*; the designation *Patriarchium* does not appear in the *L P* before the notice of Sergius (*ibid*, p 371, l 10)

[5] *Lib Pontif*, vol i p 376

§ 2.—Gallican Books.

7. *The Missale Gothicum* [1]

This valuable manuscript bears the number 317 in Queen Christina's collection in the Vatican. It came from the Petau Library. From certain details which it contains,[2] we are able to ascertain that it was drawn up for the Church of Autun. Tommasi, who was the first to edit it, and Mabillon, who published it after him, were incorrect in thinking that its *provenance* was the province of Narbonne, then subject to the Visigothic kings. This opinion appears to have been suggested to them by a note written in the fifteenth century as a heading to the manuscript: *Missale Gothicum*. We must also be cautious in accepting Mabillon's opinion that it represents the *purus ordo gallicanus*. As a fact, this Sacramentary contains many Roman elements.

Two Masses are missing at the beginning, to judge by the numeration of those which follow. The series, as it stands, begins with the Mass for Christmas Eve. After the Epiphany, we find certain Masses in honour of various saints, then follow Lent and Easter, the festivals of the Invention of the Holy Cross, of St. John the Evangelist, the Rogation Days, the Ascension, and Whitsuntide, and finally other Masses in honour of saints, either special for certain festivals or for the common of saints, and six Masses for Sundays

---

[1] Delisle, *Sacramentaires*, No 3. See editions by Tommasi, Mabillon, Muratori, *op. cit* Cf Neale and Forbes, *The Ancient Liturgy of the Gallican Church*, p 32 The *De Liturgia Gallicana* of Mabillon has been reprinted in vol lxxii of Migne's *Pat Lat*, with all the texts edited or re-edited by the illustrious Benedictine

[2] It contains special Masses for the festivals of St Symphorian and St Leger

The volume, which is mutilated towards the end, breaks off in a *missa cotidiana Romensis*, of which only the first prayer is given. With the exception of this latter, all the formularies are arranged in the order followed in the Gallican Mass, but many among them, especially the Masses in honour of saints, are Roman formularies.

This Missal contains a Mass in honour of St Leger, in which his relics are spoken of as being distributed throughout Gaul. St. Leger, Bishop of Autun, died in 680. The manuscript cannot therefore be earlier than the final years of the seventh century. In Mons. Delisle's opinion, its date should not be placed later than the beginning of the following century.

8. *The Missale Gallicanum Vetus*.[1]

This Sacramentary, which is of the same date as the preceding, is known as No. 493 in the Palatine collection in the Vatican Library. It is much mutilated. The fragments even are not in their right order in the manuscript, but Tommasi, their first editor, arranged them as they ought to be.

The first document we find in it is a Mass in honour of St. Germain of Auxerre, which is followed by prayers for the benediction of virgins and widows. After a break come two Masses *in Adventum Domini*, one for Christmas Eve, and the prayers for the following night, interrupted by another gap. Further on, we find ourselves in the midst of the rites of the catechumenate and of the *Traditio symboli*, belonging to the Sunday before Easter, according to the Gallican use. After a third gap follow the ceremonies for

[1] Delisle. No 5 Cf the editions by Tommasi, Mabillon, Muratori, Neale and Forbes

Holy Week, the festivals of Easter, and the continuation of the proper of the time up to the Mass for Rogationtide, where the text breaks off.

In the passages where this Sacramentary can be compared with the preceding one, many identical formularies are met with. Neither of these Sacramentaries is complete. In order to reconstruct certain series of prayers, it is necessary to supply the omissions of one from the other. There is, moreover, here, as in the Autun Sacramentary, a large proportion of Roman elements.

9. *Masses published by Mone*.[1]

In 1850, Herr Mone[2] published a collection of Gallican Masses, deciphered in a palimpsest manuscript found at Reichenau. The older script, that of the Masses, is uncial, of the end of the seventh century.[3] According to a note added at a later date to the end of the manuscript, it belonged, even then re-written, to John II., Bishop of Constance (760–781).

These texts have this advantage over the preceding Sacramentaries, they are entirely Gallican, without any admixture of Roman elements. Unfortunately, with the exception of a Mass in honour of St. Germain of Auxerre,[4] all the others are Masses for ferial days, or Sundays, without ascription to any special festival. There are two *contestationes*, or prefaces, to each Mass, offering an alternative to the officiating priest. One of the Masses is in hexameter verse throughout, a peculiarity unique in the whole of the liturgical texts known up to the present time.

---

[1] Delisle, No. 8, § 1.

[2] *Lateinische und griechische Messen aus dem zweiten bis sechsten Jahrhundert*, Frankfort, 1850. Cf Migne, *P. L.*, vol. cxxxviii. p. 863 Neale and Forbes, *op. cit*, p 1. See note on p 574.

[3] Delisle, *op cit.*, p. 82

[4] This Mass is quite different from that of the *Missale Gallicanum.*

154 CHRISTIAN WORSHIP: ITS ORIGIN AND EVOLUTION.

To this fragment of a Sacramentary should be added a few palimpsest leaves published by Peyron, Mai, and Bunsen. The fragments of Mai and Peyron appear to have belonged to the same manuscript in the Ambrosian Library.[1] Those of Bunsen were deciphered from a manuscript at St. Gall [2] All these remains are of a well-marked Gallican character. We cannot say the same of a fragment more recently published by Herr Bickell from a manuscript at Cambridge.[3] It contains part of a Christmas Mass, composed almost entirely of Roman prayers.

10 *The Lectionary of Luxeuil.*

This manuscript, numbered 9427 in the Bibliothèque Nationale, contains the lections of the Mass for the ecclesiastical year. It is written in minuscules of the seventh century. Mabillon found it at the Abbey of Luxeuil, and published it in his *De Liturgia Gallicana.* He did not give the complete text, as he did not consider it necessary to reproduce, in their entirety, the portions known from other sources. He therefore prints merely the beginning and end of each lection, with the necessary references, but he gives the whole of the rubrics, which are of much greater importance.

The Lectionary of Luxeuil is a purely Gallican book,

---

[1] M. 12 (or 14) *supp* Those of Peyron are to be found in his book entitled, *M. T. Ciceronis Orationum Fragmenta Inedita*, Stuttgard, 1824, p 226; those of Mai, in his *Script. Vett*, vol iii, 2nd part, p. 247. Mr. C. E. Hammond has reprinted the first in his pamphlet, *The Ancient Liturgy of Antioch*, p 51; the others in his *Liturgies Eastern and Western*, p. lxxxi. The latter appear also in Migne's *Pat. Lat*, at the end of Mone's Masses, *op. cit*, p. 883.

[2] Bunsen, *Anal. Antenicaena*, vol iii. p 263 Hammond. *Liturgy of Antioch*, p 53

[3] *Zeitschrift für katholische Theologie*, 1882, p. 370.

without the slightest trace of Roman influence. It is arranged according to the order of the Gallican ecclesiastical year, and this constitutes its great interest. The festivals of the saints given are few in number, that of St. Geneviève being the only one which might furnish us with any indications as to the origin of the manuscript. Although it was discovered at Luxeuil, it contains nothing which relates particularly to that region. Dom Morin[1] is of opinion that it represents the use of the Church of Paris.

11. *The Letters of St. Germain of Paris.*

Among the most valuable documents for the study of the Gallican Liturgy, we must include two letters published by Martene[2] from a manuscript at Autun. The first bears as its title the words *Germanus episcopus Parisius scripsit de missa.* I do not believe that there is the slightest reason to doubt the authenticity of this heading.[3] St. Germain of Paris, who flourished from 555–576, is well known[4] for the zeal he displayed for the worthy celebration of the divine Service, and it is therefore not surprising that he should have been careful to devote a few pages to the symbolical meaning of the ritual of the Liturgy. This is, in fact, the subject dealt with in the two letters. The first deals with the Mass, the second with certain particular details, ceremonies for special occasions, and liturgical vestments. In order to explain the ritual, the venerable author is obliged to give a summary description of it, and in this lies the peculiar interest for us of his explanation.[5]

[1] *Revue Bénédictine*, 1893, p. 438
[2] *Thes Anecdot.*, vol. v. Cf. Migne, *P L*, vol lxxii. p. 89.
[3] See note, p. 574
[4] Fortunatus, *Carm*, ii. 9
[5] We may reconstruct from the letters of St. Germain a kind of *Ordo*

12. *British and Irish Books, etc.*

The ancient liturgical manuscripts found in the British Isles are all, with one or two exceptions, books of a mixed character—in the main Roman, but with certain Gallican details. The most important is the Stowe Missal,[1] which contains, at the end of St. John's Gospel, an Ordinary [and Canon] of the Mass,[2] followed by prayers belonging to three Masses for special occasions, an *Ordo Baptismi*, an *Ordo ad infirmum visitandum*, and finally a treatise in Irish on the ceremonies of the Mass. All are not in the same handwriting. The Latin texts are partly of the eighth and partly of the tenth century. Nearly all the rubrics are in the later hand, in which also are many additions in the blank spaces left in the original text, and even over the lines, which have been previously erased. The beginning of the Canon is in the later writing, as is also the rubric *Canon dominicus papae Gilasi*, to which too much confidence should not be given. We have here, in fact, the usual Roman Canon in its Gregorian form, that is to say, with the final *diesque nostros*, etc., in the *Hanc igitur*. There are, however, interpolations in various places, sometimes in the earlier, sometimes in the later hand. Among these interpolations, one of the most curious is that of the *Memento* for the departed (in the earlier hand); we find

Gallicanus. The fourth Council of Toledo (c. 25) decreed that bishops should furnish every priest to whom they entrusted the care of a parish, with a *libellus officialis* to direct them in performing the ceremonies connected with public worship. No book of this nature has come down to us.

[1] Published by F E. Warren, *The Liturgy and Ritual of the Celtic Church*, Oxford, 1881, pp 207-248 Cf Whitley Stokes, *The Irish Passages in the Stowe Missal*, Calcutta, 1881.

[2] This Mass, when due allowance is made for the long interpolations from Irish sources, presents a striking resemblance in general outline to the *Missa quotidiana Romensis* of the Bobbio Missal, with which we shall presently have to deal Attention has been drawn to this similarity by Dom Cagin in *Paléographie Musicale*, vol. v. p 128.

mentioned in it a long list of the righteous, from Abel down to the Irish saints of the sixth century. We find in it, moreover, the names of Pope St. Gregory, and of the three first successors of St. Augustine in the see of Canterbury—Laurence, Mellitus, and Justus.

A few fragments, Gallican in character, are to be found (1) in the book of Deer, an Evangeliarium belonging to Scotland, but now in the University Library at Cambridge,[1] (2) in the Irish books of Dimma[2] and Mulling,[3] and (3) in a manuscript of St. Gall[4] Mr. Bannister has recently published some fragments of the same type from two MSS. belonging to Reichenau, and from another at Piacenza, which must have come from Bobbio.[5] These texts present some analogy to the Masses in the Stowe Missal. They come under the category of combinations of the old Irish books, of the Gallican type, with those of the Roman use.

We possess, on the other hand, an Irish liturgical book entirely free from any trace of Roman influence. This is the Antiphonary of Bangor.[6] This manuscript, now preserved in the Ambrosian Library, is dated by the list which terminates it. This gives the names of the abbots of the monastery of Bangor[7] from Comgill, its founder, down to Cronan, the abbot then living, whose rule extended from 680 to 691. The manuscript also contains a number of hymns for the office of Matins, various prayers connected with the same office, and a few antiphons and other small pieces.[8]

---

[1] Warren, *op cit*, p 164.   [2] *Ibid*, p 167   [3] *Ibid*, p 171
[4] No 1394, Warren, *ibid*, p 177
[5] *The Journal of Theological Studies*, October, 1903, p 49.
[6] Published by Muratori, *Anecdota bibl. Ambrosianae*, vol. iv. p. 121, an edition reprinted in Migne's *Pat. Lat.*, vol. lxxii. p 582. A new edition has been lately published by the Henry Bradshaw Society [with complete facsimiles. Edited by F E Warren. Pt 1., 1892, pt. ii., 1895 —Tr.]
[7] This monastery of Bangor, situated in co. Down, Ireland, must not be confounded with the monastery of Bangor in Wales, mentioned by Bede, *Hist. Eccl*, ii. 2.
[8] See note, p 574.

13. *The Bobbio Missal.*[1]

One book remains to be described, which, like most of the ancient liturgical manuscripts, has received from its original editor an incorrect title. This is the *Sacramentarium Gallicanum* of Mabillon. As the *Missale Gothicum* and the *Missale Gallicanum* are thus designated, although they are not Missals, but Sacramentaries, so the *Sacramentarium Gallicanum* bears this name, although it is not a Sacramentary, but a Missal. Mabillon found it at Bobbio, and published it in his *Musaeum Italicum*.[2] The manuscript, which was sent to St. Germain des Prés at the time of publication, has remained at Paris ever since. It is now in the Bibliothèque Nationale (No. 13, 246). Mons. Delisle believes it to be a work of the seventh century.

In spite of its great antiquity, the Bobbio Missal is but an indifferent source of information on the Gallican use. It begins by a *missa Romensis cottidiana*, in which the Roman and Gallican uses are combined in a peculiar fashion. Up to the Preface, all the ritual is Gallican; from the Preface onwards all is Roman. This is followed by the Masses and ritual of the ecclesiastical year. The series begins with three Masses *in Adventum Domini*, before the Vigil of Christmas. The Saints' Days are few in number. There is a Mass in honour of St. Sigismond for those who are suffering from the quartan ague. In each Mass we find, first the text of the three Gallican lections, then the four prayers before the Preface, and finally the latter under the rubric *Contestatio*. None of the Masses goes beyond the *Sanctus*, which implies that they all terminated in the same way as the *missa Romensis cottidiana* at the beginning of the Missal.

[1] Delisle, No 6
[2] Vol i, part 2. Cf. Migne's *Pat Lat*, vol lxxii. p. 451; Muratori, *Lit Rom*, vol ii col 775, Neale and Forbes, *op cit*, p 205

In the part before the Preface, the prayers are mostly arranged according to the Gallican use, and placed under Gallican rubrics; in nearly one-third of the Masses, however, the prayers are preceded by Roman rubrics, and are arranged according to the Roman method. The compiler, nevertheless, has shown such a want of skill, that in the Masses of Roman type the prayers are mostly Gallican, and *vice versâ*. He even places purely Gallican invitatories under the rubrics belonging to Roman prayers. In short, all we have in this text is a very bad attempt to combine the two uses.[1]

Mabillon is of opinion that the Bobbio Missal may have come from the province of Besançon, wherein was situated Luxeuil, which was the mother house of the Italian Convent. He regards the Mass of St. Sigismund as being an indication in favour of this conjecture. I am unable to say whether this is so or not. The Mass of St. Sigismund is not a Mass for the anniversary of this saint, but one for the cure of the fever-stricken, of whom he was regarded as the patron, and that not only in the Seine valley and Burgundy, but in other districts I should rather be inclined to lay stress on the place from whence the manuscript came, and on the fact that the name of St. Ambrose occurs in the Canon of the Mass, a peculiarity not met with in any other Gallican or Frankish Sacramentary. The Roman rite, moreover, is here combined with the Gallican in a peculiar fashion, quite different from that which obtains in the systems of combination which we find in the Frankish manuscripts of late Merovingian times. It is not exactly the Ambrosian Liturgy, but it is somewhat analogous to it.

---

[1] The Benedictines of Solesmes have announced an edition of this book. One of them, Dom Cagin, has explained his theory in the *Paléographie Musicale*, vol. v. p. 97, *et seq*; but I cannot share his opinions I have given my reasons in the *Revue d'Histoire et de Littérature Religieuses*, vol v. (1900), p 38

The Roman Canon is frankly adopted, more completely, indeed, than in the Ambrosian rite, which has in this portion of the service retained a few peculiarities.

14. *Ambrosian Books.*

We find a considerable number of liturgical manuscripts, compiled for Churches using the Ambrosian rite, preserved in the collections of North Italy, particularly in the Ambrosian collection at Milan, and in the treasury of the cathedral of that town. The most ancient are of the tenth century. The first of the series is the Sacramentary of Biasca,[1] which is somewhat coarse in execution, as might be expected, since it was a book for the use of a country parish. In the Ambrosian books, the ecclesiastical year begins on St. Martin's Day (November 11), and we find the Ordinary of the Mass placed after Whit Week, in the middle of the volume. Besides the Sacramentaries, there are also a few Antiphonaries.[2]

---

[1] Ambros., A 24 *bis* inf ; Delisle, No 71. It is not within the scope of this book to describe, even briefly, the manuscripts of the Ambrosian Liturgy, and I have not studied them for a long enough period to be competent to do so. I have learnt much in the short time which I have been able to devote to them, owing to the fact that I had as my guide the Abbé Ceriani, the most learned expert on the Milanese Liturgy. It is to be regretted that he died (1906) without publishing the results of his long and conscientious researches. Meanwhile the description of the most ancient Ambrosian Sacramentaries will be found in the memoir of Mons. L Delisle, p. 198, *et seq* See also article "Ambrosien" (*rit*) in Dom Cabrol's *Dict. d'Archéologie chrétienne*, etc., Paris, 1904

[2] The Benedictines of Solesmes have published (1896) in volume v. of their *Paléographie Musicale*, an Ambrosian Antiphonary of the twelfth century. They have also brought out (1900) a Sacramentary of Bergamo of the eleventh century, with three capitularies of the Gospels. This publication forms the first part of their liturgical supplement to Migne's *Patrology*. Dr. Magistretti edited in 1894 the *Beroldus*, a ceremonial representing the customs of the same period; he has, moreover, begun a collection entitled, *Monumenta veteris Liturgiae Ambrosianae*, the first number of which (1897) contains a Pontifical of the ninth century. Attention may also be drawn to the studies of Signor Mercati in No. 7 of the *Studi e Testi* of the Vatican Library.

15. *Mozarabic Books.*

The liturgy in use in Visigothic Spain was retained throughout the Arab domination; it was not until after the re-conquest of Toledo (1085) that it came into conflict with the Roman use, introduced by the monks of Cluny. It disappeared soon after. Of its later state a few ancient books have come down to us, but not all of them have been published.[1]

1. A Sacramentary of the tenth century for the use of the Cathedral of Toledo (*Toletanus*, xxxv. 3), unpublished. This is the only Sacramentary known so far.
2. The *Comes* or *Liber Comicus*, containing the lections of the Mass, with interesting rubrics. There are several MSS. of it extant; one of them has been published by Dom G. Morin.[2]
3. The Antiphonary of the Cathedral of Leon, copied in 1066 from a MS. dated in the first year of King Wamba (672); also unpublished.
4. The *Liber Ordinum*, a kind of Euchologion of ritual, containing the order of various Ceremonies and a certain number of Votive Masses. It has been published by Dom Férotin from a MS. from Silos of 1052.[3]

---

[1] This enumeration is made from the information given by Dom Férotin in his introduction to the *Liber Ordinum*.

[2] *Anecdota Maredsolana*, vol 1. (1893). The MSS are:—
  1. *Toletanus*, xxxv. 8, of the ninth or tenth century.
  2. *Parisinus*, recently acquired 2171, from Silos, eleventh century (before 1067). This is the MS. published by Dom Morin.
  3. A MS of the Cathedral of Leon, written shortly before 1071
  4. *Matritensis*, Acad. d'histoire, 22; its provenance is S. Millan de la Cogolla.

[3] Other MSS., less complete, have been made use of by him; two other copies from Silos, one of 1039, the other of uncertain date, though of the eleventh century and of less important content; finally one of Madrid (Acad. d'histoire, No 56), having S. Millan for provenance.

The old Visigothic Use had been obsolete for four centuries when Cardinal Ximenes undertook to revive it and caused a Mozarabic Missal and Breviary to be drawn up. For this purpose, although the ancient books were used, they were supplemented by additional matter from Roman sources.[1]

[1] The *editio princeps* is that of Toledo, 1500. The best is that of Lesley, Rome, 1755, reproduced in vol. lxxxv. of Migne's *Latin Patrology*.

CHAPTER VI.

THE ROMAN MASS.

THE *Ordines Romani* describe to us the stational Mass as celebrated by the Pope in person in the great liturgical assemblies to which all the clergy and people were convoked, and at which it was taken for granted that they were present. The priests, in their titulary churches, in the churches and chapels of cemeteries, in the oratories of monasteries, of deaconries, and of private houses, were accustomed to celebrate according to a form fundamentally the same, but without the solemn ceremonial. The cardinal priest had at his disposition only clerics of an inferior order —the acolytes—and he was obliged to take upon himself many functions which in a solemn Mass would be assigned to the deacons. The disparity in the ceremonial was not occasioned by the difference in rank between the priest and a bishop, for it often happened that when the Pope could not celebrate, the stational Mass was taken by a simple priest, and the ceremonial in this case was not less imposing and complicated than if the Pope himself were present. It was not, moreover, the place of the station which made the difference. Private Masses might be said at St. Peter's, or at Constantine's basilica at the Lateran, or at Santa Maria Maggiore; and, on the other hand, it often happened that the stational Mass, in all its ceremony, was celebrated in a simple presbyteral church. We may even safely say that all such churches, or almost all, had, at least once in each year, the honour of being designated for the stational Mass. The difference in place depended on the character of the congregation. At the Masses celebrated in chapels, cemeteries, presbyteral churches, and even in the great basilicas, there were present, the stational days excepted, only a private congregation, consisting of a family, or a corporation, or the inhabitants of a quarter, or any kind of association of the faithful, whether resident or pilgrims. The Mass said on such occasions was a private Mass. The public Mass, that is to say, the stational Mass, was that in which the whole Roman church was considered to take part.

This public Mass is that which agrees best with the primitive type of the institution, and on that account its study is the more important. As we find it described in the *Ordines* of the eighth or ninth century, it implied a ceremonial which corresponded more with the exigencies of a later date than with those of primitive times. The pontifical court, which had then reached a considerable development, played in it an important part. The different classes of the clergy, arranged according to their orders and to their regions, the corporation of cantors, the crucifers of the quarter, the military and civil rulers, and, in fact, everybody, had his part in these high ceremonials of worship. I will put on one side everything in the *Ordo* which has to do with this high ceremonial, and will confine myself to those rites which are essential, and which are common to the Roman and other liturgies.

1. *The Entry of the Officiating Priest.*

The congregation of the faithful having assembled, the priests, accompanied by the bishops then in Rome, took their places in the apse of the church which was reserved for the superior clergy. The pontiff and his deacons set out from the *secretarium*, or sacristy (which was situated close to the entrance of the church), and proceeded to the altar.

The *Ordines* of the eighth century represent them as wearing their liturgical vestments, and as preceded by the sub-deacons, one of whom swings a censer,[1] and by seven acolytes carrying tapers.[2] During this procession the choir (*schola cantorum*) sings the antiphon *ad introitum*. Originally this antiphon consisted of the singing of a complete psalm, or, at least, of several verses of it. It continued to be sung until the pontiff had reached the altar. Before he did so, he was met by a cleric, who brought to him a fragment of consecrated bread, which was reserved from a previous Mass. This eucharistic portion was intended to be placed in the chalice before the ceremony of the "fraction of the bread." On entering the sanctuary the Pope gave the kiss of peace to the senior bishop and senior priest, and then to all his deacons. He thereupon proceeded to prostrate himself before the holy table. A few minutes before his arrival there, the book of the Gospels had been solemnly brought and placed upon the altar. After the Pope's prostration, the deacons proceeded two by two and kissed the altar on its sides. The pontiff also, drawing near, kissed the altar, as well as the book of the Gospels.

It is difficult to assign a precise date to this ceremony. In all rituals the entry of the officiating minister was from an early time associated with some pomp. We shall not go far wrong, however, if we refer to the fifth

[1] Judging from the *Ordines* and other liturgical books, as well as from the inventories of Church furniture which we find in the *Liber Pontificalis*, the portable censer was used at Rome, up to the ninth century, only in processions. The route which the *cortège* had to follow was thus made sweet-smelling with incense. As for censing the altar, or the church, or the clergy or congregation, such a thing is never mentioned.

[2] I fancy that there must have been some connection between the custom of carrying, on certain occasions, tapers before the Pope and before the book of the Gospels, and the tapers figuring among the insignia of the highest dignitaries of the Roman Empire in the *Notitia dignitatum imperii*.

century, at the earliest, the majority of the details which have just been described.

2. *Introductory Chants*

The *Kyrie eleison* may be considered as a remnant of the Litany form of prayer, or dialogue between one of the sacred ministers and the whole congregation. This form of prayer occupies, as we have seen, a prominent place in the Greek liturgies. The Liturgy of Constantinople, for instance, contains a litany to be said at the beginning of the Mass, before the entry of the celebrants. It would appear also that at Rome, in early times, it formed the initial portion of the Liturgy. It was customary in the eighth century on the Litany days, that is, the days on which the people went in general procession to the church of the station, to sing neither *Kyrie* nor *Gloria*. The service at the church began directly with the *Pax vobis* and the first prayer. The *Kyrie*, in like manner, was omitted on the days appointed for ordinations, because on such occasions the Litany was sung after the gradual. Even at the present time the *Kyrie eleison* in the Mass for Easter Eve is nothing more than the conclusion of the Litany with which that Mass commenced.[1] St. Gregory[2] is the authority for the statement that in his time the words *Kyrie eleison* and *Christe eleison* were accompanied, except in the daily Masses, by other formularies. These formularies were, doubtless, a litany more or less elaborated.

The Litany of the Saints at present in use has preserved this ancient form of dialogue-prayer as it was accustomed to be said in the Roman Church. It has, doubtless, been

---

[1] This correlation of the *Kyrie* and Litany is still clearly manifest in the *Ordines* of the twelfth century.

[2] Ep. ix. 12 (26): "In quotidianis missis aliqua quae dici solent tacemus, tantummodo *Kyrie eleison* et *Christe eleison* dicimus, ut in his deprecationis vocibus paulo diutius occupemur."

subject to considerable development, especially in the first part of it, which contains the invocation of Saints. But the conclusion, in which the response occurs, *Te rogamus, audi nos*, has quite an ancient ring about it, and possesses a great resemblance to the petitions in the litanies used in the Greek Church. Although the earliest text in which it occurs goes back only to the eighth century, it is probable that it is much more ancient.

It is evident, moreover, that the place assigned to the *Kyrie eleison* in the Roman Litany is not that given to it in the Eastern Churches. In the Roman Litany it occurs at the beginning and the end, and is said alternately by the precentor and the congregation. In the East it formed the people's response to the petitions in the Diaconal Litany. St. Gregory was already aware of this difference.[1] It arose from the fact that the *Kyrie* was adventitious in the Roman Church, as it was throughout the entire West.[2] The formulary *Te rogamus, audi nos*, however, could not be omitted, since it occupies in the Roman Litany the same place as the *Kyrie eleison* in the Greek. Another place had to be found for the latter. It is a somewhat singular thing that the *Kyrie*, which is of later date at Rome than the Litany, should now be preserved in

---

[1] Ep ix 12: "*Kyrie eleison* autem nos neque diximus neque dicimus sicut a Graecis dicitur, quia in Graecis simul omnes dicunt, apud nos autem a clericis dicitur et a populo respondetur; et totidem vicibus etiam *Christe eleison* dicitur, quod apud Graecos nullo modo dicitur"

[2] Council of Vaison (529), c 3: "Et quia tam in sede apostolica quam etiam per totas orientales atque Italiae provincias dulcis et nimium salutaris consuetudo est intromissa ut *Kyrie eleison* frequentius cum grandi affectu et compunctione dicatur," etc The Council agreed to the introduction of this custom into the Churches of the province of Arles, in which it was still unknown The word *intromissa* cannot have any reference to the Eastern Churches, which, as we know, used the *Kyrie* from the remotest times. The drawing up of the Canon is somewhat defective on this point, but it is clear that the Council of Vaison regarded the *Kyrie* then in use at Rome and in Italy (Milan) as an importation of somewhat recent date.

the Mass, whereas from the Litany, a more ancient service, it has been almost eliminated.

The *Gloria in excelsis*.—This hymn, like the *Kyrie*, is of Greek origin. We find it, in a slightly different form, however, in the *Apostolic Constitutions*[1] (vii. 47), and in the appendices to the Bible at the end of the *Codex Alexandrinus*, which belongs to the fifth century. It was a morning hymn, and formed part of the office for Matins, and did not belong to the Liturgy properly so called. It was originally introduced at Rome into the first Mass of the Nativity, which was celebrated before daybreak. Pope Symmachus extended its use to Sundays and the feasts of martyrs,[2] but only in the case of episcopal Masses. Priests were allowed to say it only on Easter Day, when they were regarded as taking the place of the absent Pope, or on the day of their first performance of sacerdotal functions.[3]

3. *The First Prayer.*

After saluting the congregation, the celebrant calls upon them to pray with him in the introductory prayer, which

---

[1] The following is the text in the *Constitutions*: " Δόξα ἐν ὑψίστοις Θεῷ καὶ ἐπὶ γῆς εἰρήνη, ἐν ἀνθρώποις εὐδοκία.

" Αἰνοῦμέν σε, ὑμνοῦμέν σε, εὐλογοῦμέν σε, δοξολογοῦμέν σε, προσκυνοῦμέν σε διὰ τοῦ μεγάλου ἀρχιερέως, σὲ, τὸν ὄντα Θεὸν, ἀγέννητον ἕνα, ἀπρόσιτον μόνον, διὰ τὴν μεγάλην σου δόξαν,

" Κύριε, βασιλεῦ ἐπουράνιε, Θεὲ Πάτερ παντοκράτορ,

" Κύριε ὁ Θεὸς, ὁ πατὴρ τοῦ Χριστοῦ, τοῦ ἀμώμου ἀμνοῦ, ὃς αἴρει τὴν ἁμαρτίαν τοῦ κόσμου, πρόσδεξαι τὴν δέησιν ἡμῶν, ὁ καθήμενος ἐπὶ τῶν Χερουβὶμ, ὅτι σὺ μόνος ἅγιος, σὺ μόνος κύριος Ἰησοῦ Χριστοῦ, τοῦ Θεοῦ πάσης γενητῆς φύσεως, τοῦ βασιλέως ἡμῶν, δι' οὗ σοι δόξα, τιμὴ καὶ σέβας."

The printed editions give at the end 'Ἰησοῦς Χριστός; which is evidently an error, and must be corrected as I have done. This text breathes the spirit of "subordinationism." It has been carefully revised before insertion in the Roman Liturgy.

[2] *Lib. Pontif.*, vol. i. p. 129 (Telesphorus), and 263 (Symmachus)

[3] *Ord. Rom.* 1. 25 Cf. in the *Ordo* of the manuscript of Saint-Amand (printed in the appendix of the present work) the chapter dealing with the ordination of priests

was called the *collecta*, because it was said as soon as the people had fully assembled.[1] This is the first of the three "collective prayers,"[2] or collects, allowed in the Roman Mass. The other two are the prayer *super oblata* (*secreta*), and that called the *post communio*.

4. *The Lections and the Chanting of Psalms.*

From the beginning of the sixth century there were in use in Rome only two lections, viz. the Epistle and Gospel.[3] The first was taken, sometimes from the Old Testament and sometimes from the New (the four evangelists excepted), but most frequently from the Epistles of St. Paul, or from the General Epistles, from whence its name.

Originally the lections were more numerous. In the existing use, indeed, more than one trace is found of the *prophetic* lection, which has now disappeared. This form of lesson, indeed, is still employed on certain days—for instance, on the Ember days and in Lent. The most remarkable thing in this connection is the arrangement of the chants between the Epistle and Gospel. These chants are always two in number, a *psalmus responsorius*, or respond, which is entitled the *Gradual*, and the *Alleluia*,[4] to which there is still attached a verse

---

[1] *Colligere plebem* is the ordinary expression for calling the people together to worship. The meaning of the word *collecta* (= *collectio*, as *missa* = *missio*) is made perfectly clear in the rubrics of the Gregorian Sacramentary relating to the Litany days. The prayer prescribed for use at the Church whence the procession sets out is called "*ad collectam*" It is needless to point out that the Greek words σύναξις, συνάγειν, are the equivalents of the Latin terms *collecta* and *colligere*.

[2] See above, p 107.

[3] *Lib Pont*, Celestine, vol i p 230.

[4] The singing of the *Alleluia* is a very ancient practice in the Church.

of a psalm. During Lent and other penitential seasons, and at Masses for the dead, the *Alleluia* is replaced by a psalm, with a melody of a special character, called the *Psalmus tractus*, or tract.[1] There is in every case a second chant after the gradual. Whence this duality? The reason will occur to us if we consider that in the few Masses which have preserved the "prophetic" lection, the gradual is sung between that lection and the Epistle, whilst the *Alleluia*, or the tract, is used between the Epistle and Gospel. The two chants were at first thus inserted respectively between the lections, but when the first of the latter was removed, both chants were united and sung between the Epistle and Gospel.

The suppression of the prophetic lection must have taken place at Rome in the course of the fifth century.[*] About the same time it suffered similar treatment at Constantinople.[2] The Armenian Liturgy, which is an ancient form of the Byzantine, still retains the three lections, but in the most ancient books of the Byzantine use which have come down to us there are but two.

I have already pointed out that the practice of chanting psalms between the lections in the Mass is as old as these lections themselves, and that both go back in direct line to the religious services of the Jewish Synagogue. In the Christian Liturgy these psalms constitute the most

---

but its exact place in divine service varies according to the different uses In the Gallican use the *Alleluia* was sung after the Gospel, at the procession of the oblation This is also the place it occupies in the East The placing of the *Alleluia* before the Gospel is a peculiarity of the Roman use Before the time of St Gregory it was sung at Eastertide only (Ep ix. 12 [26]) It would even appear that it was originally sung on Easter Day only (Sozomen, *Hist Eccl*, vii. 19).

[1] See above, p. 114.

[2] I find it mentioned, however, at the beginning of the seventh century in the life of St. Theodorus Siceotes. *Acta SS*, April 22, § 16.

[*] See Appendix, *infra*, p. 577B.

ancient and most solemn representation of the Davidic Psalter. We must take care not to put them on the same footing as the other chants, the Introit, Offertory, and Communion, which were introduced later, and then merely to occupy attention during long ceremonies. The gradual and similar chants had an intrinsic value, and during the time in which they were sung there was nothing else going on.[1] This was the ancient chanting of the psalms, which in the primitive Church alternated with the lections from Holy Scripture.[2]

The *gradual*, as has been said, was so called because it was sung at the *gradus*, or ambo, where the lections also were read. It was sung always by a single cantor, and the office of the choir was confined to taking up the final musical phrase.[3] The other chants were executed *in plano* by the choir, or *schola cantorum*. It was also customary, up to the time of St. Gregory, that the gradual and its additions should be sung like the Gospel, by deacons only; and this function had quite a special importance in the ministry of that order. Mention of it frequently occurs in epitaphs:

> "*Psallere et in populis volui modulante propheta
> sic merui plebem Christi retinere sacerdos*,"

says a bishop, explaining in this manner how the faithful,

---

[1] St Augustine refers to this frequently. Cf *Paléographie Musicale*, vol. v. p. 30.

[2] We see from this what a heresy it is to replace these chants by organ solos.

[3] The choir-rules continue to prescribe this method of executing the ending of the chant This practice is very ancient, for mention is made of it in the *Apostolical Constitutions*: "Τὶς τοὺς τοῦ Δαβὶδ ψαλλέτω ὕμνους καὶ ὁ λαὸς τὰ ἀκροστίκια ὑποψαλλέτω" (ii 57) Cf above, pp 113, 114.

being ravished by his singing, had raised him to the episcopate.[1] We read also in the epitaph of the deacon Redemptus, a contemporary of Pope Damasus—

> *Dulcia nectareo promebat mella canore*
> *prophetam celebrans placido modulamine senem;*

and in that of the archdeacon Deusdedit (fifth century)—

> *Hic levitarum primus in ordine vivens*
> *Davitici cantor carminis iste fuit;* [2]

and in that of the archdeacon Sabinus (fifth century)—

> [Ast eg]*o qui voce psalmos modulatus et arte*
> [dive]*rsis cecini verba sacrata sonis.*[3]

Thus the possession of a good voice and of a thorough knowledge of music was a necessary qualification for a deacon.

In the pursuit of this knowledge, many other more essential things were neglected. St. Gregory thought to obviate this evil by suppressing the monopoly of deacons in regard to chanting the psalms.[4] But if the gradual came to be no longer sung by the deacons, it still continued to be executed as a solo.

The reading of the lections was formerly prefaced by an injunction to silence, of which the formulary is preserved in the order of the ceremony called "Opening of the Ears," or "Traditio Symboli," one of the ceremonies preparatory to baptism. The deacon said in a loud voice, *State cum silentio, audientes intente!*

After the lections we ought to find the homily. But

---

[1] De Rossi, *Bull.*, 1864, p. 55.
[2] De Rossi, *Roma Sotteranea*, vol. III. pp 239, 242.
[3] De Rossi, *Bull*, 1864, p. 33.
[4] Council of 595, can. 1.

the homily appears to have fallen into disuse at Rome at a somewhat early period. St. Gregory, and St. Leo before him, were the only early Popes who left homilies behind them, or, indeed, seem, as far as we know, to have preached them. The homilies of St. Leo are, moreover, short, and restricted to certain solemn festivals. Roman priests had no authority to preach, and the Popes looked askance at the permission to do so granted to their clergy by other bishops.[1] Sozomen, who wrote about the time of Pope Xystus III., tells us that no one preached at Rome.[2]

There is no trace to be found in the liturgical books of the eighth century of the dismissal of catechumens and penitents. This is owing to the fact that they were drawn up at a time when discipline in regard to catechumens and penitents had been largely modified. There were no longer any adult catechumens, and public penitents were usually shut up in monasteries. The ancient formularies of the *missa catechumenorum* and of the *missa paenitentium* were preserved, notwithstanding, and occur respectively in the order of baptism already referred to, and in one of St. Gregory's dialogues. On the day of the "Opening of the Ears" the deacon dismissed the candidates for baptism with the words, *Catechumeni recedant! Si quis catechumenus est recedat! Omnes catechumeni exeant foras!* St. Gregory[3] relates that two nuns, who had been excommunicated by St. Benedict, were buried in a certain church, and that whenever the deacon cried out, at each Mass celebrated there, the words, *Si quis non communicat, det locum!* their foster mother used to see them arise from their graves

---

[1] Letter from Pope Celestine to the Bishops of Provence. Jaffé, 381.
[2] Sozomen, *Hist. Eccles.*, vii. 19.
[3] *Dial*, ii. 23.

and go out of the holy place. The manner in which St. Gregory explains *Cumque* . . . EX MORE *diaconus clamaret*, seems to indicate that this form of dismissal, or one equivalent to it, was still in use in his time, that is, at the end of the sixth century.

5. *The Prayer of the Faithful.*

After the Mass of the catechumens had been said, that of the faithful began.[1] The bishop, having once more saluted the congregation with the words *Dominus vobiscum!* calls upon them to pray: *Oremus!* It is a strange thing that this exhortation was as barren of result in the eighth century as it is in the present day. No one prayed. The Pope and his assistants proceeded to collect the offerings of the people and clergy, the choir executed some chant or other, but no prayer was provided by the liturgical books, and there was no rubric implying that any prayer was to be said privately or secretly. There is, therefore, a hiatus here; something has disappeared, and that something is nothing else than the "Prayer of the Faithful," which, in all other liturgies, occurs at this place.

I am inclined to believe that the disappearance is not altogether complete, and that the form used in ancient times in the Roman Church is still preserved in the series of solemn prayers employed on Good Friday.

In the eighth century these prayers were said, not only on the Friday, but also on the Wednesday in Holy Week. There is nothing in their tenor which connects them especially with the solemnities of the Passion and of Easter.

---

[1] The custom of chanting the *Creed* at this place in the Mass was not introduced at Rome until the first half of the eleventh century. Bernon, Abbot of Reichenau, relates that in his presence the emperor Henry II. induced Pope Benedict VIII. (1012–1024) to adopt this custom; before this it was unknown to the Roman Church (*De off. Missae*, c. 2; Migne, *Pat. Lat.*, vol. cxlii. p. 1060).

They are prayers for the ordinary needs of the Church, for peace, for the bishop, for the whole hierarchy down to the confessors (*ascetae*), virgins, and widows; for the Roman emperor; for the sick, the poor, captives, travellers, sailors; for heretics, schismatics, Jews, and heathen. These are the same petitions which we encounter, frequently repeated, in the daily liturgies of the Eastern Church. I am of opinion, therefore, that these prayers once formed part of the ordinary Roman Mass, and that they were said after the lections, that is, at the place in which they long continued to be recited on Wednesday and Friday in Holy Week [1]

6. *The Offering.*

If the Roman Liturgy was deprived at an early date of the Prayer of the Faithful, it still preserved in the ninth century, as a compensation, that of the oblation, which had disappeared at an early date from all other liturgies.[2] The faithful, including not only the laity, but also the priests and other clerics, together with the Pope himself, brought each their gifts of bread and wine, for each was obliged to make his own offering. The Pope himself, assisted by the bishops and priests, received the loaves; the archdeacon and his colleagues the *amulae*, or phials of wine. This distinction of functions was observed throughout the entire ceremony, the species of wine being considered as within the special province of the deacons.

During the offering the choir chanted a responsory psalm, called the *Offertorium*. This chant is of ancient use. It was

---

[1] The prayers used now between the Gospel and the Homily or Sermon, called Prayers of the *Praeconium*, correspond with this ancient prayer of the faithful. [Bidding Prayer.—Tr.]

[2] At present it is no longer in use in the Church at Rome, but it is still preserved at Milan, and in certain places in France.

introduced into Carthage while St. Augustine was yet alive. As is the case with all novelties, this introduction was adversely criticised. A certain Hilary, an individual of the rank of a tribune (*vir tribunitius*), made such a stir over the matter that the Bishop of Hippo was asked to write a treatise to confute him. This was the occasion of the book, now lost, called *Contra Hilar*[i]*um*, in which the celebrated doctor defended *morem qui tunc esse apud Carthaginem coeperat, ut hymni ad altare dicerentur de Psalmorum libro,*[1] *sive ante oblationem, sive cum distribueretur populo quod fuisset oblatum.*

The *Offertory* at present consists of a single verse without response, but in the ancient antiphonaries it presents a longer and more complicated form.

The offerings having been made, the archdeacon chooses from the loaves those which are to be employed in the communion, and places them upon the altar. He places there also the vessel (*scyphus*) containing the wine for the communion of the faithful, the two loaves offered by the Pope himself, and lastly the chalice, which, together with these two loaves, is to serve for communicating the pontiff and the higher clergy. He takes care to pour into this chalice, together with the wine offered by the Pope, a little of that offered by the priests and deacons, and of that which is contained in the *scyphus* which represents the offering of the faithful. He adds, last of all, a small quantity of water.

No prayer accompanies these ceremonies. The Pope takes no part in them, but sits all the time in his seat at

---

[1] *Aug., Retract.*, ii. 11.—Take note of the employment of the word *Hymnus* to designate a psalm, and also of the custom of taking the text of the Offertory from the Book of Psalms. This does not exclude the use of forms taken in the course of time from other sacred books, or even from other sources, but it throws light on the origin and primitive character of this ecclesiastical chant.

the end of the apse. The offertory prayers now in use are not indicated in the ancient books. They are, however, complete counterparts, as far as the meaning is concerned, of those employed by the Greek priests, and, doubtless, also by the Gallican priests, before the beginning of the Mass at the table of Prothesis.[1]

7. *The Consecration Prayers.*

As the preparation of the oblation takes place, according to the Roman custom, at the altar itself, and during the time of Mass, there is no room in it for the solemn entry with the oblation previously prepared, of the Oriental and Gallican ritual. The kiss of peace and the reading of the diptychs are relegated to a later place. As soon as the archdeacon has finished placing on the altar the loaves and chalices to be consecrated, the Pope, after washing his hands, proceeds to the altar and begins the consecration prayers.[2] He calls the faithful, in the first place, to join in a prayer, which is the second of the two *collective* prayers of the Roman Mass, and is known by the appellation *super oblata,* or *Secreta*. It is preceded by an invitatory of a special form:

---

[1] For the peculiarity of the custom of the Dominicans on this point see the following chapter

[2] From several texts of the *Liber Pontificalis* (especially vol i. p 139, note 3; and p 246, note 9), compared with a passage in the *Ordo I* of Mabillon (c. 48), it would seem that the titular priests made use here of a special rite at the outset. Some of the *oblatae* were held before them on patens They said the Canon at the same time as the Pope, and thus celebrated the Eucharistic Liturgy with him. If I have rightly interpreted the passages in question, this custom must have existed at the beginning of the sixth century, as far as the stational Masses are concerned. In the eighth century this custom was observed only on the feasts of the Nativity, Easter, Pentecost, and of St Peter. On other days the co-operation of the priests was limited to the offering, the fraction, and the communion.

Orate, fratres, ut meum ac vestrum sacrificium acceptabile fiat apud Deum Patrem omnipotentem. The form of prayer which follows, and which at the beginning was merely the conclusion of the prayer offered up in silence by the faithful, was said in a low voice, and hence its name of *Secreta*. It was terminated by an *ecphony*, that is, by an ending on a high note, to which *Amen* was responded.

At this point came the eucharistic prayer which corresponded to the *Anaphora* of the Greek liturgies.[1] It was divided by the chanting of the *Sanctus* into two parts of unequal length, of which the first, sung on a high note, was called the *Preface,* and the second, recited in a low tone, named the *Canon.* The Roman *Anaphora* possesses testimony to its great antiquity. The form at present in use existed already, word for word, at the beginning of the seventh century. St. Gregory gave to it its final touch, adding to the prayer *Hanc igitur* the following words: *diesque nostros in tua pace disponas,*[2] *atque ab eterna damnatione nos eripi et in electorum tuorum jubeas grege numerari.* The author of the *Liber Pontificalis,* which dates from the beginning of the sixth century, speaks of the Canon as fixed in form, and of known content. He implies also that it had been a long time in existence, for he relates that St. Leo (440-461) had added some words to it.[3] But we can go

---

[1] The grouping of the *collective* and *eucharistic* prayers is not a peculiarity, in the Roman use, of the liturgy of the Mass It is met with in all the solemn benedictions and consecrations. See note, p. 574.

[2] It is possible that this prayer for temporal peace was occasioned by the incessant troubles brought about by the Lombardic invasion. Cf. *Liber Pontif*, vol. i. p. 312.

[3] The words are *sanctum sacrificium, immaculatam hostiam,* which stand in apposition to the mention of Melchisedec's sacrifice in the prayer *Supra quae propitio.* I think that St. Leo must have intended to introduce by them a protest against the Manicheans who did not allow the use of wine in their liturgy. Cf *Lib Pontif*, vol i. p 239.

still further back, and show conclusively that the prayer to which St. Leo added four words was already in being in the time of Pope Damasus. The proof is to be found in a criticism levelled at it by the author of the *Quaestiones Veteris et Novi Testamenti*,[1] who was a contemporary of Damasus. In the misleading theology of this writer, Melchisedec is identified with the Holy Spirit, and, while he is still recognised as the priest of God, Melchisedec's priesthood is considered as inferior to that of Christ: *Similiter et Spiritus sanctus quasi antistes sacerdos appellatus est excelsi Dei, non summus, sicut nostri in oblatione praesumunt. Quia quamvis unius substantiae Christus et Spiritus sanctus, uniuscujusque tamen ordo observandus est.* The words *non summus sicut nostri in oblatione praesumunt* have evidently in view the form of the Roman Epiclesis, *summus sacerdos tuus Melchisedech.*

We find, furthermore, in a work not much later than the time of Damasus—the *De sacramentis* of the pseudo-Ambrose—large portions of the Roman Canon. Although we cannot assign a precise date to this work, or give the name of its author, it would seem, in my opinion, to have been drawn up in some North Italian Church, where the Roman use was combined with that of Milan, probably at Ravenna. As it assumes that the population of the towns is still made up of pagans and Christians, and as it is, moreover, partly borrowed from a similar work of St. Ambrose, we cannot go far wrong in fixing its date as somewhere about 400. The portions of the Roman Canon which appear in it run as follows [2]:—

---

[1] Migne, *Pat Lat.*, xxxv p 2329.

[2] *De Sacram*, iv 5, Migne, *Pat. Lat.*, vol xvi. p. 443. Pamelius, a canon of Bruges, in his work entitled *Liturgica Latinorum* (vol. i p. 301), published at Cologne, in 1571, introduces this fragment into the middle of the prayers of the Ambrosian Mass, and from this fact it has been usually cited as the "Ambrosian Canon." There never was, in fact, an Ambrosian Canon. Before the

Vis scire quia' verbis caelestibus consecratur? Accipe quae sunt verba. Dicit sacerdos: *Fac nobis, inquit, hanc oblationem ascriptam, ratam, rationabilem, acceptabilem, quod figura est corporis et sanguinis Iesu Christi. Qui pridie quam pateretur, in sanctis manibus suis accepit panem, respexit in caelum ad te, sancte Pater omnipotens, aeterne Deus, gratias agens, benedixit, fregit, fractumque apostolis suis et discipulis suis tradidit, dicens: "Accipite et edite ex hoc omnes: hoc est enim corpus meum, quod pro multis confringetur." Similiter etiam calicem, postquam caenatum est, pridie quam pateretur, accepit, respexit in caelum ad te, sancte Pater omnipotens, aeterne Deus, gratias agens, benedixit, apostolis suis et discipulis suis tradidit, dicens: "Accipite et bibite ex hoc omnes: hic est enim sanguis meus. . . . Quoties cumque hoc feceritis, toties commemorationem mei facietis, donec iterum adveniam."*

Et sacerdos dicit: *Ergo memores gloriosissimae ejus passionis et ab inferis resurrectionis et in caelum ascensionis, offerimus tibi hanc immaculatam hostiam, hunc panem sanctum et calicem vitae aeternae; et petimus et precamur, ut hanc oblationem suscipias in sublimi altari tuo per manus angelorum tuorum, sicut suscipere dignatus es munera pueri tui justi Abel et sacrificium patriarchae nostri Abrahae et quod tibi obtulit summus sacerdos Melchisedech.*

This text, while it does not correspond word for word, agrees very closely with that of the present Roman Canon from the conclusion of the formulary of the diptychs up to and including the *Epiclesis*.

But let us return to our consideration of the Roman *Anaphora*.

After the injunction to lift up the heart to God, and to render thanks to Him,[1] the officiating priest goes on: *Vere*

---

adoption of the Roman Canon at Milan, the consecration prayers were of variable tenor there, as in the Gallican books. When the Roman Canon was adopted it was taken from the form in use in the seventh century, with the addition introduced by St Gregory. The Ambrosian Mass of Pamelius is, in many respects, an artificial text drawn up by the author himself. It is not to be found in any of the manuscripts of the Ambrosian rite.

[1] The *Sursum corda* is attested by St. Cyprian (*De Domin. Oratione*, 31): "Adeo et sacerdos ante orationem praefatione praemissa parat

dignum et justum est, etc. In the Sacramentary of Adrian, this form, that is to say, the *Preface*, admits only a small number of variations for the chief festivals. Previously these variations were much more numerous. We would gather from the Leonian Sacramentary that improvisation, or at the least the intercalation of certain sentences previously composed by the officiating priest, was still the practice in the sixth century. The Preface ends with an ascription to the glory of God, and the *Sanctus*.

After the *Sanctus* the Roman Canon, instead of proceeding at once to the account of the Last Supper, intercalates a long passage appropriated to the enumeration of the persons in whose name the oblation is made—the whole Catholic Church, the Pope (or, if occasion requires it, the bishop of the locality), and all the orthodox bishops; then the Sovereign and the congregation; and finally, as representing the Communion of Saints, all the righteous who have already attained the heavenly beatitude—the Virgin Mary, the Apostles, and their successors the Popes, martyrs, and other saints. The oblation is thus made by the whole Christian family, and God is asked to accept it, and to transform it into the Body and Blood of Christ.

The existing texts for this part of the Canon[1] give forms which are definitely fixed, but not so much so, however, that provision has not been made for additions with the object of commemorating the festival of the day or for the enumeration of certain persons or classes of persons. Thus, there is no doubt that the names of the four patriarchs of the East, and possibly of certain Western primates, were formerly mentioned in the *Te igitur* after

---

fratrum mentes dicendo · *Sursum corda*, ut, dum respondet plebs *Habemus ad Dominum*, admoneatur," etc These versicles appear already in the "Apostolic Tradition" of Hippolytus (see Appendix 6).

[1] That is, the prayers which begin with the words, *Te igitur, Memento, Communicantes, Hanc igitur,* and *Quam oblationem.*

that of the Roman pontiff The *Memento*, which follows it, admits of a break where many names and petitions might have been intercalated. As for the prayer beginning with *Communicantes*, the Sacramentary of Adrian furnishes variations suited to the solemnity of the day. Later in the same prayer the list of Popes, now reduced to the first three names, Linus, Cletus, and Clement, must have been recited at length.[1] It is not impossible that the ancient pontifical catalogue, of which we have a relic in the Hieronymian Martyrology, was extracted from some copy of the Canon. The names of martyrs which follow are also merely a selection. The Churches which adopted the Roman Liturgy were within their rights in completing that list by adding to it the names of the saints which they held in special honour.[2] Finally, the *Hanc igitur* admits the insertion at the festivals of Easter and Pentecost of a commemoration of the newly baptised. Formerly the names of the candidates for baptism were therein recited on the days of the scrutiny, while those of their godfathers and godmothers found a place in the *Memento*.[3] Similar additions were made in Masses for ordinations.

All this part of the Canon corresponds, on the whole, with the recitation of the diptychs prescribed in the Gallican and Eastern liturgies, but which are placed in these liturgies before the beginning of the Preface. This latter disposition may seem the more natural one, and we may perhaps admit that the former is not altogether primitive.[4] It is at the same time certain, that from the beginning of the fifth century the order of the Roman Canon was already

---

[1] *Liber Pontificalis*, vol i. p lxx.; De Rossi, *Roma Sott*, vol i p. 114

[2] In France, the names of St. Hilary and St. Martin are always found at this point.

[3] *Ordo Rom*, vii. 3.

[4] *Revue d'Hist. et de Litt. Relig*, vol. v. (1900), p. 43. See Appendix p. 577B.

that which it is to-day. The final formulary, in fact, in all this series of enumerations, namely, that which appears before the *Qui pridie*, is already met with in the *De sacramentis*, in terms almost identical with those of the present *Quam oblationem*. The letter of Pope Innocent to Decentius assumes, moreover, that the recitation of the diptychs occupied at Rome in 416, and for a long time previously, the place which it holds at present.

The account of the institution (*Qui pridie*) and the *Anamnesis* (*Unde et memores*), which follows it, present nothing peculiar. The same may be said of the *Epiclesis*.

This portion of the Canon runs as follows :—

Supra quae (the oblations) propitio ac sereno vultu respicere digneris et accepta habere, sicuti accepta habere dignatus es munera pueri tui justi Abel et sacrificium patriarchae nostri Abrahae, et quod tibi obtulit summus sacerdos tuus Melchisedech [sanctum sacrificium, immaculatam hostiam]. Supplices te rogamus, omnipotens Deus, jube haec perferri per manus sancti angeli tui in sublime altare tuum, in conspectu divinae majestatis tuae, ut quotquot ex hac altaris participatione sacrosanctum Filii tui corpus et sanguinem sumpserimus, omni benedictione caelesti et gratia repleamur.

This prayer is far from exhibiting the precision of the Greek formularies, in which there is a specific mention of the grace prayed for, that is, the intervention of the Holy Spirit to effect the transformation of the bread and wine into the Body and Blood of Jesus Christ. It is true, nevertheless, (1) that it occupies, in regard to the subject-matter and the logical connection of the formulary, the exact place of the Greek *Epiclesis;* and (2) that it also is a prayer to God for His intervention in the mystery. But whilst the Greek Liturgies use here clear and simple terms, the Roman Liturgy embodies its meaning in symbolical forms It prays that the angel of the Lord may take the oblation from the visible altar and bear it to the highest heaven, to the invisible altar, before the shrine of the Divine Majesty. This symbolical transference is in a contrary sense to that implied in the Greek formulary; it involves not the descent of the Holy Spirit upon the oblation, but the elevation by God's angel of the oblation to heaven. But in both cases alike it is after it has been brought near to, and has participated in, the Divine Virtue that it is called the Body and Blood of Christ.

The prayers which follow correspond with the Great Intercession of the Greek Liturgies, and occupy the same place as that assigned to it in the Syro-Byzantine rite.

It is certain that this formulary has been much curtailed. It begins with the commemoration of the faithful departed (*Memento*)[1] for whom it requests eternal beatitude. This is also asked for those still living (*Nobis quoque*) by the mention of the saints into whose society it desires they should be admitted. After this prayer . . . *largitor admitte, per Christum Dominum nostrum*, there is apparently a *hiatus*. The text continues: *per quem haec omnia, Domine, semper bona creas, sanctificas, benedicis et praestas nobis*. It is clear that the words *haec omnia bona* have no reference to what immediately precede them; if we take the word *omnia*, moreover, into account it is difficult to make them apply to the consecrated oblation. The easiest explanation of the difficulty is that there was formerly here a mention of the fruits of the earth, with an enumeration of the various kinds—wheat, wine, oil, etc. This view is confirmed,

---

[1] The *Memento* of the departed is wanting in several ancient copies of the Canon as, for instance, in the *Gelasian Sacramentary*. This omission arose, I believe, from the fact that this formulary served as a framework for the diptychs of the dead, which were read from a special text, a roll, a tablet, or something of this kind. It is a mistake to suppose that in its primitive state the *Memento* must have been separated from the *Nobis quoque*. These two prayers constitute a whole; the second is merely the natural continuation of the first.

moreover, by the fact that the blessing of aliments took place, on certain days, at this point in the Mass, as, for instance, the drink made of water milk and honey, which was given to the neophytes at Easter and Pentecost. I append the formulary of this benediction, according to the Leonian Sacramentary, for the first Mass at Pentecost [1]—

> Benedic, Domine, et has tuas creaturas fontis, mellis et lactis [2] et pota famulos tuos ex hoc fonte aquae vitae perennis qui est Spiritus veritatis, et enutri eos de hoc lacte et melle, quemadmodum patribus nostris Abraham, Isaac et Jacob [promisisti] [3] introducere te eos in terram promissionis, terram fluentem melle et lacte. Conjunge ergo famulos tuos, Domine, Spiritui sancto, sicut conjunctum est hoc mel et lac, quo caelestis terrenaeque substantiae significatur unitio in Christo Jesu Domino nostro, per quem haec omnia, etc.

It was also at this place that the new beans were blessed on Ascension Day, and the new grapes on the day of St. Sixtus (August 6).[4]

> *Benedic, Domine, et has fruges novas fabae, etc.*
> *Benedic, Domine, et hos fructus novos uvae, etc.*

Finally, it was at this point that the oil for the unction of the sick was blessed, and still is blessed, on Maundy Thursday.

There is no doubt, therefore, that the formulary *per quem haec omnia* was originally preceded, and that, too, apart from these extraordinary occasions, by a prayer for the fruits of the earth. This furnishes a further instance of the resemblance of the Roman Canon to the corresponding portion of the Greek and Eastern Liturgies.

---

[1] Muratori, vol. i p. 318
[2] See note, p. 575.
[3] I supply this word, omitted in the manuscript.
[4] Muratori, vol. i p 588, p. 746; vol. ii. p. 109. Cf. *Lib. Pontif.*, vol. 1. p. 159

8. *The Fraction of the Bread.*

The Canon having come to an end, the *Pater noster* follows. According to universal custom, it has a short introductory preface, and at the end an elaboration of the last petition (*Libera nos*).

Before the time of St. Gregory, the fraction of the bread followed immediately upon the Canon. It was he who transferred the *Pater noster* to this place, on the ground that it was hardly proper that the formulary of the Canon, the work of some unknown scholar, should alone be recited over the oblation, to the exclusion of the prayer composed by our Lord Himself.[1] This transposition, although St. Gregory defends himself from the accusation of having followed any authority in introducing it, had the effect of bringing the Roman use into conformity with that of Constantinople.

The ceremony which follows is seemingly complicated. It begins with the kiss of peace, which is placed immediately after the salutation, *Pax Domini sit semper vobiscum.* The Pope places in the chalice the fragment of consecrated bread which had been brought to him at the beginning of the Mass; he then breaks one of his own two *oblatae*, and places one half of it upon the altar. We have not yet come to the fraction of the bread, properly speaking, but as all the loaves upon the altar

---

[1] Ep. ix. 12 (26). "Orationem vero dominicam idcirco mox post precem dicimus, quia mos apostolorum fuit ut ad ipsam solummodo orationem oblationis hostiam consecrarent Et valde mihi inconveniens visum est ut precem quam scholasticus composuerat super oblationem diceremus, et ipsam traditionem quam Redemptor noster composuit super ejus corpus et sanguinem non diceremus. Sed et dominica oratio apud Graecos ab omni populo dicitur, apud nos vero a solo sacerdote." We are not obliged to believe, in spite of the authority of this text, that the Apostolic Liturgy knew of no other formulary but the *Pater noster*, but it is difficult to argue against St. Gregory's having thought so.

intended for the Communion are about to be removed, and as it was customary to observe the prescription, *dum missarum solemnia peraguntur, altare sine sacrificio non sit*,[1] the half-loaf placed on the altar by the Pope is meant to maintain this idea of permanence.

It was a matter of importance in the Roman Church that the ritual of the Communion should contain a clear and striking expression of ecclesiastical unity. Hence the custom of the *fermentum*, that is, of sending consecrated bread from the bishop's Mass to the priests whose duty it was to celebrate in the *Tituli*;[2] hence also the significance of the rite of the *Sancta*, that is, of putting into the chalice at the *Pax Domini* a fragment consecrated at the preceding Mass and brought forth at the beginning of the present one. Thus, in all the Churches at Rome, and at every assembly there for liturgical worship past or present, there was always the same Sacrifice, the same Eucharist, the same Communion. Thus, in order to show clearly that the bread broken and distributed away from the altar was the same as that which had been consecrated on the altar, a fragment of it was allowed to remain on the holy table.

The other half of the first *oblata* and the second in its entirety were placed on the paten and brought before the Pope, who, after the *Pax Domini*, had returned to his seat. As for the other consecrated loaves, the archdeacon had caused them to be brought before the bishops and priests by acolytes, who carried them in linen bags suspended from their necks. Thereupon followed the fraction of the bread by the whole *presbyterium*. The Pope also took part in it, but only through his intermediaries the deacons, whose office it was to break the

---

[1] *Ordo Rom* of Saint-Amand. See Appendix
[2] For this rite see the *Lib Pontif*, vol 1 p 169, note 4

oblata and demi-*oblata* placed upon the paten. From the time of Pope Sergius (687–701) this ceremony was accompanied by the chanting of the *Agnus Dei*. It is probable that before the time of St. Gregory the *Pater noster* was said at this time, that is, after the fraction.[1]

9. *The Communion.*

The fraction having been performed, the deacons present to the Pope the paten, from which, taking a fragment, he detaches a particle and consumes the rest. He then puts the detached portion into the chalice, which the archdeacon, who has brought it from the altar, holds before him. This is the rite of the *Commixtio*. The Pope thereupon drinks from the chalice, which is presented to him and held by the archdeacon.

Then comes the communion of the superior clergy. The bishops and priests approach the Pope, who puts into the hands of each a fragment taken from the paten. They then proceed to the altar, and each one, putting on the holy table his hand containing the consecrated bread, then communicates. The deacons do the same after them. The archdeacon brings back the chalice to the altar and puts it into the hands of the senior bishop present, who, after having drunk from it, presents it to the other bishops, and then to the priests and deacons. The communion of the congregation then follows. The Pope and the bishops and priests distribute the Eucharist under the species of bread. The

---

[1] I am induced to believe this by the fact that in the ancient Roman books there is no prayer preparatory to the communion. In the Gallican Liturgy we find in this place the benediction, and in the Greek Liturgies prayers of similar import are prescribed here. The *hiatus* which appears here in the Roman Mass must have been occasioned by the removal of the *Pater noster* to another place. This *hiatus* is at the present time filled up by the private prayers of the priest.

archdeacon, following the Pope, and the other deacons following the bishops and priests, administer the chalice. As the Pope's chalice is used only for communicating the higher clergy, the archdeacon takes care to pour, beforehand, into the vessels containing the consecrated wine for the communion of the people, some drops from that used by the Pope, and, afterwards, what remains in it after the communion of the bishops, priests, and deacons. By this it is intended to show, that, although all do not touch with their lips the same vessel, yet they all drink the same spiritual drink. The rite of the *Commixtio*, having been performed by the Pope in the principal chalice, is repeated by the bishops and priests in all the other chalices, from which the faithful are communicated under the species of wine.

Before the communion of the people, the archdeacon announces the day and place of the next Station. There was an object in choosing this moment for the announcement. Those who did not communicate were, doubtless, accustomed to go out before the communion began. While the faithful were communicating, the choir chanted the antiphon *ad communionem*. At present it is chanted after communion, and is restricted to the anthem [*antienne*, see p. 115], which is sung only once. But the liturgical books of the ninth century still presuppose here a *real* antiphon, the psalm being chanted either in its entirety, or in part, according as the time occupied in the communion is long or short. It was terminated by the doxology *Gloria Patri*, etc , and the antiphon [*antienne*] was repeated. This chant, like that of the offertory, must go back to somewhere about the end of the fourth century.[1]

The communion having ended, the pope returns to the altar, and salutes the congregation, inviting them to join

---

[1] See above, p 174.

in an act of thanksgiving, the *post communio*. This is the third of the *collective* prayers of the Roman Mass. It is followed by a final salutation, whereupon the deacon announces the dismissal in a special formulary: *Ite missa est*. The procession is then reformed in the same order as it had at entrance, and as it proceeds to the sacrarium the Pope gives his blessing successively to the different groups of clergy and the faithful which he encounters on his way.

CHAPTER VII.

THE GALLICAN MASS.

THE Gallican use having almost entirely disappeared, it would be difficult to picture to ourselves from experience the ancient ceremonies of a solemn Mass in the Churches of this rite. Fortunately, St. Germain of Paris († 576) has left us a sufficiently clear account of it, and one much more ancient than that afforded by the Roman *Ordines*. I will restrict my description of it, therefore, to that given by this venerable author, and in reproducing his text[1] will compare it with other documentary sources for reconstructing the Gallican use—that is, the Mozarabic books, the liturgical books of Merovingian Gaul, of Britain, and of North Italy. As the Gallican texts are less known and less accessible than the Roman, I have thought it necessary to introduce in my description all the formularies for prayers and chants which the Gallican Mass contained. With this purpose in view, I have selected those for the festival of the Nativity, and I take the text from the *Missale Gothicum*.

---

[1] In this reproduction I restrict myself to the sentences or parts of a sentence in which the rite is *described*. As for the symbolical signification of the rites, as they do not enter directly into my aims, I refer the reader to Martene's edition (*Thesaurus*, vol v ; Migne, *Pat. Lat*, vol lxxii) Here and there I venture to correct the most glaring errors of the copyist.

As this work does not contain the parts sung, I have taken the latter from the Mozarabic Missal.

By following my description, it will be possible to gain an approximate idea of what a solemn Mass would have been in the sixth century, say, at Milan, or Arles, or Toledo, or Paris.

1. *Entry of the Officiating Bishop.*

GERMAIN: *Antiphona ad praelegendum canitur. . . . Psallentibus clericis procedit sacerdos in specie Christi de sacrario.*

This Antiphon was specially intended to enhance the dignity of the entry of the sacred ministers. It corresponds in the Byzantine Liturgy, to the chanting of the Μονογενής, and in the Roman Liturgy, to the Introit. At Milan it was called the *Ingressa,* and at Toledo the *Officium.* The following is the Mozarabic *Officium* for the Mass of the Nativity [1] :—

Alleluia ! Benedictus qui venit, alleluia, in nomine Domini. Alleluia! Alleluia!
℣. Deus Dominus et illuxit nobis.
℟. In nomine Domini.
℣. Gloria et honor Patri et Filio et Spiritui sancto in saecula saeculorum. Amen.
℟. In nomine Domini.

GERMAIN: *Silentium diaconus annuntiat. . . . Sacerdos ideo datur populo ut dum ille benedicit plebem, dicens:* Dominus sit semper vobiscum, *ab omnibus benedicatur dicentibus:* Et cum spiritu tuo.

---

[1] The psalm is reduced here, as in the Roman books, to a single verse. Observe also the form *Gloria et honor Patri,* etc. The words *et honor* were already in the seventh century characteristic of the Spanish use (*Conc. Tol.,* iv 14).

THE GALLICAN MASS.

The deacon enjoins silence; for which the Mozarabic formulary is *Silentium facite*.[1] The bishop salutes the congregation in a formulary preserved by St. Germain and identical with that given in the Mozarabic Liturgy. At Milan it was the custom to use *Dominus vobiscum*, as at Rome. St. Germain speaks of the salutation only in this place, that is, before the introductory canticles. This is the place also assigned to the first salutation in the Ambrosian Liturgy. In the Mozarabic it is said only after the collect. In these two liturgies the salutation follows each of the three lections.[2]

2. *The Introductory Canticles.*

GERMAIN: *Ajus vero ante prophetiam pro hoc canitur in graeca lingua quia. . . . Incipiente praesule ecclesia Ajus psallit, dicens latinum cum graeco. . . . Dictum Amen ex hebraeo. . . . Tres autem parvuli qui ore uno sequentes Kyrie eleison. . . . Canticum autem Zachariae pontificis in honorem sancti Johannis Baptistae cantatur . . .; ideo prophetiam quam pater ejus ipso nascente cecinit alternis vocibus ecclesia psallit.*

There are three canticles: first, the Trisagion (*Ajus* = Ἅγιος), which was intoned by the bishop, at first in Greek, and afterwards in Latin; second, the *Kyrie eleison*, sung by three boys; and third, the *Benedictus*, or "prophecy." In the Mozarabic and Milanese uses the Trisagion is not found,

---

[1] In the Mozarabic Missal we do not encounter it at this place. With regard to the demand for silence, cf. Gregory of Tours, *Hist. France*, vii. 8: "Quadam die dominica, postquam diaconus silentium populis ut missae abscultarentur indixit. . . ." Cf. Isidore, *De Eccl. Officiis*, i. 10.

[2] With this difference that in the Mozarabic Liturgy it precedes, and, in the Ambrosian, follows the response chanted after the first lection.

192   CHRISTIAN WORSHIP: ITS ORIGIN AND EVOLUTION.

at least not in this place. It is evidently an Eastern importation, or rather Byzantine. At the time of the second Council of Vaison (529), it was used only at "public Masses." This council decreed (c. 3) that it was to be sung at all Masses without distinction.

In place of the Trisagion we find in the Mozarabic and Ambrosian Missals the *Gloria in excelsis*, which is here [1] a Roman importation.

The second chant, that of the *Kyrie*, is preserved in the Ambrosian Liturgy, but has disappeared from the Mozarabic. It was customary at Milan, as in Gaul, to restrict the number of *Kyries* sung to three. The *Kyrie* was introduced in imitation of Eastern usage, but in the Oriental liturgies it is only employed as the response of the people to the petitions of the Diaconal Litany, and even at Rome it had at first a strict connection with that litany. In the Gallican use it was a species of chant absolutely unconnected with the Litany.

In the time of the Council of Vaison [2] the *Kyrie* was

---

[1] I say *here*, for it is certain that the *Gloria in excelsis*, as a chant in the *Office*, was known in Spain and Northern Italy from the seventh century at latest (*Conc Tol*, iv. 12; *Sacrament Gall*, p 780, Muratori). The Trisagion is mentioned in the life of St. Gery, Bishop of Cambrai in the seventh century. "*Ajus, ajus, ajus*, per trinum numerum imposuit in nomine Trinitatis" (*Anal. Boll*, vol. vii. p 393)

[2] *Concil. Vasense*, c. 3: "Et quia tam in sede Apostolica quam etiam per totas Orientales atque Italiae provincias dulcis et nimium salutaris consuetudo est intromissa ut *Kyrie eleison* frequentius cum grandi affectu et compunctione dicatur; placuit etiam nobis ut in omnibus ecclesiis nostris ista tam sancta consuetudo et ad matutinum et ad missas et ad vesperam, Deo propitio intromittatur. Et in omnibus missis, seu in matutinis, seu in quadragesimalibus, seu in illis quae pro defunctorum commemoratione fiunt, semper *Sanctus, Sanctus, Sanctus*, eo ordine quo modo ad missas publicas dicitur, dici debeat; quia tam sancta et tam dulcis et desiderabilis vox, etiamsi die noctuque possit dici, fastidium non possit generare" The *Sanctus* here referred to is evidently the Trisagion, and not the *Sanctus* after the Preface. Observe that the council does not name Spain among the countries where it was customary to use the *Kyrie*.

still almost unknown in Gaul, while it was already in use at Rome and "in Italy," that is, at Milan.

After the *Kyrie* came the "Prophecy,"[1] that is, the canticle *Benedictus Dominus Deus Israel* (Luke i. 68–79) In the Mozarabic Liturgy it is still ordered to be sung once every year, that is, on the Sunday *in adventu S Johannis Baptistae.* It has disappeared completely from the Ambrosian Liturgy.[2]

The Trisagion and the Prophecy were not used during Lent, at least at Paris, but a special canticle, which began with the words *Sanctus Deus Archangelorum,* was substituted for them.[3]

After the Prophecy the bishop said a prayer, which had either some analogy with the canticle itself or a bearing upon the festival of the day. This is what is called the *Collectio post Prophetiam.* The following is the text of it, taken from the *Missale Gothicum* for the festival of the Nativity :—

Ortus es nobis, verus Sol justitiae, Jesu Christe; venisti de caelo

---

[1] Mabillon, and many others after him, have confounded the "Prophecy" with the Prophetic Lection It is evident that it is to the first, that is, to the Canticle of the *Benedictus,* that Gregory of Tours is referring in *Hist Franc*, viii 7, where Palladius, Bishop of Saintes, is introduced as beginning the chanting of the Prophecy: "Quo incipiente prophetiam. . . ." The officiating bishop precented the canticles, but he did not read the lections, that was the business of the lectors or deacons.

[2] It had a place there originally, to judge from the Sacramentary of Bobbio, in which the rubric *Collectio post Prophetiam* occurs several times.

[3] Germain, Ep ii : "*Sanctus Deus Archangelorum* in Quadragesimo concinitur et non canticum Zachariae . . Nec *Alleluia* in nostra ecclesia, *Sanctus,* vel *Prophetia,* hymnus trium puerorum, vel canticum Rubri maris illis diebus decantantur." I think we ought to understand *Sanctus* here as meaning the Trisagion There was a previous reference to a canticle *Sanctus de Caelis,* which was resumed at Easter, with the song of Moses and the *Alleluia,* after having been omitted during Lent.

humani generis Redemptor; erexisti nobis cornu salutis,[1] et celsi Genitoris Proles perpetua, genitus in domo David propter priscorum oracula vatum, propriam volens absolvere plebem et vetusti criminis delere chirographum, ut aeternae vitae panderes triumphum. Ideoque nunc te quaesumus ut in misericordiae tuae viscera nostris appareas mentibus, salus aeterna; et nos eripiendo ab iniquo hoste justitiae cultores efficias; omnique mortis errore spreto pacis viam recto itinere gradientes, tibi recte servire possimus, Salvator mundi, qui cum Patre et Spiritu sancto vivis, dominaris et regnas Deus in saecula saeculorum.[2]

3. *The Lections and the Psalms.*

GERMAIN: *Lectio vero Prophetica suum tenet ordinem Veteris videlicet Testamenti, corripiens mala et adnuncians futura, ut intelligamus ipsum Deum esse qui in Prophetia tonuit quam qui et in Apostolo docuit et in Evangelico splendore refulsit. Quod enim propheta clamat futurum, apostolus docet factum. Actus autem Apostolorum vel Apocalypsis Johannis pro novitate gaudii paschalis leguntur, servantes ordinem temporum, sicut historia Testamenti Veteris in Quinquagesimo, vel gesta sanctorum confessorum ac martyrum in solemnitatibus eorum, ut populus intelligat quantum Christus amaverit famulum, dans ei virtutis indicium, quem devota plebicula suum postulat patronum. Hymnum autem trium puerorum, quod post lectiones canitur. . . . Ecclesia servat ordinem ut inter Benedictionem et Evangelium lectio non*[3] *intercedat, nisi tantummodo responsorium quod a parvulis canitur.*

There were always two lections in the Mass besides the Gospel. The first (*Lectio Prophetica*) was taken from

---

[1] This is an allusion to the canticle *Benedictus*. The whole prayer is full of reminiscences of this character.

[2] In the present Milanese use the Collect is placed before the Canticles. The Sacramentary of Bobbio implies that it was said after them. Besides certain collects *post Prophetiam*, it contains others that are said after the trisagion (*post Ajus*), or after the *Gloria in excelsis*.

[3] I have inserted here the negative, which is required by the text.

the Old Testament, and the second from the Apostolical Epistles. During Eastertide the Apocalypse and the Acts of the Apostles were also read, and in Lent the "Histories" of the Old Testament. On the festivals of the Saints their biographies were included in the lections. This information, which is furnished by St. Germain, is in full agreement with the arrangement in the Luxeuil Lectionary, with that in the present Mozarabic use,[1] and with the distribution of lections in the Sacramentary of Bobbio.[2] The use of Constantinople in the time of St. Chrysostom made provision also for this threefold arrangement of lections—the Prophetic, the Apostolic, and the Evangelical.[3]

After the reading of the two first lections, the Hymn of the Three Children, according to St. Germain, was sung. It was known also by the name of the Benediction (*Benedicite*), because in it the word *Benedicite* is continually repeated. Then came the Respond. The order in which these various portions were arranged was not the same everywhere. In the Mozarabic Liturgy the chants were placed between the first two lections, while in the Merovingian Liturgy they came after the reading of the Apostolical Epistles.[4] The Milanese Liturgy still makes use of the

---

[1] The reading of the Apocalypse in the Eastertide Masses was a very ancient custom in Spain. The fourth Council of Toledo (c. 16) threatens with excommunication those who would omit it.

[2] The Ambrosian Liturgy has discontinued the Prophetic Lection, except on certain days. It was still included there in the twelfth century; and it was customary to use it with the *Gesta Sanctorum* on the festivals of saints This is to be inferred from the letters of Paul (Bernried) and Gebehard published by Mabillon (*Mus. Ital*, vol 1, part 2, p 97): "Gestis Sanctorum quae missarum celebrationibus apud vos interponi solent," etc. These letters were written about the year 1130.

[3] *Hom.* xxix. *in Act*, *App*, p 229 The Armenian Liturgy has preserved the Prophetic Lection, which had fallen into disuse at Constantinople.

[4] The Luxeuil Lectionary, however, prescribes for the Nativity, "*Daniel cum Benedictione*," that is, the Hymn of the Three Children before the Apostolical Lection. It is true that in the Mass of the *Clausum Paschale* it places it after this lection.

Benedicite on certain days, and provides for a respond, called the *Psalmulus*, after the Prophetic Lection, and a verse accompanied by the *Alleluia* after the Apostolic Lection. The following is the introduction to the *Benedicite* in the Mozarabic rite [1]:—

> Daniel Propheta. Tunc illi tres quasi ex uno ore hymnum canebant et benedicebant Dominum de fornace, dicentes: Benedictus es Domine, etc.

This is almost the actual text of Daniel iii 51. The respond for the Nativity in the Mozarabic Missal is arranged as follows:—

> Dominus dixit ad me: Filius meus es tu, ego hodie genui te.—℣. Pete a me et dabo tibi gentes haereditatem tuam et possessionem tuam terminos terrae.—℟. Ego hodie genui te.

According to St. Germain, this respond was sung by boys (*parvuli*). Gregory of Tours assigns the singing of it to a deacon. The use at Tours [2] may possibly have differed from that of Paris on this point. The Roman use in this respect underwent an important change at the end of the sixth century.[3]

4. *The Gospel.*

GERMAIN: *Tunc in adventu sancti Evangelii claro modulamine denuo psallit clerus Ajus. . . . Egreditur processio sancti Evangelii velut potentia Christi triumphantis de morte, cum praedictis harmoniis et cum septem candelabris luminis, quae sunt septem dona Spiritus sancti vel v(eteris) legis lumina mysterio crucis confixa ascendens in tribunal analogii,[4] velut Christus sedem regni paterni, ut inde intonet*

---

[1] I take this from the first Sunday in Lent
[2] Or of Orleans, for it was at Orleans where this service took place (*Hist. Franc*, viii 3).
[3] See above, p 170.
[4] The ambo

dona vitae, clamantibus clericis: Gloria tibi Domine! ...
Sanctus *autem quod redeunte sancto Evangelio clerus cantat, etc.*

St. Germain is the only writer who mentions the chanting of the Trisagion as accompanying the procession of the Gospel, both on going and returning. But in all the Latin liturgies the exclamation by the congregation, *Gloria tibi Domine,* is prescribed as the response to the announcement of the Gospel lection: *Lectio sancti Evangelii secundum N.*

5. *The Homily.*

GERMAIN: *Homiliae autem sanctorum quae leguntur pro sola praedicatione ponuntur, ut quicquid Propheta, Apostolus vel Evangelium mandavit, hoc doctor vel pastor Ecclesiae apertiori sermone populo praedicet, ita arte temperans ut nec rusticitas sapientes offendat, nec honesta loquacitas obscura rusticis fiat.*

The custom of having the Homily after the Gospel was better observed in Gaul than in Rome. The priests, as well as the bishops, were accustomed to preach. This usage is denounced by Pope Celestine in a letter which he addressed to the Bishops of Provence.[1] But instead of being abolished on that account, it was confirmed and extended even to rural parishes by the second Council of Vaison (529). This council was the Provincial Council of the Metropolis of Arles, and it is well known what a zealous advocate of preaching its bishop, St. Cæsarius of Arles, was. His homilies have exactly the qualities of clearness and simplicity which St. Germain claims for them.[2]

---

[1] Jaffe, 381
[2] C. 2: "Hoc etiam pio aedificatione omnium ecclesiarum et pro

6. *The Prayers.*

GERMAIN: *Preces vero psallere levitas pro populo ab origine libri Moysacis ducit exordium, ut audita Apostoli praedicatione levitae pro populo deprecentur et sacerdotes prostrati ante Dominum pro peccata populi intercedant, etc.*

The Prayer of the Faithful begins with a diaconal litany. The Merovingian liturgical books, which furnish only the part for the celebrant, have preserved no text of this litany. A prayer in the form of a litany, but drawn up for the use of public penitents, occurs in the Mozarabic Liturgy for the Sundays in Lent between the Prophecy and the Epistle.[1] The Ambrosian Liturgy also preserves a trace of the Litany after the Gospel in the threefold *Kyrie eleison,* which continues to be said in this place. The Litany itself is still in use at Milan in the Masses for the Sundays in Lent, but it is placed at the beginning of the Mass, after the *Ingressa* and the *Dominus vobiscum.* The following is the text of the Sacramentary of Biasca (tenth century):—

Incipit letania. Dominica I de Quadragesima. Divinae pacis et indulgentiae munere supplicantes, ex toto corde et ex tota mente precamur te, Domine, miserere.

utilitate totius populi nobis placuit, ut non solum in civitatibus, sed etiam in omnibus parochiis verbum faciendi daremus presbyteris potestatem; ita ut si presbyter aliqua infirmitate prohibente per seipsum non potuerit praedicare, sanctorum Patrum homiliae a diaconibus recitentur. Si enim digni sunt diacones quod Christus in Evangelio locutus est legere, quare indigni judicentur sanctorum Patrum expositiones publice recitare?"

[1] This prayer is mentioned in the decrees of the Council of Lyons in the year 517 (c. 6); permission is given to penitents, as a special favour, to remain in the church, "usque ad orationem plebis quae post evangelia legeretur."

Pro Ecclesia tua sancta catholica, quae hic et per universum orbem diffusa est, precamur, etc.

Pro papa nostro *illo*[1] et omni clero ejus omnibusque sacerdotibus ac ministris, precamur . . .

Pro famulo tuo *illo* imperatore et famula tua *illa* imperatrice et omni exercitu eorum, precamur . . .

Pro pace eclesiarum, vocatione gentium et quiete populorum, precamur . . .

Pro plebe hac et conversatione ejus omnibusque habitantibus in ea, precamur . . .

Pro aerum temperie ac fructuum et fecunditate terrarum, precamur . . .

Pro virginibus, viduis, orfanis, captivis ac penitentibus, precamur . . .

Pro navigantibus, iter agentibus, in carceribus, in vinculis, in metallis, in exiliis constitutis, precamur . . .

Pro his qui diversis infirmitatibus detinentur, quique spiritibus vexantur inmundis, precamur . . .

Pro his qui in sancta tua Eclesia fructus misericordiae largiuntur, precamur . . .

Exaudi nos Deus, in omni oratione atque deprecatione nostra, precamur . . .

Dicamus omnes: Domine miserere. Ky(rie eleison), Ky(rie eleison), Ky(rie eleison).

In the Stowe Missal, representing the Irish use, there is a very similar litany between the Epistle and Gospel. It is as follows[2]:—

Dicamus omnes: "Domine exaudi et miserere, Domine miserere," ex toto corde et ex tota mente.

Qui respicis super terram et facis eam tremere.—Oramus [te Domine, exaudi et miserere].[3]

1. Pro altissima pace et tranquillitate temporum nostrorum, pro-

---

[1] The Archbishop of Milan. [The term "papa," or pope, was not restricted to the Bishop of Rome till the time of Gregory VII., 1073-85.—Tr]

[2] F. E. Warren, *The Liturgy of the Celtic Church*, p. 229.

[3] In the Stowe Missal each verse is followed by the word *Oramus* only. A Fulda manuscript, quoted by Bona (*Rer Liturg.*, ii. 4, § 3), contains the same Litany, with a few slight variations. In it it is seen that the formulary of the Response ought to be completed as I have here given it (cf. Warren, p. 252).

sancta Ecclesia catholica quae a finibus usque ad terminos orbis terrae.—Oramus.

2. Pro pastore n ¹[ostro] episcopo et omnibus episcopis et presbyteris et diaconis et omni clero.—Oramus.

3. Pro hoc loco et inhabitantibus in eo, pro piissimis imperatoribus et omni Romano exercitu.—Oramus.

4. Pro omnibus qui in sublimitate constituti sunt, pro virginibus, viduis et orfanis.—Oramus.

5. Pro peregrinantibus et iter agentibus ac navigantibus et paenitentibus et catechumenis.—Oramus.

6. Pro his qui in sancta Ecclesia fructus misericordiae largiuntur, Domine Deus virtutum, exaudi preces nostras.—Oramus.

7. Sanctorum apostolorum ac martyrum memores simus, ut orantibus eis pro nobis veniam mereamur.—Oramus.

8. Christianum et pacificum nobis finem concedi a Domino precemur. —Praesta, Domine, praesta.

9. Et divinum in nobis permanere vinculum caritatis sanctum Dominum deprecemur.—Praesta.

10. Conservare sanctitatem et catholicae fidei puritatem Dominum deprecemur.—Praesta.

Dicamus, etc.

By comparing[2] this litany with those found in the Oriental liturgies, from that of the Apostolic Constitutions onwards, we shall see that they are all absolutely of the same type. We may go even further and say that the examples given are nothing more than translations from a Greek text. The beginning is precisely the same as in the Litany of Constantinople[3]: "Εἴπωμεν πάντες ἐξ ὅλης τῆς ψυχῆς καὶ ἐξ ὅλης τῆς διανοίας ἡμῶν εἴπωμεν."

We may say the same of the form of the response, Δεόμεθά σου, ἐπάκουσον καὶ ἐλέησον. As for the petitions of the Litany, the text does not correspond exactly with any known Greek litanies, but they are arranged in the same order and drawn up in the same manner as the Greek. There is less difference between the Latin Litany and those contained in the Greek liturgies of St. James,

---

[1] [N here stands probably for the name of the unnamed bishop.—Tr.]
[2] For note, see p. 575.
[3] Brightman, p 373

St. Chrysostom, etc., than there is between the latter and those of the Apostolical Constitutions [1]

The Litany was followed by a prayer said by the bishop. This was the *Collectio post precem*. It sums up the petitions already recited. The following is the form for use on the Nativity from the *Missale Gothicum* :—

Exaudi, Domine, familiam tibi dicatam et in tuae ecclesiae gremio in hac hodierna solemnitate Nativitatis tuae congregatam ut laudes tuas exponat. Tribue captivis redemptionem, caecis visum, peccantibus remissionem ; quia tu venisti ut salvos facias nos. Aspice de caelo sancto tuo et inlumina populum tuum, quorum animus in te plena devotione confidit, Salvator mundi, qui vivis, etc.

This collect corresponds with the prayer Κύριε παντοκράτορ, in the Liturgy of the Apostolical Constitutions, and with the shorter formulary, Κύριε ὁ Θεὸς ἡμῶν, τὴν ἐκτενῆ ταύτην;[2] in the Liturgy of Constantinople. It has disappeared from all the Latin liturgies.[3]

---

[1] I add here the most noteworthy coincidences (CP = Byzantine Liturgy; Jac = the Liturgy of St James; Cl = the Liturgy of the Apostolical Constitutions): 1. Ὑπὲρ τῆς ἄνωθεν εἰρήνης (Jac CP), ὑπὲρ τῆς ἁγίας καθολικῆς καὶ ἀποστολικῆς ἐκκλησίας τῆς ἀπὸ περάτων ἕως περάτων (Cl.).— 2 Ὑπὲρ τοῦ ἐπισκόπου ἡμῶν, τοῦ τιμίου πρεσβυτερίου, τῆς ἐν Χριστῷ διακονίας, παντὸς τοῦ κλήρου (CP)—3. Ὑπὲρ τῆς ἁγίας μονῆς ταύτης, πάσης πόλεως καὶ χώρας, καὶ τῶν πίστει οἰκούντων ἐν αὐταῖς (CP)—Ὑπὲρ τοῦ εὐσεβεστάτου καὶ φιλοχρίστου ἡμῶν βασιλέως, παντὸς τοῦ παλατίου καὶ τοῦ στρατοπέδου καὶ νίκης αὐτῶν (Jac)—4 Ὑπὲρ βασιλέων καὶ τῶν ἐν ὑπεροχῇ (Cl), ὑπὲρ.. παρθένων, χηρῶν τε καὶ ὀρφανῶν (Cl)—5. Ὑπὲρ πλεόντων καὶ ὁδοιπορούντων (Cl, CP, Jac), ξενιτευόντων (Jac)—6. Ὑπὲρ τῶν καρποφορούντων ἐν τῇ ἁγίᾳ ἐκκλησίᾳ καὶ ποιούντων τοῖς πένησι τὰς ἐλεημοσύνας (Cl.).—7. Τῆς παναγίας . . . Μαρίας καὶ πάντων τῶν ἁγίων καὶ δικαίων μνημονεύσωμεν, ὅπως εὐχαῖς καὶ πρεσβείαις αὐτῶν οἱ πάντες ἐλεηθῶμεν (Jac).— 8 Χριστιανὰ τὰ τέλη τῆς ζωῆς ἡμῶν, ἀνώδυνα, ἀνεπαίσχυντα . . . αἰτησώμεθα (Jac)—9, 10 Τὴν ἑνότητα τῆς πίστεως καὶ τὴν κοινωνίαν τοῦ παναγίου Πνεύματος (Jac)

[2] Brightman, *op cit*

[3] But as it belongs to the Litany which precedes it, it is worth while to recall what has been said above at p 173, note 1, in regard to the corresponding part of the Roman Mass

7. *The Dismissal of the Catechumens.*

GERMAIN : *Catechumenum ergo diaconus ideo clamat juxta anticum Ecclesiae ritum, ut tam judaei quam haeretici vel pagani instructi, qui grandes ad baptismum veniebant et ante baptismum probabantur,*[1] *starent in ecclesia et audirent consilium Veteris et Novi Testamenti; postea deprecarent pro illos levitae, diceret sacerdos collectam, post precem exirent postea foris qui digni non erant stare dum inferebatur oblatio, et foras ante ostium auscultarent prostrati ad terram magnalia. Quae cura ad diaconum vel ad ostiarium pertinebat, ut ille*[2] *eos admoneret exire, iste provideret ne quis indignus retardaretur in templo, dicendo :* "*Nolite dare Sanctum canibus, neque mittatis margaritas ante porcos.*"

By the second half of the sixth century the catechumenate had become merely a reminiscence. It was necessary then to explain the *missa* (dismissal) *catechumenorum*, of which the rite, however, continued to be preserved.[3] This ceremony took place after the prayer, as in the Liturgy of Constantinople. In the Apostolic Constitutions it is placed before the prayer. We cannot gather precisely from the text of St. Germain whether it was accompanied by special prayers. I am inclined to believe that its text has in view the prayers which I have just dealt with, but that at the beginning there were special prayers, which disappeared with the disappearance of the catechumens. Thus, at the end of the sixth century, at least in the Church of Paris, nothing more was said than some such formulary as *Ne quis catechumenus, catechumeni recedant*, etc.

[1] *Probantur*, in the printed edition.
[2] Ille eos] *illis*, in the printed edition.
[3] The Council of Epaon (517), c. 29, still mentions: "Cum catechumeni procedere commonentur."

The dismissal of the penitents, which is not alluded to by St. Germain, was still in use shortly before his time. The Council of Lyons, held about the year 517, makes express mention of it (c. 6). According to this, the penitents must have been sent away ordinarily before the Prayer of the Faithful.[1]

8. *Procession of the Oblation.*

GERMAIN: *Spiritualiter jubemur silentium facere observantes ad ostium, id est ut tacentes a tumultu verborum . . . hoc solum cor intendat ut in se Christum suscipiat.*

De sono. Sonum autem quod canitur quando procedit oblatio, hinc traxit exordium. Praecepit Dominus Moysi, . . . Nunc autem procedentem ad altarium corpus Christi non jam tubis irreprehensibilibus, sed spiritalibus vocibus praeclara Christi magnalia dulci modilia psallit Ecclesia Corpus vero Domini ideo defertur in turribus quia . . . Sanguis vero Christi ideo specialiter offertur in calice quia . . . Aqua autem ideo miscetur vel quia . . .

Patena autem vocatur ubi consecratur oblatio, quia . . . Palla vera linostima . . . Corporalis vero palla ideo pura linea est super quam oblatio ponitur, quia . . . Coopertum vero sacramentorum ideo exornatur quia . . . Sirico autem ornatur aut auro, vel gemmis.

Laudes autem, hoc est Alleluia, Johannes in Apocalypsi post resurrectionem audivit psallere. Ideo hora illa Domini pallio quasi Christus tegitur caelo,[2] ecclesia solet angelicum canticum [cantare]. Quod autem habet ipsa Alleluia prima et secunda et tertia, signat tria tempora ante legem, sub lege, sub gratia.

The ceremony begins by an injunction to silence and by the appointment of a watch at the doors. St. Germain

---

[1] See above, p 198, note L.
[2] A corrupt passage.

interprets this as applying to the gates of the soul, that is, the senses, but the true signification is furnished by the Liturgy of St. James, when the deacon exclaims: Μή τις τῶν κατηχουμένων, μή τις τῶν ἀμυήτων, μή τις τῶν μὴ δυναμένων ἡμῖν συνδεηθῆναι! 'Αλλήλους ἐπίγνωτε! Τὰς θύρας! 'Ορθοὶ πάντες! It has evidently reference to the doors of the church, which had to be guarded in order that no profane person might enter the assembly.

The oblation was prepared beforehand, and there was bestowed on it by anticipation the same honour which it had after consecration. It was even already designated by the terms Body and Blood of Christ. The preparation took place before the entrance of the celebrant,[1] and was performed with rites and prayers, of which no traces remain in the Merovingian manuscripts. Some relics of it are to be found in the Irish books, the Stowe Missal, and the Lebhar Breac.[2] The Mozarabic Missal contains the whole ceremony down to the most minute details. It even repeats it at the end of the Procession of the Oblation, after having previously prefixed it to the entry of the celebrant. Its place after the Procession of the Oblation is that which this rite occupies in the Ambrosian Missal, and it is that of its counterpart, the Offertory, in the present Roman use. The preparation of the oblation in this place can be regarded only as a modification suggested by the Roman use. We may still recognise the latter in the ceremony of the *Vecchioni* of Milan, who make at this point the offering of bread and wine; a custom observed also in many Churches of France. The offering by the people at this point in the Mass, is a ceremony of Roman origin, and is incompatible with that of the *processio oblationis*, a custom common to the Gallican and Oriental rite.

[1] This Gallican peculiarity has passed into the special use of the Order of St. Dominic.
[2] Whitley Stokes, *The Irish Passages in the Stowe Missal*, Calcutta, 1881, pp 8, 14.

The bread is brought in a vessel having the form of a tower,[1] and the wine, mixed with water, in a chalice. Besides these two eucharistic vessels, the paten also was employed, in which the consecrated bread was placed, either at the time of the preparation, or at the altar during the consecration. There were also, as it appears, three veils, one of which, the *corporalis palla*, was of linen, without any admixture (*pura linea*). This was the cloth for the altar. The other was of silk, and was ornamented with gold, and even with gems. It was used to cover the oblation after it had been placed upon the corporal. I am at a loss to know the purpose served by the *palla linostima*, of which Germain speaks first of all. In the Byzantine rite there was one veil to cover the paten and the bread, and another to cover the chalice, and a third to cover both together.

During the procession a chant, similar to the Byzantine *Cheroubicon*, was sung by the choir, and ended, like it, with the *Alleluia*. This is what St. Germain calls the *Sonus*. In the Mozarabic Liturgy it bore the name of *Laudes*, a word already met with in the seventh century.[2] At Milan it was called the *Antiphona post Evangelium*. When the sacred elements were placed upon the altar, they were covered by the precious veil.[3] The choir then

---

[1] Cf. Greg. Tur., *Glor Mart*, 85 The event is taking place at Riom, and on the day of St Polycarp. "Lecta igitur passione (S. Polycarpi) cum reliquis lectionibus quas canon sacerdotalis invexit, tempus ad sacrificium offerendum advenit Accepta quoque turre diaconus, in qua mysterium Dominici corporis habebatur, ferre cepit ad ostium; ingressusque templum ut eam altari superponeret, elapsa de manu ejus ferebatur in aera, et sic ad ipsam aram accedens, nunquam eam manus diaconi potuit adsequi; quod non alia credimus actum de causa, nisi quia pollutus erat in conscientia" Krush, in dealing with this passage, is wrong in confounding the use of this tower with that of the Capsa, in which the Eucharist was carried in the Roman Mass.

[2] Isidore, *De Eccl Off.*, i. 13; *Conc Tol*, iv. 11.

[3] This veil is mentioned several times by Gregory of Tours (*Hist Fr.*,

sang a sacred chant, which St. Germain calls *Laudes*, or *Alleluia*. This was the *Sacrificium*, or *Offertorium*, of the Mozarabic Liturgy,[1] and the *Offerenda* of the Milanese. I append the Mozarabic text of these two chants for the Nativity:

Laudes:
Alleluia! Redemptionem misit Dominus populo suo: mandavit in aeternum testamentum suum; sanctum et terribile nomen ejus. Alleluia!
Sacrificium:
Parvulus natus est nobis et filius datus est nobis; et factus est principatus ejus super humeros ejus. Alleluia! Alleluia!

There are ordinarily in the Mozarabic Liturgy two verses in the *Sacrificium*, so by combining these two chants the triple *Alleluia* was obtained of which St. Germain speaks. The idea of grouping these arose naturally from the fact that they originally followed each other immediately. The prayers, which are at present interposed between them in the liturgies of Milan and Toledo, are, as I have already said, not in their original place—at least some of them; the others are secret prayers, which were recited privately by the officiating priest whilst the choir was engaged in the chant.

9. *The Prayer of the Veil.*

St. Germain does not speak of this. It was preceded by a kind of preface, or invitatory, addressed, not to God, but to the congregation.

---

vii. 22; *Virtutes S. Martini*, ii 25; *Vitae PP.*, viii. 11). We see from this last text that the stuff out of which it was made could not have been transparent, for the veil was meant to hide the *mysterium corporis sanguinisque dominici*.

[1] *Sacrificium* is the term employed in the liturgical books; *offertorium* is found in St. Isidore (*loc cit*, 14)· "De offertoriis Offertoria, quae in sacrificiorum honore canuntur," etc.

PRAEFATIO MISSAE.

Sacrosanctum beatae Nativitatis diem, in quo, nascente Domino, virginalis uteri arcana laxata sunt, incorruptorumque genitalium pondus saeculi levamen effusum est, sicut exoptavimus votis ita veneremur et gaudiis. Hic namque ortus die splendidior, luce coruscantior est. In hoc omnipotentem Deum qui terrenam fragilemque materiam causa nostrae redemptionis adsumpsit, Fratres dilectissimi, supplices deprecemur, uti nos, quos ortu corporis visitavit, societate conversationis edocuit, praecepto praedicationis instituit, degustatione mortis redemit, participatione mortis amplexus est, divini Spiritus infusione ditavit, sub perpetua devotione custodiat; et in his beati famulatus studiis permanere concedat qui cum Patre et Spiritu Sancto vivit et regnat Deus in saecula saeculorum.

COLLECTIO SEQUITUR.

Deus, qui dives es in misericordia, qua mortuos nos peccatis convivificasti Christo filio tuo, ut formam servi acciperet qui omnia formavit, ut qui erat in deitate generaretur in carne, ut involveretur in pannis qui adorabatur in stellis, ut jaceret in praesepio qui regnabat in caelo; invocantibus nobis aurem majestatis tuae propitiatus adcommoda, donans hoc per ineffabilem tuae misericordiae caritatem, ut qui exultavimus de nativitate Filii tui, qui vel ex virgine natus vel ex Spiritu sancto regeneratus est, pareamus praeceptis ejus quibus nos edocuit ad salutem. Praesta, per dominum nostrum Jesum Christum Filium tuum, qui tecum, etc.

In the Ambrosian and Mozarabic liturgies these formularies are preceded by a salutation.[1] St. Isidore gives them as the two first prayers of the Mass. They form, in fact, only one prayer, and that not the first; but St.

---

[1] It was at this point that the Kiss of Peace occurred formerly in the Milanese use. The deacon gave the signal for it by the words, *Pacem habete!* He then added: *Erigite vos ad orationem!* to which the response, *Ad te Domine*, was given. Cf. the Σοὶ Κύριε, a frequent response in the Greek liturgies At the present day the words *Erigite vos ad orationem* are omitted from the liturgical books, and the response *Ad te Domine* has no longer, consequently, its natural sense.

Isidore understood that the Mass did not begin until after the singing of the Offertory.¹ At Milan this prayer was called the *Oratio super sindonem*. In the other Gallican liturgies it has no special name. It is evidently the counterpart of the prayer *Super oblata*, or *Secreta*, in the Roman Missal. In the Mozarabic Liturgy the invitatory is separated from the prayer in the following manner: the priest, having said *Oremus*, the choir sings the trisagion, Ἅγιος, ἅγιος, ἅγιος, *Domine Deus, rex aeterne, tibi laudes et gratias!* Then the priest proceeds: *Ecclesiam sanctam catholicam in orationibus in mente habeamus; ut eam Dominus fide et spe et caritate propitius ampliare dignetur; omnes lapsos, captivos, infirmos atque peregrinos in mente habeamus, ut eos Dominus propitius redimere, sanare, et confortare dignetur.* The choir answers: *Praesta, aeterne, omnipotens Deus!* and then follows the prayer.

10. *The Reading of the Diptychs.*²

GERMAIN: *Nomina defunctorum ideo hora illa recitantur qua pallium tollitur, quia tunc erit resurrectio mortuorum quando adveniente Christo caelum sicut liber plicabitur.*

A formulary for the diptychs is preserved in the Mozarabic Liturgy—

Offerunt Deo Domino oblationem sacerdotes nostri, papa Romensis

---

¹ *De Eccl. Off*, i 15· "Ordo autem missae et orationum quibus oblata Deo sacrificia consecrantur primum a sancto Petro est institutus, cujus celebrationem uno eodemque modo universus peragit orbis (this ought to be interpreted). Prima earumdem oratio admonitionis est erga populum, ut excitentur ad exorandum Deum; secunda invocationis ad Deum est, ut clementer suscipiat preces fidelium oblationesque eorum"

² See note, p. 575.

³ The Bishops of Spain. The name of the Pope ought always to be given. Council of Vaison (529), c. 4 " Et hoc nobis justum visum est

et reliqui, pro se et pro omni clero ac plebibus ecclesiae sibimet consignatis vel pro universa fraternitate.

Item offerunt universi presbyteri, diaconi, clerici ac populi circumastantes, in honorem sanctorum, pro se et pro suis.

R⁊. Offerunt pro se et pro universa fraternitate.

Facientes commemorationem beatissimorum apostolorum et martyrum, gloriosae[1] sanctae Mariae Virginis, Zachariae, Joannis, Infantum, Petri, Pauli, Johannis, Jacobi, Andreae, Philippi, Thomae, Bartholomaei, Matthei, Jacobi, Simonis et Judae, Matthiae, Marci, et Lucae.—R⁊. Et omnium martyrum.

Item pro spiritibus pausantium, Hilarii, Athanasii, Martini, Ambrosii, Augustini, Fulgentii, Leandri, Isidori, etc.—R⁊. Et omnium pausantium.[2]

I will quote also a formulary for the reciting of the diptychs according to the use of an Irish Church. It is to be found in the Stowe Missal, inserted in the middle of the *Memento* of the dead used in the Roman Mass.[3]

Cum[4] omnibus in toto mundo offerentibus sacrificium spiritale Deo Patri et Filio et Spiritui sancto sanctis ac venerabilibus sacerdotibus,

ut nomen domni Papae quicumque sedi apostolicae praefuerit, in nostris ecclesiis recitetur."

[1] The words *gloriosae* ... *infantum* must have been a later addition. They are not provided for in the formulary which goes before: *apostolorum et martyrum*. The names of the martyrs have disappeared.

[2] This formulary must differ widely from its primitive text. It has, nevertheless, preserved certain vestiges of antiquity, notably the grouping of the holy confessors with the ordinary dead Mabillon compares it with the commemorative formulary, which appears at the end of the Rule of Aurelian, Bishop of Arles, of the sixth century (Migne, *Pat Lat.*, vol. lxviii. p 395). The *Liber Ordinum* contains (p. 235) a text of similar form to that of the present Missal.

[3] Warren, *loc. cit*, pp 237, 240. The formulary is interrupted by a litany and a prayer of which we need not take account. These pieces occupy two intercalated leaves (29, 30) (Warren, p 200), in a later handwriting The names in the Litany, both Latin and Irish, are all in the vocative, and are preceded by the word *Sancte*, and followed by *Ora pro nobis* In the primitive list—the only one which I cite here—the Latin and Irish names are all isolated, and in the genitive case, as the construction of the sentence requires.

[4] I have restored the usual orthography for the ordinary text, but not for the proper names.

offert senior noster N. presbyter, pro se et pro suis et pro totius ecclesiae coetu catholicae, et pro commemorando anathletico gradu venerabilium patriarcharum, prophetarum, apostolorum et martyrum et omnium quoque sanctorum, ut pro nobis dominum Deum nostrum exorare dignentur: Ablis,[1] Zeth, Enoc, Noe, Melchsedech, Abrache, Isac, Jacob, Joseph, Job, Mosi, Essu,[2] Samuelis, David, Heliae, Helessiae, Essaiae, Heremiae, Ezechelis, Danielis, Hestre,[3] Osse, Johel, Amos, Abdiae, Jonae, Michiae, Nauum, Ambacuc, Sophoniae, Agiae, Sachariae, Malachiae, Tobiae, Ananiae, Azariae, Misahelis, Machabeorum;

item Infantium,[4] Johannis Baptiste et Virginis Mariae, Petri, Pauli, Andriae, Jacobi, Johannis, Pilipi, Barthalomae, Tomae, Mathei, Jacobi, Simonis, Tathei, Madiani,[5] Marci, Lucae, Stefani, Cornili, Cipriani et ceterorum martirum;

Pauli, Antoni, et ceterorum patrum heremi Sciti[6]:

item episcoporum: Martini, Grigori, Maximi, Felicis, Patrici, Patrici, Secundini, Auxili, Isernini, Cerbani, Erci, Catheri, Ibori, Ailbi, Conlai, Maicnissae, Moinenn, Senani, Finbarri, Cuani,[7] Colmani, Cuani, Declach, Laurenti, Melleti, Justi,[8] Aedo, Dagani, Tigernich, Muchti, Ciannani, Buiti, Eogeni, Declani, Carthain, Maileruen[9];

Item et sacerdotum: Vinniani, Ciarani, Oengusso, Endi, Gilde, Brendini, Brendini, Cainnichi, Columbe, Columbe, Colmani, Comgelli, Coemgeni;

et omnium pausantium, qui nos in dominica pace praecesserunt ab Adam usque in hodiernum diem, quorum Deus nomina nominavit et novit.[10]

---

[1] Abelis.
[2] Jesu = Joshua.
[3] Esdrae.
[4] The Holy Innocents.
[5] Matthias. His name is repeated twice in error.
[6] The desert of Scaete.
[7] [Partly erased.—Tr.]
[8] The three immediate successors of St. Augustine in the see of Canterbury. Augustine himself is omitted, clearly owing to an oversight of the editor, or of the copyist [or from Celtic antipathy to him.—Tr.].
[9] "If, as is probable, the Maelruen here mentioned was Maelruain of Tallaght, this part of the manuscript must have been written after A D 792, in which year this bishop died." Whitley Stokes, *op. cit.* p. 5.
[10] So manuscript.

The recitation of the diptychs was followed by the prayer *Post nomina* :—

COLLECTIO POST NOMINA.

Suscipe, quaesumus, Domine Jesu omnipotens Deus, sacrificium laudis oblatum quod pro tua hodierna Incarnatione a nobis offertur; et per eum sic propitiatus adesto ut superstitibus vitam, defunctis requiem tribuas sempiternam. Nomina quorum sunt recitatione complexa scribi jubeas in aeternitate, pro quibus apparuisti in carne, Salvator mundi, qui cum coaeterno Patre vivis et regnas, etc.

This is the third of the prayers of the Mass according to St. Isidore.[1]

11. *The Kiss of Peace.*

GERMAIN: *Pacem autem ideo Christiani*[2] *mutuo proferunt ut per mutuum osculum teneant in se caritatis affectum.*

The following prayer accompanied the ceremony of the Kiss of Peace [3] :—

COLLECTIO AD PACEM.

Omnipotens sempiterne Deus, qui hunc diem Incarnationis tuae et partus beatae Mariae virginis consecrasti, quique discordiam vetustam per transgressionem ligni veteris cum angelis et hominibus per Incarnationis mysterium, lapis angularis, junxisti; da familiae tuae in hac celebritate laetitiam; ut qui te consortem in carnis

---

[1] *Op. cit* "Tertia autem effunditur pro offerentibus sive pro defunctis fidelibus, ut per idem sacrificium veniam consequantur."

[2] *Christi*, in the printed edition.

[3] Isidore, *op cit :* "Quarta post haec infertur pro osculo pacis, ut charitate reconciliati omnes invicem digne sacramento corporis et sanguinis Christi consocientur, quia non recipit dissensionem cuiusquam Christi indivisibile corpus."

propinquitate laetantur, ad summorum civium unitatem, super quos corpus adsumptum evexisti, perducantur; et [1] semetipsos per externa complexa jungantur, ut jurgii non pateat interruptio, qui te auctorem gaudent in sua natura per carnis venisse contubernium. Quod ipse praestare digneris, qui cum Patre, etc.

In the Mozarabic Liturgy, which alone has preserved both the order and formularies of this ceremony, the prayer *ad Pacem* is said before the Kiss of Peace; then follows the long Salutation, which in the Syro-Byzantine liturgies precedes the Eucharistic prayer—

Gratia Dei Patris omnipotentis, pax ac dilectio domini nostri Jesu Christi, et communicatio Spiritus sancti sit semper cum omnibus vobis.[2]

℟. Et cum hominibus bonae voluntatis.

Quomodo astatis pacem facite.

During the giving of the Kiss of Peace the choir sings a respond—

Pacem meam do vobis; pacem meam commendo vobis; non sicut mundus dat; pacem do vobis.—℣. Novum mandatum do vobis ut diligatis invicem.—Pacem meam, etc.—℣. Gloria et honor Patri et Filio et Spiritui sancto.—Pacem meam, etc.

In the present Ambrosian rite the Kiss of Peace occurs, as at Rome, immediately before the Communion, but this was not its original position. From Pope Innocent's letter to Decentius, written at the beginning of the fifth century, we see that the custom of giving the Kiss of Peace before the consecration

---

[1] Some such expression as *sic inter* must be here supplied

[2] *Clem* "Ἡ χάρις τοῦ παντοκράτορος Θεοῦ καὶ ἡ ἀγάπη τοῦ κυρίου ἡμῶν Ἰησοῦ Χριστοῦ καὶ ἡ κοινωνία τοῦ ἁγίου Πνεύματος ἔστω μετὰ πάντων ὑμῶν" The Latin adds only the words *Patris* and *Pax*; the whole of the remainder being nothing more than a translation from the Greek The formularies of the Greek and Oriental liturgies depart more widely from the text of the Apostolical Constitutions.

prayers (*ante confecta mysteria*) was in full observance in North Italy. A vestige of this custom is to be found in the invitatory of the deacon, *Pacem habete*, which occurs in the Milanese Liturgy before the prayer *super sindonem*. As for the reading of the diptychs, we see from the same document that it also took place before the Preface and the Canon. It has now, owing to the adoption of the Roman Canon, disappeared from the Ambrosian Liturgy.

12. *The Eucharistic Prayer.*

GERMAIN: *Sursum corda ideo sacerdos habere admonet ut nulla cogitatio terrena maneat in pectoribus nostris in hora sacrae oblationis*, etc.

After the long salutation given above, the Mozarabic Liturgy furnishes the following text for the initial versicles:—

Introibo ad altare Dei.
— Ad Deum qui laetificat juventutem meam.
Aures ad Dominum!
— Habemus ad Dominum.
Sursum corda!
— Levemus ad Dominum.
Deo ac Domino nostro Jesu Christo filio Dei, qui est in caelis, dignas laudes dignasque gratias referamus!
— Dignum et justum est.

Then the celebrant begins the Eucharistic prayer, called *contestatio*,[1] or *immolatio* in Gaul, and *illatio* in Spain. This last designation, to which St. Isidore witnesses,[2] ought to be compared with the analogous Greek

---

[1] Greg Tur, *Vit S Martini*, ii 14. This is the term most frequently employed in the Merovingian liturgies, and in the Bobbio Sacramentary, but we find somewhat frequently in the *Missale Gothicum* and *Missale Gallicanum*, the term *immolatio*

[2] *Op. cit.*: " Quinta denique infertur illatio in sanctificatione oblationis,

term ἀναφορά. The Gallican *contestatio* is the equivalent of the Roman Preface.

> Vere dignum et justum est, aequum et salutare est, nos tibi gratias agere, Domine sancte, Pater omnipotens, aeterne Deus; quia hodie dominus noster Jesus Christus dignatus est visitare mundum, processit de sacrario corporis virginalis et descendit pietate de caelis. Cecinerunt angeli "Gloria in excelsis" cum humanitas claruit Salvatoris. Omnis denique turba exultabat angelorum, quia terra regem suscepit aeternum. Maria beata facta est templum pretiosum portans dominum dominorum. Genuit enim pro nostris delictis vitam praeclaram ut mors pelleretur amara. Illa enim viscera quae humanam non noverant maculam Deum portare meruerunt. Natus est in mundo qui semper vixit et vivit in caelo, Jesus Christus Filius tuus dominus noster. Per quem majestatem tuam laudant Angeli, etc.

Here follows the singing of the *Sanctus*, which is common to all the liturgies. The text of the Mozarabic Missal varies in no respect from that of the Roman text at present in use.

The prayer that follows, *Collectio post Sanctus*, serves merely to connect the *Sanctus* with the account of the institution of the Eucharist. As in the Oriental liturgies,[1] it begins regularly with the words *Vere Sanctus*. St. Isidore does not distinguish it from the prayer which precedes it, but in the liturgical books it is clearly separate. As a rare exceptional instance, the words *Vere Sanctus* do not appear in the *Missale Gothicum* at this point in the Mass for the Nativity.

POST SANCTUS.

> Gloria in excelsis Deo et in terra pax hominibus bonae voluntatis!
>
> in qua etiam et ad Dei laudem terrestrium creaturarum virtutumque caelestium universitas provocatur et *Hosanna in excelsis* cantatur, quod Salvatore de genere David nascente salus mundo usque ad excelsa pervenerit."

[1] "Ἅγιος γὰρ εἶ ὡς ἀληθῶς, καὶ πανάγιος ... (Cl. C P.)—Ἅγιος εἶ, βασιλεῦ τῶν ἁγίων καὶ πάσης ἁγιωσύνης κύριος ... (Jac.).—Πλήρης γὰρ ἐστιν, ὡς ἀληθῶς, ὁ οὐρανὸς καὶ ἡ γῆ τῆς ἁγίας σοῦ δόξης (Alex.)."

Quia adpropinquavit redemptio nostra, venit antiqua expectatio gentium, adest promissa resurrectio mortuorum, jamque praefulget aeterna expectatio beatorum; per Christum dominum nostrum. Qui pridie quam pro nostra omnium salute pateretur. . . .

The Ambrosian Liturgy of the present day follows here the order and text of the Roman Canon, but there still remains in it a remarkable trace of its original conformity with the Gallican arrangement. In the Mass for Saturday in Holy Week the *Sanctus* is connected with the *Qui pridie* by a single and unusual formulary of an unmistakably Gallican type:

POST SANCTUS.

Vere sanctus, vere benedictus dominus noster Jesus Christus filius tuus. Qui, cum Deus esset majestatis, descendit de caelo, formam servi qui primus perierat suscepit, et sponte pati dignatus est ut eum quem ipse fecerat liberaret. Unde [1] et hoc paschale sacrificium tibi offerimus pro his quos ex aqua et Spiritu sancto regenerare dignatus es, dans eis remissionem omnium peccatorum, ut invenires eos in Christo Jesu domino nostro; pro quibus tibi, Domine, supplices fundimus preces ut nomina eorum pariterque famuli tui imperatoris scripta habeas in libro viventium. Per Christum dominum nostrum, qui pridie quam pro nostra et omnium salute pateretur, accipiens panem, etc.[2]

In the ancient Gallican books the account of the institution of the Eucharist is always omitted, or is merely indicated by the first words of it. The celebrant must have known it by heart. The following is the Ambrosian text :—

Qui pridie quam pro nostra et omnium salute pateretur, accipiens

---

[1] This sentence is somewhat analogous to the *Hanc igitur* of the Mass for Easter in the Roman use.

[2] It is hardly necessary to draw attention to the fact that the printed Missals, and even the late manuscript Missals of the Middle Ages, have adopted here the first part of the Roman Canon, although this leads to its double employment. I refer to the Sacramentary of Biasca and those of a similar age.

panem elevavit oculos ad te, Deum Patrem suum omnipotentem, tibi gratias agens benedixit, fregit, deditque discipulis suis dicens ad eos: "Hoc est enim corpus meum." Simili modo, postea quam caenatum est, accipiens calicem elevavit oculos ad caelos, ad te, Deum Patrem suum omnipotentem, item tibi gratias agens, benedixit, tradidit discipulis suis, dicens ad eos : " Accipite et bibite ex eo omnes ; hic est enim calix sanguinis mei, novi et aeterni testamenti, mysterium fidei, qui pro vobis et pro multis effundetur in remissionem peccatorum." Mandans quoque et dicens ad eos : " Haec quotienscumque feceritis, in meam commemorationem facietis, mortem meam praedicabitis, resurrectionem meam adnuntiabitis, adventum meum sperabitis, donec iterum de caelis veniam ad vos.

The following is the text of the Mozarabic Missal :—

[Adesto,[1] adesto, Jesu, bone pontifex, in medio nostri, sicut fuisti in medio discipulorum tuorum ; sanctifica hanc oblationem ut sanctificata sumamus per manus sancti angeli tui, sancte domine ac redemptor aeterne.]

Dominus noster Jesus Christus in qua nocte tradebatur accepit panem et gratias agens benedixit ac fregit, deditque discipulis suis, dicens : " Accipite et manducate: hoc est corpus meum quod pro vobis tradetur. Quotiescumque manducaveritis, hoc facite in meam commemorationem." —R︎. Amen.—Similiter et calicem postquam caenavit, dicens : " Hic est calix novi testamenti in meo sanguine, qui pro vobis et pro multis effundetur in remissionem peccatorum. Quotiescumque biberitis, hoc facite in meam commemorationem."—R︎. Amen —Quotiescumque manducaveritis panem hunc et calicem istum biberitis, mortem Domini annuntiabitis, donec veniet in claritatem de caelis.—R︎. Amen.

The last sentence in each of these formularies is suggested by a passage from St. Paul (1 Cor. xi. 26). A similar adoption appears in the Liturgy of the Apostolical Constitutions, and in those of St. James, St. Basil, St. Cyril, and of St. Basil as used by the Copts.

The agreement of the Mozarabic and Ambrosian liturgies with each other, and with the Eastern liturgies, in a detail of this importance, is a remarkable coincidence.

---

[1] The prayer *Adesto* cannot be primitive, for in the Merovingian Missals of the seventh and eighth centuries the *Vere Sanctus* always precedes immediately the words of institution. This prayer, however, is not found either in the *Liber Ordinum* (p 238) or in the (unpublished) Sacramentary of Toledo.

13. *The Epiclesis.*

Then follows a prayer[1] in which there is an elaboration of two themes, one of the commemoration of the Lord, and the other of the Eucharistic change effected by the operation of the Holy Spirit. It sometimes happens, moreover, that neither of these ideas is found expressed. I will give here two specimens, both of them taken from the *Missale Gothicum,* the first for the Mass of the Nativity, and the second for that of the *Circumcision.* The prayer is prefaced by a rubric, which appears in the different forms, *Post secreta, Post pridie, Post mysterium.*[2]

POST SECRETA.—*Christmas.*

Credimus, Domine, adventum tuum; recolimus passionem tuam. Corpus tuum in peccatorum nostrorum remissionem confractum est, sanguis sanctus tuus in pretium nostrae redemptionis effusus est; qui cum Patre et Spiritu sancto vivis et regnas in saecul[a saeculorum].

Circumcision.

Haec nos, Domine, instituta et praecepta retinentes, suppliciter oramus uti hoc sacrificium suscipere et benedicere et sanctificare digneris: ut fiat[3] nobis eucharistia legitima in tuo Filiique tui nomine et Spiritus sancti, in transformationem corporis ac sanguinis domini Dei nostri Jesu Christi, unigeniti tui, per quem omnia creas, creata benedicis, benedicta sanctificas et sanctificata largiris, Deus, qui in trinitate perfecta vivis et regnas in saecula saeculorum.

Here is another Mozarabic *Epiclesis* taken from the *Liber Ordinum*[4] :—

---

[1] Isidore, *op. cit* · "Porro sexta ex hinc succedit, conformatio sacramenti, ut oblatio quae Deo offertur, sanctificata per Spiritum sanctum, Christi corpori ac sanguini conformetur"

[2] The rubric *Post pridie* is peculiar to the Mozarabic books. It is remarkable that the text *Dominus noster Jesu Christus in qua nocte tradebatur* does not contain the word *pridie.* The rubric must belong to a more ancient time when in the Spanish, as in the other Latin books, the words of institution were introduced by the phrase *qui pridie quam pateretur.*

[3] The words which follow are a sort of customary phrase, characteristic of the Gallican Epiclesis

[4] Edited by Dom Férotin, p. 265. (Firmin-Didot, Paris, 1904)

Memores sumus, eterne Deus, Pater omnipotens, gloriosissime passionis domini nostri Iesu Christi Filii tui, resurrectionis etiam et eius ascensionis in celum; petimus ergo maiestatem tuam, Domine [ascendant] preces humilitatis nostre in conspectu tue clementie, et descendat super hunc panem et super hunc calicem plenitudo tue diuinitatis. Descendat etiam, Domine, illa sancti Spiritus tui incomprehensibilis maiestas, sicut quondam in Patrum hostiis mirabiliter descendebat, ac presta, Domine, ut huius panis uinique substantia sanis custodiam adhibeat, languentibus medicinam infundat, discordantibus insinuet reconciliationem et supereminentem pacis augeat karitatem, stultis infundat sapientiam et sapientibus ne extollantur tribuat disciplinam, omnibusque ad te confugium facientibus plenissimam conferat sospitatem et regni celestis plebem tuam faciat coheredem. Amen.

These short formularies have been replaced in the Milanese use by the *Unde et memores*, etc., continuing the Roman Canon. But even here also we can distinguish in the most ancient manuscripts a trace of conformity with the Gallican use. In these manuscripts the prayers *Unde et memores, Supra quae, Supplices te rogamus, Memento,* and *Nobis quoque,* are omitted on Maundy Thursday, and are replaced by the following formulary[1]:—

Haec facimus, haec celebramus, tua, Domine, praecepta servantes et ad communionem inviolabilem hoc ipsum quod corpus Domini sumimus mortem dominicam nuntiamus.

14. *The Fraction.*

GERMAIN: *Confractio vero et commixtio corporis Domini tantis mysteriis declarata . . . In hac confractione sacerdos vult augere; ibidem debet addere, quia tunc caelestia terrenis miscentur et ad orationem sacerdotis caeli aperiuntur. Sacerdote autem frangente, supplex clerus psallit antiphonam, quia [Christo] patiente dolore mortis, omnia* [2] *trementis testata*

---

[1] The Canon for Maundy Thursday was published by Muratori (*Lit. Romana Vetus*, vol. i. p 133) from a manuscript which now belongs to the Marquis Trotti (described by Mons. Delisle, *op cit*, p. 205). A better edition of it was put forth by Sig. Ceriani, in his *Notitia Liturgiae Ambrosianae*, 1895.

[2] *Sic.* I have supplied *Christo;* something more seems wanting.

sunt elementa. Oratio vero dominica pro hoc ibidem ponitur ut omnis oratio nostra in dominica oratione claudatur.

The Fraction was a complicated matter; a certain amount of superstition was imported into this ceremony at an early date. The particles of the Host were arranged upon the paten in such a manner as to represent the human form. The Council of Tours (567) denounced this practice, and decreed that the portions should be arranged in the form of a cross.[1] This is still, with a slight variation, the Mozarabic custom. The particles of the Host are disposed as follows, each having its special designation corresponding to a mystery in the life of Christ:—

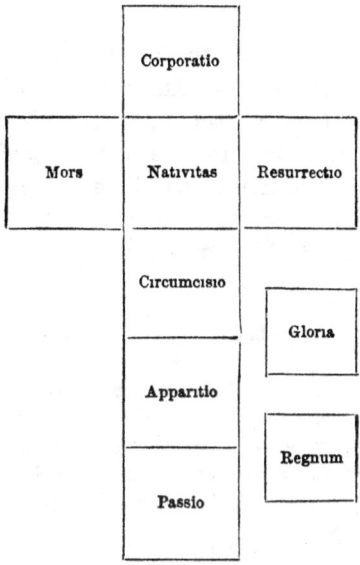

[1] "Ut corpus Domini in altari non in imaginario ordine, sed sub crucis titulo componatur" (*Conc. Tur.*, ii. c. 3). It was to correct the same abuse, I believe, that Pope Pelagius I. wrote (about 558) a letter to Sapaudus, Bishop of Arles (Jaffé, 978): "Quis etiam illius non excessus, sed sceleris dicam, redditurus est rationem, quod apud vos idolum ex similagine, ve iniquitatibus nostris! patienter fieri audivimus, et ex ipso idolo fideli

In Ireland the Host was divided in seven different manners, according to the festivals;[1] at ordinary Masses into five particles, on the festivals of saints (confessors) and virgins into seven, on the festivals of martyrs into eight, on Sundays into nine, on the festivals of the Apostles into eleven, on the kalends of January and on Thursday in Holy Week into twelve, on the Sunday after Easter and on Ascension Day into thirteen, and on the festivals of the Nativity, Easter, and Pentecost, into sixty-five. They were arranged in the form of a cross, with certain additional complications when they were numerous. At the communion each of the parts of the cross, or of its additions, was distributed to a special group of persons, that is, priests, monks, etc.

During this ceremony the choir chanted an antiphon, which was called in the Ambrosian Liturgy the *Confractorium*. A chant of this character is implied in the Mozarabic Liturgy, but in the books now in use it is replaced by the recitation of the Creed. The following text occurs only in the Stowe Missal; and it is to be noted that it is not an antiphon, but a respond.

Fiat, Domine, misericordia tua super nos quemadmodum speravimus in te.
Cognoverunt Dominum, alleluia, in fractione panis, alleluia.
Panis quem frangimus corpus est domini nostri Jesu Christi, alleluia.
Calix quem benedicimus, alleluia, sanguis est domini nostri Jesu Christi, alleluia, in remissionem peccatorum nostrorum, alleluia.
Fiat, Domine misericordia tua super nos, alleluia, quemadmodum speravimus in te, alleluia.
Cognoverunt Dominum, alleluia.

populo, quasi unicuique pro merito, aures, oculos, manus ac diversa singulis membra distribui?"

[1] A treatise in Irish on the Mass (tenth century) in the Stowe Missal, *Whitley Stokes*, p 10 [Warren, *l.c*, p. 241.—Tr.] Cf above, p. 148, note 2.

When the chant was ended, the Lord's Prayer,[1] with, as in all the liturgies, a short preface at the beginning and an elaboration of the *Libera nos a malo* at the end, was then said I append the text of the latter from the *Missale Gothicum* for Christmas Day—

> Non nostro praesumentes, Pater sancte, merito, sed domini nostri Jesu Christi Filii tui obedientes imperio, audemus dicere:
> Pater noster, etc.
> Libera nos, omnipotens Deus, ab omni malo, ab omni periculo, et custodi nos in omni opere bono, perfecta veritas et vera libertas, Deus, qui regnas in saecula saeculorum.

The *Pater noster* was said, not only by the priest, but also by the congregation.[2] At present the participation of the congregation is confined, in the Mozarabic rite, to the reciting of *Amen* to each of the petitions in the *Pater noster*.

Then came the rite of the Commixtio. The celebrant dipped one or more of the consecrated particles into the chalice. In the Mozarabic rite of the present day it is the particle *regnum* which is used for this purpose. The celebrant holds it over the chalice and says thrice—

> Vicit leo de tribu Juda, radix David, alleluia.

To which is said the response—

> Qui sedes super Cherubim, radix David, alleluia.

---

[1] This is the last of the seven prayers enumerated by St Isidore (*op cit*) "Harum ultima est oratio qua Dominus noster discipulos suos orare instituit," etc In Spain it was customary to recite the Nicene Creed before the *Pater noster* This custom was instituted by a decree of the third Council of Toledo (589), c 2 (cf Isidore, *op cit*, c 16)

[2] Greg. Tur., *Vit S Martini*, ii 30. This is the Greek custom, cf. Greg M, *Ep*, ix. 12 (26).

He then lets the particle fall into the chalice, saying—

Sancta sanctis ! Et conjunctio corporis domini nostri Jesu Christi sit sumentibus et potantibus nobis ad veniam, et defunctis fidelibus praestetur ad requiem.

The order of the ceremonies, according to the Mozarabic rite, is attested by the fourth Council of Toledo, c. 17, which mentions, in the first instance, the Lord's Prayer, then the Commixtio (*conjunctionem panis et calicis*), then the Benediction, and finally the Communion.

In the Ambrosian rite the *Pater noster* is recited after the Fraction, but the Commixtio follows immediately after the latter, as in the Roman use from the time of Gregory. The *Sancta sanctis* has also disappeared.

15. *The Benediction.*

GERMAIN[1]: *Benedictionem vero populi sacerdotibus fundere Dominus per Moysen mandavit. . . . Propter servandum honorem pontificis sacri constituerunt canones ut longiorem benedictionem episcopus proferret, breviorem presbyter funderet, dicens*[2]: "Pax, fides et caritas et communicatio corporis et sanguinis Domini sit semper vobiscum."

The Benediction was the occasion of the introduction of a great number of formularies, varying with the festivals of the year, formularies which survived in France even after the adoption of the Roman Liturgy. They are still found, at the moment I write, in the ritual of the Church of Lyons. The deacon calls upon the faithful to bow their heads for the blessing of the bishop. The formulary which

---

[1] Cf Isidore, *op cit*, c 17
[2] *Dicit*, in the printed editions

he employed, as attested by St. Cæsarius of Arles,[1] is still used in the Mozarabic rite: *Humiliate vos benedictioni!* This is the counterpart of the Greek formulary : Τὰς κεφαλὰς ἡμῶν Τῷ Κυρίῳ κλίνωμεν! After the ordinary salutation,[2] the bishop pronounces a blessing in several sentences, to each of which the congregation reply, *Amen.* The following is the text of the *Missale Gothicum* :—

> Deus, qui adventum tuae majestatis per angelum Gabrihelem priusquam descenderes nuntiare jussisti,
> Qui dignanter intra humana viscera ingressus, ex alvo virginis hodie es mundo clarificatus,
> Tu, Domine, benedic hanc familiam tuam, quam hodierna solemnitas in adventu tuo fecit gaudere ;
> Da pacem populo tuo, quem pretiosa nativitate vivificas et passionis tolerantia a morte perpetua redemisti,
> Tribue eis de thesauro tuo indeficientis divitias bonitatis ; reple eos scientia, ut impollutis actibus et puro corde sequantur te ducem justitiae, quem suum cognoscunt factorem ;
> Et sicut in diebus illis advenientem te in mundo perfidia Herodis expavit et periit rex impius a facie regis magni, ita nunc praesenti tempore celebrata solemnitas peccatorum nostrorum vincla dissolvat ;
> Ut cum iterum ad judicandum veneris, nullus ex nobis ante tribunal tuum reus appareat ; sed discussa de pectoribus nostris caligine tenebrarum, placeamus conspectui tuo et perveniamus ad illam terram quam sancti tui in requiem possidebunt aeternam.

The following short formulary for the use of priests is found, almost as St. Germain gives it, in the Irish Stowe Missal and in the Ambrosian Liturgy. The Stowe Missal[3] has—

> Pax et caritas domini nostri Jesus Christi et communicatio sanctorum omnium sit semper nobiscum.

---

[1] "Rogo, fratres, quoties clamatum fuerit ut *vos benedictioni humiliare* debeatis, non vobis sit laboriosum capita inclinare, quia non homini, sed Deo humiliatis" (Aug serm , 285, No. 2).
[2] Mozarabic.
[3] Warren, *loc. cit.*, p 242.

The Ambrosian Missal gives—

Pax et communicatio domini nostri Jesu Christi sit semper vobiscum.

The Ambrosian rite places here the ceremony of the Kiss of Peace, in conformity with the Roman custom.

16. *The Communion.*

GERMAIN: *Trecanum vero quod psallitur signum est catholicae fidei de Trinitatis credulitate procedere. Sic enim prima in secunda, secunda in tertia et rursum tertia in secunda et secunda rotatur in prima. Ita Pater in Filio mysterium Trinitatis complectit: Pater in Filio, Filius in Spiritu sancto, Spiritus sanctus in Filio et Filius rursum in Patre.*

In Gaul the faithful, in order to communicate, entered the sanctuary and came up to the altar.[1] The same custom was not observed in Spain. There the priests and deacons communicated at the altar, the other clergy in the choir (before the altar), and the laity outside the choir.[2] The men received the Host into the bare hand, the women into the hand covered with a linen cloth, called the *dominical*, which they brought with them for the purpose.[3] During the communion a

---

[1] *Conc. Turon*, II 4: "Ad orandum et communicandum laicis et feminis, sicut mos est, pateant sancta sanctorum." Cf. Greg Tur, *H. Fr.*, ix. 3; x. 8· "Ad altarium"

[2] *Conc Tol*, iv c 17

[3] S Caesarius (serm. 252 *de Tempore*, Migne, *Pat Lat*, vol xxxix p. 2168). "Omnes viri, quando ad altare accessuri sunt, lavant manus suas, et omnes mulieres nitida exhibent linteamina ubi corpus Christi accipiant" Synod of Auxerre, about 578, c 36, 37, 42· "Non licet mulieri nuda manu eucharistiam accipere. Non licet mulieri manum suam ad pallam dominicam (the linen cloth on the altar) mittere. Ut unaquaeque mulier

short chant was sung, which St. Germain calls the *Trecanum*, and which seemed to him to be an expression of the doctrine of the Trinity. The following is the chant, according to the Mozarabic formulary :—

Gustate et videte quam suavis est Dominus. Alleluia! Alleluia! Alleluia!
Benedicam Dominum in omni tempore, semper laus ejus in ore meo. Alleluia! Alleluia! Alleluia!
Redimet Dominus animas servorum suorum, et non derelinquet omnes qui sperant in eum. Alleluia! Alleluia! Alleluia!
Gloria et honor Patri et Filio et Spiritui sancto in saecula saeculorum. Amen. Alleluia! Alleluia! Alleluia!

The two first verses are found in the chants for the Communio in the Stowe Missal and in the Bangor Antiphonary. The latter are much longer than that just given, but, like it, they are broken up by repeated alleluias.[1] It is remarkable that the three verses of the Mozarabic *Trecanum* should be singled out from that psalm (33) which in St. Cyril of Jerusalem, and in the liturgies of the Apostolic Constitutions and of St. James, is prescribed as the chant for the Communio.[2]

I think it worth while to give here, as a specimen of Gallican liturgical poetry, a hymn provided as a substitute for the psalm at the Communio.

quando communicat dominicalem suum habeat; quod si qua non habuerit, usque in alium diem dominicum non communicet"

[1] A chant with alleluia inserted at intervals, like this, is also met with in the Armenian, the Syriac, and St James's liturgies. The Ambrosian Liturgy has here a chant called *Transitorium*.

[2] The verse prescribed in the Mozarabic Missal before the Post Communio must have originally been attached to the *Gustate* It runs as follows: *Refecti Christi corpore et sanguine te laudamus, Domine.* Alleluia! Alleluia! Alleluia!

It is found in the Bangor Antiphonary.[1] The measure is in Iambic trimeter—

> Sancti venite, Christi corpus sumite,
> sanctum bibentes quo redempti sanguinem.
>
> Salvati Christi corpore et sanguine,
> a quo refecti laudes dicamus Deo.
>
> Hoc sacramento corporis et sanguinis
> omnes exuti ab inferni faucibus.
>
> Dator salutis Christus, Filius Dei,
> mundum salvavit per crucem et sanguinem.
>
> Pro universis immolatus Dominus
> ipse sacerdos existit et hostia.
>
> Lege praeceptum immolari hostias
> qua adumbrantur divina mysteria.
>
> Lucis indultor et salvator omnium
> praeclaram sanctis largitus est gratiam.
>
> Accedant omnes pura mente creduli,
> sumant aeternam salutis custodiam.
>
> Sanctorum custos rector quoque Dominus
> vitae perennis largitor credentibus.
>
> Caelestem panem dat esurientibus
> de fonte vivo praebet sitientibus.
>
> Alfa et Omega[2] ipse Christus Dominus
> venit, venturus judicare homines.

17. *The Thanksgiving.*

The communion being ended, the bishop calls upon the congregation to thank God, he himself reciting the

---

[1] Migne, *Pat Lat*, vol lxxii p 587; Warren, *op. cit*, p. 187 The title is *Ymnum quando commonicarent sacerdotes* (See Version in Hymns Ancient and Modern, 313)

[2] ω in the printed edition. The metre requires something more than the sound *o*. I fancy there is something omitted between *Alfa* and *et*.

prayer of thanksgiving. I append the two formularies taken from the *Missale Gothicum* for Christmas Day—

POST COMMUNIONEM.

Cibo caelesti saginati et poculo aeterni calicis recreati, Fratres karissimi, Domino Deo nostro laudes et gratias indesinenter agamus, petentes ut qui sacrosanctum corpus domini nostri Jesu Christi spiritaliter sumpsimus, exuti a carnalibus vitiis, spiritales effici mereamur, per dominum nostrum Jesum Christum Filium suum.

COLLECTIO SEQUITUR.

Sit nobis, Domine, quaesumus, medicina mentis et corporis quod de sancti altaris tui benedictione percepimus, ut nullis adversitatibus opprimamur qui tanti remedii participatione munimur. Per dominum nostrum Jesum Christum Filium tuum.

The invitatory formulary has disappeared from the Ambrosian and Mozarabic Liturgies. In the former the prayer is both preceded and followed by the ordinary salutation; in the latter it is only followed by this.

According to the Mozarabic rite, the formulary of dismissal is as follows:—

Solemnia completa sunt in nomine domini nostri Jesu Christi. Votum nostrum sit acceptum cum pace.—R⁊. Deo gratias!

The Ambrosian Liturgy prescribes here a triple *Kyrie eleison*, and then the benediction, *Benedicat et exaudiat nos Deus*—R⁊. *Amen.* Then follows—

Procedamus in pace.—R⁊. In nomine Christi.
Benedicamus Domino.—R⁊. Deo gratias!

The Stowe Missal furnishes the most simple text: *Missa acta est.—In pace.*

CHAPTER VIII.

THE CHRISTIAN FESTIVALS.

§ 1.—USUAL OBSERVANCES OF THE WEEK.

THE Church inherited from the Jews the custom of keeping the week holy. In addition to the Sabbath, the religious observance of which was commanded by the Law, the pious Jews kept two other days in the week, namely, Monday and Thursday. The Sabbath was observed by a cessation from work and by meetings for worship; the Monday and Thursday were days of fasting. Traces of this practice are found in the Gospel. The words of the Pharisee are familiar to us[1]: "I fast twice on the Sabbath," that is, twice in the week.

The Church substituted the Sunday for the Sabbath, but not without certain modifications in its observance with regard to the strictness of the prescribed rest. This substitution had already taken place in apostolic times.[2] In very early times also we find that the Wednesday and Friday fasts had superseded those of the Jews. The *Doctrine of the Apostles* expressly mentions them,[3] and the *Pastor* of Hermas[4] also speaks of fasts under the

---

[1] *St. Luke* xviii. 12.
[2] 1 *Cor.* xvi. 2; *Acts* xx. 7; *Rev.* i. 10.
[3] viii. 1; cf. Epiphan¡us, *Haer.*, xvi. 1.
[4] *Simil.*, v. 1

name of *Stations*, without indicating the days; this omission is, however, supplied by Clement of Alexandria,[1] Tertullian,[2] and a number of later writers. The fasts of the Stations were not prolonged fasts, as they did not extend beyond the ninth hour, that is, until the middle of the afternoon.

From the point of view of worship in its strict sense, the services on these holy days were not all alike. Sunday was essentially the day for liturgical worship in common. The liturgical service took place in the early hours of the morning; but this service was preceded by another, held before daybreak, which consisted of lections, homilies, the singing of chants, and the recital of prayers This nocturnal meeting, or *vigil*, is mentioned at an early date, namely, in the letter in which Pliny speaks of the customs of the Christians.[3] This service was combined later on with the office of Matins, which gradually superseded it. The two services were still distinct, although mentioned together, in the description of the ritual at Jerusalem given in the *Peregrinatio Etheriae (Silviae)*. At Rome the Vigil was retained for certain solemn seasons, such as Easter, Whitsuntide, the Sundays of the Ember Days. The offices for Easter Eve and Whitsun Eve, in that part which precedes the benediction of the baptismal water, still preserves the type of the ancient vigils as they were celebrated every Sunday in the first centuries of Christianity.[4]

---

[1] *Strom*, vi 75.

[2] *De Jejun.*, 14.

[3] *Rel.*, 96: "Adfirmabant . . . quod essent soliti stato die ante lucem convenire, carmenque Christo quasi deo dicere secum invicem . . . ; quibus peractis morem sibi discedendi fuisse, rursusque coeundi ad capiendum cibum, promiscuum tamen et innoxium."

[4] The same may be remarked of the sequence of lections, responses, and prayers with which the Mass for Saturday in the Ember Days begins. This Mass is, in reality, the early Mass of the following day, Sunday.

The two stational days were also marked by meetings for worship. But these were held in different manners in different localities. In some places the liturgy properly so called was used, that is, the Eucharist was celebrated. This was the custom in Africa in the time of Tertullian,[1] and at Jerusalem towards the end of the fourth century. In the Church of Alexandria, on the other hand, the Station did not include the liturgy. Socrates tells us that on these days "the Scriptures were read and were interpreted by the doctors; in short, all was done as in the Synaxes, except the celebration of the Mysteries."[2] I believe that on this point, as on many others, the use at Rome was similar to that at Alexandria. It is certain, at least, that about the beginning of the fifth century, the celebration of the Mysteries (*Sacramenta*) did not take place at Rome on Fridays. There is no record as to what took place on Wednesdays.[3]

Saturday, of which the observance had at first fallen into desuetude, was later on assigned a special place. In the East, during the fourth century, it was a day of Synaxes,[4]

It will be seen that Saturday in the Ember Days has no special Mass assigned to it

[1] *De Oratione*, 14.

[2] Socrates, *H E*, v 22 On the other hand, a Vigil was observed there, and it was during a Friday Vigil that St. Athanasius was attacked in the Church of Theonas, the night of Feb 8th-9th, 356.

[3] Letter of Innocent to Decentius, c 4. "Non dubium est in tantum eos (the apostles) jejunasse biduo memorato ut traditio Ecclesiae habeat isto biduo sacramenta penitus non celebrari; *quae forma utique per singulas tenenda est hebdomadas*, propter id quod commemoratio diei illius semper est celebranda" This only applies to public, and not to private Masses.

[4] *Conc Laodic*, c. 16. *Constit Ap*, ii. 59; v. 20; vii. 27; viii. 33; Epiphanius, *Exp fid*, 24. St. Epiphanius does not seem to consider these Synaxes as a universal custom: "ἔν τισι δὲ τόποις καὶ ἐν τοῖς σάββασι συνάξεις ἐπιτελοῦσιν." The *Pilgrimage of Etheria* (*Silvia*) mentions the liturgical Synaxes of Lent, but does not speak of those at other times of the year The Council of Laodicea (*loc cit*.) decrees that the reading of the Gospel shall be combined with that of other Scriptures. It is impossible to

and even of liturgical Synaxes. At Alexandria, however, the Synaxes were not liturgical. This omission of the liturgy was peculiar to the city of Alexandria itself, for in the interior of Egypt the liturgy was said in the evening, and was preceded by an agape.[1] It might be imagined that this observance of Saturday was a primitive attempt to reconcile the Jewish and Christian uses. But as these Saturday services are not mentioned by any author before the fourth century, and as, moreover, they were unknown at Rome, it is more natural to suppose that they were a later institution. Besides this, the Eastern Church, while adopting the observance of Saturday, was extremely careful to eliminate from it the chief characteristic of the Jewish Sabbath, namely, the obligation to observe it as a day of rest [2]

In the West, and particularly at Rome, Saturday became a day of fasting. As early as the time of Tertullian, there were Churches in which the Friday fast was occasionally prolonged to the Saturday. This was called *continuare jejunium*,[3] an expression which was superseded later on by the term *superponere jejunium*, which is merely an unsatisfactory attempt to translate into Latin the Greek word ὑπερτίθεσθαι (to protract). These prolonged fasts were very common at the end of the third century. Reference is made to them in one of the writings of Victorinus,[4] Bishop of Pettau. The Council of Elvira enjoins the observance of one such fast every month, except in July and August, and at the same time abolishes the weekly "superposition," which had up till then been observed

say whether the use which it aimed at reforming included the liturgy after these lections or not. St Basil (*Ep* 289) speaks of liturgical Synaxes

[1] Socrates, *op cit.*
[2] *Conc. Laod*, cf. 29; c pseudo-Ignatius, *Ep ad Magnes*, 9.
[3] *De Jejun*, 14.
[4] *De Fabrica Mundi* (Migne, *Pat. Lat*, vol v pp. 304, 306).

every Saturday.¹ The origin of the Roman Saturday fast is usually referred to this weekly prolongation of the Friday. The fast on Friday must in early times have trenched on the Saturday, and when the practice of prolonging it was found to be too severe, it was probably replaced by another fast or semi-fast, distinct from that of the Friday.²

However this may be, it is certain that at Rome there was no celebration of the Eucharist on Saturdays. Sozomen, who on this point confirms the statement made by Pope Innocent,³ adds that in this matter the Alexandrians were in agreement with the Church of Rome.

We may sum up by saying that in addition to the two meetings on Sunday, one for the Vigil, and the other for the Mass, services were everywhere held on Wednesdays and Fridays, but these services did not in all places include the celebration of the Eucharist. At Rome and Alexandria these were non-liturgical, but in all parts of the East, Alexandria excepted, the liturgy was used. As to the Synaxis of Saturday, it was peculiar to the East, and was a later institution than those of the Wednesday and Friday.

§ 2.—THE EMBER DAYS.

The arrangement of the services in the Ember weeks still preserves some features of the early religious weekly observances as practised by the Church at Rome. It still contains three fast days, the Wednesday, Friday, and

---

[1] C. 23: "Jejunii superpositiones per singulos menses placuit celebrari, exceptis diebus duorum mensium julii et augusti, propter quorundem infirmitatem" C. 26: "Errorem placuit corrigi ut omni sabbati die superpositiones celebremus"

[2] Canon 26 of the Council of Elvira was at an early date given a title which does not correspond with its contents, but with the modification that I have here pointed out. *Ut omni sabbato jejunetur.*

[3] *Hist Eccl*, vii 19

Saturday. The ancient formularies of indiction, however, which are given in the homilies of St. Leo, mention the fast of the Wednesdays and Fridays only. That of the Saturday being merely a "superposition," or prolongation of that of the Friday, is not taken into account.[1] The distinguishing feature of the Saturday was the Solemn Vigil, which on this day was always observed at St. Peter's: *Quarta igitur et sexta feria jejunemus; sabbato autem ad beatum Petrum apostolum pariter vigilemus.* The Vigil was always followed by the Mass in the early hours of the Sunday.

The Ember-day fasts, which are met with in those countries only which followed the Roman use, and which even in Rome did not take their rise till the fifth century, appear to me to be none other than the weekly fast, as observed at the beginning, but made specially severe, as well by the retention of the Wednesday, which had disappeared early from the weekly Roman use, as by the substitution of a real fast[2] for the semi-fast of the ordinary Stations. The choice of the weeks in which the fast was thus increased in rigour was determined by the commencement of the four seasons of the year. It is probable that from the first institution of the Ember Days the Synaxes of the Wednesdays and Fridays, or at all events those of the Wednesdays, were liturgical. This appears to me to be suggested by the archaic arrangement of the Mass for the Wednesday in Ember Week, in which the prophetic lection was still preserved, although it had fallen into disuse in most Masses in the course of the fifth century.

---

[1] The author of the *Liber Pontificalis* (vol. i p. 141), on the contrary, mentions this one only. The reason is that he is dealing with it as a matter of practice, and not like St Leo, as a matter of tradition. The Saturday fast was the most severe, as no food could have been eaten since the Thursday night.

[2] There was a much greater difference in the strictness with which the fast was observed than in the methods of fixing the fasting days themselves.

§ 3 — HOLY WEEK.

Similar observations may be made on the subject of Holy Week. The most ancient of its peculiar features is the festival of Maundy Thursday, devoted to the solemn commemoration of the institution of the Eucharist, to which was added, at all events at Rome, the consecration of holy oils and the reconciliation of penitents, ceremonies which invest it with the character of an immediate preparation for the Christian Easter. With the exception of the Thursday, there are no ancient Stations in Holy Week except those of the Wednesday and Friday. Saturday never had, and even now has not, any Station assigned it, properly speaking, since the present service for that day is merely the Easter Vigil anticipated. The liturgical Stations for Monday and Tuesday are certainly later than the time of St. Leo. It was, in fact, the custom of this Pope to give a yearly exposition on the Passion of our Lord, and as it was impossible for him to do so in one sermon, he began on the Sunday before Easter, and continued his exposition at the Station on Wednesday. Had there been any meetings between the Sunday and the Wednesday, St. Leo would not have waited till the latter day to resume his discourse. In the present service for Good Friday, if we except the ceremonies connected with the Adoration of the Cross, which are certainly not an essential part of it, and also the Mass of the Presanctified, we have the exact order of the ancient Synaxes without a liturgy, namely, lections alternating with chants, and followed by prayers for all the necessities of the Church. The lections are still three in number, separated by two *psalmi responsorii* in the form of the gradual and the tract.

I am inclined to believe that the ancient service for Wednesday in Holy Week was of exactly the same type, and that the present liturgical Station is as much an innovation as those of Monday and Tuesday in the same week. In the eighth century there were two services on the Wednesday; one in the morning, when the same prayers for the necessities of the Church as those now reserved for Good Friday were recited, and another in the evening at the hour of vespers, for the liturgy properly so called. The morning service, restricted to the recital of solemn prayers, appears to me to be the residuum or vestige of the ancient Station without the liturgy, while the lections and chants which formed part of it have been transferred to the new liturgical Station in the evening.

We see, therefore, that before the institution of the Stations in Lent, which cannot be regarded as primitive, Divine Service in Holy Week at Rome was identical with that in other weeks, always excepting the festival of Maundy Thursday, and was composed of Synaxes without the liturgy on Wednesday and Friday, and of a Solemn Vigil in the night between Saturday and Sunday.

§ 4.—Movable Feasts.

In the matter of festivals, as in many other things, the Church is, up to a certain point, indebted to the Synagogue. The ecclesiastical year is nothing but the combination of two calendars, the one Jewish, the other Christian. The movable feasts correspond to the Jewish, the fixed to the Christian calendar. We must not, however, press this analogy too strongly. The Christians did not take over all the Jewish festivals, and to those which they did retain they attached, at an early date, a significance in harmony with their own belief. Thus, for instance, the feasts of the seventh month, those of the Day of Atonement and of Tabernacles, and the feast of Purim at the end of the year, were completely disregarded. Only those of Easter and

Pentecost were retained. In adopting, moreover, these ancient festivals, the Church intended to employ them to commemorate respectively Christ and the Holy Spirit, the two terminating points of the Divine evolution which were characteristic of the new belief. The festival of Easter is devoted to the commemoration of the work of Christ in this world, accomplished in His Passion, sealed by His Resurrection, while the Feast of Pentecost is that of the first manifestation of the Holy Spirit in the disciples of Jesus Christ, and consequently that of the foundation of the Church. Historically speaking, the events commemorated had coincided in time with the Jewish feasts of the first and third months, and it was therefore quite natural to connect them with those festivals.

1. *The Computation of Easter.*

The festivals of the Jews were determined by a lunar calendar, the twelve months of which fell a little short of the length of the solar year. From time to time, therefore, the intercalation of a supplementary month was arranged, but rather in accordance with the state of the seasons at the end of the twelfth month than from the consideration of well-established astronomical laws. Easter fell on the full moon of the first month, otherwise called the 14th of Nisan. But when did this first month, Nisan, begin? Was it at the end of the twelfth or at the end of a thirteenth supplementary month? The Jews came to an agreement on this question, and the Christians at the outset accepted their solution. There was, however, much discussion on the subject even within the Church itself; because, in the first place, the Christians were divided on the question as to how far the new Easter should coincide as a ceremony and in date with the older feast, and in the second place, because they could not agree as to the mode of fixing the month and the week in which the festival should be kept. The most noteworthy of these controversies with regard to the keeping of Easter may be thus briefly enumerated:—

1. The contention which arose at Laodicea in the province of Asia, about 165, as to whether certain points of Jewish ritual in the celebration of the Christian Festival should be retained or abandoned.[1]

2. The conflict between the Churches of the province of Asia as a whole and those of other parts of the Empire with regard to the day of the week on which the paschal fast should terminate. The Asiat Christians made it end on the 14th of Nisan, the others on the Sunday following. This divergence of view continued till nearly the close of the second century, when it degenerated into an open strife, which ended in the defeat of the ancient Asiat custom. The Churches of the province of Asia adopted the general custom of keeping Easter on the Sunday. Those who still clung to the local custom, quartodecimans, organised themselves into a separate sect, which maintained an existence down to the fifth century.

3. The conflict occasioned by the different methods of computation at Antioch and Alexandria, was settled by the Council of Nicæa. At Antioch the Resurrection of Christ was commemorated on the Sunday following the Jewish Easter, without questioning whether the Jews had rightly or wrongly fixed their Easter and first month. At Alexandria, on the other hand, calculations were specially made for finding Easter, and it was considered imperative that it should always fall after the vernal equinox. The Alexandrians having won their cause at the Council of Nicæa, the old custom of Antioch was followed merely by small

---

[1] Cf. my *Early History of the Christian Church*, vol. i p 209.

sects (Audiani, Protopaschites), and all the Churches of the East conformed to the paschal computation as proposed by the Bishop of Alexandria.[1]

4. Numberless difficulties again cropped up in the fourth and fifth centuries, owing to the differences between the Alexandrian and Roman computations. These difficulties arose from certain differences in calculation and custom. The determination of the age of the moon, as it was calculated at Rome, was founded on imperfect lunar cycles. It was often at variance with that of Alexandria, which was based on the cycle of nineteen years. On the other hand, the Romans did not admit that Easter Sunday could fall, in the lunar month, before the 16th of that month, whereas at Alexandria Easter might be kept on the 15th. Finally, a tradition was supposed to exist at Rome according to which Easter could not be observed after the 21st of April. This limitation was unknown at Alexandria, where it might be held up to the 25th. The conflicts arising from these differences were, for the most part, amicably settled between the Pope and the Greek Church, and when Rome adopted the Alexandrian computation, under the form given to it by Dionysius Exiguus[2] (525), they at length finally disappeared.

5. Mention must also be made of the divergence between the paschal tables of Victorius of Aquitaine and Dionysius Exiguus. The table of the former, drawn up at Rome in 457, was not long in use there, if indeed it ever was employed, but it was adopted by the Churches of Frankish Gaul, and was used by them till the Carlovingian period. In certain cases it offered two solutions by giving two paschal dates, that of the Alexandrians and that arrived at

---

[1] See my memoir *La Question de la Pâque au Concile de Nicée*, in the *Revue des Questions Historiques* for July, 1880.

[2] See De Rossi, *Inscr. Christ*, vol. 1 pp lxxxii.-xcvii.; Br Krusch, *Der 84jahrige Ostercyclus und seine Quellen*, Leipzig, 1880; *Bulletin Critique*, vol 1 p. 143.

THE CHRISTIAN FESTIVALS. 239

by the application of the old Roman rules. This dual result was necessarily the cause of much uncertainty.[1]

6. Finally, we have the quarrel with regard to the Celtic computation in the British Isles. The British Church, and consequently the Irish Church, had preserved an old method of keeping Easter, in use at Rome about the beginning of the fourth century, according to which Easter Sunday could occur from the 14th to the 20th of Nisan [2] The Roman computation having been subjected to several modifications since the time when the British adopted it, the Roman missionaries of the seventh century found themselves, consequently, at variance with the Insular Church in their method of calculating Easter. Hence the quarrels which for some time played so important a part in the history of the country. Both sides appealed to alleged apostolic traditions, and the Celtic clergy did not scruple to quote apocryphal books composed expressly to defend their national custom.

2. *Eastertide.*

The Christian Easter was preceded by a fast and followed by seven weeks of rejoicing Thus defined, Lent and Eastertide may claim attestation of their observance from extreme antiquity. For the fast before the festival, it will suffice to cite in a general way the documents relating to the paschal controversy at the end of the second century. In these documents, whatever may have been their *provenance,* the festival of Easter is regarded primarily as

---

[1] For this and the following controversy, see the memoir by Herr Bruno Krusch, *Die Einfuhrung des Griechischen Paschalritus im Abendlande,* in the *Neues Archiv,* vol ix. p 99

[2] This rule differs from that subsequently (and even previously) in use at Rome, in so far that the limits assigned by the former for the variation of the date of Good Friday are in the other applied to the variation of the date of Easter Sunday.

the end of a fast. It could not then have been of recent institution, for besides the evidence of its antiquity in the unanimity of so many traditions, otherwise divergent, we have the testimony of Irenæus, in dealing with fasting at Rome, as to the practice of the Popes Telesphorus and Xystus, who were contemporaries of the Emperor Adrian. For the observance of Pentecost, understood as associated with a period of fifty days, we have the attestation of St. Irenæus,[1] of Tertullian,[2] and of Origen,[3] who in their agreement on this point serve to establish the great antiquity of the custom.

The festival of Pentecost, the end of this time of rejoicing, is implied rather than explicitly mentioned in early Christian writings.[4] It is possible that there was not at first much outward ceremony in its observance. The Council of Elvira (*circ.* 300) considered it necessary to bring to remembrance the obligation of observing it.[5] The writers and councils of the second half of the fourth century speak of it as a festival already of long standing.

This last observation applies also to the festival of the Ascension, but it is impossible to find a trace of it before the middle of the fourth century [6]

---

[1] In a book (now lost) on the Passover, but cited by the pseudo-Justin, *Quaest. ad Orthodoxos.*

[2] *De Idol*, 14; *De Baptismo*, 19; *De Corona*, 3.

[3] *Adv. Celsum*, viii. 22

[4] Origen appears, however (*op cit*), to distinguish between the two meanings of Pentecost; he evidently connected it with the commemoration of the descent of the Holy Spirit.

[5] Can. 43: "Pravam institutionem emendari placuit, juxta auctoritatem Scripturarum, ut cuncti diem Pentecostes celebremus; ne, si quis non fecerit, quasi novam haeresem induxisse notetur"

[6] In Cappadocia this festival was entitled Ἐπισωζομένη (*Greg. Nyss.*, Migne, *Pat. Gr*, vol. xlvi. p. 690). The same name was given at Antioch to the Sunday before or after it (Chrys, vol. ii. p 188). This designation has not yet been satisfactorily explained. ["Any day specially retained for solemn celebration over and above the great festivals." "A holiday secured in addition." *Dict. Chr. Ant.*, i. 145 --Tr.]

3. *Lent.*

As for Lent, it has been the subject of many vicissitudes as well in the matter of its duration as in the rigour with which it was observed. It is certain that the fast before Easter, in the time of Irenæus, was for a very short period; some fasted only for a day, others for two, and others again for a number of days. Some, moreover, ate nothing for forty hours. These periods must be considered, 1 think, as continuous and uninterrupted fasts.[1] Tertullian was unacquainted with any solemn fast, prescribed by the Catholic Church, except that of the day of the *Pascha*, a term which he uses in a special sense here for Good Friday. He declares that the time of fasting included only the days *quibus ablatus est sponsus*, that is to say, from Good Friday to Easter Sunday morning[2] In Alexandria it was customary about the middle of the third century to fast the whole week before Easter Day, some continuously, and others at intervals. The letter of St. Dionysius of Alexandria to Basilides,[3] in which this question crops up, is the most ancient authority which we possess for the observance of Holy Week, or the week of Xerophagy. Before that time the Montanists observed a fast of two weeks' duration instead of one, and this custom was continued amongst them until the fifth century, when their boasted fast of longer duration than that of others was surpassed.[4]

---

[1] Οἱ μὲν γὰρ οἴονται μίαν ἡμέραν δεῖν αὐτοὺς νηστεύειν, οἱ δὲ δύο, οἱ δὲ καὶ πλείονας · οἱ δὲ τεσσαράκοντα ὥρας ἡμερινάς τε καὶ νυκτερινὰς συμμετροῦσι τὴν ἡμέραν αὐτῶν Eusebius, *Hist Eccl* , v 24. There is no need to take into consideration here the blunder of Rufinus, who preoccupied by the discipline prevailing in his own time, misconstrued the end of this text.

[2] *De Jejunio*, 2, 13, 14, *De Oratione*, 18

[3] Migne, *Pat Gr* , vol. x. p 1277.

[4] Tertullian, *De Jejuniis*, 15, cf. Eusebius, *H E*, v 18; Sozomen, *H E.*, vii. 19.

Of the *Quadragesima* (Τεσσαρακοστή, Lent) no traces are found before the fourth century.[1] The fifth canon of the Council of Nicæa (325) contains the earliest mention of it. From this time forward it is frequently referred to, but at first chiefly as a time of preparation for baptism, or for the absolution of penitents, or as a season of retreat and recollection for the faithful living in the world. Among the duties of these sacred weeks fasting naturally occupied an important place, but the practice varied in different countries. In the "festal letters" of St. Athanasius[2] we are able to follow the progress of the observance of Lent in Egypt. St. Athanasius speaks, in the beginning, of the *time* of Lent and of the *week* of

---

[1] Origen's homily on Luke x, which is sometimes cited as an earlier witness, exists only in the revised Latin text of Rufinus, and cannot therefore be regarded as evidence of a custom contemporary with the great doctor of Alexandria. What it says of the fast of forty days is manifestly in contradiction with the sequence of ideas in this fragment

[2] See especially those of the years 329, 330, 340, 341, 347. In the first (329) it is merely dealt with as a preparation for the festival of Easter, and that, too, in a general way without any mention of the Quadragesima · the fast is indicated in the index as commencing on the Monday in Holy Week In 330 the Quadragesimal period is mentioned as lasting for six weeks, but the fast, strictly speaking, is always that of Holy Week. It was well understood that fasting was among the number of necessary exercises preparatory to the observance of Easter, it was not, however, prescribed as of strict obligation, or as a custom accepted everywhere The Egyptians maintained, for the most part, only the fast of Holy Week While St Athanasius was at Rome in 340 and the following years, he was the subject of reproach in respect of this practice He complains of this in a note appended to his festal letter of 341. It was dated at Rome, and addressed to his friend Serapion, Bishop of Thmuis, who was charged with the supervision of the Churches of Egypt in his absence He exhorts him in impressive terms to enjoin upon the Egyptians the observance of the fast, saying that they make themselves the laughing-stock of the world. From this time forward the index mentions regularly the fast of the Forty Days and of Holy Week Previously St Athanasius spoke of them as the time of Lent and the week of the fast In the festal letter of 347 it is formally declared that he "who shall neglect the observance of Lent shall not celebrate Easter," or, in other words, shall be excommunicated for a time.

the fast, but later on uses the terms "the *fast* of Lent and the Holy Week of Easter." At Rome it was the custom to observe the fast for only the last three weeks before Easter.[1]

Various endeavours were made in various countries to combine the Quadragesima with the Holy Week. At Antioch and in the Churches following this great centre, the two periods were more distinctly defined than elsewhere. In one of his homilies[2] St. Chrysostom expresses himself somewhat as follows: "We have at length come to the end of Quadragesima, and we are now about to enter on the great week." In the *Apostolic Constitutions* also[3] it is formally declared that the fast of Lent is finished when that of the great paschal week is begun. At Rome, on the other hand, and at Alexandria, and even at Jerusalem,[4] Holy Week was included in the Quadragesima in such a manner that the whole fast lasted only six weeks, but at Constantinople and in the East properly so called, that is, the countries following the ancient custom of Antioch, the fast was observed for seven weeks. The Sundays only were excepted at Rome, but at Constantinople both the Sundays and Saturdays, with the exception of Saturday in Holy Week, were exempt

---

[1] Socrates, *H E*, v. 22 This passage, however, inspires me with some distrust, for it says that in these three weeks the Sundays and Saturdays were excepted The exception of the Saturdays is far from being conformable to Roman usage I am inclined to believe that the three weeks of fasting, following the primitive custom of Rome, were not continuous, but broken by intervals, that is, the fast was observed on the first, the fourth, and the sixth week. The first is now assigned to the spring Ember Days, the fourth, called formerly *mediana*, has preserved certain liturgical peculiarities, and the sixth is Holy Week. These three weeks are weeks for ordination

[2] *Hom*, xxx *in Gen*, 1.

[3] Bk V 13

[4] As to Jerusalem, there were fluctuations, for the *Peregrinatio* of Etheria (Silvia) speaks of a Lent of eight weeks' duration (cf *infra*, pp 499, 554).

from the observance of fasting. The fast in both places, therefore, lasted in reality only thirty-six days. There were, moreover, Churches in which, up to the fifth century, Lent consisted of only three weeks of fasting. These, whether broken up by intervals or not, always occurred in the sacred period of six or seven weeks.[1] About the middle of the fifth century the greater number of divergences had disappeared; the two usages of Rome-Alexandria and Antioch-Constantinople had absorbed all others into their respective domains, and taken definite shapes

Certain supplemental days came, however, to be added. The thirty-six days of actual fasting seemed at first to form a perfect number, that of the tenth of the whole year.[2] The inconsistency of this period with the name of Quadragesima, however, came to be noted. The author at Rome of the *Liber Pontificalis* sought to enforce, even in his time, the necessity of a seventh week, which would, according to the Roman usage, have increased the number of fasting-days to forty-two. In the seventh century[3] four days were added, by what Pope we cannot say, and from that time forward these have been universally accepted throughout the West. It was about this time also that the stational Masses for the three Sundays *in Septuagesima, in Sexagesima,* and *in Quinquagesima,* were

---

[1] Socrates, *H E*, v 22; Sozomen, *H E*, vii. 19 Socrates cannot explain how, while some fast for thirty-six days, and others for fifteen, everybody should speak of Quadragesima. He did not know that the period of forty days had been at first introduced for another purpose than that of fasting, and that it was only by a sort of continuous expansion that the fast succeeded in extending itself over the whole Quadragesima.

[2] Cassian, *Coll*, xxi 30.

[3] St Gregory in his time knows of only the thirty-six days (*Hom* 16 *in Evang*) The Gelasian Sacramentary drawn up at the beginning of the eighth century has already the stational Masses for the supplementary days

instituted, and the cycle of paschal solemnities thus extended to the ninth week before Easter. At Constantinople also three Sundays were added, and associated with the festival of Easter in the same way as the seven Sundays in Lent properly so called.[1] The first two are designated by the names of the Gospels read at Mass on these days, that is, the Sunday of the Pharisee and the Publican (κυριακὴ τοῦ Τελώνου καὶ τοῦ Φαρισαίου), and the Sunday of the Prodigal Son (τοῦ 'Ασώτου). The third is the Sunday of the Carnival ('Απόκρεω).[2]

These innovations did not extend to the countries following the Gallican rite. The latter continued to observe the six weeks prescribed by the ancient Roman custom,[3] but I believe that this ancient custom itself had been preceded by a Lent of seven weeks' duration, the Saturdays being exempt, that is to say, a Lent similar to that observed at Constantinople. At Milan, in the time of St. Ambrose, the Saturdays were not kept as fasting days.[4] The Council of Agde (506)[5] and the fourth Council of Orleans (541),[6] which were posterior

[1] These ten weeks comprise that which is called in the office books the Τριῴδιον, the paschal season, including the octave of Pentecost, forms the Πεντηκοστάριον; the remaining weeks of the year constitute the 'Οκτώηχος.

[2] From this Sunday forward no meat is eaten, although Lent has not yet been reached The following Sunday is called, for a similar reason, the Cheese Sunday (τῆς Τυροφάγου), because from this day forward the Lenten fast excludes milk-products

[3] This is still the custom in the Church of Milan. Lent begins at Milan not on Ash Wednesday, but on the Sunday following.

[4] *De Elia et Jejunio*, 10. "Quadragesima, totis praeter sabbatum et dominicam jejunamus diebus"

[5] C 12· "Placuit etiam ut omnes ecclesiae, exceptis diebus dominicis, in quadragesima, etiam die sabbati, sacerdotali ordinatione et districtionis comminatione jejunent."

[6] C 2: "Hoc etiam decernimus observandum ut quadragesima ab omnibus ecclesiis aequaliter teneatur; neque quinquagesimam aut sexagesimam ante Pascha quilibet sacerdos praesumat indicere. Sed neque

to the introduction of the Roman usage, were obliged to insist upon the observance of fasting on the Saturdays in Lent. The last-named council also condemns the prolonging of Lent by the Quinquagesima or Sexagesima. These decrees imply that the Eastern custom was still maintaining its ground on some points.

There were some peculiarities in Divine Service during Lent. In the East, wherever it was customary to celebrate the Eucharist at the Synaxes of Wednesday and Friday, this usage was omitted.[1] As a compensation the ordinary Synaxes became more numerous. St. Chrysostom preached at Antioch every day in Lent. In the West, on the other hand, the liturgical Synaxes became multiplied, but by slow degrees.

The Mozarabic Missal contains Masses for the Wednesdays and Fridays in Lent, and the Gelasian Sacramentary has them for every day in the week, Thursdays excepted.[2] It is difficult to trace this institution to its origin. Several of the Roman Churches noted as places for Stations in the Sacramentary of Adrian had been founded in the course of the seventh century, but it is possible that the Stations may have been assigned in the outset to other Churches. However this may be, there is no evidence earlier than the seventh century or thereabout for the Roman Stations for Lent. What I have already said[3] in regard to those

per sabbata absque infirmitate quisquam solvat quadragesimae jejunium, nisi tantum die dominico prandeat, quod sic fieri specialiter patrum statuta sanxerunt Si quis hanc regulam irruperit, tanquam transgressor disciplinae a sacerdotibus censeatur"

[1] See for Asia Minor, the Council of Laodicea, c. 49: "Ὅτι οὐ δεῖ ἐν τῇ τεσσαρακοστῇ ἄρτον προσφέρειν, εἰ μὴ ἐν σαββάτῳ καὶ κυριακῇ μόνον;" and for Jerusalem, *Peregrin Etheriae* (Silv), cf *infra*, pp 501, 556

[2] The Mass for the Thursday was added by Gregory II. (715-731). See *Lib Pontif*, vol 1 p 402; cf p 412, note 19

[3] P 234

for the Monday and Tuesday of Holy Week would lead us to believe that they were instituted after the time of St. Leo.

4. *Holy Week.*

Holy Week, at the end of Lent, begins on a Sunday, which, both in the Greek and Latin Churches, is called Palm Sunday, or the Sunday of branches. The Mass on this day is preceded by a procession in which each one carries a branch, previously blessed, in remembrance of the triumphal entry of Jesus, six days before his death, into Jerusalem. This ceremony, like many others of the same kind, was at first peculiar to Jerusalem. It is described in the *Peregrinatio* of Etheria (Silvia).[1] Cyril of Scythopolis, a writer of the sixth century, also makes mention of it.[2] It was introduced into the West at a relatively late date, that is, about the eighth or ninth century. The ancient Latin liturgical books make no mention of it whatever. Amalarius speaks of it, but in terms showing that the custom of observing it was not universal.[3] St. Isidore, however, without explicitly mentioning the procession, speaks of the *dies Palmarum*,[4] and seems to refer to the custom of carrying palm branches to church and of crying *Hosanna*.

Maundy Thursday, which, in the cycle of movable feasts, commemorates the anniversary of the institution of the Eucharist, could not fail to be observed liturgically. In Africa the Eucharist was celebrated—as a thing unusual—after the evening meal, with the view of establishing a closer

---

[1] See *infra*, pp 505, 559.
[2] *Vita S Euthymii*, c 11, 103 (*Acta SS*, vol ii, 20th January)
[3] *De Off*, i 10 "In memoriam illius rei nos per ecclesias nostras solemus portare ramos et clamare Hosanna"
[4] *De Off*, i. 28.

conformity with the circumstances of its institution at the Last Supper[1]

On Good Friday, commemorating the Passion and death of the Saviour, there was no liturgical celebration of the Eucharist anywhere. I have previously stated that the service of this day, as it is found in the Roman use, has preserved for us in its first part an exact type of the ancient meetings for worship without liturgy. It became complicated about the seventh or eighth century, by the introduction of two ceremonies, the Adoration of the Cross and the Mass of the Presanctified The former of these came from Jerusalem, where we have evidence of it as early as the fourth century. The wood of the cross was solemnly presented to the faithful in the Holy City on that day, in order that they might approach and kiss it.[2]

The ancient Latin liturgical books, almost without exception,[3] speak of the Adoration of the Cross as forming part of the religious service on Good Friday, but they differ considerably as to the manner in which this ceremony was connected with the rest.[4] The chants which are sung at the present day during the Adoration of the Cross have

---

[1] Council of Carthage, of 397, c 29 " Ut sacramenta altaris non nisi a jejunis hominibus celebrentur. excepto uno die anniversario quo caena Domini celebratur" St Augustine also speaks of this custom in his *Ep.* 118, *ad Januarium*, c 7. He says even that, as certain persons did not fast at all on this day, the *oblation* was celebrated twice, once in the morning, and once in the evening In this way those who did not fast could partake of it after the morning meal, and those who did after the evening meal The omission of fasting was owing to the custom of taking a bath on this day. Bathing and fasting were considered incompatible.

[2] *Peregrin. Etheriae (Silviae)*, cf *infra*, pp 510, 564.

[3] The Sacramentary of Adrian preserves no trace of it, doubtless owing to the fact that it gives only the prayers said by the celebrant, the pope The *Ordo* of the manuscript of St Amand indicates the ceremony in the title-page, but it makes no mention of it in the description of the papal Station.

[4] Compare the three *Ordines* described, p. 146 *et seq*, and the Gelasian Sacramentary, i 41

certainly an ancient, but rather Gallican,[1] ring about them. They are not found in the ancient Roman books.[2]

The "Mass of the Presanctified" is not marked by any greater prominence. It is merely the Communion, separated from the liturgical celebration of the Eucharist properly so called. The details of the ceremony are not found earlier than in books of the eighth or ninth century, but the service must belong to a much earlier period. At the time when Synaxes without liturgy were frequent, the "Mass of the Presanctified" must have been frequent also.

In the Greek Church it was celebrated every day in Lent except on Saturdays and Sundays, but in the Latin Church it was confined to Good Friday. The ceremony at Rome was of the most simple character. The *capsa* containing the consecrated bread was placed upon the altar; the *Pater noster*, with its introductory and concluding formularies, was said; a particle of the consecrated bread was placed in a chalice containing ordinary wine, and everybody communicated by partaking of the consecrated bread in the *capsa* and of the wine sanctified as described. It is probable that the faithful, when they administered the communion to themselves in their houses, observed a similar ceremonial.[3]

---

[1] For instance, the Trisagion, in Greek and Latin, the Reproaches, and the hymn *Pange Lingua* I do not quote in this respect the Gregorian Antiphonary, a book which is far from being homogeneous and free from Gallican influence.

[2] The Appendix to the *Ordo I* of Mabillon mentions only the anthem [antiphon] *Ecce lignum Crucis*, combined with the long psalm *Beati immaculati*. According to the *Ordo* of Einsiedeln, this antiphon was sung during the procession, both going and coming, from the Lateran to the Sessorian basilica. The Adoration of the Cross took place during the lections of the Synaxis.

[3] Communion at home, a very frequent custom in the time of the persecutions, was maintained among solitaries in monasteries where there were no priests, and, generally, in the case of those who lived at a great

On the Saturday in Holy Week there was no special meeting for worship. The ceremonies of the Easter Vigil had already been transferred in the eighth century to the afternoon of the Saturday. At the present day they are performed in the morning. Apart from the rites in it which bear upon baptismal initiation, and which shall be described later on, this solemn Vigil was distinguished by certain peculiarities, namely, by the blessing of the new fire, and of the candle, and by the Mass itself, in which certain archaic features were preserved.

A very natural symbolism led to the adoption of these ceremonies. The death of Christ, followed quickly by His resurrection, found an expressive image in the fire, candle, or lamp, which being extinguished, can be lit again. We know what importance is still attached in our own days to the ceremony of the new fire in the Easter ritual of the Greek Church at Jerusalem. In the East, however, this ceremony does not extend beyond the Holy City. It is not found in the ordinary Byzantine ritual.

In the West, we learn from the legend of St. Patrick that it was customary for the Irish, as early as the sixth century, at latest, to kindle great fires at nightfall on Easter Eve. It appears from the correspondence between St. Boniface and Pope Zacharias[1] that these fires were lighted not from other fires, but from flints. They were really new fires. This custom appears to have been peculiar to the British or Irish, and to have been conveyed, through the Anglo-Saxons, to the Continent by

distance from a church, even after the Church was free from persecution In 519, Dorotheos, the Bishop of Thessalonica, fearing that persecution was about to descend upon his flock, caused the elements for communion to be distributed among them in basketsful, *canistra plena, ne imminente persecutione communicare non possent* (Thiel, *Epp Rom Pont.*, vol 1 p 902).

[1] Jaffé, 2291.

missionaries of the eighth century. There is no trace of it in the ancient Merovingian books.[1]

It was not known, moreover, at Rome. A rite, however, of similar import was observed here. On Maundy Thursday, at the time of the consecration of the holy chrism, sufficient oil was collected from all the lamps of the Lateran basilica to fill three great vessels, which were placed in a corner of the church. The oil thus collected was allowed to burn by means of wicks until the Vigil of Easter. It was at these three great lamps that the candles and other lights were lit which were used on the night of the Vigil of Easter to illuminate the ceremony of baptism.[2] It is possible that the taking of the light on this occasion was a matter of some solemnity, for Pope Zacharias assigned the office to a priest, or even to a bishop (*per sacerdotem*). But there is no trace of this either in the *Ordines* or in the Sacramentaries.

The custom, furthermore, of solemnly blessing the Easter candle, and the lights of the church generally, at the beginning of the holy night, was one foreign to Rome. It is needless to say that this custom has the closest relation to that in which a spark, as it were, of the ancient fire was preserved, or that in which there was a

---

[1] In the Mozarabic Missal now in use, there is, as in the Roman Missal, a blessing of the fire at the beginning of the Easter Vigil. The fire is obtained from a flint and steel. I do not know whether the ceremony is really primitive in the Mozarabic Missal. It is certainly not so in the Roman.

[2] Zacharias to Boniface (*loc cit.*): "De igne autem paschali quod inquisisti . . , quinta feria Paschae, dum sacrum chrisma consecratur, tres lampades magnae capacitatis ex diversis candelis ecclesiae oleo collecto in secretiori ecclesiae loco, ad figuram interioris tabernaculi insistente, indeficienter cum multa diligentia ardebunt, ita ut oleum ipsum sufficere possit usque ad tertium diem. De quibus candelis sabbato sancto pro sacri fontis baptismate sumptus ignis per sacerdotem renovabitur. De crystallis autem, ut asseruisti, nullam habemus traditionem"

solemn production of the new. At Rome, where the ceremony of blessing the paschal candle was not in use, the great lamps prepared on Maundy Thursday were used on the Friday and Saturday to light the two candles which in these latter days were borne in procession before the Pope, in place of the seven candles which ordinarily preceded him.

Outside Rome, that is, in Northern Italy, Gaul, and Spain,[1] the blessing of the paschal candle was an ancient custom. The same may be said perhaps of Africa also: St. Augustine (*Civ. Dei*, xv. 22) furnishes some verses which he had composed *in laude quadam cerei*. We are not sure whether that *Laus Cerei* may not have been composed for some deacon at Milan or of a neighbouring Church. This ceremony was so popular that the Popes, although they did not adopt it in their own church, were obliged to permit of its use in those of the "suburbicarian" diocese. The middle of the sixth century, according to the *Liber Pontificalis* (second edition), is the date of that concession, which is attributed therein to Pope Zosimus. The Easter candle is met with at Ravenna in the time of St. Gregory, and at Naples in the eighth century.[2] It is in Southern Italy, moreover, that the blessing of the candle has left the most striking traces in liturgical paleography.

The formulary of the blessing, wherever it was in use, was said, not by a bishop,[3] or a priest, but by the archdeacon, who for the purpose ascended the ambo, close to which the candle to be blessed was placed. He began, in a sort of invitatory, to announce the beginning of the

---

[1] Formulary published from a MS of the seventh century by P Ewald and G Lowe, *Exempla scripturae Wisigothicae*, pl. ii. iii , cf. Mercati (and Bannister) fasc. 12 of *Studi e texti*, Rome, 1904, p 40

[2] *Lib. Pont.*, vol i p 225, St. Gregory, *Ep* xi 33, (31); *Gesta Epp. Neap.*, p 426 of the edition of Waitz (*Mon. Germ Script. Lang*).

[3] At Ravenna, however, these prayers were said by the bishop (St. Gregory, *loc cit*). They were so long as to weary the officiating bishop.

great festival, then adopting the tone and style of the most solemn prayer—the Eucharistic—he called for the Divine blessing on that luminous pillar which was about to shed its radiance on the mysteries of the Christian Passover, as in like manner of old the pillar of fire had gone before the children of Israel to guide them in their wanderings in the desert. He dwelt poetically upon the elements composing it, the papyrus,[1] which furnished the wick, and the virgin oil and the beeswax, which formed the material. Here occurred a curious eulogy of the bee, chaste and fecund like the Virgin mother, and which in the manner of its generation furnished a type of the eternal origin of the Divine Word.[2]

The following is the formulary now in use. I reproduce it here from the earliest manuscripts,[3] without taking into consideration later revisions.

[1] See the two blessings of the candle, contained in the *Opuscula* of Ennodius, Nos 9 and 10.

[2] The following is the passage in the formulary *Deus mundi conditor* of the Gelasian Sacramentary: "Apes vero sunt frugales in sumptibus, in procreatione castissimae; aedificant cellulas cereo liquore fundatas, quarum humanae peritiae ars magistra non coaequat Legunt pedibus flores et nullum damnum in floribus invenitur. Partus non edunt, sed ore legentes concepti foetus reddunt examina, sicut exemplo mirabili Christus ore paterno processit. Fecunda est in his sine partu virginitas, quam utique Dominus sequi dignatus carnalem se matrem habere virginitatis amore constituit Talia igitur, Domine, digna sacris altaribus tuis munera offeruntur, quibus te laetari religio christiana non ambigit" The general subject of the *Praeconium Paschale* is described, and somewhat caricatured, in a letter attributed to St Jerome, but certainly of the year 384 (Migne, *Pat. Lat.*, vol xxx p 182) This is addressed to a deacon of Placenza, called Praesidius, who had asked the writer to draw up for him his *Praeconium*

[3] This is the formulary which appears in the three Gallican Sacramentaries, from whence it passed into the supplement to the Sacramentary of Adrian, which was probably compiled by Alcuin (see above, p. 121). This supplement contains also the formulary *Deus mundi conditor*, peculiar to the Gelasian Sacramentary. Ennodius (*Opusc*, 9, 10) has left us two formularies of this kind, drawn up, doubtless, for his own use, whilst he was Deacon of the Church of Pavia

Exultet jam angelica turba caelorum! exultent divina mysteria! Et pro tanti regis victoria tuba intonet salutaris! Gaudeat[1] et tellus tantis inradiata fulgoribus, et aeterni regni splendore lustrata, totius orbis se sentiat amisisse caliginem! Laetetur et mater Ecclesia tanti luminis adornata fulgore, et magnis populorum vocibus haec aula resultet!

Quapropter, adstantibus vobis, Fratres karissimi, ad tam miram sancti hujus luminis claritatem, una mecum, quaeso, Dei omnipotentis misericordiam invocate; ut qui me non meis meritis intra levitarum[2] numerum dignatus est adgregare, luminis sui gratia infundente, cerei hujus laudem implere praecipiat. Per resurgentem filium suum dominum nostrum, etc.

Sursum corda!—R͞. Habemus ad Dominum!

Gratias agamus Domino Deo nostro!—R͞. Dignum et justum est!

Vere, quia dignum et justum est invisibilem Deum omnipotentem Patrem, Filiumque ejus unigenitum, dominum nostrum Jesum Christum, toto cordis ac mentis affectu et vocis ministerio personare. Qui pro nobis aeterno Patri Adae debitum solvit et veteris piaculi cautionem pio cruore detersit. Haec sunt enim festa Paschalia, in quibus verus ille Agnus occiditur, ejusque sanguis postibus consecratur. In qua[3] primum patres nostros filios Israhel educens de Aegypto Rubrum mare sicco vestigio transire fecisti. Haec igitur nox est quae peccatorum tenebras columnae inluminatione purgavit. Haec nox est quae hodie per universum mundum in Christo credentes, a vitiis saeculi segregatos et caligine peccatorum, reddit gratiae, sociat sanctitati. Haec nox est, in qua destructis vinculis mortis Christus ab inferis victor ascendit. Nihil enim nasci profuit nisi redimi profuisset.

O mira circa nos tuae pietatis dignatio! O inaestimabilis dilectio caritatis! Ut servum redimeres filium tradidisti! O certe necessarium Adae peccatum, quod Christi morte deletum est! O felix culpa, quae talem ac tantum meruit habere redemptorem! O beata nox, quae sola meruit scire tempus et horam, in qua Christus ab inferis resurrexit! Haec nox est de qua scriptum est: *Et nox sicut dies inluminabitur, Et nox inluminatio mea in deliciis meis.* Hujus igitur sanctificatio

---

[1] The three Gallican Sacramentaries have: *Gaudeat se tantis illius inradiata.*

[2] *Sacerdotum*, in the *Miss. Goth.* This is a variant which depends on the question whether the officiating minister is a priest or a bishop.

[3] This pronoun, like the verb *fecisti*, at the end of the sentence, does not fall in easily with what follows. Something must have fallen out, as in the case of the words *Nihil enim*, a little lower down.

noctis fugat scelera, culpas lavat, reddit innocentiam lapsis et maestis laetitiam; fugat odia, concordiam parat, et curvat imperia.

In hujus igitur noctis gratia, suscipe, sancte Pater, incensi[1] hujus sacrificium vespertinum, quod tibi in hac cerei oblatione solemni per ministrorum manus de operibus apum sacrosancta reddit Ecclesia. Sed jam columnae hujus praeconia novimus quam in honorem Dei rutilans ignis accendit; qui licet divisus in partes mutuati luminis detrimenta non novit. Alitur liquantibus ceris, quas in substantiam pretiosae hujus lampadis apis mater eduxit.

Apis[2] caeteris quae subjecta sunt homini animantibus antecellit. Cum sit minima corporis parvitate, ingentes animos angusto versat in pectore; viribus imbecilla, sed fortis ingenio. Huic,[3] explorata temporum vice, cum canitiem pruinosa hyberna posuerint et glaciale senium verni temporis moderatio[4] deterserit, statim prodeundi ad laborem cura succedit, dispersaeque per agros, libratis[5] paululum pinnis, cruribus suspensis insidunt, parte[6] ore legere flosculos, oneratae[7] victualibus suis ad castra remeant; ibique aliae inaestimabili arte cellulas tenaci glutino instruunt, aliae liquantia mella stipant, aliae vertunt flores in ceram, aliae ore natos fingunt, aliae collectis e foliis nectar includunt. O vere beata et mirabilis apis! Cujus nec sexum masculi violant, foetus non quassant, nec filii destruunt castitatem! Sicut sancta concepit virgo Maria: virgo peperit et virgo permansit.

O vere beata nox, quae expoliavit Aegyptios, ditavit Hebraeos! Nox, in qua terrenis caelestia junguntur!

Oramus te, Domine, ut cereus iste in honorem nominis tui consecratus, ad noctis hujus caliginem destruendam indeficiens perseveret, et in odorem suavitatis acceptus supernis luminaribus misceatur. Flammas ejus Lucifer matutinus inveniat; ille, inquam, Lucifer, qui nescit occasum; ille, qui regressus ab inferis humano generi serenus inluxit.

---

[1] *Incensi* has here a figurative meaning. The *sacrificium vespertinum incensi* (cf. *Ps.* 141, v. 2) is nothing else than the candle itself. The word *incensi*, however, has given origin to the ceremony of the five grains of incense, which being blessed together with the new fire, are here inserted into the body of the candle.

[2] This eulogy of the bee, full of Virgilian reminiscences, is no longer to be found in the text now in use.

[3] *Haec*, in the manuscripts.

[4] *Moderata*, manuscripts.

[5] *Libratim p pinnibus*, manuscripts.

[6] *Raptim* (?).

[7] *Oneratis*, manuscripts. Something must have fallen out here. The whole passage is very corrupt.

Precamur ergo te, Domine, ut nos famulos tuos,[1] omnem clerum et devotissimum populum, quiete temporum concessa, in his Paschalibus gaudiis conservare digneris.

These formularies were said, in Italy at least, from separate rolls, which it was customary to decorate as sumptuously as possible. The text was ornamented here and there with miniatures illustrative of various passages, such as the angelic choir, the earth illuminated with celestial light, the church, the officiating deacon, bees, etc. The name of the sovereign at the end was sometimes accompanied by his portrait.[2] In the ornamentation of these rolls the figures were placed upside down, so that the reader observed them turned in the opposite direction from the text. This custom finds its explanation in the fact that each roll, as it was read, was allowed to fall over the side of the ambo, so that its end could be seized by members of the congregation, and the miniatures contemplated while the deacon continued his chanting of the remainder.

The Mozarabic Liturgy contains here, besides the blessing of the new fire, which is not, perhaps, primitive in this place, a twofold benediction, namely, that of the lamp and that of the candles. There were two officiating ministers —deacons—who must either have composed the necessary formularies themselves, or have known them by heart

[1] The local community. We find here, in the copies, formularies in which the pope, the bishop, and the sovereign, are named

[2] This was the case in one of the *Exultets* preserved among the archives of the Cathedral of Bari; we see depicted on it the portraits of two emperors of the East, Basil II and Constantine IX, then rulers of the country. This roll furnishes a formulary which varies somewhat from the usual text. The Benedictines of Monte Cassino have undertaken the publication of the miniatures in some of these rolls, especially those of Gaeta, Fondi, Capua, and Mirabella (*Le Miniature nei rotoli dell' Exultet*, Monte Cassino, 1899) A more complete work on the same subject has just been published by Mons E. Bertaux, *L'art dans l'Italie méridionale*. Paris, 1903, p 213, *et seq* For the text of the *Exultet*, see *infra*, p 543.

These preliminary ceremonies were followed by a long series of lections, chants, and prayers, constituting the Vigil service, and by the blessing of the Fonts, the rites of baptism and confirmation, and finally the Mass, which was said in ancient times at dawn. This first Easter Mass still continues to preserve at Rome its primitive arrangement. It begins, after the litany, with the *Gloria in excelsis* (originally sung on the Nativity only), and excludes the other chants introduced at the end of the fourth century, viz. the introit, the offertory, and the antiphon of the communion. The same is the case, as we might naturally anticipate, with the *Agnus Dei*, which was not introduced until three centuries later. The only other chants occurring in this Mass—the *gradual* and the *sanctus*—go back to the earliest times.

§ 5.—The Immovable Feasts.

1. *Christmas and Epiphany.*

The second of the cardinal points on which the ecclesiastical year turns is the Nativity of Christ. Once fixed, this festival, like Easter, determined a great number of others.

There is no authoritative tradition bearing on the day of the birth of Christ. Even the year is uncertain. The latter, however, was determined at an early date from a consideration of two texts, Luke iii. 1, and Luke iii. 23, which imply a synchronism between the thirtieth year of Jesus[1]

---

[1] Ὡσεὶ ἐτῶν τριάκοντα. This figure is given as approximate by the Evangelist himself. It is irreconcilable with the statement common to St Matthew and St. Luke, that Jesus was born while Herod the Great was yet alive. The first year of Jesus began, on this hypothesis, in the year 2 or 1 before our era (752–753 A.U.C.), whilst Herod died in the spring of the fourth year before A.D. (i.e 750 A.U.C.).

and the fifteenth year of the rule of Tiberius (28-29). As for the month and the day, Clement of Alexandria[1] speaks of calculations which result in fixing these as the 18th or 19th of April, or even as the 29th of May. But these were private calculations upon which no festival observance could be made to depend. The book called *De Pascha Computus*, put forth in 243, either in Africa or in Italy, states that our Lord was born on the 28th of March[2] Those who proposed such figures evidently knew nothing of the existence of the festival of the Nativity. If we are to give credence to a text of very doubtful authenticity, then Hippolytus at the beginning of the third century in Rome fixes, in his Commentary on Daniel (iv. 23), the date as Wednesday, the 25th of December, in the forty-second year of the Emperor Augustus[3] Even if such were the fact we should not as yet have reason to conclude from this that the festival of Nativity had been already instituted in the time of St. Hippolytus.

The most ancient authority for the observance of the Nativity is the Philocalian Calendar, drawn up at Rome in the year 336. We read in it, in the table called *Depositio Martyrum: viii. kal. jan., natus Christus in Betleem Judee*.[4] The table of episcopal anniversaries, moreover, implies that

---

[1] *Strom.*, 1. 145, 146 (Pharmouthi, 24 or 25 Pachon, 25)

[2] This curious document will be found in the appendices to Hartel's edition of St. Cyprian, p 267.

[3] This text was recently discovered by Mons. Basil. Georgiades, vol i p 242, of the edition of Bonwetsch and Achelis, Berlin, 1897. Cf. Vacandard, *Etudes de critique*, third series, p 8

[4] Usener (*Rhein. Mus*, vol. lx. p 489) recognised this, but he refuses to see in this note *VIII. Kal. ian* anything more than an historical statement It would not prove that the festival had been kept anterior to this But why should an historical note figure in such a meagre calendar? And how could an event not commemorated by a festival, form the starting-point of the religious year?

the beginning of the liturgical year was between the 8th and 27th of December.[1]

Christmas was originally a festival peculiar to the Latin Church. St. John Chrysostom states, in a homily delivered in 386, that it had not been introduced into Antioch until about ten years before, that is, about 375 [2] At this time there was no observance of this feast either at Jerusalem,[3] or at Alexandria. It was adopted at the latter place about 430.[4] The Armenians did not observe it either.[5] These Churches, however, had a festival of the same import as that of the Latin festival of the 25th of December. They called it the festival of "the Manifestations," τὰ 'Επιφάνια, or Epiphany, and celebrated it on the 6th of January. The most ancient indication of it is to be found in Clement of Alexandria. He states that the Basilidians celebrated the day of Christ's baptism by a festival which was preceded by a Vigil, or Watch, spent in hearing lections[6] There was a variation, however, as to the date. Some kept this festival on the 10th, others on the 6th of January. It is not possible to say at what date this custom was introduced into the orthodox Churches of the East, but it is certain that in the course of the fourth century the 6th of January was universally observed among them. Three events were commemorated in this festival—the birth of Christ, the adoration of the Magi, and the baptism of our Lord. The most

[1] Cf *Bulletin Critique*, 1890, p 41.
[2] Migne, *Pat Gr*, vol xlix p. 351.
[3] This is borne out by the *Pereg. Etheriae*, and also by a sermon of St. Jerome at Bethlehem early in the fifth century This sermon has been dealt with by G. Morin (*Revue d'Hist et de Litter. Religieuses*, vol. 1., 1896, p. 414). See Appendix, p 577B.
[4] Cassian. *Coll.* x 1, Gennadius, *De Viris*, 59. Paul, Bishop of Emesa, preached a sermon on Sunday, the 25th of December (29 Khoiak) A.D. 432, at Alexandria, from which it appears that the birth of our Lord was observed there on that day (Hardouin, *Conc*, vol 1 p 1693).
[5] Cf above, p 74, n. 2
[6] Τοῦ βαπτίσματος αὐτοῦ τὴν ἡμέραν ἑορτάζουσι προδιανυκτερεύοντες ἀναγνώσεσι (*loc. cit.*).

ancient mention of this feast is found in the Passion of St. Philip, Bishop of Heraclea in Thrace, where there is mention of an incident which occurred in the time of the Diocletian persecution.[1] It was also observed in the countries following the Gallican rite. Ammianus Marcellinus[2] relates that, in 361, Julian, who was already ill-disposed towards Constantius, but who continued to disguise his pagan leanings, was publicly present at the Christian religious service in Vienne on the day of the Epiphany. The Council of Saragossa (380) mentions it also (c. 4) as a very high festival.[3]

At Rome and in Africa the 6th of January was as little observed as the 25th of December among the Orientals.[4] The Epiphany does not occur in the Philocalian Calendar, and the Donatists did not keep it. St. Augustine reproaches them with this in terms which imply that the festival had been imported from the East.[5] The two festivals were accepted everywhere in the West from cir. 400, except among the Donatists.

It is thus clear that towards the end of the third century the custom of celebrating the birthday of Christ had spread throughout the whole Church, but that it was not observed everywhere on the same day. In the West the 25th of December was chosen, and in the East the 6th of January. The two customs, distinct at first, were finally both adopted, so that the two festivals were universally observed, or almost so.

---

[1] Ruinart's edition, cap. 2.

[2] "Feriarum die quem celebrantes mense januario christiani Epiphania dictitant" (xxi 2).

[3] "A xvi. kal jan. usque in diem Epiphaniae qui est viii id jan. continuis diebus, nulli liceat de ecclesia absentare." If the festival of the 25th of December had been observed in Spain at this date, it ought, apparently, to have been mentioned in this canon.

[4] St Epiphanius (*Haer*., li. 16, 24, *Exp. Fidei*, 22) is exclusively for the 6th of January.

[5] "Quia nec unitatem amant, nec orientali ecclesiae . . . communicant" (Sermon 202).

What were the influences, we may ask, which led to the adoption of these dates? Several answers have been proposed, which I will here enumerate.

First, the *Saturnalia* of the Roman Calendar were considered to have been a determining motive. An endeavour was made, it was thought, to turn away the faithful from the observation of this popular festival by directing their piety to the remembrance of Christ. This motive must be discarded, for there is no coincidence between the two festivals. The *Saturnalia* began on the 17th of December, and were not prolonged beyond the 23rd.

A better explanation is that based on the festival of the *Natalis Invicti,* which appears in the Pagan Calendar of the Philocalian collection under the 25th of December. The *Invictus* is the Sun, whose birth coincides with the winter solstice, that is, with the 25th of December, according to the Roman Calendar. The worship of Mithras, or, speaking more generally, of the Sun, was widespread and popular in the third and fourth centuries. One is inclined to believe that the Roman Church made choice of the 25th of December in order to enter into rivalry with Mithraism.[1] This reason, however, leaves unexplained the choice of the 6th of January. The following solution has the advantage of explaining both festivals at the same time.

The date of the birth of Christ was fixed by taking as a starting-point that which was believed to be the day of His death.

The latter date cannot be determined with historical accuracy. The information given in the Gospels and furnished by tradition is insufficient to enable us to come to a definite solution of the question. Attempts were made, however, at an early date to solve the problem. Clement of Alexandria[2] mentions certain private calculations which

---

[1] See the texts quoted by Mommsen (*Corp. Inscr. Lat.*, vol i p 410.
[2] *Loc. cit.*

262 CHRISTIAN WORSHIP: ITS ORIGIN AND EVOLUTION.

resulted—as far as the day was concerned—in assigning the 21st of March or the 13th or 19th of April for the day of Christ's death. The *De Pascha Computus*, previously referred to, gives the 9th of April. Lactantius[1] assigns it to the 23rd of March, but a solution more generally accepted makes it the 25th. Tertullian is the first to mention the subject; he says:—*Passio perfecta est sub Tiberio Caesare, consulibus Rubellio Gemino et Fufio Gemino* [29], *mense martio, temporibus Paschae, die viii. kal. april, die prima azymorum*[2] Hippolytus, in his Paschal Table, refers the Passion of Christ to a year in which the 14th of Nisan fell on Friday, the 25th of March In his Commentary on Daniel[3] he definitely assigns the Passion to Friday, the 25th of March, in the consulate of the two Gemini.[4] The Philocalian Catalogue of the Popes gives the same day and year. It must be remembered that both the Cycle of Hippolytus and the Philocalian Catalogue are based upon official documents, and that they may be regarded as indicating the Roman ecclesiastical reckoning. This same date—the 25th of March—appears also in certain Acts of Pilate, which, about the beginning of the fourth century at latest, were widely known, and enjoyed a considerable reputation. It was from this document, which was well known throughout Asia Minor, that the Quartodecimans of Phrygia obtained their date of the 25th of March for Easter. In Cappadocia the adherents of this sect were divided as to the fixing upon the 25th of March, or the 14th of Nisan, but they were at one in refusing to celebrate Easter on a Sunday.[5] In the fifth and sixth centuries the traditional date of the 25th of March

[1] *De mort. Pers*, 1; *Divin. Inst*, iv. 10.
[2] *Adv Judaeos* (written about 207), c. 8. These dates are irreconcilable with each other. On the 25th of March, in the year 29, the moon was in its last quarter. The Passover could not therefore fall on this day.
[3] *Loc. cit*, p. 242.
[4] Side by side with these Consuls those of 41 have been interpolated in his text.
[5] Epiphanius, *Haer*, 1 1; cf Philastrius, *Haer*, 58

was so firmly established in Gaul, that it gave rise to not only a celebration of the Passion of our Lord on that day, but also a festival of His Resurrection on the 27th of the same month, without interfering, however, with the movable feasts of Good Friday and Easter Sunday.[1]

These festival observances imply an inveterate tradition We are not, on this account, to assume that this tradition had an historical basis. The Passion certainly did not occur on a 25th of March[2] This date must have been arbitrarily chosen, or rather suggested, from its coincidence with the (official) spring equinox. The death of Christ was thus made to fall on the same day as that on which, according to an universal belief, the world had been created.

This date having once been determined, and determined, too, from astronomical and symbolical considerations, it was not unnatural that it should be used to establish another coincidence. 'Christ must have lived upon earth, it was thought, for only a complete number of years. Fractions are imperfections which do not fall in with the demands of a symbolical system of numbers, and hence they must be got rid of as completely as possible. The Incarnation must, therefore, like the Passion, have taken place on the 25th of March, and as the Incarnation was reckoned from the first moment of the conception of Mary, the birth of Christ must have taken place on the 25th of December

This explanation would be the more readily received if

[1] Calendar of Perpetuus, Bishop of Tours († *circ* 490), in Greg Tur, *Hist Fi*., x 31, Hieronymian Martyrology, 25th and 27th of March. Cf Martin de Braga, *De Pascha* 1 (Migne, *Pat. Lat*, vol xxxii p 50). "A plerisque Gallicanis episcopis usque ante non multum tempus custoditum est ut semper viii kal april diem Paschae (inexact) celebrarent, in quo facta Christi resurrectio traditur" There is some confusion here *Passio* should be read for *resurrectio*, unless Martin meant to write *vi kal* in place of *viii kal*

[2] In the years 29 and 35 the 25th of March fell on a Friday, but this Friday could not have been either the day of the Jewish Passover, or the day following it The age of the moon is opposed to this In the interval between the years 29 and 35, the 25th of March does not occur on a Friday

we could find it fully stated in some author.[1] Unfortunately we know of no text containing it, and we are therefore compelled to put it forward as an hypothesis, but it is an hypothesis which falls in with what we may call the recognised methods in such matters.

I will adduce, moreover, a coincidence which increases its probability. Up to the present we have been dealing only with the date of the 25th of December. That of the 6th of January still remains to be explained.

Sozomen[2] makes mention of a sect of the Montanists who celebrated Easter on the 6th of April in place of the 25th of March, because the world having been created at the equinox, that is, according to their reckoning, on the 24th of March, the first full moon of the first month took place fourteen days later, that is, on the 6th of April.[3] Now, between the 6th of April and the 6th of January there are just nine months, the same interval as between the 25th of March and the 25th of December. The Greek day for the observance of the Nativity, the 6th of January, is thus found to be connected with a paschal computation, based on astronomical and symbolical considerations exactly similar to those from which we have endeavoured to deduce the date of the 25th of December.

It is possible, from what has preceded, that the date

---

[1] It is indeed found, but at too late a date, that is, when the festival of the Nativity had been observed for a long time. Thus St. Augustine blames the Jews for having transgressed against the command *non coques agnum in lacte matris suae* The lamb is Jesus Christ, crucified the 25th of March, that is, on the same day in which His mother began to have milk: ‹ Dicuntur enim feminae ex quo conceperint lac colligere " (*In Heptat.*, ii. 90).

[2] *H. E*, vii. 18.

[3] This reasoning would not be conclusive for the date of the Passion, an event separated from the Creation by an interval of some thousands of years; but it is understood that the Passover of Christ, being the true Passover, must fall due at typical maturity reckoned from the origin of all things. The Passion could not possibly have taken place on the 6th of April; for no Friday, the 6th of April, can be found in the interval of years from which we have to choose, as coinciding with the full moon.

for the birth of Christ was fixed from the assumed starting-point of His Passion. Among all the solutions proposed this seems to me the most satisfactory, but I would not venture to say, in regard to the 25th of December, that the coincidence of the *Sol novus* exercised no direct or indirect influence on the ecclesiastical decisions arrived at in regard to the matter.

The festival of Christmas is at the present day [1] characterised in the Roman use by the celebration of three Masses; one at cockcrow, *i.e.* before daylight (*ad galli cantum*), another at dawn, and the third in the morning. This custom was in existence as early as the end of the sixth century, and St. Gregory mentions it in one of his homilies.[2] It arose as follows. At the beginning of the fifth century there was only one Mass—that of the morning—and it was celebrated at St. Peter's. Pope Celestine received, on the morning of Christmas Day, 431, the imperial letters which informed him of the result of the Council of Ephesus, and he caused them to be read " at the assembly of all the Christian people, at St. Peter's." [3] Celestine's successor, Xystus [Sixtus] III., rebuilt the Liberian Basilica on the Esquiline, and dedicated it to St. Mary. It is only from that time forward that we hear of a Station or nocturnal Mass on Christmas Day, and it has always been celebrated in that church. Here, I believe, we have an imitation of the use at Jerusalem, which permitted a night Station at Bethlehem and a day Mass in Jerusalem itself. The Basilica of Santa Maria Maggiore was, as it were, the Roman equivalent of Bethlehem, and later on a *Praesepe* [manger or *crèche*],

---

[1] Before the sixth century it was not the custom at Rome to sing the *Gloria in excelsis* except at the Feast of Christmas, and then only at the nocturnal Mass (see *infra*). It is to Pope Symmachus (498-514) that we owe its use on Sundays and festivals (cf. *supra*, p 166).

[2] *Hom* viii. 1

[3] Jaffé, 386.

on the model of that of Palestine, was established there. With regard to the Mass at dawn, it was originally in honour of St. Anastasia of Sirmium, a saint who became popular at Constantinople after the translation of her relics under the Patriarch Gennadius (458–471). About the same time her cult was introduced at Rome and was installed in the old *titulus Anastasiae*, a church situated at the foot of the Palatine. As this building constituted a sort of special metropolitan church for the Greek quarter, and was in close proximity to the official staff of the Palatine, the festival of St. Anastasia assumed an extraordinary importance, and continued to be observed in spite of its coinciding with the celebration of Christmas. A third Station was thus formed, and was intercalated between the two others. In other places than Rome, where there was neither a church of St. Anastasia nor a Byzantine colony, no reason existed for celebrating a solemn Mass on the anniversary of the Martyr of Sirmium.[1] The custom of having three Masses was, however, preserved; but the Mass at dawn, like the two others, was said in honour of our Lord's Nativity, and St. Anastasia no longer figures in it, except in a mere commemoration.[2]

---

[1] It is a somewhat remarkable fact that this Byzantine cultus should have succeeded in establishing itself, notwithstanding the dominant claims of the festival of Christmas Various Roman saints also, of whom the best-known was St Eugenia, had their anniversaries on the 25th of December, and they are still marked in the Leonine Sacramentary, but in course of time they were all eliminated

[2] On this subject, cf my work on the Church of St Anastasia in the *Mélanges de l'École française de Rome*, vol vii. (1887) p 405, *et seq*, cf. also G. Bonnacorsi, *Il Natale*, Rome, 1903.

[NOTE ON THE ROMAN NIGHT —The Romans divided the night into three parts; the first began in the evening and lasted till the hour when all noises ceased (*conticinium*), the third began at cockcrow.

Between these two was the night of undefined length (*intempesta nox*). The modern custom of celebrating Mass exactly at midnight is not quite in accordance with the ancient Roman method of reckoning the hours]

2. *The Festivals after Christmas.*

The festival of the Nativity having been once fixed, there were associated with it, and that too from an early date, certain commemorations connected with the greatest saints of the New Testament. St. Gregory of Nyssa, in his funeral oration over St. Basil, preached at the Cappadocian Cæsarea in 379, states that it was customary after Christmas and before the 1st of January to celebrate the festivals of St. Stephen, St. Peter, St. James, St. John, and St. Paul. This statement is confirmed by the Syriac Menologion published by Mr. Wright from a manuscript of the date 412.[1] I have made a study of the text of the latter, and have shown that it is merely an abridgment of a Greek Martyrology of Asia Minor, of which a more complete form was embodied in the Latin compilation called the Hieronymian Martyrology. The Greek Martyrology must have been drawn up within the last three decades of the fourth century; it is even possible that the first redaction may have been a little earlier[2] It is, therefore, in the main, of the same date and country as St. Basil and St. Gregory of Nyssa. There is nothing to prove, however, that the festivals which we are about to mention were inscribed in it from the beginning. We have on this point merely the testimony of the Syriac abridgment, of which the provenance was Edessa, or some other oriental locality, where Syriac was the current language in ecclesiastical use. The following are the days after Christmas which it contains[3]:—

---

[1] *Journal of Sacred Lit.*, vol. viii., London, 1865–66, pp. 45, 423
[2] *Les Sources du Martyrologe Hiéronymien*, in the *Mélanges de l'École de Rome*, 1885. Since the appearance of the first edition I have published this Syriac Menologion in the *Acta SS Novembris*, vol. ii. p. [lii].
[3] I follow here the Syriac Menologion. In the Hieronymian Martyrology the festivals of St Peter and St. Paul have been transferred, according to Roman custom, to the 29th of June

December 26, St. Stephen.
„ 27, SS. James and John.
„ 28, SS. Peter and Paul.

The coincidence is complete. It is not, moreover, an isolated instance. The Nestorian and Armenian Churches furnish in their respective calendars evident traces of the same custom. The Armenians have not the festival of Christmas in their calendar,[1] yet, before they begin on the 29th of December to make immediate preparation for the observance of the Epiphany, they celebrate the four following festivals:—

December 25, St. David, and St. James, the brother of the Lord.[2]
„ 26, St. Stephen.
„ 27, SS. Peter and Paul.
„ 28, SS. James and John.

The Nestorian Calendar arranges these festivals somewhat differently. The custom in that Church is to commemorate saints on a Friday. The order is as follows:—

1st Friday after the Epiphany, St. John Baptist.
2nd „ „ „ SS. Peter and Paul.
3rd „ „ „ The Four Evangelists.[3]
4th „ „ „ St. Stephen.

---

[1] The Uniat Armenians have adopted this festival, but they still continue to celebrate the four festivals I have mentioned, and that also in the same order, except that SS David and James are placed before Christmas

[2] These two saints are introduced here as relations of Christ David is θεοπάτωρ, and James ἀδελφόθεος. Photius (*Bibl. Cod.*, 275) speaks of a sermon by Hesychius of Jerusalem (fifth century) in honour of James, the brother of the Lord, and of David, "ancestor of God" It is certain that this festival is of Palestinian origin Cosmas Indicopleustes testifies that it was still celebrated in his time at Jerusalem (Migne, *Pat. Gr.*, vol lxxxviii p. 197).

[3] This festival is, I think, a transformation of the primitive festival of the two sons of Zebedee St John must have attracted to him the three

It is manifest that these anniversary dates were fixed arbitrarily, and that there was no historical support for their adoption. St. James, son of Zebedee, is the only one among them whose death may be assigned to one period of the year more than another. But, he was beheaded about the time of the Passover,[1] and not in the month of December.

The most ancient of these festivals are those given in the list of St. Gregory of Nyssa and in the Syriac Menologion. The festival of St. Stephen goes back, as we know, to a period considerably earlier than that of the discovery of his tomb, which took place in 415, and gave a great impulse to his commemoration. It is mentioned, moreover, in the Apostolic Constitutions.[2] All Western calendars and liturgical books,[3] from the fifth century onwards, give this festival with its Eastern date.[4]

The festival of the 27th of December was at first

---

other evangelists, and the festival having thus changed its character, St James would have been omitted.|

[1] Acts xii 1–5.

[2] viii 33. The day is not noted, but it could only have been on the 26th of December.

[3] The Leonian Sacramentary presents an apparent anomaly. In this collection, which is in much disorder, the Masses in honour of St Stephen, the first martyr, instead of being placed at the 26th of December, are ranged under the rubric of the 2nd of August, along with the Pope, St Stephen It is, doubtless, because of the identity of the name of the Pope and the deacon, that the festival of the Invention of the body of St Stephen has been assigned to August 3 This festival is noted in the Hieronymian Martyrology, but not in all the manuscripts Its interpolation, therefore, could have only been made so far back as the revision of Auxerre (*circ* 595) No ancient liturgical work, Latin, Gallican, or Roman (except the Leonian Sacramentary), contains a festival of the deacon, St Stephen, in the month of August. On the other hand, the festival of the ἀνακομιδὴ τῶν λειψάνων τοῦ ἁγίου Στεφάνου appears on the 2nd of August in the Byzantine Calendars, at least from the end of the tenth century (Martinov, *Annus Ecclesiasticus Graeco-Slavicus*, p 192) It is also celebrated by the Armenians

[4] The Church of Constantinople transfers it to the 27th, for it assigns the day after Christmas to the commemoration of the Blessed Virgin and St. Joseph

T

commemorative of both St. James and St. John. It is inserted as such in the Carthage Calendar, the Hieronymian Martyrology, and the Gallican liturgical books. In this, as in many other respects, the Gallican usage agrees with the Oriental.

At Rome, on the other hand, the commemoration of St. John alone was adopted. At Constantinople the two apostles were transferred to two other days in the calendar.

As for the apostles Peter and Paul, their common festival was celebrated in the West on the 29th of June, a practice which goes back at least to the time of Constantine. The Eastern anniversary of these saints, the 28th of December, could not disturb such a deeply rooted tradition. At Constantinople also the Roman date was adopted from an early period.[1] In other Eastern countries it was found practicable to combine them [2]

The festival of the Holy Innocents must have been instituted at an early date, that is, some time in the fifth century. It is found on the 28th of December in all the ancient Latin calendars and liturgical books from the sixth century [3] onwards. The Church of Constantinople has also this festival, but places it a day later, that is, on the 29th of December.[4]

[1] *Cod Theod*, xv. v, 5; the law belongs to the year 425, its terms are somewhat vague, but they seem to point to the festival of the month of June It was celebrated at Constantinople at the end of the fifth century (Theod Lect, ii 16)

[2] The festival was still celebrated at Jerusalem in the month of December, in the seventh century, as we learn from a homily of Bishop Sophronius (Migne, *Pat Gr*, vol lxxxvii p 3361) The festival of St. Stephen took place on the 27th, and that of the apostles Peter and Paul on the 28th

[3] My remarks here are about the festival, and not of the mention of the Innocents in hymns, as in Prudentius, or in homilies, as in those of St. Peter Chrysologus

[4] The term *Innocents* is peculiar to Roman liturgical language. The Calendar of Carthage and the Gallican books employ the word *Infantes*.

3. *The Festivals of the Virgin and of St. John Baptist.*

We have seen that the Armenian Calendar provides in the last days of December for a special festival in honour of the two relatives of Christ, King David, and James, "the brother of the Lord." The person who has in this respect an incontestable right to a special commemoration among the festivals of the Nativity is assuredly the Blessed Virgin. We need not, therefore, be astonished that her festival finds a place immediately after Christmas in the Nestorian Calendar. A similar festival appears also in the Coptic Calendar on the 16th of January, almost immediately after the solemnities of the Epiphany, which came to an end on the 14th

In Gaul also we find, in the sixth century, a festival of the Blessed Virgin in the month of January : *mediante mense undecimo*, says Gregory of Tours [1] The Hieronymian Martyrology, in its revised Auxerre form (*circ.* 595), assigns this festival to the 18th of January.[2] It appears also in the liturgical books in this part of the calendar, but with somewhat less precision.

Her festival was celebrated in Spain, but at various dates in various places. The tenth Council of Toledo (656) enjoins a fixed and universal date, the 18th of December, eight days before Christmas [3]

---

[1] *Glor Mart*, 8 There is no earlier attestation as far as Gaul is concerned The festival does not appear in the Calendar of Perpetuus (Greg Tur , *Hist Fr* , x 31)

[2] In the Luxeuil Lectionary it follows the 2nd Sunday after Epiphany, before the festival of *Cathedra Petri*, which was then celebrated on the 18th of January. In the *Missale Gothicum* it occurs between Epiphany and St. Agnes (21st January), in the Sacramentary of Bobbio, between Epiphany and Lent, with (and after) the festival of the Chair of St. Peter. The Hieronymian Martyrology gives the two festivals on the same day.

[3] Can 1 From the terms employed by the council it has been wrongly inferred that it was cognisant of the festival of the 25th of March as in vogue in certain Churches This was not the case The council confined itself

The Church of Rome seems to have celebrated no festival of the Virgin before the seventh century, when it adopted the four Byzantine festivals, of which I will speak presently.[1]

The Gospel[2] furnishes, in regard to the festival of St. John Baptist, a fragment of information which has not been neglected The birth of the Forerunner of our Lord must have preceded that of the Saviour by six months. I suspect, notwithstanding, that the festival of the 24th of June was preceded, at least in the East, by another commemoration, which was observed about Christmastide. We have seen what the Nestorian use was in this respect, and we find that in the Armenian Church also the festival of the Forerunner of our Lord was the first which was observed after Epiphany.[3] The Calendar of Perpetuus, Bishop of Tours (461–490), places the *Natale S. Johannis* between the Epiphany and *Cathedra Petri*, that is, exactly at the same period in the year [4]

This festival was replaced later on by another, that of the *Passion*, or *Decollation* of St. John, observed on the 29th of August, which was adopted in Gallican regions and in Constantinople before it was followed at Rome.[5]

to stating that this date, which is that of the Incarnation, would be most suitable for the festival of the Blessed Virgin, but that the exigencies of Lent and of the paschal festivals did not allow of its adoption.

[1] See, however, what is said on page 273 of the significance of the festival of the 1st of January at Rome.

[2] St. Luke i 36.

[3] Nilles, *Kalend. Manuale*, vol. ii. pp 564, 566

[4] In the Calendar of Carthage, under the 27th of December we read, *S. Johannis Baptistae et Jacobi Apostoli quem Herodes occidit*, but we have every reason to believe that this was an error of the copyist, who read *Baptistae* in place of *Evangelistae*.

[5] For Constantinople see Martinov, *Annus Eccl. Graeco-Slavicus*, p. 210. In the Hieronymian Martyrology and the Gelasian Sacramentary the festival is placed on the 29th of August. All the Gallican liturgical books have a Mass for the Passion of St. John, which they place at a greater or less distance after that of the Nativity of the same saint, but without

As for the festival of the 24th of June, it appears to have been of Western origin, like that of the 25th of December.[1] The earliest witness to its observance is to be found in the sermons of St. Augustine.[2] From the middle of the fifth century onwards the existence of this festival is attested in all our sources of information as to Western usages. It appeared also at a very early date at Constantinople and in the Byzantine East. There were, however, places in which the ancient festival of January held its own against the innovation. The Calendar of Tours, belonging to the sixth century, represents a kind of compromise; the *Natale* of St. John is still retained in the month of January, but the festival of June is also adopted, and, strange to say, as the anniversary of the *Passio* of the saint.

The festivals of the Blessed Virgin, as they are now observed both in the Latin and Greek Churches, have a different origin and a different history from that of the primitive commemoration which I have just dealt with.

The most ancient of these is that of the Presentation of Christ in the Temple, which is generally called in the West the festival of the Purification of the Blessed

precisely indicating the date The genuine Roman books have no mention of this festival. its appearance in the Gelasian Sacramentary is an indication of one of the many revisions by Gallican hands to which this collection has been subjected

[1] It is to be noted that the festival is on the 24th, and not the 25th of June; and we may well ask why the latter figure was not adopted, since it would have given the exact interval of six months between the Baptist and Christ The reason is that the calculation was made according to the Roman Calendar, the 24th of June is the *viii. kal jul*, just as the 25th of December is *viii kal jan.* At Antioch, where the calculation was made, from the beginning to the end of the month the 25th would undoubtedly have been chosen.

[2] *Serm* 196 and 287. It is not to be found in either the Philocalian Calendar, or in that of Polemius Silvius (448) Owing to the present condition of the Syriac Menologion, we cannot say whether it was there or not

Virgin.* Its date results from that assigned to the birth of Christ, which it must follow at an interval of forty days. The first notice we have of its institution is in the second half of the fourth century, and that too in Jerusalem. The *Peregrinatio* of Etheria (Silvia) describes it under the name *Quadragesimae de Epiphania*. As the festival of Christmas had not yet been adopted there, the Presentation was celebrated on the fortieth day after the Epiphany, that is, on the 14th of February.[1] In the description of the festival furnished by Etheria, we remark no indication of a special association with the Blessed Virgin. An edict of Justinian, of the date 542,[2] enjoins the solemnisation of this festival at Constantinople

The observance of the festival of the Annunciation, on the 25th of March, is attested by the *Chronicon Paschale* (first half of the seventh century), which speaks of it (*ad ann.* 5506) as an established institution.[3] Like the preceding festival, this is also dependent on that of Christmas.

About the time of the Council *in Trullo* (692), which mentions all four festivals, a document at Rome attested, not only to the observance of the two preceding festivals, but also to two other commemorations of the Blessed Virgin, viz. that of her *Nativity* (8th September), and that of her *Dormitio* (15th August).[4] These four festivals are recorded in the Gelasian Sacramentary at the beginning of the eighth century. They had passed, therefore, into Roman usage as

* [An early Greek form of the *Ave Maria*, probably for use on this festival, will be found on p 540.—TR]

[1] This is the date adopted, and for the same reason, in the Armenian Calendar.

[2] Theophanius, A.M 6034

[3] There is a homily of St. Sophronius, Bishop of Jerusalem, on the Mystery of the Annunciation (Migne, *Pat. Gr.*, vol lxxxvii p 3217) Some earlier (?) evidences have been collected by S. Vailhé, in the *Echos d'Orient* (1906, pp. 138–145). None of them are absolutely conclusive, but it is possible that the Festival was observed, at least in some localities, as early as the fifth century See note, p 576

[4] *Liber Pontif*, vol 1 p 376 (*Life of Sergius I*) It was about this time that Andreas of Crete delivered his homilies on the Nativity, Annunciation, and Dormitio of the Blessed Virgin (Migne, *Pat Gi* , vol xcvii)

century. They had passed, therefore, into Roman usage as early as the seventh century.[1] I am unable to say, or even to conjecture, where and how the two dates the 15th of August and the 8th of September were arrived at.

These four festivals of the Blessed Virgin Mary are Byzantine importations. They were introduced in the first place at Rome The countries of the Gallican rite knew nothing of them until they adopted the Roman Liturgy.[2]

4. *The Festival of the 1st of January.*

The festival of the Circumcision, as we understand it, is not of Roman origin. There was, from the seventh century onward, a solemn Station at Rome on the 1st of January in the basilica of St Mary *ad Martyres*, but the liturgical texts prescribed for this day make no mention of the Circumcision.[3] The official designation of the festival was *Octavas Domini*.[4] It was a sort of renewal of the solemnity of Christmas, with

---

[1] It is certain that they were not yet in existence in the time of St. Gregory. Not only does he never make mention of them, but the same is true of all the documents bearing on the Roman usage prior to, or considered to be prior to, the seventh century, such as the Calendar of Carthage, the Leonian Sacramentary, etc But what is still more conclusive, these festivals were still unknown to the Anglo-Saxon Church at the beginning of the eighth century

[2] They do not appear either in the Auxerre recension of the Hieronymian Martyrology, or in the Gallican liturgical books An inscription (Le Blant, No 91) mentions the dedication of a church in the diocese of Coutances—the celebrated dedication *mense augusto medio* The church had been built *in honore Alme Maria* It must not, however, be assumed from this that the festival of the 15th of August was then observed in Neustria The festival in the middle of August referred to in the inscription, and described as being celebrated every year on the same day, was not that of the *Dormitio S Mariae*, but the dedication of the Church of Ham This dedication took place in 679 (*Bull des Antiquaires de France*, 1886, p 287)

[3] This word appears, it is true, in the Preface of the Gelasian Sacramentary, but not as associated with the commemoration of the circumcision of the child Jesus It meant simply the Jews collectively, just as the word *praeputium*, its antithesis, meant the Gentiles collectively

[4] Cf. The Capitularies of Capua for the Epis of St. Paul (sixth century) and those of Naples for the Gospels (seventh century), published by Dom Germain Morin (*Analecta Maredsolana*, vol. 1. pp 437, 428, 430)

274   CHRISTIAN WORSHIP : ITS ORIGIN AND EVOLUTION.

a special consideration of the Virgin Mother. The most ancient Byzantine calendars,[1] on the other hand, give us for the 1st of January the twofold festival of the Circumcision of Christ and of the anniversary of St. Basil. In ancient authorities on the Gallican custom the Circumcision appears alone; and it is mentioned at a tolerably early date, as, for instance, at the Council of Tours in 567 (can. 17), in the Auxerre recension of the Hieronymian Martyrology (*circ.* 595), and in the liturgical books of the seventh and eighth centuries.[2] There was, moreover, in countries of the Gallican rite at this period of the year a solemn fast, which had been instituted with the object of turning away the faithful from the observance of certain riotous festivals celebrated on the 1st of January.

5. *The Festivals of the Holy Cross.*[3]

Holy Cross Day, the 14th of September, like that of the Presentation in the Temple, is a festival of Palestinian origin. It was the anniversary of the dedication of the basilicas erected by Constantine on the sites of Calvary and the Holy Sepulchre. This dedication festival was celebrated in 335 by the bishops attending the Council of Tyre, who had pronounced upon St. Athanasius the sentence of deposition. There was associated with it also the commemoration of the discovery of the true cross. As early as the end of the fourth century it was celebrated at Jerusalem with much solemnity, and attracted thither a great concourse of bishops, monks, and pilgrims.[4] Like

---

[1] That of Morcelli (Kal CP, Rome, 1788), attributed to the eighth century, that of Naples (ninth century), the Menologion of Basil, etc

[2] *Missale Goth*, Sacramentary of Bobbio, and the Luxeuil Lectionary

[3] In addition to the texts referred to, consult Isidore, *De Off*, i 41; *Conc Tol.*, iv, c 10

[4] *Peregrinatio, infra*, pp 522, 576

the festivals of Easter and Epiphany, it lasted eight days. From Jerusalem it passed to Constantinople, and at length to Rome, where it was introduced as late as the seventh century.[1]

The Gallican Churches, to which this festival was unknown, had another of the same significance, at least in regard to the discovery of the true cross. They celebrated it on the 3rd of May. It is found on this date in several early manuscripts of the Hieronymian Martyrology.[2] In the Mozarabic Calendars and in the two Gallican Sacramentaries of Autun (*Missale Gothicum*) and Bobbio respectively it appears between the octave of Easter and the Rogation days, without a more precise indication of date. In the Gelasian Sacramentary it is noted on the 3rd of May, but, as it is not found in the earliest documents bearing on the Roman usage—the Sacramentaries of Leo and of Pope Adrian—its presence here may be attributed to a Gallican revision of this text. It seems even to have been introduced into Gaul somewhat late, that is, in the course of the seventh century, and it is possible that it was not universally observed there when the Roman usage was adopted.[3] The assignation of the date seems to have been occasioned by the legend of the invention of the cross, in which a certain Judas-Cyriacus figured [4]

---

[1] *Lib Pont*, vol 1 p 374

[2] For instance, those of Berne and Wolfenbuttel, the latter of the year 772, and the former somewhat later. In the Epternach manuscript (*Parisinus*, 10837) of the beginning of the eighth century there is no mention of this festival It is also lacking in the Luxeuil Lectionary, and Gregory of Tours does not mention it either, in a passage (*Gl. Mart.*, 5) where we might expect to find a notice of it.

[3] See the preceding note A Festival called *Inventio Crucis est* given in the Naples Capitulary (seventh century), published by Dom G. Morin (*Anal. Maredsolana*, vol. i p. 427); but the day is uncertain, so that it is impossible to know if it is the Festival of May 3 or that of September 14.

[4] *Lib. Pont*, vol. 1 p cviii

6. *St. Michael and the Maccabees.*

The only angel of whom we find a commemoration before the ninth century is St. Michael Festivals of this kind can be attributed only to the dedications of churches. This was the case, in fact, with the Byzantine festival of the 8th of November, relative to the Church of St. Michael in the baths of Arcadius;[1] also with the festival of the 8th of May, relative to the celebrated sanctuary of Monte Gargano, and with that of the 29th of September, relative to a church (destroyed long ago) in the suburbs of Rome at the sixth milestone on the Via Salaria. This festival of St. Michael is the only one of the kind which appears in the early Roman liturgical books. It is found in an authority as early as the Leonian Sacramentary, that is, of the sixth century. The Gallican books and calendars make no mention of a day especially assigned to the commemoration of St Michael the archangel.[2]

The festival of the Maccabees (August 1) seems to have been universally observed in the Church about the fifth century. It is mentioned in all the calendars, beginning with the most ancient form of the Hieronymian Martyrology.[3] It does not occur, however, in any of the Gallican or Roman liturgical books, except the Gelasian Sacramentary. The commemoration of the Maccabees, occurring, as it does, in the kalends of August, must have been eclipsed by the festival of St. Peter *a vinculis*.

[1] Martinov, *Annus Eccl Graeco-Slavicus*, p. 273.

[2] It is only in the Mozarabic Calendars of the tenth and eleventh centuries that we find the Festival of the 29th of September evidently imported from Rome

[3] Syriac Menologion (412); calendars of Polemius Silvius (448), and of Carthage (fifth to sixth century), all the manuscripts of the Hieronymian Martyrology; homilies of St Gregory Nazianzen, St Chrysostom, St. Augustine, St. Gaudentius of Brescia, St. Leo, St. Cæsarius of Arles etc, the inscriptions of Arles in De Rossi, *Bull*, 1874, p. 148, Mozarabic Calendars.

7. *The Festivals of the Apostles.*

I have already mentioned certain festivals of the apostles celebrated at Christmastide. I proceed now to deal with some other festivals of the same nature, confining myself to the notice of those which were celebrated at an early date in the West. The most important of these is that of St. Peter and St. Paul, on the 29th of June. It appears in the Philocalian Calendar of the year 336, coupled with the consular date 258. I have elsewhere [1] shown how this date may serve to determine the origin of the festival. We have here, not the anniversary of the martyrdom of either of the apostles, or of them both together, but merely the commemoration of the translation of their relics to the place called *ad Catacumbas*, at the third milestone on the Appian Way. At the beginning of the fourth century, when the calendar of the Roman Church was drawn up, from which calendar the text of the Philocalian is derived, the bodies of the two apostles were still reposing in this place. They were removed from it later on to be deposited in the basilicas raised to their honour by the Emperor Constantine on their original burying-places at the Vatican and the Ostian Way respectively. These translations brought about no change in the date of the celebration of their festival, the observation which had doubtless become rooted in the customs of the Christian population in Rome

The same calendar contains, under the date of the 22nd of February, a festival entitled *Natale Petri de Cathedra*. It was intended to be a commemoration of the beginning of the episcopate or apostolate of St. Peter. Its connection with the festival of the 29th of June was exactly the same as that which exists between the anniversaries

[1] *Liber Pontif*, vol 1 p civ

of the *natalis* and of the *depositio* of each bishop—anniversaries which the Popes, at least, were accustomed to commemorate, and that, too, as early as the first half of the fourth century. The choice of the day was not suggested by any Christian tradition. The reason will be clear if we glance at the ancient calendars of pagan Rome,[1] wherein we see that the 22nd of February was devoted to the celebration of a festival, popular above all others, in memory of the dead of each family. The observance of this festival and the participation in its ceremonies were considered as a thing incompatible with the profession of a Christian; but it was very difficult to uproot such ancient and cherished habits. It was, doubtless, to meet this difficulty that the Christian festival of the 22nd of February was instituted.

This festival was of more special interest to the Church of Rome than to others. Hence we see that it was never adopted in the East. It has not left, moreover, any trace in Africa.[2] In Gaul, however, it is found at a somewhat early date. As early as 448 it is mentioned in the Calendar of Polemius Silvius[3] Several homilies bear testimony to its existence and to its identification with the pagan festival of the *Cara Cognatio*.[4] The Council of Tours of the year 567[5] is also a witness to it. From these authorities we may gather how difficult it must have been to suppress the ancient funeral repast of the 22nd of February. This funeral repast was observed

[1] Mommsen, *Corp Ins Lat*, vol. i. p. 386.
[2] The Calendar of Carthage makes no mention of it. The sermons on this festival attributed to St Augustine are now known to be apocryphal.
[3] Under the incorrect title of *Depositio sancti Petri et Pauli*.
[4] See, especially, sermons 190–192 in the appendix to the sermons of St. Augustine.
[5] Can 22: "Sunt etiam qui in festivitate cathedrae domni Petri apostoli cibos mortuis offerunt, et post missas redeuntes ad domos proprias ad gentilium revertuntur errores, et post corpus Domini sacratas daemoni escas accipiunt."

in the West up to the twelfth century at least. I have been a witness of this custom among the orthodox Greeks in Epirus, and also among the Mahometans.

The *Natale Petri de Cathedra* was the subject of another coincidence, of which the inconvenience came at length to be recognised. It occurred often in Lent. In countries observing the Gallican rite, where Lenten observance was considered incompatible with the honouring of saints,[1] the difficulty was avoided by holding the festival on an earlier date. The liturgical books place it in the month of January, alongside the festival of the Blessed Virgin, which was celebrated on the 18th of that month.[2] The Hieronymian Martyrology, in its Auxerre recension, is more precise. It gives the 18th of January as the day of the festival of the Chair of St. Peter *at Rome*. The Auxerre editor was accommodating himself here to the custom of his country, but as the text before him noted a *Natale S. Petri de Cathedra* on the 22nd of February, the idea occurred to him of preserving the two commemorations by attributing the latter to Antioch, a see which was believed to have been also occupied by the prince of the apostles.

This combination was not at first received with favour. Only the feast of the 18th of January continued to be observed in Gaul. This is seen from the mention of it

---

[1] *Conc. Tol.*, x. c 1

[2] The Luxeuil Lectionary reckons only two Sundays between Epiphany and the festival of the *Cathedra*, and places three between the latter and Lent. The Sacramentary of Bobbio puts the festival of the *Cathedra* immediately before that of the Virgin (January 18); as for the *Missale Gothicum*, it intercalates between the festival of the *Cathedra* and that of the Virgin masses for St. Agnes (January 21), St. Cecilia (November 22), St. Clement (November 23), St. Saturninus (November 29), St Andrew (November 30), St Eulalia (December 10), and for the Conversion of St Paul (January 25) It is clear from this that it does not follow here the order of the calendar, and that it cannot consequently be adduced as a witness against the unanimity of the other documents

in the ancient Sacramentary of Gellona (eighth to ninth century), where it is accompanied by the explanation Se&*un-dum Gallos*. As far as Rome was concerned, the festival of the 22nd of February was maintained to the exclusion of the other, and that, too, down to the sixteenth century.[1]

A third festival of St. Peter was celebrated at Rome on the 1st of August. This was the festival of the Dedication of the Church of the Apostles,[2] on the Esquiline, which was rebuilt in the time of Xystus [Sixtus] III. (432–440) at the cost of the Imperial family of the East. In this church were preserved, as much-venerated relics, the chains of St. Peter, by which name the basilica itself was frequently designated.[3]

---

[1] De Rossi, *Bull*, 1867, p 38. The conclusions arrived at in this learned memoir differ from mine The difference must not be attributed to a superficial examination on my part of the reasons alleged and of the solutions set aside I am unable to admit, in particular, that there was any connection, before the later Middle Ages, between the *Notule Cathedrae S Petri* and the cult of the relic venerated at Rome under the name of Chair of St Peter. The texts adduced to prove that this chair was in existence as early as the fourth century in the baptistery of the Vatican have not the meaning assigned to them They speak of the *Sedes Petri*, or *Sedes Apostolica*, only in a metaphorical sense The statement of Ennodius as to a *sella gestatoria*, has reference to the *sella* on which the consuls were carried in the consular processions (*Revue de Philologie*, vol vii (1883), p. 81) The most ancient mention of a relic thus called is in the catalogue of Monza, of the time of St. Gregory and Queen Theodelinda (De Rossi, *Roma Sott*, vol i. p. 176)· *Oleo de sede ubi prius sedit S Petrus* This oil had been obtained on the Via Salaria, or Via Nomentana, far from the Vatican. Here was a cemetery called sometimes *Ad Nymphas S Petri*, where, it is said, St Peter baptised This tradition is referred to early in the sixth century in the *Gesta Liberii papae* and the *Passio Marcelli*. There was in that place, doubtless, a movable chair, or perhaps a chair cut in the tufa, which was regarded as a *Sedes S Petri*. As to that of the Vatican, unlike in shape and size to anything in the Catacombs, I know of no mention of it before 1217 (*Nerini, De templo S. Alexii*, p 209) Peter Mallius, writing of the basilica of St Peter (1159–1181), does not allude to it, and considering how constantly he enlarges on the relics therein, his silence shows that no chair of St. Peter was venerated then.

[2] Philip, a priest of this church, was a legate at the Council of Ephesus (431) (Hard, vol. 1 p. 1483). It existed, therefore, before Xystus III.

[3] This designation, *a vinculis S Petri*, is first met with in the *Lib Pont*, vol. i. p. 261, in the account of an event in 501, and in an inscription of 533 (*ibid.*, p 285). The poem of Arator, read in this basilica in 544, mentions the chains.

This festival was peculiar to Rome, and was never imported into the East,[1] or into the countries of the Gallican rite. It is certain that it was intended to commemorate the dedication of the basilica on the Esquiline. This dedication, therefore, had taken place on the 1st of August. As the 1st of August, from the time of Augustus, was a day of pagan religious observance and rejoicing,[2] it is possible that it was designedly chosen.

The special festival of St. Paul (January 25) was of much less importance than those just mentioned. In the Auxerre recension of the Hieronymian Martyrology it is called *Translatio S. Pauli Apostoli*, without any indication as to where this translation had taken place. In the *Missale Gothicum* there is a mass *in Conversione S. Pauli*, which appears to have been assigned to the same date.[3] In the ancient Roman books there is absolutely no mention of this festival.[4]

The festival of St. John the Evangelist (May 6) must have been the anniversary of the dedication of the church near the Porta Latina, which had been consecrated in his honour. This church is mentioned for the first time in the *Liber Pontificalis*, in the passage dealing with Pope Adrian I. (772-795).[5] The festival of St. John *ante Portam Latinam* has no earlier testimony than the Sacramentary of the same Pope. We ought, however, to take note of the fact that the Greeks celebrate on the 8th of May [6]

[1] In the East there are festivals in honour of the chains of St Peter, or of the deliverance of St Peter (Acts xii), but they have no connection with the Roman festival under consideration.

[2] The vulgar still observe at Rome the day of the *felice Agosto*

[3] Cf p 279, note 2

[4] We must bear in mind, however, that the Roman mass for Sexagesima Sunday is really a mass in honour of St. Paul The station was held on that day in the basilica of this apostle on the Ostian Way There are sermons of St. Augustine on the Conversion of St. Paul, but we must not conclude from this that the festival existed in his time.

[5] Vol. i p 508, l. 23. *Johannis Baptistae* is an error.

[6] Martinov, *op. cit.*, p. 124.

a festival in commemoration of a miracle which was performed on the tomb of the apostle at Ephesus. This miracle was known in Gaul, for Gregory of Tours makes mention of it.[1] In the *Missale Gothicum* there is a Mass *S. Johannis Apostoli et Evangelistae* between the festival of the Invention of the Cross (May 3) and the Rogation days. The connection is closer, I think, between this festival and that observed in the Greek church than between it and the Roman Commemoration. But there is nothing to prevent our believing that the latter, which must have been instituted when Rome was under Byzantine influence, had been itself determined by some consideration of the solemnity at Ephesus.[2]

The festival of the 1st of May in honour of SS. Philip and James was also an anniversary of the dedication of a church, namely, of that called the Holy Apostles at Rome. This church, originally founded by Pope Julius (337–352), was rebuilt about 561 by the Popes Pelagius I. and John III., and placed under the names of the two apostles Philip and James. The 1st of May was fixed upon for the day of the dedication, because the festival of St. Philip was commemorated on this date.[3] I am unable to single out from the two or three apostles so named, the James who was here associated with St. Philip. The Hieronymian Martyrology mentions the festival of St. Philip at Hierapolis in Phrygia, and an interpolation occurs here of the name of St. James, who is thus placed under a false topographical rubric. The Gallican liturgical books contain no mention of any festival commemorating either St. Philip alone or associated with St. James.

[1] *Glor. Mart.*, 30.
[2] In the Martyrology of Ado, the *Porta Latina* is given as the locality of the cauldron of boiling oil, in which, according to a tradition already in existence in the second century, St. John was said to have been plunged (Tertullian, *Praesc.*. 36).
[3] *Lib Pont*, vol. i. p. 306, note 2.

In the East there were festivals of St. Philip the Apostle and St. James the Deacon, but these have no connection with the festivals previously mentioned.

The festival of St. Andrew (November 30) was of much greater importance, and was more widely celebrated. It occurs on this day in all the calendars from the sixth century onwards.[1] It is difficult to trace out its origin, or at least to suppose, as would seem to follow from the celebrated letter (apocryphal) on the martyrdom of the apostle, that this was the day of his festival at Patras. In any case, this was not the day on which his translation was observed at Constantinople (March 3), neither was it that of the second dedication of the Church of the Holy Apostles in this city (July 28), nor of that of the dedication of the first church consecrated to him at Rome (November 3).[2]

8. *The Martyrs and other Local Festivals.*

Whatever may have been the dignity of the individuals in whose honour the immovable festivals of which I have just been writing were instituted, these festivals, without exception, yield in point of antiquity to the anniversaries of the martyrs. The latter go back to the second century. The anniversary of the martyrdom of St. Polycarp († 155) was instituted at Smyrna immediately after his death[3] I could not instance, in the case of Rome, a commemoration as ancient. It is a remarkable thing even that the martyrs of the second century at Rome—I mean genuine martyrs,

---

[1] It is not found in the Calendars of Philocalus, or of Polemius Silvius, or of Perpetuus It appears in that of Carthage, in all the Roman and Gallican liturgical books, and in the Byzantine Calendar, etc.

[2] *Lib. Pont*, vol. 1. p 250; *Hier. Mart*, 3rd November

[3] *Martyr Polyc*, 18. "Παρέξει ὁ Κύριος ἐπιτελεῖν τὴν τοῦ μαρτυρίου αὐτοῦ ἡμέραν γενέθλιον"

and indubitably of the second century, like Pope Telesphorus and St. Justin Martyr—were not inscribed in the ecclesiastical calendars of the time of Constantine. The anniversaries inserted in these calendars refer to martyrs of the third century at the earliest. The Christian epitaphs at Rome, moreover, belonging to a date earlier than the third century, contain no indication of the day of the death of the deceased, whether they were martyrs or not. The case would have been different if, as early as this, the funeral anniversary had become the subject of a religious commemoration, and, as far as the martyrs were concerned, of an ecclesiastical solemnisation. From the beginning of the third century, on the other hand, the celebration of the anniversary became a matter of universal observance.

The anniversaries of martyrs were, naturally, local festivals. Each Church honoured its own saints. Sometimes, owing, it may be, to the lack of special festivals for each martyr, or in the way of addition to these festivals, a general commemoration of all the martyrs of a locality was celebrated.

The practice soon arose of one Church adopting the commemorations of another, and thus the festivals of the most distinguished saints were celebrated elsewhere, as well as in their own country. Some even attained an almost œcumenical veneration, such as St. Xystus [Sixtus] and St. Laurence of Rome, and St. Cyprian of Carthage, etc. The translation of relics, real or representative, gave, from the fourth century onwards, a great impulse to this form of veneration, and to the festivals associated with it.

There soon came to be associated with the martyrs the holy confessors, that is, the ascetæ, using the term in its fourth-century significance, such as St. Martin, St. Anthony, St. Simeon Stylites, etc.

Among the local festivals there must also be mentioned the anniversaries of the dedications of churches, and of the ordination (*natale*) and burial (*depositio*) of bishops.

9. *Fasts, Octaves, and Litanies.*

Besides festivals, properly so called, the ecclesiastical year embraced also fasting and litany days.

At the outset, the fasts before Easter and those of the weekly stations were the only public, common, and obligatory observances. The bishops, however, were accustomed to prescribe extraordinary fasts, as the occasion demanded. These arbitrary appointments, which seem to have been very frequent, and for this reason somewhat burthensome, were gradually replaced by fixed observances on certain prescribed days. It was for this reason, as we have seen,[1] that the Council of Elvira restricted the custom of weekly *superpositions* to once a month. At Rome, from the time of St. Leo, no more than four were provided in each year, but fifty years previously they appear to have been more numerous.[2]

The Ember days, as I have previously said, were a special feature of Roman usage in the matter of fasts observed at other seasons than Lent. Elsewhere than in Rome, the days at the end of, or immediately following, the paschal solemnities were observed as fasts everywhere. At Milan, in the fourth century, the ten days between Ascension and Pentecost were reckoned as days of fasting.[3] St. Isidore[4] makes mention of this custom, and explains it. But it was a more general practice to put off this fasting until after Pentecost. This was the custom in the East, in

---

[1] See above, p. 231.
[2] St Augustine, *Ep.*, 46: "Christianus qui quarta et sexta feria et ipso sabbato jejunare consuevit quod *frequenter* plebs Romana facit."
[3] Philastrius, *Haer.*, 119.
[4] *De Off*, i. 38.

Gaul, and in Spain,[1] allowing for certain differences in the number of days and in the time fixed for the beginning of the fast.

The summer Ember days at Rome offered some points of resemblance to the Pentecostal fast.

In Gallican regions the fast of the kalends of January was also observed. It is to this, possibly, that Philastrius, writing in the fourth century, refers when he speaks of the fast of the Epiphany.[2] The aim of this observance in Gaul and Spain[3] was to detach the faithful from the pagan masquerades and ceremonies of the 1st of January—ancient heathen customs, of which traces remain until the present day. It is possible, however, that this custom was adopted at the very beginning as a preparation for the observance of the Epiphany.[4] From the example of the fast which precedes Easter, it was concluded that every high festival ought to have a preparatory fast immediately before it. Such was the origin of the fast before Christmas, which is mentioned by Philastrius in the passage just referred to, and which was adopted later on in Gaul.[5] This was the fast

---

[1] *Const Apost*, v. 20; cf Athanasius, *Apol de fuga sua* (vol i p 323); the Council of Gerona (517), c. 2; Isidore, *loc cit*; Council of Tours (567), c 17 (in reference to monks only). In the East it was not begun until after the octave of Pentecost. This was the fast which, having been extended up to the festival of SS. Peter and Paul (June 29), became the Greek fast of the Holy Apostles.

[2] In Epiphania (*loc. cit*).

[3] Council of Tours (567), c 17; Isidore, *De Off*, i. 41, 42

[4] We have previously seen (p. 260) that the festival of the Epiphany seems to have been regarded, in Gallican countries, as of more importance than that of Christmas.

[5] Calendar of Perpetuus: Council of Tours, *can cit*; Council of Mâcon (581), c. 19. I find no trace of it in Spain It was more especially observed by monks (Bede, *H. E*, iii 27; iv. 30). It is worthy of note that in the system referred to by Philastrius there were, as at Rome, four solemn fasts every year: those of Lent, Pentecost, Christmas, and Epiphany; but the appointment of the special weeks and months did not originate from one and the same considerations

which gave rise to the special solemnisation of the four weeks before the festival of Christmas referred to in the Roman liturgical books of the eighth century.

The same idea was at the bottom of the custom of fasting on the vigils of the high festivals, that is, of those in which the ancient *pervigilium* or nocturnal Synaxis had been preserved. But these fasts were not generally observed until a somewhat late period. That which is ancient about them is not the fast, but the vigil.[1]

The festival of Easter was truly a model festival, and was an object of imitation in the case of all others. Before the latter had been provided with preparatory fasts they already possessed octaves, which were a reproduction of Easter Week.[2] In the fourth century it was customary at Jerusalem to solemnise the Epiphany and dedication festivals for eight days. This custom was very generally followed everywhere at an early date, and applied also to other festivals.

Litanies were solemn supplications, instituted to implore the blessing of Heaven on the fruits of the earth It was customary to recite them in the spring, that is, in the season of late frosts, so much dreaded by the cultivators of the soil. It is not a matter of wonder that Christian practice on this point should coincide with customs anterior to it. The same necessities, the same apprehension of dangers, and the same trust in Divine help, inspired rites mutually resembling each other. The practice was based on the idea of a kind of *lustration* of the cultivated lands, in which the future harvest was giving indications of its promise. The people marched in procession to the spot, chanting the while that dialogue

---

[1] See above, p. 229.

[2] It is needless to point out that this was derived from the ceremonies of the Jewish Passover.

prayer which we call a litany, elaborated, according to circumstances, into a long series of invocations addressed to God and to angels and saints.

The day set apart for this purpose at Rome was the 25th of April, a traditional date, being that on which the ancient Romans celebrated the festival of the *Robigalia*. The principal ceremony of the latter was a procession, which, setting out from the Flaminian Gate, made its way towards the Milvian Bridge, and arrived at length at a suburban sanctuary some distance off, that is, at the fifth milestone on the Claudian Way.[1] The Christian procession which replaced it followed the same route as far as the Milvian Bridge. It set out from the Church of St. Laurence *in Lucina*, the nearest to the Flaminian Gate, held a station at St. Valentine outside the walls, and afterwards at the Milvian Bridge. From thence, instead of proceeding along the Claudian Way, it turned to the left towards the Vatican, stopped at a cross, of which the site is not given, and again in the paradise or atrium of St. Peter, and finally in the basilica itself, where the station was held.[2]

The most ancient authority for this ceremony is a formulary for convoking it found in the Register of St. Gregory the Great,[3] which must have been used in the first instance for the year 598.

In Gaul, from the end of the fifth century, the three days before Ascension were adopted for using this litany. Bishop Mamertus (*circ.* 470) of Vienne was the first to introduce this custom, and it was extended to the whole

---

[1] Ovid, *Fasti*, iv. 901. The *flamen Quirinalis* sacrificed in this temple a dog and a sheep.

[2] These stations are noted in the Sacramentary of Pope Adrian.

[3] Jaffé, 1153; *Ep app*, 3. We must not confound this annual litany with the extraordinary litany of 590, described by Gregory of Tours, *Hist. Fr.*, x. 1.

of Frankish Gaul[1] by the first Council of Orleans (511).[2] These litany prayers were called *Rogations*.[3] The Rogation days were days of very strict fasting. They were introduced into Rome in the time of Pope Leo III., about the year 800.[4]

The litanies for springtime were not employed in Spain, but litanies were used there in the beginning of November,[5] at the time of sowing the seed. These were not the only litanies in use. They were also employed, according to the locality, on the fast of Pentecost,[6] and at the autumnal equinox.[7]

Litanies were as much in use in the East as in the West, but they seem not to have been connected with prescribed days.

10. *Calendars and Martyrologies*

The festivals celebrated every year were noted in the local calendar. Each Church must have possessed its own. The most ancient which have come down to us are those of Rome, Tours, and Carthage.[8]

The Roman Calendar has come down to us in two different forms. The most complete form is that presented

---

[1] Without disturbing, it must be understood, the litanies already in use in certain Churches. There was, at Auxerre, a litany at the beginning of each month (*Gesta Epp. Autissiod*, c. 19; Migne, *Pat Lat*, vol cxxxviii. p 233)

[2] Sidonius Apollinaris, *Ep*, v. 14; vii. 1; Council of Orleans, c. 27.

[3] This is the term used by Sidonius, and also by Avitus, the successor of Mamertus, in his homily *in Rogationibus*. The Council of Orleans also mentions *Rogationes id est litanias*.

[4] See on this subject the *Liber Pontificalis*, vol ii. p. 35, note 17, and p 40, note 58.

[5] Council of Gerona (517), c. 3; Isidore, *De Off.*, i. 40.

[6] Council of Gerona, c. 2.

[7] Isidore, *De Off*, i. 39.

[8] I must not neglect to mention here the fragment of a Gothic calendar published by Mai, *Script Vet.*, vol. v. p. 66

in the Hieronymian Martyrology. The Roman Calendar in this collection is not, it is true, given by itself. It is mixed up day by day with many other analogous documents, and it requires considerable critical ability to disengage it from its context. The other form is that given in the two tables called *Depositiones Episcoporum* and *Depositiones Martyrum*, which are contained in the collection known as the Philocalian. This collection, or, at least, the part of it containing these two tables, was drawn up in 336. The calendar preserved in the Hieronymian Martyrology exhibits indications of certain revisions, of which the latest are of the time of Pope Xystus III (432–440); but it also furnishes traces of an editing in the time of Pope Miltiades (311–314). From this circumstance, and from certain other considerations, we may conclude that the two forms of it were derived from a text in existence about the year 312, immediately after the last persecution.[1]

The Calendar of fasts and vigils in the Church of Tours has been preserved to us by Gregory, bishop of that town, in his *Historia Francorum* (x. 31). He mentions only the most solemn festivals, that is, those which were preceded by a vigil. This arrangement had been drawn up by Bishop Perpetuus (461–490).

The Calendar of the Church of Carthage, published by Mabillon,[2] and reproduced by Ruinart at the end of his *Acta Martyrum Sincera*, is somewhat less ancient. It contains the name of St. Eugenius, who died in 505.

By combining the calendars of different Churches, espe-

---

[1] See my memoir on *Les Sources du Martyrologe Hiéronymien*, in the *Mélanges de l'École de Rome*, vol. v. (1885), p. 137, *et seq.* Cf. *Lib. Pont.*, vol 1 pp. ix., cxlviii

[2] *Analecta*, vol iii p 398; folio edition, p. 163 Mabillon discovered it in the binding of a manuscript of the seventh century, or thereabout, at Cluny. The title runs as follows. *Hic continentur dies nataliciorum martyris et depositiones episcoporum quos ecclesia Carthagenis anniversaria celebrant* (sic).

cially those of great cities like Rome, Carthage, Alexandria, Antioch, and Nicomedia, the so-called martyrologies were formed. The most ancient collections of this nature seem to have been drawn up about the middle of the fourth century, in Africa and Asia Minor respectively. They have not come down to us in their primitive form. We know them only as they appear in the Hieronymian Martyrology, which was compiled about the middle of the fifth century in Italy, and thence carried to France, where, about the year 595, it was subjected, at Auxerre, to a revision, from which revised text all existing manuscripts of it are derived. In addition to the Hieronymian Martyrology, there has been preserved to us the primitive martyrology of Asia Minor in a much abridged Syriac translation [1]

The Hieronymian Martyrology had attained, from the seventh to the ninth century, a widespread celebrity; but, owing to its complexity, and the many errors made by copyists, who were embarrassed by the multitude of proper names both of persons and places, it was held in less esteem than abridged texts, which, while containing fewer saints, furnished certain historical details concerning them, together with extracts from their acts. These are what is known as historical martyrologies. The most ancient and best known examples are those of Bede, Florus, Rabanus Maurus, Ado, and Usuard. The latter, which was drawn up at St. Germain des Prés about the year 875, enjoyed much popularity during the Middle Ages. The existing Roman Martyrology is nothing more than a new edition of the latter, revised and completed by Cardinal Baronius.[2]

[1] In regard to all this, see the edition of the Hieronymian Martyrology, which I published in 1894 in concert with M. de Rossi, in vol. ii. of the *Acta Sanctorum Novembris*

[2] Cf. on this point Dom H. Quentin, *Les Martyrologes historiques du moyen age*, Paris, Lecoffre, 1900.

CHAPTER IX.

CEREMONIES OF CHRISTIAN INITIATION.

THE ceremonies of Christian initiation, such as they are described in authorities from the end of the second century onwards, consisted of three essential rites—Baptism, Confirmation, and First Communion. These could not be entered upon—at least, ordinarily—without a more or less lengthy preparation. As early as the end of the second century the increasing number of Christian candidates rendered it necessary to systematise this preparation, to lay down definite rules for its performance, and to determine the period of probation. Hence arose the discipline of the catechumenate.

The catechumenate was a period during which converts learned and put into practice their essential duties in regard to belief and conduct. The catechumens were looked upon as members of the Christian community, and were regarded as Christians, the entrance of converts into this lower category being effected by rites which appear in the ancient liturgical books under the heading *ad Christianum faciendum*, or under one of a similar significance. Catechumens could remain in their probationary stage as long as they liked. The Emperors Constantine and Constantius, in the fourth century, continued catechumens until they were at the point of death. The system of prolonging the catechumenate considerably lightened the burden of disciplinary obligations, and was much in vogue with the aristocracy, who largely availed themselves of it.

If a catechumen was desirous of completing his initiation, and the rulers of the Church deemed him worthy to receive baptism, he passed into the category of the *elect*, or *competents*.[1] At the beginning of Lent the names of those who were to be baptised on Easter Eve were written down. During these solemn forty days they were obliged to be present frequently at church, in order to undergo exorcisms and to hear preparatory instruction on baptism.

It was at Easter, in fact, that baptism was ordinarily administered, and that, too, from the earliest times [2] The vigil of Easter Sunday was devoted to this ceremony. If this did not allow sufficient time of probation, or if the neophyte for any reason could not participate in the initiation on this day, it was postponed to a later date in Eastertide. The last day for this purpose, that of Pentecost, as much on account of its being the last as for its own special solemnity, came soon to be regarded as a second baptismal festival.

The Roman Church restricted baptism to this period. In the East, the Epiphany, the great festival of the birth of Christ and of His baptism, appeared to be naturally indicated for the second birth, the regeneration, the baptism of Christians. The Greek Fathers of the end of the fourth century are witnesses to the custom in their respective countries of blessing the baptismal waters on this day, and of baptising the neophytes. The example of the East was followed by several Western Churches, and it became gradually the custom to put Christmas and several other

---

[1] Herr Fr. X. Funk (*Theologische Quartalschrift*, 1883, p. 41, *et seq*) shows clearly that these were the only subdivisions of the catechumens, and that the view of their having been distributed into four classes is based on a wrong interpretation of the ancient texts.

[2] Tertullian, *De Baptismo*, 19.

festivals on the same footing as the Epiphany[1] in this respect. The Popes, however, urgently insisted upon, and succeeded in securing—not, it is true, without difficulty—the observance by the Latin Churches of the ancient Roman custom, which had its origin at a period long anterior to the institution of the festival of the Nativity.

The rites observed in regard to the catechumenate, baptism, and confirmation, varied, as was the case with the Eucharistic Liturgy, according to the country. I will describe in the following pages the various customs.

§ 1.—Baptism according to the Roman Usage.

The documents from which we gather the baptismal ceremonies of the Roman Church are as follows:—[2]

1. The *Ordo Baptismi*, published by Mabillon as No. VII. This *Ordo*, as far as the text is concerned, goes back, at least, to the time of Charlemagne. We find it almost in its entirety, and word for word, in an instruction on baptism given by Jesse, Bishop of Amiens, to the clergy of his diocese, probably in 812.[3]

2. The Sacramentary of Pope Adrian, which furnishes but few details, except in regard to the final ceremony.

---

[1] Cf. letter from Siricius to Himerus of Tarragona, c 2 It appears to have had no effect, for the Council of the Province of Tarragona still recognised, in 517, Christmas as a baptismal festival (*Conc. Gerund*, c 4); the letter of St Leo to the Bishops of Sicily (Jaffé, 414, c. 1); the letter of Gelasius to the Bishops of Lucania, etc, c. 12. Victor Vitensis, *Hist. Persec Vandal*, ii. 47; *Synodus Patricii*, n. 19 (Hardouin, vol i. p. 1795) From these last two authorities it would appear that the Epiphany was a baptismal festival both in Africa and in Ireland. The Councils of Mâcon (585) c 3, and Auxerre (*circ* 585), show that the Roman custom prevailed in Gaul towards the end of the sixth century. For the East, see especially Gregory Nazianzen, hom. 40; various homilies of St. John Chrysostom, vol ii. pp. 268, 433; vol. xi p. 25, Theodoret, *Hist. Eccl*, ii 27.

[2] Cf. also the "Apostolic Tradition" of Hippolytus, Appendix 6.

[3] Migne, *Pat. Lat.*, vol cv p 781. Cf. above, p. 149.

3. The Gelasian Sacramentary, which agrees generally with the *Ordo;* but here, also, possible Gallican revision has to be taken into account.

The almost complete agreement between the Gelasian Sacramentary and the *Ordo Baptismi* proves that the latter represents the custom of the seventh century at the latest. From certain details, such as the bilingual formularies, the employment of the Nicene Creed, the substitution of acolytes for exorcists, we are forced to the conclusion that this ritual was not finally drawn up until the course of the seventh century, that is, in Byzantine times.

At this period the baptism of adults had become exceptional, and the rites of initiation were ordinarily confined to infants. Thus the *Ordo* and the rubrics of the Sacramentary speak of infants in arms, who are accompanied by godfathers and godmothers to answer in their names. It is clear, however, that the formularies were composed for adults, and that the ceremonies themselves have only their full significance where persons of riper years are concerned. It is necessary, therefore, in order to place the whole in its true light, to regard the details which limit the ceremony to infants, and thus cause a chronological transposition of the whole text, as indications of the work of a reviser. I will endeavour, therefore, to take this into consideration in the following description.[1]

1. *Rites of the Catechumenate.*

The entrance into the catechumenate was accompanied by the following ceremonies:—

[1] Most of the rites here described are still in use when baptism is solemnly administered to adults; but everything takes place at the one service. In the case of infants, the ceremonies are fundamentally the same, but considerably abridged.

The insufflation, with a formulary of exorcism;
The signing with the cross on the forehead;
The administering of salt.

The convert presents himself before the priest, who, after blowing in his face,[1] marks him on the forehead with the sign of the cross, saying, *In nomine Patris et Filii et Spiritus sancti*. This ceremony is followed by a prayer, which the priest recites, holding his hand extended over the candidate:[2]

> Omnipotens, sempiterne Deus, Pater domini nostri Jesus Christi, respicere dignare super hunc famulum tuum quem ad rudimenta fidei vocare dignatus es. Omnem caecitatem cordis ab eo expelle; disrumpe omnes laqueos Satanae quibus fuerat conligatus. Aperi ei, Domine, januam pietatis tuae, et signo sapientiae tuae imbutus omnium cupiditatum foetoribus careat, et suavi odore praeceptorum tuorum laetus tibi in Ecclesia deserviat, et proficiat de die in diem, ut idoneus efficiatur accedere ad gratiam baptismi tui, percepta medicina.

Then follows the administering of the salt,[3] which had been previously exorcised:—

---

[1] This ceremony is not given in the *Ordo* or in the Sacramentaries, but it is attested by John, the Roman deacon, in his letter to Senarius, an official of the time of Theodoric (Migne, *Pat. Lat.*, vol. lix. p. 402). He says even that it was followed by an exorcism, *ut exeat et recedat (diabolus)*. These words are also found in the formularies for exorcism which were prescribed according to the custom of the seventh century for the scrutiny at Lent.

[2] I give the text of the Gelasian Sacramentary, i. 30, using the singular for the plural number. The two other formularies which follow this prayer seem to be variants. This prayer is also found in the Gregorian Sacramentary, p 60 (Muratori), but it is incomplete towards the end. Beside the ritual given in i. 30-32, the Gelasian Sacramentary furnishes another, i. 71, which has supplied much of the material of the ritual of the present day. I think, however, that this second ritual is Gallican, with the exception of the administering of the salt, which is decidedly Roman, but which is accompanied in this case by no formulary The formularies i. 71, or something like them, are found in the *Missale Gothicum* and in the Gallican Sacramentary.

[3] The administering of salt is mentioned by John the Deacon.

Exorcizo te, creatura salis, in nomine Dei Patris omnipotentis et in caritate domini nostri Jesu Christi et in virtute Spiritus sancti. Exorcizo te per Deum vivum et per Deum verum, qui te ad tutelam humani generis procreavit et populo venienti ad credulitatem per servos suos consecrari praecepit. Proinde rogamus te, domine Deus noster, ut haec creatura salis in nomine Trinitatis efficiatur salutare sacramentum ad effugandum inimicum. Quam tu, Domine, sanctificando sanctifices, benedicendo benedicas; ut fiat omnibus accipientibus perfecta medicina, permanens in visceribus eorum, in nomine domini nostri Jesu Christi qui venturus est judicare vivos et mortuos et saeculum per ignem.

The priest then puts a particle of salt in the mouth of the candidate, saying, *Accipe N., sal sapientiae, propitiatus in vitam aeternam.* He concludes with a prayer—

Deus patrum nostrorum, Deus universae conditor veritatis, te supplices exoramus, ut hunc famulum tuum respicere digneris propitius; ut hoc primum pabulum salis gustantem non diutius esurire permittas quominus cibo expleatur caelesti, quatenus sit semper, Domine, spiritu fervens, spe gaudens, tuo semper nomini serviens. Perduc eum ad novae 're-generationis lavacrum, ut cum fidelibus tuis promissionum tuarum aeterna praemia consequi mereatur.

After this ceremony the candidate was regarded as a catechumen, and was admitted to religious assemblies, but not to the Eucharistic Liturgy, properly so called. The catechumens had a special place assigned to them in the church, and were dismissed before the beginning of the holy mysteries.[1]

Accipiet jam catechumenus benedictum sal. It would appear that at the beginning this ceremony was frequently repeated. A canon of the Council of Hippo (393) implies that the catechumens were accustomed to receive the salt all through the year, even at Easter (*Conc Carth*, III. c. 5). The administering of salt is a characteristic of the Roman rite.

[1] See above, pp 58, 171, 202.

2. *Preparation for Baptism.*

The preparation for baptism, at Rome as elsewhere, consisted of a series of instructions and exercises during the season of Lent. The meetings for this purpose were called *scrutinies;* and in the seventh century amounted to seven in number. No Roman collection of catechetical instructions is now in existence which might be compared with those of St. Cyril of Jerusalem, but the latter is sufficient to give us an idea of the nature and form of the teaching given preparatory to baptism.[1]

As the name suggests, the scrutinies were designed to test the preparation of the candidates, and especially to present them to the faithful, who, if the occasion arose, could protest against the admission of such as might be unworthy. Upon this matter the documents are necessarily mute. They contain nothing beyond the prayers and the rites. The latter had in view the gradual casting out of the evil spirit by forcing him to relinquish his hold over those who were about to pass into the kingdom of Christ.

In the seventh century[2] the scrutinies began in the third week of Lent. At the Stational Mass on the Monday an announcement[3] was made from the ambo of the first of these meetings—

Scrutinii diem, dilectissimi Fratres, quo electi nostri divinitus instruantur, imminere cognoscite. Ideoque sollicita devotione, succedente

---

[1] The sermons of St Augustine addressed *ad competentes* (Nos. 56-59, 112-116) may be regarded as representing the Latin custom, and even the Roman, for Africa followed, both in baptismal and other rites, the order prevailing at Rome.

[2] See Appendix, p 577c.

[3] *Gel*, 1. 29. The Gelasian Sacramentary gives after this the rites of the catechumenate such as have been just described The *Ordo* also assigns them to the first scrutiny, but this may not have been their original place.

sequente *illa* feria, circa horam diei sextam convenire dignemini, ut caeleste mysterium quo diabolus cum sua pompa destruitur et janua regni caelestis aperitur, inculpabili, Deo juvante, ministerio peragere valeamus.

At the first scrutiny the elect gave in their names, which were inscribed in a register. Then the sexes were separated, the men being placed on the right, and the women on the left.

The Mass then began. After the collect and before the lections, a deacon called upon the catechumens to prostrate themselves in prayer. The prayer was concluded by all of them saying in a loud voice, *Amen*. Always at a signal from the deacon they signed themselves with the sign of the cross, saying, *In nomine Patris*, etc. The exorcisms took place at this point in the service. One of the clergy,[1] whose duty it was, approached the male candidates, and having made the sign of the cross on the forehead of each, imposed his hands upon each and pronounced the formulary of exorcism. He then proceeded to the female candidates, and repeated the ceremony. A second exorcist followed him, and then a third, performing the same act. I give here one of the formularies used—

Deus Abraham, Deus Isaac, Deus Jacob, Deus qui Moysi famulo tuo in monte Sinai apparuisti et filios Israel de terra Aegypti eduxisti, deputans eis angelum pietatis tuae qui custodiret eos die ac nocte; te quaesumus, Domine, ut mittere digneris sanctum angelum tuum ut similiter custodiat et hos famulos tuos et perducat eos ad gratiam baptismi tui.

Ergo,[2] maledicte diabole, recognosce sententiam tuam et da honorem Deo vivo et vero, et da honorem Jesu Christo Filio ejus et Spiritui sancto; et recede ab his famulis Dei, quia istos sibi Deus et dominus

---

[1] The *Ordo* and the *Sacramentary* mention acolytes in this place, but it is certain that as long as there were exorcists in office, this was not the duty of acolytes.

[2] This portion of the formulary is invariable. It is repeated at each of the six exorcisms

noster Jesus Christus ad suam sanctam gratiam et benedictionem fontemque baptismatis dono[1] vocare dignatus est. Et hoc signum sanctae crucis frontibus eorum quod nos damus, tu, maledicte diabole, numquam audeas violare.

After each of the exorcists had performed his function in turn, the catechumens were invited to prostrate themselves and pray, signing themselves with the sign of the cross. A priest then approached, and repeated the ceremony of the signing and the imposition of hands, while saying—

> Aeternam ac justissimam pietatem tuam deprecor, domine sancte, Pater omnipotens, aeterne Deus luminis et veritatis, super hos famulos et famulas tuas, ut digneris eos inluminare lumine intelligentiae tuae. Munda eos et sanctifica; da eis scientiam veram, ut digni efficiantur accedere ad gratiam baptismi tui. Teneant firmam spem, consilium rectum, doctrinam sanctam, ut apti sint ad percipiendam gratiam tuam.

It is to be noted that the priest, instead of following the exorcists in conjuring the devil, merely makes his prayer to God. It was not his office—at least, at this moment—to conjure the demon. After a final prostration, the catechumens resume their places, and the Mass proceeds in their presence up to the Gospel. Before the reading of this they were dismissed. Their relations or sponsors, however, took part in the offering. The names of the latter were recited in the *Memento*, but those of the elect were included in the *Hanc igitur*, with a special recommendation.[2]

These exorcisms were repeated in the same manner, and with the same accompaniments, on the other days of the scrutiny, except the seventh. The third day possessed a special importance. It was on this day that the candidate was officially instructed in the Gospel, the Creed, and the

---

[1] *Donum* in the manuscript. Cf. below, p. 303. The same manuscript has, however, given *per* in place of *et*.

[2] Cf. above, p. 180.

CEREMONIES OF CHRISTIAN INITIATION. 301

Lord's Prayer. In other countries the initiation at this stage was limited to the Creed, and the ceremony was called *Traditio Symboli*. At Rome it was customary to make known to the initiated not only the Creed, but also the *instrumenta sacrosanctae legis*,[1] that is, a summary of the Christian Law. The name by which this ceremony was known there had also a wider import. It was called the "Opening of the Ears."

On this day the catechumens were not dismissed immediately after the gradual. As soon as this chant was finished, four deacons proceeded from the sacristy with an imposing ceremonial, each carrying one of the four Gospels. Approaching the altar, they placed thereon the sacred volumes, one at each of the corners of the holy table. A priest then began a discourse, in which he explained the nature of the Gospel. The elect were thereupon ordered[2] to stand up, in order to hear, in an attentive and respectful manner, one of the deacons read the first page of St. Matthew's Gospel, to which the priest added a short commentary. The same ceremony was repeated in the case of the three other evangelists.

After the *traditio* of the Gospel came that of the Creed, which was preceded and followed by an address from the priest. In Byzantine times the Nicæo-Constantinopolitan Creed was used, and provision was also made for its being recited, first in Greek, and then in Latin. The population of Rome at that time was bilingual, and the catechumens were grouped according to their language, to hear the recitation of the Creed. Each group in turn was led up to the priest by an acolyte[3] set apart for this

---

[1] In Africa, where the Roman rite was followed, we find also a *traditio* of the *Pater noster*, but not that of the Gospel Aug, *Serm*, 57, 58, Ferrandus, *Ep. ad Fulgentium* (Migne, *Pat. Lat.*, vol. lxv. p 379).

[2] Cf. p. 170.

[3] The acolyte in this case is probably a substitute for the exorcist, or possibly for the reader.

purpose. The priest then asked: *Qua lingua confitentur dominum nostrum Jesum Christum?* The acolyte replies, as the occasion requires, either *Graece* or *Latine*, and is then ordered by the priest to teach the catechumens, in their proper language, the formulary of the faith.

There is no doubt that the formulary employed originally at Rome was the Apostles' Creed, which is, properly speaking, the Roman symbol. This was the creed dealt with by St. Augustine in his explanation of this ceremony.[1]

Then followed the *traditio* of the *Pater noster*. The priest himself assumed this function. He began with a general exhortation, and then proceeded to recite clause by clause the text of the Lord's Prayer, accompanying his recitation with a running commentary. After the last petition there was a short address, which concluded the ceremony.[2]

This simple, but very imposing, ceremony must have produced a lively impression on the candidates for baptism. I am inclined to believe that this ceremony finds artistic expression in the representation of the giving of the Law which we find on many early Christian monuments, such as pictures, sarcophagi, decorated vases, and especially the apsidal mosaics of the basilicas. Christ is there depicted as seated on a splendid throne placed on the summit of a mountain from whence flow the four rivers of Paradise. Around him are assembled the apostles. St. Peter, their chief, receives from the hands of the Saviour a book—emblem of the Christian Law—on which is inscribed

---

[1] With regard to the Roman symbol and its history, and also the use of Greek in the Roman liturgy, see Caspari, *Quellen zur Geschichte des Taufsymbols*, etc., vol. iii, Christiania, 1875. Cf A. Harnack, *Patres Apostolici*, No 1, part 2 (2nd edition), p. 115.

[2] Several sermons of St. Augustine (56-59) bear upon the *traditio* of the *Pater noster*, and are explanatory of the latter. In Africa the *traditio* of the Pater took place eight days after that of the Creed (Aug. *Serm. ad compet*, lviii, lix ; *Pat Lat*, vol. xx , xviii. pp 393, 400) It is possible that at Rome in early times, each *traditio* was delivered on a separate occasion Cf. the Naples Capitulary referred to on p 275, note 3.

DOMINUS LEGEM DAT, or some similar device. Above this group there appear in the azure of the sky the four symbolical animals with the four books of the Gospel. I would not take upon myself to say that this scene was expressly depicted from the ritual of the *Traditio legis Christianae*, but there is such a striking resemblance between the two things, that the likeness could not fail to have been remarked. Many of the faithful, when casting their eyes upon the paintings which decorated the apses of their churches, must have had thus brought before them one of the most beautiful ceremonies of their initiation.

The seventh and last scrutiny was almost immediately before baptism. It took place on the vigil of Easter, and, according to the manuscripts of the eighth century, at the hour of *tierce;* but it is probable that in more ancient times it was held in the afternoon. As no Mass was celebrated on the Saturday in Holy Week, the ceremony had no connection with any stational assembly. On this occasion the exorcism was no longer assigned to the inferior clergy; a priest performed the duty of adjuring Satan on this the last function of the series. Passing down the ranks of the candidates, he made upon each the sign of the cross, and having placed his hand on the head of each, pronounced the last exorcism in the following terms:—

> Nec te latet, Satanas, imminere tibi paenas, imminere tibi tormenta, imminere tibi diem judicii, diem supplicii, diem qui venturus est velut clibanus ardens, in quo tibi atque universis angelis tuis aeternus veniet interitus. Proinde, damnate, da honorem Deo vivo et vero; da honorem Jesu Christo Filio ejus et Spiritui sancto, in cujus nomine atque virtute praecipio tibi ut exeas et recedas ab hoc famulo Dei, quem hodie dominus Deus noster Jesus Christus ad suam sanctam gratiam et benedictionem fontemque baptismatis dono vocare dignatus est, ut fiat ejus templum per aquam regenerationis in remissionem omnium peccatorum, in nomine domini nostri Jesu Christi qui venturus est, etc.

Then followed the rite of the *Effeta* [*Ephphatha*]. The

priest, having moistened his finger with saliva,[1] touched the upper part of the lip (*nares*)[2] and the ears of each of the candidates. This mode of anointing, after the manner of our Lord's healing of the deaf-mute in the Gospel, was accompanied by the following formula :—

> Effeta, quod est adaperire, in odorem suavitatis. Tu autem effugare, diabole, adpropinquavit enim judicium Dei.

The candidates, having then laid aside their garments, were anointed on the back and breast with exorcised oil. The whole ceremony had a symbolical meaning. The critical moment of the strife with Satan had arrived. The candidates were now to renounce him solemnly in order to bind themselves to Jesus Christ. Their senses were loosed that they might be able to hear and speak, and they were anointed with oil as athletes about to enter the arena for the strife. The anointing having been finished, each of them presented himself to the priest—

> Abrenuntias Satane ?—Abrenuntio.
> Et omnibus operibus ejus ?—Abrenuntio.
> Et omnibus pompis ejus ?—Abrenuntio.

Once the renouncing of Satan had been accomplished, the new disciple pronounced the formulary of the faith by reading the text of the Creed.[3] This was the so-called

---

[1] This was not primitive. We see by the Epistle of John the Deacon (*Pat. Lat*, vol lix. p. 402) that early in the sixth century it was the custom at Rome to use, not saliva, but consecrated oil The change must have been inspired by the subject-matter of the Gospel, John ix 6.

[2] In spite of the words *in odorem suavitatis* of the formulary, there is no doubt that the nostrils were here substituted for the mouth. The author of the *De Sacramentis* gives the reason. "Quia mulieres baptizantur" (i. 3).

[3] According to the books of the eighth century, it was the priest who recited it, holding his hand over the children, as if he were acting in their name. At Rome, in the time of St Augustine, the neophytes ascended an elevated place to make their profession, *in loco eminentiore, in conspectu populi fidelis* (*Conf.* viii. 5).

recitation of the symbol (*Redditio symboli*).[1] The ceremony being over, the candidates prostrated themselves in prayer, and were dismissed by the archdeacon.

3. *Blessing of the Holy Oils.*

It is necessary here to go back a little. While the candidates were completing their preparations, the Church was making its arrangements to receive them. On the Thursday in Holy Week the *chrismal Mass* was celebrated, at which the holy oils were consecrated for use in the ceremony of initiation. They were prepared in two separate vessels (*ampullae*), one of which contained nothing but pure oil, and the other oil rendered fragrant by a mixture of balsam. It was the Pope himself who poured the balsam into the oil in the sacristy before the Mass. During the ceremony the two vessels were held by clergy of the minor orders standing before the altar.

The Mass was celebrated [2], with a high ceremonial on account of the solemnity of the day. Towards the end of the Canon the faithful brought small vessels of oil to be blessed for their own use. This was the oil for anointing the sick, and the faithful could make use of it themselves. It served also for extreme unction. The vessels containing it were placed on the balustrade, or *podium*, which separated the sacred precincts from the rest of the building. From this place some of these vessels were taken by the deacons and brought to the altar, where the Pope blessed them, using the following formulary [3]:—

---

[1] This *Redditio symboli* was a ceremony; in Africa (see Aug., *Serm.*, 58, 59) and in Jerusalem (*Peregrinatio*) it was preceded by a private rehearsal, in order to make certain before the solemn ceremony of Thursday in Holy Week that the candidates knew the Creed by heart.

[2] See note, p 576.

[3] It is common to both the Gelasian Sacramentary and that of Adrian.

Emitte, quaesumus Domine, Spiritum sanctum Paraclitum de caelis in hanc pinguedinem olei, quam de viridi ligno producere dignatus es ad refectionem mentis et corporis; et tua sancta benedictione sit omni ungenti, gustanti, tangenti, tutamentum mentis et corporis, animae et spiritus, ad evacuandos omnes dolores, omnem infirmitatem, omnem aegritudinem mentis et corporis, unde unxisti[1] sacerdotes, reges et prophetas et martyres, chrisma tuum perfectum a te, Domine, benedictum, permanens in visceribus nostris in nomine Domini nostri Jesu Christi.

The blessing being ended, the bishop proceeded with the Mass from the *Per quem haec omnia*, etc., at the end of the Canon.[2] The deacons returned the vessels of oil to the place whence they had brought them. Those that had not been brought to the altar were blessed where they stood on the balustrade, by either bishops or priests, who made use of the formulary employed by the Pope.

The consecration of the greater vessels took place immediately after the communion of the Pope and before that of the clergy and congregation. The deacons brought back to the altar the paten and chalice, and spread over them a white linen cloth. The acolytes who held the *scyphi* containing the wine for the communion of the faithful, covered these in the same manner. The sub-deacons, having brought the *ampullae* to the archdeacon and to one of his colleagues, the archdeacon took the one containing the fragrant oil and presented it to the Pope. The Pope, having breathed thrice upon it, signed it with the sign of the cross, saying, *In nomine Patris et Filii et Spiritus sancti*. He then, having saluted the congregation as at the Preface, with the *Sursum Corda* and the *Gratias agamus*, recited the following eucharistic prayer:—

Vere dignum . . . aeterne Deus, qui in principio, inter caetera bonitatis et pietatis tuae munera, terram producere fructifera ligna jussisti,

---
[1] See note, p. 576.
[2] Cf. above, p. 182.

inter quae hujus pinguissimi liquoris ministrae oleae nascerentur, quarum fructus sacro chrismati deserviret. Nam David prophetico spiritu gratiae tuae sacramenta praenoscens vultus nostros in oleo exhilarandos esse cantavit. Et cum mundi crimina diluvio quondam expiarentur effuso, in similitudinem futuri muneris columba demonstrans per olivae ramum pacem terris redditam nuntiavit. Quod in novissimis temporibus manifestis est effectibus declaratum, cum baptismatis aquis omnium criminum commissa delentibus, haec olei unctio vultus nostros jucundos efficiat et serenos. Inde etiam Moysi famulo tuo mandata dedisti ut Aaron fratrem suum prius aqua lotum per infusionem hujus unguenti constitueret sacerdotem. Accessit ad hoc amplior honor cum Filius tuus dominus noster Jesus Christus lavari a Johanne undis Jordanicis exegisset, et Spiritu sancto in columbae similitudine desuper misso Unigenitum tuum in quo tibi optime complacuisse testimonio subsequentis vocis ostenderes, hoc illud esse manifestissime comprobares, quod eum oleo laetitiae prae consortibus suis ungendum David propheta cecinisset. Te igitur deprecamur, Domine sancte, Pater omnipotens, aeterne Deus, per Jesum Christum Filium tuum dominum nostrum, ut hujus creaturae pinguedinem sanctificare tua benedictione digneris et in sancti Spiritus immiscere virtutem per potentiam Christi tui; a cujus sancto nomine chrisma nomen accepit, unde unxisti sacerdotes, reges, prophetas et martyres tuos; ut sit his qui renati fuerint ex aqua et Spiritu sancto chrisma salutis, eosque aeternae vitae participes et caelestis gloriae facias esse consortes.

The ampulla containing the pure oil was then presented to the Pope, and consecrated with the same ceremony. It was breathed upon and signed with the cross in the manner followed in the case of the holy chrism, but the blessing was recited in an ordinary tone of voice. The text is as follows:—

Deus incrementorum et profectuum spiritalium munerator, qui virtute sancti Spiritus tui imbecillarum mentium rudimenta confirmas; te oramus, Domine, ut venturis ad beatae regenerationis lavacrum tribuas per unctionem istius creaturae purgationem mentis et corporis; ut si quae illis adversantium spirituum inhaesere reliquiae, ad tactum sanctificati olei hujus abscedant. Nullus spiritalibus nequitiis locus, nulla refugis virtutibus sit facultas; nulla insidiantibus malis latendi licentia relinquatur; sed venientibus ad fidem servis tuis et sancti Spiritus operatione mundandis sit unctionis hujus praeparatio utilis ad salutem quam etiam per caelestis regenerationis nativitatem in sacramento sunt baptismatis adepturi.[1]

4. *Baptism*.

The "elect" were present at the solemn vigil of Easter. The lections[2] chosen for the occasion were meant to present a summary of the relations between man and God, and to form, as it were, a final instruction at the moment of the accomplishment of the mystery of initiation. These lections are practically the same in all the Latin rituals. Some of the finest passages in the Old Testament are presented in them—such as the account of the Creation, the Deluge, the Sacrifice of Isaac, the Passage of the Red Sea, the Vision of Ezekiel, the History of Jonah, the account of the image set up by Nebuchadnezzar; then some passages from the prophets, as, for instance, that in which Isaiah predicts baptism, and extols the vine of the Lord; also that dealing with the covenant of Moses and the institution of the Passover. Each one of these lections is followed by a prayer.[3] Canticles of a like import are

---

[1] I have given here the prayers common to the Gelasian Sacramentary and that of Adrian, but using the text of the former, on account of its better preservation. As for the ritual, I have described that in the *Ordines*, with which the Sacramentary of Adrian is in full agreement. In the Gelasian Sacramentary there is found in the first place the prayer *Deus incrementorum*, and the consecratory formulary *Deus qui in principio*, both of which therefore seem to have reference to the same ampulla, that of the holy chrism. But the former of these prayers is evidently out of place, for it was drawn up in reference to the oil intended for the anointing which precedes baptism, whilst the other has in view the anointing which follows it. After the consecrating formulary comes an exorcism of the oil together with a eucharistic prayer. These two do not seem to fall in with the ritual of the *Ordines*, and it is possible that they are Gallican, and not Roman, in origin.

[2] At first there were twelve lections, as we see from the Gelasian Sacramentary. Only four are found in the Sacramentary of Adrian, but the ancient custom, which had been maintained in France, was restored later on at Rome.

[3] In support of this description of the vigil of Easter, there is a very

interspersed between the lections, as, for instance, the song of Miriam, the sister of Moses, *Cantemus Domino;* that of Isaiah, *Vinea facta est;* that in Deuteronomy, *Attende, caelum, et loquar;* and, finally, the psalm *Sicut cervus desiderat ad fontes.*

At the appointed hour the Pope and his clergy accompanied the "elect" to the baptistery.

The main structure of the baptistery of the Lateran still exists. It opens on to the courtyard which extends [1] behind the basilica, and is entered by a portico, at the end of which on either side are two apses. In one of these the original mosaics of the fourth century or thereabouts are still preserved. The subject represented is the vine, as typical of our Lord, and its leaves are here and there interspersed with golden crosses. Passing through this portico, we enter the baptistery itself, an octagonal building, having in its centre a large font of the same shape. Eight massive columns of porphyry support the upper part of the baptistery, which formerly terminated in a dome above the font, the aisle being roofed with a barrel vault. On the architrave may still be read the inscription which Pope Xystus III. (432–440) caused to be engraved there—

> *Gens sacranda polis hic semine nascitur almo*
> *quam fecundatis Spiritus edit aquis.*

curious epigraphic inscription found at Chiusi, belonging to the fourth century or thereabouts, in which there is mention of the death of a child that occurred during the vigil, and at the moment of the fifth prayer: *Aurelius Melitius cristeanus* (sic) *fidelis peregrinus hic positus est, qui vixit annis IIII. dies duo; qui defunctus est diae Saturni Pascae; noctis ipsius pervigilatio, oratione quinta, vita privatus est et sepultus diae solis VI kal. april* (*C. I. L*, vol. xi, No. 2551; cf De Rossi, *Inscr. Christ*, vol. i. p. 326).

[1] "Which extended," for, owing to the additions made to the old basilica of late, this courtyard has been considerably restricted in area. For an account of these buildings see the *Liber Pontif*, vol. i. pp. 191, 192, 236, 245. Cf. Rohaut de Fleury, *Le Latran au moyen âge*, pl. xxxiii.–xxxv.

310   CHRISTIAN WORSHIP: ITS ORIGIN AND EVOLUTION.

> *Virgineo fetu genitrix Ecclesia natos*
> *quos spirante Deo concipit, amne parit.*
> *Coelorum regnum sperate, hoc fonte renati;*
> *non recipit felix vita semel genitos.*
> *Fons hic est vitae qui totum diluit orbem*
> *sumens de Christi vulnere principium.*
> *Mergere, peccator, sacro purgande fluento:*
> *quem veterem accipiet proferet unda novum.*
> *Insons esse volens isto mundare lavacro*
> *seu patrio premeris crimine seu proprio.*
> *Nulla renascentum est distantia, quos facit unum*
> *unus fons, unus spiritus, una fides.*
> *Nec numerus quemquam scelerum nec forma suorum*
> *terreat: hoc natus flumine sanctus erit.*

Facing the entrance is a door, opening formerly[1] on to an oblong courtyard, at the end of which was the chapel of the Cross, built in the time of Pope Hilary (461-468). It is to the same Pope that we owe the erection of the two other oratories on the right and left of the baptistery, respectively dedicated to the two St. Johns, the Baptist and the Evangelist. These oratories are still standing.

From the middle of the water in the baptistery arose a tall candelabrum of porphyry, ending in a golden bowl full of balsam, in which burnt a wick of amianthus, diffusing at the same time both light and fragrance. On one of the sides of the font stood two silver statues, one of Christ and one of St. John, having between them a golden lamb, with the legend, *Ecce Agnus Dei, ecce qui tollit peccata mundi*. From beneath this lamb a jet of water issued into the font, while from the seven remaining sides as many streams of water poured forth from the heads of stags.

It was in this building that the Pope officiated at the

---

[1] It now opens on to the piazza of S. Giovanni in Laterano, and by it access is usually gained to the baptistery. The oratory of the Cross, or of St. Andrew, with its own atrium, has disappeared since the sixteenth century.

CEREMONIES OF CHRISTIAN INITIATION.   311

"Easter baptism," the most imposing of all the pontifical ceremonies. He entered at the head of a procession before which two great tapers were borne, the litany, meanwhile, being sung. When this was ended, the Pope, standing by the font, saluted the congregation and called upon them to join in the *collective* prayer, which was immediately followed by a prayer of *eucharistic* character. The following are the formularies of the ancient Sacramentaries, which are still in use :—

Omnipotens, sempiterne, Deus, adesto magnae pietatis tuae mysteriis, adesto sacramentis; et ad creandos novos populos quos tibi fons baptismatis parturit spiritum adoptionis emitte; et quod humilitatis nostrae gerendum est ministerio tuae virtutis compleatur effectu.

Vere dignum . . . aeterne Deus, qui invisibili potentia tua sacramentorum tuorum mirabiliter operaris effectum. Et licet nos tantis mysteriis exequendis simus indigni, tu tamen gratiae tuae dona non deserens etiam ad nostras preces aures tuae pietatis inclina. Deus, cujus spiritus super aquas inter ipsa mundi primordia ferebatur, ut jam tunc virtutem sanctificationis aquarum natura conciperet; Deus, qui nocentis mundi crimina per aquas abluens regenerationis speciem in ipsa diluvii effusione signasti, ut unius ejusdemque elementi mysterium et finis esset vitiis et origo virtutis; respice, Domine, in faciem Ecclesiae tuae et multiplica in ea generationes tuas, qui gratiae tuae effluentis impetu laetificas civitatem tuam fontemque baptismatis aperis toto orbe terrarum gentibus innovandis, ut tuae majestatis imperio sumat Unigeniti tui gratiam de Spiritu sancto, qui hanc aquam regenerandis hominibus praeparatam arcana sui luminis admixtione fecundet; ut sanctificatione concepta ab immaculato divini fontis utero in novam renata creaturam progenies caelestis emergat; et quos aut sexus in corpore aut aetas discernit in tempore omnes in unam pariat gratia mater infantiam. Procul ergo hinc, jubente te, Domine, omnis spiritus immundus abscedat; procul tota nequitia diabolicae fraudis absistat. Nihil hic loci habeat contrariae virtutis ammixtio; non insidiando circumvolet, non latendo subripiat, non inficiendo corrumpat. Sit haec sancta et innocens creatura libera ab omni impugnatoris incursu, et totius nequitiae purgata discessu. Sit fons vivus aquae regenerans, unda purificans, ut omnes hoc lavacro salutifero diluendi, operante in eis Spiritu sancto perfecti, purgationis indulgentiam consequantur. Unde benedico te, creatura aquae, per Deum vivum, per Deum sanctum, per Deum qui te in principio verbo separavit ab arida et in quatuor fluminibus totam terram rigare praecepit, qui te in deserto amaram suavitate indita fecit esse potabilem et sitienti populo de petra produxit. Benedico te et per Jesum Christum, Filium ejus unicum, dominum nostrum, qui te in Cana Galileae signo admirabili sua potentia convertit in vinum, qui pedibus super te ambulavit et a Johanne in Jordane in te baptizatus est, qui te una cum sanguine de latere suo produxit et discipulis suis jussit ut credentes baptizarentur in te, dicens: Ite, docete omnes gentes, baptizantes eos in nomine Patris et Filii et Spiritus sancti. Haec nobis praecepta servantibus tu, Deus omnipotens, clemens adesto, tu benignus aspira, tu has simplices aquas tuo ore benedicito; ut praeter naturalem emundationem quam lavandis possunt adhibere corporibus, sint etiam purificandis mentibus efficaces. Descendat in hanc plenitudinem fontis virtus Spiritus tui et totam hujus aquae substantiam regenerandi fecundet effectu. Hic omnium peccatorum maculae deleantur; hic natura ad imaginem tuam condita et ad honorem sui reformata principii cunctis vetustatis squaloribus emundetur; ut omnis homo hoc sacramentum regenerationis ingressus in vera innocentia nova infantia renascatur.

According to the ritual directions of the eighth century three breaks were to be made in this long prayer, that is, at the making of the sign of the cross over and in the water, and again at the insufflation, or breathing over it. When the Pope came to the words, *Descendat in hanc plenitudinem fontis virtus Spiritus tui*, the two dignitaries who carried the tapers plunged them into the font. The Canon being ended, the Pope took an ampulla full of chrism and poured it crosswise on the water, which he then stirred with his hand.[1]

All being then ready, the baptisms began. Completely divested of their garments,[2] the "elect" approached the

---

[1] The same *Ordines* tell us that the Pope then sprinkled the assembly with holy water, and that the faithful were permitted at that moment to take some of it away as a phylactery. This can scarcely be primitive.

[2] In the Appendix to Mabillon's *Ordo I*, one of the lateral chapels of the baptistery is called *ad S. Johannem ad Vestem*. It was probably there that the candidates divested themselves of their garments. As there are two similar chapels, it is possible that they were both used, one for the men, the other for the women. It is scarcely necessary to remark that, in spite of this direction to remove all clothing, precautions were taken so that decency, as it was then understood, should not be offended. The

font. The archdeacon presented them, one by one, to the Pope, who put to them the three questions, which epitomised the whole Creed—

Credis in Deum Patrem omnipotentem?
Credis et in Jesum Christum, Filium ejus unicum, dominum nostrum, natum et passum?
Credis et in Spiritum sanctum, sanctam Ecclesiam, remissionem peccatorum, carnis resurrectionem?

After his threefold reply in the affirmative, the candidate was thrice immersed, while the Pope pronounced the formula, *Baptizo te in nomine Patris et Filii et Spiritus sancti.*

Baptismal immersion did not imply that the person baptised was entirely plunged in the water. He entered the font, in which the water would not reach beyond the middle of an adult, and was placed under one of the openings from which a stream issued, or else the water was taken from the font itself and poured over his head. It is thus that baptism is represented on the ancient monuments.

The actual ceremony of baptism was not performed by the Pope alone. Priests, deacons, and even clerics of inferior order, entered the water, clothed in long linen tunics, and administered the sacred washing to the crowd of neophytes.

deaconesses had here an important part to play in connection with the baptism of the women (*Const. Ap*, III. 15, 16). It must not be thought, however, that propriety in ancient times was as easily offended as it would be now. The author of *De singularitate clericorum* (Cyprian, App., p. 189, Hartel) does not understand that *in ipso baptismate cujusquam nuditas erubescat, ubi Adae et Evae renovatur infantia, nec exponit sed potius accipit tunicam.* Cf. the curious story related by John Moschus in his *Prat. Spir.*, ch. 3.

5. *Confirmation.*

While the baptisms were proceeding, the Pope withdrew to the *consignatorium*, where the neophytes were brought to him for the ceremony of the Consignation [signing]. The place set apart for this was, from the time of Pope Hilary (461–468), the chapel of the Cross, behind the baptistery. Before entering the chapel, the newly baptised first presented themselves before a priest, who anointed them on the head with the fragrant oil of the holy chrism, saying—

> Deus omnipotens, Pater domini nostri Jesu Christi, qui te regeneravit ex aqua et Spiritu sancto, quique dedit tibi remissionem omnium peccatorum, ipse te linit chrismate salutis in vitam aeternam.

The baptised then resumed their garments, or rather they put on new white ones, being assisted in this operation by their godfathers and godmothers. Having been brought before the bishop, they stood in groups, over each of which the pontiff first pronounced the invocation of the Holy Spirit [1]—

> Omnipotens, sempiterne, Deus, qui regenerare dignatus es hos famulos et famulas tuas ex aqua et Spiritu sancto, quique dedisti eis remissionem omnium peccatorum, emitte in eos septiformem Spiritum sanctum tuum Paraclitum de caelis: Spiritum sapientiae et intellectus, Spiritum consilii et fortitudinis, Spiritum scientiae et pietatis; adimple eos Spiritu timoris tui et consigna eos signo crucis Christi in vitam propitiatus aeternam.[2]

The Pope then made the sign of the cross with his

---

[1] Gregorian text.

[2] According to the *Ordo* of St Amand, this prayer is accompanied by the imposition of hands first upon the men, and then upon the women.

thumb, previously dipped in the chrism, upon the forehead of each neophyte, saying to each separately, *In nomine Patris et Filii et Spiritus sancti. Pax tibi.*

6. *First Communion.*

The Consignation being ended, the procession again formed to return to the basilica. The *schola cantorum* had already been there for some time. During the long ceremonies which had taken place in the baptistery, they had continued to sing the litanies, repeating the invocations first seven times, then five, then thrice. At the end of the threefold litany the Pope made his entry, and approaching the altar, prostrated himself before it. He then arose and began to sing *Gloria in excelsis*, thus commencing the first Easter Mass. Before the end of the Canon, he blessed the drink, composed of honey, water, and milk, which was given to the neophytes after their communion.[1] The newly initiated participated in the holy mysteries for the first time. It was daybreak before this solemn ceremony came to any end.

The octave of Easter was, as we have already remarked, one unbroken festival. There was a Stational Mass every day, at which the neophytes were present in their white garments, and at which they communicated. They met at the basilica of the Lateran every evening for the office of Vespers. In the basilica three antiphons were sung, accompanied by alleluias and responds. This part of the office ended by the chanting of the evangelical

---

[1] Cf. p. 175. This potion, mentioned in the sixth century by Johannes Diaconus in his letter to Senarius, and in the Leonian Sacramentary, does not appear in the later documents of the Roman Liturgy. Herr H Usener (*Rhein. Museum*, vol. lvii. p 189) conjectures that it was suppressed about the time of St. Gregory, and perhaps by that Pope himself.

hymn, that is to say, the *Magnificat*, and by prayer. The neophytes were then conducted to the baptistery and the chapel of the Cross, thus accomplishing a kind of pilgrimage to the scene of their baptism and confirmation. This double procession was accompanied by singing, sometimes in Latin, sometimes in Greek.[1]

§ 2.—The Gallican Baptismal Rite.

It is somewhat difficult to reconstruct the baptismal ritual of the Gallican Church. The documents we possess are all more or less incomplete, and, moreover, if they agree on most points, they reveal here and there certain differences peculiar to this or that country. I will class them according to their geographical order.

North Italy.—The treatise *De Mysteriis* of St. Ambrose, the anonymous treatise *De Sacramentis*, the sermons of St. Maximus of Turin, and the Sacramentary of Bobbio.

Gaul.—A few details given in the second letter of St. Germain of Paris; the *Missale Gothicum;* the *Missale Gallicanum vetus.*

Spain.—The *De Officiis* of St. Isidore, and the *De cognitione Baptismi* of St. Ildefonsus.

---

[1] On the two last days, instead of repairing directly to the baptistery, they went, on the Friday, to Santa Croce in Gerusalemme, and on the Saturday to Santa Maria Maggiore. On these days the station at the chapel of the Cross did not take place All these stations are given in the Sacramentary of Pope Adrian. They have long since ceased to be observed at Rome, but in some countries they are still in use—in the diocese of Paris, for instance, on Easter Day Few persons, however, know their origin or understand their peculiar significance The *Liber Ordinum*, published by Dom Férotin, contains, pp. 24-35, a rite for private baptism— *Ordo babtismi celebrandus quolibet tempore* As for Solemn Baptism, some of the ceremonies are given on Palm Sunday (p. 184) and on Easter Eve (p 217).

1. *The Catechumenate.*

The ritual of the catechumenate consisted of three ceremonies—exorcism, unction, and insufflation.

Exorcism is mentioned by Isidore and Ildefonsus. One rather curious formulary, preserved in the *Missale Gallicanum*, probably refers to this ceremony [1]:

> Adgredior te, immundissime, damnate spiritus, etc.

The unction, mentioned also by Spanish writers, is specially that of the ears and mouth. In this respect it corresponds to the Roman *Effeta*, but it was also applied to other parts of the body, and in this case it corresponds to the unction of the breast and shoulders, which, in the Roman rite, follows immediately after the *Effeta*. We have here, then, at the very beginning of the catechumenate, the ceremony which, according to the Roman use, terminates that period of probation, and immediately precedes the renunciation of the devil.[2] Finally, this anointing is accompanied by the

---

[1] St. Isidore, *De Off.*, ii. 21, adds to exorcism the administration of salt: "Exorcizantur, deinde sales accipiunt et unguntur." But this ceremony was not universal in Spain, as Ildefonsus (*De cognit baptismi*, 26) says it was observed in some places, but that he disapproved of the custom. It was used, perhaps, in the province of Boetica, and was a vestige of the Roman use, which in that country had preceded the Gallican.

[2] St. Ildefonsus mentions the unction as immediately following the exorcism (*op. cit.*, c 21, 27, 28). He refers the origin of this custom to the healing of the deaf and dumb by the *Ephphatha* and the anointing with the saliva, citing in support St. Mark vii. 32, 33; he says also that this passage from the Gospel was read at the Mass during which the exorcism took place. All this shows that it is clearly the Gallican *Effeta* which is in question. The same writer, indeed, specifies (c. 29) that "post exorcismos tanguntur auriculae oleo . . . tangitur et os," and all this before the *traditio* of the Creed, at the moment when from being *gentilis* the person became *catechumenus*.

imposition of the sign of the cross, and, from this point of view, it corresponds with the Roman ceremony of the signing with the cross in the ritual of the catechumenate.

At Milan, the anointing and the *Effeta* were relegated, as at Rome, to Easter Eve.[1] This difference in the order of the ceremonies appears to go back to a considerable antiquity. It was a subject of discussion about the year 400, for we see in a document of that period[2] that the bishops of Gaul had consulted the Pope on the matter. At Rome, provided the unction took place after the third scrutiny, the day was not considered of any moment. We see that on this point the Church of Milan conformed her use to that of Rome, but in Spain it was otherwise. We have no documentary evidence to show which course was adopted in Gaul.[3]

---

[1] There are, however, differences, for at Rome the *Effeta* and the renunciation of the devil took place in the morning, at a service quite distinct from the actual baptism, while at Milan these ceremonies occurred immediately before the neophyte entered the font Moreover, the *Effeta* at Milan was made with consecrated oil, and not with saliva

[2] *Canones ad Gallos*, 11; Coustant, *Epistolae Rom Pont* , p. 693.

[3] In the *Missale Gothicum*, the ritual of the catechumenate, under the rubric *Ad Christianum faciendum*, is placed on Easter Eve. In the *Missale Gallicanum*, it is true, this ritual precedes the *Traditio Symboli;* but there is, at that place, a lacuna which prevents us from ascertaining whether the unction occurred there or not. Its use is not indicated on Easter Eve. I give here two formularies for this ceremony, the first of which figures in the *Missale Gothicum ;* the other, which is still in use, is common to the Gelasian Sacramentary (cf. *supra*, p 295) and to that of Bobbio.

Signo te in nomine Patris et Filii et Spiritus sancti, ut sis christianus oculos, ut videas claritatem Dei , aures, ut audias vocem Domini ; nares, ut odores suavitatem Christi ; conversus, ut confitearis Patrem et Filium et Spiritum sanctum ; cor, ut credas Trinitatem inseparabilem. Pax tecum.

Accipe signum crucis, tam in fronte quam in corde ; sume fidem caelestium praeceptorum ; talis esto moribus ut templum Dei esse jam possis ; ingressusque Ecclesiam Dei evasisse te laqueos mortis laetus agnosce. Horresce idola, respue simulacra, cole Deum Patrem omnipotentem et Jesum Christum Filium ejus qui vivit cum Patre et Spiritu sancto per omnia saecula saeculorum.

Then follows, in the Gelasian Sacramentary, the prayer *Te deprecor*, still in use (for adults), and another prayer, *Deus qui es et qui eras*, etc.

The insufflation appears also in the rites enumerated by St. Isidore. It is also found in the Bobbio Sacramentary, and according to this authority it was administered three several times on the face of the candidate, the officiating minister saying, *Accipe Spiritum sanctum et in corde teneas*. The most natural place for it, however, is at the beginning of the ceremony, with the exorcism. This is where it occurs in the Mozarabic Rite.[1]

2. *Preparation for Baptism.*

We have no information with regard to the number and order of the Gallican scrutinies. All that remains of this part of the ritual are the two formularies of prayer in the *Missale Gallicanum*, where they appear under the title of *Praemissiones ad scrutamen.*

On the other hand, the *Traditio Symboli* is often mentioned. It took place on the Sunday before Easter. We have the testimony of St. Ambrose on this point, besides trustworthy attestations in Gaul and Spain.[2] The Bishop himself presided at this ceremony, which was placed between the Mass of the catechumens and that of the faithful. He began by an address, and then, having recited the Apostles' Creed three times, he proceeded to give an exposition of it article by article.[3]

---

[1] *Liber Ordinum*, p. 21.

[2] Ambr., *Ep.*, 20: "Sequenti die, erat autem dominica (Sunday before Easter), post lectiones atque tractatum, dimissis catechumenis, symbolum aliquibus competentibus in baptisteriis tradebam basilicae." Council of Agde (506), c. 3: "Symbolum etiam placuit ab omnibus ecclesiis una die, id est ante octo dies dominicae Resurrectionis, publice in ecclesiis competentibus tradi." St Germain of Paris and all the liturgical books, together with Isidore and Ildefonsus (*loc cit.*), mention the same Sunday. Cf. Mabillon, *Mus Ital.*, vol i p. 95; see also the *Liber Ordinum*, p. 184, and the Mozarabic Missal for Palm Sunday.

[3] The *Missale Gallicanum* contains two formularies for the *Traditio Symboli*, one entire, the other imperfect owing to a *lacuna;* and there is a third in the Bobbio Sacramentary. These two books contain, besides, with some slight abbreviations, the Roman ceremony of the *Apertio aurium*. Their

St. Germain of Paris describes this ceremony as connected with the benediction of the holy oils. It was only natural to choose the Sunday which was called *dies unctionis* for the blessing of the oils.[1]

Having been taught to the catechumens on the Sunday before Easter, the Creed was rendered, that is to say, recited publicly, on Maundy Thursday.[2] By this means its recitation was separated from the renunciation of the devil, which in the other rites precede it.

3. *Baptism and Confirmation.*

The observances for Easter Eve were much the same as those in use at Rome. The passages from Holy Scripture which constituted the lections were almost identical, and were, like the Roman lessons, interspersed with hymns and prayers. At the appointed hour, all concerned proceeded to the baptistery,[3] where the ceremony of initiation began by the blessing of the water.

---

complexity on this point agrees with the general character of their redaction, which is throughout a combination of Roman and Gallican elements.

[1] *Ep. II.*; cf Ildef, *loc cit*, c. 34. This appellation owes its origin to the fact that the Gospel for that day contains the anointing of Christ at Bethany.

[2] Martin of Braga, can 49; Ildefonsus, *loc. cit.*, c. 34. Direct attestation comes from Spanish sources only, but in all other Gallican countries, contrary to the Oriental and Roman uses, we find that the renunciation of the devil is not followed by the recitation of the Creed. This omission concurs with the testimony from Spanish sources, and goes to prove that we have here not simply a Spanish peculiarity, but one that is Gallican in the widest sense of the word. This conclusion is also confirmed by the fact that the Council of Laodicea fixes Thursday, and that probably Maundy Thursday, for the *Redditio Symboli*: "Ὅτι δεῖ τοὺς φωτιζομένους τὴν πίστιν ἐκμανθάνειν καὶ τῇ πέμπτῃ τῆς ἑβδομάδος ἀπαγγέλλειν τῷ ἐπισκόπῳ ἢ τοῖς πρεσβυτέροις" (c. 46). This canon was confirmed by the Council *in Trullo* (c. 78).

[3] The oldest Mozarabic books of the eleventh century, the *Liber Comicus* and the *Liber Ordinum*, place the beginning of the Baptismal ceremonies

The officiating priest first recited a collective prayer, which was preceded by a somewhat lengthy invitatory of the usual Gallican type.[1] The following is one of the formularies which have been preserved:—

Deum immortalium munerum et salutarium gratiarum, Fratres dilectissimi, concordi mente et humili oratione poscamus, ut per Verbum, Sapientiam et Virtutem suam, dominum nostrum Jesum Christum Filium suum, concurrenti ad baptismum salutarem plebi suae gratiam novae regenerationis indulgeat; atque accessus hinc penitus malignae contagionis avertens infundat vitali lavacro Spiritum suum sanctum; ut dum sitiens fidem populus aquas salutares ingreditur, vere, ut scriptum est, per aquam et Spiritum sanctum renascatur, et consepultus in lavacro Redemptori suo, in similitudinem sacri divinique mysterii, cui commoritur per Laptismum eidem conresurgat in regno.

Benedic, Domine, hanc aquam salutaris et sanctifica eam, omnipotens Trinitas, qui humanum genus formare creareque jussisti, quique etiam dedisti nobis per tui baptismatis mysterium [2] gratiam renascendi. Respice

---

during the third Lection Several authors speak of baptismal fonts, which were miraculously filled during the night of Easter Eve One of these was in Sicily, and is mentioned by Paschasinus, Bishop of Lilyboeum, in a letter addressed to Pope St Leo (Ballerini, vol 1 p 607); there was another at Marcelliana, near Consilinum, in Lucania (Cassiodorus, *Var.*, viii. 33); and others in Asia Minor (Moschus, *Prat. Spir*, 214, 215) The most celebrated was that of Osset [Osset Constantia,? Salteras,—Tr.], near Seville, in Spain, frequently mentioned by Gregory of Tours (*Hist Fr*, v. 17; vi 43, *Glor. Mart*, 23, 24; cf. Ildefonsus, *De Baptismo*, 105, 106). He was careful to ask, in those years when there was uncertainty as to the date when Easter should fall, whether the miraculous font had filled itself on the day on which he had kept the festival

[1] This is one of the two given in the *Missale Gallicanum* The other has a Gallican invitatory, followed by the Roman prayer quoted on p. 311. In the *Missale Gothicum*, the invitatory is so badly copied that it is unintelligible After the sentence *Stantes, fratres karissimi, super ripam vitrei fontis*, come several words which have no sense whatever, then the text continues. *Navigantes pulsent mare novum non virga sed cruce, non tactu sed sensu, non baculo sed sacramento. Locus quidem parvus sed gratia plenus*, etc. The formulary of the Bobbio Sacramentary has been curiously cut out of the Roman rite. The Mozarabic Missal does not contain any formulary of this kind On the other hand, the *Liber Ordinum* contains two invitatories, one of which is the *Deus immortalium* given above.

[2] Mysteriis, *printed edition*.

322   CHRISTIAN WORSHIP: ITS ORIGIN AND EVOLUTION.

propitius super istius aquae creaturam religionis mysterio[1] procuratam, spiritalem tuam benedictionem perfunde, ut sit eis qui in ea baptizandi sunt fons aquae salutaris in remissione veterum criminum, te, Domine, largiente, in vitam aeternam.

After this introductory prayer, the bishop proceeded to exorcise the water.[2]

Exorcizo te, creatura aquae, exorcizo te omnis exercitus diaboli, omnis potestas adversaria, omnis umbra daemonum. Exorcizo te in nomine domini nostri Jesu Christi Nazarei, qui incarnatus est in Maria virgine, cui omnia subjecit Pater in caelo et in terra. Time et treme, tu et omnis malitia tua; da locum Spiritui sancto, ut omnes qui descenderint in hunc fontem fiat eis lavacrum baptismi regenerationis in remissionem omnium peccatorum. Per Dominum nostrum Jesum Christum, qui venturus est in sede majestatis Patris sui cum sanctis angelis suis judicare te, inimice, et saeculum per ignem, in saecula saeculorum.

There is very ancient evidence for this part of the ceremony, quite apart from its existence in the liturgical books. It is mentioned by the author of the *De Sacramentis*,[3] and by Gregory of Tours.[4]

Then follows the *Contestatio*, or eucharistic prayer.[5]

Dignum et justum est, vere aequum et justum est, nos tibi gratias

---

[1] Mysterium, *printed edition*.
[2] I give here the formulary of the *Missale Gothicum* There are others in the *Missale Gallicanum*, in the Bobbio Sacramentary, and in the Mozarabic Missal. That of the *Missale Gallicanum* is partly borrowed from the Roman canon of consecration.
[3] I. 5: " Ubi primum ingreditur sacerdos, exorcismum facit secundum creaturam aquae, invocationem postea et precem defert ut sanctificetur fons et adsit praesentia Trinitatis aeternae "
[4] *Glor. Mart*, 23.
[5] I give the formulary of the *Missale Gallicanum*, which is identical with that of the Mozarabic Missal In the two other Sacramentaries are others of different tenor.

agere, Domine Deus aeterne, qui solus habes immortalitatem, eamque ne solus possideas nobis quoque renovata aetate tribuisti; qui humano generi amissam per transgressionem pristinae originis dignitatem reformare in melius tam pretioso quam felici baptismatis munere voluisti. Adsiste, quaesumus, ad invocationem nominis tui; sanctifica fontem hunc, sanctificator generis humani; fiat locus iste dignus in quem Spiritus sanctus influat. Sepeliatur illic Adam vetus, resurgat novus; moriatur omne quod carnis est, resurgat omne quod spiritus; exuantur sordentes vitiis, et discissis criminis amictibus, splendoris et immortalitatis indumenta sumantur. Quicumque in Christo baptizabuntur induant Christum; quicumque hic renunciaverint diabolo da eis triumphare de mundo; qui te in hoc loco invocaverit tu eum cognoscas in regno. Sic in hoc fonte extinguantur crimina ne resurgant, sic invalescat aquae istius beneficium ut aeterni ignis restinguat incendium. Mitte fonte[1] altaribus tuis quos altaria regnis tuis mittant. Totus hic horror mortis intereat; quicumque hic tuus esse ceperit tuus esse non desinat; quicumque hic se sibi negaverit te lucrifaciat, et per ministerium nostrum et misterium tuum consecratus tibi populus aeternis ad te praemiis consecretur.

At this point the infusion of the chrism into the font takes place. The bishop pours it crosswise into the water,[2] saying—

Infusio chrismae salutaris domini nostri Jesu Christi, ut fiat fons aquae salientis cunctis descendentibus in ea, in vitam aeternam.[3]

He then recites a final prayer, imploring the grace of

---

[1] Fontis, *printed edition*.

[2] The *Missale Gallicanum* states that this infusion is made in three distinct acts. The *Missale Gothicum* here mentions a triple insufflation, but as it places at this point the exorcising of the water, which all other documents put before the *Contestatio*, it is possible that this rite refers to the exorcism itself, and not to the consecration properly so called.

[3] This formulary is met with in the *Missale Gothicum*, and in the Bobbio Sacramentary. It is omitted in the *Missale Gallicanum*. The Mozarabic Missal contains another · *Signo te, sacratissime fons*, etc.

God for those who are about to enter the consecrated water—

> Deus ad quem sitientes animae vivendi[1] immortalitatis amore festinant, da eis famulis tuis supplicantibus invenire munus quod cupiunt, adipisci gratiam quod merentur; ingrediantur fontem regenerationis auctorem, in quo lethiferam illam primi parentis offensam, mutata in novum hominem caducae carnis fragilitate, deponant.[2]

The blessing of the water doubtless took place before the candidates were admitted. At the appointed moment the doors of the baptistery were opened to them. Each one presented himself, completely divested of his garments.[3] The candidate took up his position facing west, and was thrice called upon to renounce the devil, his pomps and his pleasures.[4] Having made a threefold reply, he was made to enter the font, and was there thrice required to make a confession of the Christian faith.[5] Thrice he replied *Credo*.

---

[1] Bibendique, *printed edition*.

[2] This is the formulary in the *Missale Gallicanum*. There are others in other Sacramentaries; the *Missale Gothicum* omits it.

[3] At Milan, it was at this point that the ceremony of the *Effeta* and of the anointing took place.

[4] "Abrenuntias Satanae, pompis saeculi et voluptatibus ejus? (*Missale Gallicanum*) Abrenuncias Satanae, pompis ejus, luxuriis suis, saeculo huic?" (Bobbio Sacram) The formulary is not given in the *Missale Gothicum*. "Abrenuntias diabolo et angelis eius, operibus eius, imperiis eius?" (*Lib Ord*).

[5] This formulary also is omitted in the *Missale Gothicum*. That in the Bobbio Sacramentary is merely the Apostles' Creed in an interrogatory form, arranged into three articles. Cf the formulary cited by the anonymous Arian mentioned above, p. 88, note : *Credis in Deum, Patrem omnipotentem, creatorem caeli et terrae? Credis et in Christo Jesu filio ejus?* The following is that of the *Missale Gallicanum*.—
Credis Patrem et Filium et Spiritum sanctum unius esse virtutis?
Credis P. et F. et Sp s. ejusdem esse potestatis?
Credis P. et F. et Sp s. trinae veritatis una manente substantia, Deum esse perfectum?
This formulary, evidently prompted by a hatred of Arianism, cannot be older than the fourth century, at a time when the barbarian Arians were living in Gaul among the Catholics St Maximus of Turin (*De Baptism*

He is then plunged three times in the consecrated water. This was not the case in Spain, where single immersion was considered as a protest against Arianism.[1]

The baptismal formularies which are given in the Gallican books all have something additional to the text as used at Rome. With all their variations, they agree in introducing the words *ut habeas vitam aeternam*.[2]

As he left the water the neophyte was led to the bishop, who made the sign of the cross on his head with fragrant oil,[3] reciting meanwhile the formulary—

Deus omnipotens, qui te regeneravit ex aqua et Spiritu sancto concessitque tibi peccata tua, ipse te ungat in vitam aeternam.[4]

---

tract 2) gives the following formulary: "Credis in Deum Patrem omnipotentem? Credis et in Jesum Christum, Filium ejus, qui conceptus est de Spiritu sancto et natus est ex Maria Virgine? Credis et in Spiritum sanctum?" Further on he adds: "Credis in sanctam Ecclesiam et remissionem peccatorum?"

[1] *Conc. Tol.*, iv., can. 5. The Eunomians, who were extreme and obstinate Arians, also practised single immersion (Sozom., *Hist Eccl.*, vi. 26), though contrary to the custom of all the Catholic Churches of the East. We see from this that the symbolism is entirely arbitrary. the rite has no other meaning than that attached to it

[2] *Miss Goth.*: "Baptizo te, in nomine P. et F. et Sp s in remissionem peccatorum ut habeas vitam aeternam" *Miss. Gall.*: "Baptizo te credentem in nomine P. et F. et Sp. s ut habeas vitam aeternam in saecula saeculorum" *Bobb Sacram*: "Baptizo te in nomine P. et F. et Sp. s., unam habentem substantiam, ut habeas vitam aeternam, partem cum sanctis" *Lib Ord.*: "Te baptizo in nomine P. et F et Sp s., ut habeas vitam aeternam"

[3] The Bobbio Sacramentary specifies: *Suffundis chrisma in fronte ejus.*

[4] This formulary is given in the *De Sacramentis*; it is found with some slight variations in the *Missale Gallicanum* and in the Bobbio Sacramentary. It is almost identical with the Roman formulary of the *Chrismatio*, and strongly resembles that given by the anonymous Arian (*l. c.*): *Deus et pater domini nostri Jesu Christi qui te regeneravit ex aqua ipse te linet* (read: *linat*) *Spiritu Sancto* etc. The *Missale Gothicum* here contains a formulary which appears to be corrupt and to have been amalgamated with that of the giving of the white garment. "Perungo te chrisma sanctitatis, tunicam immortalitatis, quam D. N. Jesus Christus traditam a Patre primus accepit, ut eam integram et inlibatam perferas ante tribunal Christi et

He then received a white garment, which the bishop handed to him, saying—

> Accipe vestem candidam quam immaculatam perferas ante tribunal domini nostri Jesu Christi.[1]

Before or after[2] this ceremony the washing of the feet must have taken place. The bishop, having his loins girt, washed the feet of the neophytes, saying to each of them—

> Ego tibi lavo pedes, sicut dominus noster Jesus Christus fecit discipulis suis, ut tu facias hospitibus et peregrinis, ut habeas vitam aeternam.[3]

The ceremony of the feet-washing was observed in Gaul and at Milan, but not in Spain, where it had been officially proscribed by the Council of Elvira.[4] We find no traces of it in the East, and it is quite certain that it was not practised at Rome. It was a local peculiarity, introduced at an early date into the Churches of Southern Gaul or Northern Italy.

The initiation ended by the imposition of hands upon the neophytes, accompanied by a special prayer. In the texts of the ancient Milanese use, this prayer comprises a petition for the sevenfold gifts of the Holy Spirit. The

---

vivas in saecula saeculorum." As there is, farther on, however, a special formulary for the giving of the white robe, it is possible that this latter may be the correct one In that case the former would have a special symbolism, according to which the chrism would be considered as a garment.

[1] This is the formulary in the *Missale Gothicum* and in the Bobbio Sacramentary. The *Missale Gallicanum* omits this ceremony.

[2] Before, according to the *Missale Gothicum*; after, according to the Bobbio Sacramentary.

[3] Text of the *Missale Gothicum* The words in the other Sacramentaries have nearly the same import St. Cæsarius (Serm. 160, *De temp*) implies an identical formulary. The same may be said of St Maximus of Turin (*De Bapt*, tract. 3).

[4] Can. 48. [It was observed in Ireland. See Stowe Missal, Warren's edition, p 217 —Tr]

Spanish writers also appear to refer to some invocation of this nature. It is found very explicitly in the *Liber Ordinum*.[1] The other liturgical books contain merely a prayer for the perseverance of the newly baptised.[2]

After this prayer, the bishop returned to the church and began the Mass, at which the neophytes communicated. The paschal festival does not seem to have been marked by any particular observance beyond that of the double Mass on Easter Sunday and the daily celebration of the liturgy during the following week.[3]

§ 3 —The Initiatory Rites in the Churches of the East.

We possess a considerable amount of information as to the baptismal ritual in the Eastern Church, properly so called. Among the documents of the fourth century we have the Catecheses of St. Cyril of Jerusalem, the descriptions in the Apostolic Constitutions,[4] and those of the *Peregrinatio*, or Pilgrimage of Etheria (Silvia).[5] From the beginning of the sixth century we have the writings of the pseudo-Dionysius the Areopagite. We may add to these important central texts the scattered information gleaned from other writers, and that which we deduce from the liturgical books now in use. As the scope of the present work does not permit of my dealing with this subject in a detailed manner, or

---

[1] *Lib. Ord.*, p 33.

[2] The *Missale Gothicum* contains two invitatories, but no text of any prayer; the *Missale Gallicanum* has a prayer without invitatory. Both invitatory and prayer are found in the Bobbio Sacramentary.

[3] The Ambrosian Liturgy provides two Masses for every day in Easter Week, one of which implies the presence of the neophytes.

[4] III. 15, 16.

[5] See *infra*, pp 518, 541.

at any great length, I will confine myself to dealing with the four documents above mentioned.

With St. Cyril as our guide, we can follow the whole series of preparatory rites and those of the initiation itself. His catecheses are divided into two groups, one dealing with the ceremonies which precede, the other with those which follow, the initiation. The first, which is a kind of preliminary discourse, entitled pro-Catechesis, describes the catechumens as presenting themselves at the beginning of Lent to be enrolled as candidates for baptism. The *Pilgrimage of Etheria* gives a similar account of this preparatory stage. The names having been inscribed, a day was appointed on which the bishop, assisted by his priests and all the other clergy, proceeded to make a general scrutiny. The candidates, accompanied by their relatives, appeared before him one by one. The bishop made inquiries of the neighbours of each catechumen as to his conduct; if the candidate were a stranger, he had to show commendatory letters. In the case of his not being considered worthy to present himself for baptism, he was made to wait until a subsequent occasion. If the information given was satisfactory, he was accepted, and was thenceforth placed among the number of the competents (*competentes*, φωτιζόμενοι).

During the whole of Lent the competents were summoned every morning to church, to be exorcised, and to hear a sermon from the bishop,[1] or from some one appointed by him. The exorcisms were performed by the inferior clergy, and were accompanied by insufflation. Cyril seems to say that while the words of conjuration were being pronounced, the candidates had their faces covered.

At the end of a stated time [2] the *Traditio Symboli*, or

---

[1] The *Peregrinatio* takes for granted that it is the bishop who preaches; but it is clear that he could appoint a deputy. Cyril himself was only a priest when he delivered his catecheses.

[2] In the series of the Catecheses of St Cyril, that of the *Traditio*

delivery of the Creed, took place. As it was the universal custom for the Creed to be taught by word of mouth, and not learned from a written copy, Cyril has not inserted the text of it in his Catecheses. After the *Traditio*, the teaching dealt with the articles of the Creed, and was continued till the beginning of Holy Week. It was then that the *Redditio*, or recital of the Creed, took place, each candidate presenting himself before the bishop and reciting the Belief, which he had learned by heart. The catecheses during Lent were devoted to instruction in the doctrines of the Eucharist and Baptism; and these also formed the theme of the teaching which the neophytes received during Easter Week.

At Jerusalem, the commemoration of the Passion was of too great an importance, and engaged too much time, to permit of the candidate for baptism receiving instruction during Holy Week, but they presented themselves on the night of Easter Eve for the ceremonies of initiation. They were received in the vestibule of the baptistery, and the service began by the renunciation of the devil.[1] The candidate turned to the west, the region of darkness, and extending his hand, pronounced the formulary of rejection, addressing himself to the evil one, as if he were present—

"I renounce thee, Satan, thy works, thy pomps, and all thy worship."[2] He then turned to the east, the

---

Symboli occupies the fifth place Etheria relates that the first five weeks of Lent were devoted in a general manner to the explanation of the Scriptures and to doctrine, and that the *Traditio* took place at the beginning of the sixth week. This was also the case in the Gallican rite; but as Lent at Jerusalem in Etheria's time lasted eight weeks, the *Traditio* occurred three weeks before Easter.

[1] According to Dionysius, the candidate divested himself previously of nearly all his garments.

[2] This formulary is that of St. Cyril, who mentions expressly the use

region of light, and recited the Creed for the second time. This ceremony, with its two corresponding parts, constituted what is called in the Greek, the ἀπόταξις and the σύνταξις.[1]

The candidate then put off his garments and entered the baptistery. He was immediately anointed,[2] from head to foot, with exorcised oil. In the case of the women, this anointing was performed by deaconesses.

After this anointing, the neophyte entered the font, which had been previously blessed by the bishop.[3] He once more confessed his faith, replying to the threefold questioning of the officiating minister, and was then plunged three times in the consecrated water.

Having quitted the font, the candidate[4] was anointed with perfumed unguents (μύρον, chrism). According to St. Cyril's account, this was administered on the forehead, ears, nose, and breast. He then turned to the east and recited the Lord's Prayer.[5] The ceremony ended with the celebration of the Eucharist, in which the neophytes took part for the first time. In the countries which followed the Alexandrian use, the first communion was followed by the reception of the draught of milk and honey, as at Rome [6]

---

of the second person. In the *Apostolic Constitutions*, the candidate thus expressed himself. "I renounce Satan, his works, his pomps, his worship, his customs, his inventions, and all that belongs to his kingdom."

[1] Dionysius here places a prayer which accompanied the laying-on of hands

[2] According to Dionysius, the bishop himself begins this anointing by a threefold consignation, and the priests conclude it.

[3] Dionysius notes that the benediction was accompanied by a triple infusion of chrism in the form of a cross.

[4] It is here, according to Dionysius, that he resumes his garments

[5] This prayer is not mentioned either by Cyril or by Dionysius.

[6] This custom which, even at Rome, fell into disuse at an early date, is still retained in the Coptic and Ethiopian communities.

CEREMONIES OF CHRISTIAN INITIATION. 331

The Euchologion of Sarapion gives several formularies which correspond to these various ceremonies: namely, first a formulary for the consecration of the water, followed by a prayer over the neophytes before baptism; then another prayer after the *Abrenuntio;* a fourth at the approach to the font; and a final one when they have quitted it. It also contains prayers for the blessing of the oil for the first unction, and for that of the chrism used after baptism.[1]

§ 4.—Comparison of Rites, and their Antiquity.

Amid this diversity of ritual, we have no difficulty in recognising the chief ceremonies which were common to all. They may be divided into two series. Before baptism, there was first a ceremony of admission to the catechumenate, followed by a preparation which consisted of several exorcisms, instructions, the delivery and recital of the Creed, an anointing, and the renunciation of the devil. The initiation itself included the profession of faith, immersion,[2] the anointing with perfumed unguents (chrism), the consignation or signing with the cross, and the imposition of hands.

The rite of admission to the catechumenate contained the insufflation, the ceremony connected with exorcism, and the signing with the cross. At Rome, in addition to these, there was the administering of the salt; while in Spain, and

---

[1] "Ἁγιασμὸς ὑδάτων (7), Εὐχὴ ὑπὲρ βαπτιζομένων (8), Μετὰ τὴν ἀποταγὴν (9), Μετὰ τὴν ἀνάληψιν (10), Μετὰ τὸ βαπτισθῆναι καὶ ἀνελθεῖν (11), Προσευχὴ Σαραπίωνος ἐπισκόπου Θμούεως, Εὐχὴ εἰς τὸ ἄλειμμα τῶν βαπτιζομένων (15), Εὐχὴ εἰς τὸ χρῖσμα ἐν ᾧ χρίονται οἱ βαπτισθέντες (16)."

[2] For the import of the word *immersion*, see *supra*, p. 313, and also what I have said on the subject in my *Eglises Séparées*, p. 93.

probably in Gaul, there was at this point the anointing, which in other countries was relegated to the day of baptism itself.

The immediate preparation of the competents, or φωτιζόμενοι, took place universally during Lent.[1] On a given day the candidates were solemnly taught the symbol of the Christian faith, and at Rome this tradition of the symbol was accompanied by the tradition of the Gospel and the Lord's Prayer.

Immediately before their baptism (except in Spain, and perhaps in Gaul) the candidates received the preparatory anointing with the signing of the cross upon the organs of sense, particularly on the ears and mouth. At Rome the signing of the organs of sense is now made with saliva; formerly, as in the East, and in the countries observing the Gallican use, the same oil was employed with which the body was anointed. In all Latin countries this ceremony precedes the renunciation of the devil; in all others it immediately follows it.

The threefold renunciation of Satan, or the abjuration of paganism, is also common to all the rites. Everywhere, except in Gallican countries, it is followed by the recitation of the Creed,[2] in which the candidate expresses his adherence to his new Master, Jesus Christ.

The last profession of faith, under the form of a reply to a triple interrogation, is of universal use. So is also the triple immersion, except in Spain, where immersion took place only once. A special peculiarity is found in Gaul and North Italy [and in Ireland—TR.] in the washing of the feet after baptism.

[1] It is indeed, in all probability, that from this same preparation Lent derived its origin. See *supra*, p. 242.
[2] In the East there are two "redditions" of the Creed (see p. 329)· one before the day of the renunciation, the other immediately after that ceremony. The Gallican rite has retained the first of these only.

The anointing with unguents, the signing with the cross, and the imposition of hands,[1] were also ceremonies of universal observance. The signing with the cross was made with the same fragrant oil as that used for the anointing itself. At Rome and at Alexandria the unction, or *chrismatio*, was separate from the consignation. It was performed by a priest, whereas the signing with the cross was reserved for the bishop. In the East, and in Gallican countries, the signing took place at the same time as the *chrismatio*, and was made by the bishop when present, or by an ordinary priest in his absence. Another Romano-Alexandrian peculiarity, unknown to the Oriental and Gallican rites, was the drink of milk and honey given to the neophytes after their first communion.

All these ceremonies were in use at the beginning of the fourth century; on this point there cannot be the slightest doubt. They must, therefore, have been introduced before the Church was free from persecution, and even before that of Diocletian. It now remains to be seen how far we can trace them back into the three preceding centuries.

The New Testament [2] sets before us, in the earliest times an initiation composed of two acts, by virtue of one of which, viz. baptism with water, the converted person is washed from his sins, while by the other the gift of the Holy Spirit is imparted to the soul of the neophyte.[3] Baptism was absolutely indispensable; the imparting of the

---

[1] The Greek rituals do not actually mention the laying-on of hands, but it is certain that it was originally connected with the prayer that accompanies the signing of the cross, a prayer in which the Holy Spirit is invoked. Cf. *infra*, p. 340, note 3. It also occurs in the Apostolic Traditions of Hippolytus.

[2] Particularly *Acts of the Apostles*, viii. 12-17; xix. 5, 6.

[3] These passages imply that the Holy Spirit then manifested His Presence in the initiated by signs similar to those mentioned on p 48.

Holy Spirit was merely the completion of the initiation. While, however, baptism might be performed by the inferior members of the Christian community, the imparting of the Holy Spirit was reserved to the chief rulers, to the apostles, and to those invested with apostolic powers. The method of procedure was by imposition of hands, there being no mention whatever in the earliest times of the rite of unction.

The Apostolic Fathers and the apologists of the second century furnish us with no additional information. St. Justin, in his description of the initiation of the neophytes,[1] speaks only of the first act, that is, baptism with water; the *Doctrine of the Apostles* does the same.

We must come down to the time of Severus, about the year 200, before we find any definite mention of the anointing.[2] Tertullian and St. Hippolytus,[3] especially the former, speak with a precision which leaves nothing to be desired. Tertullian describes the rites of initiation in several places, and wrote a special treatise upon baptism. He states that this rite should be administered by a bishop, or, with his delegated authority, by priests and deacons, and that in certain cases it might even be conferred by a lay person. The candidate had to prepare himself for it by prayer, fastings, and holy vigils. It was usually administered at Easter or during the fifty days following. Before entering the font, which had been previously blessed, the neophyte solemnly renounced the devil, his pomps, and his angels[4]

---

[1] Apol., i 61-65

[2] Cf., however, in Theophilus, *Ad Autolycum*, i 12, an allusion which, if not certain, is nevertheless quite a probable one

[3] *In Dan*, v. 17; *De Christo et Antichristo*, 59.

[4] This detail is not found in the treatise *De Baptismo*, but in the *De Corona Militis*, c. 3. This renunciation, as well as the exorcisms, presupposes that the ceremony is taking place over a heathen convert. In the case of a Jew being baptised it would have been otherwise, and a special ritual should have been drawn up. This, however, was not done, and the baptismal ceremony of to-day, as formerly, is applicable only to the general case, viz. that of the infidel

CEREMONIES OF CHRISTIAN INITIATION. 335

After the sacred washing, conferred in the Name of the Father, the Son, and the Holy Ghost, he received an unction of consecrated oil and the imposition of hands, during which the bishop prayed that the Holy Spirit might be given to him. In his treatise on the resurrection of the flesh, the same writer sums up in a few words the whole of the baptismal ritual, and he mentions not only the anointing with chrism, but the signing with the cross,[1] and also the first communion: *Caro abluitur, ut anima emaculetur; caro ungitur, ut anima consecretur; caro signatur, ut et anima muniatur; caro manus impositione adumbratur, ut et anima spiritu illuminetur; caro corpore et sanguine Christi vescitur, ut et anima Deo saginetur.*[2] Finally, in his treatise against Marcion,[3] he speaks of the drink of milk and honey administered to the neophytes. Testimony is also borne to this custom in Alexandrian documents subsequent to Hippolytus.[4]

We have here nearly all the rites incidental to baptism and confirmation, at all events those which, in the fourth century, were universally practised. There is only one rite, apparently, which is not mentioned, and that is the unction previous to baptism, which is clearly indicated in the "Apostolic Tradition" of Hippolytus.

Tertullian speaks of all these things as being universally

---

[1] Cf *Prescript.*, 40.
[2] *De Resurr*, 8.
[3] I 14.
[4] Herr H. Usener, who has recently given his attention to this rite (*Milch und Honig*, in the *Rheinisches Museum*, vol. lvii. p. 177), endeavours to connect it with the pagan legend of Dionysus. He is, however, mistaken. The symbolism of the Promised Land, with its streams "flowing with milk and honey," and that of the nourishment of the new-born babe, is amply sufficient to account for the introduction of this ceremony, without its being necessary to admit improbable borrowing from paganism.
[5] It is possible that this rite may be much less ancient than the others At the end of the fourth century it still had a somewhat uncertain position in the Western ritual. Cf. *supra*, p. 318.

received and as of long standing. In his controversy with Marcion,[1] he witnesses to the fact that the followers of this heretic used the same baptismal ritual as that of the Church Catholic, and specifies the baptism with water, the unction, the signing on the forehead, and the drink of milk and honey. Besides this, we are aware that the Valentinians and other Gnostic sects attached great importance to unction, more so, indeed, than did the Catholic Church itself.[2] It is difficult to believe[3] that these very early sects did not borrow the customs in question from a ritual already established at the time of their separation from the Church, whatever may have been the subsequent modifications which they introduced into it in other respects.

Whatever view may be taken of this chronological discussion of the ceremonies of unction, the signing of the cross, and the drink of milk and honey, it is certain that the division of the initiation into two distinct acts. such as we find already in the New Testament, was maintained in use. The distinction became much more sharply defined when the controversy arose with regard to the baptism of heretics.

It is clear that ceremonies of such importance were presided over by the bishop. As, however, they might have become interminable had the bishop himself performed all the rites in connection with the initiation, a division of functions was made at an early date. The bishop blessed the holy oils and the font, and baptised with his own hand some of the neophytes. The priests, assisted by ministers

---

[1] *Loc. cit.*; cf iii. 22.

[2] Irenæus, i. 18–22; see also the apocryphal Acts of St. Thomas (Max Bonnet's edition), and the curious Gnostic epitaph found at Rome (*Corp. Inscr Graec*, No. 9595a)

[3] It is easy to state the contrary (Renan, *l'Église Chrétienne*, p. 154), but not to prove it.

of lower rank, continued the administration of baptism, but the subsequent ceremonies—the anointing, signing with the cross, and imposition of hands—were reserved for the bishop. At Rome, however, and at Alexandria, doubtless on account of the length of the service, the priests first poured the perfumed unguents (holy chrism) on the head of the neophyte, thus reducing the Pope's function to the signing with the cross and the imposition of hands.

When the local Churches became more numerous, and dependent parishes had been thus created outside the episcopal city, it was necessary to cede to the priests of these parishes the right of conferring holy baptism. But this privilege was nowhere extended to them in its entirety. The blessing of the chrism, and of the oils employed in baptismal unction in general, was in all places interdicted to priests, and they were therefore obliged to have recourse to the bishop to obtain these elements ready consecrated.[1] This restriction expressed symbolically the idea that none could enter the Christian community without the personal intervention of its supreme ruler.

Baptism with water, which, from the earliest times, had been considered valid even when conferred by a Christian layman, was reckoned among the offices of a parish priest. The same was the case with regard to the benediction of fonts, and even, in countries using the Roman rite, to the anointing with chrism. In these countries, the signing with the cross only, together with the laying-on of hands, was reserved for the bishop, who performed these functions either in the episcopal town or on the occasion of his diocesan visitations. In the

---

[1] Innocent, letter to Decentius, c. 3; third Council of Carthage (397), c 36; first Council of Toledo (400), c 20; first Council of Vaison (442), c. 2, etc. In the Eastern Church, the blessing of the holy chrism is now performed by the patriarchs only.

Eastern Church, as there was no distinction between the anointing with chrism and the signing with the cross, the priests possessed the right to perform the whole ceremony.[1] There is ground for belief that this was also the case in countries using the Gallican rite, and that, too, for the same reason; but the influence of Roman discipline appears to have introduced some restrictions.[2]

§ 5.—The Reconciliation of Heretics.

The question as to how far Christian initiation was valid when it was performed by an heretical sect had been a subject of discussion even before the close of the second century. Tertullian deals with it in his treatise on baptism, or, rather, he refers to the solution of the question which he had already given in a special book on the subject, drawn up in Greek.[3] According to him, initiation performed by heretics separated from the Church has no validity. A man who has been converted from paganism[4] to an heretical sect, who has been initiated by the leaders

---

[1] In Egypt also, where, however, this distinction existed (*Ambrosiaster, In Eph*, iv 21; *Quaest. Vet. et Nov Testamenti*, 101, in Migne, *P. L*, vol. xvii. p. 388, and vol xxxv p 2302)

[2] The letter of Innocent to Decentius, c 3, bears testimony to, while inveighing against, the custom which allowed priests the right to confirm; this custom is shown to have existed in Gaul by the Councils of Orange (441, c. 1, 2) and of Epaone (517, c 16); and in Spain by the first Council of Toledo (400, c. 20) and by the *Capitula Martini*, c 52. For the contention which took place in the Island of Sardinia, probably owing to the clashing of the two uses, see Greg. M , *Ep* , iv. 9, 26; cf. the epitaph of Mareas (*Lib Pontif.*, vol. i. p. 302, note 34)

[3] *De Baptismo*, 15

[4] This is the only case here taken into account. That of the child born of heretical parents and baptised in infancy into their sect must have been fully covered by it. As to those Christians who, having left the Church to enter a sect, returned to their first faith and asked to be received back into the community, they were made to do penance.

CEREMONIES OF CHRISTIAN INITIATION. 339

of that sect, and who then leaves it to enter the Catholic Church, should be treated as a pagan, that is, as one not initiated. He must be baptised, since the baptism he has already received is not valid.

Tertullian's view was that of the African Church, and in particular that of the Metropolitan Church of Carthage. The same practice was observed by the Churches of Syria and of Asia Minor. This was not the case, however, at Rome and Alexandria. In these two great Churches, and in those following their direction, a distinction was made. Baptism with water was admitted to be valid, whoever had administered it and in whatever sect it had been conferred, so long as the essential forms had been observed. As to the remaining part of the initiation, it was rejected, and had therefore to be repeated in the case of the heretic who demanded entrance into the Church.

In the year 256, the divergence between the African and Roman practice was the cause of an animated discussion between Pope Stephen and St. Cyprian, Bishop of Carthage; but the conflicting customs, notwithstanding, remained unmodified. It was not until the Council of Arles, in 314, that the Catholic Church in Africa gave up her ancient practice.[1] It was, nevertheless, obstinately persisted in by the Donatists, who even applied it to the Catholic Church, which was treated by them as a dissentient sect. The Eastern Church also continued to regard the baptism of heretics as invalid.[2] Distinctions, however, soon came to be introduced. We find the Council of Nicæa decreeing the adoption of a different treatment towards the Novatians and the partisans of Paul of Samosata.[3] The seventh canon

---

[1] *Conc. Arelat.*, c. 8; cf *Conc. Carthag*, i (347), c. 1.
[2] *Const. App*, vi. 15; *Can. App*, 46, 47; St. Cyril of Jerusalem, *Procatech.*, 7. The rebaptism so long practised by the Gothic Arians was an instance of that custom.
[3] Cf. St. Basil, ep. 188.

of Constantinople, which, although not emanating from the Œcumenical Council of 381, bears witness, nevertheless, to the use of the Church at Constantinople in the fifth century, divides the heretical sects into two categories, those whose baptism, but not confirmation, was accepted, and those whose baptism and confirmation were both rejected.[1] The Monophysites, who separated from the Church in the fifth and sixth centuries, were treated with less severity, and were admitted upon a mere profession of the orthodox faith.[2]

The Western Church remained faithful to the old Roman custom, which was often enjoined by the Popes. Councils, accounts of conversions of heretics, and even liturgical books themselves, all bear testimony to its persistence.[3]

---

[1] This canon was inserted in the Council *in Trullo* (c. 95), and thus found a place in Byzantine canonical law.

[2] Greg. M , *Ep.*, xi. 67 (52).

[3] Jaffé, 255 (Siricius; cf. the Roman Council of 386, c. 8), 286, 303 (Innocent), 536, 544 (Leo); Greg M , *Ep* , xi 67 (52); Council of Orange (441), c. 1; of Toledo (589); Gregory of Tours, *Hist. Fr.*, ii 31, 34; iv. 27, 28; v. 38; ix. 15; *Virt. S Martini*, i. 11; Gelasian Sacramentary, i. 85, 86, etc. It may here be useful to point out a difference of expression which is constantly found in the texts when the rite of imparting the Holy Spirit is in question, depending on whether it is regarded as occurring in the celebration of an ordinary baptism, or in connection with the reconciliation of heretics. Sometimes it is unction, or the *chrismatio*, that is spoken of, at other times the laying-on of hands. But we have only to compare the texts to see that the one hardly ever goes without the other As a rule, the Roman texts employ the term *consignatio* when it is a question of ordinary confirmation, and that of *manus impositio* for the reconciliation of heretics. It is even possible that, in countries where the Roman rite was followed, the whole ceremony was not repeated for converted heretics. Certain passages of St. Optatus and St Augustine give colour to this, and the same may be said of the text of St Gregory the Great (*Ep.*, xi. 67 (52): 'Arianos per impositionem manus Occidens, per unctionem vero sancti, chrismatis. . . . Oriens reformat " But the letters of St Leo and of other Popes above cited leave no room for doubt that, if this really were so, they made the essential part of the rite—the imparting of the Holy Spirit—to lie in the imposition of hands. In Gallican countries it is

always the *chrismatio*, and not the imposition of hands, that is mentioned in the texts. As to the Eastern Church, St. Gregory's phrase entirely agrees with the rule laid down by the seventh canon of Constantinople; but all the same, the liturgical books expressly mention the imposition of hands when it is a question of dealing with heretics. On the other hand, they do not mention it in connection with ordinary confirmation, although writers like Chrysostom, Theodoret, Gennadius, and Photius, when they comment on the text *Heb.*, vi 1, never fail to speak expressly of it. Indeed, the author of the *Apostolic Constitutions*, viii. 28, desiring to enunciate the theory that a priest has the power to confirm, but not to ordain, thus expresses himself: "Πρεσβύτερος . . . χειροθετεῖ οὐ χειροτονεῖ." He also calls (iii. 15) the ceremony in which the bishop applies the perfumed unguents after baptism imposition of hands (χειροθεσία). We must therefore be somewhat cautious here in dealing with isolated expressions, and in every case consider the thing itself rather than the term used to denote it.

CHAPTER X.

ORDINATION.

§ 1.—The Ecclesiastical Hierarchy.

THE ecclesiastical hierarchy, in its earliest stage, comprised, as we have seen above, three orders, those of the episcopate, the priesthood, and the diaconate. The functions of the first two orders could be exercised by men only, but women had been admitted, to a certain extent, to share the duties of the diaconal ministry. Beside the deacons of the male sex, the ancient Church recognised deaconesses,[1] who also bore the name of Widows, χῆραι, *viduae*, or even

---

[1] The following inscription, discovered in the cemetery of Priscilla, is perhaps the most ancient Christian inscription which mentions a member of the ecclesiastical hierarchy. It is the epitaph of a deaconess (χήρα):—

Φλάβια · ΑΡΚΑC · ΧΗΡΑ · ΗΤ C
ἔζησεN · ΑΙΤΗ · ΠΕ · ΜΗΤΡΙ ·
γλυκυΤΑΤΗ · ΦΛΆΒΙΑ · ΘΕΟΦΙΛΑ
θυγάτΗΡ ἐπΟΙΗCΕΝ.

"Flavia Arcas, widow, who lived eighty-five years. To her beloved mother Flavia Theophila, her daughter, has made (this tomb)." It is hardly possible that this person was an ordinary widow. At eighty-five years of age widowhood is not so unusual a state as to require special mention of it on an epitaph (De Rossi, *Bull.*, 1886, p. 90; cf. *Bull. Critique*, vol. viii. p. 255).

Virgins, *virgines canonicae.* They occupied themselves chiefly in works of charity and hospitality, but they had also some liturgical functions to perform in the administration of baptism and at the agapes. The service of the altar was reserved for the deacons, and we find no instance (except as an abuse) of the deaconesses having had any share in it.

The diaconate of women maintained an existence down to the fifth or sixth century. By that time the baptism of adults had become more and more exceptional, and the deaconesses had thus no longer the opportunity of exercising their liturgical functions; besides which monasteries for women gradually began to attract within their walls such holy persons as lived in that age of the "religious" life. There was therefore less need of this special and somewhat exceptional order, and as early as the middle of the third century we find the deaconesses at Rome taking a place in the *canon*, that is to say, in the group of persons assisted by the Church, and not among the *clergy* properly so called.[1]

While the diaconate of women thus declined in importance, that of men developed rapidly. The functions of the deacons were distributed among the grades of a more or less complicated hierarchy. In the East there were only two degrees, that of deacon and that of subdeacon. At Rome the subdiaconate was itself subdivided, and in addition to the subdeacons there were acolytes, or attendants. The reading of the sacred books in meetings for worship had at first been entrusted to any person whom the president thought fit to appoint. It was soon raised to an office, and from the end of the second century we note the existence of *lectors*, who are also ranked among

---

[1] On the subject of deaconesses, see Thomassin, *Discip de l'Église*, I, i. 52; II, i 43.

the clergy. In the same way, at Rome, we remark the appearance of exorcists and doorkeepers. In the West the exorcists had somewhat active functions in the preparations for baptism, but in the East these functions devolved on other clerics, the exorcists being regarded rather[1] as persons endowed with unusual supernatural powers received direct from God, and not through the medium of the Church. For this reason, therefore, they were not included in the ecclesiastical hierarchy. As to the doorkeepers, it was not thought suitable to rank among the clergy persons engaged in so humble an employment.[2]

There were, therefore, two types of hierarchy, one embracing five, and the other eight grades.

In the letter written by Pope Cornelius[3] to Fabius, Bishop of Antioch, in 251, we find a definite enumeration of the Roman clergy. There existed at that time forty-six priests, seven deacons, seven subdeacons, forty-two acolytes, and fifty-two minor clerks (exorcists, lectors, doorkeepers); besides these there were more than fifteen hundred widows or persons "assisted." We have here, including the Pope himself, the eight orders of the Latin ecclesiastical hierarchy.[4] Fabian, the predecessor of Cornelius, had constituted the

---

[1] *Const. Ap*, viii. 26

[2] Beneath the rank, however, of subdeacon and lector, or rather outside the hierarchy properly so called, the Eastern Churches recognised other categories, some common to all Churches, the others varying according to the localities and their special needs—confessors, virgins, widows, psalmists, doorkeepers, interpreters, *copiatae, parabolani*, etc. *Ap. Const.*, viii. 23-28; pseudo-Ignatius, *Ad Antioch.*, 12; Epiphanius, *Expos. fid.*, 21; Council of Antioch, c. 10; Council of Laodicea, c. 23, 24.

[3] Eusebius, *H. E*, vi. 43.

[4] The correspondence of St. Cyprian proves that at Carthage also, and in the middle of the third century, all these different minor orders were known, except perhaps that of doorkeeper, which I do not find mentioned. But the omission of this order is explained by the few occasions which St. Cyprian and his correspondents had of mentioning it.

seven ecclesiastical regions,[1] and had apportioned them among the same number of deacons. This apportioning involved soon afterwards a redistribution of the clergy, which continued to exist for a long time afterwards, namely, the distribution according to the seven regions. John the Deacon, at the beginning of the sixth century, expressly mentions this: *Septem regionibus ecclesiastica apud nos militia continetur.*[2] The *Ordines Romani* of the eighth and ninth centuries are still clearer on this subject. It should be noted, moreover, that the number of the regions was, from the outset, not only equal to that of the deacons and subdeacons, but that it also evidently affected that of the acolytes, of whom there were forty-two, that is, six to each region. If we add to these the subdeacon, we have in each region seven clerics under the rank of deacon, namely, the six acolytes and the subdeacon, who was a kind of head acolyte.

We have, therefore, ground for regarding the ministry of subdeacon and acolyte as a development of that of the deacon. These three categories of clergy, moreover, have this in common, that they are all attached to the service of the altar, which is not the case with the inferior ministers.[3]

We note the existence of acolytes at Rome and Carthage from the middle of the third century onwards. But we must not conclude from this that, even in the West, all the Churches, and more especially the smaller,

---

[1] Liberian Catal.; see my edition of *Liber Pontif*, vol. i. p. 5.
[2] *Ep. ad Senarium*, 11 (Migne, *Pat Lat*, vol lix. p 405).
[3] This is very well put by John the Deacon, *loc. cit*, 10: "Acolythi autem exorcistis hoc ordine differunt quod exorcistis portandi sacramenta eaque sacerdotibus ministrandi negata potestas est, tantumque manus impositioni vacent, propter quod exorcistae dicuntur, vel caetera quae intra acolythorum ordinem esse probantur explere festinent. Acolythi vero sacramentorum portanda vasa suscipiunt et ministrandi sacerdotibus ordinem gerunt. Ideoque exorcista fieri potest acolythus; iste vero ad exorcistarum officium nulla penitus promotione descendit"

were provided with clerics of that order. While the offices of exorcist and lector are met with nearly everywhere, that of the acolyte is lacking in some countries of the extreme West.¹ After the foundation of the *schola cantorum* at Rome, the acolytes, being then the only minor order engaged in active ministry, acquired a much greater importance than they had hitherto enjoyed. They are constantly mentioned in the *Ordines* of the eighth and ninth centuries. The cardinal priests had no other assistants in their titular Churches. In the pontifical ceremonies, all the inferior offices, becoming increasingly complicated, were delegated to them. During Lent, and at the solemnisation of baptism, they fulfilled all the functions which hitherto had devolved on the exorcists, just as the subdeacons had absorbed those of the lectors.

With regard to doorkeepers, lectors, and exorcists, Pope Cornelius classes all three categories together, merely giving us the total number. Each category contained a less number than there were of the acolytes. Their number would be in proportion to the various services they had to render, and of these we have no precise information.²

The doorkeepers are rarely mentioned in Roman documents.³ Lectors, on the other hand, are very frequently

---

¹ Cf. *infra*, p. 365 In the Christian epigraphy of Gaul, as far as I know, mention is made of only one acolyte, viz at Lyons, in 517 (Le Blant, 36). The *Statuta* prove that this order was known in the province of Arles

² Figuring in the trial concerning the seizure of the Church of Cirta, in 303, we find, besides the bishop, three priests, three deacons, four subdeacons, and *fossores* in greater number, but of whom six only are named. Besides these ecclesiastics, who were present at the seizure, there were seven lectors. Neither acolytes, exorcists, nor doorkeepers are mentioned (Migne, *P. L.*, vol. viii p. 731). Notice the conformity in the number of priests and deacons with the prescriptions of the Egyptian Apostolic Constitutions (Funk, *Doctrina Apostolorum*, pp. 62, 66; cf. *Bulletin Critique*, vol. vii. p. 366).

³ The most ancient, to my knowledge, was that *Romanus Ostiarius*, whom the *Liber Pontificalis* (vol 1 p 155) assigns as a companion in martyrdom

referred to. The series of their epitaphs begins as early as the second century on monuments which are probably anterior to Tertullian, who is the first writer to mention them.[1] In the fourth century this order was pre-eminently the first of the ministry, and constituted a sort of probationary stage. Young clerics began their career in it, and remained lectors until they had reached an adult age, which was a necessary qualification for receiving superior orders[2] Most of the ecclesiastical careers of which the details are known to us began with the lectorate. Such was the case with St. Felix of Nola, St. Eusebius of Vercelli, the father of Pope Damasus, the Popes Liberius and Siricius, Messius Romulus the Deacon of Fiesole, St. Epiphanius of Pavia, and many others.[3] It need not therefore excite surprise that this order was extremely

---

to St Laurence, in 258 The decretals of Popes Siricius, Zosimus, and Gelasius (Jaffé, 255, 339, 636), bearing on promotion in the ecclesiastical career, do not speak of doorkeepers as a step to entering that calling Gelasius who alone mentions this order, raises a distinction between it and the others, by saying that a knowledge of letters is obligatory before entering orders and that without it, *vix fortassis ostiarii (quis) possit implere ministerium* The *Liber Pont* contains (vol 1 pp. 164, 171) two enumerations of the ranks of the hierarchy; the order of doorkeepers figures only in the second; the *Constitutum Silvestri* omits it five times out of seven in enumerations of the same nature I know of no Roman inscription which mentions this office. It is met with in a law of 337 (*Cod. Theod*, XVI, xii 24); see also the Treves inscription, Le Blant, 292, and the letter of SS Lupus and Euphronius (Hardouin, *Conciles*, vol II p. 791). The doorkeepers were superseded at an early date at Rome by the *mansionarii*, a kind of sacristan not in orders, who appear as early as the sixth century.

[1] For the epitaphs of the lectors *Favor* and *Claudius Atticianus*, see De Rossi, *Bull*, 1871, p 32; Tertullian, *Praescr.*, 41.

[2] See the decretals cited above, p 346, note 3. Those who entered the ranks of the clergy when of adult age could begin their career by being exorcists; children were always placed among the lectors.

[3] For Felix of Nola, see Paulinus, *Nat IV. Fel*, v. 104, for Eusebius, St. Jerome, *De Viris*, 96; for the father of Damasus, for Liberius, Siricius, and Romulus, see inscriptions published in my edition of the *Liber Pont*, vol. i. pp 213, 210, 217; in the *Bull* of De Rossi, 183, p 17; for Epiphanius, see his life by Ennodius (p. 332, Hartel)

numerous in the fourth and fifth centuries.[1] Those whose epitaphs have come down to us had, as a general rule, reached the age of adults, but there were many young children in the corporation. Their silvery voices penetrated the vast spaces of the basilicas, and were heard by the most distant portions of the congregation. In the fulfilment of their duties, which were of a serious nature for those so tender in years, they were exposed to the temptation of playing tricks. The epitaph of Pope Liberius does not omit to call attention to the good behaviour of which he gave evidence at this stage of his career; never had he been heard to read wrong words wilfully, or to change the holy text for the amusement of his giddy companions. The lectors were distributed among the parochial Churches,[2] but this did not prevent their being grouped according to regions. They came even to be constituted as a corporation (*schola lectorum*) at an early date, though the existence of this body at Rome, it is true, is not attested by any specific document.[3] These *scholae*, however, were to be found in other Churches,[4] and, at Rome, the *schola cantorum*, of which there is clear evidence from the

---

[1] The *Constitutum Silvestri* gives ninety as the number at Rome. In 484, the clergy of Carthage comprised about five hundred persons *inter quos quam plurimi erant lectores infantuli* (*Victor Vit.*, III. 34). See De Rossi, *Bull.*, 1883, pp. 17-22.

[2] See the passage in which I have dealt with this subject in the *Mélanges de l'École de Rome*, vol vii. pp 55-57.

[3] The *Constitutum Silvestri*, after having mentioned the ninety lectors at Rome, says that their relatives accompanied them to the council This does not point to a resident corporation

[4] A *primicerius scholae lectorum* existed at Lyons (Le Blant, 667A, inscription of 552); at Tongres or at Rheims, a *primicerius scholae clarissimae, militiaeque lectorum* (Letter of St Remigius, in Migne, *Pat. Lat*, vol lxv p. 969); at Perrē (Pirūn), in the province of the Euphrates, a *primicerius lectorum* (*Conc Chalced*, sess. xiv), at Carthage (*Victor Vit*, loc cit), a master of these boys is mentioned. Cf. the epitaph of a *princeps cantorum sacrosancte aeclisiae Mirtilliae* (Myrtilis, in Lusitania), published by Mons de Laurière, in the *Bulletin des Antiquaires de France*, 1882. p. 217

seventh century onwards, consisted mainly of lectors. The latter, it is true, were no longer employed in their liturgical functions. As the vigils had fallen into desuetude from an early date, and as the lections in the Mass had also been reduced, as early as the fifth century, to the Epistle and Gospel, the reading of the Gospel being confined at the same time to the deacons, the lectors had but rare occasions of exercising their ministry. Such lections as were of less importance than the Gospel, and still remained in use, were assigned to subdeacons. The adult lectors consequently disappeared, and the children of the *schola cantorum* had no longer any other function than that of singing Hence the name *schola cantorum*.[1]

The office of exorcist was also one in which an ecclesiastical career could be begun, but it could be exercised only by adults.[2] It appears that the function of exorcist was more frequently exercised before than after the fifth century. The Roman epitaphs of exorcists all belong to the third or fourth century. At the Council of Arles we find among nine clerics of the inferior orders, who came thither with their bishops, seven exorcists and two lectors.[3] The functions of these clerics were strictly confined to

---

[1] The *schola cantorum* obtained its recruits, especially about the eighth and ninth centuries, from among orphans (*Liber Diurnus*, vii 19, Garnier; *Lib Pont*, vol ii pp 92, 195) It occupied a building situated on the Via Merulana, between the Churches of St Matthew and St Bartholomew (Urlichs, *Codex U R. Topogr*., p 173) The site of only the former of these churches is known. We see from the *Ordines Romani* that the *schola* had at its head several subdeacons The *prior* or *primicerius*, the *secundus* or *secundicerius*, the *tertius* and the *quartus*, or *archiparaphonista*, were the dignitaries of the corporation Below these were the heads of divisions, or *paraphonistae* During the ceremonies the children were arranged in two rows, with the dignitaries at their head, and the *paraphonistae* bringing up the rear.

[2] See the celebrated epitaph of Fl Latinus, Bishop of Brescia (*Corp I. Lat*, vol. v, No. 4846) St Martin began by being an exorcist

[3] According to the *Constitutum Silvestri*, the term in the functions of an exorcist lasted only one day; but according to the *Lib Pont*. (SILVESTRE)

the preparation of candidates for baptism, and they became obsolete with the disappearance of the catechumenate. The inscriptions in which they are mentioned do not anywhere connect them with the titulary churches or regions of Rome, although they ought to have been grouped, like the other clerics, according to the latter. From the beginning of the sixth century we hear but little of them;[1] if there continued to be still exorcists at Rome, they must have been among the minor clerics of the *schola cantorum*.

§ 2.—LATIN CEREMONIES OF ORDINATION.

The authorities which have come down to us on the rites of ordination in the Latin Church are as follows:—

1. The *Statuta Ecclesiae Antiqua*, a collection of disciplinary and liturgical canons drawn up in Gaul, in the province of Arles, about the beginning of the sixth century.[2] We find in them the principal ceremonies of ordination for all the orders. It is evident from these ceremonies that the use was Gallican. It is probably the only text in which that use is preserved free from any admixture, for the Gallican liturgical books do not contain the ceremonies of ordination.

2. The *Roman Sacramentaries.*—We must confine our

---

it was a month. The second pseudo-Silvestrian Council requires for it ten years. As to the actual discipline, see the decretals cited above, p 346, note 3. The *Constitutum*, which mentions eighty lectors and forty-five acolytes, enumerates only twenty-two exorcists at Rome

[1] The inscriptions, moreover, mention an exorcist, who died in 511, at Eclana; and another at Como, in 526 (*Corp. Inscr Lat*, vol ix, No 1381, vol v, No. 6428).

[2] Maasen, *Quellen*, vol. i p 382, Malnory, *S. Césaire*, p. 50. This collection was inserted, under the title *Concilium Carthaginiense quartum*, in the Spanish body of canons (*Hispana*), from whence it passed into that of the pseudo-Isidore It is still quoted by many under the latter title, and, what is more serious, pronounced as an authority for African ecclesiastical usages in the fourth century.

notice here, in general, to the Leonian Sacramentary and that of Pope Adrian. They contain identically the same prayers for the ordination of deacons, priests, and bishops, and nothing else. There is no mention in them of any of the orders below the diaconate.

3. The *Ordines Romani.*—I have three of these to specify: (*a*) that of the manuscript of St. Amand,[1] which contains only the Roman ordinations at the Ember seasons, that is, those of deacons and priests; (*b*) the *Ordo VIII.* of Mabillon, which contains in addition the ordination of the inferior orders, together with that of bishops; (*c*) the *Ordo IX.* of Mabillon, in which are given the ceremonies in regard to deacons, priests, bishops, and the Pope himself. The three *Ordines* agree in the main with each other, and the ceremonies which they describe fall in exactly with those implied in the two Sacramentaries.

4. The Gelasian Sacramentary and the *Missale Francorum.*—These two compilations furnish us with the complete ritual for all the orders; but a slight examination is enough to convince us that they contain many things derived from widely different sources. We find therein (*a*) a passage of a letter from Pope Zosimus on the intervals of time between the orders;[2] (*b*) Chapters I. to X. of the *Statuta Ecclesiae Antiqua*;[3] (*c*) ordination prayers for the five inferior orders;[4] (*d*) prayers for the ordination of deacons, priests, and bishops.[5] In the last portion, the Roman prayers, that is, those found in the Leonian Sacramentary and the Sacramentary of Adrian, are embodied

---

[1] See Appendix.
[2] This is found only in the Gelasian Sacramentary, i. 95.
[3] In the *Missale Francorum* the chapters bearing on the lectors and subdeacons are wanting.
[4] Gelas, i. 96.
[5] Gelas, i 20, 99

in other prayers, which suggest a ritual widely different from that of Rome.

From this description it will be seen that the Roman usage must be gathered from the Leonian and Gregorian Sacramentaries as well as from the *Ordines*. The *Statuta* and the non-Roman portions of the Gelasian Sacramentary and of the *Missale Francorum* represent the Gallican use.

§ 3.—ORDINATIONS AT ROME.

1. *The Minor Orders.*

From what has already been said, it is natural that we should find in the Roman books no ceremony for the ordination of the three minor orders. If this ceremony ever existed, it must have been of an entirely private character, that is, it must have taken place in the interior of the *schola cantorum*, and not in public.

Even in the cases of the acolytes and subdeacons there was no solemn ordination. At the time of the communion, at any ordinary Mass, even when it was not stational, the future acolyte approached either the Pope, if he were present, or one of the bishops of the Pontifical Court, holding the linen bag—a symbol of the highest function of these clerics, that of carrying to the priests the *oblatae*, or consecrated hosts, at the moment of the fraction of the bread,—and then prostrated himself while the pontiff pronounced over him his blessing, in these words: *Intercedente beata et gloriosa semperque virgine Maria, et beato Apostolo Petro, salvet et custodiat et protegat te Dominus.* If it were the case of a subdeacon, he held, in place of a linen bag, an empty chalice, which had been handed to him by the archdeacon, or by the bishop himself; but the whole ceremony consisted of a simple blessing, of the same tenor as that just given, and without any special reference to the conferring of either honour or authority. This formulary of blessing, moreover, has no very ancient ring about it. I do not think it is older than the seventh century. John, the Roman deacon, speaks at the beginning of the sixth century of the *traditio* of the chalice as constituting the whole ceremony in the ordination of subdeacons.[1]

2. *The Ordinations at the Ember Seasons—that is, of Priests and Deacons.*

The ordinations of deacons and priests were also performed with a very simple ritual, but they were celebrated with great publicity at a solemn station. There was not an ordination every year, but when the necessity arose one of the Saturdays of the Ember weeks was always chosen.[2]

The candidates for ordination, chosen by the pope, were at first presented to the faithful during the Stational Masses of Wednesday and Friday in Santa Maria Maggiore and in the Church of the Holy Apostles. Shortly after the beginning of Mass, a notary, mounting the ambo, announced the names of those who had been elected, and called upon those who had anything to say against them to do so without fear—

Auxiliante Domino Deo Salvatore nostro Jesu Christo, elegimus in ordine diaconi (sive presbyteri) *illum* subdiaconum (sive diaconum) (de titulo *illo*). Si quis autem habet aliquid contra hos viros, pro Deo

---

[1] "Cujus hic apud nos ordo est ut accepto sacratissimo calice . subdiaconus jam dicatur" (Migne, *Pat Lat.*, vol. lix p 405).

[2] It appears that, at the beginning, and up to the end of the fifth century, the December Ember days were chosen by preference, for the *Liber Pontificalis* mentions the ordinations as celebrated almost always *mense decembri.*

et propter Deum cum fiducia exeat et dicat. Verumtamen memor sit communionis suae.

This is the formulary of the Gelasian Sacramentary (i. 20); the other two do not contain it. The *Ordo IX.* and that of St. Amand have formularies almost identical. According to the rubric of the Gelasian Sacramentary, it is the Pope who delivers the address: *adnunciat pontifex in populo, dicens.* One of the *Ordines* assigns this duty to a lector, while the other refers it to a *scriniarius*, or notary. These two terms must be considered as meaning the same thing, for in the first case the word *lector* does not designate a cleric of that order, but the person who is performing the function at the moment. We may conclude, moreover, that, although the formulary is given in the Gelasian *Ordo* as pronounced by the Pope and drawn up in his name, it was always read, by some one acting on his behalf.

The candidates for ordination were stationed at a certain place where they could be well seen and their identity well established. This public probation had been preceded by a declaration, made before the highest dignitaries of the Church, in which the candidate had to swear that he had never committed any of the four heinous sins, the commission of which, according to the discipline of the time,[1] was an impediment to the reception of orders.

[1] These sins are enumerated in the *Ordo VIII.* of Mabillon; they were: sodomy, bestiality, adultery, violation of consecrated virgins. This enumeration does not include all the sins, whether secret or open, which in the ancient discipline were subject to public penance, and constituted thus a bar to orders There is, therefore, a difficulty here which, as far as I am aware, has never been satisfactorily solved I consider, for my part, that these interrogatories preliminary to ordination go back to a time when baptism was received at adult age, and that it had not in view the present condition of the conscience of the candidate, but his conduct before having received baptism While proclaiming the remission of sins, however heinous they might be, by virtue of the sacrament of baptism

It was on a Saturday evening, at the Mass of the Vigil, that ordinations took place. The eighth-century texts imply that this Mass had already been transferred to an earlier hour, and celebrated in the course of the afternoon. At the outset it was celebrated at night, like the Mass of Holy Saturday.[1] It was begun by the antiphon *ad Introïtum*, which was followed by a long series of lections—both in Greek and Latin—with chants and prayers between. Shortly before the reading of the Gospel, the archdeacon took the candidates and presented them to the Pope. The pontiff, arising, called upon the congregation to pray—

Oremus, dilectissimi, Deum Patrem omnipotentem, ut super hos famulos suos quos ad officium diaconii vocare dignatur benedictionem gratiae suae clementer effundat et consecrationis indultae propitius dona conservet.

This is the formulary prescribed in the Leonian and Gelasian Sacramentaries for the ordination of deacons—a slightly different one was used for the ordination of priests. In the Sacramentary of Adrian, with which Mabillon's *Ordo VIII.* agrees, the formulary is so drawn up that it can be applied at the same time to either the diaconate or the priesthood. This *Ordo*, like the two others of a similar character, implies that deacons and priests were ordained at the same time, the subdeacons intended for the priesthood receiving, in the first place, the benediction for the diaconate, and then immediately afterwards that for the priesthood.[2]

the Church might have special requirements in the cases of persons who intended to take orders. It was owing to this that digamists were excluded, without a discussion of the question whether the first marriage had been contracted before or after baptism

[1] St Leo, in a letter to Dioscorus, Bishop of Alexandria (Jaffé, 406), insists strongly on this point

[2] The custom of conferring simultaneously the diaconate and the

At the invitation of the Pope, the whole congregation prostrated themselves, including the Pope himself, the candidates, and the clergy, while the *schola cantorum* sang the Litany. When this was ended, the Pope arose, and, placing his hands on the head of each of the candidates, recited a double form of prayer, consisting of an ordinary prayer[1] and a consecratory canon (*eucharistic* prayer), as follows:—

Deus,[2] conlator sacrarum magnifice dignitatum, quaesumus, ut hos famulos tuos quos ad officium levitarum vocare dignaris, altaris sancti ministerium tribuas sufficienter implere, cunctisque donis gratiae redundantes et fiduciam sibi tuae majestatis acquirere et aliis praebere facias perfectae devotionis exemplum.

Vere dignum. . . . Adesto[3] quaesumus, omnipotens Deus, honorum dator, ordinum distributor officiorumque dispositor. Qui in te manens innovas omnia, et cuncta disponens per Verbum, Virtutem Sapientiamque tuam, Jesum Christum, Filium tuum, dominum nostrum, sempiterna providentia praeparas et singulis quibusque temporibus aptanda dispensas. Cujus corpus Ecclesiam tuam caelestium gratiarum varietate distinctam, suorumque connexam distinctione membrorum, per legem totius mirabilem compagis unitam, in augmentum templi tui crescere dilatarique largiris, sacri muneris servitutem trinis gradibus ministrorum nomini tuo militare constituens; electis ab initio Levi filiis qui mysticis operationibus domus tuae fidelibus excubiis permanentes, haereditatem benedictionis aeternae sorte perpetua possiderent. Super hos quoque

---

priesthood explains why the pontifical biographers of the ninth century, in describing the *cursus honorum* of the Popes chosen from among the cardinal priests, never make mention of the diaconate, but pass always from the subdiaconate to the priesthood. Cf., in the *Lib Pont.*, the description of the early phases of the ecclesiastical careers of Leo III, Pascal I., Gregory IV, Sergius II, Leo IV., Benedict III., Adrian II., and Stephen V.

[1] This prayer must have been considered as the end of the *collective* prayer, which was said after the invitatory *Oremus, dilectissimi*. The prayer, which was usually offered up in silence by the congregation (see above p 107), was here replaced by the Litany.

[2] This formulary is peculiar to the Leonian Sacramentary   I have corrected the *consolator* of the manuscript into *conlator*.

[3] This formulary is common to the three Sacramentaries.

famulos tuos, quaesumus, Domine, placatus intende, quos tuis sacris altaribus servituros in officium diaconii suppliciter dedicamus. Et nos quidem, tanquam homines, divini sensus et summae rationis ignari, horum vitam quantum possumus aestimamus. Te autem, Domine, quae nobis sunt ignota non transeunt, te occulta non fallunt. Tu [1] cognitor peccatorum, tu scrutator es animarum, tu veraciter in eis caeleste potes adhibere judicium, et vel indignis donare quae poscimus. Emitte in eos, Domine, quaesumus, Spiritum sanctum, quo in opus ministerii fideliter exsequendi munere septiformi tuae gratiae roborentur. Abundet in eis totius forma virtutis, auctoritas modesta, pudor constans, innocentiae puritas et spiritalis observantia disciplinae. In moribus eorum praecepta tua fulgeant, ut suae castitatis exemplo imitationem sanctae plebis acquirant, et bonum conscientiae testimonium praeferentes in Christo firmi et stabiles perseverent, dignisque successibus de inferiori gradu per gratiam tuam capere potiora mereantur.

When these prayers are ended the new deacons receive the kiss of peace from the Pope, the bishops and priests, and take their place, by the side of the Pope, among the other deacons.

The candidates for the priesthood—whether they have long since been promoted to the diaconate [2] or have just been promoted—are then presented. They prostrate themselves before the pontiff, who recites over them two other prayers of a similar form to those just given. After this they are embraced by the Pope, bishops, and priests, and then take their place at the head of the latter.

I append here the formularies,[3] with the exception of the Litany, used in the ordination of priests:—

---

[1] *Greg*: "Tu cognitor secretorum, tu scrutator es cordium; tu eorum vitam caelesti poteris examinare judicio quo semper praevales et admissa purgare et ea quae sunt agenda concedere. Emitte . ."

[2] This must have been rare. The progress from the diaconate to the priesthood was not an easy matter. For this would have, in fact, involved exclusion from the road leading to the episcopate

[3] These formularies are common to the three Sacramentaries.

Invitatory —

Oremus, dilectissimi, Deum Patrem omnipotentem, ut super hos famulos suos quos ad presbyterii munus elegit caelestia dona multiplicet, quibus quod ejus dignatione suscipiunt ejus exsequantur auxilio.

Litany.

Prayer—

Exaudi nos, Deus salutaris noster, et super hos famulos tuos benedictionem sancti Spiritus et gratiae sacerdotalis effunde virtutem, ut quos tuae pietatis aspectibus offerimus consecrandos perpetua muneris tui largitate prosequaris.

Eucharistic Prayer—

Vere dignum. . . . Deus, honorum omnium et omnium dignitatum quae tibi militant distributor, per quem proficiunt universa, per quem cuncta firmantur, amplificatis semper in melius naturae rationabilis incrementis per ordinem congrua ratione dispositum. Unde sacerdotales gradus et officia levitarum sacramentis mysticis instituta creverunt: ut cum pontifices summos regendis populis praefecisses, ad eorum societatis et operis adjumentum sequentis ordinis viros et secundae dignitatis eligeres. Sic in eremo per septuaginta virorum prudentum mentes Moysi spiritum propagasti; quibus ille adjutoribus usus in populo, innumerabiles multitudines facile gubernavit. Sic in Eleazaro et Ithamar filiis Aaron paternae plenitudinis abundantiam transfudisti, ut ad hostias salutares et frequentioris officii sacramenta sufficeret meritum sacerdotum. Hac providentia, Domine, Apostolis Filii tui Doctores fidei comites addidisti, quibus illi orbem totum secundis praedicatoribus impleverunt. Quapropter infirmitati quoque nostrae, Domine, quaesumus, haec adjumenta largire, qui quanto magis fragiliores sumus tanto his pluribus indigemus. Da, quaesumus, Pater, in hos famulos tuos presbyterii dignitatem; innova in visceribus eorum spiritum sanctitatis; acceptum a te, Deus, secundi meriti munus obtineant, censuramque morum exemplo suae conversationis insinuent. Sint probi cooperatores ordinis nostri; eluceat in eis totius forma justitiae, ut bonam rationem dispensationis sibi creditae reddituri aeternae beatitudinis praemia consequantur

3. *The Ordination of Bishops.*

We have seen that in the ordination of deacons and priests the entire rite, according to Roman usage, consists of prayers—some offered in common by the whole congregation, and others recited by the Pope over the prostrate candidate. The ceremonial in the case of bishops was not more complex.

The bishops consecrated by the Pope were almost always those of his own metropolitan province. They were not chosen by him, but elected in their several localities. The election being over, an official report or decree is drawn up, which is signed by the notables of the place, both clerical and lay, and the future bishop thereupon sets out, accompanied by some representatives of his Church, for Rome, where the election is verified and the candidate examined. If the election is found to have been regular, and the Pope approves of the choice of the electors, the consecration follows. There was no special time in the year assigned to this ceremonial, but it had always to take place on a Sunday.

As was the case in the ordinations at the Ember seasons, the Litany and *Kyrie* were deferred until after the Gradual. When this had been sung, the Pope called on the congregation to pray, and then all present prostrated themselves while the Litany was being chanted. After the Litany, the Pope arose and recited over the candidate a prayer composed of two formularies, of exactly the same type as that used for deacons and priests. The new bishop then arose, and having received the embrace of the Pope, bishops, and priests, took his place at the head of the bishops. The choir then sang the *Alleluia*, or Tract, and the Mass was continued in the usual manner. I append here the special formularies used for the ordination of bishops:—

Invitatory[1]—

Oremus, dilectissimi nobis, ut his viris ad utilitatem Ecclesiae provehendis[2] benignitas omnipotentis Dei gratiae suae tribuat largitatem.

Litany.

Prayer—

Propitiare, Domine, supplicationibus nostris, et inclinato super hos famulos tuos cornu gratiae sacerdotalis benedictionis tuae in eos effunde virtutem.

Eucharistic Prayer—

Vere dignum. . . . Deus honorum omnium, Deus omnium dignitatum quae gloriae tuae sacratis famulantur ordinibus; Deus qui Moysen famulum tuum secreti familiaris affatu, inter cetera caelestis documenta culturae de habitu quoque indumenti sacerdotalis instituens, electum Aaron mystico amictu vestiri inter sacra jussisti; ut intelligentiae sensum de exemplis priorum caperet secutura posteritas, ne eruditio doctrinae tuae ulli deesset aetati, cum et apud veteres reverentiam ipsa significationum species obtineret et apud nos certiora essent experimenta rerum quam aenigmata figurarum. Illius namque sacerdotii anterioris habitus nostrae mentis ornatus est, et pontificalem gloriam non jam nobis honor commendat vestium sed splendor animarum. Quia et illa quae tunc carnalibus blandiebantur obtutibus ea potius quae in ipsis erant intelligenda poscebant. Et idcirco his famulis tuis quos ad summi sacerdotii ministerium delegisti, hanc quaesumus, Domine, gratiam largiaris, ut quidquid illa velamina in fulgore auri, in nitore gemmarum, in multimodi operis varietate signabant, hoc in horum moribus actibusque clarescat. Comple in sacerdotibus tuis mysterii tui summam, et ornamentis totius glorificationis instructos caelestis unguenti fluore sanctifica. Hoc, Domine, copiose in eorum caput influat, hoc in oris subjecta decurrat, hoc in totius corporis extrema descendat, ut tui Spiritus virtus et interiora horum repleat et exteriora circumtegat. Abundet in his

---

[1] This and the following formulary are common to the three sacramentaries.

[2] In the Gelasian only I correct *providendis* into *provehendis*

constantia fidei, puritas delectionis, sinceritas pacis. [Sint[1] speciosi munere tuo pedes horum ad evangelizandum pacem, ad evangelizandum bona tua. Da eis, Domine, ministerium reconciliationis in verbo et in factis, et in virtute signorum et prodigiorum. Sit sermo eorum et praedicatio non in persuasibilibus humanae sapientiae verbis, sed in ostensione Spiritus et virtutis. Da eis, Domine, claves regni caelorum; utantur, nec glorientur, potestate quam tribuis in aedificationem, non in destructionem. Quodcumque ligaverint super terram sit ligatum et in caelis et quodcumque solverint super terram sit solutum et in caelis. Quorum detinuerint peccata, detenta sint, et quorum dimiserint tu dimittas. Qui benedixerit eis sit benedictus et qui maledixerit eis maledictionibus repleatur. Sint fideles servi, prudentes, quos constituas tu, Domine, super familiam tuam, ut dent illis cibum in tempore necessario, ut exhibeant omnem hominem perfectum. Sint sollicitudine impigri, sint spiritu ferventes. Oderint superbiam, diligant veritatem, nec eam umquam deserant aut lassitudine aut timore superati. Non ponant lucem ad tenebras, nec tenebras [ad] lucem. Non dicant malum bonum, nec bonum malum. Sint sapientibus debitores et fructum de profectu omnium consequantur.] Tribuas eis cathedram episcopalem ad regendam Ecclesiam tuam et plebem universam. Sis eis auctoritas, sis eis potestas, sis eis firmitas. Multiplices super eos benedictionem et gratiam tuam, ut ad exorandam semper misericordiam tuam, tuo munere idonei, tua gratia possint esse devoti.

In this ceremony, as in that of the ordination of deacons and priests, the Pope alone officiated. He might have bishops around him—and in general this was the case— but he was the sole administrator in the ceremony. This departure from the rule that a single bishop could not consecrate another is mentioned in the sixth century, in the *Breviarium* of Ferrandus.[2]

---

[1] The passage in brackets is not found either in the Leonian or Gregorian Sacramentaries, but it occurs in the Gelasian, and also in the *Missale Francorum*, which also contains this formulary. The style and character of this passage is completely in harmony with the rest. This circumstance induces me to believe—notwithstanding a conflict of paleographic authorities—that it must have formed part of the original Roman formulary

[2] Cap. 6: *Ut unus episcopus episcopum non ordinet, excepta ecclesia Romana.* This canon is one of those passed at the Roman Council of 386

4. *Ordination of the Pope*

The ceremonial followed in the consecration of the Pope was not much more complex, but it had some special features. The ceremony, as in the case of bishops, took place on a Sunday, but always in St. Peter's, where Roman deacons and priests were ordained. It was a matter of obligation that all the higher clergy of Rome should receive ordination in the sanctuary of the apostle himself.[1] The elected bishop[2] put on, in the *secretarium*, the papal liturgical vestments, with the exception of the pallium. At the chanting of the Introit he proceeded to the altar and prostrated himself as usual before it. But instead of rising immediately and proceeding to his throne, he remained prostrate all the time the Litany was being sung. After the Litany he partly raised himself while the Bishops of Albano, Porto, and Ostia respectively recited over him three prayers, of which the last was a eucharistic prayer. During the saying of the latter by the Bishop of Ostia, certain deacons held over the head of the ordinand an open book of the Gospels. The benediction having come to an end, the archdeacon placed the

but the words in it, *excepta ecclesia Romana*, were added by Ferrandus himself, and are indicative of the usage in the sixth century.

[1] The choice of the Vatican basilica was not, however, primitive. We can gather from the documents dealing with the ordination of Popes Damasus, Boniface I, and Boniface II, that the Lateran basilica, in the time of the Christian emperors and Gothic kings, was the *locus legitimus*, at least in the case of the Pope. The privilege of St. Peter's dates no further back than Byzantine times.

[2] He was always a deacon or priest of Rome, but preferably the former. Prior to the last years of the ninth century, no bishop was promoted to the papacy. The disorders and controversies occasioned by the election of Formosa, Bishop of Porto, to the papacy, are well known. In the tenth century there were frequent breaches of the ancient rule, and from this time forward it ceased to be considered as obligatory

pallium upon the new pontiff, who, going up to his throne, at once began the *Gloria in excelsis*.¹ The Mass was proceeded with as usual; and when it was over, the Pope was conducted back to the Lateran with great pomp. The formularies of blessing were the same as those employed for other bishops, but the *Et idcirco*, in which the dignity conferred on the ordinand is mentioned, was modified as follows:—

> Et idcirco huic famulo tuo, quem Apostolicae sedis praesulem et primatem omnium qui in orbe terrarum sunt sacerdotum ac universalis Ecclesiae tuae doctorem dedisti et ad summi sacerdotii ministerium elegisti, etc.

§ 4.—Ordinations according to the Gallican Rite.

The ordination ceremonies according to the Gallican rite are summarily described in the *Statuta Ecclesiae Antiqua*. In Lib. II. of the *De Officiis Ecclesiasticis* of St. Isidore there is an account of them which is in conformity with the latter, and there is also a reproduction of the text. The Mozarabic *Liber Ordinum* has preserved for us the ritual and the formularies for the ordination of Sub-Deacons, Deacons and Priests, but it is not certain that all it contains is primitive.² In the Gelasian Sacramentary and *Missale Francorum* we encounter both the ceremonies of the *Statuta* and the Roman prayers which have just been described, together with certain other prayers, which are either incompatible with Roman usage, or so completely identical with the Roman prayers in their import as to become pleonastic. This concerns, however, only the three superior

---

¹ This ceremony is mentioned in the *Liber Diurnus*, n. 8 (Garnier), as well as in the *Ordo IX.* of Mabillon.

² The formulary for the benediction of Deacons, p. 49, appears to have been inspired by the Roman formulary given, *supra*, p. 356, as also on p. 55 of the formulary relating to Priests, where the portion entitled *completoria* reproduces a phrase of the Roman formulary for the Bishops. Cf. *supra*, p. 360

orders. As to the five inferior orders, there is not a single feature common to the two liturgical books. The ceremonies of the *Statuta* and of the two liturgical books are entirely different from those which we meet with in the Roman usage. I will here describe them seriatim, furnishing at the same time the formularies as we find them in the two Merovingian Sacramentaries.

Doorkeepers.—The doorkeeper is first instructed by the archdeacon as to his conduct in the "House of God," and is then presented by him to the bishop, who, taking the keys of the church from the altar, hands them to the candidate, saying [1]—

Sic age quasi redditurus Deo rationem pro his rebus quae istis clavibus recluduntur.[2]

Then, in place of the blessing, preceded, according to the Gallican custom, by an invitatory or preface, the following prayer is used—

Deum Patrem omnipotentem suppliciter deprecemur ut hunc famulum suum *nomine Illum* benedicere dignetur, quem in officium ostiarii eligere dignatus est, ut sit ei fidelissima cura in diebus ac noctibus ad distinctionem horarum certarum ad invocandum nomen Domini.

Domine sancte, Pater omnipotens, aeterne Deus, benedicere digneris hunc famulum tuum ostiarium *nomine Illum*, ut inter janitores ecclesiae paret obsequia et inter electos tuos partem mereatur habere mercedis.

Lectors.—The bishop, addressing himself to the candidate, says—

Eligunt te fratres tui, ut sis lector in domo Dei tui; et agnoscas

---

[1] This and the following formularies, except where the contrary is specified, appear with slight modifications in the Pontifical now in use, which, like all the Roman books posterior to the ninth century, contains, as far as ordinations are concerned, a mixture of the two ancient rituals, the Roman and the Gallican.

[2] This formulary, as well as the analogous formulary used for the ordination of lectors (*Accipe et esto*) and that for exorcists (*Accipe et commenda*), are to be found in the *Statuta*, which fact implies that they were in use, at Arles at least, as early as the end of the fifth century.

officium tuum ut impleas illud: potens est enim Deus ut augeat tibi gratiam.

These words imply[1] that there had previously been an election. The election having been announced, the pontiff delivers an address to the congregation,[2] in which he dwells upon the faith and ability of the candidate, and then, in sight of all the people, puts into his hand the book from which he was to read, saying—

Accipe, et esto verbi Dei relator, habiturus, si fideliter et utiliter impleveris officium, partem cum his qui verbum Dei ministraverunt.

Then follows the prayer—

Domine sancte, Pater omnipotens, aeterne Deus, benedicere digneris famulum tuum *nomine Illum* in officio lectoris, ut assiduitate lectionum distinctus atque ornatus curis modulis spiritali devotione resonet ecclesiae.[3]

---

[1] They appear in the two Sacramentaries under the title *Praefatio Lectoris*, thus forming a counterpart to the invitatories employed for the other orders, but their form is widely different I have been inclined to place them at the beginning of the ceremony, that is, at the moment indicated by the sense of the formulary. The blessing would thus appear without an invitatory Perhaps the address of the bishop took its place; but this is not very probable The Pontifical now in use has a special invitatory.

[2] Our manuscripts give us no formulary for this address There is one in the existing Pontifical, as well as for the three other minor orders, porter, exorcist, and acolyte I am not certain as to the exact date of their origin; but it must be very early

[3] This text, which is that of the Gelasian Sacramentary, is corrupt and unintelligible at the end That of the *Missale Francorum* is not in a better state. *Ut assiduitate electionum distinctus atque ordinatus curis modolis spiritali devotione lingua resonet Ecclesiae.* In the existing Pontifical a lucid text is found here, derived from the foregoing, but it clearly betrays the fact of having been touched up

Exorcists.—The bishop hands to the candidate the book of exorcisms, saying—

> Accipe et commenda, et habeto potestatem imponendi manum super energumenum, sive baptizatum sive catechumenum.

Then follows the blessing—

> Deum Patrem omnipotentem supplices deprecemur, ut hunc famulum suum *nomine Illum* benedicere dignetur in officium exorcistae, ut sit spiritalis imperator ad abiciendos daemones de corporibus obsessis cum omni nequitia eorum multiformi.
>
> Domine sancte, Pater omnipotens, aeterne Deus, benedicere digneris famulum tuum hunc *nomine Illum* in officio exorcistae, ut per impositionis manuum et oris officium eum eligere digneris, et imperium habeat spiritus immundos coercendi[1] et probabilis sit medicus Ecclesiae tuae, gratiae curationum virtute confirmatus.

Acolytes.—The order of acolytes seems not to have been everywhere in use in Gallican countries. The *Statuta*,[2] doubtless, describe their ordination like that of the other orders, but the Gelasian Sacramentary omits the formularies of blessing. In the *Missale Francorum* a prayer only is found, and that, too, without an invitatory, and in an unusual place, viz. between the blessing of the doorkeepers and that of the lectors. At Rheims, in the fifth century, there were no acolytes.[3] In the collection of Irish canons, the acolyte is not reckoned among the seven ecclesiastical degrees; he is placed with the psalmist and cantor, outside the ordinary

---

[1] The two manuscripts have *spirituum immundorum coercendo* (*coercendum*, Miss. Fr.) I correct it from the Pontifical and the *Missale Fr.* The Gelas. Sacr. has higher up *oris in officium* The words *eum eligere digneris et* seem superfluous They do not occur in the Pontifical.

[2] The *Statuta*, drawn up at Arles, give us the usage of the most important Churches in Gaul

[3] The will of Bishop Bennadius, predecessor of St. Remigius, gives all the categories of clerics except this one (Flodoard *Hist Rem*, i. 9).

hierarchy.¹ According to the *Statuta*, the candidate was first instructed by the bishop in the duties of his office, and then a candlestick with a candle was placed in his hands by the archdeacon, as a sign that the lights of the church would be in his care; moreover, an empty *urceolus*, or cruet, was given to him as a symbol of his function of presenting at the altar the eucharistic wine. The blessing was as follows ² :—

Domine sancte, Pater omnipotens, aeterne Deus, qui Moysi et Aaron locutus es ut accenderetur lucerna in tabernaculo testimonii, sic benedicere et sanctificare digneris hunc famulum tuum ut sit acolitus in Ecclesia tua.

Subdeacons.—The candidate received from the hands of the bishop the paten and chalice, and from those of the archdeacon the basin and ewer, together with a napkin. Before the *traditio* of these objects the bishop delivered a short address to the candidate, of which a formulary, preserved in the *Missale Francorum*, is as follows:—

Vide cujus ministerium tibi traditur. Et ideo si usque nunc fuisti tardus ad ecclesiam, amodo debes esse assiduus; si usque nunc somnolentus, amodo vigil; si usque nunc ebriosus, amodo sobrius; si usque nunc inhonestus, amodo castus.³ Oblationes quae veniunt in altario, panes propositionis appellantur. De ipsis oblationibus⁴ tantum debet

---

[1] Wasserschleben's edition, pp 23, 26

[2] The invitatory, which is wanting in the *Miss Fr.*, is found in the existing Pontifical. Like all these prayers, it is Gallican in style

[3] This is a very extraordinary address It implies that men who might be *inhonesti* could be admitted into the ranks of the clergy, that is, men who might have committed sins entailing public penance and irregularity. The instructions following have a somewhat commonplace technical character. I should not be astonished if the whole passage was less ancient than those preceding and following it.

[4] This portion of the instruction is incompatible with Roman usage, in which the choice of the *oblatae* is the business of the deacons, and not

in altario poni quantum populo possit sufficere, ne aliquid putridum in sacrario maneat. Pallae vero quae sunt in substraturio in alio vase debent lavi, in alio corporales pallae. Ubi pallae corporales lavatae fuerint, nullum linteamen ibidem aliud debet lavi; ipsa aqua in baptisterio debet vergi. Ideo te admoneo, tu ita te exhibe ut Deo placere possis.[2]

Here came the *traditio* of the instruments, followed by a call to prayer from the bishop—

Oremus Deum et Dominum nostrum, ut super servum suum *Illum* quem ad subdiaconatus officium evocare dignatus est infundat benedictionem et gratiam suam, ut in conspectu suo fideliter serviens destinata sanctis praemia consequatur.

Then came the blessing, as follows :—

Domine sancte, Pater omnipotens, aeterne Deus, benedicere digneris famulum tuum hunc *Illum*, quem ad subdiaconatus officium eligere dignatus es, uti eum sacrario tuo sancto strenuum sollicitumque caelesti militiae instituas, et sanctis altaribus fideliter subministret. Requiescat super eum Spiritus sapientiae et intellectus, Spiritus consilii et fortitudinis, Spiritus scientiae et pietatis; repleas eum Spiritu timoris tui ut eum in ministerio divino confirmes, ut obediens atque dicto parens, tuam gratiam consequatur.

Deacons.—The formularies of the *Missale Francorum* imply that the candidate, previously chosen by the bishop, was presented to the people, who had to testify their acceptance of him by an acclamation. At Rome, the silence of the congregation was regarded as an expression of their approbation of the choice made by the bishop.[2] In the Gallican ritual this approbation had to be openly expressed. The Ember seasons, moreover, being unknown in countries of the Gallican rite, the presentation to the people took

of the subdeacons In the Gallican ritual, this choice, being effected in the vestry, could be confided to subdeacons.

[1] This address appears in the existing Pontifical, but a number of sentences have been added to it

[2] See note, p 576.

place only on the day of ordination itself. The following is the address delivered by the bishop to the people in presenting the candidate :—

Dilectissimi fratres, quamlibet possint ad ordinationem ecclesiastici ministerii promovendam sibi ipsa sufficere privilegia sacerdotum, attamen quia probabilior et nostra apud Dominum conversatio est et eorum quorum honor augetur major est gratia si id quod arbitria nostra eligunt etiam vestrae confirmet dilectionis adsensus, idcirco filium nostrum *Illum* cupio ad officium diaconatus in consortium nostrum divinitatis auxilio promovere; an eum dignum hoc officio censeatis scire desidero; et si vestra apud meam concordat electio, testimonium quod vultis vocibus adprobate.

The congregation then exclaimed, *Dignus est!* [1] Thereupon the bishop calls upon the people to pray—

Commune votum communis prosequatur oratio, ut hic totius Ecclesiae prece qui in diaconatus ministerio praeparatur leviticae benedictionis [2] et spiritali conversatione praefulgens gratia sanctificationis eluceat.

The bishop then pronounces [3] the blessing, holding his hand extended on the head of the candidate—

Domine sancte, spei, fidei, gratiae et profectuum munerator, qui in caelestibus et terrenis angelorum ministeriis ubique dispositis per

[1] This exclamation, as well as the address, to which it serves as a response, was not in the books from which the existing Pontifical was taken, but the beginning of the prayer which follows, *Commune votum* implies that the announcement of the suffrages of the people had just been made. These words have no longer a meaning in the present arrangement of the ceremony.

[2] Corrupt text. The *Liber Ordinum*, which also contains this formulary, gives as follows *leviticae benedictionis clarescat officio, atque inter vernantia sacri altaris lilia spiritali cum benedictione praefulgens*, etc.

[3] The existing Pontifical has here the Gallican invitatory *Commune votum*, followed by a Roman invitatory, which is composed of two Roman formularies of this nature, and ending with the Roman consecratory canon, *Deus honorum dator* (see above, p. 356).

omnia elementa voluntatis tuae defendis affectum, hunc quoque famulum, tuum *Illum* speciali dignare inlustrare aspectu, ut tuis obsequiis expeditus sanctis altaribus minister purus adcrescat, et indulgentia purior, eorum gradu quos Apostoli tui in septenario numero, beato Stephano duce ac praevio, sancto Spiritu auctore elegerunt dignus existat, et virtutibus universis quibus tibi servire oportet instructus compleat.

Priests.—The continuation of the ceremonies was exactly the same for priests as for deacons, except that the former were anointed on the hands. This was also a custom in certain places in regard to deacons.[1] The following is the formulary for the address :—

Quoniam, dilectissimi fratres, rectori navis et navigio deferendis eadem est vel securitatis ratio vel timoris, communis eorum debet esse sententia quorum causa communis existit. Nec frustra a Patribus reminiscimur institutum ut de electione eorum qui ad regimen altaris adhibendi sunt consulatur et populus ; quia de actu et conversatione praesenti quod nonnumquam ignoratur a pluribus scitur a paucis, et necesse est ut facilius quis obedientiam exhibeat ordinato cui adsensum praebuerit ordinando. Fratris nostri et conpresbyteri conversatio, quantum nosse mihi videor, probata ac Deo placita est, et digna, ut arbitror, ecclesiastici honoris augmento. Sed ne unum fortasse vel paucos aut decipiat adsensio aut fallat affectio, sententia est expetenda multorum. Itaque, quid de ejus actibus aut moribus noveritis, quid de merito censeatis, Deo teste, consulimus. Debet hanc fidem habere caritas vestra quam secundum praeceptum Evangelii et Deo exhibere debetis et proximo, ut huic testimonium sacerdoti magis pro merito quam pro affectione aliqu[a][2] tribuatis. Et qui devotionem omnium expectamus,

---

[1] Gildas (*Liber Querulus*, iii 21) speaks of a blessing *qua initiantur sacerdotum vel ministrorum manus*. This expression seems to have reference to a special ceremony, probably the anointing of the hands of priests and deacons. The anointing of the hands in case of both these orders is met with in the Anglo-Saxon books of the tenth and eleventh centuries It appears from the letter of Nicolas I to Rodulph, Bishop of Bourges (Jaffé, 2765), that about the time of Charles the Bald the anointing of deacons was in process of being introduced into **France**.

[2] *Aliqua* · the MS has *aliquid*.

intelligere tacentes non possumus ; scimus tamen, quod est acceptabilius Deo, aderit per Spiritum sanctum consensus unus omnium animarum. Et ideo electionem vestram debetis voce publica profiteri.

After the exclamation *Dignus est !* [1] the bishop proceeded to say—

Sit nobis, fratres, communis oratio, ut hic qui in adjutorium et utilitatem vestrae salutis eligitur presbyteratus benedictionem divini indulgentia muneris consequatur : ut sancti Spiritus sacerdotalia dona privilegio virtutum, ne impar loco deprehendatur, obtineat.

Then came the blessing, during which not only the bishop, but all the priests present, extended their hands over the head of the candidate—

Sanctificationum omnium auctor, cujus vera consecratio, plena benedictio est, tu, Domine, super hunc famulum tuum *Illum* quem presbyterii honore dedicamus manum tuae benedictionis [2] infunde ; ut gravitate actuum et censura vivendi probet se esse seniorem, his institutus disciplinis quas Tito et Timotheo Paulus exposuit ; ut in lege tua die ac nocte, Omnipotens, meditans, quod legerit credat, quod crediderit doceat, quod docuerit imitetur ; justitiam, constantiam, misericordiam, fortitudinem, in se ostendat, exemplo probet, admonitione confirmet, ut purum atque immaculatum ministerii tui donum custodiat, et per obsequium plebis tuae corpus et sanguinem Filii tui immaculata benedictione transformet, et inviolabili caritate in virum perfectum, in

---

[1] The address which precedes this has been preserved in the present Pontifical, but its ending has been replaced by the Roman admonition given above, p. 353 The *Dignus est* is also omitted, together with the invitatory *Sit nobis*, which forms a conclusion to the formulary *Commune votum*, in the ordination of deacons. In place of the invitatory *Sit nobis*, and the prayer *Sanctificationum*, the Roman formularies given above (p. 358) occur.

[2] The *Miss. Fr.* adds here *eum*, the Gelas Sacram, in which the formulary is in the plural, has "his" in the same place. This is a further instance of the passage being corrupt

mensuram aetatis plenitudinis Christi, in die justitiae aeterni judicii, conscientia pura, fide plena, Spiritu sancto plenus persolvat.

Then came the anointing[1] of the hands, which was accompanied by the recitation of the following formulary:—

Consecrentur manus istae et sanctificentur per istam unctionem et nostram benedictionem ; ut quaecumque benedixerint benedicta sint, et quaecumque sanctificaverint sanctificentur.

Bishops.—In countries which followed the Gallican usage the consecration of a bishop was usually effected in the Church over which he was called to preside.[2] The metropolitan and bishops of the province, having proceeded thither, presided over the election and conducted the ordination. The first business, which had nothing in it of a liturgical character, was the choice of a candidate. When it was found that one of these had practically obtained the unanimous suffrages of the electors, the president of the assembled bishops presented him to the clergy and people in the church. This presentation[3] was accompanied by an

---

[1] This anointing, and its accompanying formulary, have been adopted from the Gallican ritual into the Roman Pontifical

[2] The electors of the Bishop of Milan betook themselves to the metropolitan city (Ennodius, *Vita Epiph*, p 341, Hartel) The Metropolitans of Milan and Aquileia consecrated each other, but the ceremony had to be held in the city of him who was to be consecrated (Letter of Pelagius I, Jaffé, 983, *Pat Lat*, vol lxix p 411) The fourth Council of Toledo (633) left the choice of the place to the metropolitan, as far as his suffragans were concerned, but he himself had to be consecrated in his cathedral city In Gaul the ceremony was usually performed in the church of the candidate bishop, except when it took place at the royal palace

[3] When the Frankish kings came to reserve to themselves the approval of the election, or even of the choice of the bishop, this presentation became merely ceremonial · but it was not so at the beginning

address, of which a formulary [1] has come down to us in the liturgical books—

> Servanda est, dilectissimi Fratres, in excessu sacerdotum lex [2] antiqua Ecclesiae ut decedentibus pastoribus alii [3] dignissimi subrogentur, per quorum doctrinam fides catholica et religio christiana subsistat; ne ovili Domini praedo violentus inrumpat, et dispersas absque pastore oves fur nocturnus invadat. Recepto itaque dispensatione Dei sacerdote vestro, sollicite vobis agendum est ut in locum defuncti talis successor praeparetur ecclesiae, cujus pervigili cura et instanti sollicitudine ordo ecclesiae et credentium fides in Dei timore melius convalescat; qui, praecipiente Apostolo, in omni doctrina formam boni operis ipse praebeat, cujusque habitus, sermo, vultus, incessus, doctrina, virtus sit; qui vos ut pastor bonus fide instruat, exemplo patientiae doceat, doctrina religionis instituat, in omni opere bono confirmet caritatis exemplo. Secundum voluntatem ergo Domini in locum sanctae memoriae *Illius nomine* virum venerabilem *Illum* testimonio presbyterorum et totius cleri et consilio civium ac consistentium [4] credimus eligendum; virum, ut nostis, natalibus nobilem, moribus clarum, religione probum, fide stabilem, misericordia abundantem, humilem, justum, pacificum, patientem, caritatem habentem, tenacem, cunctis quae sacerdoti [5] eligenda sunt, bonis moribus exuberantem. Hunc ergo, dilectissimi fratres, testimonio boni operis electum, dignissimum sacerdotio consonantes laudibus clamate et dicite: Dignus est.

When the people had pronounced the *Dignus est,*[6] the consecrating bishop called upon the congregation to pray—

---

[1] This formulary, which is incompatible with Roman usage, did not find its way into the Roman Pontifical

[2] *Sacerdotum et antiquae,* Miss Fr

[3] *Decidentibus aliis quidem dignissime,* Miss Fr

[4] The *cives* are the citizens of the place; the *consistentes* are those present who have come from another town.

[5] *Sacerdos.,* Miss. Fr. Lower down, *testimonii.*

[6] This acclamation is often referred to in the accounts of episcopal elections Cf. Gregory of Tours, ii. 13; Sidon. Apoll, *Ep*, vii. 9; Life of St Gery, Bishop of Cambrai (*Anal Boll.,* vol vii p. 391) The discourse pronounced by Sidonius on the occasion of the ordination of Simplicius of Bourges is the exact equivalent of that here given.

Deum totius sanctificationis ac pietatis auctorem, qui placationem suam et sacrificia et sacra constituit, Fratres dilectissimi, deprecemur, uti hunc famulum suum quem exaltare in Ecclesia et seniorum cathedrae, concordibus sua inspiratione judiciis et effusis super plebem suam votis fidelibus ac vocum testimoniis, voluit imponi, conlocans eum cum principibus populi sui; ad eorum nunc precem universam eundem summo sacerdotio debita honoris plenitudine, charismatum gratia sanctificationum ubertate, ac praecipue humilitatis virtute locupletet: ut rector potius non extollatur, sed in omnibus se quantum est major humilians, sit in ipsis quasi unus ex illis; omnia judicia Domini nostri non pro se tantum sed et pro omni populo qui sollicitudini suae creditur contremiscens. Ut qui meminerit de speculatorum manibus omnium animas requirendas, pro omnium salute pervigilet, pastorali erga creditas sibi oves Domini diligentia ejus[1] semper se flagrantissimum adpiobans mandatorum. Ut igitur praefuturus omnibus, electus ex omnibus, universis sacris sacrandisque idoneus fiat, sub hac, quae est homini per hominem postrema benedictio, consummata atque perfecta, suae consecrationis, nostrae subplicationis, adtentissimis concordissimisque omnium precibus adjuvemur; omnium pro ipso oratio incumbat, cui exorandi pro omnibus pondus imponitur. Impetret ei affectus totius Ecclesiae virtutem, pietatem, sanctificationem, et caeteras summi sacerdotii sacras dotes universae Ecclesiae profuturas, Domino Deo nostro, qui sacrorum munerum profluus fons est, qui dat omnibus adfluenter, quod sacerdoti pio affectu poscitur, ad exundandam in omnibus sanctificationem suorum omnium, promptissime ac plenissime conferente.[2]

Then followed the consecrating prayer. The *Missale Francorum* and the Gelasian Sacramentary agree in giving here the Roman text *Deus honorum omnium*, but with a long additional passage, which is wanting in the

---

[1] This passage is very corrupt in the *Miss Fr*, which reads: *pastorali erga creditas sibi oves Domini diligentiae ejus semper se flagrantissimum adprobans. Te delictorum adigitur praefuturus, ex omnibus electus, ex omnibus universis* . .

[2] This formulary, which is also incompatible with Roman usage, did not find its way into the Pontifical, which has here the formulary given above, at p. 360 Construe. *Domino . . . conferente, ad exundandam . . quod poscitur sacerdoti (consecrando).*

Leonian and Gregorian Sacramentaries.[1] It implies, like the remainder of the formulary, that several bishops are consecrated at the same time, whilst the two addresses quoted above are always in the singular number.[2] Elsewhere than in Rome the simultaneous consecration of several bishops must have been a rare occurrence. I am therefore inclined to believe that the formulary is thoroughly Roman, and that no Gallican form for this part of the ceremony has been preserved.

While the presiding bishop—that is, the metropolitan—is saying the consecrating prayer, two bishops hold over the head of the candidate the open book of the Gospels and each of the bishops present places his hand upon him.

After the consecrating prayer came the anointing of the hands,[3] which ceremony was accompanied by the following prayer [4]:—

> Unguantur manus istae de oleo sanctificato et chrismate sanctificationis, sicut unxit Samuel David in regem et prophetam; ita unguantur et consummentur in nomine Dei Patris et Filii et Spiritus sancti, facientes imaginem sanctae crucis Salvatoris domini nostri Jesu Christi qui nos a morte redemit et ad regna caelorum perducit. Exaudi nos, pie Pater, omnipotens aeterne Deus, et praesta quod te rogamus et oramus.

---

[1] See above, p 361

[2] The same must be said of the Roman introductory prayers which the *Missale Francorum* places before the address. The formularies after the consecrating canon in the ordination Mass are, on the contrary, all in the singular number.

[3] The anointing of the hands is the only method of unction mentioned in the ancient Merovingian books That of the head is not found there; but in the time of Louis the Pious it was the customary usage in France (Amalarius, *De Eccl. Officiis,* ii 14)

[4] It is found only in the *Missale Francorum* following that of the priests (see above, p. 372), under the rubric *item alia*. I think that this is not a simple variant, but a special formulary for bishops This distinction is conformable with present usage, according to which the formulary *Consecrentur* is used for priests, and that of *Unguantur* for bishops.

§ 5.—ORDINATIONS IN THE EAST.

In dealing with the Eastern ceremonies, I will confine my descriptions to those furnished by the *Apostolic Constitutions* (viii, 4 *et seq.*), and by the *De Ecclesiastica Hierarchia* of Dionysius the Areopagite (c. 5).[1]

If the ordination is that of a bishop, the candidate is presented to the congregation, at which several bishops, surrounded by the local clergy, preside. The principal bishop—that is, by right, the metropolitan or his substitute—interrogates the congregation as to the identity of the candidate and his qualifications. Is he the man of their choice? Has he such and such a qualification for his position? These questions are thrice repeated, and at the third time with additional solemnity. The people were expected to reply in a loud voice, "He is worthy! Ἄξιός ἐστιν."

Then three of the bishops approach the altar The candidate kneels down, and while two deacons hold the open book of the Gospels on his head, the presiding bishop recites a consecrating prayer, eucharistic in form, at the end of which comes the response, *Amen.*

The newly made bishop is then conducted to his seat, receives the kiss of peace, and then celebrates the Mass himself.

The same form (except the imposition of the Gospels) is observed in the case of priests, deacons, deaconesses, subdeacons, and readers, with the exception that the diocesan bishop alone presides at the ceremony. The consecrating prayers are always accompanied by the imposition of hands.

Such is the ritual of the *Apostolic Constitutions.*[2] The

---

[1] The Euchologion of Sarapion has only the formularies Χειροθεσία καταστάσεως διακόνων (12) . πρεσβυτέρων (13) . ἐπισκόπου (14).

[2] After the reciting of the consecrating canon over the bishop, the author of the *Ap Const* adds "Εἷς τῶν ἐπισκόπων ἀναφερέτω τὴν θυσίαν ἐπὶ τῶν χειρῶν τοῦ χειροτονηθέντος" These words have no clear meaning to me.

ceremonies given in Dionysius are fundamentally the same, but there are some more precise details. For instance, the deacon kneels on only one knee during the reciting of the consecrating prayer. After this prayer, the officiating minister signs the forehead of the newly ordained with the sign of the cross, and announces solemnly his name.

We see that in all these rites the ceremony of ordination consists especially of a prayer recited over the candidate in a public and solemn assembly. This prayer is accompanied by the imposition of hands.[1] In this general form the ritual is that which we find in the New Testament.[2] We see, moreover, that the choice of the rulers and ministers of the Church was from the beginning reserved to the apostles or to their representatives. This authority came naturally to be passed on to the bishops, their successors and continuers of their work, as far as the rule of the local Christian communities was concerned. As for the installation of the bishops themselves, it was considered indispensable that it should be entrusted to a more exalted authority than the individual bishop. This authority could be no other than the superior jurisdiction of the Church, that is, the collective episcopal hierarchy. As it was impossible to bring together at each ordination all the members of this hierarchy, it was arranged that it should be represented by a group of neighbouring bishops, or, in certain places, by the metropolitan bishop.

---

[1] It is worth while citing here the words of St Augustine: "Quid aliud est manuum impositio quam oratio super hominem?" This observation is so true that the imposition of hands in express terms is frequently omitted in the books of ritual It was considered to be implied in the *oratio super hominem* It is necessary also to note that in almost all the known formularies of prayer the degree to which the candidate is promoted is mentioned I say "almost all," for this indication is not found in the prayer for the ordination of a priest in the Euchologion of Sarapion

[2] Acts vi 6, xiii 3; 1 Tim iv 14, 2 Tim i 6

Hence the obligation of having three bishops for a consecration to the episcopate, an obligation universally accepted from the beginning of the fourth century, except where a consecrator sufficiently qualified to represent in himself the collective episcopate is in question.[1]

Besides this intervention of three bishops at the least, episcopal ordination was characterised, with the same universality, by the ceremony of the open book of the Gospels being placed on the head of the candidate.[2] This rite, which was already widely observed in the fourth century, cannot have been altogether primitive, but it is certainly very ancient.

The anointing peculiar to the Gallican rite must have been suggested by the Old Testament, where we have frequent mention of the anointing of priests. It would seem not to have been very ancient. Certain indications would lead us to look for its origin in the Churches of Britain,[3] where it was practised as early as the sixth century.

It was about this period, or rather shortly after it, that the *traditio* of liturgical vestments and other similar insignia began to take their place among the ceremonies of ordination. I have passed over in silence up to the present the indications furnished on this subject in the Roman *Ordines* and other ritual authorities. This seems the proper moment to discuss the matter.

[1] This is the case of the Pope. I should not be astonished if it were found that a similar usage existed in Alexandria; but I have no proof of it The Patriarch of Alexandria, like the Pope, was the only bishop in his province at whose ordination the rite of the imposition of the Gospel was used.

[2] See, however, the restrictions pointed out in the preceding note These departures, however, do not attain the same universality as the observance of the rite.

[3] Gildas is the earliest author who mentions it. The *Statuta* know nothing of it. The same is the case, I believe, with the Frankish writers of the sixth century, and the Spanish up to Isidore inclusive It was always more widely practised in Great Britain than elsewhere Cf above, p 370, note 1.

CHAPTER XI.

LITURGICAL VESTMENTS.

1. *The Tunicle* and the Planeta.*

IN the fifth century the outdoor costume worn at Rome by official persons consisted essentially of two garments—an under tunic, with or without sleeves, and a *paenula*, or immense cloak, which was sleeveless and without any opening in front. The head was passed through an aperture made in the centre of the garment, and it was lifted in folds over the arms when the wearer required to make use of his hands. We find this costume prescribed by a law of 397,[1] which forbids senators to appear at Rome wearing the military chlamys, and permits only the use of the *colobium*, a sleeveless tunic, together with the *paenula*. This is the costume which we see portrayed in a painting of about the fifth century, representing a *Praefectus annonae* with his son.[2] When, however, they were engaged in the exercise of their functions, the magistrates continued to wear the toga. The *officiales* (apparitors, attendants), when in full dress, also donned the *paenula* over the tunic; but in this case the undergarment was confined at the waist by a girdle.

---

[1] Cod. Theod., XIV., x. 1
[2] *Annali dell' Instituto*, 1885, pl. 1.
* [I have translated the word "tunique" of the French original, by "tunic", when it denotes the classical garment, and "tunicle" when the liturgical vestment is in question. There is only one word for both in French.—TR.]

In addition to these, they had to wear conspicuously a bright-coloured *pallium*, as a badge of their office.[1] This *pallium* was a sort of scarf; the two figures 1914 and 1915 in *Saglio's* Dictionary of Antiquities exhibit the manner in which it was worn, either over the *paenula*, or merely over the tunic.

With the exception of the *pallium*, of which we shall have occasion to speak later on, the dress of the Roman clergy was absolutely identical with the dress of a civilian of the time having some position. Pope Celestine, in a letter[2] addressed to the Bishops of Provence, condemns the use of any special ecclesiastical costume, which is clearly a proof that none existed in his own Church or in the countries under his immediate jurisdiction.[3] The documents, liturgical or otherwise, dealing with the Roman use, take for granted that all ecclesiastics, from the Pope down to an acolyte, or even beneath him wore the planeta, or *paenula*, with the tunic under it. The planeta was usually dark in hue, either brown or violet (*purpurea*), while the tunic was of a light colour. This costume was still used in the sixth century by laymen of distinction. The biography of St. Fulgentius relates that

---

[1] "Discoloribus palliis pectora contegentes conditionis suae necessitatem ex hujusmodi agnitione testentur." This scarf is merely a curtailed form of the *pallium*, or ancient mantle. Everything is possible in these kinds of transformations. The religions of certain congregations of regular clerks (at Mount St. Bernard, for instance, at Klosterneuburg and elsewhere) still wear over their habits a linen band depending in front and behind. It is not three inches in width. This is no other, however, than a rochet, that is to say, a long tunic with sleeves. After this we shall scarcely be surprised to find a mantle becoming reduced to a scarf.

[2] Jaffé, 369.

[3] The elaboration of the meaning attached to the priestly vestments of the Old Dispensation which is found in the prayer for the ordination of bishops (cf. *supra*, 360), also presupposes that at the time that prayer was drawn up there were not any clearly defined liturgical vestments.

when the saint disembarked on the coast of Africa, after his return from exile, the nobles spread out their planetas over his head to shelter him from the rain which was falling at the time. John, the deacon, in his Life of St. Gregory, describes the costume of that Pope and his father Gordianus from contemporary pictures;* both are dressed alike, and each wears over the dalmatic a chestnut-coloured planeta.

The under-tunic has become the albe, from which have been derived, through various modifications, the canon's rochet and the surplice; both of these garments may be worn by clerks of different orders. The planeta has become the chasuble, now scarcely ever worn[1] except by priests and bishops. It was a costly garment, and the inferior clergy gave up its use at an early date.

Beyond the limits of Rome, the liturgical dress comprised much the same garments, namely, the albe (*tunica linea, alba, στιχάριον*) and the planeta, called also *casula* (chasuble) or *amphibalum*,[2] and in Greek *phelonion* (φελόνιον). The albe of the deacon, although not of the shape of the dalmatic, which was peculiar to the Roman use, was, however, of a more costly material than that worn by the ordinary clerk. It was not confined to the waist by a girdle, but fell straight from the shoulders.[3]

---

[1] In Lent and other penitential seasons, it is still worn by the deacons and subdeacons.

[2] These two terms are met with for the first time to denote a liturgical vestment in the treatise of St. Germain of Paris. At Rome, the word *planeta* was used, but its origin is unknown. The term *casula*, or rather *casulis*, appears there for the first time in the Life of Stephen II. (*Lib. Pon.*, vol i. p. 443, I. 18), and again under a very corrupt form (*quodsulis*).

[3] It is thus described by St Germain of Paris; the Greek deacons have always worn it in this manner.

* [A reproduction of a picture agreeing with this description is given in Marriott's *Vestiarium Christianum*, Plate XXV.—Tr.]

2. *The Dalmatic.*

Besides these two essential vestments, common to all the clergy, the Pope and his deacons wore, on festivals, between the ordinary tunic (*linea*) and the planeta, a second tunic with large sleeves, called a dalmatic. This combination of the three garments was used considerably anterior to the time when the ecclesiastical costume became stereotyped. On the day of his martyrdom (258) St. Cyprian wore a linen tunic, a dalmatic, and an over-garment, answering to the *paenula*, or planeta.[1] As early as the end of the fifth century the dalmatic, which had passed out of fashion as an ordinary article of clothing, had become the distinguishing badge of the Pope and his clergy.[2] The Pope sometimes granted it as an honorary decoration to bishops and deacons of other Churches. Pope Symmachus (*circ.* 513) conferred this privilege on the deacons of Arles; St. Gregory made a similar gift (599) to the Bishop of Gap and his archdeacon.[3] The bishops and deacons of Ravenna,

---

[1] *Acta procons*, 5: "Se lacerna byrro exspoliavit et genu in terra flexit et in orationem se Domino prostravit. Et cum se dalmatica exspoliasset et diaconibus tradidisset, in linea stetit et coepit speculatorem sustinere."

[2] The *Lib Pontif.* (vol. i. p 171, of my edition) attributes the introduction of it to Pope Silvester. The legendary life of St. Silvester, written at the end of the fifth century, does not make it go back so far, but implies that it had been in use for about a century. It should be noted that, according to the author of this document, the Roman diaconal tunicle was at the outset the same as the *colobus*, which the emperor Honorius commanded his senators to wear as their outdoor tunic (see *supra*, p. 379).

[3] *Vita St. Caesarii*, c. 4 (Migne, *Pat. Lat*, vol. lxvii. p. 1016); Greg. M, *Ep.*, ix. 107 (219). St. Gregory was even careful to send dalmatics ready made to Gap, which shows that they were not usually worn in that country. We often see quoted a similar concession by Pope Zacharias to Austrobert, Bishop of Vienne; but the document which contains it is an apocryphal letter (Jaffé, 2258).

who are represented in the mosaics of the sixth century, also wear the dalmatic, doubtless in virtue of some similar concession.

3. The "Mappula" and the Sleeves.

Besides the dalmatic, the *Liber Pontificalis*, at the beginning of the sixth century, mentions another garment peculiar to the Roman deacons, and also to those of the suburbicarian diocese.[1] This is the *pallium linostimum*, which is worn on the left arm. This *pallium linostimum*, woven of wool and linen, is merely a variety of the napkin, or *mappula*, which formed part of some ceremonial costumes—that, for instance, of the consul who presided over the *Ludi circenses*. The *Ordines* of the ninth century speak of the *mappula* of the Pope. This article of apparel is, however, never found at Rome on the mosaics or other monuments representing persons before the twelfth century. This was, no doubt, owing to the fact that the *mappula* was only used on certain occasions, and being liable to be constantly laid aside and resumed, it was not considered as constituting part of the costume. On the other hand, when we have a representation of persons in the act of presenting or receiving an object, a napkin of some costly material, unfolded, almost always lies across their hands. Some ancient monuments,[2] which have no connection with liturgical vestments, show us how the *mappula* was carried when it was not in use for presenting or receiving some object. It was folded together and placed over the right

---

[1] Vol i. pp. 171, 189, note 62; p. 225, note 2.
[2] A Syracusan painting, published by De Rossi, *Bull*, 1877, pl xi.; cf. the bas-relief found at Travaux (Jura), and published by Père Thédenat in the *Bulletin des Antiquaires de France*, 1887, p. 178.

arm with the extremities hanging down, much as we now see the Latin priests, deacons, and subdeacons wearing the maniple, which is, indeed, none other than a modification of the ancient *mappula*.

As a distinguishing liturgical badge, the *mappula* is not met with outside Rome.[1] In the East, however, and in Gallican countries,[2] sleeves of some costly material were worn (*manualia, manicae, ἐπιμανίκια*), which extended over the edge of the tunic at the wrists.

The various liturgical vestments which we have hitherto mentioned were merely the ordinary garments of daily use, which were gradually invested with a sacred character. We now come to the ecclesiastical insignia properly so called.

4. *The Pallium.*

As early as the end of the fifth century the pope wore a distinguishing badge, to which the name of *pallium* was applied. It was a long band of white woollen stuff, draped over the shoulders with the two ends depending, one before, one behind.

The Bishop of Ostia also wore it by special privilege as the usual consecrator of the pope, and the Bishops of Ravenna shared this honour, as is seen on the mosaics in which they figure. Pope Symmachus also conceded it to St. Cæsarius of Arles, a concession which was renewed in

---

[1] It is possible that the ἐπιγονάτιον, or kind of lozenge-shaped purse, which the Greek bishops wear hanging from the right side of their girdle, may also be a relic of the *mappula*.

[2] St. Germain, *Ep.* 2 [In the manuscript known as "The Bible of Charles the Bald," the *mappula* is apparently represented. See chromolithograph in Planché, *Cyclopaedia of Costume*, vol. ii., plate opposite p. 31.—Tr.]

the case of his successors. We see St. Gregory conferring the *pallium* on the Bishops of Syracuse, Messina, Milan, Salona, Nicopolis, Corinth, Justiniana Prima, Autun, Seville, and Canterbury.

This mark of honour appears to derive its origin from an Imperial gift. In the eighth century this was the opinion of the forger of the Donation of Constantine, when he makes that emperor bestow upon St. Silvester the *superhumerale, videlicet lorum qui imperiale circumdare assolet collum*. In the sixth century, when the Popes granted the *pallium* to bishops who were not subjects of the Greek Empire, it was customary for them to first ask the authorisation of the emperor.[1] The latter, moreover, claimed the right of bestowing it directly, for in the seventh century we find Maurus, Archbishop of Ravenna, asking the Emperor Constans II. for it, and obtaining it. But thenceforward such a step was regarded as equivalent to a revolt against the Pope's supremacy. The Roman *pallium* gradually acquired a symbolic significance. It was regarded as a relic, that is, as a sort of replica of the mantle of St. Peter. Before despatching it to its destination, it was deposited for the whole of the previous night in the sanctuary of the *Confessio*, immediately above the tomb of the apostle. St. Peter was regarded as having slept a night under this mantle, and it thus became his own. By a very slight extension of ideas it came to connote a kind of transmission of power, like that symbolised by the mantle of

---

[1] This was what Vigilius did in the case of Auxanius and Aurelian, Bishops of Arles; in the case of the other bishops, Sapaudus, Virgilius, and Florian, no permission is recorded, and it is possible that in the end the authorisation was granted in perpetuity for the Bishops of Arles. St. Gregory asked it in the case of the Bishop of Autun, but does not appear to have done so for those of Seville and Canterbury. The latter was, however, a Roman monk, a subject of the Emperor Maurice, and Leander of Seville had stayed at the Court of Constantinople, where he was well known.

Elijah, passed on to his successor Elisha.[1] The *pallium* thus became the natural sign of a superior jurisdiction, that is, of a species of participation in the *Pasce oves meas* As early as the sixth century the Bishops of Arles, and in the following century those of Canterbury, wore it as a mark of the special powers which they had received from Rome.

On the conclusion of the alliance between the Pope and the Carlovingian princes, when the Frankish Church found itself more closely related to Rome, the metropolitans accepted the Roman *pallium* with the symbolism attached to it.

This conception of the *pallium* as a mantle was suggested rather by the word itself than by the thing denoted. The article designated by this term was not in the form of a garment, but of a scarf. In the last analysis this scarf was, no doubt, a relic of the short mantle which had been brought into fashion in the Roman Empire by the Greeks. But the *discolora pallia* of the Theodosian Code were evidently scarves, and scarves of office, which were worn over the *paenula*, as the pontifical *pallium* was worn over the planeta. The Theodosian Code mentions this sign of office only in connection with functionaries of a comparatively humble rank, but the monuments represent it on the shoulders of consuls, a fact which gives ground for belief that the Imperial Government conferred, in reality, a very great mark of honour on the ecclesiastical dignitaries upon whom they bestowed it.

A glance at a consular diptych [*] will illustrate what I mean. The consul is there represented in the most solemn act of his inauguration, viz. at the moment when he gives the signal to start the horses in the arena.

---

[1] As early as the sixth century a similar meaning was attached to the *pallium* of Alexandria (Liberatus, *Brev.*, 20).

[*] [For example, No. 368—1871 in the South Kensington Museum, representing Anastasius, Consul of the East, A D 517.—TR.]

Over his garments we distinguish a long scarf arranged in the following manner. One end passes over the left shoulder and hangs down in front almost to the feet; this extremity is folded, and has the appearance of a long vertical orphrey; from the left shoulder the scarf passes across the back, under the right arm, and is brought up diagonally over the breast towards the left shoulder, where it can be spread out at will over the upper part of the back, and passes again under the right arm to terminate at the left hand, with a slight curve of drapery below the girdle; the end is either held in the left hand or thrown over the left wrist. In the diptychs of the sixth century, instead of falling from the left shoulder, the first end depends from the right shoulder, but care is first taken to bring it forward towards the middle of the breast, in such a manner that the end falls straight down the centre of the body, between the legs. This is kept in place either by means of a fibula, which secures the orphrey on the breast, or by merely skilfully tightening the scarf.

This draped scarf, which is not so much a modification of the classical *pallium* as of the Roman toga, presents a striking similarity to the appearance of the pontifical *pallium* as it is represented on the ancient monuments. The latter, however, is not nearly so wide. It is not a piece of drapery richly embroidered and terminated by an orphrey, but a long narrow band of white woollen material, of the same width throughout, without any other ornament than a small black cross at each extremity. Otherwise it is draped in exactly the same way as the consular scarf, except that the second end, instead of being brought round in front to terminate in the left hand, is left free, and falls down behind. To prevent it from dragging on the ground, it is cut short at the ankles, or even rather higher.

Thus, by its scarf-like form and its arrangement, the pontifical *pallium* reveals its official origin. It is to be regretted, as far as the Roman Church is concerned, that we have no document relating to its *provenance* or use earlier than the beginning of the sixth century. At the time when it first comes before us, that is, under Pope Symmachus, the Roman Church was separated from Constantinople by a schism; it was therefore not the moment for her to enjoy Imperial favours. This had been the situation since the year 484. For several years before the latter date Rome had ceased to owe allegiance to the emperors, and had passed under the rule of barbarian princes. We must therefore go back well into the fifth century to find a favourable time for its institution. On the other hand, the Bishops of Gaul and Spain [1] had, apart from the Roman *pallium*, which had been granted to some of them from the sixth century onward, a *pallium* which they used as a sign of office, and which appears to have had the same shape as that worn by the Pope. This would lead us to believe that the Imperial grant of this ornament went back to a time when the whole of Gaul was still Roman, that is to say, to the first half of the fifth century. The African bishops also wore the *pallium* as a sign of their office.[2] If they held it from the emperor, they must have received it before the invasion of the Vandals. It is to the same period that we must refer the most ancient mention of the *pallium* found in

---

[1] St. Germain of Paris, *Ep* 2. The first Council of Mâcon (581) forbade bishops to celebrate Mass without the *pallium: Ut episcopus sine pallio missas dicere non praesumat*. The reading *archiepiscopus*, which is found in the printed texts, is merely the editor's correction; the manuscripts read *episcopus*. Cf. Loening, *Deutsch. Kirchenrecht*, vol. ii. p. 94. For Spain, see *infra*, p 391.

[2] Life of St Fulgentius, ch 18. St. Fulgentius, out of humility, forbore to wear it: "Orario quidem sicut omnes episcopi numquam utebatur." The term *orarium* has no different import; it is used in Spain (*Conc. Tol.*, iv. c 27), and even at Rome (*Lib. Pont*, vol. i. p. 472, l. 3), to denote the episcopal *pallium*.

the ecclesiastical literature of the East. St. Isidore of Pelusium [1] is already familiar with this sign of office under its Greek name of *omophorion;* he attaches to it also a symbolic significance, which leads us to think that its introduction was not of recent date.

I should, therefore, be inclined to believe that its origin must be sought rather in the fourth century than in the century following.

In these early times, the *pallium* was the distinctive mark of episcopal authority in full exercise. When a Pope or patriarch was deposed, his *pallium* was taken from him. When Pope Felix IV. desired to invest his successor before his own death, he delivered up to him his *pallium*.[2] It would seem that in the East, and also in countries following the Gallican use, the *pallium* was worn indiscriminately by all bishops, and it is impossible to say whether or not they needed to be invested with it by their metropolitans or patriarchs. The Roman custom of reserving this mark of honour for certain bishops only, and of sending it to them from Rome, appears to be a modification of the primitive institution. I am rather inclined to believe that it had some connection with the change of ideas and of language which transformed an official badge into a relic of the apostle Peter.

Although originally derived from the same source as that of other bishops, the Pope's *pallium* acquired guadually a different and more exalted significance. One circumstance which must have added considerably to its prestige, was the fact that, with the exceptions of those of Ostia and Ravenna, the suffragan bishops of Rome had not the right to wear it, either because the Pope, from the first, was opposed to their receiving it, or else—which would be

---

[1] *Ep.* i. 136 Cf Palladius, *Dial.* c. 6.
[2] See *Lib Pontif.*, vol. 1. p. 282, note 4; p. 293, l. 2; p. 353, l. 2, 3, p. 472, l. 3; Theophanius, A. M. 6221; cf. *infra*, 395, note 4.

most unlikely—because he had subsequently[1] deprived them of it.*

5. *The Stole.*

The bishops were not the only ecclesiastical dignitaries to receive a special distinguishing mark. The priests and deacons had also their respective insignia. Here, however, we must pause to distinguish between the Roman custom and that of other countries. At Rome, the wearing of insignia seems to have met with little favour, as we have already seen from the letter of Pope Celestine to the Bishops of Provence.[2] This is more clearly accentuated by the fact that the *orarium* of the priest and deacon, considered as a conspicuous mark of distinction, was unknown there, certainly as late as the tenth century, whereas elsewhere it was universally adopted. The *orarium* is doubtless mentioned in the *Ordines* of the ninth century, but we see there also that this vestment was worn by acolytes and subdeacons as well as by the superior orders, and that its place was under the outer garment, whether dalmatic or planeta, and not over it. This *orarium* was merely the ancient *sudarium* (hand-

---

[1] The bishops of the suburbicarian diocese were in a much more subordinate position with regard to the Pope than other bishops were with their metropolitans They were obliged to come to Rome to be consecrated, and the consecration was performed by the Pope alone, without the concurrence of other bishops. They had not the right also to found rural Churches without the Pope's authorisation An examination of the registers of Gelasius, Pelagius, and St. Gregory will suffice to show the difference in the administration of the Roman province and that of Arles, for instance, or Milan. Like the African bishops, the prelates of South Italy strike us as occupying the position of important parish priests, rather than that of actual rulers of dioceses.

* [Probably the earliest representation of an English archbishop wearing the *pallium* (besides the stole) is in Abbot Elfnoth's Book of Prayers (Harleian Manuscript, No. 2908), an Anglo-Saxon manuscript of the tenth or eleventh century in the British Museum, where the abbot is depicted offering a book to St. Augustine —Tr.]

[2] J. 369 of the year 428.

kerchief, or neckcloth), which came finally to take a special shape, and to become even an accessory of ceremonial dress,[1] but not a distinguishing mark. I know of no Roman representation of it before the twelfth century. The priests and deacons whom we see in the mosaics never exhibit this detail of costume.

Elsewhere it was not so. Towards the end of the fourth century the Council of Laodicea in Phrygia forbade the minor orders (subdeacons, lectors, etc) to usurp the *orarium*. St. Isidore of Pelusium[2] regarded it as something analogous to the episcopal *pallium*, except that it was of linen, whereas the *pallium* was of wool. The sermon on the Prodigal Son, attributed to St. John Chrysostom, uses the same term ὀθόνη, and adds that this article of dress was worn over the left shoulder, and that its fluttering recalled that of angels' wings.

The Greek deacons still wear the stole in this manner; it is thus quite conspicuous, being over the upper garment, and secured on the left shoulder. Its ancient name of *orarium* (ὡράριον) still clings to it. As to the priestly *orarium*, it is worn, like the stole of the Latin priests, around the neck, with the two ends falling in front almost down to the feet. This is what is called the *epitrachelion* (ἐπιτραχήλιον).

These distinctions are also found in Spain and Gaul. The Council of Braga, in 561,[3] decreed that deacons were not to wear their *oraria* under the tunicle, lest they might not

[1] It at length received (like the Pope's *pallium*) a kind of consecration, which conferred upon it the nature of a relic. The *oraria* given to the candidates for ordination on Ember Saturdays had been deposited during the preceding night in the *Confessio* of St Peter. It is curious that the biographers of Popes Agatho and Stephen III. use the word *orarium* to designate the patriarchal or pontifical *pallium* (*Lib Pont*, vol. i pp 354, 472).

[2] *Loc. cit.*: " Ἡ ὀθόνη μεθ' ἧς λειτουργοῦσιν ἐν ἁγίοις οἱ διάκονοι "

[3] "Item placuit ut quia in aliquantis hujus provinciae ecclesiis diacones absconsis infra tunicam utuntur orariis, ita ut nihil differri a subdiacono videantur, de cetero superposito scapulae, sicut decet, utantur orario."

be distinguishable from subdeacons, but above it, and over the shoulder. The Council of Toledo, in 633, defined (c. 27) the *orarium* as a distinguishing mark, common to the three major orders, bishops, priests, and deacons. It specified (c. 39) that the deacon should wear it over his left shoulder, and that it should be white, without admixture of colours or gold embroidery. Another Council of Braga, held in 675, forbade priests (c. 3) to celebrate Mass without having an *orarium* passed round the neck and crossed on the breast, exactly as the Latin priests wear it at the present day. St. Germain of Paris speaks of episcopal and also of diaconal insignia; he gives to the first the name of *pallium*, stating that it is worn round the neck, that it falls over the breast, and is terminated by a fringe. He calls the diaconal distinguishing mark a stole (*stola*), and says that the deacon wears it over the albe. This fashion of wearing the diaconal stole spread, during the Middle Ages, over nearly the whole of Italy, and even to the gates of Rome.[1] In Rome itself the ancient custom seems to have been retained, but with a compromise. When the diaconal stole was at length adopted there, it was worn, indeed, across the left shoulder, but always under the dalmatic or planeta.[2]

The presbyter's stole was also adopted, and in the mosaics of Santa Maria in Trastevere (twelfth century) we see a priest wearing that vestment. It is to be noted that the four Popes who appear in the same mosaic are wearing the *pallium*, but not the stole. The one seems to exclude the other. In fact, the *Ordines* of the ninth century, when describing the dress of the Pope, always omit the stole. On those monuments, moreover, where both

---

[1] See the costume of St. Laurence in the illustrations of the Tivoli *cartularium* (Bruzza, *Il regesto di Tivoli*, pl iv)

[2] This accounts for it having to be caught together at the waist, that it might be worn bandolier-fashion.

are represented, we observe a striking resemblance between the two. To be convinced of this, it is merely necessary to glance at the mosaic which I have just mentioned, or at the miniatures of the Tivoli *cartularium*. In the latter we see grouped together the Pope, with his *pallium* over his planeta, and the suburbicarian bishops, with their stoles under the same vestment. Both stoles and *pallium* are of exactly the same shape and colour, and are ornamented with the same little black crosses. It is therefore quite conceivable that whoever wore one of these two insignia might not wear the other.[1]

In the end, however, a combination of the two was effected. At Ravenna, where a love for decorations was always evinced, we see in the mosaics of San Vitale, Bishop Ecclesius (sixth century) wearing both the priestly stole and the Roman *pallium*. This picture seems to be an isolated instance,[2] the other Bishops of Ravenna, successors of Ecclesius, being represented with the *pallium* only. Both are seen worn together in a Sacramentary of the ninth century[3] from Autun, and on the *paliotto* [altar covering] of San Ambrogio of Milan; and such appears to have been the custom thenceforward among the Frankish clergy.

If we take these facts into consideration, and also the differences and modifications, we are thus led to trace the history of the insignia known under the names pallium, omophorion, orarium, stole, and epitrachelion. All have a common origin. They are distinguishing marks of dignity, introduced into ecclesiastical use during the fourth century,

---

[1] Cf the painting in San Clemente (De Rossi, *Bull*, 1865, p 2) representing Pope Nicholas translating the remains of St. Clement The Pope wears the *pallium*, but no stole St. Methodius and another bishop, who are assisting at the ceremony, have the stole, but not the *pallium*. The painting is of the twelfth century.

[2] It should be ascertained whether this is a restoration or not.

[3] See the reproduction published by Mons. L. Delisle in the *Gazette Archéologique* of 1884, pl 20.

and resembling those prescribed by the Theodosian Code for certain classes of functionaries. The Roman Church, for one reason or another, refused to accept them, or rather confined itself to the adoption of the papal *pallium*, which soon acquired a distinctly special significance. Elsewhere, this vestment was adopted for the three superior orders of the hierarchy, introducing slight differences according to the ecclesiastical rank to which the wearer belonged. The deacon wore it over one shoulder, the priest and bishop around the neck; the deacon over the tunicle, which was his upper garment, the priest under the planeta, the bishop above it.[1]

The *pallium*, with the exception of the crosses which ornamented its extremities, was always white in colour, as was also the stole of the deacon and that of the priest or bishop. The *pallium* has universally and from all time been made of wool. In the East the diaconal stole was of linen, but I am unable to say of what material either it or that of the priest was composed in the countries of the West.[*]

---

[1] We have, however, very little information as to this method of differentiating priest and bishop. The Canon of the third Council of Braga (see *supra*, p. 391), decreeing that priests should cross the *orarium* over the breast, presupposes thereby that it was worn under the planeta. The council does not say that this method of wearing it was to be peculiar to priests only, and that bishops should follow some other fashion The term *sacerdotes*, which it employs, may include bishops as well as priests. Beyond this, we can glean no information from the ancient ecclesiastical literature of Spain. In Gaul, St. Germain of Paris speaks of the episcopal *pallium* after having described the chasuble, which might lead us to believe that the *pallium* was worn above it. I have already mentioned that Bishop Ecclesius of Ravenna is represented with the stole, or *orarium*, hanging down in front, under the planeta, while at the same time he wears the *pallium* over it, and that this custom was adopted in France in the Carlovingian period The Greek bishops also wear simultaneously the *epitrachelion* and the *omophorion*. This accumulation of insignia was forbidden in Spain in the seventh century (*Conc. Tol*, iv. c. 39), and we note that the Pope abstained from wearing both vestments till about the twelfth century, having previously used the *pallium* only, without the stole.

[*] [St. Cuthbert's stole at Durham is of linen, completely covered with embroidery.—Tr]

6. *Shoes and Head-dress.*

Shoes and head-dress also were used as distinguishing marks of ecclesiastical rank. Not all the clergy had the right to wear the *campagi,* a sort of slipper which covered only the heel and toes. As early as the sixth century this constituted the ceremonial covering of the feet for the clergy of higher rank in Rome and Ravenna.[1] Permission to wear them had to be obtained from the Pope.[2] In the histories of the depositions respectively of Pope Martin and the anti-Pope Constantine,[3] we see that in such cases not only was the wearer deprived of the *pallium,* but the straps of his *campagi* were cut.[4]

The tiara, in early times, seems to have been a costume peculiar to the Pope. At all events, it is not met with elsewhere in the West. There is no mention of it in any document earlier than the life of Pope Constantine (708–715),[5] which describes the pope making his entrance into Constantinople *cum camelauco, ut solitus est Roma*

---

[1] We may see them represented in the mosaics of the time, particularly in those of San Vitale of Ravenna, where they are worn by the emperor, the officers of his Court, the Bishop of Ravenna and his deacons One of the *Ordines Romani* mentions them as used by the Roman priests and deacons; the author of the false Donation of Constantine also speaks of them, but not in very definite terms

[2] St Gregory (*Ep*, viii. 27) forbids the Deacons of Catania to use the *campagus;* he says that the deacons of Messina are those alone in the whole of Sicily who have the privilege of wearing them, a privilege granted to them by his predecessors.

[3] It seems that the *campagus* of the Pope had something special about it, for the Greek author of the *scholion* to the letter of Anastasius the Apocrisarius (Migne, *Pat. Lat*, vol. cxxix. p. 685) says that he had received as a relic one of the *campagi* of Pope Martin · *uno de campagis ejus, id est caligis, quos nullus alius inter homines portat, nisi sanctus papa Romanus.*

[4] "Cum incidisset psachnion (pallium) beati viri excubitor et corrigiam compagiorum ejus . . ." (Hardouin, *Conc.*, vol. iii. p. 682; *Lib. Pont.*, vol. i. p. 472).

[5] *Lib Pont*, vol. i. p 390, l 15.

procedere. The similarity of the word *camelaucum* to the Greek term καμηλαύκιον shows that a covering for the head is here meant. Sixty years later, the author of the false Donation of Constantine gives a description of it and explains its origin. The Emperor Constantine desired to give his Imperial crown to St. Silvester, but the saint having out of humility refused it, the emperor placed on his head a white Phrygian cap,[1] *frigium candido nitore*, and granted to him and his successors the right to wear it in processions after the manner of a sovereign. This distinguishing head-dress does not appear, as far as I am aware, upon any monument prior to the twelfth century, when we find it in the paintings of the ancient Church of San Clemente at Rome. In these frescoes, the cap, which is conical in form, rises from a jewelled circlet; but this crown must have been added subsequently to the eighth century, for the false Donation of Constantine implies that it was not then in use. The second crown is not met with in any representations before the time of Boniface VIII.; the third was added by one of the Popes of Avignon.

7. *The White Saddle-cloth of the Roman Clergy.*

The Donation of Constantine mentions another distinguishing mark, not peculiar to the Pope alone, but to members of the Roman clergy in general—that is, the white covering (*mappula* or *mappulum*)[2] of linen of a silky texture, which the clergy had the right of placing over the saddles of their horses on the days when processions

---

[1] The papal tiara and the Phrygian cap have thus a real though somewhat distant connection. The mitre of the bishops, which is only a glorified hood, takes its origin from a cowl (*cucullus*), which in olden times was an article of apparel of the working classes and the poorer peasantry.

[2] "Decernimus et hoc ut clerici ejusdem sanctae Romanae ecclesiae mappulis et linteaminibus, id est candidissimo colore decorari equos et ita equitari"

took place. The Roman ecclesiastics were very jealous of this privilege. In the time of St. Gregory[1] they protested vigorously against the usurpations of the clergy of Ravenna in this respect. The biographer of Pope Conon[2] (687) severely reproaches him for the great crime of having authorised a deacon of Syracuse to use the *mappulum*. At Rome, the lessers clerks, even before entering the minor orders, had the enjoyment of this privilege.

8. *The Crozier and Ring.*

The crozier and ring are mentioned in the Canons of the fourth Council of Toledo (c. 27) and in the *De Ecclesiasticis Officiis* (II., 5) of St. Isidore as insignia of the episcopal office. They must, therefore, have been in use in Spain as early as the beginning of the seventh century. In the eleventh century they were almost universally used, as is shown by the history of the strife concerning investiture. Indeed, long before this date, some of the lives of the saints drawn up in countries conforming to the Gallican rite, give us ground for belief that the use of them was not peculiar to Spain. Further support of this belief is found in the employment of the crozier, under the name of *cambuta*, in the dedication rites according to the Gallican Church. At Rome, on the other hand, this sign of office was unknown. When the episcopal crozier, with its very natural symbolism, had been everywhere adopted, it was a cause of surprise that the Pope, the shepherd of the shepherds, was the only one not to make habitual use of the pastoral staff. In order to explain this peculiarity, which was merely the ancient

---

[1] *Ep*, iii 56 (54), 57 (66).
[2] *Lib. Pont*, vol. i. p. 369.
[3] *Ordo Rom*, ix. 1: " Accipient primam benedictionem ab archidiacono, ut liceat eis super linteum vellosum sedere, quod mos est ponere super sellam equi."

Roman custom, better observed at Rome than elsewhere, recourse was had to legends without any foundation.[1]

As to the mitre, we have no reason to treat of it here, as it does not come into question till the eleventh century. Indeed, neither in the eleventh century nor at the present time can it be said to constitute an episcopal sign of office, properly speaking.

The *traditio* of vestments or ecclesiastical insignia had its place in the ritual of ordination. The texts of St. Isidore and of the fourth Council of Toledo, cited above, make express mention of it, but do not state at what moment in the ceremony it took place. The other documents of the Gallican ritual are silent on this point. In the Roman *Ordines* of the eleventh century we find the archdeacon clothing the candidates in the vestments of the order about to be conferred on them, and presenting them to the Pope thus apparelled to receive the blessing for the diaconate, the priesthood, or the episcopacy. This ceremony took place in front of the altar, in the special enclosure, or *presbyterium*, beyond the apse, where the pontiff, surrounded by the higher clergy, was enthroned. The vestments thus solemnly conferred were—the orarium with the dalmatic for deacons, and the planeta for priests. Bishops were invested with both dalmatic and planeta, the latter being worn over the former.

---

[1] The story, for instance, of the staff of St Peter, which was confided to a missionary bishop, that he might restore life to one of his companions who had died on the journey Innocent III. (*De Alt. Myst.*, i. 62) is the first to have given this explanation He connects it with the legend of St. Eucherius of Treves At the time that he wrote, the same story was related about several other saints.

CHAPTER XII.

THE DEDICATION OF CHURCHES.

§ 1.—Buildings consecrated to Christian Worship.

THE primitive churches were ordinary houses suited specially for Christian worship, or rather for all the services of the Christian community. The houses of that period were very easily adapted to this purpose. They comprised, as a rule, an entrance from the public road, a courtyard surrounded by a colonnade (*atrium*), and at the back another court, or enclosed hall, a bath-room, living-rooms, cellars, and offices of all kinds, arranged around the inside courtyards. This kind of building supplied what was required for the accommodation of the various classes of persons of which the Christian meetings were composed, namely, the catechumens, the faithful, and the penitents. It also provided a dwelling for the bishop and the clergy who assisted him in his office, and could be used as a depository for papers, books, and the sacred vessels, and as a storehouse for the clothing, bedding, and provisions for the use of the poor and strangers. A *domus ecclesiae* in those early times comprised all that we have just enumerated.[1] It was a somewhat complicated institution,

---

[1] Cf. the official report relating to the seizure of the Church of Cirta in 303, in the *Gesta apud Zenophilum* (Migne, *Pat. Lat.*, vol. viii. p. 731).

being at the same time a church, an episcopal residence, a refectory, a dispensary, and an almshouse. The place specially chosen for worship, however, assumed from an early date a special importance. The other parts of the building came gradually to be detached, and participated in no respect in its sacred character. The *domus ecclesiae* became the *domus Dei*, the place where Christians met the Lord—the *dominicum* [1]

The idea of associating a particular solemnity with the taking possession of one of these sacred buildings was too natural to be overlooked, and we find, consequently, an expression of it at an early date. Immediately after the persecution of Diocletian we have notices of the dedication of churches performed with a certain degree of pomp. Eusebius describes that of Tyre, which was celebrated in the year 314. A special ritual did not yet exist. The neighbouring bishops were called together, and an immense concourse of people assembled, giving solemnity to the first celebration of the holy mysteries. Addresses bearing on the subject were delivered. Eusebius, who was elected to deliver the discourse at the dedication of the Church of Tyre, did not neglect to insert in his history his address on this occasion.

The Church of Tyre was a city church, or rather the church *par excellence*, the Cathedral of Tyre. It is possible that there may have been none other there at the time of its inauguration. In such great cities as Rome, Alexandria, and Carthage, there were at an early date several churches, a single one being insufficient to contain the whole Christian population. These churches had their own special priests, but they were none the less considered

---

[1] Κυριακόν, in Greek. Hence the term in use among Germanic nations, *kirche, kirk, church*. In the Neo-Latin language the ancient term ἐκκλησία is the source of the designations in present use.

as belonging to the collective community, and the bishop proceeded frequently from one to another. They represented the expansion of the cathedral rather than distinct parishes in the sense we now attach to them.

Besides the urban churches, there were cemetery chapels,[1] situated in burying-places and used for funeral services and Masses, and for anniversaries and other commemorations, as well as for the funeral *agape*, the observance of which continued for a long time. Sometimes these were nothing more than covered buildings, capable of sheltering the priest, the altar, and a small congregation. If the congregation were numerous, it assembled in the open air within the bounds of the cemetery. It often happened, however, that the cemetery chapel was built near or over the tomb of a martyr. In such a case popular devotion attracted thither a multitude, who did not, however, limit the festival to a commemorative anniversary. The faithful loved to hold meetings, either liturgical or otherwise, on the sites where the heroes of the faith reposed. In order to shelter such assemblies, and with the desire of honouring the memory of those who were the occasion of them, edifices of considerable size and grandeur were constructed over the tombs of martyrs and apostles. If for any reason the relics of the martyr were not already contained within the sacred precincts, they were transferred to their new resting-place with a solemn ceremonial.[2] This was, so to speak, a further interment—a *depositio*—but a triumphal one. On such occasions, besides the ordinary liturgical service, that is, the taking possession of the place for Christian worship, the festival of the dedication was

---

[1] Upon this subject, see De Rossi, *Roma Sott*, vol iii. p. 454, *et seq.*

[2] I confine my notices here to the translation of relics mentioned by St. Ambrose.

associated with the translation of the relics of the saint, that is, with his taking possession of the monument which he was henceforward to occupy.

There were, therefore, two kinds of churches, namely, the ordinary churches, which were merely places of meeting for liturgical worship, and those in which the bodies of the saints rested. The town churches belonged chiefly to the former category, as did also many of the country places of worship. The second type must have been represented by but a small number of Christian edifices, if they were limited to those actually constructed over the tombs of the martyrs, relatively few in number, whose memory and cult had been preserved. By a sort of ritualistic fiction, however, it came soon to be recognised that a single saint could have a great number of tombs. Any relic whatever—a piece of linen saturated with his blood, a vessel containing oil drawn from the lamps in his sanctuary, a fragment of stuff detached from the pall of his sarcophagus — was sufficient to represent him at a distance from his resting-place. To possess an object of this nature was to possess the body of the saint itself. To translate it and depose it in a church was equivalent to interring the body there.[1] Thus representative tombs could be multiplied to any extent that might be desired. In this way the churches with relics

[1] The history has been known for a long time of the *Basilica Romana* of Milan, dedicated by St Ambrose with the *pignora* of St. Peter and St. Paul, which were brought from Rome This dedication was prior to the year 386 (*Ambros. Ep*, 22; cf. Paulinus, *Vita Ambr.*, 33). We must recall also the basilica of the same apostles constructed by Rufinus in his Villa of the Oak, near Chalcedon, and solemnly consecrated in the year 394 with relics also from Rome But these instances are considerably less ancient than that of which an African inscription of the year 359 tells us This was the case of a *memoria* in which there had been placed, in addition to the relics of certain local martyrs, *de ligno crucis, de terra promissionis ubi natus est Christus*, *(pignora) apostoli Petri et Pauli* (Audollent, in the *Mélanges de l'École de Rome*, vol. x. p. 441).

became soon as numerous as the rest—nay, even more numerous—until, their reputation having altogether excelled that of the others, it was impossible to think of a church without relics in its altar. When relics (*pignora, sanctuaria*) of the saints were not to be had, portions of the Gospel, and even consecrated hosts, were employed for the purpose.[1]

§ 2.—Roman Dedication Rites.

Formularies for the dedication of churches are not found in either the Leonian Sacramentary or that of Adrian.[2] The Gelasian Sacramentary, as is always the case, is more complete, but we cannot say beforehand whether it corresponds in this respect with Roman or Gallican usage, or whether it is a mixture of the two. The same may be said of the liturgical works of Frankish origin from the eighth century onwards. There is, moreover, so little agreement among them, that the question naturally arises whether the whole of the dedication formulary was fixed when they were copied. There must have still been a wide latitude in this respect.

If we carry our researches further back than the eighth century, we find the earliest authority for Roman usage to be the letter from Pope Vigilius to Profuturus of Braga

---

[1] English Council of Celichyth [Chelsea—Tr], held in 816, c 2: "Eucharistia . . . cum aliis reliquiis condatur in capsula ac servetur in eadem basilica. Et si alias reliquias intimare non potest, tamen hoc maxime proficere potest, quia corpus et sanguis est domini nostri Jesu Christi"

[2] A dedication Mass occurs in the Leonian Sacramentary, i. 34 (Muratori, p. 308), but we must not confound such a Mass with the rites and formularies peculiar to the dedication itself, which must have taken place before the Mass.

(538). We learn from this that about the middle of the sixth century the Roman Church had not yet a ritual for the dedication of churches. A church was dedicated by the simple fact that Mass had been solemnly said within it. In the case, however, of a church having relics, these had to be deposited in it before the saying of the first Mass. Aspersions with holy water, which form so important a part in the existing ritual, are only mentioned to be excluded.[1] They found no place in Roman usage.

About sixty years later the letters of St. Gregory mention the dedication of churches [2] somewhat frequently. In the metropolitan diocese of the Pope no rural church could be consecrated without his authorisation, and to this circumstance we owe the frequent mention of these ceremonies in the papal correspondence. The *Liber diurnus* contains a score of formularies of the Roman usage.[3] I can discover nothing in these documents which implies, everything considered, another ritual than that referred to by Pope Vigilius.[4]

---

[1] "De fabrica vero cujuslibet ecclesiae, si diruta fuerit et si in eo loco consecrationis solemnitas debeat iterari in quo sanctuaria non fuerint, nihil judicamus officere si per eam minime aqua exorcizata jactetur: quia consecrationem cujuslibet ecclesiae in qua sanctuaria non ponuntur celebritatem tantum scimus esse missarum. Et ideo, si qua sanctorum basilica a fundamentis etiam fuerit innovata, sine aliqua dubitatione, cum in ea missarum fuerit celebrata solemnitas, totius sanctificatio consecrationis impletur. Si vero sanctuaria quae habebat ablata sunt, rursus earum depositione et missarum solemnitate reverentiam sanctificationis accipiet."

[2] Greg M., *Ep*, i 56 (54); ii. 5 (9); iii 19; vi. 22, 45 (43), 49 (48); viii 4 (5), ix. 25 (45) cf. *Dialog*, iii 30.

[3] Garnier's edition, chap. v.; Rozière, 10–31.

[4] We meet sometimes with celebrated dedications *absque missis publicis*; but these are cases of monastic oratories not open to the public, and where, consequently, *missae publicae* could not be celebrated. As the edifice was never to serve for public Masses, it is quite natural that these should not be said at the dedication.

We find a confirmation of this in comparing together the two most ancient *ordines* of dedication according to the Roman usage. The first has been hitherto unpublished,[1] and the second was edited by F. Bianchini in vol. iii. of his Anastasius, p. xlviii. The ceremony described in both of them is fundamentally the same, the differences between them arising from the fact that while one inserts the musical portions and omits the prayers, the other does the reverse. On the whole they supplement each other. Their titles are significant. There is no mention of the dedication; the translation of relics takes its place, and, in fact, almost the whole ceremony is taken up with it. Apart from these two rituals, we find in the Gelasian Sacramentary[2] a convocation formulary entitled *Denunciatio cum reliquiae ponendae sunt martyrum*, which corresponds to the ceremony in question. I will briefly describe it.

The bishop, accompanied by his clergy, proceeds to the place where are the *sanctuaria*. The choir, having sung a respond, the litany is said, followed by a prayer of the bishop. The latter then places the relics[3] on a paten on which a linen cloth was spread, and covers the whole with a silk veil. The procession then sets out for the church to be consecrated. The relics are borne either by the bishop himself or by a priest. During the progress of the procession a psalm is chanted by the choir, and on approaching the church the litany is begun.

The bishop consigns the relics to the hands of the priests, and, accompanied by only two or three clergy, enters the church. He begins with the exorcism of the water; having

[1] This is the manuscript of St. Amand. It will be found at the end of the present volume.
[2] II. 2; Muratori, vol. i. p. 635.
[3] The relics were usually placed in a box of precious metal. See De Rossi, *Bull*, 1872, pl. x.-xii ; de Laurière, *Bulletin Monumental*, vol. liv. (1888), *Note sur deux reliquaires*, etc.

mixed with it some drops of chrism, he uses this to make the mortar with which he will presently seal the altar-stone. With a sponge previously dipped in the exorcised water he washes the altar once only. Then leaving the church, he concludes the litany with a second prayer. Before re-entering the church, he asperses the people with what remains of the lustral water.[1]

The bishop now takes the relics, the door of the church is opened, and while he enters, followed on this occasion by all the people, a third litany is sung, and concluded by another prayer. When this is finished, and while the choir is chanting an antiphon, he divests himself of his planeta and proceeds alone to the altar, upon which he deposits the *sanctuaria*. Before closing the cavity (sepulchre, confession), he anoints the four internal angles of it. Then placing in position and sealing the stone of the tomb, he recites a prayer and anoints the stone once more at its centre and at its four corners.

The altar is then covered, and the bishop, resuming his vestment, recites a final prayer. The linen and sacred vessels, together with the altar cross, are then brought to him to be blessed. He proceeds thereupon to the *sacrarium*, where the doorkeeper awaits him, holding a lighted taper in his hand. The bishop blesses this taper, and by it the whole lights of the church, which are immediately lit, and the Mass begins.

It is easy to see that this ritual is exclusively funerary. The tomb of the saint is prepared for him; he is brought thither, enclosed within it, and the interior and exterior of the sepulchre is anointed with a fragrant unguent. The idea of an embalmment is still more clearly expressed in the subsequent ceremonies, in which the anointing with fragrant oil is accompanied by fumigation with incense.

---

[1] This water is called, in the later rituals, *Gregorian*.

The *Ordo* of Verona mentions the aspersion of the church at the end of the ceremony, but this passage is suspected to be an interpolation. In any case there is nothing like it in the other *Ordo;* even in that of Verona the aspersion is a mere afterthought added to the ceremony of the *depositio*.[1]

There would be, indeed, nothing extraordinary in the fact if it had been customary to asperse the walls of a new edifice. As early as the time of Pope Vigilius the faithful at Rome were in the habit of sprinkling holy water in their houses. The *Liber Pontificalis* testifies to the practice.[2] From the existing authorities, however, we cannot, I believe, conclude that this custom had been then, or even for a long time, extended to edifices consecrated for worship.

§ 3.—Gallican Dedications.

Having reconstructed, at least in its main outlines, the Roman ritual for the dedication of churches, I will endeavour to do the same in regard to the Gallican usage.[3] It is no easy task, for no description has come down to us, and no liturgical text, if we do not take into account

[1] As the *Ordo* of Verona has no reference elsewhere to the aspersion of the people with the remains of the exorcised water, before the door of the church, it is possible that it may here have that in view. The people and not the walls, are aspersed, and this in the interior instead of the exterior In the other rituals, that which remains of the lustral water is simply poured out at the foot of the altar It would appear that some importance was attached to its disappearance, probably to prevent its being used for some superstitious purpose.

[2] Vol 1 p 127.

[3] As early as the beginning of the sixth century we find traces of a Gallican ritual for the dedication of churches. *Conc Aurel.* [511], c. 10: "Ecclesias [Gothorum] simili quo nostrae innovari solent placuit *ordine* consecrari" Dom Férotin asserts (*Liber Ordinum*, p. 506) that he has not been able to find in the Mozarabic books any rite for the dedication of churches. We gather, however, by some scattered fragments that the ritual included the use of salt and the anointing of the altar, two peculiarities which are found in the Gallican rite as I give it here.

books in which the Roman and Gallican rituals are more or less combined.

An ancient commentary on the ritual of a dedication, published in the first instance by Martène, was attributed by him to Remigius of Auxerre, the head of the Episcopal School at Rheims at the end of the ninth century. Although this attribution is not certain, the text to which the commentary is attached was assuredly in use in the ninth century, for it is found, almost word for word, in another *Ordo*, that of the Verona manuscript, of which I have spoken above.[1] It immediately precedes there the Roman ritual which I have just described.

The Sacramentary of Angoulême [2] of the end of the eighth or beginning of the ninth century contains, in regard to the dedication of churches, an *Ordo* fundamentally similar to the ritual of Remigius. It differs from it in only one important point, to which I will shortly refer. The prayers and other formularies contained in this Sacramentary and in that of Gellona, which is of nearly the same date,[3] are the same as those of which the ritual of Remigius furnishes the series and the first words.

Finally, the two ancient manuscripts, called respectively the Gelasian Sacramentary and the *Missale Francorum*, contain the majority of these prayers, and even some rubrics which are absolutely identical with those implied or expressed in the Remigius ritual and the *Ordo* of Verona. We may therefore conclude that the whole of

---

[1] Dr. Magistretti has published the text of it, taken by him from a Milanese Pontifical of the ninth century, and from a Maintz Pontifical a little less ancient (*Mon. Lit. Ambr.*, vol. i.). The *Ordo Ambrosianus*, published by the Rev. Father Mercati (*Studi e Testi*, part 7, p. 21), from a Lucca manuscript of the eleventh century, gives indications, like the present Pontifical, of having been rehandled.

[2] *Parisinus*, 816. See this *Ordo* in the Appendix.

[3] Delisle, *Anciens Sacramentaires*, Nos. 7 and 15 (*Mém de l'Acad. des Inscr.*, vol. xxxii. part 1).

this ritual was in use in France at the beginning of the eighth century.

1. *Entrance of the Bishop. Introductory Prayers.*

The relics of the saints are in a place apart; an all-night vigil is kept before them. The church to be consecrated is empty, but twelve candles are burning, ranged along the walls. A cleric shuts himself inside in order to open the church when the occasion arises. The bishop presents himself before the door, and touches the lintel with his pastoral staff (*cambuta*), while saying the antiphon (anthem), *Tollite portas, principes, vestras,* etc. The choir then chants a similar psalm, *Domini est terra,* at the end of which the door is opened, and the bishop enters, saying, *Pax huic domui!* Proceeding to the altar, the clergy following, all prostrate themselves there, while through the empty church the chant of the litany is heard resounding for the first time. The bishop then rises and recites the first prayer—

Magnificare, Domine, Deus noster, in sanctis tuis; et hoc in templo aedificationis appare, ut qui omnia in filiis adoptionis operaris, ipse semper in tua haereditate laudens.

2. *The Ceremony of the Alphabet.*

The bishop then proceeds to the eastern corner on the left-hand side, and, passing in a diagonal line across the church, traces on the pavement with the end of his pastoral staff the letters of the alphabet. Then going to the right eastern corner, he repeats the ceremony in another diagonal line across the pavement.[1]

---

[1] The present custom is to trace the alphabet in Greek characters in the first line, and in Latin in the second. The ninth-century rituals do not note this distinction. The pavement is previously covered with ashes along the two diagonals, in order that the letters may be rendered visible.

3. *Preparation of the Lustral Water.*

Returning to the altar, the bishop implores the help of God, *Deus in adjutorium meum intende,* and then proceeds to the blessing of the lustral water. This ceremony begins with the exorcism and blessing, repeated separately over the water first, and then over the salt. The salt is then mixed with ashes, and the mixture sprinkled on the water in the form of a cross in three separate acts. The bishop then pours in wine, and recites the following prayer:—

> Creator et conservator humani generis, dator gratiae spiritalis, largitor aeternae salutis, tu permitte Spiritum tuum super vinum cum aqua mixtum; ut armata virtute caelestis defensionis ad consecrationem hujus ecclesiae vel altaris proficiat.

4. *Lustration of the Altar.*

Having dipped his finger into the lustral water, the bishop traces a cross at each of the four angles of the altar, and then makes the circuit of it seven times while aspersing it with a bunch of hyssop. The choir in the mean time chants the *Miserere.*

5. *Lustration of the Church.*

Still holding the bunch of hyssop, the bishop makes the circuit of the church thrice, sprinkling the lustral water on the walls, while the choir chant the three psalms, *Miserere, Exurgat Deus, Qui habitat in adjutorio Altissimi.* Certain clerics despatched by him proceed to asperse the church on the exterior walls.[1] The bishop then

---

[1] The *Ordo* of Verona says once only. At present this lustration is repeated three times. It is the bishop himself who now performs it before entering the church.

asperses the pavement while proceeding from the altar to the door, and then on a line at right angles to this across the middle of the church.

6. *The Consecrating Prayers.*

The bishop takes up a position in the middle of the church, and, facing the altar, recites two prayers, the latter being eucharistic in character—

Deus qui loca nomini tuo dicata sanctificas, effunde super hanc orationis domum gratiam tuam, ut ab omnibus hic invocantibus te auxilium tuae misericordiae sentiatur.
Dominus vobiscum.—Sursum corda —Gratias agamus, etc.
Vere dignum et justum est, aequum et salutare, nos tibi semper et ubique gratias agere, Domine sancte, Pater omnipotens, aeterne Deus, sanctificationum omnipotens dominator, cujus pietas sine fine sentitur; Deus, qui caelestia simul et terrena complecteris, servans misericordiam tuam populo tuo ambulanti ante conspectum gloriae tuae; exaudi preces servorum [tuorum], ut sint oculi tui aperti super domum istam die ac nocte; hancque basilicam in honorem sancti *illius* sacris mysteriis institutam clementissimis dedica, miserator inlustra, proprio splendore clarifica; omnemque hominem venientem adorare in hoc loco placatus admitte, propitius dignare respicere; et propter nomen tuum magnum et manum fortem et brachium excelsum in hoc habitaculo supplicantes libens protege, dignanter exaudi, aeterna defensione conserva; ut semper felices semperque tua religione laetantes constanter in sanctae Trinitatis fide catholica perseverent.

7. *The Anointing of the Altar.*

While the anthem *Introibo ad altare Dei* and the psalm *Judica me Deus* are being sung, the bishop proceeds to the altar and pours out at its foot the remainder of the lustral water. Having censed the altar, he anoints it three times—in the centre, and at the four corners—the first two with the ordinary blessed oil, and the third time with the holy chrism. During this ceremony the choir chant three antiphons suited to the rite—

Erexit Jacob lapidem in titulum, fundens oleum desuper, etc.—Psalm: *Quam dilecta tabernacula tua.*

Sanctificavit Dominus tabernaculum suum, etc.—Psalm: *Deus noster refugium.*

Ecce odor filii mei, etc.—Psalm: *Fundamenta ejus.*

During the anointing a priest makes continual circuits around the altar, swinging a censer, thus continuing the censing begun by the bishop.

8. *The Anointing of the Church.*

The bishop, having completed the anointing of the altar, proceeds round the church, and anoints the walls once with holy chrism.

9. *Consecrating Prayers.*

Returning to the altar, upon which he places in the form of a cross kindled grains of incense, he recites, while these are burning, a consecrating prayer of the Gallican type, preceded by an invitatory—

Dei Patris omnipotentis misericordiam, dilectissimi Fratres, deprecemur; ut hoc altarium sacrificiis spiritalibus consecrandum, vocis nostrae exorandus officio praesenti benedictione sanctificet; ut in eo semper oblationes famulorum suorum studio suae devotionis impositas benedicere et sanctificare dignetur; et spiritali placatus incenso, precanti familiae suae promptus exauditor adsistat.

Deus omnipotens, in cujus honorem altarium sub invocatione tui consecramus, clemens et propitius preces nostrae humilitatis exaudi, et praesta ut in hac mensa sint tibi libamina accepta, sint grata, sint pinguia et Spiritus sancti tui semper rore perfusa, ut omni tempore in hoc loco supplicantis tibi familiae tuae anxietates releves, aegritudines cures, preces exaudias, vota suscipias, desiderata confirmes, postulata concedas.

10. *Blessing of Objects used in Worship.*

The subdeacons afterwards brought the linen, the sacred vessels, and the ornaments of the church, to the bishop to bless them. Special formularies are found for the blessing of the linen and the paten and chalice, the latter being consecrated by an anointing with the holy chrism.

11. *Translation of Relics.*

The clergy, headed by the bishop, then left the church and proceeded to the locality where the people were gathered together around the holy relics. These were translated with high ceremonial during the chanting of triumphal hymns: *Ambulatis sancti Dei, ingredimini in civitatem,* etc. The people followed the solemn *cortège* into the church, but when the bishop had reached the sanctuary, a veil was let fall behind him. He went alone to the *depositio* of the *pignora,* and while he was enclosing them in the altar the choir sang, as an antiphon to the psalm *Cantate domino canticum novum,* the antiphon *Exultabunt sancti in Gloria.* When the ceremony was over [1] the lights of the church were lit, and the bishop proceeded to make his preparation in the *sacrarium* for celebrating Mass.

This ritual is in the main clear and logical. It follows the line prescribed for initiation into the Christian mysteries. Just as the Christian is dedicated by water and oil, by baptism and confirmation, so the altar in the first place, and the church in the second, are consecrated by ablutions and anointing. When the church had been consecrated, the saints, represented by their *pignora,*

---

[1] Remigius mentions here the prayer, *Deus qui ex omni coaptione*

were introduced into it, and then, in their turn, the assembly of the faithful. The latter portion corresponds with the Roman ceremony of the *depositio*, but it contains certain details which resemble those in the consecration of the altar by water and anointing. The Frankish liturgiologists of the eighth and ninth centuries, who took to meddling with the two rituals by combining them, were not always clever enough to avoid confusions and repetitions. More complications were the result in this case than in that of the ordination ritual. The same procedure was not everywhere adopted, and the *Ordines* which I publish exhibit different modes of combination. As for the existing Pontifical, it is the result of a still more complex operation. Taken as a whole, however, we recognise in it clearly the coexistence of the two rituals which I have described seriatim.

The former of the two, a ritual of a funerary type, is purely and decidedly Roman, as we readily gather both from the documents themselves and by its agreement with what we know of ancient Roman practice in such matters. But the other ritual—a ritual of a baptismal character—can we say with certainty that it is purely of a Gallican type?

We must make here, I think, some distinctions. At the beginning and in the middle of this ceremony we meet with prayers which are more Roman than Gallican in type and style. I refer to the prayer *Magnificare*, the consecrating prayers recited by the bishop in the middle of the basilica, the prayer *Deus qui loca*, and the eucharistic formulary *Deus sanctificationum*. It is possible that these were borrowed from the Roman Liturgy.[1] I would remark here, in the first place, that the prayer *Magnificare* is unknown to the Gelasian Sacramentary

---

[1] From some dedicatory Mass, and not from a specific ritual, because, as I have pointed out above, the Roman dedication did not consist of prayers of this nature apart from the Mass.

(No. lxxxviii.) and the *Missale Francorum*, and, in the second, that the latter document does not begin the series of prayers assigned to the officiating minister until the *Creator et Conservator*, whose frequent repetitions are in the Gallican style; and thirdly, that it omits altogether the two consecrating prayers, *Deus qui loca* and *Deus sanctificationum*. We have reason, therefore, to believe that these prayers were foreign to the original Gallican ritual. The elimination of them, however, does not in any way affect the character of the ceremony. The principal prayer, *Deus omnipotens, in cujus honorem*, is transferred, it is true, to the end, but this serves to give only more unity to the ritual, for in place of two consecrating prayers we have only one.

As for the remaining portion, we find it touched upon —lightly, it is true—in a passage of Gregory of Tours,[1] where the dedication of an oratory in honour of St. Allyre (Illidius) is dealt with. Gregory himself presided at the ceremony in his cathedral town. On the previous night the relics had been "watched" in the basilica of St. Martin. The bishop proceeded in the morning to the oratory, where he consecrated the altar.[2] He then returned to the basilica, and, having taken the relics, translated them in procession to the oratory. The ceremonies assume here the same order as those in our second ritual. At Rome the ceremony would have begun by the fetching of the relics from the basilica where they had been provisionally placed.

A most remarkable coincidence is found between the ceremony described and the Byzantine ritual published by Goar.[3] In this ritual the dedication and the

---

[1] *Glor. Conf*, 20.
[2] "Mane vero, venientes ad cellulam, altare quod erexeramus sanctificavimus"
[3] *Euchol.*, p. 832, *et seq.*, following the text of the Barberini manuscript.

deposition of the relics are quite distinct ceremonies, and took place usually on different days. The bishop began by sealing the table of the altar, which was placed either on columns or on a solid base. He made upon it the sign of the cross, and washed it, in the first instance, with baptismal water, and then with wine. He then anointed it with chrism (μύρον),[1] and finally fumigated it with incense. When the altar had been consecrated, he made a circuit of the church, swinging the censer, while a priest, walking behind him, anointed, in the form of a cross, the walls, columns, etc. The ceremony came to an end with the blessing of the linen, sacred vessels, lamps, and other objects used in worship.

The *depositio*, which was preceded by a solemn vigil, was accomplished with all the ceremony possible.[2] On arrival at the church, the chant *Tollite portas, principes, vestras* was sung. Before closing the tomb of the relics the bishop anointed it with chrism.

This summary is sufficient to impress upon us the relationship existing between the Greek ritual and our second Latin ritual. After all that we have seen of the relations between the Byzantine and Gallican Liturgies,

---

[1] Dionysius the Areopagite (*Eccl Hier.*, iv. 12) mentions the use of μύρον in the consecration of the altar.

[2] At Constantinople the emperor took part in the procession, walking on foot behind his state chariot, in which the patriarch was seated holding the relics on his knees. Theophanius (pp. 217, 227, 228, 238, De Boor) describes in the same way dedications celebrated at Constantinople in the time of Justinian, in the years 537, 550, 551, 562. He also mentions the chant Ἄρατε πύλας, οἱ ἄρχοντες, ὑμῶν An ivory, preserved at Treves, represents one of these ceremonies, possibly that of St. Irene, at Galata, which was celebrated in 551. My reason for supposing this date is the presence of two patriarchs in the Imperial chariot. Now, Theophanius says that the dedication of 551 was presided over by the two patriarchs Menas of Constantinople and Apollinaris of Alexandria See a representation (a bad one) of this object in the *Revue de l'Art Chrétien*, vol xxxi. p. 122.

there can hardly be any doubt that it is a Gallican ritual we have before us.[1]

A question still remains to be answered. What is the origin of the ceremony of the alphabet? It is unknown in the East; and in the West, as we have seen, it is not attested before the ninth century, even in the Frankish Liturgy. From that date it is difficult to trace it back to its true source, and to say whether it is Roman or Gallican. Sig. de Rossi[2] points out interesting relations between this singular rite and certain Christian monuments on which the alphabet appears to have a symbolical signification. He has removed all doubt as to the idea which suggested the ceremony. It corresponds with the taking possession of land and the laying down its boundaries. The saltire, or St. Andrew's cross (*crux decussata*), upon which the bishop traces the letters of the alphabet, recalls the two transverse lines which the Roman surveyors traced in the first instance on the lands they wished to measure. The letters written on this cross are a reminiscence of the numerical signs which were combined with the transverse lines in order to determine the perimeter. The series formed by these letters, moreover, that is, the entire alphabet, is only a sort of expansion of the mysterious contraction $A\Omega$, just as the *decussis*, the Greek X, is the initial of the name of Christ. The alphabet traced on a cross on the pavement of the church is thus equivalent to the impression of a large *signum Christi* on the land which is henceforward dedicated to Christian worship.

This profound symbolism, as well as the ancient custom on which it is grafted, must go back to a time when

---

[1] But it is to be well understood that the portions indicated above as Roman must be omitted in order to reconstitute it in its original form.

[2] *Bull.*, 1881, p. 140.

barbarism was not yet dominant, and consequently far beyond the eighth century. This is all that can be said. There were Roman surveyors in other places besides Rome and Italy, and there is no indication that this curious transference of their practices originated in Italy rather than in Gaul or Spain.

CHAPTER XIII.

THE CONSECRATION OF VIRGINS.

§ 1.—THE PROFESSION OF VIRGINS.

THE different forms taken by the ascetic life in Christian antiquity succeeded one after another in the following sequence.[1] In the earliest times individual asceticism was practised without its involving separation from the ecclesiastical community and family life, or absence from the city and ordinary avocations. Experience having subsequently shown the difficulty of reconciling such conflicting duties, ascetics "retired from the world," and sought silence and solitude away from human habitations. This second stage is that of *monks,* or isolated *anchorites.* Finally, these ascetics or anchorites conceived the idea of living together, of forming groups of individuals drawn exclusively from persons of their own calling, isolated from the "world," and even from ordinary Christians. It was thus that the cœnobitic life took its origin.

It is merely with the first stage that I have to deal here, namely, that of the ascetics attached to the local church without segregation of any kind. Their ranks were recruited from both sexes, even at an early period; we note their presence even in the second century under various names, such as *ascetae,* eunuchs, *continentes, encratitae,* etc. The

---

[1] I have given the logical, which is, in the main, also the chronological order

term "ascetic," or "monk" (ἀσκήτης, μόναχος), in the fourth century was more frequently used in Greek-speaking countries to denote men; whereas in Latin, when these same terms were not employed, the word "confessor," or, later on, "religious," was used (*confessor, religiosus*).[1] The women were designated by the name of *virgins*, or *sacred virgins* (πάρθενοι, *virgines sacrae*).

This term, like the majority of those that preceded it, expressed the kind of renunciation which was most highly esteemed and sought after. We must be cautious in drawing comparisons between the modern "religious" of both sexes and their forerunners of a remote antiquity. The earlier examples cultivated ascetism for its own sake, and not as a favourable condition for meditation,[2] or for the exercise of works of charity, of preaching, and teaching. The Christian virgin who remained a virgin had performed the essential part of her supererogatory obligations. No special fervour was demanded of her, no extraordinary assiduity in attending meetings for worship, nor any particular devotion to good works. It was only at a later date, when the first fervour of the Christian communities in general had somewhat abated, that an exceptional piety was looked for in those that practised continency. It is true that this idea developed rapidly, and ecclesiastical

---

[1] *Confessor* is the term used in the Roman Liturgy; see *infra*, p. 421, note 2: an epitaph (De Rossi, *Bull.*, 1874, pl. VI.) of Tarquinii mentions a *Euticius confessor;* it is in this sense that the term is employed in the Councils of Elvira (c. 25), Arles (314, c. 9), and Toledo (400, cc. 6, 9).

[2] St. Paul (1 Cor. VI.) adopts a standpoint more in harmony with our own. It should be noted that what he says with regard to virginity is in connection with the immediate coming of Christ: *tempus breve est, praeterit figura hujus mundi.* We should be careful to realise that Christian asceticism is in no way derived from this teaching of the apostle. Asceticism is anterior to Christianity, and is certainly not peculiar to it.

THE CONSECRATION OF VIRGINS.

legislation in that direction was upheld by or even prompted by the tendency of general opinion. Those who have given way to laxity do not regard with disfavour the small body of courageous souls who undertake to bear the burdens which they themselves will no longer attempt to lift. With regard to charitable works, the performance of such was considered incumbent either on the faithful in general, or on the community as represented by the clergy and their assistants—bishops, priests, deacons, deaconesses, and humbler ministers.

The principal motive of the profession of virginity was the assumption that such a manner of life, being superior to the forces of nature, reflected special honour on Christianity.[1] The virgins of both sexes—but especially the women, on account of their peculiar frailty—were regarded as an honour to the Church, the most precious jewels in her crown. Thus, far from hiding them behind walls and gratings, special delight was taken by the Church in putting them forward. The confessors and the sacred virgins, to whom were added the widows who, after a short marriage, had remained steadfast in their profession of widowhood, constituted a sort of aristocracy in the community of the faithful, obtained special mention in their prayers,[2] and had a distinct place reserved for them in the church. Marks of respect were voluntarily shown them, and the matrons did not leave the sacred place of assembly without coming to ask the holy kiss of the consecrated virgins.

The greatest freedom prevailed in regard to entering upon

---

[1] St. Ambrose draws a comparison between the Christian virgins and the Roman vestals. He points triumphantly to the inconsiderable number of the latter, and to the occasional and enforced nature of their occupations.

[2] In the Roman formulary of the prayer of the faithful, as it is preserved in the liturgy for Good Friday (cf. above, p. 175), the *ascetae* of both sexes are mentioned immediately after the clergy: "*Oremus et pro omnibus episcopis . . . ostiariis, confessoribus, virginibus, viduis et pro omni populo Dei.*"

the virginal state. Its adoption was not marked by any special ceremony. A change was made in costume, garments of a more sober shape and colour being worn; and if the person had the true spirit of her vocation, a more retired mode of life was adopted. Christianity was practised with seriousness and severity, without indulgence in any authorised or tolerated relaxations, and to the sacrifice of the pleasures of the flesh were added special austerities in the use of food, baths, and sleep.[1]

At a later date virgins, on entering upon their calling, were the objects of a special ceremony, which consisted of the bestowal of the veil, or *velatio*, to which was attached the idea of a kind of mystical marriage with Christ.[2] After this ceremony the engagement was regarded as irrevocable, and it was no longer possible to contract a marriage, any violation of the vow constituting a sort of sacrilegious adultery. In the fourth century Imperial legislation confirmed ecclesiastical opinion on this point.[3] The age for the reception of the *velatio* was not at first definitely prescribed. It varied according to the judgment of the bishop,[4] or the custom of the country. In Africa, at the end of the fourth century, the veil was

---

[1] This was the practice of the earnest ascetics; but there were others, alas, too numerous, whose lives were not so orderly. The Fathers of the Church constantly inveigh against the consecrated virgins who compromised their profession by a most worldly exterior. Some were found who, having lost their parents, or who for some reason were not living with their family, allowed themselves a "protector," who shared their dwelling, to say the least. Public opinion appears to have been very tolerant of these disorders, for they had often to be denounced in sermons of the time.

[2] This conception of virginal consecration explains why this ceremony should take place only in the case of women.

[3] *Cod Theod.*, Bk. IX., vol. 25.

[4] Ambr , *De Virg* , 7. His sister Marcellina was still young when she was consecrated by Pope Liberius. The words which St. Ambrose attributes to Liberius on this occasion would lead us to believe that the Roman virgins usually received consecration before advanced age.

given as early as the twenty-fifth year;[1] in Spain about the same time, the woman had to wait till her fortieth year.[2] This latter limit helped to obviate many difficulties, and a law of 458[3] officially sanctioned it. In this manner the *velatio* lost much of its significance. Instead of being the inaugural act of a career, it was merely its crowning-point. Under the pretext of securing the fidelity of the spouses of Christ, they were only dedicated to Him at an advanced age. Popular opinion, it must be remembered, favoured this arrangement, and had even gone further in that direction, since some apocryphal writings protest that the age should be sixty or even seventy-two years.[4]

The performance of the ceremony of the *velatio* was, like ordination, reserved for the bishop. It took place with great pomp on some solemn festival. In the curious discourse entitled *Ad virginem lapsam*, which appears among the works of St. Ambrose,[5] the bishop reminds a virgin, who has lapsed, of her solemn consecration on Easter Day, surrounded by the white-robed neophytes holding lighted tapers. At Rome the solemn festivals chosen for the purpose were Christmas Day or the Epiphany, Easter Monday, and St. Peter's Day,[6] on which occasions the Station was held at the basilica of the Vatican.

---

[1] *Cod can*, 16.
[2] Council of Saragossa (held in 800), c 8
[3] *Nov Majoriani*, vi 1
[4] The age of sixty is mentioned by the writer of the *Lib Pont* (vol i. pp. 239, 241), that of seventy-two by the false *Constitutum Silvestri* (*ibid.*).
[5] Migne, *Pat Lat*, vol. xvi p 367
[6] Decretal of Gelasius (Jaffé, 636), ch 12, compared with a rubric of the Gelasian Sacramentary (i 103). These texts do not mention the festival of Christmas; Marcellina was, however, consecrated on that day. It is possible that when the observance of the Epiphany was introduced at Rome, which was not, I believe, till after Liberius, that the ceremony of the *velatio virginum* was transferred to that festival.

§ 2.—The Rites of the Velatio Virginum.

1. *The Roman Use.*

No ancient ritual of the *velatio* according to the Roman use is extant, but the prayers for it are given in the Sacramentaries. The following are those of the Leonian Sacramentary,[1] and they were, doubtless, preceded by a litany :—

> Respice, Domine, propitius super has famulas tuas, ut virginitatis sanctae propositum quod te inspirante suscipiunt, te gubernante custodiant.
> Vere dignum ... aeterne Deus, castorum corporum benignus habitator et incorruptarum Deus amator animarum, Deus qui humanam substantiam, in primis hominibus diabolica fraude vitiatam, ita in Verbo tuo per quod omnia facta sunt reparas ut eam non solum ad primae originis innocentiam revoces, sed etiam ad experientiam quorumdam bonorum quae in novo saeculo sunt habenda perducas, et obstrictos adhuc conditione mortalium jam ad similitudinem provehas angelorum ; respice, Domine, super has famulas tuas quae in manu tua continentiae suae propositum collocantes, ei devotionem suam offerunt a quo ipsa vota sumserunt. Quando enim animus mortali carne circumdatus legem naturae, libertatem licentiae, vim consuetudinis et stimulos aetatis evinceret, nisi tu hanc flammam[2] clementer accenderes, tu hanc cupiditatem[3] benignus aleres, tu fortitudinem ministrares? Effusa namque in omnes gentes gratia tua ex omni natione

---

[1] Muratori, vol. i. p 444. That of the Gelasian Sacramentary (*ibid.* p. 629) is rather longer, as is pointed out farther on; that of the *Missale Francorum* is similar to that of the Gelasian Sacramentary, except for an omission of a few lines (vol ii. p. 674). In the supplements of the Gregorian Sacramentary (vol. ii. p. 184) we find a much shorter formulary, but derived from that of the Leonian, with a termination resembling that of the Gelasian Sacramentary and the *Missale Francorum.* This circumstance leads me to believe that the formulary has been shortened at the end in the Leonian Sacramentary.

[2] "*Hanc flammam* per liberum arbitrium hunc amorem virginitatis." *Gel. M. Fr.*

[3] "Cupiditatem in earum corde." *Gel. M. Fr.*

quae est sub caelo in stellarum innumerabilem numerum Novi Testamenti haeredibus adoptatis, inter ceteras virtutes, quas filiis tuis non ex sanguinibus neque ex voluntate carnis sed de tuo Spiritu genitis indidisti, etiam hoc donum in quasdam mentes de largitatis tuae fonte defluxit. Ut cum honorem nuptiarum nulla interdicta minuissent ac super sanctum conjugium initialis benedictio permaneret, existerent tamen sublimiores animae quae in viri ac mulieris copula fastidirent connubium, concupiscerent sacramentum, nec imitarentur quod nuptiis agitur, sed diligerent quod nuptiis praenotatur. Agnovit auctorem suum beata virginitas, et aemula integritatis angelicae illius thalamo, illius cubiculo, se devovit, qui sic perpetuae virginitatis est sponsus quemadmodum perpetuae virginitatis est filius. Implorantibus ergo auxilium tuum, Domine, et confirmari se benedictionis tuae consecratione cupientibus, da protectionis tuae munimen et regimen: ne hostis antiquus qui excellentiora studia subtilioribus infestat insidiis ad obscurandam perfectae continentiae palmam per aliquam serpat mentis incuriam, et rapiat de proposito virginum quod etiam moribus decet inesse nuptarum. Sit in eis, Domine, per donum Spiritus tui, prudens modestia,[1] sapiens benignitas, gravis lenitas, casta libertas. In caritate ferveant et nihil extra te diligant; laudabiliter vivant, laudarique non appetant. Te in sanctitate corporis, te in animi sui puritate glorificent. Amore te timeant, amore tibi serviant. Tu eis honor sis, tu gaudium, tu voluntas, tu in maerore solatium, tu in ambiguitate consilium, tu in injuria defensio, in tribulatione patientia, in paupertate abundantia in jejunio cibus, in infirmitate medicina. In te habeant omnia quem elegere super omnia.[2] Et quod sunt professae custodiant, scrutatori pectorum non corpore placiturae sed mente. Transeant in numerum sapientium puellarum; ut caelestem sponsum accensis lampadibus cum oleo praeparationis expectent, nec turbatae improvisi regis adventu praecedentium choro jungantur; occurrant, nec excludantur cum stultis; regalem januam cum sapientibus virginibus licenter introeant; et in Agni tui perpetuo comitatu probabiles mansura castitate permaneant.

2. *Gallican Use.*

The Gallican form is obtained by the comparison of those texts of undoubted Roman origin with the *Missale*

---

[1] What follows, as far as *elegere super omnia*, is wanting in the *Missale Francorum*.

[2] What follows is not found in the Gelasian Sacramentary and the *Missale Francorum*.

Francorum, which contains a mixture of the two forms, and with the *Missale Gallicanum Vetus*. The service began with a prayer, preceded by its invitatory [1]:—

> Faventes, dilectissimi Fratres, his virtutibus quas praestare paucorum est, Deum semper pudicitiae castitatisque custodem acceptis eidem precibus oremus, ut hanc famulam suam omnibus saeculi inlecebris liberam carnalibus ac spiritu integram, Regis aeterni thalamo reservandam addita caelestis propositi virtute corroboret, et ad sexagesimum fructum quem propria devotione praesumit addat sua liberalitate centesimum.
>
> Omnium quidem laudum atque virtutum sed praecipue castitatis adsertor, custos, auxiliator, effector dicatae tibi in sanctis corporibus pariter ac mentibus puritatis; qui virginitatem ideo plus intueris et diligis quia tibi origo virginitas; quique in hunc mundum natus ex virgine id in aliis probas quod in matre elegisti, atque adeo aptissime tibi sponso viro sponsam virginem dedicamus; tu, Domine, tribue hanc puellae jam tuae semper optabilem magno proposito perseverantiam, et contra multiformis inimici instantia spiritum agitantes insidias indeflexam inexpugnabilemque constantiam, ut tibi debeat consummatione quae jam ante habuit bona voluntate.

Then came the giving of the veil, accompanied by the benediction:—

> Accipe, puella, pallium, quod perferas sine macula ante tribunal domini nostri Jesu Christi, cui flectit omne genu caelestium et terrestrium et infernorum.
>
> Benedicat te conditor caeli et terrae, Deus Pater omnipotens, qui te eligere dignatus est ad instar   nctae Mariae matris Domini nostri Jesu Christi ad integram et immaculatam virginitatem, quam professa es coram Deo et angelis sanctis. Idcirco serva propositum, serva castitatem per patientiam, ut coronam virginitatis tuae accipere merearis. Nunc exoro

---

[1] I give here the formulary of the *Missale Gallicanum Vetus*, Muratori, vol ii p. 701. In the *Missale Francorum* (*ibid.*, p 673) the Roman canon *Deus castorum* is preceded by a formulary of similar import, but having the invitatory placed after the prayer.

domini nostri Jesu Christi divinam misericordiam ut hanc virginem consecrare ac sanctificare dignetur usque in finem. Benedicat te Deus Pater et Filius et Spiritus sanctus omni benedictione spiritali, ut maneas sine macula sub vestimento sanctae Mariae matris domini nostri Jesu Christi.

CHAPTER XIV.

THE NUPTIAL BLESSING.

TERTULLIAN[1] extols the happiness of that marriage which is cemented by the Church, confirmed by the oblation, sealed with the benediction, which the angels proclaim, and which is ratified by the Heavenly Father. Many other ancient writers also speak of marriages celebrated before the Church and blessed by her with more or less solemnity. No ecclesiastical law, however, obliged Christians to seek a blessing on their marriage. The benediction was a matter of custom or propriety, and although it subsequently became the rule, it was never a condition of validity. The marriage is independent of the rite.

The rite has been subjected to many variations, according to the times and countries in which it was celebrated.[2] Nothing can be gleaned on this point either from the *Ordines* or from the ancient liturgical books, except the prayers of the nuptial Mass and those of the nuptial blessing. We must come down as far as the time of Pope Nicolas I. to find a description with any details of the

---

[1] *Ad Uxor.*, ii. 9.

[2] The Roman ritual now in use, after having given a minimum of ceremonies and formularies, adds that, if there are any other praiseworthy customs or ceremonies in this or that country, the Council of Trent desires that they should be retained

rites of marriage in the Latin Church.[1] The description occurs in his celebrated conference with the Bulgarians, held in 866. The acts which he mentions are divided into two categories, those which precede and those which accompany the *nuptialia foedera*. The first category contains—

1. The betrothal, or espousal (*sponsalia*), the expression of the consent of the couple to be married and of their parents, to the projected marriage.

2. The *subarrhatio*, or delivery of the ring by the bridegroom to the bride.

3. The delivering over of the dowry, by written document, in the presence of witnesses.

These are the preliminaries. The marriage ceremony itself comprises—

1. The celebration of Mass in the presence of the newly married, who take part in the offering and are communicated.

2. The benediction pronounced while a veil is held above their heads.

3. The coronation on leaving the church.[2]

---

[1] *Responsa ad consulta Bulgarorum*, c 3: "Post *sponsalia*, quae futurarum sunt nuptiarum promissa foedera, quaeque consensu eorum qui haec contrahunt et eorum in quorum potestate sunt celebrantur, et postquam *arrhis* sponsam sibi sponsus per digitum fidei a se annulo insignitum desponderit, *dotem* utrique placitam sponsus ei cum scripto pactum hoc continente coram invitatis ab utraque parte tradiderit, aut mox aut apto tempore . . . ambo ad nuptialia foedera perducuntur. Et primum quidem in ecclesia Domini cum oblationibus quas offerre debent Deo per sacerdotis manum statuuntur, sicque demum benedictionem et velamen caeleste suscipiunt . . . Verumtamen velamen illud non suscipit qui ad secundas nuptias migrat. Post haec autem de ecclesia egressi coronas in capitibus gestant, quae semper in ecclesia ipsa sunt solitae reservari. Et ita festis nuptialibus celebratis, ad ducendam individuam vitam Domino disponente de caetero diriguntur" The Pope goes on to say that nothing of all this is essential to the marriage, that consent is sufficient, and is the only thing indispensable.

[2] The Pope takes note that these crowns are usually kept in the church. No doubt care was taken to prevent the wearing of crowns which had been profaned by some superstitious use.

All these rites are still found in modern uses. The nuptial ceremony at the present time comprises the ceremonies of the betrothal, as well as those of marriage properly so called. It begins by the declaration of consent, which, as the marriage follows immediately after, has here the character of an engagement *de praesenti*.[1] The contracting parties, interrogated by the priest, publicly express their intention of being united in marriage. Then follows the *subarrhatio*, performed by the bridegroom, with a ring previously blessed, followed, in many places, by the conveyance of the dowry, represented by a medal or piece of money.

The whole of this constitutes the ancient ritual of the betrothal, which formerly took place in the family circle, and without the intervention of the priest. As to the ritual of the marriage itself, the present use and that of the ninth century both agree with that implied in the most ancient liturgical books. The nuptial Mass is met with in all the Roman Sacramentaries.[2] The formularies of the prayers in them are naturally suited to the circumstances. It should be remarked that they presuppose the oblation to be made for the bride. The following is that of the *Hanc igitur* in the Leonian Sacramentary[3]:—

---

[1] At this point, in the Middle Ages, occurred the formulary *Ego conjungo vos in matrimonium*, etc, which is, as may be seen, a sort of interpolation in the primitive ceremony. This formulary, of which the literal sense goes beyond the fact, has considerably contributed to a false idea of the nature of the religious marriage, and has given rise to the belief that the matrimonial tie depends on the authority of the priest. The Council of Trent (*Sess.* xxiv, *De ref. mar.*, c 1) mentions it without enforcing its use.

[2] The Gallican books give no Mass I find in them merely a *benedictio thalami super nubentes*, comprising an invitatory and a prayer, in the Bobbio Sacramentary (Murat., ii. p 956)

[3] Cf. the formularies of the Gelasian Sacramentary (Murat. i. p 722) and of the Gregorian Sacramentary (added part, *ibid.*, vol ii. p. 245).

Hanc igitur oblationem famulae tuae *illius*, quam tibi offerimus pro famula tua *illa*, quaesumus, Domine, placatus aspicias; pro qua majestatem tuam supplices exoramus, ut sicut eam ad aetatem nuptiis congruentem pervenire tribuisti, sic consortio maritali tuo munere copulatam desiderata sobole gaudere perficias, atque ad optatam seriem cum suo conjuge provehas benignus annorum.

The nuptial benediction takes place after the *Pater noster*, before the fraction of the consecrated bread. A veil is held over the bride and bridegroom, and the officiating minister recites, first a simple prayer, then one of *Eucharistic* character.

Adesto,[1] Domine, supplicationibus nostris, et institutis tuis quibus propagationem humani generis ordinasti benignus assiste; ut quod te auctore jungitur te auxiliante servetur.

Vere dignum. . . . Pater,[2] mundi conditor, nascentium genitor, multiplicandae originis institutor; qui Adae comitem tuis manibus addidisti, cujus ex ossibus ossa crescentia parem formam admirabili diversitate signarent. Hinc ad totius multitudinis incrementum conjugalis thori jussa consortia, quo totum inter se saeculum colligarent, humani generis foedera nexuerunt. Sic enim tibi placitum necessario; ut quia longe esset infirmius quod homini simile quam quod tibi deo feceras, additus fortiori sexus infirmior unum efficeret ex duobus, et pari pignore soboles mixta manaret, dum per ordinem flueret digesta posteritas, ac priores ventura sequerentur, nec ullum sibi finem in tam brevi termino quamvis essent caduca proponerent. Ad haec igitur venturae hujus famulae tuae, Pater, rudimenta sanctifica, ut bono et prospero sociata consortio legis aeternae jura custodiat. Memineritque se, Domine, non tantum ad licentiam conjugalem sed ad observantiam Dei sanctorumque pignorum custodiae delegatam. Fidelis et casta nubat in Christo, imitatrixque sanctarum permaneat feminarum. Sit amabilis ut Rachel viro, sapiens ut Rebecca, longaeva et fidelis ut Sarra. Nihil ex hac subcisivus ille auctor praevaricationis usurpet; nixa fidei mandatisque permaneat; muniat infirmitatem suam robore disciplinae; uni thoro juncta contactus vitet illicitos. Sit verecundia gravis, pudore venerabilis, doctrinis caelestibus erudita. Sit fecunda in sobole, sit probata et innocens, et ad beatorum requiem atque ad caelestia regna perveniat.

---

[1] Leonian Sacramentary, Muratori, vol i. p. 446.
[2] Leonian and Gelasian Sacramentaries, *ll. cc.*

This ceremony is the principal religious rite. It is by the name of the *velatio nuptialis* that the nuptial benediction is known in the old Leonian Sacramentary; at the end of the fourth century Pope Siricius[1] speaks of the *velatio conjugalis*. St. Ambrose[2] says also that the marriage ought to be sanctified *velamine sacerdotali et benedictione*. Not long since it was still the custom in France to hold the veil (*pallium, paleum, poêle*) extended over the married pair during the blessing, but this custom, not being mentioned in the Roman ritual, is fast disappearing.[3]

The coronation of the newly wedded, which still occupies such an important place in the Greek rite, has also been given up in the West.

I have already stated that the old Merovingian books do not contain the marriage rite. The Gallican use, however, has, I believe, left a trace of it in the later Missals, in the benediction which is pronounced over the bride and bridegroom after the communion.[4] Of the three ancient Roman Sacramentaries, the Gelasian, in which we so often find Gallican prayers, is the only one which contains a formulary of this nature. We have seen, moreover, that benedictions at the time of communion form an important feature in the Gallican liturgical system. The following is the formulary in the Gelasian Sacramentary:—

---

[1] Decretal at Himera, c. 4.
[2] *Ep*, xix. 7.
[3] This is one of those ancient Roman rites which were better preserved in France than in Italy, and which disappeared when the modern Roman use was of late years adopted.
[4] The formulary *Deus Abraham* . . . is now pronounced after the *Ite missa est*, at the moment prescribed for the blessing of the people in the Roman use. In the Gelasian Sacramentary the benediction of the newly married is placed immediately after the communion, before the prayer *post communionem*.

Domine sancte, Pater omnipotens, aeterne Deus, iteratis precibus te supplices exoramus, pro quibus apud te supplicator est Christus: coniunctiones famulorum tuorum fovere digneris, benedictiones tuas excipere mereantur, et filiorum successibus fecundentur. Nuptias eorum sicuti primi hominis confirmare dignare; avertantur ab eis inimici omnes insidiae, ut sanctitatem Patrum etiam in ipso coniugio imitentur, qui providentia tua, Domine, coniungi meruerunt.

It is interesting to note that the nuptial ritual described by Pope Nicolas is neither more nor less than the ancient Roman marriage rite, without the sacrifice, or rather with the substitution of the Mass for the pagan sacrifice. The Romans themselves distinguished between the preliminary engagement or betrothal and the nuptial ceremony proper. Their rite began by the mutual engagement, which was contracted by both parties in presence of each other in a set form of words. This engagement was marked by the delivery of the ring, or *subarrhatio;* then followed the drawing up of the marriage contract, accompanied by gifts from the bridegroom to the bride. All this took place in the presence of the friends of the family, who were afterwards entertained at a banquet.

On the morning of the marriage the gods were at first consulted by the taking of auspices. At a later date the divination of the haruspex, which presupposed a sacrifice, was substituted for the auspices. On the previous evening the woman had laid aside her maiden dress and had assumed the garments of a bride. Her head was covered with the *flammeum,* or red-coloured veil, which, with the exception of the colour, was the same as that worn by all married women. It is from this *obnubilatio capitis* that the terms *nubere, nuptiae, nuptials,* are derived. The bride's hair was divided into six plaits, and her head crowned with flowers which she herself had gathered. A similar floral crown was also worn by the bridegroom.

The invited guests having assembled, the haruspices came to announce the result of their divinations. The bride and bridegroom then expressed their consent to the union, and the contract was signed (*tabulae nuptiales*); the *pronuba* then caused them to take each other's hands. At this point came the unbloody sacrifice of the *confarreatio*, an offering of fruits and of a wheaten loaf. While this was proceeding, the married couple were seated on two chairs bound together and covered with the skin of the sheep which had been slaughtered for the divination. While the priest recited the prayer the bride and bridegroom made the circuit of the altar, walking towards the right. A bloody sacrifice then took place, an ox or a pig being immolated on the altar of a temple. The guests then shouted *Feliciter!* and the bride's father gave a great feast. At nightfall the bride was conducted with much ceremony to the house of her husband.

From this cursory description it will be evident that, with the exception of the rites of a purely religious character, especially those of the haruspex and the sacrifices, the whole of the Roman marriage ritual has been preserved in the Christian ceremony. Even the *flammeum* and the crowns have found their place in it. This instance of the adoption of a pagan custom does not stand alone. Essentially conservative, the Church in these matters merely modified that which was incompatible with her faith.

CHAPTER XV.

THE RECONCILIATION OF PENITENTS.

SINNERS who had been excluded by ecclesiastical authority from the society of the faithful, either for faults which they themselves had acknowledged to the Church with more or less publicity, or which had been brought home to them in some other manner, could only regain admission by the way of penance. The first step in that direction was the petition for rehabilitation, that is to say, for admission into the number of the penitents. It was not easily granted; sometimes, even when it was accorded, the penitent was given to understand that the expiation for his fault must be continued till the day of his death. It was never granted more than once to the same individual. Throughout the whole time of his penance the sinner had to live under much the same conditions as the professed ascetics. He could neither marry nor fulfil the conditions of a marriage already contracted. He had to renounce his military or ecclesiastical career, as the case might be, as well as participation in public functions; he was made to practise austerities in eating, drinking, dress, and in the use of the bath; he had to be frequently at church, and his life, in short, was that of a monk. The whole difference between the state of a monk in the world and that of a penitent lay in the fact that a monk had freely chosen his manner of life, whereas for the penitent it was a condition of rehabilitation.[1]

Such was the discipline with regard to offenders in the fourth and fifth centuries, but it was not long before it was mitigated and so modified that, except in extremely rare cases, the penance lost all its external formalities, and ceased to have any place assigned to it in public worship.

In early times it had its accompanying ritual, the forms of which closely resembled those of Christian initiation. The penitent was regarded in the main as a Christian who had lost his initiation and was labouring to recover it. Penance was, as it were, a beginning again of the novitiate, or the catechumenate, except that the questionings, the scrutinies, and the exorcisms were replaced by ascetic exercises. Just as there was a *doctor audientium,* or head catechist, assisted by a staff of exorcists, so there was, in certain churches, at all events, a penitentiary priest, with clerks under him, who were entrusted with the care of the penitents, and were responsible for the sincerity of their expiation. In church, the penitents, like the catechumens, constituted a group by themselves, and were dismissed at the same time as the latter, that is, before the celebration of the holy mysteries. When at length their time of probation

---

[1] It should be noted that the monastic state did not, like the penitent, preclude the taking of Holy Orders. The three or four stages of penitential discipline in the East were never observed in Latin countries (Funk, *Theol. Quartalschrift,* 1886, p 373, *et seq.*). We may even question, if in the East they were of universal observance. The Apostolic Constitutions and Canons do not mention them, neither does the Council of Antioch (341) nor St. John Chrysostom. In Syria we see, both by the writings of St. John Chrysostom and Book II. of the Apostolic Constitutions, that great leniency was shown towards penitent sinners. The Constitutions (ii. 16) assign, in proportion to the offence, a greater or lesser duration for the penitential exercises; but the maximum length of time is seven weeks. This duration is that of the Oriental Lent, and also of that apparently observed in Rome during the seventh century. Cf. *infra,* p. 438.

was ended, they were solemnly readmitted into the body of the faithful, just as they had been solemnly introduced into it at the time of their baptismal initiation. There was even a coincidence of time in the two ceremonies, for both took place immediately before the Easter festival.

But few traces have come down to us from these early times of the ritual in use for the admission to the number of the penitents. It was necessary first to have acknowledged the faults for which the penance was sought. We gather from the life of St. Hilary of Arles[1] († 447) that the bishop gave an address, laid his hands on the penitents, and recited a prayer. The Council of Agde (506) also mentions the imposition of hands,[2] to which was added the giving of the hair-shirt. After this ceremony, the penitents were obliged to wear mourning, the form of which differed according to the customs of the country in which they lived.[3]

At Rome, the purely unmixed liturgical books, that is, the Leonian Sacramentary and that of Adrian, are absolutely silent with regard to the penitential rites.[4] The Gelasian Sacramentary takes for granted that, at the beginning of Lent, the penitents entered a monastery, which they did not quit till Maundy Thursday.[5]

---

[1] III. 17.

[2] "Paenitentes, tempore quo paenitentiam petunt, impositionem manuum et cilicium super caput a sacerdote, sicut ubique constitutum est, consequantur" (can 15)

[3] In Gaul, by shaving the head (Council of Agde, *loc cit.*); in Spain both hair and beard were allowed to grow (Isidore, *De Eccl. Off.*, ii. 17).

[4] In the Leonian Sacramentary, this may be owing to the mutilation of the manuscript.

[5] It may well be asked, seeing the silence of the two other Sacramentaries on the subject, if we are not here confronted with a ritual which is Gallican rather than Roman. But this hypothesis is set aside by the diction of the prayers, and by the mention of the Wednesday *in capite jejunii*, which, at the time of the transcription of the Gelasian Sacramentary, was still characteristic of Roman usage.

On the Wednesday[1] *in capite jejunii,* which we now call Ash Wednesday,[2] the penitent presented himself before the priest in the early morning, that is, before the procession to the stational Mass, and received from him a hair-shirt, in which he was clothed during the recital of a prayer, the text of which is not given. This is in the main the same ceremony as that prescribed by the Council of Agde. There is no reason to doubt that in Rome this ceremony may not have been in use much earlier than the seventh century. The more modern element in it is the choice of Ash Wednesday for its performance, and also the seclusion of the penitent in a monastery. As late as the middle of the fifth century the penitents at Rome were left to themselves, and were neither secluded nor subjected to official supervision.[3]

The custom of seclusion naturally obviated the solemn dismissal of the penitents (*missa paenitentium*) at the public Mass. The Latin Sacramentaries have preserved no vestige of this usage, but in the Greek books, and especially in the Apostolic Constitutions, it is otherwise, for in them we note the group of penitents, present

---

[1] *Sacram. Gel*, i 16. *Ordo agentibus publicam paenitentiam Suscipis eum IIII. feria mane, in capite Quadragesimae, et cooperis eum cilicio, oras pro eo et inclaudis usque ad Caenam Domini Qui eodem die in gremio praesentatur ecclesiae; et prostrato eo omni corpore in terra, dat orationem pontifex super eum ad reconciliandum, in quinta feria Caenae Domini, sicut ibi continetur.*

[2] Neither the Gelasian Sacramentary nor the *Ordo I.* of Mabillon, which describes the station of the Wednesday *in capite jejunii*, mentions the benediction or the imposition of ashes; but the existing ceremony is given at length in the *Ordines* of the twelfth century. It corresponds with a wider conception of penance All the faithful, clergy and laity, adopt the attitude of penitents for the Lenten season, and receive the imposition of ashes, which are, like the hair-shirt, the symbol of a state of penitence. Such an idea, particularly in relation to the clergy, is irreconcilable with the ancient penitentiary legislation observed in Rome down to the ninth century.

[3] Sozomen, *H. E.*, vii. 16.

at the beginning of the meeting, as coming forward at the summons of the deacon, and as leaving the sacred building after a special prayer, followed by the bishop's blessing. This custom was still observed at Rome in the middle of the fifth century, as we have Sozomen's[1] express authority for this.

The final ceremony—that of reconciliation—is found in the Gelasian Sacramentary,[2] with very copious formularies.

By the help of this text we can imagine ourselves at Rome on Maundy Thursday, the day specially set apart in that city for the reconciliation of penitents.[3] Mass begins without any singing—that is to say, without the chanting of the Introit[4]—and without the Pope's salutation of the congregation by the *Dominus vobiscum*. He recites an introductory prayer,[5] after which a deacon brings before him the penitents,[6] who prostrate themselves full length in the centre of the church. The deacon then addresses the Pope as follows:—

Adest, o venerabilis pontifex, tempus acceptum, dies propitiationis divinae et salutis humanae, qua mors interitum et vita accepit aeterna principium, quando in vinea Domini Sabaoth sic novorum plantatio

---

[1] *Loc cit.* Cf *supra*, p 171.

[2] I. 38 · " *Orat in quinta feria.* Eodem die non psallitur, nec salutat, id est non dicit *Dominus vobiscum;* et reconciliatio paenitentis." Three prayers follow, then: " *Ordo agentibus publicam paenitentiam* Egreditur paenitens de loco ubi paenitentiam gessit et in gremio praesentatur ecclesiae, prostrato omni corpore in terra, et postulat in his verbis diaconus "

[3] Letter of Innocent to Decentius, c. 7; cf. *Lib Pont*, vol 1 p. cxi.

[4] The *Kyrie Eleison* is no doubt suppressed because it comes so shortly after; the same applies to the *Gloria in excelsis*. All these details, more or less definitely given, are contradicted by the *Ordines* of the ninth century, which imply that the Mass began in the usual way. The latter contain, moreover, no vestige of the reconciliation of penitents on Maundy Thursday. It is possible that this ceremony may have been abandoned in the course of the eighth century.

[5] The Gelasian Sacramentary gives three different forms of it, which are evidently alternatives.

[6] The rubric and the formularies are always in the singular.

facienda est ut purgetur et curatio (?) vetustatis. Quamvis enim a divitiis bonitatis et pietatis Dei nihil temporis vacet, nunc tamen et largior est per indulgentiam remissio peccatorum et copiosior per gratiam adsumptio renascentium. Augemur regenerandis, crescimus reversis; lavant aquae, lavant lacrymae; inde gaudium de adsumptione vocatorum, hinc laetitia de absolutione paenitentium. Inde est quod supplex tuus, postea quam in varias formas criminum neglectu mandatorum caelestium et morum probabilium transgressione cecidit, humiliatus atque prostratus prophetica ad Deum voce clamat, dicens: *Peccavi, impie egi, iniquitatem feci, miserere mei Domine*, evangelicam vocem non frustratoria aure capiens: *Beati qui lugent, quoniam ipsi consolabuntur.* Manducavit, sicut scriptum est, panem doloris; lacrymis stratum rigavit; cor suum luctu, corpus adflixit jejuniis, ut animae suae reciperet quam perdiderat sanitatem. Unicum itaque est paenitentiae suffragium, quod et singulis prodest et omnibus in commune succurrit. Hic ergo dum ad paenitudinis actionem tantis excitatur exemplis, sub conspectu ingemiscentis ecclesiae, venerabilis Pontifex, protestatur et dicit: *Iniquitates meas ego agnosco et delictum meum contra me est semper. Averte faciem tuam a peccatis meis, Domine, et omnes iniquitates meas dele. Redde mihi laetitiam salutaris tui et spiritu principali confirma me.* Quo ita supplicante et misericordiam Dei adflicto corde poscente, redintegra in eo, apostolice Pontifex, quicquid diabolo scindente corruptum est; et orationum tuarum patrocinantibus meritis, per divinae reconciliationis gratiam fac hominem proximum Deo; ut qui antea in suis perversitatibus displicebat, nunc jam placere se Domino in regione vivorum [1] devicto mortis suae auctore gratuletur.

The Pope [2] then admonishes the penitent, either in person or through a priest, and after that recites a prayer, followed by another of Eucharistic character [3]—

Adesto, Domine, supplicationibus nostris et me, qui etiam misericordia tua primus indigeo, clementer exaudi; ut quem non electione

---

[1] Here the Sacramentary adds *cum*, which has no sense

[2] *Post hoc admonetur ab episcopo sive alio sacerdote ut quod paenitendo diluit iterando non revocet. Inde vero has dicit orationes sacerdos super eum.*

[3] This part of the formulary is found among the supplements of the Gregorian Sacramentary (No. 99), the variants of which are noted on the next page.

meriti sed dono gratiae tuae constituisti operis hujus ministrum, da fiduciam tui muneris exequendi, et ipse in nostro ministerio quod tuae pietatis est operare.[1]

[Vere dignum . . . aeterne] Deus, humani generis benignissime conditor et misericordissime reformator; qui hominem invidia diaboli ab aeternitate dejectum unici Filii[2] tui sanguine redemisti, vivifica hunc famulum tuum[3] quem tibi nullatenus mori desideras, et qui non derelinquis devium, adsume correptum. Moveant pietatem tuam, quaesumus, Domine, hujus famuli tui lacrymosa suspiria. Tu ejus medere vulneribus, tu jacenti manum porrige salutarem, ne Ecclesia tua aliqua sui corporis portione vastetur, ne grex tuus detrimentum sustineat, ne de familiae tuae damno inimicus exultet, ne renatum lavacro salutari mors secunda possideat. Tibi ergo, Domine, supplices preces, tibi fletum cordis effundimus. Tu parce confitenti, ut[4] in imminentes paenas sententiamque futuri judicii te miserante non incidat. Nesciat quod terret in tenebris, quod stridet in flammis; atque ab erroris via ad iter reversus justitiae, nequaquam ultra novis vulneribus saucietur; sed integrum sit ei atque perpetuum et quod gratia tua contulit et quod misericordia reformavit.[5]

The Gallican books furnish us merely with a single prayer, with its invitatory, for the reconciliation of penitents. It is preserved at the end of the Bobbio Sacramentary,[6] but the manuscript is in a very bad condition. At the time when these books were drawn up, the penitential discipline, especially in Gaul, had been subjected to very considerable external modifications.[7]

I may here make a passing reference to an ancient

---

[1] There is a second prayer here; but the general character of the Roman ceremonies leads us to regard it as an alternative

[2] *Filii* supplied from the Gregorian Sacramentary.

[3] *Hunc famulum tuum* Greg : *itaque* Gel.

[4] *Ut . . . incidat*] Greg.: "Ut sic in hac mortalitate peccata sua te adjuvante defleat qualiter in tremendi judicii die sententiam damnationis aeternae evadat, et nesciat, etc."

[5] Here the Gelasian Sacramentary gives a fresh group of formularies, three prayers, and a Eucharistic prayer; these alternatives do not appear in the Gregorian supplement.

[6] Muratori, vol ii. p. 966

[7] For the variations of the penitential discipline in Gaul and in the British Isles, see Malnory, *Luxovienses Monachi*, p. 62, *et seq* (Paris, 1894).

office known as the ceremony of Indulgence, which took place in Spain on Good Friday, the same day on which apparently the solemn reconciliation of penitents was held from very early times at Milan.[1] This ceremony was prescribed by the fourth Council of Toledo (633),[2] and all the details of it are found in the Mozarabic Missal.

After a few preliminaries, among which are the reproaches, *Popule meus, quid feci tibi*, now forming part of our Good Friday service, the office begins by three lessons, one drawn from the Prophets (Isa. lii. 53), one from the Epistles (1 Cor. v. 6), and one from the Gospels. It was the Gallican custom, as we see also from the Lectionary of Luxeuil, to read the Passion from a composite text, a sort of *Diatessaron*, in which the narratives of the four evangelists were combined. This consecutive account was distributed between the various offices of Maundy Thursday and Good Friday. At the service of Indulgence this lection began by the words, *Mane autem facto, cena pura, consilium inierunt.*[3] After these lections followed the actual ceremony called the Indulgence.[4] Those present, who are indiscriminately described as penitents, are thrice invited to

---

[1] This follows, I think, from St. Ambrose's twentieth letter · "Erat autem dies quo sese Dominus pro nobis tradidit, quo in Ecclesia paenitentia relaxatur."

[2] Can. 6: "Oportet eodem die mysterium crucis, quod ipse Dominus cunctis annuntiandum voluit, praedicare atque indulgentiam criminum clara voce omnem populum postulare, ut paenitentiae compunctione mundati venerabilem diem dominicae Resurrectionis remissis iniquitatibus suscipere mereamur, corporisque ejus et sanguinis sacramentum mundi a peccato sumamus"

[3] Matt xxvii. 1. The words *cena pura*, which do not form part of the text of Holy Scripture, are a very ancient designation of Good Friday. They are met with in a book on the paschal computation drawn up at Rome in the fourth century (Krusch, *Der 84jahrige Ostercyclus*, p 234). The text *Mane autem facto* is assigned in the Luxeuil Lectionary to the office of *Secunda*, a morning office, corresponding to that of *Prime*, in the Roman hours.

[4] The *Liber Ordinum* itself contains this service, but it is not there given with such precision and clearness as in the Mozarabic Missal.

prostrate themselves and invoke the Divine mercy. The formularies preserved closely resemble that of the *Missa paenitentium* in the liturgy of the Apostolic Constitutions.

The archdeacon, then addressing the assembly, both clergy and laity, calls upon them to cry out, *Indulgentia!*[1] When these cries have ceased, the archdeacon directs the minds of all present to the "Good Shepherd who giveth His life for the sheep," and then invites them to unite in prayer. The bishop then begins a kind of rhythmical litany, to which the congregation respond by fresh cries of *Indulgentia!*

> Te precamur, Domine,—Indulgentia!
> Procedat ab Altissimo—Indulgentia!
> Succurrat nobis miseris—Indulgentia!
> Delicta purget omnibus—Indulgentia!
> Praestetur paenitentibus—Indulgentia!
> Patrona sit lugentibus—Indulgentia!
> Errantes fide corrigat—Indulgentia!
> Lapsos peccatis erigat—Indulgentia!
> Te deprecamur, Domine,—Indulgentia!

A prayer in the form of a collect follows, pronounced by the bishop in the name of all present, in which he appeals to the Divine mercy in favour of the penitents.

The cries of *Indulgentia* arise afresh, followed by the litany, and the bishop's prayer, with other formularies, but in the same order. This series being terminated, it is taken up a third time; but at the end of the latter the final prayer is omitted, and the service is continued by the Adoration of the Cross and the Mass of the Presanctified, much as in the present use.

---

[1] The rubric of the present Mozarabic Missal takes for granted that these cries are regulated, and not spontaneous; the first time they are not to be repeated more than three hundred times; the second, not more than two hundred; and the third, not more than one hundred times.

The ceremony of the Indulgence is easily separated from the other parts of the service. It comprises three acts: the prayer of the penitents themselves, the intercession of the congregation in their favour, the prayer addressed in his own person by the bishop to the Divine mercy. The liturgical books do not distinguish clearly between the penitents and the general body of the congregation. At the opening of the service every one[1] appears to be in the position of a penitent; but, later on, in that of an intercessor. But the parts must be distinguished if we wish to trace back this ritual to its primitive meaning. In early times the penitent could not re-enter the community of the faithful without their expressed consent. When it was not spontaneously manifested, it was the office of the bishop to evoke it. The scene is described in a passage of Tertullian[2] narrating the procedure of Pope Callixtus at the reconciliation of a repentant sinner—

"Thou dost usher into the church the penitent adulterer, who comes to petition the assembly of the faithful. Behold him, clad in a hair-shirt, covered with ashes, in garments of mourning such as to excite horror. He prostrates himself in the midst of the congregation, before the widows, before the priests. He lays hold on the hem of their garments, he kisses their footprints, he clasps them by the knees. Meanwhile, thou dost address the people, thou dost excite public pity for the sad lot of the suppliant. Good shepherd, blessed Pope, thou dost relate the parable of the lost sheep, that they may bring thee back thy wandering she-goat;[3] thou dost promise that it shall no more escape from the flock," etc.

[1] Compare this with what has been stated on p. 438, note 2, as to the origin of the ceremony of the Ashes.
[2] *De Pudicitia*, 13
[3] We must not forget that this description is a caricature. Tertullian, who was a bitter opponent of Pope Callixtus and his decree concerning penitence, is here doing his best to turn it into ridicule.

THE RECONCILIATION OF PENITENTS. 445

Between this picture and the ritual of the Mozarabic Missal there is the difference which in matters of this nature separates the third century from the sixth.[1] But the cries of *Indulgentia* which on Good Friday once rang through the Churches of the Visigothic kingdom are directly descended from the cries of pity which the persevering faithful of old times raised, either spontaneously, or at the exhortations of the bishop, when a repentant sinner came to beg for readmission into the Christian assembly.

[1] A theory has been put forward of late (Hugo Koch, *Theolog Quartalschrift*, 1900, p. 481) that the dismissal (*missa*) of the Penitents was never customary in the West. It is deduced from Sozomen and from the silence of Western documents. But, on the contrary, Sozomen clearly describes a *missa paenitentium* He shows us the penitents in the place set apart for them in the Church, and adds that they are dismissed πληρωθείσης τῆς τοῦ Θεοῦ λειτουργίας, μὴ μετασχόντες ὧν μύσταις θέμις In this expression, the accent must be put, I think, on the final words, which convey a distinction between the part of the service which is accessible to the initiated only, and that to which the non-initiated, that is the catechumens, are admitted. Thus the beginning of the phrase. "At the end of the Service" must apply to the mass of the catechumens Sozomen thus says the very opposite of what is attributed to him. Besides this the Canons of Agde (60), Epaone (39), Lyons (6), and of Valencia in Spain (1) prove that the *missa paenitentium* was still in use at the beginning of the sixth century

CHAPTER XVI.

THE DIVINE OFFICE.

WE have seen in Chapter VIII. what was the organisation of the ancient Church in regard to the sanctification of the week and the year. The meetings for worship on Sunday, Wednesday, Friday, and the festivals, with their nocturnal and diurnal services, did not exhaust all the pious resources of the faithful, nor even all their obligations. The ideal of the Christian life was that of a constant communion with God, maintained by as frequent prayer as possible. A Christian who did not pray every day and even frequently, would not have been considered a Christian at all. No doubt prayer in common, made collectively in the same place by the whole of the local Church, was confined to those days and hours fixed for assembly. But prayer could be made in private, apart from the stated times of meeting, either alone, or in the family, or in conjunction with friends and neighbours. The custom was established at an early date of devoting the last moments of the night, the time between cock-crow and sunrise, to private prayer, and also the end of the day, the gloomy hour when the sun disappears, when shadows fall, and the household lamps are lit. These were the fundamental prayers universally in use—the morning and evening prayer, or matins and vespers. During the day certain times were also singled out, either in accordance with Holy Scripture, or Jewish tradition, or even in agreement with the customs of ordinary and civil life. It was natural to take advantage of the moment when the family met together for the midday meal, and later on, when they again separated, to continue the avocations of their daily life. Two regular times of prayer were thus obtained—two *hours*, observed privately, but habitually. Others, calling to mind that Daniel prayed three times a day, concluded that it would be profitable to follow his example. The three hours were indicated in the Acts of the Apostles, where we see the disciples gathered together for prayer at the hour of *tierce*, when the Holy Spirit came upon them on the Day of Pentecost; St. Peter goes up to the roof of the house to pray, at the hour of *sext*, before partaking of his meal; and finally, the apostles Peter and John enter the temple for prayer at the hour of *none*. These hours, moreover, constituted the principal divisions of the day; they were observed for business, and were marked by the call of the city bells.[1]

It is from Tertullian that we learn the observance of these three "hours" of the day, and it is he who thus explains their origin. Clement of Alexandria was also aware[2] of this division of the Christian day. In his *Cathemerinon* Prudentius appears to take his inspiration from a somewhat different custom, that which I first described, but with the hours of matins and vespers doubled. There is a hymn for the hour when the cock crows, *Ales diei nuntius*, another for the dawn, *Nox et tenebrae et nubila;* others are written for before and after the midday meal, *O crucifer bone, lucis sator, Pastis visceribus ciboque sumpto;*

---

[1] *De Jejunio*, 10. Cf. Cyprian, *De Orat*, 34.
[2] *Strom.*, vii. 40.

and others for the evening, *Inventor rutili, dux bone luminis*,[1] and for the hour of sleep, *Ades Pater supreme*.

We must repeat again that these prayers, distributed over the course of the day in somewhat different fashions, are essentially private prayers. The bishop and the clergy, no doubt, were those who particularly observed them; but before the fourth century we do not see them transferred to the edifices where the public meetings of Sunday and the stational days were held. They are not the spiritual exercises of the community, that is, of the whole Christian community of a particular locality. In the fourth century the fact that they were adopted by the congregations of ascetics, that is, the monasteries, attracted special attention to them. There was no monastery that did not have its hours of prayer in common. As in many other matters, there were in this respect, at first, great differences between the religious houses themselves as well as between those of different countries.[2] In the fifth century the Egyptian monks had merely the two primitive hours of morning and evening, the *Gallicinium* and the *Lucernarium*. The monks of Syria and Mesopotamia met together, in addition to these, at the three day-hours of *tierce, sext*, and *none*. At Bethlehem, another office was added at the first hour of day, to prevent the monks from retiring to bed after the night office and sleeping during part of the morning. This custom spread beyond the town of its origination, and thus occasioned six hours being set apart for prayer. A verse of Psalm cxviii.,* in which the psalmist says to God that he prays to Him seven times a day, provides a sort of ideal which it was attempted to realise by making a distinction between the two parts of the office of Matins,

---

[1] It is a mistake to regard this daily prayer, as some have done, as a poem composed in honour of the paschal candle.

[2] For all this, see Book III. of the *Institutions* of Cassian.

* [Ps cxix. 164 of the Prayer-book version.—TR.]

the prayers at cock-crow and those at dawn (*Lauds*). At a much later date the same result was attained by the introduction of the office of Compline,[1] between the evening meal and the time of retiring to rest. It is the system of Prudentius combined with that of Tertullian.

The study of these diversities leads us into the special history of monastic discipline. A point of more general interest was the introduction of daily prayers into ecclesiastical use proper. The author of the Apostolic Constitutions insists even in his day that the bishop should require the faithful to attend the morning and evening offices, and even those of the three day-hours.[2] He takes for granted that these offices are said in the church, and that the bishop and his clergy take part in them. The Pilgrimage of Etheria (Silvia) furnishes very definite information on this point as far as the special usage of the Church of Jerusalem is concerned.[3] Except during Lent, when the hour of *tierce* was recited in public, there were four daily meetings in the Church of the Holy Sepulchre—at cockcrow, at *sext*, at *none*, and at vespers (*lucernarium*). The sacred edifice, which was not, be it remarked, the mother church or cathedral of Jerusalem, but merely a sanctuary of relatively restricted dimensions, was open to every one who wished to enter. As a matter of fact, the congregation was principally composed of ascetics of both sexes (*monazontes* and *parthenae*). These pious persons sang psalms, either according to the ancient method of responds, or by means of two choirs, antiphonally. Two or three

[1] This office has not any earlier attestation than the rule of St. Benedict. When once *compline* was admitted, it was possible, even by distinguishing Matins from Lauds, to point to the *Septies* IN DIE *laudem dixi tibi*, without reckoning Matins, which was a night office.

[2] II 59; viii. 34–39. In the first of these texts the day-hours do not yet come into question; the other text merely gives the formularies for morning and evening, while at the same time recommending the three hours of *tierce*, *sext*, and *none*

[3] See *infra*, pp. 492 and 547.

priests and as many deacons took their turn in reciting the prayers, for it was an understood thing that, in assemblies of a certain importance, the general prayers, litanies, and other devotions, could be conducted only by the higher clergy. Any other practice would have been considered somewhat perilous, from the standpoint of ecclesiastical unity. But this was not the only part taken by the clergy in the office of the ascetics. When the psalms, interrupted by prayers, were drawing to a close, the bishop and clergy entered the church. From this point onwards the service became definitely ecclesiastical. Prayers were said, first with the catechumens present, then with the faithful only, the catechumens being dismissed after a certain time, as in the liturgical Synaxes. The congregation did not break up without receiving the bishop's blessing, and it was even customary that all should kiss his hand before leaving the church.

On Sundays and festivals the ancient Synaxes were again resumed. The private office followed, and took place, if time permitted, in the interval between the Vigil and the Mass. At cock-crow all the clergy, headed by the bishop, were present at the night office, which was attended by far greater numbers than on week-days. At daybreak Mass was said in the great basilica (*Martyrium*) close to the Holy Sepulchre. The service was a very long one, so that there was only time after it for the *lucernarium*, *sext* and *none* having to be omitted.

It is needless to say that regular attendance at such frequent offices could not be expected of every one. St. J. Chrysostom[1] mentions some of the objections made on this score by the laity of his time. "Is it possible" (he makes his hearers say) "that a man of the world, engaged in the business of the tribunals, can be interrupted three times

[1] *Hom IV. de Anna*; Migne, *Pat. Gr.*, vol. liv. p. 667.

a day to go to church for prayer?" To which the saint replies, that it is possible to pray in private, wherever one may be. His words, however, testify to the fact, as do those of many other contemporary writers, that the offices were said daily in the churches, at the canonical hours, in the presence of the clergy and under their direction. This is the important point. Having once found a place in the church, private prayer was thenceforth to be retained in it. The isolated ascetics, and the virgins living in the world, soon disappeared or became attached to the monasteries, in the oratories of which the occupants performed their offices. The habit, however, had been formed. The faithful, although not attending them, felt it was right that the offices should be said by the clergy in their churches, and the clergy themselves were obliged to agree to the continuation of a practice, the regular performance of which was somewhat onerous, all the more so because in early times it had not been obligatory. The obligation to say the offices, like the duty of celibacy, was a legacy left to the clergy by asceticism. We might almost say that, on these two points, a sort of tacit agreement had been arrived at. The popularity enjoyed by the "perfect," the *continentes*, the "men of God," as they were called, had been, and continued to be, so great, that the right of the clergy to direct the Christian communities might have been called into question, had not the latter hastened to adopt, in its main features, the curriculum of the monks, and thus stopped short in a decisive and visible manner in the downward path of general relaxation.

Thus was laid upon the clergy the obligation of saying the canonical offices, both day and night, in the public churches, in the cathedrals of the towns, and the parish churches of the country. Great variety, however, existed in the precise arrangement of these offices,—in the distribution of the psalms, antiphons and responds, in the prayers, litanies or "collects," even in the lections, and the hours of saying the offices and the times of the year to be observed. In these, as in the primitive services for Sundays and the stations, the suffragan churches followed the usage of the great metropolitan cathedrals. Provincial councils did their best to regulate the details and obtain some sort of uniformity. On the other hand, the order of the offices constituted one of the principal features of the monastic rules. The important religious houses followed on this point the rules which they had adopted; others accepted the diocesan or provincial usage, as laid down by the bishops. In the West, down to the ninth century, there existed no uniformity in this sphere. When at length uniformity was arrived at, it was due to the influence of the Benedictine rule, and specially [1] to that of the great Roman monasteries which had sprung up around the basilicas of the Lateran, the Vatican, and Santa Maria Maggiore. These eventually became chapters, first of regular, then of secular monks, but they represented in the main the *principium et fons* of the whole Latin development of ecclesiastical and monastic offices.[2]

[1] I shall confine myself to pointing out a few facts which may be of interest to those who study the ancient office books At Rome, at all events down to the twelfth century, hymns were still unknown, chants, psalms, and other Scriptural canticles alone being used. The lections, at first reserved for the ancient services of the Vigil and the Mass, were not introduced into the offices until some time had elapsed, *i.e.* about the seventh century. The offices, therefore, were entirely composed of psalms, antiphons and responds, and prayers. This primitive Roman usage agrees exactly with what was observed at Jerusalem in the time of Etheria (Silvia). The rule of St. Benedict, on the other hand, admits of hymns and lections. See the letter of Theodemar, Abbot of Monte Cassino, to Charlemagne, in Jaffé, *Monum Carolina*, p. 360; cf. *Lib. Pont*, vol. i. p. 231, note 1, where I have made the mistake of placing the responds of the offices in the category of later additions.

[2] This applies, of course, to times posterior to the seventh century in the case of Gaul, and to the tenth and eleventh in the case of Spain.

It will be easily understood that, when confronted with so vast a subject, I have been obliged to abstain from entering upon it in detail, and can touch upon it only superficially.[1]

In these countries, we must take note of an indigenous development, which took its rise under the direct influence of the Oriental uses, and which owed little to that of the Roman monasteries.

[1] Among the books in which parts of this subject have been treated of late, I may mention *Histoire du Bréviaire Romain*, by Mgr. Battifol, and the *Geschichte des Romischen Breviers*, by the lamented Dom Suitbert Baeumer.

APPENDIX.

1.

THE ROMAN "ORDINES" FROM THE MANUSCRIPT OF ST. AMAND.

THE manuscript of the ninth century (*Parisinus* 974), from which I have taken these texts, contains the following treatises of St. Augustine: *De libero arbitrio et gratia Dei libri II.; Altercatio Feliciani arriani et beati Augustini, liber I.; De praedestinatione, liber I.* The *provenance* of the manuscript is St. Amand en Puelle, as is shown by the following note, written at the end: *Almae ecclesiae sancti Amandi in Pabula liber.* Before and after the text of St. Augustine, a few blank sheets remained, and advantage was taken of these for transcribing the *Ordines*.

These are drawn up in vulgar Latin (*non grammatico sermone*), which would, if the writer were a Frankish clerk, make them of a date anterior to 800 or thereabouts. If it were a Roman clerk who transcribed them, then the date might be rather later. The manuscript is certainly not an original. It is a copy from an original which was full of abbreviations, all of which have not been deciphered by the copyist with equal skill. I reproduce it as it stands, with the exception of a few manifest errors which were easily corrected; in these cases the reading of the manuscript is given at the bottom of the page.

I.

In nomine Domini nostri Jesu Christi incipit ordo qualiter in sancta atque apostolica ecclesia Romana missa caelebratur, quam nos cum summo studio atque cum diligentia maxima curavimus, non grammatico sermone, sed aperte loquendo veritatem indicare, id est qualiter pontifex procedit in die sollemni cum honore magno; sicut investigatum est a sanctis patribus.

Primitus enim procedit omnis clerus ad ecclesiam vel omnis populus ubi missa caelebranda est, et ingreditur pontifex in sacrario et induit se vestimentis sacerdotalibus. Quando dalmaticas induit, et diaconi similiter induunt se, et subdiaconi involvunt se anagolagio circa collo et induunt se tonicas albas quales habent, sericas aut lineas. Et si pontifex dalmaticas non induerit, diaconi vel subdiaconi non se involvunt anagolagio, sed cum tonicis albis et planitis ambulant. Et interim dum pontifex sedit in sacrario in sede sua, custodit evangelium diaconus qui eum lecturus est, et postea tradit ad subdiaconum. Deinde portans eum subdiaconus per medium presbiterio, et non presumat sedere quisquam quando eum viderint pretereuntem; et pertransiens subdiaconus ponat eum super altare. Et interim stat quartus de scola ante pontificem et dicit [I] ad subdiacono regionario [II]: "Talis psallit responsorium et talis Alleluia." Deinde dicit pontifex scolae: "Intrate." Et renuntiat ad primum scole, et dicit: "Jubete." Deinde venit subdiaconus suprascriptus ad auriculam pontificis et dicit secreto: "Talis legit, talis et talis psallit."

(i) diaconus.
(ii) regionaria.

Deinde oblationarius inluminat duos cereos ante secretario pro luminaria pontificis,[1] quod est consuetudo omni tempore, et antecaedit ante pontificem,[ii] et ponit eos retro altare, in duo candelabra, dextra levaque. Deinde inluminant acolithi cereostata [iii] ante secrarium et aegreditur pontifex de secrario cum diaconibus, tenentes eum duo dextra levaque, et VII. caereostata procaedunt ante eum et subdiaconus[1] temperita [iv] cum thimiamasterium ante pontificem. Et ipsi diaconi planitas habeant indutas super dalmaticas, usque dum venerint cum pontifice ad summum presbiterium. Et cum introierint, exuent planitas quas habent, et recipiunt eas ministri ipsorum. Et dum viderit subdiaconus primus de scola eos expoliare et pontificem introeuntem in presbiterio, expoliat se planita qua est indutus, et recipit eam accolitus de scola. Et surgunt sacerdotes et stant. Et subdiaconi qui antecaedunt pontificem non transeant per medium scolae, sed dextra levaque stantes subtus cancello, hinc et inde. Et cum adpropinquaverit pontifex scola, stant ibi acolithi cum cereostata, mutantes, novissimi primi. Et transit pontifex cum diaconis per mediam scolam, et annuit primo [v] scolae ut dicatur *Gloria*. Et venit prior episcopus et prior presbiter; dat eis pacem pontifex, deinde et ad diaconos.[vi] Et si pontifex minime fuerit, similiter dat diaconus pacem qui ipsa diae lecturus est evangelium. Deinde psallit[2] ante altare, et stat inclinato capite et diaconi similiter. Dum dixerit scola *Sicut erat in principio*, erigunt se diaconi ab

        (i) pontifex.
        (ii) pontifex.
        (iii) ceor.
        (iv) teperita.
        (v) primum.
        (vi) diaconum.

[1] The subdeacon *temperita* reappears later on. I do not know the meaning of this qualification.

[2] In this text the verb *psallere*, besides its ordinary meaning to chant a psalm, signifies here to ascend.

oratione, et osculant altare hinc et inde. Et dum dixerit scola versum ad repetendum, surgit pontifex ab oracione et osculat evangelium qui est super altare, et vadit de dextra parte altaris ad sedem suam, et diaconi cum ipso hinc et inde stantes et aspicientes contra orientem.[1]

Deinde ponunt acolithi cereostata quas tenent in terram. Et dum compleverit scola antiphonam, annuit pontifex ut dicatur *Kyrie eleison*. Et dicit scola et repetunt regionarii [2] qui stant subtus ambone. Dum repetierunt tertio, iterum annuit pontifex ut dicatur *Christae eleison*. Et dicto tertio, iterum annuit ut dicatur *Kirie eleison*. Et dum compleverint novem vicibus, annuit ut finiantur. Et respiciens pontifex ad populum dicit *Gloria in excelsis Deo* et revolvit se ad orientem et diaconi cum ipso, usque dum expletur *Gloria in excelsis Deo*. Hunc expleto, respicit populum et dicit: *Pax vobis*. Respondetur: *Et cum spiritu tuo*. Deinde *Oremus*. Leventur acolithi caereostata et ponunt ea ante altare, sicut ordinem habent.

Oracione expleta, sedet pontifex in sede sua et diaconi stant hinc et inde. Et revertit scola subtus tabula qui est subtus ambone, et subdiaconi qui stant subtus cancellum psallunt circa altare ex utraque parte. Et annuit pontifex ut sedeant sacerdotes in presbyterio. Deinde legitur lectio a subdiacono in ambone, stans [3] in medium de scola, aut acolithus planita et accipit cantorium et psallit in ambone et dicit responsorium; similiter et alius *Alleluia*.

Hoc expleto, inclinat se diaconus ad pontificem, et jubet pontifex ut legatur evangelium; et vadit ad altare, et osculat

---

[1] On condition, it must be understood, that the Church lends itself to this orientation. This is the case with the two basilicas of the Lateran and the Vatican, but not with those of Santa Maria Maggiore, St. Paul, and many others.

[2] The region-defenders.

[3] The text is here corrupt Cf. the *Ordo* of Mabillon: *Subdiaconus... ascendit in ambonem et legit. Postquam legerit, cantor cum cantatorio ascendit et dicit responsum*. In our text some words are wanting; I think that the cantor was here requested to put off his planeta before mounting the ambo.

aevangelium et accipit eum. Deinde surgit pontifex a sede seu
[sua?—Tr.] et omnes sacerdotes stantes. Et antecedunt eum duo
subdiaconi, unus dextra parte, alius de sinistra, et duo acolithi
portantes ante ipsum dua caereostata. Et dum venerit subtus
ambone, porrigit ei subdiaconus qui est dextra parte brachio
sinistro et recumbit super eum diaconus aevangelium usque
dum custodit signum. Deinde psallit in ambone, et revertunt
cereostata ante ambonem et legitur aevangelium. Et suscipit
aevangelium subdiaconus, et tenens eum contra pectus suum
subtus ambone, usque dum osculantur omnes aevangelium.
Inde retrudit eum in capsa sua. Et revertit diaconus ad altare
et ipsa caereostata ante eum, et ponunt ea retro altare, seu
et reliqua caereostata. Et si fuerit pallium super altare,
replicat eum in una parte ad orientem, et expanditur corporale
super altare a diaconibus.

Deinde lavat pontifex manus suas et surgit a sede sua.
Et revertitur scola in partae sinistra praesbiterii. Deinde
descendit pontifex ad suscipiendum oblationes a populo, et
annuit archidiaconus scolae ut dicatur offertorium. Et dum
suscipit aeas pontifex, tradit a subdiacono et subdiaconus
ponit eas in sindone quos acolithi tenent, sequentes eum.
Et diaconi recipiunt amulas et portatur stationarius calix
a subdiacono regionario, et refundit diaconus ammulas in
ipso calice sancto; et dum repletus fuerit, devacuatur in
sciffo quas portant acholithi. Deinde vadit pontifex ad
partem mulierum [1] cum diaconibus et faciunt similiter.
Deinde revertitur ad sedem suam et permanent diaconi ad
amulas recipiendas. Et interim stant ante pontificem primi-
caerius, secundicaerios, notarii et regionarii, dum presbiteri
recipiant oblaciones seu et amulas infra presbyterium, tam
de parte virorum quam de muliaerum; et acolithi tenentes
sindones et sciffos ad recolligendum.

Deinde lavat archidiaconus manus suas, et vadit ante
altare, et ceteri diaconi lavant manus suas, et tenent acolithi
sindone cum oblatas quas recepit pontifex a populo in dextro
cornu altaris; et eliguntur eas a subdiacono temperita, et

(i) mulieris.

tradit eas a subdiacono regionaris et ipse porrigit eas ad archidiaconum, et ex eas facit tres aut V. ordines super altare, tantum ut sufficiat populo et exinde in crastino remaneat, secundum auctoritatem canonicam. Et interim teneatur calix a subdiacono regionario, et accipit archidiaconus amula pontificis de manu oblationaris et devacuat ea in calice sancto, similiter ammulas presbyterorum seu et diaconorum. Deinde tenet subdiaconus colatorium super calicem et mittitur de vino quod est in sciffo quos offert populus. Deinde portatur aquarum de scola fontem cum aqua munda, et datur ad oblacionarium, et oblacionarius porrigit eam archidiacono, et facit crucem de aqua in calicae sancto, tenente a subdiacono in dextro cornu altaris. Deinde descendit pontifex a sede sua, veniens ante altare, et recipit archidiaconus oblatas pontificis a subdiacono oblacionario et tradit eas pontifici, et ponit eas pontifex super altare. Et recipit archidiaconus calicem a subdiacono et ponit eum super altare.

Et annuit pontifex scola ut faciant finem; et revertitur scola subtus tabula. In Natale Domini sive in Aepyphania et in Sabbato sancto seu in Dominica sancta et in feria secunda, in Ascensa Domini et in Pentecosten vel in natale sancti Petri et sancti Pauli, stant episcopi post pontificem inclinato capite, presbiteri vero dextra levaque et tenet unusquisque corporale in manu sua, et dantur eis ab archidiacono oblatas duas ad unumquemque,[i] et dicit pontifex canon ut audiatur ab eis, et sanctificantur [1] oblaciones quas tenent, sicut et pontifex [2] . . . inclinato capite post episcopos et subdiaconi [ii] ante ipsum inclinato capite ad altare, usque dum dicit *Nobis quoque.* Et si isti dies solempni non sunt, dum calix ponitur supra altare, revertuntur presbiteri in presbiterio; similiter et alius clerus revertitur subtus tabula; et si dominica

(i) unumque.
(ii) subdiaconos.

[1] For *sanctificant.*
[2] Something is wanting here. We must add, according to Mabillon, *Ordo I.*, something like *Diaconi vero stant.*

evenerit, presbiteri inclinato capite stant, et si cotidianis diebus, genua flectant quando inchoant *Sanctus*. Et veniunt acolithi stantes ante altare post diaconos, dextra levaque, involuti cum sindonibus. Et unus ex illis involutus de palla cum cruce sirica, tenens patenam contra pectus suum, stans primus, et alii tenentes sciffos cum fontes, alii saccula. Et dum venerit pontifex ad *omnis honor et gloria*, levat duas oblatas in manus suas, et diaconus calicem tenens et levans paululum usque dum dicit: *Per omnia saecula saeculorum, amen.*

Et surgunt ab oracione diaconi seu et sacerdotes, et dum dixerit pontifex: *Pax Domini sit semper vobiscum*, accipit subdiaconus patenam ab acolitho et porriget eam archidiacono et tenet eam ad dexteram pontificis et frangit unam ex oblatis quas offert pro se et dimittit coronam ipsius super altare, et ponit unam integram et aliam mediam in patenam et reddit archidiaconus patenam ad accolitum, et pontifex vadit ad sedem suam. Deinde confranguntur alii diaconi in patena, seu et episcopi in dextra parte abside. Deinde levat archidiaconus calicem de altare et dat ad subdiaconum, et stat cum ipso ad dextro cornu altaris, et psallunt acolithi ad altare cum saccula, et stant circa altare, et ponit archidiaconus oblatas per saccula et revertuntur ad presbiteros ut confrangantur et [1] interim psallunt *Beati immaculati* secreto presbiteri vel diaconi: et si necessitas evenerit, rumpantur primitus oblatae a presbitero et sicut frangantur subdiaconi regionarii. Et revertitur scola in presbiterio, in parte sinistra, et annuit archidiaconus scola ut dicatur *Agnus Dei*. Et interim, dum confranguntur, iterum respondunt acolithi qui sciffos et amulas [(1)] tenent *Agnus Dei*. Et dum fractum habuerint, accipit archidiaconus calicem sanctum a subdiacono, et alius diaconus patenam ab acolitho, et vadunt ante pontificem.

Accipit pontifex sancta de patena, mordit ex ea particula,

(i) amalas.

---

[1] The words *et interim dum confranguntur*, at first left out, were supplied on the margin of the manuscript.

et de ipsa facit crucem super calicem, dicendo secreto: *Fiat conmixtio et consecratio* et reliqua. Deinde confirmat pontifex, tenente calicae ab archidiacono. Deinde accipiunt aepiscopi vel presbiteri sancta de manu pontificis et vadunt in sinistra parte altaris, et ponunt manus cum sancta super altare et sic communicant. Quando incipiunt episcopi vel presbiteri communicare, tunc vadit archidiaconus in dextra parte altaris, stans ante eum acolitus cum sciffo priore, et adnunciat stacione, et respondunt omnes: *Deo gracias.* Et tunc perfundit de calicae in sciffo. Deinde dat calicem ad episcopum qui prius communicavit et vadit ad pontificem et accipit sancta de manu ipsius, similiter et alii diaconi. Et vadunt in dextra parte altaris et communicant. Deinde confirmantur ab episcopo a quo et presbiteri confirmati sunt. Deinde communicat pontifex primicerios et secundicaerios. Deinde recipit archidiaconus calicem ab episcopo, et veniens subdiaconus, habens colatorio minore in manu sua, expellit sancta de calicae, et ponit ea in fonte priore unde archidiaconus debet confirmare populo, et devacuat calicem archidiaconus in secundo calice, et de ipso perfundit acolithus in fonte priorae. Deinde descendit pontifex ad communicandum populum, et annuit archidiaconus scola ut dicatur antiphona ad communionem. Et dum dixerit scola, repetunt subdiaconi de sinistra parte cancello infra thronum. Et dum communicati fuerint primati, tribuni, comites et judices et caeteros quos voluerit, vadit de parte mulierum infra cancellum, et diaconi post ipsum, confirmantes populo. Deinde quando jubet revertitur ad sedem suam, et stant sacerdotes ad communicandum vel confirmandum populum infra presbiterium. Et interim pontifex sedet in sede sua, et stat ante eum acolitus cum sancta patena, et veniunt ad eum subdiaconi, notarii vel regionarii, et communicat eos, et confirmantur a diacono.

Deinde stant notarii ante eum tenentes calamario et dhomum in manu, et cui voluerit pontifex invitare, jubet ut scribantur nomina ipsorum. Et descendunt notarii a sede et adnunciant ad ipsos qui scripti sunt.

Et interim venit sacerdos et communicat scola, et tenens quartus fontem in manu, quod impleta est de sciffo primo, et accipit eam presbiter de manu ipsius et facit crucem de sancta super fontem et ponit eam intro. Similiter et omnes presbiteri faciant quando confirmant populum et confirmat scola. Et dum viderit archidiaconus quod pauci sunt ad communicandum, annuit ut dicatur scola *Gloria.* Et repetunt subdiaconi *Sicut erat in principio* et repetit scola versum.[1]

Deinde descendit pontifex a sede et vadit ante altare et revertuntur cereostata post ipsum. Et interim lavant sacerdotes vel diaconi manus suas et osculantur se per ordinem et subdiaconi in vicem ubi stant, similiter et scola in loco quo stat. Oracione expleta, dicit diaconus *Ite missa est,* non ipse qui legit evangelium, sed alius.

Deinde descendit pontifex ab altare et diaconi cum ipso, et subdiaconi ante eum cum thimiamasteriun qui supra scriptus est, seu et cereostata ante eum ab acolitis portantes. Et transiens per medium praesbiterium, dicit subdiacono de scola: *Jube, domne, benedicere.* Et dat pontifex orationem, et respondetur *Amen.* Et cum exierit de presbiterio, iterum dicunt judices: *Jube, domne, benedicere.* Et data benedictione respondetur *Amen.* Et venientes acolithi ante pontifice cum coreostata, stant ante ostium usque dum ingreditur pontifex sacrarium, et extinguunt cerea.

Et spoliat se pontifex et recipiunt vestimenta a subdiaconibus, et ipsi tradunt eas ad cubicularios. Et diaconi spoliant se foras secretario, et accipiunt vestimenta ipsorum acholiti. Et dum sedet pontifex, venit mansionarius prior de ecclesia cum bacea argentea cum pastillos, et si non fuerit argentea, cum catino, stat ante pontificem; et veniunt per ordinem diaconi, deinde primicerius et secundicereus, sed [ii] et vicaedominus vel subdiaconi [iii] et accipiunt pastillos de manu pontificis. Deinde miscitur pontifici et ceteros suprascriptos. Omnia expleta, dat pontifex oracionem et egrediuntur de secrario.

Et hoc quod obmisimus ad memoriam reducimus, id est quod si pontifex non processerit, diaconi sic procedant sicut superius

(i) versum ii.
(ii) se quicae dominus.
(iii) subdiaconus.

dictum est. Et si diaconi minime fuerint, in loco ipsorum procedat presbiter de secrario cum cereostata ad [1] custodiendum sedem pontificis [ii] et licet evangelium legere in ambone procinctus de planita, sicut et diaconus, et descendens de ambone induit se planita. Et dum venerint ante cancellum diaconi aut presbiteri, venit episcopus aut presbiter de parte sinistra presbiterii qui ipsa die missa caelebraturus est; dat ei diaconus pacem qui evangelium lecturus est ipsa diae. Et dum finierit scola *Kirie eleison*, psallit episcopus in parte dextra throni infra cancello et dicit *Gloria in excelsis Deo*. Et si presbiter missa debet caelebrare, non dicit *Gloria in excelsis Deo*, sed tantum psallit et dicit oracione. Ipsa expleta, revertitur in locum suum, usque dum legitur evangelium. Ipso expleto, psallit ut supra, et dicit *Dominus vobiscum;* deinde *Oremus*, et sequitur omnia sicut supra scriptum est. Et dum venerit ad *omnis honor et gloria*, non levat diaconus calicem, sicut ad pontificem, sed ipse episcopus aut presbiter levat duas oblatas et tangit ex ipsis calicem et dicit *Per omnia saecula saeculorum*. Et dum dixerit *Pax Domini sit semper vobiscum*, tenet subdiaconus de sancta cum corporale ad cornu altaris quod pontifex consecravit,[iii] et accipit eam diaconus et tradit eam episcopo aut presbitero. Et exinde facit crucem super calicem, dicendo *Pax Domini sit semper vobiscum*. Et osculatur altare, et diaconus dat pacem ad subdiaconum. Deinde veniet alius episcopus de parte sinistra; tenent ambo manus super oblata et frangunt ea, et episcopus revertitur ad locum suum. Et episcopus aut presbiter qui fecit missa tradit una et media oblata qui partita est ad diacono, et ipse ponit medietate in patenam et qui integra est in sacculo, tenente acholito. Et vadit ad archipresbitero ad confrangendum; et stat episcopus in sinistra parte altaris usque dum expensae [iv] fuerint oblatae per saccula acholitorum, sicut mos est. Deinde revertitur episcopus ante altare et confrangendum medietate de oblata qui remansit. Et dum confractum habuerint, adnunciat

(i) et.
(ii) pontificem.
(iii) consecrabit.
(iv) expensa.

diaconus stacione, sicut mos est. Et veniunt tam episcopi quam presbiteri ad communicandum ante altare, et dat episcopus particulas duas ad primum ex illis episcopis in manu sua; et ipse qui eis accipit, reddit unam ex illis ad eum; et ipse particula tenit in manu dextra usque dum communicant sicut supra. Et tunc ponit manus supra altare, et communicat ipse qui missa fecit. Deinde communicant diaconi et confirmantur ab episcopo sive a presbitero qui prius communicavit et calicem tenet et complet omnia sicut supra scriptum est.

II.

Qualiter Feria V. Caene Domini agendum sit.

Media illa nocte surgendum, nec more solito *Deus in adjutorium meum* nec invitatorium, sed in primis cum antiphonis III. psalmi secuntur; deinde versus;[1] nec presbiter dat oracionem. Deinde surgit lector ad legendum, et non petat benedictionem, et non dicit *Tu autem Domine*, sed ex verbis leccionis jubet prior facere finem. III. [lectiones de lamentatione Hieremiae, III.][1] de tractatu sancti Augustini in psalmo *Exaudi* ad *Deus oracionem meam dum tribulor*, III. de Apostolo ubi ait Corinthios: *Et ego accepi a Domino quod et tradidi vobis.* VIIII. [psalmi] cum antiphonis, VIIII. lectiones, VIIII. responsoria completi sunt; et non dicit *Gloria* nec in psalmis nec in responsoriis. Sequitur matutinum. Matutino completo non dicit *Chirie eleison*, sed vadunt per oratoria psalmis psallendo cum antiphonis.

In eadem die, ora V., procedunt ad ecclesiam et mutant se

(i) u.

---

[1] I supply these words, and also *psalmi*, lower down.

vestimentis suis tam pontifex quam et diaconi [1] cum dalmaticis et subdiaconi non induunt planitas. Deinde egreditur pontifex de sacrario cum diaconibus et VII. cereostata ante eum, et cetera sicut mos est in die sollempni. Dum transierit per medium scolae, annuit primum scolae ut dicatur *Gloria.* Et antequam ascendat ad altare, dat pacem priori episcopo et priori presbitero seu et diaconibus omnibus. Et veniens ante altare et reclinans se ad oracionem prostratus in terram, usque dum dicit versum ad repetendum. Deinde psallit ad sedem. Et dum finierit *Kirie eleison* scola, dicit *Dominus vobiscum* et sequitur oracio *Deus a quo et Judas;* deinde leccio Apostoli et responsorium, deinde evangelium. Offerente populo dicit scola offertorium *Dextera Domini.*

Dum venerit ad finem, in verbis in quibus coeperit dicere *intra quorum nos consortium non aestimator meriti,*[ii] *sed veniae, quaesumus, meritis largitor admitte, per Christum dominum nostrum,* tunc vadunt diaconi et tollent ampullas cum oleo que ponuntur a diversis in podia et tenent eas super altare et benedicuntur a pontifice; residue vero quae remanent super cancellos, dextra levaque juxta altare ascendunt episcopi et priores presbiteri: ab eis benedicuntur. Qua benedictione olei completa, subjungit pontifex et dicit: *Per quem hec omnia, Domine, semper bona creas,* et revocantur ampullae a diaconibus per loca sua. Hec autem benedictio dicitur super oleum secreto, tam a pontifice [iii] quam et ab episcopis vel a presbiteris: *Emitte, Domine, Spiritum sanctum tuum Paraclitum,* et [1] oratione completa dicit pontifex: *Per quem hec omnia, Domine,* et cetera, deinde oratione dominica, et sequitur *Libera nos, quaesumus, Domine,* et dicit: *Pax Domini sit semper vobiscum.* Et vadit ad sedem et confrangunt,

(i) diaconus.
(ii) meritis.
(iii) pontificibus.

[1] Between *et* and *oratione* the manuscript inserts the words *ipse suum oleum ad unguendum infirmum,* which are a marginal reference wrongly inserted in the text. *Ipse suum* is, moreover, a wrongly deciphered abbreviation. We ought to read *ubi supra, sub verbo oleum,* etc.

sacerdotes sancta, seu et diaconi, et interim psallitur *Agnus Dei.* Deinde communicat pontifex tantum, et diaconus cooperit sancta seu et calicae super altare cum corporale ; similiter et acoliti cooperiunt sciffos cum pallas, tenentes eos.

Et venit pontifex ante altare et habens suajuva¹ duas ampullas infra presbiterium, una cum balsamo confecto et alia cum oleo purissimo, et venit ad eum regionarius secundus et accepit ab eo ampullam ⁽ⁱ⁾ cum balsamo involuta cum mafortio sirico ; et de ipso ponit super scapula sinistra caput unum qui eam recepturus est ; similiter recepit eam regionarius primus a regionario ⁽ⁱⁱ⁾ secundo. Deinde subdiaconus regionarius et archidiaconus infra cancello stans similiter recepit eam et vadet ante pontificem et stat ante eum cum ampulla. Et exalat in eam pontifex tribus vicibus, et faciens crucem super eam, dicendo : *In nomine Patris et Filii et Spiritus sancti.* Et sequitur benedictio decantando sicut et *Vere dignum.* Ipsa expleta, revocantur ampullae per ordinem sicut acceperunt. Similiter et alia ampulla cum oleo purissimo portatur ante pontificem ab alio diacono, sicut superius ; et alat in eam ter, sicut supra. Deinde benedicit eam secreto, et iterum revocat eam ad suajuva, per ordinem, sicut superius. Deinde communicat cunctus clerus seu et populi. Missa completa, dicit diaconus : *Ite, missa est.* Et reservantur sancta usque in crastinum.

III.

Feria VI. Parasceven.

Media nocte surgendum est ; nec more solito *Deus in adjutorium meum* nec invitatorium dicuntur. VIIII. psalmi

(i) ampullas.
(ii) subregionario.

¹ This is the word *subadjuva.*

cum antiphonis et responsoriis; lectiones III. de lamentacione Hieremiae, III. de tractatu sancti Augustini [i] de psalmo LXIII., tres de apostolo, ubi ait ad Aebreos : *Festinemus ergo ingredere in illam requiem.* Et non dicit *Gloria* nec in psalmis nec in responsoriis; nec lector petit benediccionem, sed sicut superius. Sed tantum inchoat ad matutinum antiphona in primo psalmo, tuta lampada de parte dextra, in secundo psalmo de parte sinistra; similiter per omnes psalmos usque VI. aut VII., aut in finem evangelii, reservetur absconsa usque in Sabbato sancto.

Ipsa autem die, hora V., procedit ad ecclesiam omnis clerus et ingreditur archidiaconus cum aliis diaconibus in sacrario et induunt se planetas fuscas, et egrediuntur de sacrario, et duo cereostata ante ipsum cum cereis accensis, et veniunt ante altarae. Osculantur altare et vadunt ad sedem pontificis secundum consuetudinem. Deinde annuit archidiaconus subdiacono ut legatur leccio prima. Sequitur responsorium *Domine audivi;* deinde alia leccio, et sequitur tractus *Qui habitat.* Deinde legitur passio Domini secundum Johannem. Hoc expleto psallit sacerdos de parte sinistra presbiterii [ii] in partem dextram altaris infra thronum et dicit oraciones sollempnes. Deinde revertuntur presbiteri per titula sua, et hora nona tam de lectionibus quam responsoriis vel evangelium seu et oraciones sollemnes faciunt similiter, et adorant sanctam crucem et communicantur omnes.

IV.

Ordo qualiter in Sabbato sancto agendum est.

Media nocte surgendum est, et sicut superius taxavimus ita fiat, excepto in luminaribus, sed tantum una lampada accendatur propter legendum.

(i) III. de ps.
(ii) presbiter.

Post hoc vero, die illa, octava hora diaei procedit ad ecclesiam omnis clerus seu et omnis populus, et ingreditur archidiaconus in sacrario cum aliis diaconibus et mutant se sicut in die sancta. Et aegrediuntur de sacrario et duae faculae ante ipsos accense [1] portantes a subdiacono, et veniunt ante altare diaconi, osculantur ipsum et vadunt ad sedem pontificis, et ipsi subdiaconi stant retro altare, tenentes faculas usque dum complentur lectiones. Deinde annuit archidiaconus subdiacono regionario ut legatur lectio prima, in greco sive in latino. Deinde psallit sacerdos infra thronum in dextra parte altaris et dicit *Oremus*, et diaconus *Flectamus genua*, et post paululum dicit *Levate*. Et sequitur oracio *Deus qui mirabiliter creasti hominem*. Deinde secuntur lectiones et cantica seu et oraciones, tam grece quam latine, sicut ordinem habent.

Lectionibus expletis, egrediuntur de ecclesia quae appellatur Constantiniana et descendit archidiaconus cum aliis diaconibus, et ipsas faculas ante ipsos, usque in sacrarium qui est juxta fontes, et ibi expectant pontificem. Et dum advenerit, quando jubet, dicit ad quartum de scola : *Intrate*. Et inchoant laetania ante fontes, repetentes ter. Qui dum dixerint *Agnus Dei*, egreditur pontifex de sacrario cum diaconibus, et ipsas faculas ante ipsum usque ad fontes. Letania expleta, dicit *Dominus vobiscum*, deinde *Oremus*, et sequitur oratio his verbis : *Omnipotens sempiterne Deus, adesto piaetatis tuae mysteriis*. Deinde sequitur benedictio his verbis : *Deus qui invisibili potentia*, decantando sicut prefatione. Ubi dixerit : *Descendat in hanc plenitudinem fontis*, ponunt faculas ipsas infra fontes. Benediccione conpleta, accipit pontifex crisma cum oleo mixto in vase ab archidiacono, et aspargit eam per medium fontis in tribus partibus, et recepit vas archidiaconus de manu pontificis et reddit eam acholitho qui eam detulit. Et pontifex aspargit cum manu de ipsa aqua super populum.

Et vadit ad locum ubi baptizare debet, et diaconi intrant infra fontes, qui denominati sunt ad baptizandum, cum sindalia in pedibus, seu et subdiaconi exuti planitas suas. Deinde accipiunt subdiaconi infantes et tradunt ad diacones et diaconi

---

(i) ancense.

ad pontificem. Et pontifex baptizat quantos voluerit. Et stans presbiter infra fontes facit crucem de oleo exorcizato in verticae, tenentes ipsos infantes subdiaconi, et reddentes per ordinem, sicut acceperunt.

Deinde revertitur pontifex in consignatorio et archidiaconus [1] cum ipso, et ipsas faculas ante eum. Et alii diaconi stant ad baptizandum. Et vestiuntur infantes ab ipsis qui susceperunt eos de fonte, et ipsi portant eos in consignatorium, et stant per ordinem, masculi in dextra parte et feminae in sinistra. Et surgit pontifex a sede de consignatorio et vadit in dextram partem masculorum, dicendo oracionem et tangendo capita ipsorum de manu; similiter et ad feminas. Deinde venit subdiaconus cum crisma in vase argenteo; stat ad dexteram pontificis et pontifex revertit ad infantes priores et facit crucem de crisma cum police in frontibus ipsorum, dicendo: *In nomine Patris et Filii et Spiritus sancti, pax tibi.* Similiter et ad feminas.

Deinde revertitur pontifex in sacrarium qui est juxta thronum, et ipsas faculas ante ipsum. Et stat unus de scola ante eum; et dum ei placuerit, dicit: *Intrate.* Et inchoant letania hoc ordine, id est prima VII. vicibus repetent. Similiter, facto intervallo, dum jusserit pontifex, dicunt tertia letania, ter repetant. Et dum dixerint *Agnus Dei*, egreditur pontifex de sacrario et diaconi cum ipso, hinc et inde, et duae faculae ante eum portantur ab eis qui eas portaverunt ad fontes. Et veniens ante altare, stat inclinato capite, usque dum repetunt *Kyrie eleison;* et osculatur altare et diaconi similiter, hinc et inde. Deinde revertit ad sedem suam, et ipsi subdiaconi regionarii tenent ipsas faculas retro altare, dextra levaque. Et dicit pontifex *Gloria in excelsis Deo.* Sequitur oratio, inde lectio et *Alleluia, Confitemini Domino* et tractus *Laudate Dominum.* Et ipsa nocte non psallit offertorium nec *Agnus Dei* nec antiphona ad communionem. Et communicat omnis populus, seu et infantes qui in ipsa nocte baptizati sunt, similiter usque in octavas paschae.

Ipsa nocte, omnes presbiteri cardinales non ibi stant, sed

---

(1) archidiaconi.

unusquisque per titulum suum facit missa et habet licentiam sedere in sede et dicere *Gloria in excelsis Deo.* Et transmittit unusquisque presbiter mansionarium de titulo suo ad ecclesiam Salvatoris, et expectant ibi usque dum frangitur sancta, habentes secum corporales. Et venit oblationarius subdiaconus, et dat eis de sancta quod pontifex consecravit, et recipiunt ea in corporales, et revertitur unusquisque ad titulum suum et tradit sancta presbitero. Et de ipsa facit crucem super calicem et ponit in eo et dicit *Dominus vobiscum.* Et communicant omnes, sicut superius.

Et dicit diaconus *Ite, Missa est.*

In vigilia Pentecoste sicut in Sabbato sancto ita agendum est; sed tantum una letania ad fontem et alia pro int[roitu]; offertorium seu Alleluia vel antiphona ad communionem sicut continet in antifonarium.

In ipsa nocte sancta Resurrectionis, post gallorum cantu surgendum est. Et dum venerint ad ecclesiam et oraverint, osculant se invicem cum silentio. Deinde dicit *Deus in adjutorium meum.* Sequitur invitatorium cum Alleluia: sequuntur III. psalmi cum Alleluia: *Beatus vir, Quare fremuerunt gentes, Domine, quid multiplicati sunt.* Sequitur versus, et orationem dat presbiter. Deinde secuntur III. lectiones et responsoria totidem, prima lectio de Actibus apostolorum; inde secunda; tertia de omiliis ad ipsum diem pertinentium. Sequitur matutinum cum Alleluia.

Infra Albas Paschae, tres psalmos per nocturno inponuntur per singulas noctes usque in Octavas Paschae, id est, feria II*a*, *Cum invocarem, Verba mea, Domine ne in furore tuo;* feria III*a*, *Domine Deus meus, Domine Dominus noster, In Domino confido;* feria IIII*a*, *Salvum me fac Domine, Usquequo Domine, Dixit insipiens;* feria V*a*, *Domine quis habitabit, Conserva me Domine, Exaudi Domine;* feria VI*a*, *Caeli enarrant, Exaudiat te Dominus, Domine in virtute tua;* sabbato, *Domini est terra, Ad te Domine levavi, Judica me Domine.* In dominica vero Octabas Paschae vigiliam plenam faciunt, sicut mos est, cum VIIII. lectionibus et totidem responsuriis.

V.

Ordo qualiter in ebdomada Pasche usque in sabbato de Albas vespera caelebrabitur.

In primis Dominica sancta, hora nona, convenit scola cum episcopis, presbiteris et diaconibus in ecclesia majore quae est catholica, et a loco crucifixi incipiunt *Chyrie eleison* et veniunt usque ad altare. Ascendentibus diaconibus in poium, episcopi et presbiteri statuuntur locis suis in presbyterio et sancto ante altare stet.[1] Finito *Chyrie eleison*, annuit archidiaconus primo scolae, et ille, inclinans se illi, incipit *Alleluia* cum psalmo *Dixit Dominus Domino meo*. Hoc expleto, iterum annuit archidiaconus secundo vel cui voluerit de scola, sed et omnibus incipientibus hoc modo praecipit et dicit iterum *Alleluia* cum psalmo CX. Sequitur post hunc primus scolae cum paraphonistis instantibus *Alleluia* et respondent paraphoniste. Sequitur subdiaconus cum infantibus versum *Dominus regnavit decore induit;* et respondent paraphonistae *Alleluia;* item versum *Parata sedes tua Deus*, et sequitur *Alleluia* a paraphonistis; item versum *Elevaverunt flumina Domine*, et reliqua. Post hos versus salutat primus scolae archidiacono, et illo annuente incipit *Alleluia* cum melodias, simul cum infantibus. Qua expleta respondent paraphoniste prima *Alleluia* et finitur. Post hanc incipit *Alleluia* tercius de scola in psalmo CXI.; post hunc sequitur *Alleluia* ordine quo supra: *Alleluia. Pascha nostrum;* versus *Aepulemur*. Hanc expletam, ordinem quo supra, incipit archidiaconus in evangelio antiphonam *Scio quod Jesum queritis crucifixum*. Ipsa expleta, dicit sacerdos orationem.

Dein descendit ad fontes psallendo antiphonam *In die resurrectionis meae*, quam ut finierint inchoatur *Alleluia;* psallitur psalmus CXII. Ipso expleto, sequitur *Alleluia, O Kyrios*

---

[1] I understand the reading to be *et sanctum ante altare stent.*

ebasileusen eupreprian, et sequitur *Alleluia* a cantoribus; item versus *Ce gar estereosen tin icummeni tis*;[1] et finitur ordine quo supra. Post hanc sequitur diaconus secundus [(i)] in evangelium antiphonam *Venite et videte locum;* deinde sequitur oratio a presbitero.

Et tunc vadunt ad sanctum Andream ad Crucem, canentes antiphonam *Vidi aquam egredientem de templo.* Post hanc dicitur *Alleluia* cum psalmo CXIII. Quo finito, primus scolae incipit *Alleluia, Venite exultemus Domino*, versus *Preoccupemus faciem ejus.* Post hanc dicit diaconus in evangelio antiphonam *Cito euntes dicite discipulis ejus;* deinde sequitur oratio a presbitero.

Deinde descendunt primatus ecclesiae ad accubita, invitante notario vicedomini, et bibet ter, de greco una, de pactisi una, de procumma [una]. Postquam biberint, omnes presbiteri et acholiti per singulos titulos redeunt ad faciendas vesperas, et ibi bibunt de dato presbitero.

Hec ratio per totam ebdomadam servabitur usque in dominica Albas.

VI.

Quando letania major debet fieri, adnuntiat eam diaconus in statione catholica et dicit: "Feria tale veniente, collecta in basilica beati illius, statio in basilica sancti illius." Et respondet omnis clerus: "Deo gratias." Die [(ii)] nuntiata, colligit se omnis clerus vel omnis populus in ecclesia suprajamdicta; et ingreditur pontifex in sacrario, seu et diaconi, et induunt se planitas fuscas.

(i) secundum
(ii) Deinde.

---

[1] These are the first words of verses 1 and 2 of Psalm 93: "'Ο Κύριος 'βασίλευσεν, εὐπρέπειαν. . . . Καὶ γὰρ ἐστερέωσεν τὴν οἰκουμένη[ν ἥ]τις . . ."

Et stat unus de scola ante pontificem et dicit: "Intrate." Et inchoant antiphonam ad introitum. Et antecedit oblationarius cum duobus cereis in manu accensos, et ponit eos retro altare, sicut mos est. Et egreditur pontifex de sacrario cum diaconibus et thimiamasterium, portante [i] eam subdiacono temperita. Dum transit per scola, jubet ut dicatur *Gloria*. Et venit ante altare, et inclinat se ad oracionem, usque dum dicit versus ad repetendum, et surgit ab oratione, osculatur altare, et diaconi similiter, hinc et inde. Ipsa antiphona expleta, non dicit scola *Kyrie eleison*, et pontifex, stans ante altare, aspiciens populum, dicit *Dominus vobiscum* et *Oremus*, et diaconus *Flectamus genua*, et facto intervallo, dicit *Levate*. Et dicit pontifex orationem. Ipsa expleta, annuit scolae [ii] ut inchoet antiphonam. Et interim egrediuntur omnes de ecclesia. Primitus enim pauperes de xenodoxio, cum cruce lignea picta, clamando *Kyrie eleison*, deinde *Christe eleison*, inde *Christe audi nos*, deinde *Sancta Maria ora pro nobis*, et ceteros. Et post ipsos egrediantur cruces VII. stacionarias, portantes ab stauroforos, habens in unaquaque III. accensos cereos. Deinde secuntur episcopi vel presbiteri et subdiaconi, deinde pontifex cum diaconibus et due cruces ante eum, portantes a subdiaconibus et timiamasteria portantur a mansionariis ecclesiae, et scola post pontificem psallendo, et [1] dum completa non repetunt presbiteri vel subdiaconi qui antecedunt pontificem: et adpropinquantes ecclesia prima, inchoant laetaniam. Et interim dum dixerint laetania ad fores ecclesiae, intrat pontifex, sacerdotes vel diaconi in ecclesia ad orationem et revertunt ad scolam. Et percompletam letaniam, dicit pontifex *Dominus vobiscum* et *Oremus;* et diaconus *Flectamus genua;* et post paululum *Levate*. Et sequitur oratio a pontifice. Oratione expleta, annuit ut dicatur alia antiphona. Similiter faciant per omnem ecclesiam ubi consuetudo est.

Cum autem adpropinquaverint atrium ecclesiae ubi statio denuntiata est, annuit pontifex in sacrario et diaconi cum ipso.

(i) portant eam subdiaconi.
(ii) scola.

[1] A corrupt passage.

Et scola complet letania infra presbyterium, *Cyrie eleison* repetentes ter, deinde *Christe audi nos, Sancta Maria, ora pro nobis, sanctae Petre, sanctae Paule, sanctae Andreas, sancte Johannes, sancte Stephane, sancte Laurenti,* vel sancto illi in cujus ecclesiae missa celebranda est; deinde *Omnes sancti orent pro nobis. Propitius esto, parce nobis Domine. Propitius esto, libera nos Domine. Ab omni malo libera nos Domine. Per crucem tuam libera nos Domine. Peccatores, te rogamus, audi nos. Filius Dei, te rogamus, audi nos. Ut pacem dones, te rogamus audi nos.* Et *Agnus Dei,* omnia ter repetentes. Deinde *Christe audi nos, Kyrie eleison,* tantum ter; et completum est.

Et ipsa die duo cereostata procedunt ante pontificem et non dicit scola *Cyrie eleison* post antiphonam, neque pontifex *Gloria in excelsis Deo.*

VII.

Ordo qualiter in sancta atque apostolica sede, id est beati Petri ecclesia, certis temporibus ordinatio fit, quod ab orthodoxis patribus institutum est, id est mense primo, IIII., VII., X., hoc est in XII. lectiones.

Primitus enim, secunda feria in ebdomada, quando XII. lectiones debent fieri, vocat pontifex electos, et jurant ante eum super reliquias sanctorum, adstante primicereo et secundicerio et archidiacono et archipresbitero et cui voluerit de IIII.[1] capitula quod canones prohibent. Deinde IIII. feria, statio in ecclesia sancte Dei genetricis Mariae; et procedunt electi seu et omnis clerus, sicut mos est, hora VI. Et inchoat scola antifona ad introitum. Et psallit sacerdos secundum consuaetudinem ad altare, et dicit *Dominus vobiscum* et *Oremus;* et diaconus *Flectamus genua;* et post paululum *Levate.* Et dicit

(1) III

sacerdos orationem et respondeant omnes *Amen.* Et stant aelecti in presbyterio, induti planitas. Deinde ascendit scriniarius in ambonem et dicit: *In nomine Domini nostri Jesu Christi. Si igitur est aliquis qui contra hos viros aliquid scit de causa criminis, absque dubitatione exeat et dicat; tanto memento communionis suae.* Et hoc tertio repetit et descendit de ambone. Et psallit subdiaconus et legit lectionem; et sequitur responsorium. Et ipso completo psallit iterum sacerdos et dicit *Oremus* et sequitur oratio, lectio et responsorium; deinde evangelium, et complent missa sicut mos est.

VI. feria veniente, stacio ad Sanctos Apostolos. Et procedunt omnes, tam clerus quam et electi, hora VI. Post antiphonam ad introitum psallit sacerdos et dicit orationem. Et iterum scriniarius in ambone sicut supra et dicit ut[1] supra tertio Deinde legitur lectio et sequitur responsorium et cetera; et complent missa.

Sabbato autem veniente in XII. lectiones, statio ad beatum Petrum apostolum. Procedit pontifex hora VII. et omnis clerus, tam presbiteri quam diaconi et electi. Deinde quando jubet pontifex inchoat scola antiphonam ad introitum, et procedit pontifex de sacrario, et diaconi, et cereostata, sicut mos est; et osculato altare psallit ad sedem, sicut mos est. Et dum conpleverit scola *Kyrie eleison,* dicit pontifex: *Dominus vobiscum;* dein *Oremus;* et diaconus: *Flectamus genua;* et post paululum: *Levate.* Et dat pontifex orationem, et legitur lectio et sequitur responsorium. Similiter facit per omnes lectiones. Et sequitur benedictio et Apostolo et tracto. Ipsa expleta, stant aelecti in presbyterio, induti dalmaticas et campages in pedibus. Et vocat pontifex vocae magna unumquemque per nomina ipsorum ad sedem, et dicit: *Talis presbiter regionis tertiae, titulo tale, ille.* Et descendat diaconus et ducit unumquemque ad sedem pontificis, et statuit eos ante aeum, sicut vocati sunt ab ipso, vestiti omnes dalmaticas et campages, stantes inclinato capite. Et dat pontifex orationem sicut continet in Sacramentorum.

Ipsa expleta, descendunt ipsi qui presbiteri futuri sunt

---

[1] dicit ut] dicitur.

ante altare, et diaconi qui ordinati sunt stant ad latus pontificis juxta sedem. Et archidiaconus induit orarios et planitas ad presbiteros, stans ante altare, et iterum ducit eos ante pontificem, et accipiunt orationem presbiterii [i] ab ipso. Ipsa expleta, ducit eos archidiaconus osculando per ordinem episcopos, deinde presbiteros; et stant in caput, supra omnes presbiteros, per ordinem, sicut vocati sunt a pontifice, eodem die. Deinde offerunt pontifici ante omnes presbiteros et communicant similiter eodem die ante omnes. Et accipit unusquisque a pontifice firmata oblata de altare, unde et communicat XL. diebus.

Missa expleta, sint parati mansionarii de titulis ipsorum cum cereostata et thimiamateriis; et procedunt de ecclesia beati Petri apostoli [ii] unusquisque in titulo suo, habens unusquisque paranymfum presbiterum secum; et stratores missi a pontifice duo ante eum euntes et tenentes caballo cum freno hinc et inde, et clamant voce magna: *Tali presbitero talis sanctus elegit!* Et respondunt mansionarii ipsum usque in titulo ipsius. Et vadit post eum sacellarius ipsius, faciendo aelimosinam, et cum pervenerit ad ecclesiam, ponitur sedes latus altare, et habet ibi licentiam sedere eodem die et in vigilia paschae tantum et dicere *Gloria in excelsis Deo*. Similiter paranimfus presbiter stat a latere ipsius et legit evangelium in ambone. Deinde presbiter supradictus [iii] facit missa. Et completa ea, aegreditur de ecclesia et epulat cum amicis suis. In alia vero diae defert pontifici presbiter X. cerea, similiter et archipresbitero.

Similiter et diaconi habent stratores dominicos duos, qui antecedunt eos clamando et dicendo: *Tali diacono sanctus Petrus elegit!* Et respondit cunctus clerus, qui eum sequitur, similiter usque in domum suam. Et ipse aepulat cum amicis suis.

(i) presbiteri.
(ii) aepi.
(iii) supra dictus est.

VIII.

Incipit ad reliquias levandas sive deducendas seu condendas.

Intrant cantores antiphonam *Ecce populus custodiens*[1] *judicium;* psalmus *Fundamenta ejus.* Dicit *Gloria,* deinde repetit *Sicut erat,* versus *Sicut laetantium omnium nostrum.* Finita autem antiphona, levat episcopus in brachia sua linteo desuper patena et mittit ibi reliquias et desuper coopertas olosyrico, et sustentant duo diaconi brachia episcopi, et tunc dat primam orationem. Et post completam orationem, accendunt cereos et egrediuntur cum ipsis et turabula cum thymiama, et cantor inchoat antiphonam *Cum jucunditate exibitis.* Si autem via longinqua fuerit ad ducendum dicit psalmum cum antiphonam.

Adpropinquantes autem prope ecclesia, faciunt laetaniam, et commendat episcopus reliquias ad presbiteros foras [ii] ecclesia, et remanent ibi cum cereis et turibula, facientes laetaniam.

Et tunc episcopus intrat in ecclesiam solus, et facit omne instrumento aqua exorcizata, lavat altare cum spungia et non mittunt chrisma. Et exit [iii] episcopus foras et dat orationem secundo. Et tunc de aqua exorcizata quod remanet asperget super populum. Et mox aperiantur januae ecclesiae, et intrat universus populus cum laetania. Finita laetania, dat tertiam orationem.

Ipsa expleta, inchoat cantor antiphonam *Sacerdos magne, pontifex summi Dei, ingredere templum Domini et hostias pacificas pro salute populi offeres Deo tuo. Hic est enim dies dedicationis sanctorum Domini Dei tui* Psalmus: *Gaudete justi in Domino; Gloria, Sicut erat.* Et exuens se episcopus planitam suam et condit reliquias ipse solus. Quas dum posuerit, cantor inchoat antiphonam *Sub altare Domini sedes accepistis, intercedite pro*

(i) Et con populus custodi.
(ii) faras.
(iii) exiit et episcopus.

nobis per quem meruistis. Psalmum : *Beati inmaculati* tamdiu [1] psallis usque dum condite fuerint reliquie. Et subsistent cum silentio nihil canentes.

+ Et accipit episcopus chrisma et tangit per quattuor angulos loci ubi reliquiae positae fuerint, similitudinem crucis, et dicit: *In nomine Patris et Filii et Spiritus sancti pax tibi.* Et respondit omnis populus: *Et cum spiritu tuo.* Sic similiter et in quattuor cornua altaris eundem sermonem repetit per unumquemque.

His expletis induit se episcopus planitam suam et procedunt levite de sacrario cum veste altaris et cooperiunt altare una cum episcopo, et dat ipse orationem ad consecrandum altare seu ipsa vestimenta, deinde omne ministerium altaris, sive patenam vel crucem.

Hec omnia expleta intrat episcopus in sacrario et venit mansionarius cum cereo accenso ante episcopum et petit orationem et dicit: *Jube, domne, benedicere.* Et dicit episcopus: *Inluminet Dominus domum suam in sempiternum.* Et respondent omnes: *Amen.* Et sic accenduntur a mansionariis candele in ecclesia. Et incipit cantor antiphonam ad introitum. Et procedit episcopus de sacrario cum ordinibus sacris, sicut mos est, et celebratur missarum sollemnia sicut in Sacramentorum continetur.

IX.

Ordo qualiter in Purificatione sanctae Mariae agendum est.

Ipsa autem die, aurora ascendente, procedunt omnes de universas diaconias sive de titulis cum letania + vel antiphonas psallendo, et cerea accensa portantes omnes in manibus per turmas suas, et veniunt in ecclesia sancti Adriani martyris et expectant pontificem. Interim ingreditur pontifex sacrario et induit se vestimentis nigris, et diaconi similiter

(i) tamdum.

planitas induunt nigras. Deinde intrant omnes ante pontificem et accipiunt ab eo singula cerea. His expletis, inchoat scola antiphonam *Exsurge Domine, adjuva nos.* Et dicto versu egreditur pontifex de sacrario cum diaconibus dextra levaque et annuit pontifex scola ut dicatur *Gloria.* Deinde ascendens ante altare, inclinans se ad orationem usque dum inchoat scola versum ad repetendum, surgit ab oratione, salutat altare et diaconi[i] similiter hinc et inde. Ipsa antiphona expleta, non dicit scola *Chyrie eleison*, sed pontifex stans ante altare dicit *Dominus vobiscum*, deinde *Oremus*, et diaconus *Flectamus genua*; et facto intervallo dicit iterum *Levate*. Et dat pontifex orationem.

Interim egrediuntur cruces VII., portantur ab stauroforo permixti cum populo. Deinde presbiteri vel subdiaconi[ii] deinde pontifex cum diaconibus; et duo cerea accensa ante eum portatur et thimiamasterium a subdiacono et duae cruces ante ipsum. Deinde subsequitur scola pontificem psallendo antiphonas. Dum finit scola antiphonam, repetit clerus qui antecedit pontificem.

Cum autem adpropinquaverint atrium sanctae Dei genetricis ecclesiae,[iii] innuit pontifex scola ut dicatur letania, repetentes ter vicissim. Postquam autem ingreditur pontifex in ecclesia, vadit in sacrario cum diaconibus suis et ceterus clerus vadit ante altare et percomplet letania sicut alibi scriptum est. Dein inchoat scola antiphonam ad introitum. Et ipsa die non psallitur *Gloria in excelsis Deo.*

(i) diaconus.
(ii) diaconi.
(iii) ecclesiam

2.

THE ROMAN ORDO FOR THE THREE DAYS BEFORE EASTER.

The celebrated manuscript of Einsiedlen (*Einsiedl.* 326) contains, among other things, a fragment of the *Ordo Romanus* dealing with the last three days of Holy Week. The description given therein of the ceremonies differs in certain respects from that found in other texts. I reproduce it here according to the edition of J. B. de Rossi in vol. ii. of his *Inscriptiones Christianae Urbis Romae,* Part I., p. 34.

Fer. V. Ad matutinum non dicunt *Domine labia mea* nec invita(to)rium neque *Gloria* ad psalmum, neque *Tu aut(em) Domine* nec orationem neque *Kirieleison* per circuitum, sed tantum *Christus factus est pro nobis.* Item ad missa. Hora quasi septima [1] egreditur apostolicus de Lateranis et descendit per sanctum Johannem ad secretarium et diac(oni) et subdiac(oni) cum planetis ante ipsum usque ad secretarium; posteaquam de secretario exeunt subdiaconi cum albis vestibus, procedunt et diaconi cum dalmaticis et ante domnum apostolicum VII. acoliti cum VII. candelabris. Et post *Kirieleyson* domnus apostolicus dicit *Gloria in excelsis deo.* Et omnia sicut in aliis festis, praeter *all(eluia)* et chrisma quod eo die benedicitur. Et cum dicit *Pax domini sit semper,* confringit unam oblatam in duas partes et dat eam archidiacono, et ille mittit eam in patenam quam tenet minister. Reliquas vero oblationes ipse archidiaconus expendit per presbiteros et postea frangit tam ipse quam omnes presbiteri. Et cum tota oblatio fracta

---

[1] The other *Ordines* prescribe, for Maundy Thursday and Good Friday, an earlier hour.

fuerit, communicat solus apostolicus   Et sic benedicit chrisma, et jubet de ipso aut de annotino oblationario aut subadjuve [i] expendere per titulos et per alias ecclesias. Similiter et de sancto sacrificio quod servant in sexta feria : et communicant et vadunt in tabernacula sua.

Fer. VI., hora quasi VIII., descendit domnus apostolicus de Lateranis in sanctum Johannem, verumtamen discalceatus tam ipse quam reliqui ministri sanctae ecclesiae, et veniunt ad altare. Et praecipit domnus apostolicus accendere lumen in ungiario, et accendit ex ipso lumen cui ipse jusserit duas faculas albas, quas portant duo clerici de cubiculo ante domnum. Et procedent de sancto Johanne psallendo *Beati immaculati*, archidiacono tenente sinistram manum domni apostolici, et ipso pontifice in dextera sua portante turibulum [ii] cum incenso et alio diacono post dorsum domni apostolici portante lignum pretiosae crucis in capsa de auro cum gemmis ornata. Crux vero [iii] ipsa de ligno pretioso desuper ex auro cum gemmis intus cavam habens confectionem ex balsamo satis bene olente. Et dum preveniunt ad Hierusalem intrant ecclesiam et ponit diaconus ipsam capsam ubi est crux super altare et sic aperit eam domnus apostolicus. Deinde prosternit se ante altare ad orationem : et postquam surgit osculatur eam et vadit et stat circa sedem. Et per ejus jussionem osculantur episcopi, presbiteri, diaconi, subdiaconi super altare ipsam crucem. Deinde ponunt eam super arcellam ad rugas et ibi osculatur eam reliquus populus   Tamen feminae ibi non introeunt : sed postea portant eam oblationarius [iv] et alii subdiaconi et osculatur a feminis. Verumtamen ut a domno apostolico fuerit osculata, statim ascendit subdiaconus in ambonem

(i) Sub ambe *cod*.

(ii) According to Latin use, neither the bishop nor the celebrating priest carries the censer in procession. The case is different in the East, and we need not be astonished to find here an Oriental detail, for the ritual of the Adoration of the Cross was imported into Rome from the East. This practice, moreover, soon disappeared.

(iii) With regard to this cross, see the *Lib. Pont.*, vol. i. p. 374 (life of Sergius I.).

(iv) Oblati, *cod*.

et incipit legere lectionem Oseae prophetae. Post cujus descensum ascendit cantor et canit gr(aduale) *Domine audivi* cum versibus suis. Et iterum ascendit subdiaconus et legit aliam lectionem Deuteronomii; post quem cantor ascendens incipit tractum [i] *Qui habitat.* Quo completo, vadit diaconus discalceatus cum evangelio, et cum eo duo subdiaconi, et legit passionem Domini secundum Johannem. Et cum completa fuerit, dicit domnus apostolicus orationem *Oremus pro ecclesia sancta Dei*, et dicit archidiaconus *Flectamus genua*, et postea dicit *Levate*, et reliqua omnia in ordine suo. Et ad finem tantum dicit *Dominus vobiscum* et respondent *Et cum spiritu tuo.* Et procedent iterum ad Lateranis psallendo *Beati immaculati.* Attamen apostolicus ibi non communicat [ii] nec diaconi; qui vero communicare voluerit, communicat de capsis de sacrificio quod V. feria servatum est Et qui noluerit ibi communicare vadit per alias ecclesias Romae seu per titulos et communicat.

Sabbato sancto, hora qua(si) VII., ingreditur clerus in aecclesiam; nam domnus apostolicus non. Evadunt ad secretarium, diaconi scilicet et subdiaconi in planetis, et accendunt duo regionarii per unumquemque faculas de ipso lumine quod de VI. feria abscunditum est et veniunt ad altare. Diaconi stant ad sedem et episcopi sedent in choro. Et ascendit lector in ambonem et legit lectionem grecam. Sequitur *In principio* et orationes et *Flectamus genua* et tractus. Et dum hoc completum fuerit, descendent ad fontes et dicit schola cantorum laetania III. vicibus, *Christe audi nos* et reliqua. Postea benedicit domnus papa fontem, et dum venit in eo loco ubi dicit *Descendat in hanc plenitudinem*, deponent faculas regionarii qui illas tenent in fontes. Et dum complet, sparget de aqua super populum et sic initiat baptizare. Et post quam baptizat IIII. vel V. infantes, exiet foras et baptizant presbiteri et duo diaconi et ille postea consignat et chrismat. Postea facit clerus et letanias II. et interea intrant ad missam jam sero, et dicit *Gloria in excelsis Deo* et *All(eluia)*, *Confitemini*

(i) Tractatum *cod.*
(ii) Cf. Amalarius, *De Off.*, i. 15.

Domino; tract(us) *Laudate Dominum.* Et *Agnus Dei* [1] cantat schola cantorum et respondent IIII. acoliti stantes ad rugas, tenentes sciphos et gimellares quae postea tenent ad confirmandum populum.

[1] The other *Ordines* say exactly the contrary. The present custom agrees with them. The *Agnus Dei* is not sung at Mass on Saturday in Holy Week.

3.

THE DEDICATION RITUAL IN THE SACRAMENTARY OF ANGOULÊME.

Manuscript 216 of the Bibl. Nationale (Delisle, No. 15) of the eighth century, or of the beginning of the ninth, f. 141. The language of this fragment is, doubtless, the Latin of later Merovingian times. Note especially the employment of the pronoun *ille* for the article.

Ordo Consecrationis Basilicae Novae.

In primis veniunt sacerdotes et clerus cum sacris ordinibus ante fores templi quod benedicendum est, et introeunt clerici et sacerdotes intra januam templi. In ipso introitu incipiunt laetania; et ipsa finita, accipiat episcopus aqua cum vino mixta et benedicat eos, post haec faciens comparsum per totam ecclesiam. Post haec benedicit eam. Nam illae cruces vel candelabra seu illae reliquiae foris stent dum altarium benedicitur. Et post benedictionem templi iterum clerici et sacerdotes accedunt prope altare, et incipiant alia laetania. Ipsa finita, accedat sacerdos et accipiat illa aqua cum illo vino quod antea benedixit et aspergat altarium secundum traditionem suam, et benedicat. Ipso benedicto, accipiat chrysma et faciat crucem in medio altaris et per cornua ipsius altaris, vel illo loco ubi reliquiae ponendae sunt. Similiter per totum templum in circuitu faciens cruces de ipsa chrysma. Post haec benedicit lenteamina vel vasa templi, et post haec revestientur altare seu et vela templi penduntur et accendunt luminaria. Post haec omnia consummata, vadunt sacerdotes cum omni clero foris, ubi sunt illae reliquiae. Et intrant cum ipsis reliquiis cum sacris ordinibus cum laetania, et veniunt ante altare et recondunt ipsas reliquias in ipso altario in suo loco, et incipiat sacerdos missa caelebrare de dedicatione basilicae novae. Quando ille comparsus benedicendus est, adferant ad episcopum aqua in uno vas, vinum in aliud ; conmiscit eos inter ipsa vasa et sic benedicit sicut ordo continet, ubi dicit oratione *Creator et conservator humanæ generis.*[1]

[1] P 410.

4.

THE DEDICATION RITUAL ACCORDING TO THE USE OF THE BISHOP OF METZ

Sacramentary of Drogo, Bishop of Metz (826–855); Delisle, No. 17; Bibl. Nationale, No. 9428, f. 100.

Ordo Dedicationis Ecclesiae.

PRIMO eundum est ad locum ubi reliquiae positae sunt priori die, in quo etiam loco vigiliae prius sollempniter implendae sunt sub honore ipsorum sanctorum quorum reliquiae in novam ecclesiam ponendae sunt. Deinde sacranda est aqua a pontifice et mittenda est chrisma in aqua cum hac benedictione—

Deus qui ad salutem humani generis maxima . . .

Et canenda est tibi interim laetania, post quam sequitur oratio

Aufer a nobis . . .

alia

Fac nos Domine . .

Hac finita subleventur reliquiae cum feretro a sacerdotibus, canente clero antifonam *Cum jocunditate exibitis* vel ceteras antifonas ad deducendas reliquias usque ad hostium novae edificationis ad occidentem, post quas dicit pontifex orationem

Deus qui ex omni coaptatione . . .

Qua finita incipit pontifex aquam aspargere consecratam a foris sequendo feretro reliquiarum, cleroque canente antifonam *Asperges me Domine* cum psalmo L^{mo}, sed uno ex clericis in nova ecclesia clausis hostiis quasi latente. Nam pontifex circumit ecclesiam ab hostio in partem aquilonarem prima vice usque iterum ad idem hostium; et cum illic perventum fuerit pulsat hostium tribus vicibus, dicendo: *Tollite portas, principes, vestras et elevamini, portae aeternales, et introibit Rex gloriae.* Ille deintus respondens dicat: *Quis est iste rex gloriae?* Iterum circumienda est ecclesia secunda vice sicut prius, cum eadem antiphona et eodem psalmo, usquedum perveniatur ad hostium, atque iterum pulsetur sicut prius eisdem verbis et idem respondente deintus latente. Tunc tertio iterum circumienda est eodem modo cum eodem cantu usque iterum ad hostium. Tunc dicenti pontifici et pulsanti respondum est ei sicut prius: *Quis est iste rex gloriae?* Pontifex respondeat: *Dominus virtutum ipse est Rex gloriae.*

Tunc aperientur hostia et canenda est antiphona *Ambulate sancti Dei, ingredimini in domum Domini,* cum psalmo *Laetatus sum in his quae dicta sunt mihi* et cetera. Et ille qui prius fuerat intus quasi fugiens egrediatur ad illud hostium foras, iterum ingressurus per primum hostium vestitus vestimentis ecclesiasticis.

Dum ingreditur pontifex ecclesiam dicit orationem

Domum tuam Domine clementer . . .

Illa finita incipit iterum ab hostio ad partem aquilonarem ab intus aspargere aquam, antiphonam canente *Beati qui habitant in domo tua, Domine,* cum psalmo *Quam dilecta tabernacula tua, Domine,* usquedum prius circumeundo sicut a foris pervenerit ad hostium, et dicit orationem

Deus qui in omni loco . . .

Et sic iterum circumienda est cum supradicta antiphona et eodem psalmo usque ad idem hostium et dicenda est oratio

Deus qui loca nomini tuo . . .

Et cum tertio lustrata fuerit ab intus sicut primo et secundo, dicenda est oratio

Deus qui sacrandorum . . .

Tunc iterum incipiet clerus laetaniam positis reliquiis extra velum quod extensum est inter aedem et altare. Quo canente ingreditur pontifex cum deputatis ministris intra velum et facit maldam de aqua sanctificata unde recludantur reliquiae in confessione. Tunc veniens ad altare, aspargens illud tribus vicibus aqua sanctificata, inde sequitur benedictio tabulae⁽¹⁾ his verbis—

Singulare illud repropitiatorium . . .

Inde asparsio confessionis simul cum unctione chrismatis per quattuor angulos confessionis. Postea ponentur reliquiae in confessione cum tribus particulis corporis Domini ac tribus particulis thimiamatis canendo antiphonam *Sub altare Domini sedes accepistis, intercedite pro nobis apud quem gloriari meruistis.*

His expletis, superponendus est lapis super quem infundendum est oleum sanctificatum et expendendum in modum crucis. Similiter per quattuor angulos altaris modus crucis de eodem oleo significandus est. Inde benedictio altaris simul cum consecratione ejusdem—

Deprecamur misericordiam tuam . . .

Consecratio altaris.

Deus omnipotens, in cujus honore . . .

Inde benedictio linteaminum altaris et aliorum indumentorum necnon et vasorum sacro ministerio usui apta his verbis—

Exaudi Domine supplicum . . .

Et post hoc velatur altare. Post velatum vero dicitur oratio

Descendat quaesumus . . .

Ad missam—

Deus qui invisibiliter .

(i) talae

5.

ORDER OF THE OFFICES AT JERUSALEM TOWARDS THE END OF THE FOURTH CENTURY.

(Extract from the *Peregrinatio* of Etheria (Silvia).)

THE following are the final pages of a curious book discovered by Signor I. F. Gamurrini in a MS. at Arezzo, and published by him in the *Biblioteca dell'Accademia storico giuridica*, vol. iv., Rome, 1887, and in the *Studi e documenti di storia e diritto*, April to Sept., 1888. It is the account of a long pilgrimage to the holy places in the East, undertaken by a great lady who addresses it to her "sisters," that is to say, probably sisters in the religious profession. Her journey seems to have taken place in the time of Theodosius, and some important indications inclined Signor Gamurrini to identify her with Silvia, the sister of the celebrated minister Rufinus. This identification was not accepted as certain by any one, but was generally adopted for convenience of quotation. The real name of the pilgrim has been discovered by Dom M. Férotin (*Revue des questions historiques*, vol. lxxiv. [October, 1903] p. 367, *et seq.*). She was a virgin called Etheria,[1] of the province of Galicia [Spain] Valerius, a monk of this same country, who lived in the seventh century, has left us a life of this lady in a letter addressed to the Religious of Vierzo, in which the *Peregrinatio* is described at length. This short epistle has been known for some time (Florez, *España Sagrada*, vol. xvi. p. 366 ; Migne, *Pat. Lat.*, vol. lxxxvii. p. 421), but no one had thought of it in connection with the text discovered by Signor Gamurrini. Dom Férotin has published an edition of it (*op. cit.*, p. 379), revised from the original MSS. Henceforward, assigned to its real author, the lady's work must be cited as the *Peregrinato Etheriae*.

Several editions have appeared[2] since Signor Gamurrini's first. I have revised the text, which I took in the first instance from that editor, making special use of the edition by M. Paul Geyer, *Itin. Hierosol. Saec. IIII.-VIII.* vol. xxxix. of the Vienna *Corpus SS. Eccles. Latin*, pp. 71-101, in which his own corrections and conjectures, as well as those of preceding writers on the subject, may be found.

I have not thought it necessary to annotate the text. I add, however, a few explanations as to the ecclesiastical topography of Jerusalem and its environs.

The primitive Church, the Cathedral of Jerusalem, is that on Mount

---

[1] For the various readings of this lady's name, see p. 547.

[2] Among others · Palestine Pilgrims' Text Society, *The Pilgrimage of St. Silvia, etc., circa* 385 A D. Translated by John H. Bernard, D.D, with an appendix by Col Sir C. W. Wilson. London, 1891. Dom Fernand Cabrol has published an interesting treatise on the *Peregrinatio*, entitled *Les Églises de Jérusalem, la Discipline et la Liturgie au Quatrième Siècle.* Paris, 1895.

Sion, now served by the Armenians. According to tradition, it was the house in which the disciples met together on the evening of Easter Day, and eight days after, when the risen Saviour appeared to them. There also took place the descent of the Holy Spirit on the day of Pentecost. In the time of Theodosius it had ceased to be the ordinary place for worship. The bishop at that time lived near the Holy Sepulchre, close to the sanctuaries built by the Emperor Constantine on the sites of the Passion and the Resurrection.

These sacred buildings were three in number, not reckoning their dependencies: (1) the *Anastasis,* or Sanctuary of the Resurrection, where was the Holy Sepulchre. (2) The Sanctuary of the Cross, where the true cross and other relics were preserved. This was a double edifice, one part being the *ante Crucem,* consisting mainly of a large courtyard surrounded by cloisters, the other a roofed-in building, of lesser proportions, known as the *post Crucem.* (3) The Great Basilica, or *Martyrium,* also situated *post Crucem.* It was in the *Anastasis* that the daily offices were said, but the Mass on Sunday, and, generally speaking, the stations, when there was a large congregation, took place in the *Martyrium.* The old church on Mount Sion was only frequented on the stations of Wednesdays and Fridays, and also on Easter Day and its octave, and on Whitsun Day.

Outside Jerusalem, the Basilica of Bethlehem was the appointed place for meeting, at an early date, on the night of the Epiphany, and afterwards on Ascension Day. Stations were much more frequently held in the sanctuaries on the Mount of Olives. The most important of these was the *Eleona* (now the Church of the Ascension), where there was a grotto, in which, according to the tradition of that day, our Lord had held frequent converse with His disciples. Beyond, in the village of Bethany, was the *Lazarium,* or the house of Lazarus; these two sanctuaries were churches, and Mass could be celebrated in them. Above the Eleona, and not far from it, was a third sanctuary, which does not appear to have been a roofed-in building. It was called the *Imbomon,* and was the traditional site of the Ascension. This was, doubtless, what is now called the *Viri Galilaei.* Other small churches were to be encountered before reaching Bethany, near to Gethsemane on the slope of the Mount of Olives.

Etheria writes in vulgar Latin, difficult to accommodate to grammatical rules, but not so barbarous in character as that of the *Ordines,* of which we have already spoken. The word *missa* has still for her its primitive meaning of dismissal; she uses it for all meetings, for the offices as well as for the liturgy, always distinguishing between the *missa* of the catechumens and that of the faithful. When she speaks of a liturgical meeting properly so called, she uses the terms *oblatio* and *procedere.*

2 K

I.

Daily Offices.

1. *Matins.*[1]

Ut autem sciret affectio vestra quae operatio singulis diebus cotidie in locis sanctis habeatur, certas vos facere debui; sciens quia libenter haberetis haec cognoscere.

Nam singulis diebus, ante pullorum cantum, aperiuntur omnia hostia Anastasis, et descendent omnes monazontes et parthenae, ut hic dicunt; et non solum hii, sed et laici preter viri aut mulieres, qui tamen volunt maturius vigilare. Et ex ea hora usque in lucem dicuntur ymni[2] et psalmi responduntur, similiter et antiphonae; et cata singulos ymnos fit oratio. Nam presbyteri bini vel terni, similiter et diacones, singulis diebus vices habent simul cum monazontes, qui cata singulos ymnos vel antiphonas orationes dicunt. Jam autem ubi coeperit lucescere, tunc incipiunt matutinos ymnos dicere. Ecce et supervenit episcopus cum clero, et statim ingreditur intro spelunca, et de intro cancellos primum dicet orationem pro omnibus; commemorat etiam ipse nomina quorum vult; sic benedicet cathecuminos. Item dicet orationem et benedicet fideles. Et post hoc, exeunte episcopo de intro cancellos, omnes ad manum ei accedunt; et ille eos uno et uno benedicet exiens jam, ac sic fit missa, jam luce.

2 *Sext and None.*

Item hora sexta denuo descendent omnes similiter ad Anastasim, et dicuntur psalmi et antiphonae, donec commonetur

---

[1] While following Signor Gamurrini's latest text, I have introduced these divisions to enable the student of the present volume to understand better Etheria's narrative.

[2] On this passage, see above, pp. 115, 452, note 1. The word *ymni* does not mean a metrical hymn, it is the same thing as psalm or biblical canticle. Cf. p. 174, note 1.

episcopus; similiter descendet, et non sedet, sed statim intrat intra cancellos intra Anastasim, id est intra speluncam, ubi et mature; et inde similiter primum facit orationem; sic benedicet fideles, et sic exiens de cancellos, similiter ei ad manum acceditur. Ita ergo et hora nona fit, sicuti et ad sexta.

3. *Vespers.*

Hora autem decima (quod appellant hic *licinicon*,[1] nam nos dicimus lucernare), similiter se omnis multitudo colliget ad Anastasim, incenduntur omnes candelae et cerei, et fit lumen infinitum. Lumen autem de foris non affertur, sed de spelunca interiori eicitur, ubi noctu ac die semper lucerna lucet, id est de intro cancellos. Dicuntur etiam psalmi lucernares, sed et antiphonae diutius. Ecce et commonetur episcopus, et descendet, et sedet susum, nec non etiam et presbyteri sedent locis suis; dicuntur ymni vel antiphonae. Et at ubi perdicti fuerint juxta consuetudinem, lebat se episcopus, et stat ante cancellum, id est ante speluncam, et unus ex diaconibus facit commemorationem singulorum, sicut solet esse consuetudo. Et diacono dicente singulorum nomina, semper pisinni plurimi stant, respondentes semper: *Kyrie eleyson*, quod dicimus nos: *Miserere Domine*, quorum voces infinitae sunt. Et at ubi diaconus perdixerit omnia quae dicere habet, dicet orationem primum episcopus, et orat pro omnibus: et sic orant omnes, tam fideles, quam et cathecumini simul. Item mittet vocem diaconus ut unusquisque, quomodo stat, cathecuminus inclinet caput: et sic dicet episcopus stans benedictionem super cathecuminos. Item fit oratio, et denuo mittet diaconus vocem; et commonet ut unusquisque stans fidelium inclinent capita sua; item benedicet fideles episcopus, et sic fit missa Anastasi. Et incipient episcopo ad manum accedere singuli. Et postmodum de Anastasim usque ad Crucem [eum] ymnis ducitur episcopus; simul et omnis populus vadet. Ubi cum perventum fuerit, primum facit orationem, item benedicet cathecuminos, item fit alia

[1] Λυχνικόν.

oratio, item benedicit fideles. Et post hoc denuo tam episcopus quam omnis turba vadet denuo post Crucem, et ibi denuo similiter fit sicuti et ante Crucem. Et similiter ad manum episcopo acceditur sicut ad Anastasim, ita et ante Crucem, ita et post Crucem. Candelae autem vitreae ingentes ubique plurimae pendent, et cereofala plurima sunt, tam ante Anastasim quam etiam ante Crucem, sed et post Crucem. Finiuntur ergo haec omnia cum tenebris.

Haec operatio cotidie per dies sex ita habetur ad Crucem et ad Anastasim.

II.

Sunday Offices.

1. *Vigil.*

Septima autem die, id est dominica die, ante pullorum cantum colliget se omnis multitudo, quaecumque [1] esse potest in eo loco ac si per Pascha, in basilica quae est loco juxta Anastasim, foras tamen, ubi luminaria per hoc ipsud pendent. Dum enim verentur ne ad pullorum cantum non occurrant, antecessus veniunt et ibi sedent. Et dicuntur ymni nec non et antiphonae, et fiunt orationes cata singulos ymnos vel antiphonas. Nam et presbyteri et diacones semper parati sunt in eo loco ad vigilias propter multitudinem quae se colliget. Consuetudo enim talis est, ut ante pullorum cantum loca sancta non aperiantur. Mox autem primus pullus cantaverit, statim descendet episcopus, et intrat intro speluncam ad Anastasim. Aperiuntur hostia omnia, et intrat omnis multitudo ad Anastasim, ubi jam luminaria infinita lucent. Et quemadmodum ingressus fuerit populus, dicet psalmum quicunque de presbyteris, et respondent omnes; post

---

[1] Etheria means, it seems to me, that the multitude which assembled there was comparable with what is seen elsewhere on Easter Day.

hoc fit oratio. Item dicit psalmum quicumque de diaconibus, similiter fit oratio. Dicitur et tertius psalmus a quocumque clerico, fit et tertio oratio, et commemoratio omnium. Dictis ergo his tribus psalmis et factis orationibus tribus, ecce etiam thimiataria inferuntur intro spelunca Anastasis, ut tota basilica Anastasis repleatur odoribus. Et tunc ibi stat episcopus intro cancellos, prendet evangelium et accedet ad hostium, et leget resurrectionem Domini episcopus ipse. Quod cum coeperit legi, tantus rugitus et mugitus fit omnium hominum et tantae lacrimae, ut quamvis durissimus possit moveri in lacrimis, Dominum pro nobis tanta sustinuisse. Lecto ergo evangelio exit episcopus, et ducitur cum ymnis ad Crucem, et omnis populus cum illo. Ibi denuo dicitur unus psalmus, et fit oratio. Item benedicit fideles, et fit missa. Et exeunte episcopo, omnes ad manum accedunt. Mox autem recipit se episcopus in domum suam. Etiam ex illa hora revertuntur [1] omnes monazontes ad Anastasim, et psalmi dicuntur et antiphonae usque ad lucem, et cata singulos psalmos vel antiphonas fit oratio; vicibus enim quotidie presbyteri et diacones vigilant ad Anastasim cum populo. De laicis etiam, viris aut mulieribus, si qui volunt usque ad lucem, loco sunt; si qui nolunt, revertuntur in domos suas, et reponent se dormito.

2. *Mass.*

Cum luce autem, quia dominica dies est, proceditur in ecclesia majore quam fecit Constantinus; quae ecclesia in Golgotha est post Crucem; et fiunt omnia secundum consuetudinem quae ubique fit die dominica. Sane quia hic [2] consuetudo sic est ut de omnibus presbyteris qui sedent quanti volunt praedicent, et post illos omnes episcopus praedicat; quae praedicationes propterea semper dominicis diebus sunt, ut semper erudiatur populus in Scripturis et in Dei dilectione; quae praedicationes

---

[1] The ecclesiastical vigil is over; the monks remain to sing Matins. Cf. pp. 229, 449.
[2] Cf. p. 58.

dum dicuntur, grandis mora fit ut fiat missa ecclesiae; et ideo ante quartam horam, aut forte quintam, missa [non] fit. At ubi autem missa facta fuerit ecclesiae juxta consuetudinem qua et ubique fit, tunc de ecclesia monazontes cum ymnis ducunt episcopum usque ad Anastasim. Cum autem coeperit episcopus venire cum ymnis, aperiuntur omnia hostia de basilica Anastasis. Intrat omnis populus, fidelis tamen; nam cathecumini non. Et at ubi intraverit populus, intrat episcopus, et statim ingreditur intra cancellos martyrii speluncae. Primum aguntur gratiae Deo, et sic fit oratio pro omnibus; postmodum mittet vocem diaconus et inclinent capita sua omnes, quomodo stant; et sic benedicet eos episcopus stans intra cancellos interiores, et postmodum egreditur. Egredienti autem episcopo omnes ad manum accedent. Ac sic est, ut prope usque ad quintam aut sextam horam protraitur missa. Item et ad lucernare similiter fit juxta consuetudinem cotidianam.

Haec ergo consuetudo singulis diebus ita per totum annum custoditur, exceptis diebus sollennibus, quibus et ipsis quemadmodum fiat infra annotavimus. Hoc autem inter omnia satis praecipuum est quod faciunt, ut psalmi vel antiphonae apti semper dicantur, tam qui nocte dicuntur, tam qui contra mature, tam etiam qui per diem vel sexta aut nona vel ad lucernare, semper ita apti et ita rationabiles, ut ad ipsam rem pertineant quae agitur. Et cum toto anno semper dominica die in ecclesia majore procedatur, id est quae in Golgotha est (id est post Crucem), quam fecit Constantinus, una tantum die dominica, id est Quinquagesimarum per Pentecosten, in Syon proceditur, sicut infra annotatum invenietis; sic tamen in Syon, ut antequam sit hora tertia et [1] illuc eatur, fiat primum missa in ecclesiam majorem.[2]

* * * * * * *

[1] I supply *et*. On this, see *infra*, p. 516.
[2] A leaf is wanting here. It contained, besides observations on the ordinary days, the beginning of the description of the festivals on the Nativity. These festivals took place at Jerusalem on the 6th of January, and not on the 25th of December (see above, p. 259). There was a night Station at Bethlehem, and a day Mass at Jerusalem. The procession started from Bethlehem. Cf. *supra*, p. 265.

III.

FESTIVALS AT EPIPHANY.

1. *Nocturnal Station at Bethlehem.*

* * * * * * *

Benedictus qui venit in nomine Domini et cetera quae secuntur. Et quoniam per monazontes, qui pedibus vadent, necesse est levius iri, ac sic pervenitur Jerusolima ea hora qua incipit homo hominem posse cognoscere, id est prope luce, ante tamen quam lux fiat. Ubi cum perventum fuerit statim sic in Anastase ingreditur episcopus et omnes cum eo, ubi luminaria jam supra modo lucent. Dicitur ergo ibi unus psalmus, fit oratio, benedicuntur ab episcopo primum cathecumini, item fideles. Recipit se episcopus, et vadent se unusquisque ad ospitium suum, ut se resumant. Monazontes autem usque ad lucem ibi sunt, et ymnos dicunt.

2. *Mass at Jerusalem.*

At ubi autem resumpserit se populus, hora incipiente secunda, colligent se omnes in ecclesia majore quae est in Golgotha. Qui autem ornatus sit illa die ecclesiae vel Anastasis, aut Crucis, aut in Bethleem superfluum fuit scribi. Ubi extra aurum et gemmas aut sirico, nichil aliud vides; nam et si vela vides, auroclava olosericae sunt; si cortinas vides, similiter auroclavae olosericae sunt. Ministerium autem omne genus aureum gemmatum profertur illa die. Numerus autem vel ponderatio de ceriofalis, vel cicindelis, aut lucernis, vel diverso ministerio, nunquid vel extimari aut scribi potest? Nam quid dicam de ornatu fabricae ipsius, quam Constantinus sub praesentia matris suae, in quantum vires regni sui habuit, honoravit auro, musivo et marmore pretioso, tam ecclesiam majorem, quam Anastasim, vel ad Crucem, vel cetera loca sancta in Jerusolima? Sed ut redeamus ad rem, fit ergo prima die missa in ecclesia majore, quae est in Golgotha. Et quoniam dum praedicant vel legent singulas lectiones vel dicunt ymnos, omnia tamen apta ipsi diei, et inde postmodum cum missa ecclesiae facta fuerit, hitur cum ymnis ad Anastasim, juxta consuetudinem : ac sic fit missa forsitan sexta hora. Ipsa autem die, similiter et ad lucernare, juxta consuetudinem cotidianam fit.

3. *Octave of the Festival.*

Alia denuo die similiter in ipsa ecclesia proceditur in Golgotha; hoc idem et tertia die; per triduo ergo haec omnis [1] laetitia in ecclesia quam fecit Constantinus celebratur usque ad sextam. Quarta die in Eleona, id est in ecclesia quae est in monte Oliveti, pulchra satis, similiter omnia ita ornantur et ita celebrantur ibi. Quinta die in Lazariu, quod est ab Jerusolima forsitan ad mille quingentos passus. Sexta die in Syon, septima die in Anastase, octava die ad Crucem. Ac sic ergo per octo dies haec omnis laetitia et is hornatus celebratur in omnibus locis sanctis quos superius nominavi. In Bethleem autem per totos octo dies cotidie is ornatus est et ipsa laetitia celebratur a presbyteris et ab omni clero ipsius loci, et a monazontes qui in ipso loco deputati sunt. Nam ex illa hora, qua omnes nocte in Jerusolima revertuntur cum episcopo, tunc loci ipsius monachi, quicumque sunt usque ad lucem in ecclesia in Bethleem pervigilant, ymnos seu antiphonas dicentes; quia episcopum necesse est hos dies

---

(1) haec omnis] homines *cod.*

semper in Jerusolima tenere. Pro sollemnitate autem et laetitia ipsius diei infinitae turbae se undique colligent in Jerusolima, non solum monazontes, sed et laici, viri aut mulieres.

4. *The Presentation* (14th February).

Sane Quadragesimae de Epiphania [1] valde cum summo honore hic celebrantur. Nam eadem die processio est in Anastase, et omnes procedunt et ordine[suo] aguntur omnia cum summa laetitia, ac si per Pascha. Praedicant etiam omnes presbyteri, et sic episcopus, semper de eo loco tractantes evangelii, ubi quadragesima die tulerunt Dominum in templo Joseph et Maria, et viderunt eum Symeon vel Anna prophetissa filia Fanuhel, et de verbis eorum quae dixerunt viso Domino, vel de oblatione ipsa qua[m] obtulerunt parentes. Et postmodum celebratis omnibus per ordinem (1) quae consuetudinis sunt, aguntur sacramenta, et sic fit missa.

IV.

Lent.

Item dies paschales cum venerint, celebrantur sic. Nam sicut apud nos quadragesimae ante Pascha adtenduntur, ita hic octo septimanas [2] attenduntur ante Pascha. Propterea autem octo septimanae attenduntur, quia dominicis diebus et sabbato non jejunantur, excepta una die sabbati qua vigiliae paschales sunt et necesse est jejunari; extra ipsum ergo diem penitus nunquam hic toto anno sabbato jejunatur. Ac sic ergo de octo septimanis deductis octo diebus dominicis et septem sabbatis (quia necesse est una sabbati jejunari, ut superius

(1) ordines *cod*.

[1] Cf p 272.
[2] Cf. p. 243.

dixi), remanent dies quadraginta et unum qui jejunantur; quod hic appellant Eortae, id est Quadragesimas.

1. *Services on Sundays.*

Singuli autem dies singularum ebdomadarum aguntur sic, id est ut die dominica de pullo primo legat episcopus intra Anastase locum resurrectionis Domini de evangelio, sicut et toto anno dominicis diebus fi[t], et similiter usque ad lucem aguntur ad Anastasem et ad Crucem quae et toto anno dominicis diebus fiunt. Postmodum mane, sicut et semper dominica die, proceditur, et aguntur quae dominicis diebus consuetudo est agi, in ecclesia majore quae appellatur Martyrio, quae est in Golgotha post Crucem. Et similiter, missa de ecclesia facta, ad Anastase itur cum ymnis, sicut semper dominicis diebus fit. Haec ergo dum aguntur, facit se hora quinta. Lucernare hoc idem hora sua fit, sicut semper ad Anastasem et ad Crucem, sicut et singulis locis sanctis fit; dominica enim die nona non [1] fit.

2. *Week-day Services.*

Item secunda feria similiter de pullo primo ad Anastasem itur sicut et toto anno, et aguntur usque ad mane quae semper. Denuo ad tertia itur ad Anastasim, et aguntur quae toto anno ad sextam solent agi: quoniam in diebus Quadragesimarum et hoc additur, ut ad tertiam eatur; item ad sextam et nonam et lucernare ita aguntur sicut consuetudo est per totum annum agi semper in ipsis locis sanctis. Similiter et tertia feria, similiter omnia aguntur sicut et secunda feria.

3. *Wednesday and Friday.*

Quarta feria autem similiter itur de noctu ad Anastase, et aguntur ea quae semper usque ad mane; similiter et ad

---

[1] I supply here *non.*

tertiam et ad sexta; ad nonam autem, quia consuetudo est
semper, id est toto anno, quarta feria et sexta feria ad nona
in Syon procedi, quoniam in istis locis, excepto si martiriorum
dies evenerit, semper quarta et sexta feria etiam et a cathecuminis jejunatur, et ideo ad nonam in Syon proceditur.
Nam si fortuito in Quadragesimis martyrorum dies evenerit
quarta feria aut sexta feria, atque ad nona in Syon proceditur. Diebus vero Quadragesimarum, ut superius dixi,
quarta feria ad nona in Syon proceditur juxta consuetudinem
totius anni, et omnia aguntur quae consuetudo est ad nonam
agi praeter oblatio: nam ut semper populus discat legem,
et episcopus et presbyter praedicant assidue. Cum autem
facta fuerit missa, inde cum ymnis populus deducet episcopum
usque ad Anastasem; inde sic venitur ut cum intratur in
Anastase jam e[s]t hora[1] lucernari: sic dicuntur ymni et
antiphonae, fiunt orationes, et fit missa lucernaris in Anastase
et ad Crucem. Missa autem lucernaris in isdem diebus, id est
Quadragesimarum, serius fit semper quam per toto anno. Quinta
feria autem similiter omnia aguntur sicut secunda feria et tertia
feria. Sexta feria autem similiter omnia aguntur sicut quarta
feria, et similiter ad nonam in Syon itur et similiter inde cum
ymnis usque ad Anastase adducetur episcopus.

4. *Saturday.*

Sed sexta feria vigiliae in Anastase celebrantur ab ea hora qua
de Sion ventum fuerit cum ymnis, usque in mane, id est de hora
lucernarii, quemadmodum intratum fuerit, in alia die mane, id est
Sabbato. Fit autem oblatio in Anastase maturius, ita ut fiat
missa ante solem. Tota autem nocte vicibus dicuntur psalmi
responsorii, vicibus antiphonae, vicibus lectiones diversae, quae

---

[1] Tota lucernari sic sic, *cod* I correct *tota* into *hora*, and I omit the first *sic*.

omnia usque in mane protrahuntur. Missa autem quae fit sabbato ad Anastase, ante solem fit, hoc est oblatio, ut ea hora qua incipit sol procedere, jam missa [1] in Anastase facta sit. Sic ergo singulae septimanae celebrantur Quadragesimarum. Quod autem dixi, maturius fit missa sabbato, id est ante solem, propterea fit ut citius absolvant hi quos dicunt hic [eb]domadarios. Nam talis consuetudo est hic jejuniorum in Quadragesimis, ut hi quos appellant ebdomadarios, id est qui faciunt septimanas, dominica die, quia hora quinta fit missa, ut manducent. Et quemadmodum prandiderint dominica die, jam non manducant, nisi sabbato mane, mox communicaverint in Anastase. Propter ipsos ergo, ut citius absolvant, ante sole fit missa in Anastase sabbato. Quod autem dixi, propter illos fit missa mane, non quod illi soli communicent, sed omnes communicant qui volunt eadem die in Anastase communicare.

5. *The Fast.*

Jejuniorum enim consuetudo hic talis est in Quadragesimis, ut alii, quemadmodum manducaverint dominica die post missa, id est hora quinta aut sexta, jam non manducent per tota septimana, nisi sabbato veniente post missa Anastasis, hi qui faciunt ebdomadas. Sabbato autem, quod manducaverint mane, jam nec sera manducant, sed ad aliam diem, id est dominica, prandent post missa ecclesiae hora quinta vel plus; et postea jam non manducent nisi sabbato veniente, sicut superius dixi. Consuetudo enim hic talis est; omnes, qui sunt, ut hic dicunt, Aputactitae, viri vel feminae, non solum diebus Quadragesimarum, sed et toto anno, qua manducant, semel in die manducant. Si qui autem sunt de ipsis Aputactites, qui non possunt facere integras septimanas jejuniorum, sicut superius diximus, in totis Quadragesimis, in medio quinta feria cenant; qui autem nec hoc potest, biduanas facit per totas Quadragesimas; qui autem nec ipsud, de sera ad seram manducant. Nemo autem exigit quantum debeat facere, sed unusquisque ut potest id facit; nec ille laudatur qui satis fecerit, nec ille vituperatur qui minus.

(i) jam missa] ad missam *cod.*

PEREGRINATIO ETHERIAE (SILVIAE).

Talis est enim hic consuetudo. Esca autem eorum Quadragesimarum diebus haec est, ut nec panem, quid liberari[1] non potest, nec oleum gustent, nec aliquid quod de arboribus est, sed tantum aqua et sorbitione modica de farina. Quadragesimarum sic fit, ut diximus.

Et completo earum septimanarum vigiliae in Anastase sunt de hora lucernarii sexta feria, qua de Syon venitur cum psalmis, usque in mane sabbato, qua oblatio fit in Anastase. Item secunda septimana et tertia et quarta et quinta et sexta similiter fiunt ut prima de Quadragesimis.

V.

HOLY WEEK AND THE FESTIVALS AT EASTER.

1. *Saturday before Palm Sunday.—Station at Bethany.*

Septima autem septimana cum venerit, id est quando jam due superant cum ipsa ut Pascha sit, singulis diebus omnia quidem sic aguntur sicut et ceteris septimanis quae transierunt. Tantummodo quod vigiliae quae in illis septimanis in Anastase factae sunt, septima autem septimana id est sexta feria, in Syon fiunt vigiliae juxta consuetudinem, ea quae in Anastase factae sunt per sex septimanas. Dicuntur autem totis vigiliis[(1)] apti psalmi semper vel antiphonae, tam loco quam dici.

At ubi autem coeperit se mane facere sabbato illucescente, offeret episcopus, et facit oblationem, mane sabbato. Jam ut fiat missa, mittit vocem archidiaconus, et dicit: "Omnes hodie hora septima in Lazario parati simus." Ac sic ergo cum ceperit se hora septima facere, omnes ad Lazarium veniunt. Lazarium

(i) toti singulis *cod.*

[1] There is, perhaps, a corruption of the text here; but I do not see why *liberari* should be corrected into *librari*, as Sig Gamurrini has done. The same editor has put lower down *Jejunium* before *Quadragesimarum*. On these fasts, see p 241, *et seq.*

autem, id est Bethania, est forsitan secundo miliario a civitate. Euntibus autem de Jerusolima in Lazarium forsitan ad quingentos passus de eodem loco, ecclesia est in strata in eo loco in quo occurrit Domino Maria soror Lazari. Ibi ergo cum venerit episcopus, occurrent illi omnes monachi, et populus ibi ingreditur; dicitur unus ymnus et una antiphona, et legitur ipse locus de evangelio ubi occurrit soror Lazari Domino. Et sic, facta oratione et benedictis omnibus, inde jam usque ad Lazarium cum ymnis itur. In Lazario autem cum ventum fuerit, ita se omnis multitudo colligit, ut non solum ipse locus, sed et campi omnes in giro pleni sint hominibus. Dicuntur ymni, etiam et antiphonae, apti ipsi diei et loco; similiter et lectiones apte diei quaecumque leguntur. Iam autem, ut fiat missa, denuntiatur Pascha, id est, subit presbyter in altiori loco, et leget illum locum qui scriptus est in evangelio: *Cum venisset Jesus in Bethania ante sex dies paschae*, et cetera. Lecto ergo eo loco et annuntiata Pascha, fit missa. Propterea autem ea die hoc agitur, quoniam sicut in evangelio scriptum est, ante sex dies Paschae factum hoc fuisset in Bethania; de sabbato enim usque in quinta feria, qua post cena noctu comprehenditur Dominus, sex dies sunt. Revertuntur ergo omnes ad civitatem, rectus ad Anastase, et fit lucernare juxta consuetudinem.

2. Palm Sunday.—(a) Mass.

Alia ergo die, id est dominica qua [1] intratur in septimana paschale, quam hic appellant septimana major, celebratis de pullorum cantu his quae consuetudinis sunt in Anastase vel ad Crucem, usque ad mane agitur. Die ergo dominica mane proceditur juxta consuetudinem in ecclesia majore, quae appellatur Martyrium. Propterea autem Martyrium appellatur quia in Golgotha est, id est post Crucem, ubi Dominus passus est, et ideo Martyrio. Cum ergo celebrata fuerint omnia juxta consuetudinem in ecclesia majore, et antequam fiat missa, mittet vocem archidiaconus, et dicit primum: "Juxta septimana omne, id est die crastino, hora nona, omnes ad Martyrium conveniamus,

[1] quae *cod*.

id est in ecclesia majore." Item mittet vocem alteram, et dicet:
"Hodie omnes hora septima in Eleona parati simus." Facta
ergo missa in ecclesia majore, id est ad Martyrium, deducitur
episcopus cum ymnis ad Anastase, et ibi completis quae consuetudo est diebus dominicis fieri in Anastase post missa
Martyrii, etiam unusquisque hiens ad domum suam festinat
manducare, ut hora inquoante septima omnes in ecclesia parati
sint quae est in Eleona, id est in monte Oliveti; ibi est spelunca
illa, in qua docebat Dominus.

(b) *Procession in the Evening.*

Hora ergo septima omnis populus ascendet in monte Oliveti,
id est in Eleona; in ecclesia sedet episcopus; dicuntur ymni et
antiphonae aptae diei ipsi vel loco, lectiones etiam similiter. Et
cum coeperit se facere hora nona, subitur cum ymnis in Imbomon,
id est in eo loco de quo ascendit Dominus in caelis, et ibi seditur:
nam omnis populus semper presente episcopo jubetur sedere;
tantum quod diacones soli stant semper. Dicuntur et ibi ymni
vel antiphonae aptae loco aut diei, similiter et lectiones interpositae et orationes. Et jam cum coeperit esse hora undecima,
legitur ille locus de evangelio, ubi infantes cum ramis vel palmis
occurrerunt Domino, dicentes: *Benedictus qui venit in nomine
Domini.* Et statim levat se episcopus et omnis populus; porro
inde de summo monte Oliveti totum pedibus itur. Nam totus
populus ante ipsum cum ymnis vel antiphonis, respondentes
semper: *Benedictus qui venit in nomine Domini.* Et quotquot
sunt infantes in hisdem locis, usque etiam qui [1] pedibus ambulare
non possunt, quia teneri sunt, in collo illos parentes sui tenent,
omnes ramos tenentes, alii palmarum, alii olivarum; et sic
deducetur episcopus in eo typo quo tunc Dominus deductus est.
Et de summo monte usque ad civitatem, et inde ad Anastase per
totam civitatem, totum pedibus omnes, sed et si quae matronae
sunt aut si qui domini, sic deducunt episcopum respondentes, et
sic lente et lente, ne lassetur populus; porro jam sera pervenitur ad Anastase. Ubi cum ventum fuerit, quamlibet sero sit,

[1] quae *cod.*

totum fit lucernare; fit denuo oratio ad Crucem et dimittitur populus.

3. *Monday in Holy Week.*

Item alia die, id est secunda feria, aguntur quae consuetudinis sunt de pullo primo agi usque ad mane ad Anastase; similiter et ad tertia et ad sexta aguntur ea quae totis Quadragesimis. Ad nona autem omnes in ecclesia majore, id est ad Martyrium, colligent se, et ibi usque ad horam primam noctis semper ymni et antiphonae dicuntur, lectiones etiam aptae diei et loco leguntur, interpositae semper orationes. Lucernarium etiam agitur ibi, cum coeperit hora esse : sic est ergo ut nocte etiam fiat missa ad Martyrium. Ubi cum factum fuerit missa, inde cum ymnis ad Anastase ducitur episcopus. In quo autem ingressus fuerit in Anastase, dicitur unus ymnus, fit oratio, benedicuntur cathecumini, item fideles, et fit missa.

4. *Tuesday in Holy Week.*

Item tertia feria similiter omnia fiunt sicut secunda feria. Illud solum additur tertia feria, quod nocte sera, postea quam missa facta fuerit ad Martyrium, et itum fuerit ad Anastase, et denuo in Anastase missa facta fuerit, omnes illa hora noctu vadent in ecclesia quae est in monte Eleona. In qua ecclesia cum ventum fuerit, intrat episcopus intra spelunca in qua spelunca solebat Dominus docere discipulos, et accipit codicem evangelii, et stans ipse episcopus leget verba Domini quae scripta sunt in evangelio in cata Matheo, id est ubi dicit: *Videte ne quis vos seducat.* Et omnem ipsam allocutionem perleget episcopus. At ubi autem illa perlegerit, fit oratio, benedicuntur cathecumini, item et fideles, fit missa, et revertuntur a monte unusquisque ad domum suam satis sera jam nocte.

5. *Wednesday in Holy Week.*

Item quarta feria aguntur omnia per tota die a pullo primo sicut secunda feria et tertia feria, sed posteaquam missa facta fuerit nocte ad Martyrium et deductus fuerit episcopus cum ymnis ad Anastase, statim intrat episcopus in spelunca quae est in Anastase, et stat intra cancellos; presbyter autem ante cancellum stat, et accipit evangelium, et legit illum locum ubi Judas Scariothes hivit ad Judeos, definivit quid ei darent ut traderet Dominum. Qui locus at ubi lectus fuerit, tantus rugitus et mugitus est totius populi, ut nullus sit qui moveri non possit in lacrimis in ea hora. Postmodum fit oratio, benedicuntur cathecumini, postmodum fideles, et fit missa.

6. *Maundy Thursday.*—(*a*) *Evening Masses.*

Item quinta feria aguntur ea de pullo primo quae consuetudinis est usque ad mane ad Anastase, similiter ad tertia, et ad sexta. Octava autem hora juxta consuetudinem ad Martyrium colliget se omnis populus: propterea autem temporius quam ceteris diebus, quia citius missa fieri necesse est. Itaque ergo collecto omni populo aguntur quae agenda sunt; fit ipsa die oblatio ad Martyrium, et facitur missa hora forsitan decima. Ibidem, antea autem quam fiat missa, mittet vocem archidiaconus, et dicet: " Hora prima noctis omnes in ecclesia quae est in Eleona conveniamus, quoniam maximus labor nobis instat hodie nocte ista." Facta ergo missa Martyrii venit[ur] post Crucem, dicitur ibi unus ymnus tantum, fit oratio, et offeret episcopus ibi oblationem, et communicant omnes. Excepta enim ipsa die una per totum annum nunquam offeritur post Crucem, nisi ipsa die tantum. Facta ergo et ibi missa, itur ad Anastase; fit oratio; benedicuntur juxta consuetudinem cathecumini et sic fideles, et fit missa.

(b) *Night Station on the Mount of Olives.*

Et sic unusquisque festinat reverti in domum suam, ut manducet; quia statim ut manducaverint, omnes vadent in Eleona, in ecclesia ea, in qua est spelunca in qua ipsa die Dominus cum apostolis fuit. Et ibi usque ad hora noctis forsitan quinta, semper aut ymni, aut antiphonae aptae diei et loco, similiter et lectiones dicuntur; interpositae orationes fiunt; loca etiam ea de evangelio leguntur in quibus Dominus allocutus est discipulos eadem die, sedens in eadem spelunca quae in ipsa ecclesia est. Et inde jam hora noctis forsitan sexta itur susu in Imbomon cum ymnis in eo loco unde ascendit Dominus in caelis. Et ibi denuo similiter lectiones et ymni et antiphonae aptae diei dicuntur; orationes etiam ipsae quaecumque fiunt, quas dicet episcopus, semper et diei et loco aptas dicet.

(c) *Stations at Gethsemane.*

Ac sic ergo cum ceperit esse pullorum cantus, descenditur de Imbomon cum ymnis et accedit[ur] eodem loco ubi oravit Dominus, sicut scriptum est in evangelio: *Et accessit quantum jactus lapidis, et oravit,* et cetera. In eo enim loco ecclesia est elegans. Ingreditur ibi episcopus et omnis populus; dicitur ibi oratio apta loco et diei; dicitur etiam unus ymnus aptus, et legitur ipse locus de evangelio, ubi dixit discipulis suis: *Vigilate, ne intretis in temptationem.* Et omnis ipse locus perlegitur ibi; et fit denuo oratio.

Et jam inde cum ymnis usque ad minimus infans in Gessamani pedibus cum episcopo descendent; ubi prae tam magna turba multitudinis, et fatigati de vigiliis et jejuniis cotidianis lassi, quia tam magnum montem necesse habent descendere, lente et lente cum ymnis venitur in Gessamani. Candelae autem ecclesiasticae super ducentae paratae sunt propter lumen omni populo. Cum ergo perventum fuerit in Gessamani, fit primum oratio apta; sic dicitur ymnus; item legitur ille locus de evangelio, ubi comprehensus est Dominus. Qui locus ad quod lectus fuerit, tantus rugitus et mugitus totius populi est cum fletu, ut forsitan porro ad civitatem gemitus populi omnis auditus sit.

(d) *Return to Jerusalem.*

Et jam ex illa hora hitur ad civitatem pedibus cum ymnis; pervenitur ad portam ea hora qua incipit quasi homo hominem cognoscere; inde totum per mediam civitatem omnes usque ad unum, majores atque minores, divites, pauperes, toti ibi parati, specialiter illa die nullus recedit a vigiliis usque in mane. Sic deducitur episcopus a Gessemani usque ad portam, et inde per totam civitate[m] usque ad Crucem.

7. *Good Friday* —(a) *Service at Daybreak.*

Ante Crucem autem at ubi ventum fuerit, jam lux quasi clara incipit esse. Ibi denuo legitur ille locus de evangelio, ubi adducitur Dominus ad Pilatum, et omnia quaecumque scripta sunt Pilatum ad Dominum dixisse aut ad Judeos, totum legitur. Postmodum autem alloquitur episcopus populum, confortans eos, quoniam et tota nocte laboraverint et adhuc laboraturi sint ipsa die, ut non lassentur, sed habeant spem in Deo, qui eis pro eo labore majorem mercedem redditurus sit. Et sic confortans eos, ut potest ipse, alloquens dicit eis: "Ite interim nunc unusquisque ad domumcellas vestras, sedete vobis et modico, et ad horam prope secundam diei omnes parati estote hic, ut de ea hora usque ad sexta sanctum lignum crucis possitis videre, ad salutem sibi unusquisque nostrum credens profuturum; de hora enim sexta denuo necesse habemus hic omnes convenire in isto loco, id est ante Crucem, ut lectionibus et orationibus usque ad noctem operam demus."

(b) *The Column of the Flagellation.*

Post hoc ergo missa facta de Cruce, id est antequam sol procedat, statim unusquisque animosi vadent in Syon orare ad columnam illam ad quam[(1)] flagellatus est Dominus. Inde reversi sedent modice in domibus suis, et statim toti parati sunt.

(c) *Adoration of the Cross.*

Et sic ponitur cathedra episcopo in Golgotha post Crucem, quae stat nunc;[1] residet episcopus hic cathedra; ponitur ante eum mensa sublinteata; stant in giro mensa diacones; et affertur loculus argenteus deauratus in quo est lignum sanctum crucis; aperitur et profertur; ponitur in mensa quam lignum crucis quam titulus. Cum ergo positum fuerit in mensa, episcopus sedens de manibus suis summitates de ligno sancto premet; diacones autem qui in giro stant custodent. Hoc autem propterea sic custoditur, quia consuetudo est ut unus et unus omnis populus veniens, tam fideles quam cathecumini, acclinant se ad mensam, osculentur sanctum lignum, et pertranseant. Et quoniam, nescio quando, dicitur quidam fixisse morsum et furasset sancto ligno, ideo nunc a diaconibus qui in giro stant, sic custoditur, ne quis veniens audeat denuo sic facere. Ac sic ergo omnis populus transit, unus et unus, toti acclinantes se, primum de fronte, sic de occulis tangentes crucem et titulum et sic osculantes crucem pertranseunt; manum autem nemo mittit ad tangendum. At ubi autem osculati fuerint crucem [et] pertransierint, stat diaconus, tenet anulum Salomonis et cornu illud de quo reges unguebantur; osculantur et cornu, attendunt et anulum minus secunda usque ad horam

(i) quem *cod*.

[1] I do not understand *quae stat nunc*.

sextam **omnis** populus transit, per unum ostium intrans, per [1] alterum perexiens, quoniam hoc in eo loco fit in quo pridie, id est quinta feria, oblatio facta est.

(d) Station at Golgotha.

At ubi autem sexta hora se fecerit, sic itur ante Crucem, sive pluvia sive aestus sit, quia ipse locus subdivanus est, id est quasi atrium valde grandem et pulchrum satis quod est inter Cruce et Anastase : ibi ergo omnis populus se colliget ita ut nec aperiri possit. Episcopo autem cathedra ponitur ante Cruce ; et de sexta usque ad nona aliud nichil fit, nisi leguntur lectiones sic ; id est, ita legitur : primum de psalmis, ubicumque de passione dixit ; legitur et de apostolo sive de epistolis apostolorum, vel de actionibus, ubicumque de passione Domini dixerunt, nec non et de evangeliis leguntur loca, ubi patitur ; item legitur de prophetis ubi passurum Dominum dixerunt ; item legitur de evangeliis ubi passionem dicit. Ac sic ab hora sexta usque ad horam nonam semper sic leguntur lectiones aut dicuntur ymni, ut ostendatur omni populo quia quicquid dixerunt prophetae futurum de passione Domini, ostendatur tam per evangelia quam etiam per apostolorum scripturas factum esse. Et sic per illas tres horas docetur populus omnis nichil factum esse quod non prius dictum sit, et nihil dictum esse[(1)] quod non totum completum sit. Semper autem interponuntur orationes, quae orationes et ipsae aptae diei sunt. Ad singulas autem lectiones et orationes tantus affectus et gemitus totius populi est ut mirum sit ; nam nullus est neque major neque minor, qui in illa die illis tribus horis tantum ploret quantum nec extimari potest, Dominum pro nobis ea passum fuisse.

Post hoc cum coeperit se jam hora nona facere, legitur jam ille locus de evangelio cata Johannem, ubi reddidit spiritum. Quo lecto, jam fit oratio et missa.

(i) esset *cod.*

[1] *Per alterum* is repeated twice in the manuscript.

(e) Evening Offices.

At ubi autem missa facta fuerit de ante Cruce, statim omnia [1] in ecclesia majore ad Martyrium aguntur ea quae per ipsa septimana de hora nona, qua ad Martyrium convenitur, consueverunt agi usque ad sero per ipsa septimana. Missa autem facta de Martyrium venitur ad Anastase; et ibi cum ventum fuerit, legitur ille locus de evangelio, ubi petit corpus Domini Joseph a Pilato [et] ponet illud in sepulcro novo. Hoc autem lecto, fit oratio, benedicuntur cathecumini; sic fit missa.

Ipsa autem die non mittitur vox ut pervigiletur ad Anastase, quoniam scit populum fatigatum esse; sed consuetudo est ut pervigiletur ibi. Ac sic qui vult de populo, immo qui possunt, vigilant; qui autem non possunt, non vigilant ibi usque in mane. Clerici autem vigilant ibi, id est qui aut fortiores sunt, aut juveniores: et tota nocte dicuntur ibi ymni et antiphonae usque ad mane. Maxima autem turba pervigilant, alii de sera, alii de media nocte qui ut possunt.

8 *Vigil of Easter.*

Sabbato autem alia die juxta consuetudinem fit ad tertia; item fit ad sexta: ad nonam autem jam non fit sabbato, sed parantur vigiliae paschales in ecclesia majore, id est in Martyrium. Vigiliae autem paschales sic fiunt quemadmodum ad nos. Hoc solum hic amplius fit quod infantes, cum baptidiati fuerint et vestiti, quemadmodum exient de fonte, simul cum episcopo primum ad Anastase ducuntur. Intrat episcopus intro cancellos Anastasis; dicitur unus ymnus; et sic facit orationem episcopus pro eis, et sic venit ad ecclesiam majorem cum eis, ubi juxta consuetudinem omnis populus vigilat. Aguntur ibi quae consuetudinis est etiam et aput nos, et facta oblatione fit missa. Et post facta missa vigiliarum in ecclesia majore, statim cum ymnis venitur ad Anastase; et ibi denuo legitur ille locus evangelii resurrectionis. Fit oratio; et denuo offeret episcopus; sed

(1) omnes *cod.*

totum ad momentum fit propter populum, ne diutius tardetur, et sic jam dimittetur populus. Ea autem hora fit missa vigiliarum ipsa die, qua hora et aput nos.

9. *Octave of Easter.*

Sero autem illi dies paschales sic attenduntur quemadmodum et ad nos, et ordine suo fiunt missae per octo dies paschales, sicut et ubique fit per Pascha usque ad octavas. Hic autem ipse ornatus est et ipsa compositio, et per octo dies Paschae, quae et per Epiphania, tam in ecclesia majore, quam ad Anastase, aut ad Crucem, vel in Eleona, sed et in Bethleem, nec non etiam in Lazariu, vel ubique, quia dies paschales sunt. Proceditur autem ipsa die dominica prima in ecclesia majore, id est ad Martyrium, et secunda feria, et tertia feria, ubi ita tamen, ut semper missa facta de Martyrio, ad Anastase veniatur cum ymnis. Quarta feria autem in Eleon[a] proceditur; quinta feria ad Anastase; sexta feria in Syon; sabbato ante Cruce; dominica autem die, id est octavis, denuo in ecclesia majore, id est ad Martyrium.

Ipsis autem octo diebus paschalibus cotidie post prandium episcopus cum omni clero et omnibus infantibus, id est qui baptidiati fuerint, et omnibus qui Aputactitae sunt viri ac feminae, nec non etiam et de plebe quanti volunt, in Eleona ascendent. Dicuntur ymni, fiunt orationes, tam in ecclesia quae in Eleona est, in qua est spelunca, in qua docebat Jesus discipulos; tam etiam in Imbomon, id est in eo loco de quo Dominus ascendit in caelis. Et posteaquam dicti fuerint psalmi et oratio facta fuerit, inde usque ad Anastase cum ymnis descenditur hora lucernae. Hoc per totos octo dies fit.

10. *Vesper Station at Sion on Easter Sunday.*

Sane dominica die per Pascha, post missa lucernarii id est de Anastase, omnis populus episcopum cum ymnis in Syon ducet. Ubi cum ventum fuerit, dicuntur ymni apti diei et loco, fit oratio, et legitur ille locus de evangelio, ubi eadem die Dominus in eodem loco, ubi ipsa ecclesia nunc in Syon est, clausis ostiis, ingressus est discipulis; id est quando tunc unus ex discipulis ibi⁽¹⁾ non erat, id est Thomas, qua reversus est, et dicentibus ei aliis apostolis, quia Dominum vidissent, ille dixit: "Non credo, nisi videro." Hoc lecto, fit denuo oratio; benedicuntur cathecumini, item fideles, et revertuntur unusquisque ad domum suam sera, hora forsitan noctis secunda.

11. *Sunday after Easter.*

Item octavis Paschae, id est die dominica, statim post sexta omnis populus cum episcopo ad Eleona ascendit. Primum in ecclesia quae ibi est aliquandiu sedetur; dicuntur ymni, dicuntur antiphonae aptae diei et loco; fiunt orationes similiter aptae diei et loco. Denuo inde cum ymnis itur in Imbomon susu similiter, et ibi ea aguntur quae et illic. Et cum coeperit hora esse, jam omnis populus et omnes Aputactitae deducunt episcopum cum ymnis usque ad Anastase. Ea autem hora pervenitur ad Anastase, qua lucernarium fieri solet. Fit ergo lucernarium tam ad Anastase quam ad Crucem; et inde omnis populus usque ad unum cum ymnis ducunt episcopum usque ad Syon. Ubi cum ventum fuerit, similiter dicuntur ymni apti loco et diei; legitur denuo et ille locus de evangelio, ubi octavis Paschae ingressus est Dominus, ubi erant discipuli, et arguet Thomam, quare incredulus fuisset. Et tunc omnis ipsa lectio perlegitur; postmodum fit oratio; benedictis [tam] cathecuminis quam fidelibus, juxta consuetudinem revertuntur unusquisque ad domum suam, similiter ut die dominica Paschae, hora noctis secunda.

(1) ubi *cod.*

VI.

FESTIVALS OF WHITSUNTIDE.

1. *Eastertide*.

A Pascha autem usque ad Quinquagesima, id est Pentecosten, hic penitus nemo jejunat, nec ipsi Aputactitae qui sunt. Nam semper ipsos dies sicut toto anno, ita ad Anastase, de pullo primo usque ad mane consuetudinaria aguntur; similiter et ad sexta et ad lucernare. Dominicis autem diebus semper in Martyrio, id est in ecclesia majore, proceditur juxta consuetudinem; et inde itur ad Anastase cum ymnis. Quarta feria autem et sexta feria, quoniam ipsis diebus penitus nemo jejunat, in Syon proceditur, sed mane; fit missa ordine suo.

2. *The Ascension.—Festival at Bethlehem.*

Die autem [1] Quadragesimarum post Pascha, id est quinta feria, pridie omnes post sexta, id est quarta feria, in Bethleem vadunt propter vigilias celebrandas. Fiunt autem vigiliae in ecclesia in Bethleem, in qua ecclesia spelunca est ubi natus est Dominus. Alia die autem, id est quinta feria Quadragesimarum celebratur missa ordine suo, ita ut et presbyteri et episcopus praedicent, dicentes apte diei et loco; et postmodum sera revertuntur unusquisque in Jerusolima.

3. *Whitsunday.—(a) Morning Station.*

Quinquagesimarum autem die, id est dominica, qua die maximus labor est populo, aguntur omnia sic de pullo quidem primo juxta consuetudinem: vigilatur in Anastase, ut legat episcopus locum illum evangelii qui semper dominica die legitur, id est resurrectionem Domini, et postmodum ea aguntur in

---

[1] eadem *cod.*

Anastase quae consuetudinaria sunt, sicut toto anno. Cum autem mane factum fuerit, procedit omnis populus in ecclesia majore, id est ad Martyrium; aguntur etiam omnia quae consuetudinaria sunt agi; praedicant presbyteri, postmodum episcopus; aguntur omnia legitima, id est offertur juxta consuetudinem qua dominica die consuevit fieri; sed eadem adceleratur missa in Martyrium, ut ante hora tertia fiat.

(b) *Station at Sion.*

Quemadmodum enim missa facta fuerit ad Martyrium, omnis populus usque ad unum cum ymnis ducent episcopum in Syon; sed [ut] hora tertia plena in Syon sint. Ubi cum ventum fuerit, legitur ille locus de Actus apostolorum, ubi descendit Spiritus, ut omnes linguae intellegerent quae dicebantur; postmodum fit ordine suo missa. Nam presbyteri de hoc ipsud quod lectum est, quia ipse est locus in Syon ubi modo ecclesia est, ubi quondam post passionem Domini collecta erat multitudo cum apostolis, qua hoc factum est, ut superius diximus legi ibi de Actibus apostolorum. Postmodum fit ordine suo missa; offertur et ibi; et jam ut dimittatur populus, mittit vocem archidiaconus, et dicet: "Hodie statim post sexta omnes in Eleona parati simus in [Im]bomon."

(c) *Station at the Mount of Olives.*

Revertitur ergo omnis populus unusquisque in domum suam resumere se, et statim post prandium ascenditur mons Oliveti, id est in Eleona, unusquisque quomodo potest, ita ut nullus christianus remaneat in civitate, qui non omnes vadent. Quemadmodum ergo subitum fuerit in monte Oliveti, id est in Eleona, primum itur in Imbomon, id est in eo loco, unde ascendit Dominus in caelis; et ibi sedet episcopus et presbyteri, sed et omnis populus. Leguntur ibi lectiones, dicuntur interpositi ymni, dicuntur et antiphonae aptae diei ipsi et loco; orationes etiam quae interponuntur semper tales pronuntiationes habent, ut et diei et loco conveniunt; legitur etiam et ille locus de evangelio, ubi dicit de ascensu Domini; legitur et denuo de Actus apostolorum ubi dicit de ascensu Domini in caelis post resurrectionem. Cum autem hoc factum fuerit, benedicuntur cathecumini, sic fideles; et hora jam nona descenditur inde, et cum ymnis itur ad illam ecclesiam, quae et ipsa in Eleona est, id est in qua spelunca sedens docebat Dominus apostolos. Ibi autem cum ventum fuerit, jam est hora plus decima; fit ibi lucernare, fit oratio, benedicuntur cathecumini, et sic fideles.

(d) *Night Procession.*

Et jam inde descenditur cum ymnis omnis populus usque ad unum toti cum episcopo, ymnos dicentes vel antiphonas aptas diei ipsi; sic venitur lente et lente usque ad Martyrium. Cum autem pervenitur ad portam civitatis, jam nox est, et occurrent candelae ecclesiasticae vel ducentae, propter populo. De porta autem, quoniam satis est usque ad ecclesia majore, id est ad Martirium, porro hora noctis forsitan secunda pervenitur; quia lente et lente itur totum, pro populo, ne fatigentur pedibus. Et apertis balvis majoribus, quae sunt de quintana parte, omnis populus intrat in Martyrium cum ymnis et episcopo. Ingressi autem in ecclesia, dicuntur ymni, fit oratio, benedicuntur cathecumini et sic fideles, et inde denuo cum ymnis itur ad Anastase. Similiter ad Anastase cum ventum fuerit, dicuntur ymni seu antiphonae, fit oratio, benedicuntur cathecumini, sic fideles; similiter fit et [(i)] ad Crucem. Et donuo inde omnis populus christianus usque ad unum cum ymnis ducunt episcopum usque ad Syon. Ubi cum ventum fuerit, leguntur lectiones aptae, dicuntur psalmi vel antiphonae, fit oratio, benedicuntur cathecumini, et sic fideles, et fit missa. Missa autem facta accedunt omnes ad manum episcopi, et sic revertuntur unusquisque ad domum suam hora noctis forsitan media.

Ac sic ergo maximus labor in ea die suffertur; quoniam de pullo primo vigilatum est ad Anastase, et inde per tota die

(i) fiet *cod.*

nunquam cessatum est; et sic omnia quae celebrantur protrahuntur, ut nocte media post missa quae facta fuerit in Syon omnes ad domos suas revertantur.

4. *Resumption of the Ordinary Service.*

Jam autem de alia die Quinquagesimarum omnes jejunant juxta consuetudinem sicut toto anno, qui prout potest, excepta die sabbati et dominica, qua nunquam jejunatur in hisdem locis. Etiam postmodum ceteris diebus ita singula aguntur ut toto anno; id est semper de pullo primo ad Anastase vigiletur. Nam si dominica dies est, primum leget de pullo primo episcopus evangelium juxta consuetudinem intro Anastase locum resurrectionis Domini, qui semper dominica die legitur; et postmodu[m] ymni seu antiphonae usque ad lucem dicuntur in Anastase. Si autem dominica dies non est, tantum quod ymni vel antiphonae similiter de pullo primo usque ad lucem dicuntur in Anastase. Aputactitae omnes vadent; de plebe autem, qui quomodo possunt, vadent; clerici autem cotidie vicibus vadent. Clerici autem de pullo primo, episcopus autem albescente vadet semper, ut missa fiat matutina cum omnibus clericis, excepta dominica die: quia necesse est illum de pullo primo ire, ut evangelium legat in Anastase. Denuo ad horam sextam aguntur quae consuetudinaria sunt in Anastase; similiter et ad nona, similiter et ad lucernare juxta consuetudinem quam consuevit toto anno fieri. Quarta autem et sexta feria semper nona in Syon fit juxta consuetudinem.

VII.

Baptism.

1. *The Inscribing of the Competents.*

Et illud etiam scribere debui quemadmodum docentur hi qui baptidiantur per Pascha. Nam qui dat nomen suum, ante diem Quadragesimarum dat, et omnium nomina annotat presbiter; hoc est ante illas octo septimanas quibus dixi hic attendi Quadragesimas. Cum autem annotaverit omnium nomina presbyter, postmodum alia die de Quadragesimis, id est qua inchoantur octo ebdomadae, ponitur episcopo cathedra media ecclesia majore, id est ad Martyrium; sedent hinc et inde presbyteri in cathedris, et stant clerici omnes. Et sic adducuntur unus et unus competens; si viri sunt, cum patribus suis veniunt; si autem feminae, cum matribus suis. Et sic singulariter interrogat episcopus vicinos ejus qui intravit, dicens: "Si bonae vitae est hic, si parentibus deferet, si ebriacus non est aut vanus," et singula vitia, quae sunt tamen graviora in homine, requiret; ut si probaverit sine reprehensione esse de his omnibus quibus requisivit praesentibus testibus, annotat ipse manu sua nomen illius. Si autem in aliquo accusatur, jubet illum foras exire, dicens: "Emendet se, et cum emendaverit se, tun[c] accedet ad lavacrum." Sic de viris, sic de mulieribus requirens dicit. Si quis autem peregrinus est, nisi testimonia habuerit qui eum noverint, non tam facile accedet ad baptismum.

2. *Preparation for Baptism.—Catechisings*

Hoc autem, dominae sorores, ne extimaretis sine ratione fieri, scribere debui. Consuetudo est enim hic talis, ut qui accedunt ad baptismum per ipsos dies quadraginta quibus jejunatur, primum mature a clericis exorcizentur, mox missa facta fuerit de Anastase matutina. Et statim ponitur cathedra episcopo ad Martyrium in ecclesia majore, et sedent omnes in giro prope episcopo qui baptidiandi sunt, tam viri quam mulieres; etiam loco stant patres vel matres, nec non etiam qui volunt audire de plebe omnes intrant et sedent, sed fideles. Cathecuminus autem ibi non intrat tunc qua episcopus docet illos legem Id est sic inchoans a Genese per illos dies quadraginta percurret omnes Scripturas, primum exponens carnaliter, et sic illud solvet spiritualiter. Nec non etiam et de resurrectione, similiter et de fide omnia docentur per illos dies. Hoc autem cathecisis appellatur.

3. "*Traditio*" *of the Creed.*

Et jam quando completae fuerint septimanae quinque a quo docentur, tunc accipient simbolum. Cujus simboli rationem, similiter sicut omnium Scripturarum ratione exponet eis, singulorum sermonum primum carnaliter, et sic spiritualiter; ita et simbolum exponet. Ac sic est ut in hisdem locis omnes fideles sequantur Scripturas quando leguntur in ecclesia, quia omnes docentur per illos dies quadraginta, id est ab hora prima usque ad horam tertiam, quoniam per tres horas fit cathecisin. Deus autem scit, dominae sorores, quoniam majores voces sunt fidelium, qui ad audiendum intrant in cathecisen ad ea quae dicuntur vel exponuntur per episcopum, quam quando sedet et praedicat in ecclesia, ad singula quae taliter exponuntur. Missa autem facta cathecisis hora jam tertia, statim inde cum ymnis ducitur episcopus ad Anastase, et fit missa ad tertia; ac sic tribus horis docentur ad die per septimanas septem. Octava enim septimana Quadragesimarum, id est quae appellatur septimana major, jam non vacat eos doceri ut impleantur ea quae superius sunt.

4. "*Redditio*" [*Recitation*] *of the Creed.*

Cum autem jam transierint septem septimanae, superat illa una septimana paschalis quam hic appellant septimana major. Jam tunc venit episcopus mane in ecclesia majore ad Martyrium; retro in absida post altarium ponitur cathedra episcopo, et ibi unus et unus vadet, vir[i] cum patre suo, aut mulier cum matre sua, et reddet simbolum episcopo. Reddito autem simbolo episcopo, alloquitur omnes episcopus, et dicet: " Per istas[ii] septem septimanas legem omnem edocti estis Scripturarum;

(i) viri *cod.*   (ii) istos *cod.*

nec non etiam de fide audistis; audistis etiam et de resurrectione carnis, sed et singuli omnem rationem, ut potuistis tamen adhuc catecumini audire; verbum autem quae sunt mysterii altioris, id est ipsius baptismi, qui adhuc cathecumini audire non potestis; et ne extimetis aliquid sine ratione fieri, cum in nomine Dei baptidiati fueritis, per octo dies paschales, post missa facta de ecclesia, in Anastase audietis. Qui adhuc cathecumini estis, misteria Dei secretiora dici vobis non possunt."

5. *Mystic Catechisings.*

Post autem venerint dies Paschae, per illos octo dies, id est a Pascha usque ad octavas, quemadmodum missa facta fuerit de ecclesia et itur cum ymnis ad Anastase, mox fit oratio, benedicuntur fideles, et stat episcopus incumbens in cancello interiore, qui est in spelunca Anastasis, et exponet omnia quae aguntur in baptismo. Illa enim hora cathecuminus nullus accedet ad Anastase: tantum neofiti et fideles qui volunt audire misteria, in Anastase intrant; clauduntur autem ostia ne qui cathecuminus se dirigat. Disputante autem episcopo singula et narrante, tantae voces sunt collaudantium ut porro foras ecclesia audiantur voces eorum. Vere enim ita misteria omnia absolvent ut nullus non possit commoveri ad ea quae audit sic exponi.

Et quoniam in ea provincia pars populi et grece et siriste novit, pars etiam alia per se grece, aliqua etiam pars tantum siriste; itaque quoniam episcopus, licet siriste noverit tamen semper grece loquitur et numquam siriste, itaque ergo stat semper presbyter, qui, episcopo grece dicente, siriste interpretatur, ut omnes audiant quae exponuntur; lectiones etiam, quaecumque in ecclesia leguntur, quia necesse est grece legi, semper stat qui siriste interpretatur, propter populum, ut semper discant. Sane quicumque hic latini sunt, id est qui nec siriste nec grece noverunt, ne contristentur, et ipsis exponitur eis, quia sunt alii fratres et sorores grec[ol]atini, qui latine exponunt eis. Illud autem hic ante omnia valde gratum fit et valde admirabile, ut semper tam ymni quam antiphonae et lectiones, nec non etiam et orationes quas dicet episcopus, tales pronuntiationes habeant, ut et diei qui celebratur, et loco in quo agitur, aptae et convenientes sunt semper.

VIII.

Dedication of Churches.

Item dies Enceniarum appellantur, quando sancta ecclesia quae in Golgotha est, quam Martyrium vocant, consecrata est Deo, sed et sancta ecclesia, quae est ad Anastase, id est in eo loco ubi Dominus resurrexit post passionem, ea die et ipsa consecrata est Deo. Harum ergo ecclesiarum sanctarum encenia cum summo honore celebrantur, quoniam crux Domini inventa est ipsa die. Et ideo propter hoc ita ordinatum est, ut quando primum sanctae ecclesiae suprascriptae consecrabantur, ea dies esset qua crux Domini fuerat inventa, ut simul omni laetitia eadem die celebrarentur. Et hoc per Scripturas sanctas invenitur, quod ea dies sit enceniarum, qua et sanctus Salomon, consummata domo Dei quam aedificaverat, steterit ante altarium Dei et oraverit, sicut scriptum est in libris Paralipomenon.

Hi ergo dies Enceniarum cum venerint, octo diebus attenduntur. Nam ante plurimos dies incipiunt se undique colligere; ubi non solum monachorum vel [Aput]acticorum [i] de diversis provinciis, id est tam de Mesopotamia vel Syria, vel de Egypto aut Thebaida, ubi plurimi monazontes sunt, sed et de diversis omnibus locis vel provinciis; nullus est enim qui non se eadem die in Jerusolima tendat ad tantam laetitiam et tam honorabiles dies; saeculares autem tam viri quam feminae fideli animo propter diem sanctum similiter se de [ii] omnibus provinciis isdem diebus Jerusolima colligunt. Episcopi autem, quando parvi fuerint, hisdem diebus Jerusolima plus quadraginta aut quinquaginta sunt; et cum illis veniunt multi clerici sui. Et

(i) actito *cod*.
(ii) sed et *cod*.

quid plura? putat se maximum peccatum incurrisse, qui in hisdem diebus tantae sollemnitati inter non fuerit; si tamen nulla necessitas contraria fuerit, quae hominem a bono proposito retinet. His ergo diebus Enceniarum ipse ornatus omnium ecclesiarum est qui et per Pascha vel per Epiphania; et ita per singulos dies diversis locis sanctis proceditur ut per Pascha vel Epiphania. Nam prima et secunda die in ecclesia majore quae appellatur Martyrium proceditur. Item tertia die in Eleona, id est in ecclesia quae est in ipso monte a quo ascendit Dominus in caelis post passionem, intra qua ecclesia est spelunca illa in qua docebat Dominus apostolos in monte Oliveti. Quarta autem die.

* * * * * * *

6.

THE *APOSTOLIC TRADITION* OF HIPPOLYTUS

AMONG the collections of Ecclesiastical Rules formerly current, whether those designated as "Apostolic," or others labelled with more or less questionable titles, we find two which bear the name of Hippolytus. One of these is the *Epitome*, an abridgment of the VIIIth Book of the Apostolic Constitutions, beginning at the 4th Chapter of that book. We possess it in the original Greek.[1] The other, the "Canons of Hippolytus," has been preserved in Arabic and Ethiopic versions only, both derived from Coptic versions taken from the original Greek. The importance of these Canons in the tradition of pseudo-apostolic regulations, and the great antiquity which had been assigned to them, had decided me to reproduce them in these Appendices in Haneberg's Latin version. Now, however, two scholars, Ed Schwartz of the University of Strasbourg, and Dom R. Hugh Connolly, an English Benedictine, have arrived independently at quite new conclusions, which I here append.[2]

The VIIIth Book of the Apostolic Constitutions, the Canons of Hippolytus and another recently discovered apocryphal writing, the Testament of our Lord, are all derived, independently, from a text which has hitherto received scant attention, that passing under the name "Egyptian Church Order"; two passages in the Epitome of the VIIIth Book of the Apostolic Constitutions are also derived from the same source. Neither this Epitome nor the Canons of Hippolytus are to be

---

[1] Funk, *Didascalia et Constitutiones Apostolorum*, vol. ii. p. 72

[2] Owing to the war, I have not been able to procure Schwartz's work, *Ueber die pseudo-apostolischen Kirchenordnungen*, which appeared in the Strasbourg series of *Schriften der wissenschaftlichen Gesellschaft* in *Strassburg*, 1910. Dom Connolly's treatment of the problem, however, which is much more detailed and exhaustive, will suffice to give an idea of the situation from the critical point of view See *Texts and Studies*, Cambridge, vol viii. No 4 (1916).

attributed to the celebrated Roman Doctor. He must be considered, on the contrary, as the author of the so-called Egyptian Church Order, the real title of which should be "The Apostolic Tradition." It is this title which figures in the Catalogue of the writings of Hippolytus, inscribed on his celebrated statue in the Lateran: 'Αποστολικὴ παράδοσις, after that of another book, περὶ χαρισμάτων.[1]

We are, then, in possession of an attempt to codify certain traditions or customs which were regarded as reaching back to Apostolic times, an attempt, the "redaction" of which is not placed under direct Apostolic patronage or some Apostolic patronage, but presents itself as the work of a man whose name and date are well known, Hippolytus.

The Greek text is lost: the Latin, Coptic, Arabic and Ethiopic versions only remain.[2] The Arabic text, derived from the Coptic as we know it, is not of great value, the Coptic omits certain formulas of prayer; of the Latin, we have only fragments, though happily they are of some length. The Ethiopic alone is complete; but as it is derived through the Coptic, which is itself a translation from the Greek, the deterioration to which the document has been exposed through such transmission is evident. This disadvantage is felt particularly by persons who do not know Ethiopic, and are obliged to have recourse to a version in some European language. Even supposing that we possessed the Greek text from which all these versions are taken, it would be advisable to use it with caution; books of this kind being constantly exposed to subsequent modifications. In spite of these drawbacks, I believe that, taken generally, the "Apostolic Tradition" may be regarded as a document of the first third of the third century, and that its author must have drawn his inspiration from Roman use, just as the author of the Didascalia and the author of the Apostolic Constitutions drew theirs from the Syrian use.

But when we come to details we must be cautious, since later editors of this class of composition are always prone to allow their ideas and tastes to modify the directions found in the document which serves as the basis of their work.

The limits of this volume must restrict me to citing from the "Apostolic Tradition" those pages which relate to Ordination and Christian Initiation. These alone present some connection with the

---

[1] In the VIIIth book of the Apostolic Constitutions, the part (c 3 and ff) which corresponds to 'Αποστολικὴ παράδοσις is preceded (c 1-2) by a little treatise on charismatic gifts, but the latter is the work of the author of the Const. Ap ; it is certainly not the περὶ χαρισμάτων of Hippolytus.

[2] The Latin has been published by Edm. Hauler, *Didascaliae Apostolorum fragmenta Veronensia latina*, Leipzig, 1900; the Oriental versions by G. Horner, *The Statutes of the Apostles or Canones Ecclesiastici*, London, 1904

descriptions given in my book. The text is taken from Dom Connolly's edition, which reproduces the Latin of the Verona MS., and where that is at fault supplements it by the Ethiopic, published by Horner, and translated by him into English.

[The first clause of the interrogatory Creed at baptism, p. 534 below, which has fallen out of the Oriental versions, is added in brackets by Dom Connolly from the Canons of Hippolytus. The Testament of our Lord has the same formula; and the agreement of these two documents here seems to show that these reproduce with fair accuracy the text of the "Apostolic Tradition."—TR.]

THE TEXT.

Ea quidem quae uerba fuerunt digne posuimus de donationibus, quanta quidem Deus a principio secundum propriam uoluntatem praestitit hominibus offerens sibi eam imaginem, quae aberrauerat. Nunc autem ex caritate, quam in omnes sanctos habuit, producti ad uerticem traditionis, quae catecizat, ad ecclesias perreximus, ut hii, qui bene ducti sunt, eam, quae permansit usque nunc, traditionem exponentibus nobis custodiant et agnoscentes firmiores maneant, propter eum qui nuper inuentus est per ignorantiam lapsus uel error, et hos qui ignorant, praestante sancto spiritu perfectam gratiam eis qui recte credunt, ut cognoscant, quomodo oportet tradi et custodiri omnia eos, qui ecclesiae praesunt.

Episcopus ordinetur electus ab omni populo, quique cum nominatus fuerit et placuerit omnibus, conueniet populum una cum praesbyterio et his qui praesentes fuerint episcopi, die dominica. Consentientibus omnibus inponant super eum manus et praesbyterium adstet quiescens. Omnes autem silentium habeant orantes in corde propter descensionem spiritus; ex quibus unus de praesentibus episcopis ab omnibus rogatus, inponens manum ei qui ordinatur episcopus, oret ita dicens·

"Deus et pater domini nostri Iesu Christi, pater misericordiarum et Deus totius consolationis, qui in excelsis habitas et humilia respicis, qui cognoscis omnia antequam nascantur tu, qui dedisti terminos in ecclesia per uerbum gratiae tuae, praedestinans ex principio genus iustorum Abraham, principes et sacerdotes constituens et sanctum tuum sine ministerio non derelinquens, ex initio saeculi bene tibi placuit in his, quos elegisti, *pr(a)edi*cari : nunc effunde eam uirtutem, quae a te est, principalis spiritus, quem dedisti dilecto filio tuo Iesu Christo, quod donauit sanctis apostolis qui constituerunt ecclesiam per singula loca, sanctificationem tuam, in gloriam et laudem indeficientem nomini tuo. Da, cordis cognitor pater, super hunc seruum tuum, quem elegisti ad episcopatum, pascere gregem sanctam tuam et primatum sacerdotii tibi exhibere, sine repraehensione seruentem noctu et die, incessantur repropitiari uultum tuum et offerre dona sancta(e) ecclesiae tuae, spiritu primatus sacerdotii habere potestatem dimittere peccata secundum mandatum tuum, dare sortes secundum praeceptum tuum, soluere etiam omnem colligationem secundum potestatem, quam dedisti apostolis, placere autem tibi in mansuetudine et mundo corde, offerentum tibi odorem suauitatis per puerum tuum Iesum Christum, per quem tibi gloria et potentia et honor, patri et filio cum spiritu sancto, et nunc et in saecula saeculorum, Amen."

Qui cumque factus fuerit episcopus, omnes os offerant pacis, salutantes eum, quia dignus effectus est. Illi uero offerant diacones oblationem, quique imponens manus in eam cum omni praesbyterio dicat gratia[n]s agens : "Dominus uobiscum"; et omnes dicant : "Et cum spiritu tuo." "Sursum corda" "Habemus ad dominum" "Gratias agamus domino." "Dignum et iustum est." Et sic iam prosequatur :

"Gratias tibi referimus, Deus, per dilectum puerum tuum Iesum Christum, quem in ultimis temporibus misisti nobis saluatorem et redemptorem et angelum uoluntatis tuae; qui est uerbum tuum inseparabilem (*sic*), per quem omnia fecisti et bene placitum tibi fuit; misisti de caelo in matricem uirginis, quique in utero habitus incarnatus est et filius tibi ostensus est ex spiritu sanctus et uirgine natus; qui uoluntatem tuam conplens et populum sanctum tibi adquirens extendit manus, cum pateretur, ut a passione liberaret eos qui in te crediderunt; qui cumque traderetur uoluntariae passioni, ut mortem soluat et uincula diaboli dirumpat et infernum calcet et iustos inluminet et terminum figat et resurrectionem manifestet, accipiens panem gratias tibi agens dixit: Accipite, manducate: hoc est corpus meum, quod pro uobis confringetur. Similiter et calicem dicens: Hic est sanguis meus, qui pro uobis effunditur; quando hoc facitis, meam commemorationem facitis. Memores igitur mortis et resurrectionis eius offerimus tibi panem et calicem gratias tibi agentes, quia nos dignos habuisti adstare coram te et tibi ministrare. Et petimus, ut mittas spiritum tuum sanctum in oblationem sanctae ecclesiae; in unum congregans des omnibus, qui percipiunt, sanctis in repletionem spiritus sancti ad confirmationem fidei in ueritate, ut te laudemus et glorificemus per puerum tuum Iesum Christum, per quem tibi gloria et honor, patri et filio cum sancto spiritu, in sancta ecclesia tua et nunc et in saecula saeculorum. Amen."

Si quis oleum offert, secundum panis oblationem et uini et non ad sermonem dicat, sed simili uirtute gratias referat dicens: "Ut oleum hoc sanctificans das, Deus, sanitatem utentibus et percipientibus, unde uncxisti reges, sacerdotes et profetas, sic et omnibus gustantibus confortationem et sanitatem utentibus illud praebeat."

Similiter, si quis caseum et oliuas offeret, ita dicat: "Sanctifica lac hoc, quod quoagulatum est, et nos conquaglans tuae caritati. Fac a tua dulcitudine non recedere fructum etiam hunc oliuae, qui est exemplum tuae pinguidinis, quam de ligno fluisti in uitam eis, qui sperant in te." In omni uero benedictione dicatur: "Tibi gloria, patri et filio cum sancto spiritu, in sancta ecclesia et nunc et semper et in omnia saecula saeculorum. (Amen.)"

And the people shall say: "As it was, is and shall be to generation of generation and to age of age. Amen."

And the bishop shall say: "And again we beseech thee, Almighty God, the Father of the Lord and our Saviour Jesus Christ, to grant us to receive with blessing this holy Mystery; and that he may not condemn any of us, but cause worthiness in all them who take the reception of the holy Mystery, the Body and Blood of Christ, Almighty Lord, our God."

The deacon shall say: "Pray ye." (And the bishop shall say): "God, Almighty, grant to us the reception of thy Holy Mystery as our strengthening; nor condemn any amongst us, but bless all through Christ, through whom to thee with him and with the Holy Spirit be glory and might now and always and for ever and ever. Amen."

The deacon shall say: "As ye stand, bow down your heads."

(The bishop shall say): "Eternal God, knower of that which is secret, to thee thy people bowed down their heads, and to thee they bent the hardness of heart and flesh; look down from thy worthy dwelling-place, bless them both men and women, incline thine ear to them and hear their prayer, and strengthen (them) with the might of thy right hand, and protect (them) from evil sickness, be their guardian for both body and soul, increase to them and to us also thy faith and thy fear, through thine only Son, through whom to thee with him and with the Holy Spirit be glory and might now and always for ever and ever. Amen."

And the deacon shall say: "Let us attend."

And the bishop: "Holiness to holy ones."

"And the people shall say. "One holy Father, one holy Son, one is the Holy Spirit."

The bishop shall say: "The Lord (be) with you all."

And the people shall say: "With thy spirit."

And then they shall lift up glory; and the people shall come in for the salvation of their souls, in order that their sin may be remitted.

The prayer after that they have communicated: "God, Almighty, the Father of the Lord and our Saviour Jesus Christ, we give thee thanks, because thou hast imparted to us the reception of thy holy Mystery: let it not be for guilt or condemnation, but for the renewal of soul and body and spirit through," etc.

And the people shall say: "Amen."

And the presbyter shall say: "The Lord be with you all."

Laying on of hand after they have received: "Eternal God, Almighty, the Father of the Lord and our Saviour Jesus Christ, bless thy servants and thy handmaids, protect and help and prosper (them) by the power of thine angel. Keep and confirm in them thy fear by thy greatness; provide that they shall both think what is thine and will what is thine; grant to them peace without sin and anger through," etc.

And the people shall say: "Amen."

And the bishop shall say: "The Lord (be) with you all."

And the people shall say: "With thy spirit."

And the deacon shall say: "Go forth in peace."

And after (that) the Ḳeddāsē is finished.

Cum autem praesbyter ordinatur, inponat manum super caput eius episcopus contingentibus etiam praesbyteris et dicat secundum ea, quae predicta sunt, sicut praediximus super episcopum, orans et dicens: "Deus et pater domini nostri Iesu Christi, respice super seruum tuum istum et inpartire spiritum gratiae et consilii praesbyteris ut adiuuet et gubernet plebem tuam in corde mundo, sicuti respexisti super populum electionis tuae et praecepisti Moysi, ut elegeret praesbyteros, quos replesti de spiritu tuo, quod donasti famulo tuo; et nunc, domine, praesta indeficienter conseruari in nobis spiritum gratiae tuae et dignos effice, ut credentes tibi ministremus in simplicitate cordis laudantes te, per puerum tuum Christum Iesum, per quem tibi gloria et uirtus, patri et filio cum spiritu sancto, in sancta ecclesia et nunc et in saecula saeculorum. Amen."

Diaconus uero, cum ordinatur, eligatur secundum ea, quae praedicta sunt, similiter inponens manus episcopus solus, sicuti et praecipimus. In diacono ordinando solus episcopus inponat manus propterea, quia non in sacerdotio ordinatur, sed in ministerio episcopi, ut faciat ea, quae ab ipso iubentur; non est enim particeps consilii in clero, sed curas agens et indicans episcopo, quae oportet; non accipiens communem praesbyteri spiritum eum, cuius participes praesbyteri sunt, sed id, quod sub potestate episcopi est creditum. Qua de re episcopus solus diaconum faciat, super praesbyterum autem etiam praesbyteri superinponant manus propter communem et similem cleri spiritum. Praesbyter enim huius solius habet potestatem, ut accipiat; dare autem non habet potestatem. Quapropter clerum non ordinat; super praesbyteri uero ordinatione consignat episcopo ordinante. Super diaconum autem ita dicat: "Deus, qui omnia creasti et uerbo perordinasti, pater domini nostri Iesu Christi, quem misisti ministrare tuam uoluntatem et manifestare nobis tuum desiderium, da spiritum sanctum gratiae et sollicitudinis et industriae in hunc seruum tuum, quem elegisti ministrare ecclesiae tuae et offerre

in thy holy of holies that which is offered to thee by thy ordained Chief Priests to the glory of thy name; thus without blame in pure life having served the degrees of ordination he may obtain the exalted and thy honour, and glorify thee, through thy Son Jesus Christ our Lord, through whom to thee with him (be) glory and power and praise with the Holy Spirit now," etc.

Concerning those who confessed and were condemned for the name of Christ. If the confessor has been in the place of punishment, in chains for the name of Christ, they shall not lay hand on him for a ministering, for that is the work of a deacon: but (as for) that of the presbyterate, though he hath the honour of the presbyterate by that which he confessed, (yet) the bishop shall ordain him, having laid his hand upon him. And if the confessor was one who came not before the judges, and if he was not punished with chains, nor was shut up in prison, nor suffered any affliction, but withal was only derided for the name of his Lord, and was condemned to the least punishment, yet he professed all the work of the priesthood which is meet for him, they shall lay hand on him and make a deacon.

And the bishop shall give thanks as we have already said. And it is (not) necessary that he should mention the things which we have already said, that he should recite clearly and carefully, according as it is possible for each to pray. And if there was one who could pray with devotion or use (make) a grand and elevated prayer, it is well; and if he prayed and speaks praise with moderation (*i.e.*? moderately, sufficiently), no one shall prevent him from praying, who is true in right (faith).

Concerning the ordination of Widows. If a widow is ordained, she shall not be sealed, but be made by the name. And if it was one whose husband died a long time, she shall be ordained. And if it was one whose husband had lately died, she shall not be trusted. But even if she is aged, she shall be tried many days, because lust will contend with those who are ordained to a place. And the widow shall be ordained by word only, and she shall (then) be joined to the rest of the widows; and they shall not lay hand upon her, because she does not offer the sacrifice, nor has she a (sacred) ministry. For the sealing is for the priests because of their ministry, but (the duty) of widows is about prayer, which is the duty of all.

Concerning the Reader and the Virgins and the Subdeacons,

and concerning the grace of healing. To the reader who is ordained the bishop shall deliver the Scripture, and shall not lay hand upon him. As for the virgin also, he shall not lay hand on a virgin; but it is with her heart alone that she became a virgin. As for the subdeacons, he shall not lay hand upon a subdeacon, but he shall make (mention) over them of the name that they may minister to the deacons. As for the grace of healing, if some one says, "I have acquired the grace of healing and prophecy," they shall not lay hand upon him until his deed make evident that he is trustworthy.

Concerning the time during which they shall hear instruction after (they have left off their) occupations. The catechumens shall remain three years hearing the word of instruction: yet if he was a good scholar and one who knows good conduct, no length of time need be required of him, but the conduct alone shall decide for him.

Concerning the prayer of him who hears instruction, and his kiss. When the teacher has finished the admonition the catechumens shall pray alone, apart from the believers. And the women shall stand in (one) place in the church; and the women believers shall pray alone and the women catechumens. And if the prayer is finished, the catechumens shall not kiss with the believers, because their kiss is not yet pure. And the believers shall kiss one another; man shall kiss man and woman shall kiss woman, and males shall not kiss females. And all the women shall have their heads veiled with a pallium or with a mantle, and not with sindon only, because this is not what is allowed to them.

Concerning the laying hand upon the catechumen. And after the prayer, when the teacher has laid his hand upon the catechumen he shall pray, and dismiss them. And if it was one belonging to the church who teaches, or a layman, he shall do likewise. And if a catechumen was arrested for the name of our Lord Jesus Christ, he shall not be doubtful about the testimony (which he gives); because if they overpower and injure and kill him before he receives baptism for the forgiveness of his sin, he shall be justified; because he was baptised in his own blood.

Concerning him who is baptised. When one has been chosen or who is ready for baptism, they shall examine their life; if they lived in the fear of God before they are baptised, if they honoured the widow, or if they visited the sick, or if they did all good, and if there is witness in their favour from those who bring them; and if they have done thus they shall hear the Gospel from the time that they were set apart, and they shall lay hand upon them every day and instruct them. And when the day draws near on which they shall be baptised, the bishop binds every one of them by oath, that he may know if they are pure. And if one was found that was not pure, they shall put him aside by himself; for he has not hearkened to the word of instruction with faith; because it is not proper to baptise (*lit.* do to) an utter alien (?). And they shall instruct those who shall be baptised that they should wash and be exorcised on the fifth day of the week; and if there was a menstruous woman among them, she shall be put aside, that she may be baptised on another day. And those who desire to be baptised shall fast on Friday, and the bishop shall assemble all those who shall be baptised on the sabbath into one place, and shall command all of them (to make) prayer and prostration; and when he has laid his hand upon them, let him exorcise every unclean spirit that he may flee away from them and not enter into them again. And when he has finished his exorcising, he shall breathe upon them, and they shall read to them and exhort them. And they who shall be baptised shall not bring with them any ornament of gold, nor ring nor gem of any kind; but every one of them shall give thanks, and it is fitting for them whom it beseems to bring their oblations also at the time.

Concerning the order of Baptism, and the profession of the Faith, and the confession of sin at baptism, and the Oblation; and concerning the milk and honey. At the time of cock-crow they shall first pray over the water. And it shall be either such as flows into the tank of baptism or is caused to flow down upon it. And it shall be thus unless there is a scarcity of water; but if there is a scarcity they shall carry water to the tank, having drawn (it from a well). And they shall put off their garments and be baptised naked. And they shall baptise the little children first; and if they can speak for themselves, let them speak. But if they cannot, their parents shall answer the word instead of them, or one of their relatives. And afterwards they shall baptise the grown-up men And afterwards all the women shall loose their hair; and they shall be forbidden to wear their ornaments and their gold; and none shall go down having anything alien with them into the water. And whenever they baptise, the bishop shall give thanks over the oil which is in a vessel, and it is named mystic oil; and he shall take other oil and exorcise in it, and it is named oil that has been exorcised from every unclean spirit. And there shall be a deacon who will carry the oil in which (Satan) was exorcised, and he shall stand on the left of the presbyter; and another deacon shall take the mystic oil, and shall stand on his right. And let the presbyter, having taken every one of those who shall be baptised, bid them renounce and say: "I renounce thee, Satan, and all thine angels and all thine unclean work." And when he has professed this, he shall anoint him with the oil which he made pure from all evil, saying: "All unclean spirits shall depart from him." Thus he shall deliver (him) to the bishop, naked, or to the presbyter—to him who stands at the water of baptism. Let the deacon go down with him to the water, and he shall say and instruct him: "I believe in one God the Father Almighty, and in his only Son Jesus Christ, our Lord and Saviour, and the Holy Spirit, giver of life to all creation, the Trinity equal in Godhead, one Lord, and one Kingdom and one Faith and one Baptism, in the holy Church Catholic, and life eternal Amen." (Tunc descendat in aquas, presbyter autem manum suam capiti eius imponat eumque interroget his uerbis: "Credisne in Deum patrem omnipotentem?") And he who shall be baptised shall say again thus: "Yea, I believe."

And thus he shall baptise him and lay his hand upon him and upon him who answers for him.

Manum habens in caput eius inpositam baptizet semel. Et postea dicat: "Credis in Christum Iesum, filium Dei, qui natus est de spiritu sancto ex Maria uirgine et crucifixus sub Pontio Pilato et mortuus est et sepultus et resurrexit die tertia uiuus a mortuis et ascendit in caelis et sedit ad dexteram patris uenturus iudicare uiuos et mortuos?" Et cum ille dixerit: "Credo," iterum baptizetur. Et iterum dicat: "Credis in spiritu sancto et sanctam ecclesiam et carnis resurrectionem? Dicat ergo, qui baptizatur: "Credo." Et sic tertia uice baptizetur. Et postea cum ascenderit, ungueatur a praesbytero de illo oleo, quod sanctificatum est, dicente: "Ungueo te oleo sancto in nomine Iesu Christi." Et ita singuli detergentes se iam induantur et postea in ecclesia ingrediantur. Episcopus uero manum illis inponens inuocet dicens: "Domine Deus, qui dignos fecisti eos remissionem mereri peccatorum per lauacrum regenerationis spiritus sancti, inmitte in eos tuam gratiam, ut tibi seruiant secundum uoluntatem tuam; quoniam tibi est gloria, patri et filio com spiritu sancto, in sancta ecclesia et nunc et in saecula saeculorum. Amen." Postea oleum sanctificatum infunde(n)s de manu et inponens in capite dicat: "Ungueo te sancto oleo in domino patre omnipotente et Christo Iesu et spiritu sancto." Et consignans in frontem offerat osculum et dicat: "Dominus tecum." Et ille, qui signatus est, dicat: "Et cum spiritu tuo." Ita singulis faciat. Et postea iam simul cum omni populo orent, non primum orantes cum fidelibus, nisi omnia haec fuerint consecuti. Et cum orauerint, de ore pacem offerant.

Et tunc iam offeratur oblatio a diaconibus episcopo et gratias agat panem quidem in exemplum, quod dicit Gr(a)ecus antitypum, corporis Christi; calicem uino mixtum propter antitypum, quod dicit Graecus similitudinem, sanguinis, quod effusum est pro omnibus, qui crediderunt in eum; lac et melle mixta simul ad plenitudinem promissionis, quae ad patres fuit, quam dixit terram fluentem lac et mel, quam et dedit carnem suam Christus, per quam sicut paruuli nutriuntur, qui credunt, in suauitate uerbi amara cordis dulcia efficiens, aquam uero in oblationem in indicium lauacri, ut et interior homo, quod est animale, similia consequa[n]tur sicut et corpus. De uniuersis uero his rationem reddat episcopus eis, qui percipiunt; frangens autem panem singulas partes porrigens dicat: "Panis caelestis in Christo Iesu." Qui autem accipit, respondeat: "Amen." Praesbyteri uero si non fuerint sufficientes, teneant calices et diacones et cum honestate adstent et cum moderatione: primus, qui tenet aquam, secundus, qui lac, tertius, qui uinum. Et gustent, qui percipient, de singulis ter dicente eo, qui dat: "In Deo Patre omnipotenti.' Dicat autem, qui accipit. "Amen." "Et domino Iesu Christo et spiritu sancto et sancta ecclesia." Et dicat: "Amen." Ita singulis fiat. Cum uero haec fuerint, festinet unusquisque operam bonam facere.

7.

THE EXULTET OF BARI.

The roll of the *Exultet*, executed for the cathedral of Bari, is still preserved there. The text, with a coloured specimen of the splendid miniatures which adorn it, has been published by Signor Fr. Nitti di Vito, in vol. i. of the *Codice diplomatico Barese* (Bari, 1897), p. 205. Some of the other miniatures have been reproduced, from photographs, in the *Compte rendus* of the Académie des Inscriptions et Belles Lettres, vol. i. (1897), p. 96 (communication from Mr. G. Schlumberger), and in Mons. E. Bertaux's work, *L'art dans l'Italie Méridionale*, plate x. The date of the roll is determined by the portraits of the Emperors Basil II. and Constantine IX. (976–1025), which appears towards the end of it. It goes back, therefore, to about the year 1000. I here reproduce the text as given in the *Codice diplomatico*; I have ventured a few corrections, but give the original in the footnotes.

Exultet iam angelica turba caelorum, exultent divina mysteria et pro tanti regis victoria tuba intonet salutaris. Gaudeat se tantis tellus inradiata fulgoribus et aeterni regis splendore lustrata totius orbis se sentiat amisisse caliginem. Laetetur et mater Aecclesia tanti luminis[(1)] adornata fulgoribus et magnis populorum vocibus haec aula resultet. Quapropter astantibus vobis, Fratres karissimi, ad tam miram sancti huius luminis claritatem, una mecum, quaeso, Dei omnipotentis misericordiam invocate. Ut qui me non meis meritis in levitarum numerum dignatus est aggregare, luminis sui gratiam infundens, cerei huius laudem implere praecipiat. Per dominum nostrum Jesum Christum filium suum viventem secum atque regnantem in unitate Spiritus Sancti Deus, per omnia, etc.

Dominus vobiscum. Et cum spiritu tuo. Sursum corda. Habemus ad Dominum. Gratias agamus Domino Deo nostro.[1]
Vere quia dignum et iustum est Patrem omnipotentem . . .[2]

(1) lumini *cod.*
[1] The response *Dignum et iustum est* is missing here.
[2] Something is missing here. Cf. the text, *supra*, p. 254.

Qui nos ad noctem istam non tenebrarum sed luminis matrem perducere dignatus est, in qua exhorta est ab inferis in aeterna die resurrectio mortuorum. Solutis quippe nexibus et calcato mortis aculeo resurrexit a mortuis qui fuerat inter mortuos liber. Unde et nox ipsa syder022 pro accelesiarum ornatu cereorum splendore tamquam dies illuminata collucet, quia in eius matutino resurgente Christo mors occidit redemptorum et emersit vita credentium. Vere tu preciosus es opifex, formator es omnium, cui qualitas in agendi non fuerat officio, sed in sermonis imperio. Qui ornatum atque abitum mundi, nec ad ampliandum quasi inops potentiae, nec ad additandum quasi egenus gloriae condidisti. Totus ac plenus in te es, qui dum per virginea viscera mundo illaberis virginitatem etiam creaturae commendas.

Apes siquidem dum ore concipiunt, ore parturiunt, casto corpore non foedo desiderio copulantur, denique virginitatem servantes posteritatem generant, sobole gaudent, matres dicuntur, intactae [i] perdurant; filios generant et viros non norunt. Flore utuntur coniuge, flore funguntur genere, flore domos instruunt, flore divitias conveunt, flore ceram conficiunt. O ammirandus apium fervor ad commune opus! Pacifica turba concurrunt et operantibus plurimis una augetur substantia. O invisibile artificium! Primo culmina pro fundamentis aedificant, et tam ponderosam mellis sarcinam pendentibus domiciliis imponere non verentur. O virginitatis insignia, quae non possessori damna [ii] sed sibi lucra convectant. Auferunt quidem praedam et cum praeda minime tollunt peccatum. Spoliant quidem florum cutem et morsuum non annotant cicatricem.

Sed inter haec quae dinumeravimus huius cerei gratiam praedicemus, cuius odor suavis est et flamma ylaris; non tetro odore arvina [iii] desudat sed iocundissima suavitate, qui peregrinis non inficitur pigmentis sed illuminatur Spiritu Sancto. Qui ut accensus proprias corporis compages depascit, ita coagulatas lacrimas in rivulos fundit guttarum.[1] Quique semiusta membra ambroseo sanguine flavea vena distollit abitum vivit ignis humorem.[1]

(i) intacte *cod.* (ii) damno *cod.* (iii) a ruina *cod.*

[1] The text here is corrupt and unintelligible.

In huius autem cerei luminis corpore te, Omnipotens, postulamus ut supernae benedictionis munus accommodes,⁽¹⁾ ut si quis hinc sumpserit adversus flabra ventorum, adversus spiritus procellarum, sit ei, Domine, singulare perfugium, sit murus ab hoste fidelibus.

Salvum fac populum tuum, Domine, et benedic hereditatem tuam, ut redeuntes ad festivitatem Paschae per haec visibilibus et invisibilibus tuis iniantes, dum praesentium usu fruuntur, futurorum desiderio accendantur, una cum beatissimo papa nostro ill[1] et antistite nostro ill,[1] sed et omnibus presbiteris, diaconibus, subdiaconibus, cunctoque clero vel plebe.

Memorare, Domine, famulorum tuorum imperatorum nostrorum ill. et ill.[1] et cunctum exercitum eorum et omnium circumadstantium, qui vivis cum Patre et Spiritu Sancto et regnas, Deus, in saecula saeculorum. Amen.

(i) accomodes *cod.*

[1] At these places, also between the lines, and at the bottom as well as on the back of the roll, certain names of Popes, Archbishops, and Sovereigns, have been inserted for the purpose of being introduced into the Commemorative formularies. I would call attention to those of Popes Alexander II (1061–1073), Gregory VII (1073–1085), the latter accompanied by the indication of the chair of Bari being vacant *et antistite nostro quem Deus providebit*, and of Archbishop Urso (1078–1089), who was nominated after this vacancy.

There occur in it also the names of the Empress Theodora (1055–1056), Argyrus, Commander of the Forces (*senioris nostri benignissimi magistri*), Constantine XI. Ducas (1059–1067) and his wife Eudocia, his sons Michael VII. and Constantine XII (1067), and finally Robert Guiscard and his wife Sikelgaita, who must have been mentioned for the first time at the Easter festival of 1071 This year the Paschal Sunday fell on the 24th of April; on the 19th of that same month Bari had fallen into the hands of the Normans The mention of all these names belongs to the second half of the eleventh century, much later, consequently, than the original script.

TRANSLATOR'S NOTE TO PAGE 272.

MONSEIGNEUR DUCHESNE has expressed a wish that I should call attention to some Greek verses on page 3 of Mr W. E. Crum's *Coptic Ostraca* (special extra publication of the Egypt Exploration Fund, 1902), a work which had not been published when Monseigneur Duchesne sent to press the third French edition of the present volume.

These verses occur on an ostracon discovered, with numerous others, by Dr. Naville, among the ruins of the Coptic Monastery which had been built on the upper terrace of the Temple of Hatasu at Dêr el-Bahri. The Rev. F E Brightman describes these lines as "approximately an Eastern form of the *Ave Maria*," to be "sung in the service, like the Psalm and Alleluia, before the Gospel and the Aspasmos at the Kiss of Peace" They are "apparently for a feast of the Blessed Virgin Mary, perhaps the Purification" Mr Crum thinks the Coptic Convent of Dêr el-Bahri was the Monastery of St Phoebammon, and that the date of the ostracon, from the handwriting, is about 600 A D The Rev. F E. Brightman, on liturgical grounds, confirms Mr. Crum's opinion as to the date.

The verses in point are as follows —

* * * * *

Χαῖρε [1] κεχαριτωμέ-
νη Μαρία ὁ Κύριος μετά σου εὐλο-
γημένη σὺ ἐν γυναιξὶ
καὶ [2] εὐλογημένος ὁ καρ-
πὸς τῆς κοιλίας σου ὅτι
Χριστὸν συνέλαβες
τὸν Υἱὸν τοῦ Θεοῦ τὸν
λυτρώτην τῶν ψυ-
χῶν ἡμῶν

TRANSLATION —"Hail, Mary, endued with grace; the Lord is with thee; blessed art thou among women, and blessed is the fruit of thy womb, because thou didst conceive Christ, the Son of God, the Redeemer of our souls."

---

[1] St. Luke i. 28.   [2] *Ibid.*, 42.

ENGLISH TRANSLATION OF THE PORTION OF THE *PEREGRINATIO ETHERIAE*[1] IN THE APPENDIX.

I.

DAILY OFFICES.

1. *Matins.*

Now that your affection may know what is the order of Service day by day in the Holy Places, I must inform you, for I know that you would willingly have this knowledge. Every day before cockcrow all the doors of the Anastasis are opened, and all the Monks and Virgins, as they call them here, go thither, and not they alone, but lay people also, both men and women, who desire to begin their vigil early. And from that hour to daybreak hymns are said and psalms are sung responsively, and antiphons in like manner; and prayer is made after each of the hymns. For Priests, Deacons, and Monks in twos or threes take it in turn every day to say prayers after each of the hymns or antiphons. But when day breaks they begin to say the Matin hymns Thereupon the Bishop arrives with the Clergy, and immediately enters into the Cave, and from within the rails

---

[1] The orthography of this name has been much discussed. *Eucheria*, upheld by Père Edmond Bouvy in the *Revue Augustinienne*, 1903-4, seems to be definitely set aside by the researches of Père Zacharie Garcia (*Anal. Boll*, vol. xxix p. 377, and vol. xxx. p 444), and by Dom A Wilmart (*Revue béné'd.*, vol. xxviii. p. 68), the former of whom proposes *Ætheria*, and the latter *Egeria*. I believe Ætheria should be retained. As to the date of the *Peregrinatio*, scholars also differ; some, as I do, maintaining that it is of the time of Theodosius, while others seek to refer it to the time of Justinian. This latter opinion has been upheld by Karl Meister in the *Rheinisches Museum*, 1909, p 337, in opposition to which the Abbé Deconinck has published a very convincing article in the *Revue Biblique* (1910, p 432). Wiegand, *Byz Zeitschrift*, 1911, pp. 1-26, *Anal Boll*, 1912, p 346.

I am firmly convinced that the *Peregrinatio* has nothing in common with the time of Justinian. Regarding it either from the general standpoint of the religious institutions mentioned, or from that of monastic or local history, there is no agreement between the situation in the Seventh Century and that described by the traveller She saw in Mesopotamia the Bishops who were Confessors for the Faith. We know they were victims of the persecution under Valens. It is impossible to place them in the time of the Emperor Anastasius. The authoress probably came from Galicia.

he first says a prayer for all, mentioning the names of those whom he wishes to commemorate; he then blesses the catechumens, afterwards he says a prayer and blesses the faithful. And when the Bishop comes out from within the rails, every one approaches his hand, and he blesses them one by one as he goes out, and the Dismissal[1] takes place, by daylight.

2. *Sext and None.*

In like manner at the sixth hour all go again to the Anastasis, and psalms and antiphons are said while the Bishop is being summoned; then he comes as before, not taking his seat, but he enters at once within the rails in the Anastasis, that is in the Cave, just as in the early morning, and as then he again first says a prayer, then he blesses the faithful, and as he comes out from within the rails every one approaches his hand. And the same is done at the ninth hour as at the sixth.

3. *Vespers.*

Now at the tenth hour, which they call here *licinicon*, or as we say *lucernare*, all the people assemble at the Anastasis in the same manner, and all the candles and tapers are lit, making a very great light. Now the light is not introduced from without, but it is brought forth from within the Cave, that is from within the rails, where a lamp is always burning day and night, and the Vesper psalms and antiphons are said, lasting for a considerable time. Then the Bishop is summoned, and he comes and takes an exalted seat, and likewise the Priests sit in their proper places, and hymns and antiphons are said. And when all these have been recited according to custom, the Bishop rises and stands before the rails, that is, before the Cave, and one of the Deacons makes the customary commemoration of individuals one by one. And as the Deacon pronounces each name the many little boys who are always standing by answer with countless voices: *Kyrie eleyson*, or as we say *Miserere Domine*. And when the Deacon has finished all that he has to say, first

---

[1] The word *Missa* has been translated "Dismissal" throughout, although it must on some occasions have meant "Mass." For the ambiguity of the meaning attached to *Missa*, see p 491.

the Bishop says a prayer and prays for all, then they all pray, both the faithful and catechumens together. Again the Deacon raises his voice, bidding each catechumen to bow his head where he stands, and the Bishop stands and says the Blessing over the catechumens. Again prayer is made, and again the Deacon raises his voice and bids the faithful, each where he stands, to bow the head, and the Bishop likewise blesses the faithful. Thus the Dismissal takes place at the Anastasis, and one by one all draw near to the Bishop's hand. Afterwards the Bishop is conducted from the Anastasis to the Cross with hymns, all the people accompanying him, and when he arrives he first says a prayer, then he blesses the catechumens, then another prayer is said and he blesses the faithful. Thereupon both the Bishop and the whole multitude further proceed behind the Cross, where all that was done before the Cross is repeated, and they approach the hand of the Bishop behind the Cross as they did at the Anastasis and before the Cross. Moreover, there are hanging everywhere a vast number of great glass lanterns and there are also a vast number of *cereofala*,[1] before the Anastasis, before the Cross and behind the Cross, for the whole Service does not end until darkness has set in. This is the order of daily Service at the Cross and at the Anastasis throughout the six days.

II.

Sunday Offices.

1. *Vigil.*

But on the seventh day, that is on the Lord's Day, the whole multitude assembles before cockcrow, in as great numbers as the place can hold, as at Easter, in the basilica which is near the Anastasis, but outside the doors, where lights are hanging for the purpose. And for fear that they should not be there at cockcrow they come beforehand and sit down there. Hymns as well as antiphons are said, and prayers are made between the several hymns and antiphons, for at the Vigils there are always both Priests and Deacons ready there for the assembling of the multitude, the custom being that the

---

[1] i e candles on tall candlesticks (*Ducange*) —Tr.

Holy Places are not opened before cockcrow. Now as soon as the first cock has crowed, the Bishop arrives and enters the Cave at the Anastasis; all the doors are opened and the whole multitude enters the Anastasis, where countless lights are already burning. And when the people have entered, one of the Priests says a psalm to which all respond, and afterwards prayer is made; then one of the Deacons says a psalm and prayer is again made, a third psalm is recited by one of the Clergy, prayer is made for the third time and there is a commemoration of all. After these three psalms and three prayers are ended, lo! censers are brought into the Cave of the Anastasis so that the whole basilica of the Anastasis is filled with odours. And then the Bishop, standing within the rails, takes the book of the Gospel, and proceeding to the door, himself reads the (narrative of the) Resurrection of the Lord. And when the reading is begun there is so great a moaning and groaning among all, with so many tears, that the hardest of heart might be moved to tears for that the Lord had borne such things for us. After the reading of the Gospel the Bishop goes out, and is accompanied to the Cross by all the people with hymns, there again a psalm is said and prayer is made, after which he blesses the faithful and the Dismissal takes place, and as he comes out all approach to his hand. And forthwith the Bishop betakes himself to his house, and from that hour all the Monks return to the Anastasis, where psalms and antiphons, with prayer after each psalm or antiphon, are said until daylight; the Priests and Deacons also keep watch in turn daily at the Anastasis with the people, but of the lay people, whether men or women, those who are so minded, remain in the place until daybreak, and those who are not return to their houses and betake themselves to sleep.

2. *Mass.*

Now at daybreak because it is the Lord's Day every one proceeds to the greater church, built by Constantine, which is situated in Golgotha behind the Cross, where all things are done which are customary everywhere[1] on the Lord's Day. But

[1] This of course includes the Celebration of the Eucharist.—TR.

the custom here is that of all the Priests who take their seats, as many as are willing, preach, and after them all the Bishop preaches, and these sermons are always on the Lord's Day, in order that the people may always be instructed in the Scriptures and in the love of God. The delivery of these sermons delays greatly the Dismissal from the church, so that the Dismissal does [not] take place before the fourth or perhaps the fifth hour. But when the Dismissal from the church is made in the manner that is customary everywhere, the Monks accompany the Bishop with hymns from the church to the Anastasis, and as he approaches with hymns all the doors of the basilica of the Anastasis are opened, and the people, that is the faithful, enter, but not the catechumens. And after the people the Bishop enters, and goes at once within the rails of the Cave [of the Martyrium.] Thanks are first given to God, then prayer is made for all, after which the Deacon bids all bow their heads, where they stand, and the Bishop standing within the inner rails blesses them and goes out, each one drawing near to his hand as he makes his exit. Thus the Dismissal is delayed until nearly the fifth or sixth hour. And in like manner it is done at *lucernare* according to daily custom.

This then is the custom observed every day throughout the whole year except on Solemn Days, as to the keeping of which we will refer later on. But among all things it is a special feature that they arrange that suitable psalms and antiphons are said on every occasion, both those said by night, or in the morning, as well as those throughout the day, at the sixth hour, the ninth hour, or at *lucernare*, all being so appropriate and so reasonable as to bear on the matter in hand. And they proceed to the greater church, which was built by Constantine, and which is situated in Golgotha, that is, behind the Cross, on every Lord's Day throughout the year except on the one Sunday of Pentecost, when they proceed to Syon, as you will find mentioned below; but even then they go to Syon before the third hour, the Dismissal having been first made in the greater church.

* * * * * * *

A leaf is wanting.

III.
Festivals at Epiphany.
1. *Nocturnal Station at Bethlehem.*

* * * * * * *

Blessed is He that cometh in the Name of the Lord, and the rest which follows. And since, for the sake of the Monks who go on foot, it is necessary to walk slowly, the arrival in Jerusalem thus takes place at the hour when a man begins to be able to recognise another, that is, close upon but a little before daybreak. And on arriving there, the Bishop and all with him immediately enter the Anastasis, where an exceedingly great number of lights are already burning. There a psalm is said, prayer is made, first the catechumens and then the faithful are blessed by the Bishop; then the Bishop retires, and every one returns to his lodging to take rest, but the Monks remain there until daybreak and recite hymns.

2. *Mass at Jerusalem.*

But after the people have taken rest, at the beginning of the second hour they all assemble in the greater church, which is in Golgotha.

Now it would be superfluous to describe the adornment either of the church, or of the Anastasis, or of the Cross, or in Bethlehem on that day; you see there nothing but gold and gems and silk. For if you look at the veils, they are made wholly of silk striped with gold, and if you look at the curtains, they too are made wholly of silk striped with gold. The church vessels too, of every kind, gold and jewelled, are brought out on that day, and indeed, who could either reckon or describe the number and weight of the *cereofala*,[1] or of the *cicindelae*,[2] or of the *lucernae*,[3] or of the various vessels? And what shall I say of the decoration of the fabric itself, which Constantine, under his mother's influence, decorated with gold, mosaic, and costly marbles, as far as the resources of his kingdom allowed him,

---

[1] *i e* candles on tall candlesticks (*Ducange*) —Tr.
[2] Probably glass lamps with oil —Tr.
[3] Lanterns, or lamps —Tr.

that is, the greater church as well as the Anastasis, at the Cross, and the other Holy Places in Jerusalem? But to return to the matter in hand: the Dismissal[1] takes place on the first day in the greater church, which is in Golgotha, and when they preach or read the several lessons, or recite hymns, all are appropriate to the day. And afterwards when the Dismissal from the church has been made, they repair to the Anastasis with hymns, according to custom, so that the Dismissal takes place about the sixth hour. And on this day *lucernare* also takes place according to the daily use.

3. *Octave of the Festival.*

On the second day also they proceed in like manner to the church in Golgotha, and also on the third day; thus the feast is celebrated with all this joyfulness for three days up to the sixth hour in the church built by Constantine. On the fourth day it is celebrated in like manner with similar festal array in Eleona, the very beautiful church which stands on the Mount of Olives; on the fifth day in the Lazarium, which is distant about one thousand five hundred paces from Jerusalem; on the sixth day in Syon, on the seventh day in the Anastasis, and on the eighth day at the Cross. Thus, then, is the feast celebrated with all this joyfulness and festal array throughout the eight days in all the Holy Places which I have mentioned above. And in Bethlehem also throughout the entire eight days the feast is celebrated with similar festal array and joyfulness daily by the Priests and by all the Clergy there, and by the Monks who are appointed in that place. For from the hour when all return by night to Jerusalem with the Bishop, the Monks of that place[2] keep vigil in the church in Bethlehem, reciting hymns and antiphons, but it is necessary that the Bishop should always keep these days in Jerusalem. And immense crowds, not of Monks only, but also of the laity, both men and women, flock together to Jerusalem from every quarter for the solemn and joyous observance of that day.

[1] Here again, although not specified, the Eucharist must have been celebrated.—Tr.
[2] *i.e.* of Bethlehem.—Tr.

4. *The Presentation* (14th February).

The fortieth day after the Epiphany is undoubtedly celebrated here with the very highest honour, for on that day there is a procession, in which all take part, in the Anastasis, and all things are done in their order with the greatest joy, just as at Easter. All the Priests preach, and then the Bishop, always taking for their subject that part of the Gospel where Joseph and Mary brought the Lord into the Temple on the fortieth day, and Symeon and Anna the prophetess, the daughter of Phanuel, saw Him, and (treating) of the words which they spake when they saw the Lord, and of that offering which His parents made. And when everything that is customary has been done in order, the Sacraments are celebrated, and the Dismissal takes place.

IV.

LENT.

And when the Paschal days come they are observed thus: Just as with us forty days are kept before Easter, so here eight weeks are kept before Easter. And eight weeks are kept because there is no fasting on the Lord's Days, nor on the Sabbath, except on the one Sabbath on which the Vigil of Easter falls, in which case the fast is obligatory. With the exception then of that one day, there is never fasting on any Sabbath here throughout the year. Thus, deducting the eight Lord's Days and the seven Sabbaths (for on the one Sabbath, as I said above, the fast is obligatory) from the eight weeks, there remain forty-one fast days, which they call here *Eortae*, that is *Quadragesimae*.

1. *Services on Sundays*.

Now the several days of the several weeks are kept thus:

On the Lord's Day after the first cockcrow the Bishop reads in the Anastasis the account of the Lord's Resurrection from the Gospel, as on all Lord's Days throughout the whole year, and everything is done at the Anastasis and at the Cross as on all Lord's Days throughout the year, up to daybreak. Afterwards, in the morning, they proceed to the greater church, called the Martyrium, which is in Golgotha behind the Cross, and all things that are customary on the Lord's Days are done there. In like manner also when the Dismissal from the church has been made, they go with hymns to the Anastasis, as they always do on the Lord's Days, and while these things are being done the fifth hour is reached. *Lucernare*, however, takes place at its own hour, as usual, at the Anastasis and at the Cross, and in the various Holy Places, but on the Lord's Day the ninth hour is [not][1] kept.

2. *Weekday Services.*

On the second weekday they go at the first cockcrow to the Anastasis, as they do throughout the year, and everything that is usual is done until morning. Then at the third hour they go to the Anastasis, and the things are done that are customary throughout the year at the sixth hour, for this going at the third hour in Quadragesima is additional. At the sixth and ninth hours also, and at *lucernare*, everything is done that is customary throughout the whole year at the Holy Places. And on the third weekday all things are done as on the second weekday.

3. *Wednesday and Friday.*

Again, on the fourth weekday they go by night to the Anastasis, and all the usual things are done until morning, and also at the third and sixth hours. But at the ninth hour they go to Syon, as is customary at that hour on the fourth and sixth weekdays throughout the year, for the reason that the fast is always kept here on the fourth and sixth weekdays even by the catechumens, except a Martyrs' Day should occur. For if a Martyrs' Day should chance to occur on the fourth or on the sixth weekday in Quadragesima, they go even then to Syon at the ninth hour. But on the days of Quadragesima, as I said above, they proceed to Syon on the fourth weekday at the ninth hour, according to the custom of the whole year, and all things that are customary at the ninth hour are done, except the Oblation, for, in

---

[1] Mgr. Duchesne supplies this *not*.

order that the people may always be instructed in the law, both the Bishop and the Priest preach diligently. But when the Dismissal has been made, the people escort the Bishop with hymns thence to the Anastasis, so that it is already the hour of *lucernare* when he enters the Anastasis; then hymns and antiphons are said, prayers are made, and the Dismissal of *lucernare* takes place in the Anastasis and at the Cross. And the Dismissal of *lucernare* is always later on those days in Quadragesima than on other days throughout the year. On the fifth weekday everything is done as on the second and third weekday. On the sixth weekday everything is done as on the fourth, including the going to Syon at the ninth hour, and the escorting of the Bishop thence to the Anastasis with hymns.

4. *Saturday.*

But on the sixth weekday the vigils are observed in the Anastasis from the hour of their arrival from Sion with hymns, until morning, that is, from the hour of *lucernare*, when they entered, to the morning of the next day, that is, the Sabbath. And the Oblation is made in the Anastasis the earlier, that the Dismissal may take place before sunrise. Throughout the whole night psalms are said responsively in turn with antiphons and with various lections, the whole lasting until morning, and the Dismissal, which takes place on the Sabbath at the Anastasis, is before sunrise, that is, the Oblation, so that the Dismissal may have taken place in the Anastasis at the hour when the sun begins to rise. Thus, then, is each week of Quadragesima kept, the Dismissal taking place earlier on the Sabbath, *i.e.* before sunrise, as I said, in order that the *hebdomadarii*, as they are called here, may finish their fast earlier. For the custom of the fast in Quadragesima is that the Dismissal on the Lord's Day is at the fifth hour in order that they whom they call *hebdomadarii*, that is, they who keep the week's (fast), may take food. And when these have taken their meal on the Lord's Day, they do not eat until the Sabbath morning after they have communicated in the Anastasis. It is for their sake, then, that they may finish their fast the sooner, that the Dismissal on the Sabbath at the

Anastasis is before sunrise. For their sake the Dismissal is in the morning, as I said; not that they alone communicate, but all who are so minded communicate on that day in the Anastasis

5. *The Fast.*

This is the custom of the fast in Quadragesima: some, when they have eaten after the Dismissal on the Lord's Day, that is, about the fifth or sixth hour, do not eat throughout the whole week until after the Dismissal at the Anastasis on the Sabbath; these are they who keep the week's (fast).

Nor, after having eaten in the morning, do they eat in the evening of the Sabbath, but they take a meal on the next day, that is, on the Lord's Day, after the Dismissal from the church at the fifth hour or later, and then they do not eat again until the Sabbath comes round, as I said above. For the custom here is that all who are *Aputactitae*, as they call them here, whether men or women, eat only once a day on the day when they do eat, not only in Quadragesima, but throughout the whole year. But if any of the *Aputactitae* cannot keep the entire week of fasting as described above, they take a meal in the middle (of the week), on the fifth day, all through Quadragesima. And if any one cannot do even this, he keeps two days' fast (in the week) all through Quadragesima, and they who cannot do even this, take a meal every evening. For no one exacts from any how much he should do, but each does what he can, nor is he praised who has done much, nor is he blamed who has done less; that is the custom here For their food during the days of Quadragesima is as follows:—they taste neither bread which cannot be weighed,[1] nor oil, nor anything that grows on trees, but only water and a little gruel made of flour. Quadragesima is kept thus, as we have said. And at the end of the week's (fast) the vigil is kept in the Anastasis from the hour of *lucernare* on the sixth weekday, when the people come with psalms from Syon, to the morning of the Sabbath, when the Oblation is made in the Anastasis. And the second, third, fourth, fifth, and sixth weeks in Quadragesima are kept as the first.

[1] See note on p. 503 —Tr.

V.

HOLY WEEK AND THE FESTIVALS AT EASTER.

1. *Saturday before Palm Sunday.—Station at Bethany.*

Now when the seventh week has come, that is, when two weeks, including the seventh, are left before Easter, everything is done on each day as in the weeks that are past, except that the vigils of the sixth weekday, which were kept in the Anastasis during the first six weeks, are, in the seventh week, kept in Syon, and with the same customs that obtained during the six weeks in the Anastasis. For throughout the whole vigil psalms and antiphons are said appropriate both to the place and to the day.

And when the morning of the Sabbath begins to dawn, the Bishop offers the Oblation. And at the Dismissal the Archdeacon lifts his voice and says: "Let us all be ready to-day at the seventh hour in the Lazarium." And so, as the seventh hour approaches, all go to the Lazarium, that is, Bethany, situated at about the second milestone from the city. And as they go from Jerusalem to the Lazarium, there is, about five hundred paces from the latter place, a church in the street on that spot where Mary the sister of Lazarus met with the Lord. Here, when the Bishop arrives, all the Monks meet him, and the people enter the church, and one hymn and one antiphon are said, and that passage is read in the Gospel where the sister of Lazarus meets the Lord. Then, after prayer has been made, and when all have been blessed, they go thence with hymns to the Lazarium. And on arriving at the Lazarium, so great a multitude assembles that not only the place itself, but also the fields around, are full of people. Hymns and antiphons suitable to the day and to the place are said, and likewise all the lessons are read. Then, before the Dismissal, notice is given of Easter, that is, the Priest ascends to a higher place and reads the passage that is written in the Gospel: *When Jesus six days before the Passover had come to Bethany*, and the rest. So, that passage having been read and notice given of Easter, the Dismissal is made. This is done on that day because, as it is written in the Gospel, these events took place in Bethany six days before the Passover; there being six days from the Sabbath to the fifth weekday on which, after supper, the Lord was taken by night. Then all return to the city direct to the Anastasis, and *lucernare* takes place according to custom.

2. *Palm Sunday.*—(*a*) *Mass.*

On the next day, that is, the Lord's Day, which begins the Paschal week, and which they call here the Great Week, when all the customary services from cockcrow until morning have taken place in the Anastasis and at the Cross, they proceed on the morning of the Lord's Day according to custom to the greater church, which is called the Martyrium. It is called the Martyrium because it is in Golgotha behind the Cross, where the Lord suffered. When all that is customary has been observed in the great church, and before the Dismissal is made, the Archdeacon lifts his voice and says first: "Throughout the whole week, beginning from to-morrow, let us all assemble in the Martyrium, that is, in the great church, at the ninth hour." Then he lifts his voice again, saying: "Let us all be ready to-day in Eleona at the seventh hour." So when the Dismissal has been made in the great church, that is, the Martyrium, the Bishop is escorted with hymns to the Anastasis, and after all things that are customary on the Lord's Day have been done there, after the Dismissal from the Martyrium, every one hastens home to eat, that all may be ready at the beginning of the seventh hour in the church in Eleona, on the Mount of Olives, where is the cave in which the Lord was wont to teach.

(*b*) *Procession in the Evening.*

Accordingly at the seventh hour all the people go up to the Mount of Olives, that is, to Eleona, and the Bishop takes his seat in the church, where hymns and antiphons suitable to the day and to the place are said, and lessons in like manner. And when the ninth hour approaches they go up with hymns to the Imbomon, that is, to the place whence the Lord ascended into heaven, and there they sit down, for all the people are always bidden to sit when the Bishop is present; the Deacons alone always stand. Hymns and antiphons suitable to the day and to the place are said, interspersed with lections and prayers. And as the eleventh hour approaches, the passage from the Gospel is read, where the children, carrying branches and palms, met the Lord, saying: *Blessed is He that cometh in the Name of the Lord*, and the Bishop immediately rises, and all the people with him, and they all go on foot from the top of the Mount of Olives, all the people going before him with hymns and antiphons, answering one to another: *Blessed is He that cometh in the Name of the Lord*. And all the children in the neighbourhood, even those who are too young to walk, are carried by their parents on their shoulders, all of them bearing branches, some of palms and some of olives, and thus the Bishop is escorted in the same manner as the Lord was of old. For all, even those of rank, both matrons and men, accompany the Bishop all the way on foot in this manner, making these responses, from the top of the mount to the city, and thence through the whole city to the Anastasis; going very slowly lest the people should be wearied; and thus they arrive at the Anastasis at a late hour. And on arriving, although it is late, the whole of *lucernare* follows, with prayer at the Cross; after which the people are dismissed.

3. *Monday in Holy Week.*

On the next day, the second weekday, everything that is customary is done from the first cockcrow until morning in the Anastasis; also at the third and sixth hours everything is done that is customary throughout the whole of Quadragesima. But at the ninth hour all assemble in the great church, that is, the Martyrium, where hymns and antiphons are said continuously until the first hour of the night, lessons suitable to the day and the place are read, interspersed always with prayers. *Lucernarium* takes place when its hour approaches, that is, so that it is already night when the Dismissal at the Martyrium takes place. When the Dismissal has been made, the Bishop is escorted thence with hymns to the Anastasis, where, when he has entered, one hymn is said, followed by a prayer; the catechumens and then the faithful are blessed, and the Dismissal is made.

4. *Tuesday in Holy Week.*

On the third weekday everything is done as on the second, with this one thing added—that late at night, after the Dismissal at the Martyrium, and after the going to the Anastasis and after the Dismissal there, then all proceed at that hour by night to the church, which is on the mount Eleona. And when they have arrived at that church, the Bishop enters the Cave where the Lord was wont to teach His disciples, and after receiving the book of the Gospel, he stands and himself reads the words of the Lord which are written in the Gospel according to Matthew, where He says: *Take heed that no man deceive you.* And the Bishop reads through the whole of that discourse, and when he has read it, prayer is made, the catechumens and the faithful are blessed, the Dismissal is made, and every one returns from the mount to his house, it being already very late at night.

5. *Wednesday in Holy Week.*

On the fourth weekday everything is done as on the second and third weekdays throughout the whole day from the first cockcrow onwards, but after the Dismissal has taken place at the Martyrium by night, and the Bishop has been escorted with hymns to the Anastasis, he at once enters the Cave which is in the Anastasis, and stands within the rails; but the Priest stands before the rails and receives the Gospel, and reads the passage where Judas Iscariot went to the Jews and stated what they should give him that he should betray the Lord. And when the passage has been read, there is such a moaning and groaning of all the people that no one can help being moved to tears at that hour. Afterwards prayer follows, then the blessing, first of the catechumens, and then of the faithful, and the Dismissal is made.

6. *Maundy Thursday.*—(*a*) *Evening Masses.*

On the fifth weekday everything that is customary is done from the first cockcrow until morning at the Anastasis, and also at the third and at the sixth hours. But at the eighth hour all the people gather together at the Martyrium according to custom, only earlier than on other days, because the Dismissal must be made sooner. Then, when the people are gathered together, all that should be done is done, and the Oblation is made on that day at the Martyrium, the Dismissal taking place about the tenth hour. But before the Dismissal is made there, the Archdeacon raises his voice and says: "Let us all assemble at the first hour of the night in the church which is in Eleona, for great toil awaits us to-day, in this very night." Then, after the Dismissal at the Martyrium, they arrive behind the Cross, where only one hymn is said and prayer is made, and the Bishop offers the Oblation there, and all communicate. Nor is the Oblation ever offered behind the Cross on any day throughout the year, except on this one day. And after the Dismissal there they go to the Anastasis, where prayer is made, the catechumens and the faithful are blessed according to custom, and the Dismissal is made.

(b) *Night Station on the Mount of Olives.*

And so every one hastens back to his house to eat, because, immediately after they have eaten, all go to Eleona to the church wherein is the Cave where the Lord was with His Apostles on this very day. There then, until about the fifth hour of the night, hymns and antiphons suitable to the day and to the place are said, lessons, too, are read in like manner, with prayers interspersed, and the passages from the Gospel are read where the Lord addressed His disciples on the same day as He sat in the same Cave which is in that church. And they go thence at about the sixth hour of the night with hymns up to the Imbomon, the place whence the Lord ascended into heaven, where again lessons are read, hymns and antiphons suitable to the day are said, and all the prayers which are made by the Bishop are also suitable both to the day and to the place.

(c) *Stations at Gethsemane.*

And at the first cockcrow they come down from the Imbomon with hymns, and arrive at the place where the Lord prayed, as it is written in the Gospel: *and He was withdrawn* [1] *from them about a stone's cast, and prayed*, and the rest. There is in that place a graceful church. The Bishop and all the people enter, a prayer suitable to the place and to the day is said, with one suitable hymn, and the passage from the Gospel is read where He said to His disciples: *Watch, that ye enter not into temptation;* the whole passage is read through and prayer is made. And then all, even to the smallest child, go down with the Bishop, on foot with hymns to Gethsemane; where, on account of the great number of people in the crowd, who are tired by the vigils and weak through the daily fasts, and because they have so great a mountain to descend, they come very slowly with hymns to Gethsemane. And over two hundred church candles are made ready to give light to all the people. On their arrival at Gethsemane, first a suitable prayer is made, then a hymn is said, then the passage of the Gospel is read where the Lord was taken. And when this passage has been read there is so great a moaning and groaning of all the people, together with weeping, that their lamentation may be heard perhaps as far as the city.

(d) *Return to Jerusalem.*

From that hour they go with hymns to the city on foot, reaching the gate about the time when a man begins to be able to recognise another, and thence right on through the midst of the city; all, to a man, both great and small, rich and poor, all are ready there, for on that special day not a soul withdraws from the vigils until morning. Thus the Bishop is escorted from Gethsemane to the gate, and thence through the whole of the city to the Cross.

7. *Good Friday.*—(a) *Service at Daybreak.*

And when they arrive before the Cross the daylight is already growing bright. There the passage from the Gospel is read where the Lord is brought before Pilate, with everything that is written concerning that which Pilate spake to the Lord

---

[1] Lat. *et accessit.*

or to the Jews; the whole is read. And afterwards the Bishop addresses the people, comforting them for that they have both toiled all night and are about to toil during that same day, (bidding) them not be weary, but to have hope in God, Who will for that toil give them a greater reward. And encouraging them as he is able, he addresses them thus: "Go now, each one of you, to your houses, and sit down awhile, and all of you be ready here just before the second hour of the day, that from that hour to the sixth you may be able to behold the holy wood of the Cross, each one of us believing that it will be profitable to his salvation; then from the sixth hour we must all assemble again in this place, that is, before the Cross, that we may apply ourselves to lections and to prayers until night."

(b) *The Column of the Flagellation.*

After this, when the Dismissal at the Cross has been made, that is, before the sun rises, they all go at once with fervour to Syon, to pray at the column at which the Lord was scourged. And returning thence they sit for awhile in their houses, and presently all are ready.

(c) *Adoration of the Cross.*

Then a chair is placed for the Bishop in Golgotha behind the Cross, which is now standing;[1] the Bishop duly takes his seat in the chair, and a table covered with a linen cloth is placed before him; the Deacons stand round the table, and a silver-gilt casket is brought in which is the holy wood of the Cross. The casket is opened and (the wood) is taken out, and both the wood of the Cross and the Title are placed upon the table. Now, when it has been put upon the table, the Bishop, as he sits, holds the extremities of the sacred wood firmly in his hands, while the Deacons who stand around guard it. It is guarded thus because the custom is that the people, both faithful and catechumens, come one by one and, bowing down at the table, kiss the sacred wood and pass on. And because, I know not when, some one is said to have bitten off and stolen a portion of the sacred wood,

---

[1] Mgr Duchesne says "I do not understand *quae stat nunc.*"

it is thus guarded by the Deacons who stand around, lest any one approaching should venture to do so again. And as all the people pass by one by one, all bowing themselves, they touch the Cross and the Title, first with their foreheads and then with their eyes; then they kiss the Cross and pass through, but none lays his hand upon it to touch it. When they have kissed the Cross and have passed through, a Deacon stands holding the ring of Solomon and the horn from which the kings were anointed; they kiss the horn also and gaze at the ring [1] . . . short of the second [1] . . . all the people are passing through up to the sixth hour, entering by one door and going out by another; for this is done in the same place where, on the preceding day, that is, on the fifth weekday, the Oblation was offered.

(d) *Station at Golgotha.* [2]

And when the sixth hour has come, they go before the Cross, whether it be in rain or in heat, the place being open to the air, as it were, a court of great size and very beautiful between the Cross and the Anastasis; here all the people assemble in such great numbers that there is no thoroughfare. The chair is placed for the Bishop before the Cross, and from the sixth to the ninth hour nothing else is done but the reading of lessons, which are read thus: first from the Psalms wherever the Passion is spoken of, then from the Apostle, either from the epistles of the Apostles or from their Acts, wherever they have spoken of the Lord's Passion; then the passages from the Gospels, where He suffered, are read. Then the readings from the prophets where they foretold that the Lord should suffer, then from the Gospels where He mentions His Passion. Thus from the sixth to the ninth hours the lessons are so read and the hymns said, that it may be shown to all the people that whatsoever the prophets foretold of the Lord's Passion is proved from the Gospels and from the writings of the Apostles to have been fulfilled. And so through all those three hours the people are taught that nothing was done which had not been foretold, and that nothing

---

[1] There is here an hiatus in the MS.—Tr.

[2] This is probably the earliest record of the Observance of the "Three Hours."—Tr.

was foretold which was not wholly fulfilled. Prayers also suitable to the day are interspersed throughout. The emotion shown and the mourning by all the people at every lesson and prayer is wonderful; for there is none, either great or small, who, on that day during those three hours, does not lament more than can be conceived, that the Lord had suffered those things for us.

Afterwards, at the beginning of the ninth hour, there is read that passage from the Gospel according to John where He gave up the ghost. This read, prayer and the Dismissal follow.

(e) *Evening Offices.*

And when the Dismissal before the Cross has been made, all things are done in the greater church, at the Martyrium, which are customary during this week from the ninth hour—when the assembly takes place in the Martyrium—until late. And after the Dismissal at the Martyrium, they go to the Anastasis, where, when they arrive, the passage from the Gospel is read where Joseph begged the Body of the Lord from Pilate and laid it in a new sepulchre. And this reading ended, a prayer is said, the catechumens are blessed, and the Dismissal is made.

But on that day no announcement is made of a vigil at the Anastasis, because it is known that the people are tired; nevertheless, it is the custom to watch there. So all of the people who are willing, or rather, who are able, keep watch, and they who are unable do not watch there until the morning. Those of the Clergy, however, who are strong or young keep vigil there, and hymns and antiphons are said throughout the whole night until morning; a very great crowd also keep night-long watch, some from the late hour and some from midnight, as they are able.

8. *Vigil of Easter.*

Now, on the next day, the Sabbath, everything that is customary is done at the third hour and also at the sixth; the service at the ninth hour, however, is not held on the Sabbath, but the Paschal vigils are prepared in the great church, the Martyrium. The Paschal vigils are kept as with us, with this one addition, that the children, when they have been baptised and clothed, and when they issue from the font, are led with the Bishop first to the Anastasis; the Bishop enters within the rails of the Anastasis, and one hymn is said, then the Bishop says a prayer for them, and then he goes with them to the greater church, where, according to custom, all the people are keeping watch. Everything is done there that is customary with us also, and after the Oblation has been offered, the Dismissal is made. After the Dismissal of the vigils has been made in the greater church, they go at once with hymns to the Anastasis, where the passage from the Gospel about the Resurrection is read. Prayer is made, and the Bishop again makes the Offering. But everything is done quickly on account of the people, that they should not be delayed any longer, and so the people are dismissed. The Dismissal of the vigils takes place on that day at the same hour as with us.

9. *Octave of Easter.*

Moreover, the Paschal days are kept up to a late hour as with us, and the Dismissals take place in their order throughout the eight Paschal days, as is the custom everywhere at Easter throughout the Octave. But the adornment (of the churches) and order (of the services) here are the same throughout the Octave of Easter as they are during Epiphany, in the greater church, in the Anastasis, at the Cross, in Eleona, in Bethlehem, as well as in the Lazarium, in fact, everywhere, because these are the Paschal days. On the first Lord's Day [1] they proceed to the great church, that is, the Martyrium, as well as on the second and third weekdays, but always so that after the Dismissal has been made at the Martyrium, they go to the Anastasis with hymns. On the fourth weekday they proceed to Eleona, on the fifth to the Anastasis, on the sixth to Syon, on the Sabbath before the Cross, but on the Lord's Day, that is, on the Octave, they (proceed to) the great church again, that is, to the Martyrium.

Moreover, on the eight Paschal days the Bishop goes every day after breakfast up to Eleona with all the Clergy, and with

---

[1] *i.e.* Easter Day itself.—Tr.

all the children who have been baptised, and with all who are *Aputactitae*, both men and women, and likewise with all the people who are willing. Hymns are said and prayers are made, both in the church which is on Eleona, wherein is the Cave where Jesus was wont to teach His disciples, and also in the Imbomon, that is, in the place whence the Lord ascended into heaven. And when the psalms have been said and prayer has been made, they come down thence with hymns to the Anastasis at the hour of *lucerna*. This is done throughout all the eight days.

10. *Vesper Station at Sion on Easter Sunday.*

Now, on the Lord's Day at Easter, after the Dismissal of *lucernare*, that is, at the Anastasis, all the people escort the Bishop with hymns to Syon. And, on arriving, hymns suitable to the day and place are said, prayer is made, and the passage from the Gospel is read where the Lord, on the same day, and in the same place where the church now stands in Syon, came in to His disciples when the doors were shut. That is, when one of His disciples, Thomas, was absent, and when he returned and the other Apostles told him that they had seen the Lord, he said: "Except I shall see, I will not believe." When this has been read, prayer is again made, the catechumens and the faithful are blessed, and every one returns to his house late, about the second hour of the night.

11. *Sunday after Easter.*

Again, on the Octave of Easter, that is, on the Lord's Day, all the people go up to Eleona with the Bishop immediately after the sixth hour. First they sit for awhile in the church which is there, and hymns and antiphons suitable to the day and to the place are said; prayers suitable to the day and to the place are likewise made. Then they go up to the Imbomon with hymns, and the same things are done there as in the former place. And when the time comes, all the people and all the *Aputactitae* escort the Bishop with hymns down to the Anastasis, arriving there at the usual hour for *lucernarium*. So *lucernarium* takes place at the Anastasis and at the Cross, and all the people to a man escort the Bishop thence with hymns to Syon. And when they have arrived, hymns suitable to the day and to the place are said there also, and lastly that passage from the Gospel is read where, on the Octave of Easter, the Lord came in where the disciples were, and reproved Thomas because he had been unbelieving. The whole of that lesson is read, with prayer afterwards; both the catechumens and the faithful are blessed, and every one returns to his house as usual, just as on the Lord's Day of Easter, at the second hour of the night.

VI.

Festivals of Whitsuntide

1. *Eastertide.*

Now, from Easter to the fiftieth day, that is, to Pentecost, no one fasts here, not even those who are *Aputactitae*. During these days, as throughout the whole year, the customary things are done at the Anastasis from the first cockcrow until morning, and at the sixth hour and at *lucernare* likewise. But on the Lord's Days the procession is always in the Martyrium, that is, in the great church, according to custom, and they go thence with hymns to the Anastasis. On the fourth and sixth weekdays, as no one fasts during those days, the procession is in Syon, but in the morning; and the Dismissal is made in its due order.

2. *The Ascension —Festival at Bethlehem.*

On the fortieth day after Easter, that is, on the fifth weekday—(for all go on the previous day, that is, on the fourth weekday, after the sixth hour to Bethlehem to celebrate the vigils, for the vigils are kept in Bethlehem, in the church wherein is the Cave where the Lord was born)—on this fifth weekday, the fortieth day after Easter, the Dismissal[1] is celebrated in its due order, so that the Priests and the Bishop preach, treating of the things suitable to the day and the place, and afterwards every one returns to Jerusalem late.

[1] Lat. *missa celebratur.*

3. *Whitsunday*—(a) *Morning Station.*

But on the fiftieth day, that is, the Lord's Day, when the people have a very great deal to go through, everything that is customary is done from the first cockcrow onwards; vigil is kept in the Anastasis, and the Bishop reads the passage from the Gospel that is always read on the Lord's Day, namely, the account of the Lord's Resurrection, and afterwards everything customary is done in the Anastasis, just as throughout the whole year. But when morning is come, all the people proceed to the great church, that is, to the Martyrium, and all things usual are done there; the Priests preach and then the Bishop, and all things that are prescribed are done, the Offering being made, as is customary on the Lord's Day, only the same Dismissal[1] in the Martyrium is hastened, in order that it may be made before the third hour.

(b) *Station at Sion.*

And when the Dismissal has been made at the Martyrium, all the people, to a man, escort the Bishop with hymns to Syon, so that they are in Syon when the third hour is fully come. And on their arrival there the passage from the Acts of the Apostles is read where the Spirit came down so that all tongues [were heard and all men] understood the things that were spoken, and the Dismissal takes place afterwards in due course. For the Priests read there from the Acts of the Apostles concerning this selfsame thing, because that is the place in Sion—there is another church there now—where once after the Lord's Passion the multitude was gathered together with the Apostles, and where this was done as we have said above. Afterwards the Dismissal takes place in due course, and the Offering is made there. Then, that the people may be dismissed, the Archdeacon raises his voice, and says: "Let us all be ready to-day in Eleona, in the Imbomon, directly after the sixth hour."

[1] Lat *eadem adceleratur missa.*

(c) *Station at the Mount of Olives*

So all the people return, each to his house, to rest themselves, and immediately after breakfast they ascend the Mount of Olives, that is, to Eleona, each as he can, so that there is no Christian left in the city who does not go. When, therefore, they have gone up the Mount of Olives, that is, to Eleona, they first enter the Imbomon, that is, the place whence the Lord ascended into heaven, and the Bishop and the Priests take their seat there, and likewise all the people. Lessons are read there with hymns interspersed, antiphons too are said suitable to the day and the place, also the prayers which are interspersed have likewise similar references. The passage from the Gospel is also read where it speaks of the Lord's Ascension, also that from the Acts of the Apostles which tells of the Ascension of the Lord into heaven after His Resurrection. And when this is over, the catechumens and then the faithful are blessed, and they come down thence, it being already the ninth hour, and go with hymns to that church which is in Eleona, wherein is the Cave where the Lord was wont to sit and teach His Apostles. And as it is already past the tenth hour when they arrive, *lucernare* takes place there; prayer is made, and the catechumens and likewise the faithful are blessed.

(d) *Night Procession.*

And then all the people to a man descend thence with the Bishop, saying hymns and antiphons suitable to that day, and so come very slowly to the Martyrium. It is already night when they reach the gate of the city, and about two hundred church candles are provided for the use of the people. And as it is a good distance from the gate to the great church, that is, the Martyrium, they arrive about the second hour of the night, for they go the whole way very slowly lest the people should be weary from being afoot. And when the great gates are opened, which face towards the market-place, all the people enter the Martyrium with hymns and with the Bishop. And when they have entered the church, hymns are said, prayer is made, the catechumens and also the faithful are blessed; after which they go again with hymns to the Anastasis, where on their arrival hymns and antiphons are said, prayer is made, the catechumens and also the faithful are blessed; this is likewise done at the Cross. Lastly, all the Christian people to a man escort the Bishop with hymns to Syon, and when they are come there, suitable lessons are read, psalms and antiphons are said, prayer is made, the catechumens and the faithful are blessed, and the Dismissal takes place. And after the Dismissal all approach the Bishop's hand, and then every one returns to his house about midnight.

Thus very great fatigue is endured on that day, for vigil is kept at the Anastasis from the first cockcrow, and there is no pause from that time onward throughout the whole day, but the whole celebration (of the Feast) lasts so long that it is midnight when every one returns home after the Dismissal has taken place at Syon

4. *Resumption of the Ordinary Services.*

Now, from the day after the fiftieth day all fast as is customary throughout the whole year, each one as he is able, except on the Sabbath and on the Lord's Day, which are never kept as fasts in this place. On the ensuing days everything is done as during the whole year, that is, vigil is kept in the Anastasis from the first cockcrow. And if it be the Lord's Day, at the earliest cockcrow the Bishop first reads in the Anastasis, as is customary, the passage from the Gospel concerning the Resurrection, which is always read on the Lord's Day, and then afterwards hymns and antiphons are said in the Anastasis until daylight. But if it be not the Lord's Day, only hymns and antiphons are said in like manner in the Anastasis from the first cockcrow until daylight. All the *Aputactitae*, and of the people those who are able, attend; the Clergy go by turns, daily. The Clergy go there at first cockcrow, but the Bishop always as it begins to dawn, that the morning Dismissal may be made with all the Clergy present, except on the Lord's Day, when (the Bishop) has to go at the first cockcrow, that he may read the Gospel in the Anastasis. Afterwards everything is done as usual in the Anastasis until the sixth hour, and at the ninth, as well as at *lucernare*, according to the custom of the whole year. But on the fourth and sixth weekdays, the ninth hour is kept in Syon as is customary.

VII.

BAPTISM.

1. *The Inscribing of the Competents.*

Moreover, I must write how they are taught who are baptised at Easter. Now he who gives in his name, gives it in on the day before Quadragesima, and the Priest writes down the names of all; this is before the eight weeks which I have said are kept here at Quadragesima. And when the Priest has written down the names of all, after the next day of Quadragesima, that is, on the day when the eight weeks begin, the chair is set for the Bishop in the midst of the great church, that is, at the Martyrium, and the Priests sit in chairs on either side of him, while all the Clergy stand. Then one by one the Competents are brought up, coming, if they are men, with their fathers, and if women, with their mothers. Then the Bishop asks the neighbours of every one who has entered concerning each individual, saying · " Does this man lead a good life, is he obedient to his parents, is he not given to wine, nor deceitful?" making also inquiry about the several vices which are more serious in man. And if he has proved him in the presence of witnesses to be blameless in all these matters concerning which he has made inquiry, he writes down his name with his own hand. But if he is accused in any matter, he orders him to go out, saying: "Let him amend, and when he has amended then let him come to the bath (of regeneration)." And as he makes inquiry concerning the men, so also does he concerning the women. But if any be a stranger, he comes not so easily to Baptism, unless he has testimonials from those who know him.

2. *Preparation for Baptism.—Catechisings.*

This also I must write, Reverend Sisters, lest you should think that these things are done without good reason. The custom here is that they who come to Baptism at this season fast for forty days, but first they are exorcised by the Clergy early in the day, as soon as the morning Dismissal has been made in the Anastasis. Immediately afterwards the chair is placed for the Bishop at the Martyrium in the great church, and all who are to be baptised sit around, near the Bishop, both men and women, their fathers and mothers standing there also. Besides these, all the people who wish to hear come in and sit down—the faithful however only, for no catechumen enters there when the Bishop teaches the others the law. Beginning from Genesis he goes through all the Scriptures during those forty days, explaining them, first literally, and then unfolding them spiritually. They are also taught about the Resurrection, and likewise all things concerning the Faith during those days. And this is called the Catechising.

3. *"Traditio" of the Creed.*

Then when five weeks are completed from the time when their teaching began, the (Competents) then are taught the Creed.[1] And as he explained the meaning of all the Scriptures, so does he explain the meaning of the Creed; each article first literally and then spiritually. By this means all the faithful in these parts follow the Scriptures when they are read in church, inasmuch as they are all taught during those forty days from the first to the third hour, for the Catechising lasts for three hours. And God knows, Reverend Sisters, that the voices of the faithful who come in to hear the Catechising are louder (in approval) of the things spoken and explained by the Bishop than they are when he sits and preaches in church. Then, after the Dismissal of the Catechising is made, it being already the third hour, the Bishop is at once escorted with hymns to the Anastasis.

---

[1] Lat. *accipient simbolum.*

So the Dismissal takes place at the third hour. Thus are they taught for three hours a day for seven weeks, but in the eighth week of Quadragesima, which is called the Great Week, there is no time for them to be taught, because the things that are [described] above must be carried out.[1]

4. *"Redditio"* [*Recitation*] *of the Creed.*

And when the seven weeks are past, [and] the Paschal week is left, which they call here the Great Week, then the Bishop comes in the morning into the great church at the Martyrium, and the chair is placed for him in the apse behind the altar, where they come one by one, a man with his father and a woman with her mother, and recite the Creed to the Bishop. And when they have recited the Creed to the Bishop, he addresses them all, and says: "During these seven weeks you have been taught all the law of the Scriptures, you have also heard concerning the Faith, and concerning the resurrection of the flesh, and the whole meaning of the Creed, as far as you were able, being yet catechumens. But the teachings of the deeper mystery, that is, of Baptism itself, you cannot hear, being as yet catechumens. But, lest you should think that anything is done without good reason, these, when you have been baptised in the Name of God, you shall hear in the Anastasis, during the eight Paschal days, after the Dismissal from the church has been made. You, being as yet catechumens, cannot be told the more secret mysteries of God."

5. *Mystic Catechisings.*

But when the days of Easter have come, during those eight days, that is, from Easter to the Octave, when the Dismissal from the church has been made, they go with hymns to the Anastasis. Prayer is said anon, the faithful are blessed, and the Bishop stands, leaning against the inner rails which are in the Cave of the Anastasis, and explains all things that are done in Baptism. In that hour no catechumen approaches the

---

[1] *i.e* the Holy Week services.—Tr.

Anastasis, but only the neophytes and the faithful, who wish to hear concerning the mysteries, enter there, and the doors are shut lest any catechumen should draw near. And while the Bishop discusses and sets forth each point, the voices of those who applaud are so loud that they can be heard outside the church. And truly the mysteries are so unfolded that there is no one unmoved at the things that he hears to be so explained.

Now, forasmuch as in that province some of the people know both Greek and Syriac, while some know Greek alone and others only Syriac; and because the Bishop, although he knows Syriac, yet always speaks Greek, and never Syriac, there is always a Priest standing by who, when the Bishop speaks Greek, interprets into Syriac, that all may understand what is being taught. And because all the lessons that are read in the church must be read in Greek, he always stands by and interprets them into Syriac, for the people's sake, that they may always be edified. Moreover, the Latins here, who understand neither Syriac nor Greek, in order that they be not disappointed, have (all things) explained to them, for there are other brothers and sisters knowing both Greek and Latin, who translate into Latin for them. But what is above all things very pleasant and admirable here, is that the hymns, the antiphons, and the lessons, as well as the prayers which the Bishop says, always have suitable and fitting references, both to the day that is being celebrated and also to the place where the celebration is being made.

VIII.

Dedication of Churches.

Those are called the days of Dedication when the holy church which is in Golgotha, and which they call the Martyrium, was consecrated to God; the holy church also which is at the Anastasis, that is, in the place where the Lord rose after His Passion, was consecrated to God on that day. The dedication of these holy churches is therefore celebrated with the highest honour, and also because the Cross of the Lord was found on this same day. And it was so ordained that, when the holy churches above mentioned were consecrated, that should (also) be the day when the Cross of the Lord had been found, in order that the whole celebration should be made together, with all rejoicing, on the self-same day. Moreover, it appears from the Holy Scriptures that this is also the day of Dedication, when holy Solomon, having finished the House of God which he had built, stood before the altar of God and prayed, as it is written in the books of the Chronicles.

So when these days of Dedication are come, they are kept for eight days. And people begin to assemble from all parts many days before; not only Monks and *Aputactitae* from various provinces, from Mesopotamia and Syria, from Egypt and the Thebaid (where there are very many Monks), and from every different place and province—for there is none who does not turn his steps to Jerusalem on that day for such rejoicing and for such high days—but lay people too in like manner, both men and women, with faithful minds, gather together in Jerusalem from every province on those days, for the sake of the holy day. And the Bishops, even when they have been few, are present to the number of forty or fifty in Jerusalem on these days, and with them come many of their Clergy. But why should I say more? for he who on these days has not been present at so solemn a feast thinks that he has committed a very great sin, unless some necessity, which keeps a man back from carrying out a good resolution, has hindered him. Now on these days of the Dedication the adornment of all the churches is the same as at Easter and at Epiphany, also on each day the procession is made in the several holy places, as at Easter and at Epiphany. For on the first and second days it is in the greater church, which is called the Martyrium. On the third day it is in Eleona, that is, the church which is on that mount whence the Lord ascended into heaven after His Passion, and in this church is the Cave wherein the Lord used to teach His Apostles on Mount Olivet. But on the fourth day . . .

NOTE TO PAGE 75.

We must, however, mention here the Liturgy of the *Apostolic Tradition* of Hippolytus, otherwise known as the *Egyptian Church Order* (Appendix 6), since this book has, not by reason of its origin, but by the use subsequently made of it, very real ties with Egypt. The Liturgy in question has given occasion to many divergencies of opinion Cf. P. Batiffol, *Revue biblique*, 1916, p 23. The Anaphora opens with a Commemoration of the Incarnation, thus omitting the Thanksgiving to God the Father and the Sanctus. Quite recently the remains of another liturgical text were found on the fragments of three leaves of papyrus, and published by Dom de Puniet, *Revue bénédictine*, vol. xxvi. 1909, p. 34 *et seq* See also for the same text a still more recent work by Th Schermann, *Der liturgische Papyrus, von Dêr Balyzeh* (*Texte und Unters.*, vol. xxxvi. fasc 1ᵇ) In this doctrine the narrative of the Institution of the Eucharist is preceded by an Epiclesis Perhaps there may have been another at the end; the fragmentary state of the papyrus prevented this from being ascertained with certainty

NOTE TO PAGE 88.

Mr W. C. Bishop in the *Journal of Theological Studies*, vol xiii. 1912, points out the resemblances which appear to him to connect the African with the Mozarabic Rite. These resemblances do not strike me. They would be more marked, were they not counterbalanced by certain clearly Roman traits, as apparent in the Liturgy of the Mass as the other parts of the Use. The Roman origin of the African Use is to be presumed, seeing the constant relations which existed between Rome and Carthage

NOTE TO PAGE 113.

This is no longer the case. Dom G. Morin has recently described (*Revue bénédictine*, vol. xxvii. 1910, p 41. Cf. vol xxviii 1911, p 297) a book of this type from a MS at Wurzburg. The same learned writer had previously drawn attention (*Revue bénédictine*, vol vii 1890, p 416, et vol. viii. 1891, p. 481) to two very ancient Lectionaries corresponding respectively to the Uses of Capua and Naples The rubrics of these books were subsequently published by him in vol. 1. of *Anecdota Maredsolana*, at the end of a Lectionary of Toledo, called the *Liber Comicus* This appellation is derived from the word *Comes*, often used to designate a Lectionary. We find it employed in this sense in a document as early as 471, viz. the *Charta Cornutiana* (*Liber pontif*, vol i. p. cxlvii *a*, 1 49). Dom Morin has also pointed out the existence in the Library at Schlestadt of a Lectionary in uncials of cir 700 (*Etudes*, vol 1. p. 440). To these books which are earlier than the Carolingian *Comes*, or at all events independent of it, we must add two very ancient collections of Lections to be found in the Bobbio Missal and in that of Monte Cassino (see *infra*, note to p. 125).

NOTE TO PAGE 115.

In certain circumstances the antiphon was repeated in the Psalm itself, either after every second verse or even after each verse. This is the case in the *Venite exultemus* at the invitation at Mattins, and in the canticle *Nunc dimittis* sung during the distribution of the candles on February 2nd

Page 122, end of note 2.

Mr. H A. Wilson published in 1915 a new edition of the Gregorianum (*The Gregorian Sacramentary under Charles the Great*, London, Bradshaw Soc) following the same MSS (Vat Reg. 337 and Ottob 313) which had been used by Muratori, with the help of one of the Cambrai MS. (No 164) belonging to the latest years of Charlemagne and directly derived from the copy of Pope Adrian and not from the revised copy corrected and supplemented by Alcuin We shall, however, do well to consult, as far as the paleography is concerned, the volume of Adolf Ebner, *Quellen und Forschungen zur Geschichte und Kunstgeschichte des Missale Romanum im Mittelalter—Iter italicum*, Freiburg im Breisgau, 1896, particularly pages 373-394, also the article by Edmund Bishop, *On some Early MSS of the Gregorianum*, in *Journal of Theological Studies*, 1903.

NOTE TO PAGE 125
The Gregorian Sacramentary

Dom André Wilmart, in the *Revue bénédictine*, 1909, pp 281-300, has drawn attention to and described a palimpsest of Monte Cassino (No 271) which contains a number of leaves in uncials, the remains of a Gregorian missa written circa 700, and consequently about a century earlier than that of Adrian This MS. comprised the Epistles and Gospels, and was; therefore, a complete missal.

It reproduces also summarily the prayers and rubrics of the Gregorian Sacramentary, as edited by Muratori Most of the Canon in it is preserved. The Chapel of St Andrew in the Lateran is mentioned in it, which leads us to suppose that the original from which this missal was copied was not older than Pope Honorius The MS is too fragmentary to permit of our discovering whether the later alterations made under Leo II, Sergius and Gregory II were contained in it or not It is impossible therefore to determine the precise moment of the Gregorian tradition to which these precious fragments bear witness, but they certainly constitute the earliest testimony which we as yet possess For a detail known to Aldhelm in the Gregorian Canon of his time, about 700, see *Revue bénédictine*, 1910, p 515, and 1911, p 90.

NOTE TO PAGE 127

For a long time regarded as lost, the triple Sacramentary of Gerbert was found by Dom Cagin in the Municipal Library (c 43) of Zurich (*Revue des bibliothèques*, 1899, p 364 and ff) Mr Bannister has published (*Journal of Theol Studies*, vol ix. p 398) a fragment of a Gelasian MS (*Paris*, 9488) of the same type as the MS of St. Gall The hand is Anglo-Saxon, and the MS. to which this fragment belonged appears to have been written in the North of England.

APPENDIX.

NOTE TO PAGE 153 (ADDITION TO NOTE 2)

Arnobius the Younger, Letter to Gregoria, c. 5, published by Dom Morin, *Etudes*, vol. 1. p. 391. Cf. particularly the work of Dom Wilmart in the *Revue bénédictine*, 1911, p. 367. Dom Wilmart was able to arrange more skilfully than Mone had done, the order of the leaves of the old Gallican book and asserted that there are in all, not eleven, but only seven masses

PAGE 155.

Even should the authenticity of this heading be contested, it could not detract from the value of the document, regarded as the expression of Gallican ritual Whether it comes from the pen of St. Germain or from that of another Merovingian clerk cannot affect its importance in the use here made of it.

NOTE TO PAGE 157.

There is reason to connect with the Bangor Antiphonary the liturgical collection of which we have six leaves left in the MS. F iv. 1 of the Turin Library, published by W. Meyer in *Nachrichten*, Gottingen (Philol. Hist), 1903, p 163 and ff.

NOTE TO PAGE 168.

The suppression was not, however, complete. Besides the exceptions already mentioned, others may be found in the Roman *Comes*, published by Dom G. Morin, *Revue bénédictine*, vol xxvii 1910. In the time of Charlemagne, the Masses of the Vigil and the night of Christmas still had the three Lections.

Page 176, note 1.

Mr. Edmund Bishop has collected and classified the variants of the most ancient and best authenticated MSS. (*Journal of Theol. Studies*, vol iv. 1903, p. 555).

NOTE TO PAGE 180.
The Commemoration of the Living and the Dead in the Canon

The incoherence of this part of the Roman Canon has, however, been much exaggerated. In my opinion, all that we can say is, that the formulary of the *Memento* of the living may be easily detached from its surroundings ; this commemoration of persons who are offering the sacrifice, or for whom it is offered, may appear adventitious—interpolated between the *Te igitur* and the *Communicantes* Perhaps we have here traces of a use in which this Commemoration may at first have been read from a special text, before it was incorporated in the Canon. It would be particularly incongruous to seek a place for it after the Epiclesis, immediately preceding the *Memento* of the departed. for in that case it would constitute a repetition of the *Nobis quoque*. The word *etiam* in the *Memento* of the departed seems indeed to indicate a co-ordination with the *Memento* of the living. it was no doubt introduced after the latter had found a place in the Canon; but co-ordination does not apply juxtaposition; the two *Mementos*, similar in form, are united in spite of the prayers that separate them But, although similar in form, the two Commemorations have by no means the same import The first deals with those persons who at the actual moment are offering the sacrifice, or at any rate are present at it, it asks for them both spiritual and temporal blessings, without direct or special reference to the life to come; the second, on the contrary, deals with the future life only; it is exclusively occupied with the departed, at the beginning with those already dead (*Memento*) and then with those who later on will join their ranks (*Nobis quoque*). Hence there is between the two *Mementos* a fortuitous and merely external resemblance.

Note to Page 183.

The "Apostolic Tradition" of Hippolytus (Appendix 6) also mentions the third element of this beverage.

Note for Page 200

Another Litany of the same kind appears in the *Officia per Ferias* of Alcuin (*P. L.*, vol ci. p. 560), W Meyer has called attention to this neglected but interesting text (*Nachrichten*, Gottingen, 1912, p. 87); Edm Bishop also noticed it (*Journal of Theol Studies*, vol. xii p. 407). The document bears as its title in the MS. (col 106) *Deprecatio quam papa Gelasius pro universali ecclesia constituit canendam esse*.

I should not place more confidence in this title than in that of *Canon papae Gelasi*, which figures in the Stowe Missal (see *supra*, p 156), although Edm. Bishop takes it seriously. His principal argument is based on the expression *qui huic ecclesiae praeficerunt catholicae*, used to denote the departed Bishops; he connects it with the title of *Episcopus Ecclesiae Catholicae* assumed by the Popes from a particular date onwards, and concludes from this that the Litany must be Roman. But I have shown (*Hist ancienne de l'Eglise*, vol. iii. p 666) that this designation is not peculiar to Rome, and that it was used wherever the presence of a dissident Community obliged the Catholic Bishop to be distinguished from a Novatian, Donatist, Arian or other colleague.

Note to Page 208

In the *Proceedings* of the *Bib Arch Soc* 1908, p 255, Mr W E Crum has published an ivory diptych, from some site in Egypt not yet ascertained, but contemporary with the Arab invasion The Liturgical formulas written on it have been examined in the *Byzantinische Zeitschrift*, vol xviii. 1909, p 625, and also in the *Journal of Theological Studies*, vol xi 1910, p. 67, by Edm Bishop.

Note on keeping Christmas and Epiphany.
(Page 259, continuation of note 3)

Eventually this older use and the Roman custom which Jerome and his followers had vigorously upheld, came into conflict Juvenal, Bishop of

Jerusalem (424–458), accepted the date of the 25th December, following doubtless the example of Cyril of Alexandria, this is clear from a contemporary homily (of Basil of Seleucia?) (Migne, *Pat. Gr*, vol lxxxv p 469). The ancient use finally, however, reasserted itself Cosmas Indicopleustes (*Pat Gr.*, vol. lxxxviii p 197), writing at Sinai, cir. 535, expressly witnesses to the fact, and we have no ground to suppose him to be mistaken In the seventh century the homilies of the Patriarch Sophronius prove that the two Festivals were again kept distinct

PAGE 272 (addition to note 3)

The Festival of the Annunciation was introduced at Ephesus about the year 500 by Bishop Abiamius, who followed in this the example of certain monastic Churches of Palestine The fact is vouched for by Abramius himself in a homily on the Hypapanti, published in 1911 at Turiev (Dorpat) by Michael Kraschenunnikov, in the Acts of the University of that town

NOTE TO PAGE 298

There were at that time seven distinct scrutinies, none of which took place on a Sunday. According to some documents it might appear that the scrutinies were at first three in number only, and took place on the 3rd, 4th, and 5th Sundays in Lent

At the beginning of the sixth century the *vir illustris* Senarius asks of John, deacon of Rome, *quare tertio ante Pascha scrutinentur infantes* (Migne, *P L.*, vol lix p 401), the Gelasian Sacramentary contains, at the 3rd, 4th, and 5th Sundays in Lent, the rubrics *pro scrutiniis pro scrutinio II*, *pro scrut.;* finally the Naples Capitulary of the eighth century (*Aneed Mared*, vol 1 pp 427, 428) shows, at these same Sundays, indications *quando psalmi (?) accipiunt, quando orationem accipiunt, quando symbolum accipiunt.*

It is, however, difficult to admit that the ritual of the scrutinies had grown more complex between the sixth and seventh and up to the eighth centuries By then it would be used merely for infants, and everything would tend to simplify, and not to develop it. This presents a problem for solution.

NOTE TO PAGE 305.

Cf *Revue bénédictine*, vol xxviii p. 304.

NOTE TO PAGE 306

The words *unde unxisti reges, sacerdotes et prophetas* are found as early as the "Apostolic Tradition" of Hippolytus, in one of the formulas of that document. (Cf. Appendix 6), Hauler, p 108. The addition of the Martyrs to this enumeration betrays an interpolation, in reality, the three categories, Kings, Priests, and Prophets, refer to actual facts mentioned in the Old Testament, the anointing of Martyrs is an imaginary anointing

PAGE 368.

In the fifth century, however, we see by a text of Arnobius the Younger (*P. L*, vol liii p 485, cf Morin, *Etudes*, vol 1 p 361), that the acclamation *Dignus et justus* was still in use

INDEX.

A

Abrenuntio, the, or Renunciation of Satan (*which see*), 304, 332
  in the Eastern Rite, 329, 331
  in the Gallican Rite, 324
Abyssinian Liturgies, 81
Accubita, 473
Acolytes, 299, 344, 345, 352, 366, 458, 469
Adaeus and Maris, SS., Liturgy of, 70
Adauctus and Felix, SS., 136
Adoration of the Cross. *See* Cross
Ad communionem, 187
Adrian, St., Church of, 124, 479. *See also* Sacramentary. *See also* Pope
Africa, Church of, appeals to Milan, 35
  bishops wear *pallium*, 385
  dedication of virgins in, 422
Agape, 49, 231
Agnus Dei, 150, 186, 257, 470, 484
Ajus in Gallican Mass, 191
Albania, 29
Albano, Bishop of, 362
Alb, 381
Alcuin, 104, 121, 129, 253
Alexandria, 16, 17, 24, 241, 243
  Use of, 54, 79, 230, 232, 332, 335
  Liturgy of, 75, 82
  Bishop of, 18, 23, 378
  computation of Easter at, 237
Alleluia, 114
  in the Roman Mass, 167, 168
  in the Gallican Mass, 196, 204, 206
  at ordination, 359
  in the *Ordines*, 456, 472
Alphabet, ceremony of, 409, 417
Altar—
  cloth, 205
  linen, 205, 306
  blessing of, 406, 413
  washing of, 406
  cross, 406
  lustration of, 410
  anointing of, 410
Amalarius, 104, 147
Amand, St., *ordo* of, 149, 455
Ambo, 114, 169, 353

Ambrose, St., 32 *et seq.*, 86, 93, 95, 105, 442
  De Mysteriis of, 316
  introduces antiphonal chanting, 115
  his name in the Canon, 159
  on Virgins, 421, 422, 423
  on marriage, 432
Ambrosian (Milanese)—
  Rite, 88, 105, 245, 285
    identical with Gallican, 88
    Eastern influence in, 93
  liturgical books, 160
  Sacramentaries, 160
  Antiphonaries, 160
  Canon, 177, 178
  Liturgy, 88, 173, 177, 190, 191, 192, 193, 194, 195, 198, 204, 205, 206, 207, 208, 212, 213, 214, 215, 217, 218, 220, 222, 223, 224, 225, 227, 327
Ammianus Marcellinus, 260
Amphibalum (or chasuble), 381
Amulae (phials of wine), 173, 459
Anagolagium, 456
Anamnesis (commemoration of Christ), meaning of, 61
  in the Nestorian Liturgy, 70
  in the Roman Mass, 181
Anaphora, the, 68, 70, 81, 110, 176
  in the Nestorian liturgies, 70
  the Roman, 176, 178
  of Bishop Sarapion, 75, 82
  of St. Basil, 81
  of St. Cyril, 81
  of St. Gregory Nazianzen, 81
Anastasia, St., 265A
Anastasis, Church of, 491
Anchorites, 419
Ancyra, Council of, 20
Andrew, St., 283
Annotinus, 482
Annunciation, Festival of, 272. *See* Virgin, the Blessed
Anointing. *See also* Chrism and *Chrismatio*, 333
  of catechumens, 304, 317, 331
  blessings of oil for, 305
  at baptism, 330, 335

Anointing (*continued*)—
  at confirmation, 314, 325, 330
  of the hands at ordination, 370, 372, 375
  of the hands in the Gallican Rite, 132, 370, 372, 375, 378
  of altar at dedication, 411
  of church, 406, 412
Anointing of the sick, 305
  with saliva, 304, 317, 332
Anthem, 116
Antioch, 16, 19
  councils and synods at, 20
  centre of influence of Greek Empire, 21
  wane of, 25
  Use of, 54
  Patriarch of, 65, 66
  ecclesiastical influence of, 71
  antiphonal chanting introduced at, 114
  Bishop of, 23
  Bishop of, Fabius, 344
  Bishop of, Sarapion, 19
  keeping of Easter at, 237
Antiphonary (*Antiphonarium*), 116
  sent by Pope Paul to Pepin, 102
  of Bangor, 157, 225
  hymn from, 226
Antiphon (Anthem), 114 *et seq.*, 187
  in the Gallican Mass, 190
  at the *post Evangelium*, 205
  at dedication of church, 406, 410
  at Matins, 492
Apostolic Constitutions, 56, 57, 216, 525
  Liturgy of, 64, 201, 202
  chanting described in, 113
  Gloria in excelsis in, 166
  Litany in, 200
  on fasting, 243
  Festival of St. Stephen in, 267
  on baptism, 327
  on ordination, 376
  on penitents, 436
"Apostolic Tradition" of Hippolytus, 57, 179, 294, 335, 524, 526, 572, 575, 576
Aput actitae, 502, 513, 514, 518, 551
Aquileia, Council of, 31
  early see of, 30, 34, 37, 88
  liturgy of, 88, 94
  Metropolitan of, 41, 372, 374
Archiparaphonista, 349
Arianism among the Goths, 29
  at Milan, 36, 93, 94
  among the Suevi, 97
  influence of, in baptismal formularies, 324, 325
  and confirmation, 340
Arles—
  origin of ecclesiastical province of, 32
  Church of, 34, 91

Arles (*continued*)—
  vicariate of, 38
  the *Statuta* of, 350, 366
  bishops of, 39, 219, 385
    wear *pallium*, 386
  St Hilary of, 437
  See also Cæsarius of Arles
Armenia—
  Church in, 26, 27
  Liturgy of, 73, 74, 168
  Christmas not observed in, 259, 266
Ascension Day, 240, 491, 515
  blessing of beans on, 183
Ascetae, 78, 284, 419, 449. *See* Confessor
Ash Wednesday, 428, 438
Ashes, sign of penitence, 438, 444
  at dedication of a church, 410
Asia (Roman province of)—
  Churches of, 16
  bishops of, 19
  diocese of, 24, 26
  Paschal Rite in, 237
Athens, Synod of, 71
Augustine of Canterbury, St., 45
  consecrated by Bishop of Lyons, 91
  St Gregory's letter to, 99
  his successors mentioned in the *Memento*, 157, 210
  pallium given to, 385, 390
Augustine of Hippo, St, 174, 260, 271, 281, 285, 298, 302, 309, 377
Autun, Church of, 151
  Bishop of, 385
  St Leger, Bishop of, 152
Auxentius, 93
Ave Maria, 540

B

Bacca, 463
Bags, linen, for carrying the Hosts, 185, 352, 461
Bangor, Antiphonary of, 157
  hymn from, 226
Baptism, 292, 308, 331 *et seq*, 337, 567
  Tertullian describes, 334
  according to Roman Use, 294
  according to Gallican Use, 316, 320
  in the Eastern Church, 327
  preparation for, 298, 568
  divesting of garments at, 312, 324, 330
  immersion at, 313, 325, 330, 331, 332
  Chrism used at, 312
  white robe at, 314, 315, 326, 561
  lay, 337
  by heretics, 338
  at Jerusalem, 512, 518, 560, 567
  in the *Apostolic Tradition* of Hippolytus, 532

INDEX. 579

Bari, *Exultet* of. *See* Exultet
Barnabas, St., tomb of, 27
Basil, St., Liturgy of, 72, 73, 80
Basilidians, the, 259
Beans, 183
Bede, the Ven., 100, 291
Bee, eulogy of, 253
Benedict Biscop, 100
Benedicite, the, in the Gall. Mass, 195, 196
Benedictine Rule, 100, 452
Benediction—
  of fonts, 257, 311, 337
  at Communion in Gall. Mass, 102, 222
  of milk and honey, 183, 315
  of ashes, 438
  of beans and grapes, 183
  of oil for anointing sick, 183
  of the holy oils, 305, 336
  of the holy oils in Gallican Rite, 320
  of objects used in worship, 413
  of the Paschal candle, 252 *et seq.*
  of the new fire, 250, 256
  of water at baptism, 324
  of water in the Gallican Liturgy, 321
  at marriage, 429, 431
Benedictus, or "prophecy" in the Gallican Mass, 191, 193
Bethany, 491
  station at, 503, 504, 552
Bethlehem—
  Basilica of, 491
  station at, 497, 513, 546
  festival at, 515, 563
  Matins originated at, 448
Bishops, 8, 359, 372, 376
Bobbio Sacramentary or Missal, 145, 158, 159, 193, 194, 195, 213, 274, 275, 279, 316, 319, 320, 321, 324, 325, 326, 327, 430, 441, 572
Boniface, St., 100, 101
  letter to, from Pope Zacharias, 102, 250
Borgian Fragments, 81
Britain, 31, 32
  Church of, 42, 43, 44
  method of keeping Easter in, 239
  liturgical books in, 120, 156
  liturgy of, 88
  Easter fires in, 250

C

Cæsarea (in Cappadocia), 24, 71
Cæsarea (in Palestine), 18
Cæsarius, St., Bishop of Arles, 39
  his Homilies, 129, 197, 326
  receives *pallium*, 384

Calamarium, 462
Calendars, 289
  of Carthage, 133, 276, 283, 290
  Philocalian, 258, 260, 261, 277, 283, 290, 291
  of Polemius Silvius, 276, 278
  of Tours, 290
Cambuta (or Gallican crozier), 397
Camelaucum (head-covering), 396
Campagus (shoes of clergy), 395, 476
Cancellum (chancel), 458, 462, 492, 493
Candle. *See* Tapers
  Paschal, 251, 252
Canon, the, 110
  Roman, 176 *et seq.*
  resemblance of Roman Canon to Eastern and Greek, 183
  names in, 343
  consecratory, in ordination, 356
  co-operation of priests with celebrant in, 175
Cantatorium, 116
Capitulary (Synaxary), 112
Capitularies—
  of Capua, 273
  of Naples, 273, 275
Capsa, 205, 249
Cara Cognatio, 278
Caralis, Bishop of, 30
Cardinales presbiteri, 470
Carnival (Sunday of), 245
Carthage, 16, 17, 22, 30, 339
  Council of. *See* Councils
  orders of clergy at, 344
  Calendar of, 289
Casula, or chasuble, 381
Cata [= κατά], 492
Catecheses (Catechising), 298, 320, 519, 520, 521, 569. *See also* St. Cyril
Catechumenate, the, 292, 331
  rites of, 295
  in the Gallican Use, 152, 317
Catechumens, 58, 79, 171, 292, 317
  dismissal of, 83, 85, 171, 297
  dismissal of, in the Gallican Mass, 202
  dismissal of, obsolete, 83, 202
Celibacy, 451
Cemetery—
  chapels, 401
  stations at, 139
Cena pura, 442
Censer—
  (swung), 163, 412, 416
  (*thimiamasterium*), 457
Cerne, Book of, 104, 122
Chaldean Nestorians, 69
Chalice—
  benediction of, 413
  used at ordination, 352

580 INDEX.

Chants, the, 113
  books of, 116
  in the Roman Mass, 167
  for the *Communio*, 225
  in the Hours, 452
Charismata (supernatural gifts), 48, 333
Charlemagne, 105, 120, 121, 452
  his *admonitio generalis*, 103, 104
  his name in the *Ordines Romani*, 150
Charta Cornutiana, 572
Chasuble (*casula*), 381. See *Planeta* and *Paenula*, 394
China—
  Church in, 28
Chlamys (the military), 379
Chrism, use of, 306, 312, 314, 315, 323, 469
  in the Eastern Rite, 330, 533
  at dedication of church, 406, 413, 416
Chrismatio, or unction, 330, 333, 341. See also Chrism *and* Anointing
Christian communities, origin of, 7
Christian hierarchy. See Hierarchy
Christmas, 257 *et seq*., 265, 293, 497, 574
  Mass for, 189, 265
  festivals after, 265B, 546
Chrodegang, St., 102
Chrysogonus, St., 133
Chrysostom, St. John, 37, 56, 258, 436, 450
  Liturgy of, 72
  preaches in Lent, 246
  on Christmas, 258
  Homilies of, 56, 391, 450
Church, early government of, 8, 342
Churches, local, 11 *et seq*
  national, 23, 26, 71
  buildings, 399
Circumcision (*Octavus Domini*), Feast of, 273
Clausum Pascha, 134
Clement of Alexandria, 259, 447
Clement, St., of Rome, 50, 51, 52
Colatorium, 460
Collecta, 167
Collectio post precem, 201
Colligere plebem, 167
Colobus (? *colobum colobium*), 379, 382
Columba, St., 43
Columbanus, St., 100
Comes Orientis, 21
Commixtio, the, 85, 184, 187, 221, 462
Communion—
  in the Roman Mass, 186
  in the Gallican Mass, 224
  Hymn from Bangor Antiphonary, 226
  fasting, single exception to, 248
  at home, 249
  first, 292, 315, 327
  in Eastern Rite, 330

Communion (*continued*)—
  antiphon for, 116, 187
  post, 188
  in Gallican Mass, 227
Competents, or candidates for baptism, 59, 83, 293, 298, 328, 331
  in the Eastern Church, 328, 518
Compline, 449
Confession (of sin), 435, 437
Confessor.
  (an ascetic), 142, 173, 284, 420
Confirmare, 462, 484
Confirmation (*Consignatio*), 292, 314, 320, 337
  various names for, 340
  prayer at, 314
  in Gallican Rite, 320, 326
  by heretics, 340
  by priests, 338
Confractorium, 220
Consignatio, or signing, 314, 315, 333, 337, 340. See also Cross, sign of, *and* Confirmation
Consignatorium, 314, 470
Constantiniana (Church), 469
Constantine, the Emperor, 274, 491, 496, 498, 546, 547
Constantinople, position of its bishops, 24, 25
  Patriarchate of, 26, 28
  influence of, 42
  Liturgy of, 71, 86
Contestatio (Preface in the Gallican Rite), 110, 158, 213
Contestatio (in Baptismal Rite), 322
Continentes, 417, 451
Corinth—
  Church of, 49
  Bishop of, 385
Cornelius and Cyprian, SS., 136
Cornu de quo reges unguebantur, 510
Corona, 461
Coronation, nuptial, 432
Corporal, 205, 460
Councils—
  Agde, 96, 245, 319, 437, 438, 445, 506
  Ancyra, 20
  Antioch (341), 20, 436
  Aquileia, 31, 33, 34
  Ariminum. See Rimini
  Arles, 339
  Braga (561), 98, 391
  ,,   (675), 392
  ,,   (3rd), 394
  Carthage (397), 35, 119, 248, 337
  ,,   (401), 35
  ,,   (407), 119
  ,,   4th of, 132
  Celichyth (Chelsea), 403
  Chalcedon, 24, 25, 65, 79, 80, 83

INDEX. 581

Councils (*continued*)—
 Chalon-sur-Saône (650), 91
 Clichy (627), 91
 Constantinople (381), 24, 340
  ,,   (553), 41
  ,,   (680), 65
 Elvira, 23, 231, 232, 240, 285, 326
 Epaone, 202, 338, 445
 Ephesus (431), 26, 27, 265, 280
 Gerona (517), 96, 286, 289
 Hippo (393), 22, 35, 297
 Iconium, 19
 Laodicea, 71, 230, 246, 320
 Lyons (517), 198, 203, 445
 Mâcon (581), 286, 294
 Milan (451), 31, 36
 Nicæa, 22, 23, 29, 237, 242, 339, 391
 Orange, 338
 Orleans, 1st (517), 289, 407
  ,, 4th (541), 245
 Paris (614), 91
 Pseudo-Silvestrian, 350
 Rimini [Ariminum] (359), 36, 93
 Rome, 30, 40, 150, 386
 Saragossa (380), 260
  ,,   (800), 423
 Syria, in, 18
 Tarragona, in the province of, 294
 Toledo, 1st (400), 33, 337
  ,, 3rd (589), 221, 269
  ,, 4th (633), 156, 222, 372, 392, 397, 398, 442
  ,, 10th (656), 269
 Tours (567), 219, 274, 276
 Trent, 428, 430
 Trullo, in, 67, 272, 340
 Turin, 34
 Tyre, 274
 Vaison, 1st (442), 337
  ,, 2nd (529), 165, 192, 197, 208
 Valencia, 445
 Vannes (*cir.* 465), 96
Crèche (*Praesepe*), 26a
Creed—
 In the Mass, 84, 172
 Recitation of, at baptism, 170, 301, 305, 319, 324, 328, 332, 526. See *Redditio symboli* and *Traditio symboli*
Cross—
 sign of, 60, 306, 533
 on catechumens, 296, 299, 300, 318
 on font, 312
 in baptism, 325, 331
 in confirmation, 314
 at dedication of church, 410, 416, 417
 made with particles of Host, 219
 on altar, 406
 in procession, 474, 480
 relics of, 482, 510

Cross (*continued*)—
 Adoration of, 234, 248, 468, 482, 510, 558
 sanctuary of, at Jerusalem, 491, 557
 festivals of the, 274, 570
 Invention of the, 133, 151, 274, 522
 Exaltation of the, 130
Crown, marriage, 433
Crozier, 397
Cubiculum (pontifical), 482
Cyprian, St., 178, 284
Cyprus, Bishops of, 26
Cyril, St., of Jerusalem—
 Catecheses of, 55, 56, 298, 327, 328
 description of anointing at baptism by, 330

D

Dacius, 92
Dalmatia, 41
Dalmatic, the, 382, 457, 476
 sent to Gap, 382
David, 266, 269
De cognitione Baptismi, 316
De Officiis, 316
De Sacramentis, 316
Deacon, John the, 296, 381
Deaconesses, or widows, 330, 342 *et seq*., 376
Deacons, 8, 170 173, 457
 institution of the Seven, 10, 161, 169, 196
 ordination of, 353
  (Gallican), 368
  (Eastern), 376
 order of, 342
 Greek, 381, 391
 of Arles, 382
 dress of, 382, 383, 395
Deaconries, 150, 161, 479
Dedication—
 of churches, 273, 276, 280, 283, 399, 478, 485, 486, 487, 522, 570
  Roman Rite, 403
  Gallican Rite, 407
 of that of Tyre, 400
 of virgins, 419, 427
Deer, book of, 157
Defensor (*civitatis*), 12
 (*regionarius*), 459
Departed, *Memento* of, 182, 577B. See *Memento*
Deposito, 284, 401, 416 See Relics
Deusdedit, Archdeacon, epitaph of, 170
dhomus (*tomus*), 462
Didache (Doctrine of the Apostles), 52, 53. 57
Didascalia of the Apostles, 56, 57

582   INDEX.

Dies unctionis, 320
Dimma, book of, 157
Dioceses, Episcopal, 11
   civil, 24
Diocletian's rulers of civil dioceses, or vicars, 24, 36
Dionysius Exiguus, 238
Diptychs, recitation of. 84. 85, 180, 181, 208
   consular, 386
Doctor (ecclesiastical), 13
   audientium, 436
Doctrine of the Apostles. *See Didache*
Dominical, 224
Dominicum, the, 400
Domumcellae, 509
Domus ecclesiae, 400
Donation of Constantine, 385
Donatists, 260, 339
Doorkeepers (or vergers, *ostiarii*), 344, 346, 364. *See also Mansionarius*
Dormitio, Festival of, 272
Dowry, delivery of, 429
Doxology, 116
   form in Spanish use, 190

E

Easter—
   baptisms at, 308
   computation of, 236-239
   Tables for finding, 238, 262
   Octave of, 513, 514
   method of keeping, 239, 287
   Roman *Ordo* for the 3 days before, 481
   at Jerusalem, 503, 513, 515
   candle, 251, 252
Easter Eve, ceremonies on, 250, 303, 308, 320, 468, 483, 512, 550
   Ordo for days after, 472
Ebdomadarii, 502
Ecphonesis, ecphony, 118, 176
Edessa, 19, 69
Effeta, the (*Ephphatha*), 303, 317, 318, 332
Ego conjungo vos, 430
Egyptian Liturgical Papyrus, 572
eicitur, 493
Einsiedeln, MS. of, 481
Elect, the (candidates for baptism), 293, 299, 300, 308, 312 *See also Competents*
Eleona (Mount of Olives), 491, 498, 505, 513, 523
Ember Days, 232, 285, 286
   ordinations at, 353
Encenia, 522
energumens, 59, 83

England—
   conversion of, 44, 98
   Roman Liturgy brought into, 98
Ennodius, 253, 280
Eortae (Quadragesimae), 500
Ephesus, 282 (Bishop of), 24
   liturgy of, 90
   Council of, 26
Ephphatha. See *Effeta*
Epiclesis—
   meaning of, 61, 110
   in Alexandrine Liturgy, 77, 82
   the Roman, 177, 181
   in the Gallican Mass, 217
Epiphany, the, 108. 257, 260, 286, 287, 293, 294, 491, 497, 546
Episcopium, 150
Epistle, the (in the Mass), 167, 195
Epitaphs—
   of cantors, 170
   of a deaconess, 342
   of a confessor, 420
   of an archdeacon, 170
Etheria, pilgrimage of (*Peregrinatio Etheriae*), 115, 229, 230, 243, 247, 248, 259, 272, 274, 327 *et seq*, 449
   extract from, 490 *et seq.*, 541 *et seq.*
Ethiopia, Church in, 28, 80
Ethnarch, 9
Eucharist—
   Justin Martyr's description of, 49 *et seq.*
   early description of, 57
   days for celebration of, 230 *et seq.*
   on Maundy Thursday, 247
   catechumens excluded from, 297. *See also Mass*
Eucheria, 541
Euchologion, or Prayer Book—
   Byzantine, 72, 110
   of Sarapion, 75, 78, 79, 330, 376, 377
Eudoxus, 71
Eunomians, 325
Euphemia, St., 133, 136
Evangelary, 112
Exorcism—
   of catechumens, 296, 299, 303, 317
   of competents, 328, 518
   at baptism (Gallican), 322
   of water at dedication, 405
   of salt, 296
Exorcists, 299, 344, 346, 349, 366
Exultet, 254
Exultet of Bari, 259, 537

F

Fasting—
   days of, 228, 231, 232, 241, 285
   calendar of, 290

INDEX. 583

Fasting (*continued*)—
  in Apostolic Constitutions, 243
  at Jerusalem, 499, 501, 502, 518
  before Baptism, 334
  Irenæus on, 240
  Communion, single exception to, 248
  See also Superpositio jejunii
Feasts or festivals—
  Jewish, 235
  movable, 235
  immovable, 257
  after Christmas, 265
  of the Apostles, 277, 281
  of Martyrs, 283, 501
  octaves of, 285, 287
Feet-washing at baptism, 326, 332
Felicissimus and Agapitus, SS., 133, 136
Felix and Adauctus, SS., 133
Fermentum (portion of Host reserved from previous Mass), 163, 184
Firmata oblata, 477
First fruits, 183
Flabellum, or fan, use of, 60
Flagellation, column of, 510, 588
Flammeum, 433
Flectamus genua, 109, 474, 483
Fons (vessel used at Mass), 460, 462
Fonts, blessing of, 257, 311, 337
  miraculously filled, 320
Fraction of the bread, 63
  in the Eastern Liturgy, 85
  in Roman Canon, 184
  by the *Presbyterium*, 185
  in the Gallican Mass, 218
Frankish Church, 32, 44
  sovereigns, relations with their bishops, 40, 103, 372
Frankish Liturgy, 104
  bishops receive *pallium*, 386
Friday, 228, 549
Funeral services, 401
Fuscae planetae, 468, 473

G

Gallican Liturgy, 83, 94, 114, 189–227
Gallican Service-books, 151–160
Gallican Use, 245
  the origin of, 86, 90 *et seq.*
  oriental features in, 92
  views with regard to the, 95
  fusion with Roman Use, 96
  abolished by Pepin, 102
  books of, 151, 158, 189
  peculiarity of, preserved by Dominicans, 204
  pallium in, 389
Gallicinium, 448

Gaul, Church of—
  metropolitan system introduced into, 31, 32
  disputes in Church of, 34
  bishops of, appeal to Milan, 34, 35, 37
  union with Breton Church, 43
  influenced by Milan, 94
Gelasian Sacramentary. *See* Sacramentary
Genevieve, St., 155
Georgia, Church of, 29, 72
Germain of Auxerre, St. (Mass of), 152, 153
Germain of Paris, St.—
  letters of, 155
  his description of Gallican Mass, 189, 319, 381, 384, 392
Gervasius and Nazarius, SS., 92
Gery, St., 192
Gethsemane, 508, 546
Gildas, 870, 378
Gimellares, 484
Gloria in excelsis, the, 166, 192, 265, 439, 481
  in the Easter Mass, 257
  at ordination of Pope, 363
Gloria Patri, 116, 190
Good Friday, 172, 234, 241, 248, 442, 467, 481, 482, 509, 557
  date of, 263
Gospel, 544 (in Mass), 58, 167, 196
Gospels—
  imposition of the, 362, 375, 376, 378
  Traditio of the, 301
Goths—
  origin of Church among the, 29
  wars of, 137
Gothic—
  Calendar, 289
  bishop at the Council of Nicæa, 29
Gradual (origin of), 114
  in the Roman Mass, 167, 169
Gradus, 114, 169
Grapes, 183
Grecum vinum, 473
Greek language (use of), 302, 316, 355
Gregorian Sacramentary. *See* Sacramentary of Adrian, 573
  water, 406
Gregorianum, 573
Gregory, St. (the Illuminator), 28
Gregory (the Great). *See under* Popes
  Sacramentary of, 120, 273, 573
  his name in the Canon, 130, 139
  alters the place of the *Pater Noster*, 150, 184
  adds *Hanc igitur* to the Canon, 176
  Mass of the Presanctified attributed to him, 72
Gregory, St., Nazianzen, Liturgy of, 80

584 INDEX.

Gregory, St., of Nyssa, 265
Gregory, St., of Tours, 134, 196, 288, 290, 321, 322, 415

H

Hadrian (Pope), Sacramentary of. *See* Adrian (*under* Popes) *and* Sacramentary
Hail Mary, 540
Hair shirt for penitents, 437, 438
Hanc igitur, 139, 176, 180
   in Stowe Missal, 156
Hands, consecration of. *See* Anointing
Helisachar, 104
Heretics—
   reconciliation of, 338
   baptism by, 338 *et seq.*
Hierarchy (Christian), 8, 19, 343, 344. *See also* Ordination
Hieronymian Martyrology, 101, 265, 267, 273, 274, 275, 276, 290, 291
Hilary. *See* Popes
Hilary of Africa, 174
Hilary of Arles, 437
Hippo—
   Council of, 35, 393
   Augustine, Bishop of. *See* Augustine
Hippolytus, Bishop, 258, 262, 334
Hippolytus and Pontianus, SS., 136
Holy Cross. *See* Cross
Holy Ghost, manifestation of, in Primitive Church, 48
Holy Innocents, festival of, 268
Holy Saturday. *See* Easter Eve
Holy water, 312, 404, 406, 407 (for lustration, 410)
Holy Week, 234, 241, 247, 465, 481
   at Jerusalem, 243, 247, 329, 503, 506, 552
   Wednesday in, 172, 234, 555
Homily. *See* Sermon
Honey, 315, 330, 333, 335, 336
Host, the—
   bags for, 185, 352
   arrangement of the particles of, 219
   in the Irish Church, 220
Hours, the Canonical, 446, 450
   influence of Benedictine Rule on, 452
   at Jerusalem, 492
Hymnus, use of word, 174
   at the Procession of the Oblation, 84
   at the *Communio*, 225
   at dedication of church, 413
   of Prudentius, 447
   absence of, 452
   at Jerusalem, 492

I

Illatio (the Preface), 110, 213
Imbomon, 491, 505, 508, 513, 516, 556

Immersion (baptismal). *See* Baptism
Immolatio, 110, 213
Imposition (of hands)—
   at exorcism and in baptism, 296, 299, 300, 303, 314, 331, 333, 337
   at confirmation, 326, 335, 340
   in penitence, 437
   at ordination, 356, 369, 371, 375, 377
   of ashes, 438
   of the Gospels (*which see*)
Incense, use of, 163, 255, 478, 482
   at Jerusalem, 495, 544
   at dedication of church, 408, 411, 412, 416
   cross of grains of, 412
Indulgence, ceremony of, 442 *et seq*
Infantes, 268, 512
Ingressa, 190. *See also* Introit
Innocentes, 268
Insufflation, or breathing on, 296, 306, 307, 312, 317, 319, 328, 331
Introit, 116, 117, 163, 190
   various names for, 190
   omitted, 439
Invention of the Cross. *See* Cross
Invitatory, 360
Invocation. *See* Epiclesis
Ireland—
   missionaries from, 98
   Church of, 43, 45
   baptism in, 294, 326, 332
   liturgy of, 88, 98
   use of diptychs in, 209
   Host in the Liturgy, 220
   method of keeping Easter, 239
   liturgical books of the, 156
   Easter Eve fires in, 250
Italy, Lombardic conquest in, 41
   Southern, sees of, 30
   early Christian communities in, 15
   Northern, few sees in, 31
Ite Missa est, 64, 188, 471
   variants of, 227

J

Jacobites, 65, 66
James, St., Feast of, 265, 266
Jerusalem, 5, 7, 14
   Patriarchate of, 27
   Juvenal, Bishop of, 27
   baptismal rites at, 329
   Churches at, 491
   offices at, 274, 490 *et seq.*, 541 *et seq.*
   Latin catechumens at, 521
Jesuyab III., 70
Jewish communities, 1 *et seq.*
   Influence, 235, 236
   Liturgy, 46

INDEX.   585

Jewish communities *(continued)*—
Sabbath, 47
Temple-worship, 46
John, Abbot of Ravenna, 120
John Baptist, St., 133, 271
oratory of, at the Lateran, 310
John, St., Evangelist, 151, 265, 266, 281, 282
Joseph, St , 267
Judices, 463
Julian the Apostate keeps Epiphany, 260
Justiniana Prima, Bishop of, receives pall, 385
Justin Martyr—
description of Eucharist by, 49, 50, 53, 284

K

Kiss of Peace, 59, 60, 84, 163, 184, 207, 211, 464 (and Collect accompanying), 212, 224, 376 (at ordination, 357)
in the East, 376
Kissing the altar, 163, 464, 468
Kissing the Cross, 510
Kissing the Gospel, 458
Kyrie Eleison, 58, 106, 164, 165, 192, 227, 359, 439, 472, 481, 493
relic of the Post-Gospel Litany, 198

L

Landulf, 105
Lateran (called Episcopium, and later *Patriarchium*), 150
Basilica, 362, 458
description of Baptistery of, 309
Easter baptisms at, 311, 315
Monastery at, 452
in the Roman *Ordo,* 481–484
Laudes, chant at procession, 205, 206
in the Mass, 208
Lauds, Office of, 448, 449
Laurence, St., 136, 284
Law, Christian emblem of, 302
Lazarium (House of Lazarus), 491, 498, 503, 513
Lebhar Breac, 204
Lectionary, the, 112, 572
of Luxeuil, 134, 154, 195, 269, 274, 275, 279, 442
Lectio prophetica, 193
Lections, the, 57, 112
in the Roman Mass, 167
in the Gallican Mass, 194, 195
at baptism, 308
in the Hours, 452
injunction to silence before, 170

Lections *(continued)* —
of first page of St. Matthew, 301
Lectors, or readers, 343, 346, 364, 376
Leger, St., 151, 152
Lent, or *Quadragesima*—
observance of, 241, 548
at Milan, 245
preparation for baptism during, 332
services in, 168, 193
at Jerusalem, 499, 518
Leon, Antiphonary of, 160A
Leonian Sacramentary. *See* Sacramentary
Leontius, Bishop, 114, 115
Liber Comicus, 160A, 320, 572
Liber diurnus, 363, 404
Liber ordinum, 160A, 217, 316, 319, 320, 327, 363, 369, 407, 442
Liber Pontificalis, 128, 163, 180, 281, 391
Liber Sacramentorum, 110, 111, 126, 175, 176
Litany, 59, 106
at the Mass, 164, 198, 200
during baptism, 315
of the Saints, 164
at Milan, 198
in the Sacramentary of Biasca, 198
in the *Ordines,* 474, 478
at Rome, 298
for the crops, 287
on Rogation Days, 289
at ordination, 357
at dedication of church, 405, 409
at the ceremony of Indulgence, 442
said by the higher clergy only, 450
Diaconal, 60, 62, 87, 111, 165
Liturgy—
four principal types of, 55
of Abyssinia, 81
of SS. Adaeus and Maris, 70
Alexandrine, the, 75–82
Ambrosian, 88, 193, 198, 215, 217
of Apostolic Constitutions, 64
of Aquileia, 88
Armenian, 73, 74, 168
of St. Basil, 72, 73, 80, 82
Byzantine, 71, 72, 82, 168. *See* Constantinople, *infra*
of St Chrysostom, 72, 201
of Constantinople, 60, 72, 201. *See* Byzantine, *supra*
Coptic, of St. Basil, 80
Coptic, of St. Cyril, 80–82
Coptic, of St. Gregory (Nazianzen), 80
Frankish, the, 104
Gallican, 55, 154 (*which see*)
Greek, of St. James, 59, 67
of St. Mark, 80, 81
Mozarabic, 88, 105, 119, 193, 217, 256
Roman, 87. *See* Mass
Suevic, the, 97, 98

586 INDEX.

Liturgy (continued)—
  Syriac, of St. James, 59, 68
  Syrian, 55, 65, 82
  of Toledo, 103
  of the Twelve Apostles, 81
Liturgies—
  Oriental, 64
  Syriac, 68, 69
  Nestorian, 70
  Coptic, 80
  Fragments of (Borgian), 81
  Syro-Byzantine, 85
Liturgical Prayer of St. Clement, 50
Love Feast, 49
Lucernarium, or *Lucernaria*, 448, 450
  at Jerusalem, 493
Lyons, Church of, 90, 101, 222, 348
  Primacy of, founded by Gregory VII., 91
  Council of, 203
  Formularies of Benediction in Church of, 101

M

Maccabees, Festival of, the, 276
Mafortium, 467
Magnificat, at Baptism, 316
Malabar, Church in, 28
Malda, 488
Manicheans, 176
Mansionarius, 347, 463, 471, 474, 477, 479. *See also* Doorkeepers
Maphrian, 69
Mappula, the, 383, 384
  (saddle-cloth, or *mappulum*), 396
Maria Maggiore, Santa, 316
  night Mass at, 265. *See also* 497
  stational Mass at, 353
Maronites, 66
Marriage, Christian, 428
  crowns, 429, 432
  pagan, 433
Martyrium, Basilica of, 450, 491, 496 *et seq.*
Martyrology, 289, 291
  the Hieronymian, 282, 290
Martyrs—
  festivals of, 283, 501
  relics of. *See* Relics
Mary (the Blessed Virgin). *See Virgin*
Mass—
  original aspect of, 49
  in the East, 46 *et seq.*
  the Roman, 161
  the Gallican, 189
  at Jerusalem, 450, 492, 495, 497, 546
  of the Prothesis, 83
  of the Presanctified, 68, 72, 234, 248, 249, 443

Mass (continued)—
  the Byzantine, 72
  the stational, 161, 244
    Ordo of, 150
  the Chrismal, 305
  at marriages, 429
  midnight, 265, 497
  three on Christmas Day, 265A
  of St. Leger, 152
  at reconciliation of penitents, 439
  dedicatory, 414. *See also* Eucharist
Masses in honour of Martyrs, 136
Masses published by Mone, 153
Matins, 447, 448, 492
Maundy Thursday, 218, 234, 247, 248, 251, 252, 439, 465, 481
  evening Masses on, 247, 507, 555
  Canon for, 218
  the Chrismal Mass on, 305
  the end of penance, 437, 439
Mauritania, 18
  Sitifensis, 22
Mediana, 243
Melchisedec (in the Mass), 176, 177
Melchites (Greek)—
  their liturgy, 65–67, 72, 80
Memento (or Great Supplication), 179
  for the Departed, 574, in the Stowe Missal, 156, 209
  godparents mentioned in, 180, 300
  in the Roman Mass, 182, 574
  position of, in Nestorian liturgies, 70
Messina, Bishop of, receives pall, 385
Metz—
  (Church of), 102
  Sacramentary of Drogo, Bishop of, 487
Michael, St., 136, 276
Milan—
  early date of, 30, 31
  Council of (451), 31
  peculiar position of, 32, 36, 93
  Councils at, 36
  appeals to, 34–36
  Auxentius, Bishop of, 93
  Use of, 88, 94, 95, 104, 285, 318, 326
  consecration of Metropolitans, 372
  pall sent to Bishop of, 385
Milanese. *See* Ambrosian
Miles, 530
Milk and honey—
  administered after first Communion, 315, 330, 333, 335, 336
  blessing of, 183
Miserere, the—
  at dedication of church, 410
Missa, 492. *See* Mass
Missa, i.e. dismissal, 491, 542
  of the catechumens, 83, 171, 202, 297
  of the penitents, 171, 203, 445

INDEX. 587

Missal—
  origin of the word, 112
  the Bobbio (*which see*)
  earliest Gregorian, 572
  the Stowe, 156, 225
    Litany in, 199
    recitation of diptychs in, 209
    Host divided in, 220
    oblation in, 204
    benediction in, 223
    Missa acta est in, 227
Missale Francorum, 134
  ordination rites in, 351, 363, 367, 374, 408
  Velatio Virginum in, 424
Missale Gallicanum Vetus, 152, 426
Missale Gothicum, 134, 151, 277, 316, 321, 322
  description of Mass in, 189
  Epiphany office from, 108
Missale of Reichenau, 153
Mithras, 261
Mitre, 368, 396
Mixed Chalice—
  in Byzantine Liturgy, 85
  in Roman Mass, 174
  in the Gallican Mass, 205
  not used in Armenia, 74
Monazontes, 449, 492, 497, 522
Monks, 417
Monophysites, the, 65, 69, 80, 84, 340
Monothelites, 65
Montanists, 241
Mozarabic, Liturgy, 88, 105, 119, 160A, 190, 191, 192, 193, 194, 195, 196, 204, 205, 206, 207, 208, 212, 213, 214, 216, 217, 219, 220, 221, 222, 223, 224, 225, 227, 246, 541
  Missal, 119, 133, 251
  ceremony of Indulgence in, 442
Mulierum (*pars*), 462
Mulling, book of, 157
Musivum, 498
Mysterium (*oratio post*), 217

N

Natale, 284
Natalis invicta, 261
Neophytes, 315, 326, 327
  white garments of, 314, 315
Nestorians, 28, 69
  Liturgy of, 70
Nicæa, Council of, 22, 23, 27, 29, 339
Nicene Creed, 221
Nicopolis, Bishop of, receives pall, 385
Nobis quoque, 182
Nomenclator, 148
Nomes, 13

None (office of), 447, 449, 450, 492
Notarii, 15
Novatians, 339
Nubia, Church of, 28
Numidia, 18, 22

O

Oblatae (loaves, or hosts), 175, 184, 185, 367
  arrangement of, 219
Oblation, the—
  in the Roman Mass, 173
  in the Gallican Mass, 204
  procession of, 84, 204
Oblationarius, 457, 460, 471, 482
Octavas Domini. See Circumcision
Offerenda, 206
Offertorium (chant at the Oblation), 173, 174, 187, 206
Offertory, 174
Officium (Mozarabic, for Christmas), 190
Oils, 304, 319, 331, 336
Opening of the Ears, 301. See *Traditio symboli*
Operatio, 492, 494
Orarium, the (or stole), 390, 394, 477
Orate Fratres, 109, 176
Orders, minor, 343, 364
Ordination, 342
  at Rome, 352 (minor Orders)
    of deacons, 353
    of priests, 353
    of bishops, 359
    of Pope, 362
  later ceremonies of, 350
  in the Gallican rite, 363
    of deacons, 368
    of priests, 370
    of bishops, 372
  in the East, 376
Ordines Romani, the, 146, 161, 351
  from the Abbey of St. Amand, 149, 351, 455
  on the seven regions, 345
  on vestments, 383, 390
  on dedications, 405
  on penitents, 438
Ordo, 111
  of the Stational Mass, 150
  Baptismi, 294
Oremus, 109, 172
Orient, Episcopate of, 21, 24, 26
Oriental Liturgies, 64
Ostia, Bishop of, 262, 384, 389
Ostiarii. See Doorkeepers

2 Q

INDEX.

P

Pactisi (wine), 473
Paenula, or *Planeta*, 379, 382
Palestine, provinces of, 27
Palla, 205, 461
Pallium, the Papal, 380, 384, 389, 391, 392, 395
  use of, at Mass, 388
  earliest English picture of, 390
  classical, the, 386
  Linostimum, 383
  of the Bishops of Gaul and Spain, 388
  the nuptial, 432
Palm Sunday (*Dies Palmarum*), 247, 504,
Pamelius of Bruges, 177   [553
Pannonian provinces, sees in, 31
Papa, 199. *See* Pope
Paranymfa (priest), 477
Paraphonistae, 472
Parthenae, 449, 492
Parvi (= *pauci*), 522
Paschal controversy, 236
Pastilli, 463
Pater Noster, the, in the Liturgy, 62, 150
  in the Eastern Liturgy, 85
  in the Roman Mass, 184
  in the Gallican Mass, 221
  in the Ambrosian Rite, 222
  in Mass of the Presanctified, 249
  traditio of, 302
  in East, 330
Patriarchates, 23, 26-28, 66, 67, 69, 71, 72, 74, 80
Patriarchium, 150. *See* Lateran
Patrick, St., 43
Paul, Apostle, Feast of, 265, 266, 277, 279, 281
Paul of Samosata, 339
Pauperes, 474
Pedilavium. *See* Feet-washing
Penitents, reconciliation of, 435
  dismissal of, 59, 83, 171, 202
Pentecost, 236, 240, 515
Pepin, 102, 103, 104
Per quem haec, 182
Peregrinatio (of Etheria, which see)
Persia, Church in, 28, 69
Peter, St.—
  festivals of, 265, 266, 277
  Natale Petri de Cathedra, 277, 279
  staff of, 398
  chains of, 280
  Confessio of, 385, 391
  pignora of, 402
Peter and Paul, SS., 277
Peter the Fuller, 26
  introduces the Creed in the Mass at Antioch, 84
Petersburg (synod of), 71

Philip of Heraclea, Passion of, 260
Philip and James, SS., 282
Philocalian. *See* Calendar
Phrygia, 11, 262
Phrygian cap, 396
Pignora of saints, 402, 413
Pisinni, 493
Planeta, the, or *paenula*, 379, 380, 381, 382, 406, 457, 480. *See Fuscae planetae*
Podium, 305, 466
Polemius Silvius. *See* Calendar
Pope—
  meaning of term, 199
  position of, 30, 38
  relations of, with Milan, 32 *et seq.*
  officiates at Easter baptisms, 311
  dress of, 382, 383, 393, 396
  Patriarch of West, 41
  ordination of, 362
  bishops ordained by, 359
  reconciles penitents, 439
  See also Rome
Popes—
  Adrian (Sacramentary of), 120 *et seq.*, 281
  Alexander II., 105. 539
  Benedict VIII., 172
  Boniface I., 362
  Boniface II., 362
  Boniface IV., 124
  Callixtus, 444
  Celestine, 115, 171, 197, 265, 390
  Clement I, 50, 180
  Cletus, 180
  Conon, 397
  Constantine, 395
  Cornelius, 29, 344, 346
  Damasus, 33, 95, 170, 362
  Fabian, 344
  Felix IV., 389
  Gelasius, 128, 347, 390. *See* Sacramentary of
  Gregory I., The Great, 72, 99, 104, 109, 120-125, 150, 160, 170, 171, 176, 197, 272, 288, 381, 382, 385, 390, 395, 404
  Gregory II., 124, 130, 246
  Gregory IV., 147
  Gregory VII., 91, 105, 539
  Hadrian. *See* Adrian
  Hilary, 140, 180, 310, 314
  Honorius, 573
  Innocent I., 37, 87, 101, 181, 212
  Innocent III., 398
  John III., 282
  Julius, 282
  Leo. I., 27, 124, 171, 176
  ,,   Homilies of, 233
  ,,   Festival of, 124
  Leo II., 124

INDEX. 589

Popes (*continued*)—
Leo III., 289
Liberius, 347, 348, 422
Linus, 180
Martin, 395
Miltiades, 290
Nicholas, 393, 428, 433
Paul, 102
Pelagius I., 219, 282, 390
Sergius, 144, 150, 186
Silvester, 382, 396
Simplicius, 137
Siricius, 347, 432
Stephen I., 133, 136, 141, 267, 339
Symmachus, 166, 382, 384, 388
Telesphorus, 166, 240, 284
Vigilius, 97, 385, 403, 407
Vitalian, 99
Xystus (Sixtus) I., 240, 284
Xystus III., 140, 171, 265, 280, 290, 309
Zacharias, 101, 250, 251, 382
Zosimus, 38, 39, 132, 140, 252, 347, 351
Porto, Bishop of, 362
Praeconium paschale, 111, 253
Praesepe. See Creche
Prayer, 46
  example of, given by St. Clement, 50
  three forms of, in early Church, 106–110
  invitatory, 107–109
  collective, 106
  of Consecration in Roman Mass, 175
  of Bishop Sarapion, 75
  eucharistic, 60, 109, 176
    in the Gallican Mass, 213
  at ordination, 356, 358, 361
  of "the Faithful," 172, 173
    in the Gallican Mass, 198
  of the *Praeconium*, or Bidding Prayer, 178
  Communicantes, 180
  for troublous times, 137
  for catechumens, 296 *et seq.*
  at baptism, 311, 321
  for Good Friday, 108
  at consecration of a church, 411
  at reconciliation of penitents, 439
  for the sovereign, 131, 256
  for the State, 135, 139
  post precem, 201
  at the canonical hours, 446
  Super Oblata, 85, 175. *See Secreta*
  Te igitur, 179
Presanctified, Liturgy of the, 72
Presentation, Feast of (*i.e.* Purification of Blessed Virgin Mary), 271, 479, 499
Pridie (oratio post), 217
Priest penitentiary, 436
Priests, 8, 353, 370

Primates, 22
Primati, 462, 473
Prime (hour of), 448
Primicerius, 348, 349, 462
Primiciarius, 148
Primus scholae, 456
Priscillianism, 83
Procedere, 491
Procession—
  before Mass, 83, 162
    Gallican Rite, 190
  on Palm Sunday, 247, 505
  of the oblation, 84
  in the Gallican Mass, 203
  to and from baptistery, 316
  at Constantinople, 416
  at dedication of church, 405, 410
  at night, 517
Procumma (wine), 473
Profuturus, 97, 98
"Prophecy," or *Benedictus*, 191
Prophetiam (oratio post), 193
Prothesis, 83
Protopaschites (Audiens), 238
Provinces, ecclesiastical, 13, 27
Prudentius, 447
Psallere (to go up), 458
Psalmulus, 196
Psalmus gradualis, 114
Psalmus responsorius, 58, 113, 114, 167, 234
Pseudo-Ambrose, *De Sacramentis*, 117
Purification. *See* Presentation

Q

Quadragesima. See Lent
Quarantain, 244
Quartodecimans, 237, 262
Quartus de Schola, 456, 462
Quinquagesima, 244, 246
Quintana parte, 517
Qui pridie, 178, 181, 215

R

Ravenna, early date of see (Classis), 30, 31, 37
  imperial residence, 36, 404
  Roll of, 144
  blessing of Paschal candle at, 252
  mosaics at, 383, 393, 395
  bishops of, wear *pallium*, 384, 385, 389, 393, 394
  clergy of, 397
Readers. *See* Lectors
Reconciliation of heretics, 338
  of penitents, 435

Redditio symboli, or recitation of the Creed, 305, 332, 569
  in the Eastern Church, 329, 332, 520
  in the Gallican Rite, 320
Redemptus, 170
Regionarius (sub-deacon), 456, 467
Regions, seven, of Rome, 345
Reichenau, 153
Relics, 478
  depositio, 401
  translation of, 402, 405, 409, 413
  Gallican, at Tours, 415
Renunciation of Satan (*see Abrenuntio*), 304, 324, 329
Reproaches, the, 442
Reservation, 185, 248, 403
Responds, or *Psalmi responsorii*, 58, 113
  in the Roman Mass, 167
  in the Gallican Mass, 195
Responduntur, 492
Rheinau MS., 125
Ring—
  Episcopal, 397
  in marriage, 429
Robigalia, 288
Rogation Days, 151, 288, 289
Roman—
  Canon, antiquity of, 177
  clergy, enumeration of, 344
  Use, 54
    origin of, 86 *et seq.*
    influence of, in Gaul, 100
  Liturgical books, 120–150
    See also Ordines Romani
Rome—
  its ecclesiastical position, 5, 15, 44
  its relation to the suburbicarian dioceses, 15, 30, 252, 390
  exceptional position of its bishop, 23
  relations with Milan, 33
  Easter baptisms at, 311
  seven regions of, 345
  suffragan bishops of, 389
  monasteries at, 452
Rotularius, 111
Rugae, 482, 484
Rugitus et mugitus, 495, 507, 509

S

Sabinus, 170
Sacellarius, 148
Sacramentary, 111, 119
  Gallican, 158
  of Angoulême, 121, 408, 485
  of Bergamo, 160
  of Biasca, 160, 198
  of Bobbio. *See* Bobbio
  of Drogo, 487

Sacramentary (*continued*)—
  Gelasian, 101, 182, 272, 275, 276, 319, 322, 323
    description of, 125–134
    Baptismal rites in, 295, 298
    ordination rites in, 351, 354, 355, 363, 366, 374
    dedication of church in, 403, 405, 408, 414
    Stational Masses in, 244
    Velatio Virginum in, 424
    marriage in, 432, 433
    reconciliation of penitents in, 437, 439
    blessing of Paschal candle in, 253
  of Gellona, 121, 280
  of Adrian, called the Gregorian. 109, 120–125, 179, 180, 248, 275, 281, 294, 315, 316, 355, 440, 573
    Velatio Virginum in, 253, 424
  Leonian, 133, 135, 138, 139, 145, 179, 267, 275, 424, 430, 431
    ordinations in, 351, 355
  of St. Remi, 121
Sacrificium, 206
St. Gall, Gelasian MS. at, 125
  MS. fragments at, 157
Saints, the—
  Litany of, 164
  lections from lives of, 195
  festivals of, 265, 269 *et seq.*, 276
Saliva, use of, 304, 317, 332
Salt, liturgical use of, 296, 317, 331, 410
Salutation, liturgical, 82, 166, 191
Sancta, rite of the, 185
Sancta sanctis, 63, 82, 222
Sanctus, the, 61, 117, 118
  in Alexandrine Liturgy, 82
  in Roman Mass, 176, 179 (*oratio post*), 215
Sanctus Deus Archangelorum, 193
Sarapion, Bishop of Antioch, 19
Sarapion, Bishop of Thmuis, 75, 79, 82, 242, 330, 376, 377. *See Euchologion of*
Saturday, 231, 233, 243, 550
Saturnalia, the, 261
Schola Cantorum (or School of Cantors at Rome), 103, 116, 163, 169, 315, 346, 348, 349, 350, 352, 456
Schola lectorum, 348
Scriniarius, 354
Scrutinies, 298, 303, 319, 328, 577c
Scyphus, 174, 459, 484
Secondiciarius, 148
Secreta (or *super oblata*), 118, 167, 175, 206, 208 (*oratio post*), 217
Secretarium, 162, 362
Seculares, 522
Secundicerius, 459

INDEX. 591

Sedes S. Petri, 280
Septimana major, 520
Septuagesima, 244
Sermons, or Homilies, 40, 170, 171, 272
  in the Gallican Mass, 197
  in Holy Week, St. Leo's, 234
  St. Chrysostom's, in Lent, 246
  to the *competents*, 328
Servia, 71
Seville, Bishop of, receives *pallium*, 385
Sexagesima, 244, 246
Sext, 448, 449, 450, 492
Shoes (for the clergy), 395
Signum Christi. See Alphabet, ceremony of
Silence, injunction to, 160, 170, 190
Silvester, St., 133
Silvia, pilgrimage of (*Peregrinatio Silviae*) See Etheria
Sindalia, 469
Sindonem (*oratio post*), 208
Sion, cathedral on Mt., 491, 496, 498, 501, 503, 510, 514
Sixtus. See Xystus
Solomon, ring of, 510
  dedication of temple by, 522
Sonus, 203, 205
Sozomen, 445
Spain—
  metropolitan system introduced in, 31
  Church of, appeals to Milan, 33-37
  Latin influence in Church of, 94
  Gallican Use in, 96
  disciplinary code of, 103
Stational churches. See Stations
Stational Mass, 161, 315, 353 See also Mass
Stations, 122, 124, 150, 160, 229, 230, 244, 474
  in Lent, 246
  in Holy Week, 234
  fasts, 229
  Statione Catholica, 478
  announced, 462
  at Bethlehem, 497, 513, 546, 563
  at Gethsemane, 508, 556
  on Mount of Olives, 508, 516, 556
  at Golgotha, 511, 549, 559
  at Sion, 516, 562, 564
Statuta Ecclesiae Antiqua, 132, 350, 351, 352, 363
Staurofori, 474, 480
Stephen, St. (Mart.), 265, 266, 267
Stephen, St. (Pope), 133, 136, 267
Stole, the (*orarium*), 390-394
Stowe Missal, the. See Missal
Strategiae, 13
Strator, 477

Subadjuva (*suajuva*), 467, 482
Subarrhatio, 429
Subdeacon, 252, 343, 344, 352, 367, 376, 457, 474
Sublinteata, 510
Sudarium, 390
Sunday, 78
  observance of, 47, 228
  services on, 229, 494, 543
Sunday in Lent, 243, 500
Superpositio jejunii, 231, 285. See Fasts
Susum, 493
Symbol, the (Creed). See *Traditio symboli* and *Redditio symboli*
Symphorian, St., 151
Synagogue—
  rulers of, 9
  worship of, 46, 47, 48, 50
  influence on Christian Liturgy, 69
  festivals of, 235
Synaxary, 112
Synaxes, the (or assemblies), 167, 230, 234, 246, 248, 249, 450
Syracuse, Bishop of, receives pall, 386
Syria in the second century, 18 *et seq.*
  provinces of, 27
  liturgy of Church of, 55, 65
  Patriarchs of, 65
  See *siriste*, 521
Syriac Menologion, 267, 276

T

Tapers, use of, 163, 252, 468, 478, 552
  at baptism, 311, 312
  at night processions, 517, 546
  at Vespers, 493, 494
  at dedications, 409
Te igitur, 179, 409
Temperita, 457, 459, 474
Te rogamus audi nos, 106, 165
Tertullian, 17, 334, 335, 338, 347, 428, 447, 448
  caricatures Callixtus, 444
Theodore, Archbishop of Canterbury, 45, 99, 100
Thessalonica, vicariate of, 42
Thrace, diocese of, 21
Thursday, 130, 246
Tiara, Papal, 396
Tiberiad, school of, 6
Tierce, 447-449
Tironian notes, 145
Toledo—
  Councils of, 96, 98, 372, 392
  centre of Visigothic Church, 103
  Liturgy of, 103
  Officium at, 190

Toletanus, Sacramentary, 160A
Tours, Calendar of, 271
Tower (*Turris*) for bread at oblation, 205
Tract (*tractus*), 114, 168, 359
Traditio of vestments at ordination, 378, 398
Traditio symboli, the, 170, 301, 319
  in Gallican Rite, 152, 319
  in the Eastern Church, 328, 520, 568
Traditio of the instruments at ordination, 368
Traditio of the Gospel, 301
Traditio of the *Pater Noster*, 302
Transitorium, 225
Trecanum, 225
Treves, Felix, Bishop of, 33, 34
Trisagion, 83
  in the Gallican Mass, 191, 193, 197
Tunica linea (alb), 381
Tunicle, 379, 456
Turin, Council of, 34
Turris. *See* Tower
Tyre, dedication of church at, 400

U

Ulfilas, Bishop, 29
Unction. *See* Anointing
Unctionis dies, 320
Ungiarium, 482
Unleavened bread, 74

V

Vecchioni of Milan, the, 204
Veil—
  across Apse, 85, 413
  for the elements, 205
  prayer of the, 206
  for covering relics, 405
  or *velatio*, taking the, 422, 424, 425
  velatio nuptialis, or pall, 432
  used at pagan marriage, 433
Vere Sanctus, 215
Vespers (*lucernaria*), 315, 449, 493
Vesper station, 513
Vestments, 163
  traditio of, 378
  enumeration of, 379, 384
  colour of, 479
Victorius of Aquitaine, tables of, 238
Vigil, 229, 287, 543
  Easter Eve, 320
Virgin, the Blessed—
  festivals of, 130, 267, 269 *et seq.*, 272, 275, 479
  church dedicated to, 273
  verses to, 540

Virgins (*virgines canonicae*), 343
  consecration of, 419, 423
Viri Galilaei, 491
Visigoths—
  Church of, 32, 98, 103
  Kings of, and their bishops, 40
Voconius, Bishop, 119

W

Washing. *See* Feet
Wednesday, 228, 233, 549
White dress, 314
Whit Sunday, 515, 564   *See* Pentecost
  Eve of, 471
Widows, 342
Wilfrid, St., 100
Women, 224, 462,
Wurzburg MS., 572

X

Xenodoxium, 474
Xerophagy, 241
Ximenes, 119, 160B
Xystus, 136. *See* Popes

Z

Zacharias. *See* Popes
Zeno, St., 107

ἀδελφόθεος, 266
ἀπόκρεω, 245
ἀπόταξις, 330
ἀσώτου, 245

ἐκφώνησις, 118
ἐπιγονάτιον, 384
ἐπιμανίκια, 384
ἐπισωζομένη, 240
ἐπιτραχήλιον, 391

θεοπάτωρ, 266

καμηλαύκιον, 396
κλάσμα, 52
κυριακόν, 400

λυχνικόν, 493

μονάζοντες, 78
μονογενής, 83, 190
μύρον, 330

ὀθόνη, 391
ὀκτώηχος, 245

πεντηκοστάριον, 245
πρόθεσις, 83
προσκομιδή, 85

σοὶ, Κύριε, 207
στιχάριον, 381
σύναξις, 167
σύνταξις, 330

τελώνου, 245
τριῴδιον, 245

τυροφάγου, 245

ὑπερτίθεσθαι, 231

φαρισαίου, 245
φελόνιον, 381
φωτιζόμενοι, 328, 332

χειροθεσία, 341
χερουβικόν, 84
χήρα, 342

ὠμοφόριον, 389
ὠράριον, 391

THE END

www.ingramcontent.com/pod-product-compliance
Lightning Source LLC
Chambersburg PA
CBHW052109010526
44111CB00036B/1577